PORSCHE

914/4 & 914/6

1970 - 1976

WORKSHOP MANUAL

A FLOYD CLYMER PUBLICATION PUBLISHED IN 2023
BY VELOCEPRESS

All rights reserved. This work may not be reproduced or
transmitted in any form without the express written
consent of the publisher

www.VelocePress.com

INTRODUCTION

Welcome to the world of digital publishing ~ the book you now hold in your hand was printed using the latest state of the art digital technology. The advent of print-on-demand has forever changed the publishing process, never has information been so accessible and it is our hope that this book serves your informational needs for years to come. If this is your first exposure to digital publishing, we hope that you are pleased with the results. Many more titles of interest to the classic automobile and motorcycle enthusiast, collector and restorer are available via our website at www.VelocePress.com. We hope that you find this title as interesting as we do.

NOTE FROM THE PUBLISHER

The information presented is true and complete to the best of our knowledge. All recommendations are made without any guarantees on the part of the author or the publisher, who also disclaim all liability incurred with the use of this information.

TRADEMARKS

We recognize that some words, model names and designations, for example, mentioned herein are the property of the trademark holder. We use them for identification purposes only. This is not an official publication.

INFORMATION ON THE USE OF THIS PUBLICATION

This manual is an invaluable resource for those interested in performing their own maintenance. However, in today's information age we are constantly subject to changes in common practice, new technology, availability of improved materials and increased awareness of chemical toxicity. As such, it is advised that the user consult with an experienced professional prior to undertaking any procedure described herein. While every care has been taken to ensure correctness of information, it is obviously not possible to guarantee complete freedom from errors or omissions or to accept liability arising from such errors or omissions. Therefore, any individual that uses the information contained within, or elects to perform or participate in do-it-yourself repairs or modifications acknowledges that there is a risk factor involved and that the publisher or its associates cannot be held responsible for personal injury or property damage resulting from the use of the information or the outcome of such procedures.

WARNING!

One final word of advice, this publication is intended to be used as a reference guide, and when in doubt the reader should consult with a qualified technician.

CONTENTS

CHAPTER ONE

GENERAL INFORMATION, SPECIFICATIONS AND TORQUE SETTINGS — 1

Identification tags & plates (all models)
914/4 General dimensions
914/4 Chassis, engine & transmission codes
914/4 Engine specifications & wear limits
914/4 General specifications & wear limits
914/4 Torque settings
914/6 Engine specifications & wear limits
914/6 General specifications & wear limits
914/6 Torque settings

CHAPTER TWO

LUBRICATION, MAINTENANCE AND TUNE-UP — 32

Routine checks
Periodic checks
Periodic maintenance
Engine tune-up
Emission control systems
914/4 & 914/6 Quick reference tune-up data

CHAPTER THREE

TROUBLESHOOTING — 49

Fuel system
Ignition system
Drive belts
Engine
Clutch
Manual transmission
Rear axle
Shock absorbers
Steering
Brakes & parking brake
Front suspension & steering linkage
Electrical - starter - alternator - regulator
914/6 Troubleshooting suplement

CHAPTER FOUR

ENGINE — 914/4 — 66

Removal and installation
Engine/transaxle separation and joining
Disassembly and reassembly
Oil cooler
Distributor drive shaft
Flywheel
Drive plate
Crankshaft end play
Rear oil seal
Front oil seal
Valve rocker assembly
Cylinder heads
Valves and valve seats
Cylinders
Pistons, pins, and rings
Single oil pump
Dual oil pump
Oil pressure relief valves
Oil strainer
Crankcase
Crankshaft
Connecting rods
Camshaft
Specifications
Tightening torques

CHAPTER FIVE

ENGINE — 914/6 98

Removal and installation
Engine/transaxle separation and joining
Disassembly and reassembly
Oil pressure relief and bypass valves
Oil strainer
Rear oil seal
Front oil seal
Valve rocker assembly
Camshaft
Cylinder heads
Chain and chain tension system
Valves and valve seats
Valve timing
Cylinders
Pistons, pins, and rings
Flywheel (Sportomatic)
Crankshaft
Connecting rods
Oil pump (engine)
Oil pump (torque converter)
Intermediate shaft
Crankcase
Specifications

CHAPTER SIX

COOLING, HEATING, AND EXHAUST 146

Fan housing
Cooling air control adjustment
Cooling fan
Cover plate
Heat exchanger
Heater control cable
Muffler replacement

CHAPTER SEVEN

FUEL INJECTION — 914/4 152

Basic principles
Principles of AFC injection
Service precautions
Air cleaner
Accelerator cable
Control unit
Relays
Fuel pump
Fuel pressure regulator
Injectors
Throttle valve switch
Auxiliary air regulator
Pressure sensor (MPC only)
Head temperature sensor
Intake air temperature sensor
Distributor trigger contacts (MPC only)
Intake manifold
Intake air distributor
Cold start system
Exhaust emission control
Fuel evaporative control system

CHAPTER EIGHT

FUEL SYSTEM — 914/6 181

Air cleaner
Weber carburetors
Intake manifold
Electric fuel pump
Fuel tank
Specifications

CHAPTER NINE

ELECTRICAL SYSTEM 189

Battery
Alternator (914)
Voltage regulator
Alternator (914/6)
Starter (914)
Starter (914/6)
Lighting system
Instruments
Directional signal systems

Fuses
Horn
Fresh air system
Windshield wiper
Ignition system
Distributor
Specifications
Wiring diagrams

CHAPTER TEN

CLUTCH 235

Clutch pedal
Clutch cable

Clutch mechanism servicing
Release bearing

CHAPTER ELEVEN

MANUAL AND AUTOMATIC TRANSAXLES 239

Manual transaxle operation
Differential operation
Gearshift housing
Main shaft oil seal
Sportomatic operation

Sportomatic clutch
Control valve
Gearshift lever microswitch
Specifications

CHAPTER TWELVE

REAR AXLE AND SUSPENSION 260

Wheel alignment
Drive shafts
Rear axle boots
Constant velocity joints

Shock absorbers
Coil springs
Trailing arm
Specifications

CHAPTER THIRTEEN

FRONT SUSPENSION AND STEERING 271

Description
Wheel alignment
Front stabilizer
Front suspension strut
Torsion bars

Wheel bearings
Steering wheel
Tie rod
Steering housing
Specifications

CHAPTER FOURTEEN

BRAKES **285**

    Master cylinder
    Brake pads
    Front calipers
    Rear calipers
    Front brake discs
    Rear brake discs

    Brake bleeding
    Handbrake
    Brake adjustment
    Brake light
    Specifications

CHAPTER FIFTEEN

BODY **300**

    Seats
    Doors
    Windows

    Hoods and locks
    Bumpers

NOTES

This page provides an excellent place to record the engine and data plate information from your Porsche for future reference.

CHAPTER ONE

GENERAL INFORMATION & SPECIFICATIONS

Unusual styling and mid-engine design combine to make the 914 an unconventional automobile. Though powered by a Volkswagen engine and built by VW production facilities, handling and performance justify the famous Porsche name.

From 1970-1973, the standard 914 uses a 1700cc 4-cylinder power plant originally used in the Volkswagen Type 4. For those demanding more performance, small numbers of the 914/6 with a 2000cc 6-cylinder engine have been imported. This optional engine is essentially the same as that offered in early 911 models. In 1973, the 914/6 was replaced by the 914S. This model contains a 2000cc version of the standard engine. For 1974, the standard engine was bored out to 1800cc. The 2000cc engine was available as an option. Both engines were used until production was halted in 1976.

All 914 models have 4-wheel disc brakes with front torsion bars and rear coil spring suspensions. Each model is available with either a 5-speed manual transaxle or 4-speed Sportomatic semiautomatic transaxle.

The chassis number is stamped on the identification plate under the luggage compartment mat and on the left windshield pillar. The manufacturer's plate is located on the right headlight housing. The engine number is stamped on the crankcase.

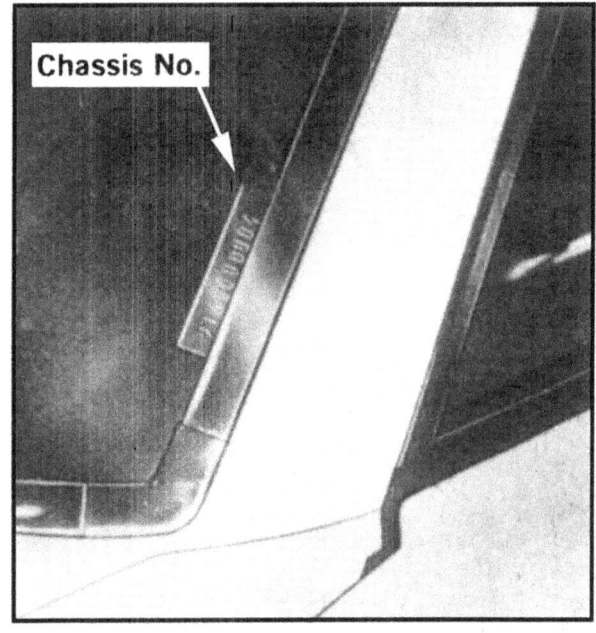

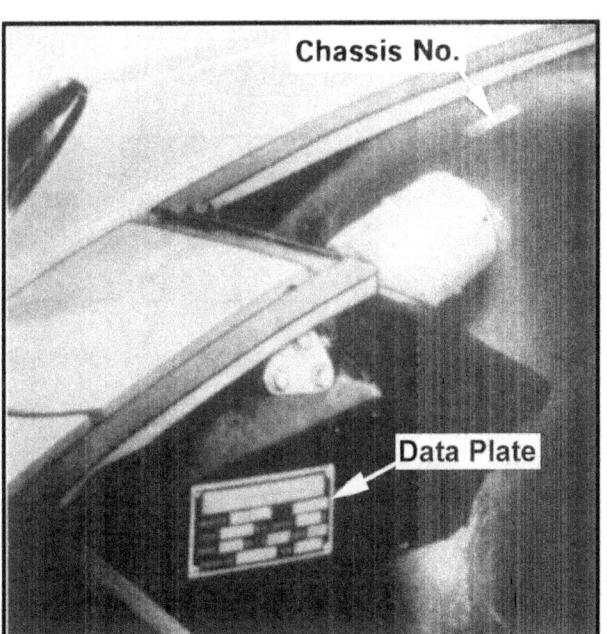

914/4

1.7 - 1.8 - 2.0 MODELS

TECHNICAL

SPECIFICATIONS

DIMENSIONS

TOLERANCES

TORQUE SETTINGS

GENERAL DIMENSIONS & WEIGHTS

Overall length	159.4" (4,050mm)
Overall width	65.0" (1,650mm)
Overall height (unladen)	48.4" (1,230mm)
Overall wheelbase	96.5" (2,450mm)
Track	
front (4½" rims)	52.4" (1,331mm)
rear (4½" rims)	53.97" (1,371mm)
Turning circle	36' (11 meters)
Ground clearance	
with 155 x 15 tires	4.7" (120mm)
with 165 x 15 tires	5.1" (130mm)
Curb weight	2,139 lbs. (970 kg)
Maximum total weight	2,780 lbs. (1,260 kg)

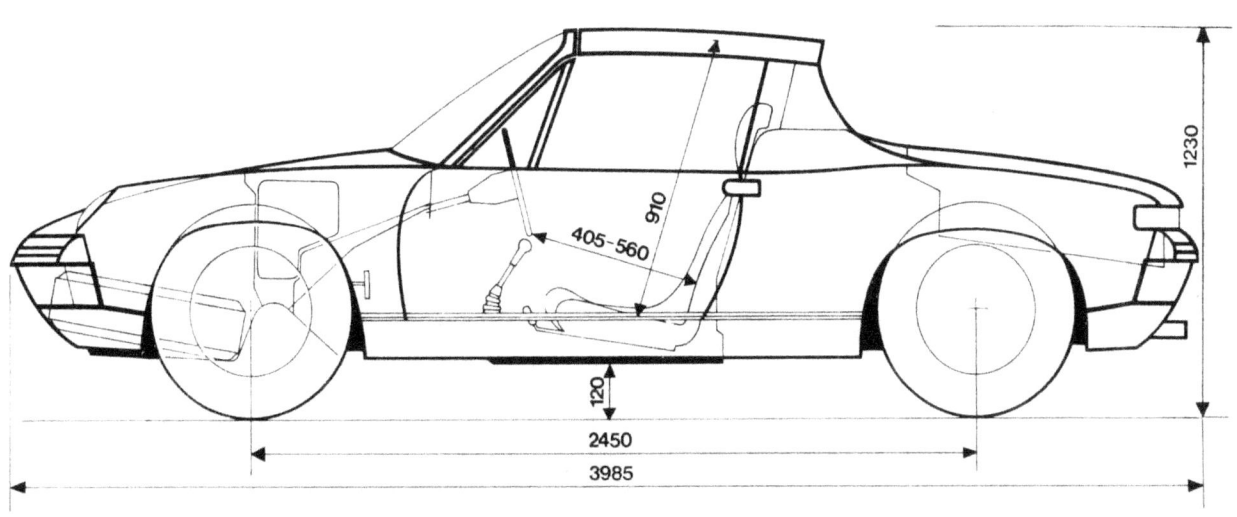

Vehicle Type Classification Codes

Year Mfd.	Model Year	Engine Code	Displ. cc.	Output DIN HP at rpm	Stroke/ Bore (mm)	Compr. Ratio	Fuel System	Transmission Type	Chassis Numbers
1969/ 1970	1970	W	1679	80/4900	66/90	8,2:1	MPC	914/11	470 29 00001–470 29 13312
1970/ 1971	1971	W	1679	80/4900	66/90	8,2:1	MPC	914/11	471 29 00001–471 29 16231
1971/ 1972	1972	EA	1679	80/4900	66/90	8,2:1	MPC	914/11	472 29 00001–472 29 21580
1972/ 1973	1973	EA	1679	80/4900	66/90	8,2:1	MPC	914/12	473 29 00001–473 29 27660
		EB	1679	72/5000	66/90	7,3:1	MPC	914/12	
		GA	1971	95/4900	71/94	7,6:1	MPC	914/12	
1973/ 1974	1974	EC	1795	76/4800	66/93	7,3:1	AFC	914/12	474 29 00001–474 29 .....
		GA	1971	95/4900	71/94	7,6:1	MPC	914/12	

Chassis Number Codes

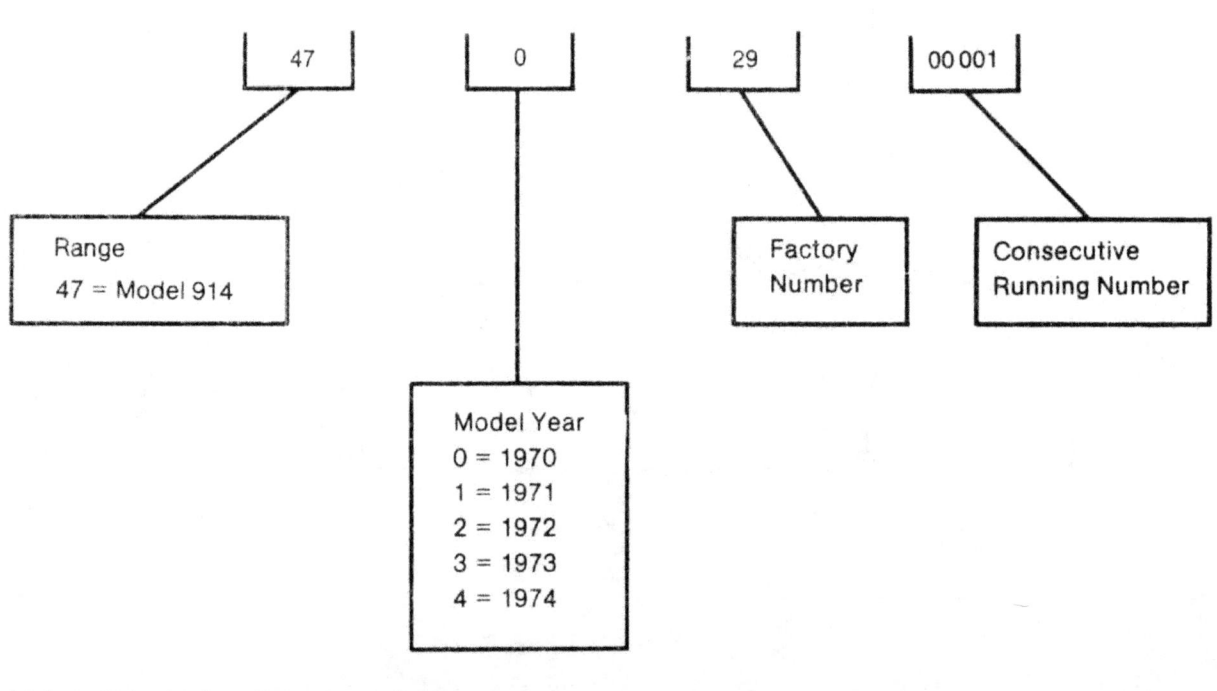

Range
47 = Model 914

Model Year
0 = 1970
1 = 1971
2 = 1972
3 = 1973
4 = 1974

Factory Number

Consecutive Running Number

Engine Number Codes

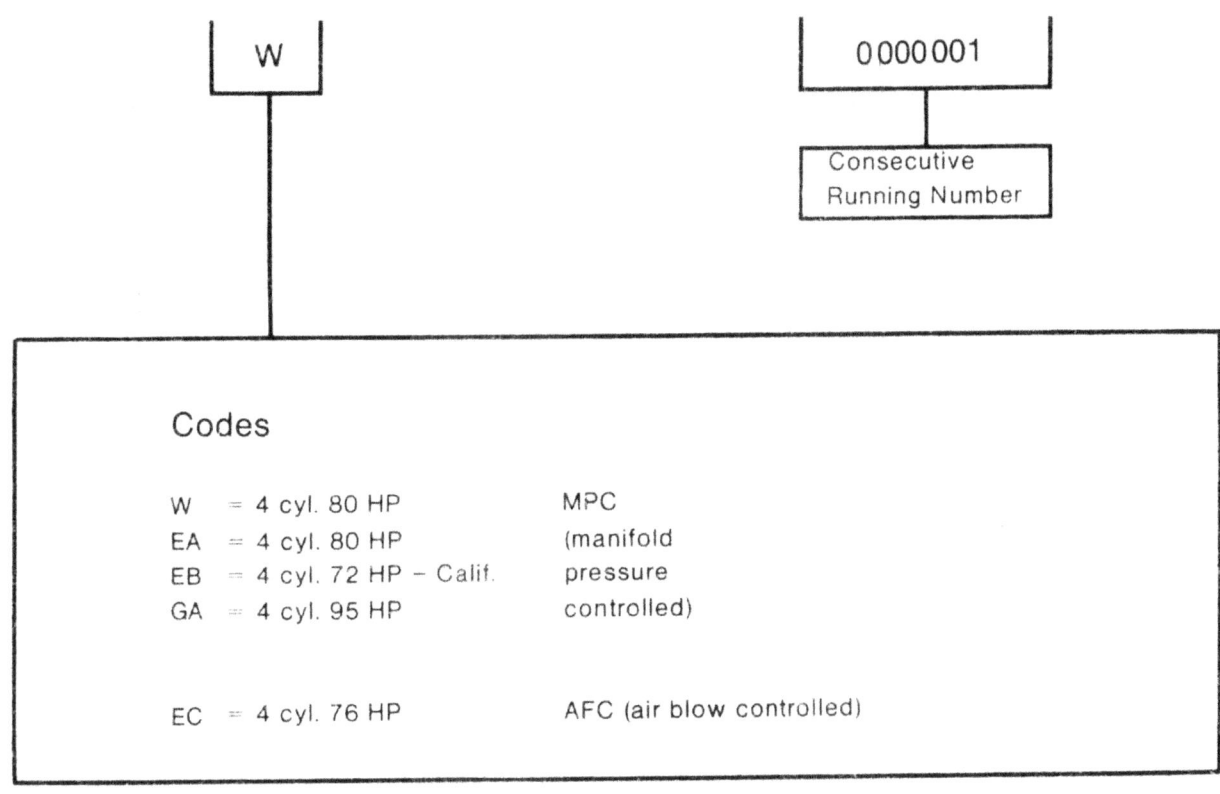

Codes

W = 4 cyl. 80 HP   MPC
EA = 4 cyl. 80 HP   (manifold
EB = 4 cyl. 72 HP – Calif. pressure
GA = 4 cyl. 95 HP   controlled)

EC = 4 cyl. 76 HP   AFC (air blow controlled)

Transmission Number Codes

Transmission numbers up to Sept. 30, 1972

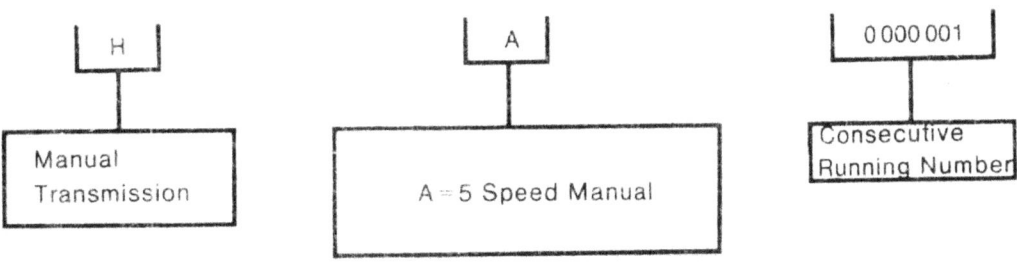

Transmission numbers from Okt. 1, 1972

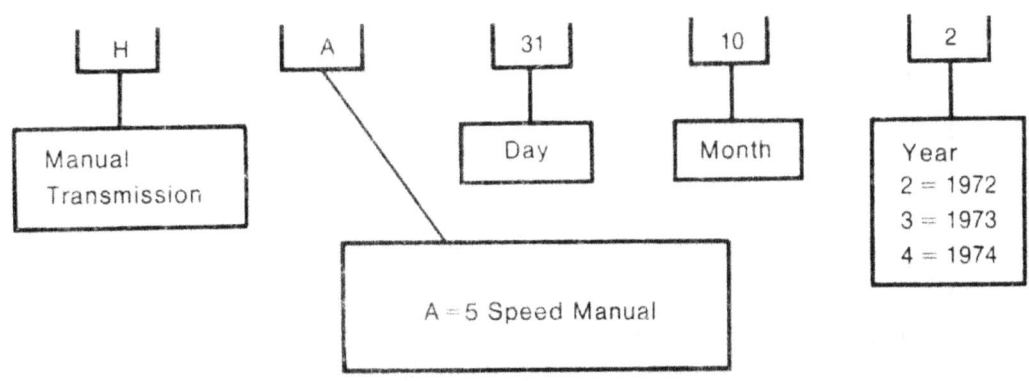

914/4 ENGINE SPECIFICATIONS 1.7L

	Tolerance (new)	Wear limit
GENERAL		
No. of cylinders	4	
Bore, in. (mm)	3.543 (90)	
Stroke	2.598 (66)	
Displacement	102.5 (1679)	
Compression ratio	8.2	
Firing order	1-4-3-2	
Output DIN hp @ rpm	72 @ 5000	
Torque foot-pounds @ rpm	99 @ 3500	
Weight (dry) lbs. (kg)	278 (126)	
CYLINDERS		
Bore, in. (mm)	3.543 (90)	
Cylinder/piston clearance	0.0016-0.0024 (0.04-0.06)	0.008 (0.20)
Out-of-round		0.0004 (0.01)
Oversize available	0.5, 1.0	
PISTONS		
Material	light alloy	
Weight (gray), grams	480-488	
(brown), grams	472-480	
Permissible weight deviation in same engine, grams	4	10
PISTON RINGS		
Number per piston	3	
Compression	2	
Oil control	1	
Ring end gap, in. (mm)		
Top compression	0.014-0.022 (0.35-0.55)	0.0354 (0.90)
Bottom compression	0.012-0.014 (0.30-0.35)	0.0354 (0.90)
Oil control	0.010-0.016 (0.25-0.40)	0.0374 (0.95)
Ring side clearance, in. (mm)		
Top compression	0.0024-0.0035 (0.06-0.09)	0.005 (0.12)
Bottom compression	0.0016-0.0028 (0.04-0.07)	0.004 (0.10)
Oil control	0.0008-0.0020 (0.02-0.05)	0.004 (0.10)
PISTON PINS		
Diameter, in. (mm)	0.9447-0.9448 (23.996-24.000)	
Clearance in rod, in. (mm)	0.0004-0.0012 (0.01-0.03)	0.0016 (0.04)
CRANKSHAFT		
Number of main bearings	4	
Main bearing journal dia., in. (mm)		
Bearings 1-3	2.3610-2.3618 (59.97-59.99)	
Bearing 4	1.5740-1.5748 (39.98-40.00)	
Connecting rod journal dia., in. (mm)	2.1646-2.1654 (54.98-55.00)	

(continued)

1700 ENGINE SPECIFICATIONS (continued)

	Tolerance (new)	Wear limit
CRANKSHAFT (continued)		
Main bearing clearances, in. (mm)		
Bearings 1 and 3	0.002-0.004 (0.05-0.10)	0.0071 (0.18)
Bearing 2	0.0012-0.0035 (0.03-0.09)	0.0067 (0.17)
Bearing 4	0.002-0.004 (0.05-0.10)	0.0075 (0.19)
End play, in. (mm)	0.0028-0.005 (0.07-0.13)	0.0059 (0.15)
Permissible out-of-round		
Main bearing journal, in. (mm)		0.0012 (0.03)
Connecting rod journal, in. (mm)		0.0012 (0.03)
CONNECTING RODS		
Weight deviation in same engine, grams	6	
Weight (black), grams	769-775	
(white), grams	746-752	
Side clearance, in. (mm)	0.004-0.016 (0.1-0.4)	0.0276 (0.70)
Connecting rod bearing clearance, in. (mm)	0.0008-0.0028 (0.02-0.07)	0.0059 (0.15)
Piston pin bushing diameter in. (mm)	0.9455-0.9458 (24.015-24.024)	
CAMSHAFT		
Number of bearings	3	
Bearing diameter, in. (mm)	0.9837-0.9842 (24.99-25.00)	
Bearing clearance, in. (mm)	0.0008-0.0020 (0.02-0.05)	0.0047 (0.12)
End play, in. (mm)	0.0016-0.0051 (0.04-0.13)	0.0062 (0.16)
TIMING GEARS		
Backlash, in. (mm)	0.000-0.002 (0.00-.0.05)	
VALVES—INTAKE		
Head diameter, in. (mm)	1.539-0.543 (39.1-39.3)	
Stem diameter, in. (mm)	0.3125-0.3129 (7.94-7.95)	
Valve guide inside diameter, in. (mm)	0.3150-0.3157 (8.00-8.02)	0.3173 (8.06)
Valve face angle	29° 30'	
Valve seat angle	30°	
Valve seat width	0.0706-0.0866 (1.8-2.2)	
VALVES—EXHAUST		
Head diameter, in. (mm)	1.286-1.299 (32.7-33.0)	
Stem diameter, in. (mm)	0.3507-0.3511 (8.91-8.92)	
Valve guide inside diameter, in. (mm)	0.3543-0.3551 (9.00-9.02)	0.3567 (9.06)
Valve face angle	45°	
Valve seat angle	45°	
Valve seat width	0.0787-0.0984 (2.0-2.5)	
VALVE SPRINGS		
Length, in. (mm)	1.18 (30)	
@ load, lbs. (kg)	160-184 (72.5-83.5)	
OIL SYSTEM		
Oil pressure (SAE 30) @ 158°F. & 2,500 rpm	43 psi (3.0 kg/cm^2)	28 psi (2.0 kg/cm^2)
Oil pressure relief valve spring		
Length, in. (mm)	1.54 (39.0)	
@ load, lbs. (kg)	15-19.4 (6.8-8.8)	

914/4 ENGINE SPECIFICATIONS 1.8L

	Tolerance (new)	Wear limit
GENERAL		
No. of cylinders	4	
Bore, in. (mm)	3.661 (93)	
Stroke	2.598 (66)	
Displacement	109.6 (1795)	
Compression ratio	7.3	
Firing order	1-4-3-2	
Output DIN hp @ rpm	72 @ 5000	
Torque foot-pounds @ rpm	99 @ 3500	
Weight (dry) lbs. (kg)	278 (126)	
CYLINDERS		
Bore, in. (mm)	3.66 (93)	
Cylinder/piston clearance	0.0016-0.0024 (0.04-0.06)	0.008 (0.20)
Out-of-round		0.0004 (0.01)
Oversize available	0.5, 1.0	
PISTONS		
Material	light alloy	
Weight (gray), grams	480-488	
(brown), grams	472-480	
Permissible weight deviation in same engine, grams	4	10
PISTON RINGS		
Number per piston	3	
Compression	2	
Oil control	1	
Ring end gap, in. (mm)		
Top compression	0.014-0.022 (0.35-0.55)	0.0354 (0.90)
Bottom compression	0.012-0.014 (0.30-0.35)	0.0354 (0.90)
Oil control	0.010-0.016 (0.25-0.40)	0.0374 (0.95)
Ring side clearance, in. (mm)		
Top compression	0.0024-0.0035 (0.06-0.09)	0.005 (0.12)
Bottom compression	0.0016-0.0028 (0.04-0.07)	0.004 (0.10)
Oil control	0.0008-0.0020 (0.02-0.05)	0.004 (0.10)
PISTON PINS		
Diameter, in. (mm)	0.9447-0.9448 (23.996-24.000)	
Clearance in rod, in. (mm)	0.0004-0.0012 (0.01-0.03)	0.0016 (0.04)
CRANKSHAFT		
Number of main bearings	4	
Main bearing journal dia., in. (mm)		
Bearings 1-3	2.3610-2.3618 (59.97-59.99)	
Bearing 4	1.5740-1.5748 (39.98-40.00)	
Connecting rod journal dia., in. (mm)	2.1646-2.1654 (54.98-55.00)	

(continued)

1800 ENGINE SPECIFICATIONS (continued)

	Tolerance (new)	Wear limit
CRANKSHAFT (continued)		
Main bearing clearances, in. (mm)		
Bearings 1 and 3	0.002-0.004 (0.05-0.10)	0.0071 (0.18)
Bearing 2	0.0012-0.0035 (0.03-0.09)	0.0067 (0.17)
Bearing 4	0.002-0.004 (0.50-0.10)	0.0075 (0.19)
End play, in. (mm)	0.0028-0.005 (0.07-0.13)	0.0059 (0.15)
Permissible out-of-round		
Main bearing journal, in. (mm)		0.0012 (0.03)
Connecting rod journal, in. (mm)		0.0012 (0.03)
CONNECTING RODS		
Weight deviation in same engine, grams	6	
Weight (black), grams	769-775	
(white), grams	746-752	
Side clearance, in. (mm)	0.004-0.016 (0.1-0.4)	0.0276 (0.70)
Connecting rod bearing clearance, in. (mm)	0.0008-0.0028 (0.02-0.07)	0.0059 (0.15)
Piston pin bushing diameter in. (mm)	0.9455-0.9458 (24.015-24.024)	
CAMSHAFT		
Number of bearings	3	
Bearing diameter, in. (mm)	0.9837-0.9842 (24.99-25.00)	
Bearing clearance, in. (mm)	0.0008-0.0020 (0.02-0.05)	0.0047 (0.12)
End play, in. (mm)	0.0016-0.0051 (0.04-0.13)	0.0062 (0.16)
TIMING GEARS		
Backlash, in. (mm)	0.000-0.002 (0.00-.0.05)	
VALVES—INTAKE		
Head diameter, in. (mm)	1.614 (41)	
Stem diameter, in. (mm)	0.3125-0.3129 (7.94-7.95)	
Valve guide inside diameter, in. (mm)	0.3150-0.3157 (8.00-8.02)	0.3173 (8.06)
Valve face angle	29° 30'	
Valve seat angle	30°	
Valve seat width	0.0706-0.0866 (1.8-2.2)	
VALVES—EXHAUST		
Head diameter, in. (mm)	1.338 (34)	
Stem diameter, in. (mm)	0.3507-0.3511 (8.91-8.92)	
Valve guide inside diameter, in. (mm)	0.3543-0.3551 (9.00-9.02)	0.3576 (9.06)
Valve face angle	45°	
Valve seat angle	45°	
Valve seat width	0.0787-0.0984 (2.0-2.5)	
VALVE SPRINGS		
Length, in. (mm)	1.18 (30)	
@ load, lbs. (kg)	160-184 (72.5-83.5)	
OIL SYSTEM		
Oil pressure (SAE 30) @ 158°F. & 2,500 rpm	43 psi (3.0 kg/cm^2)	28 psi (2.0 kg/cm^2)
Oil pressure relief valve spring		
Length, in. (mm)	1.54 (39.0)	
@ load, lbs. (kg)	15-19.4 (6.8-8.8)	

914/4 ENGINE SPECIFICATIONS 2.0L

	Tolerance (new)	Wear limit
GENERAL		
No. of cylinders	4	
Bore, in. (mm)	3.701 (94)	
Stroke	2.795 (71)	
Displacement	120.2 (1971)	
Compression ratio	7.6:1	
Firing order	1-4-3-2	
Output DIN hp @ rpm	91 @ 4900	
Torque foot-pounds @ rpm	105 @ 3500	
Weight (dry) lbs. (kg)	322 (146)	
CYLINDERS		
Bore, in. (mm)	3.701 (94)	
Cylinder/piston clearance	0.0016-0.0024 (0.04-0.06)	0.008 (0.20)
Out-of-round		0.004 (0.01)
Oversize available	0.5, 1.0	
PISTONS		
Material	light alloy	
Weight (gray), grams	—	
(brown), grams	—	
Permissible weight deviation		
in same engine, grams	4	10
PISTON RINGS		
Number per piston	3	
Compression	2	
Oil control	1	
Ring end gap, in. (mm)		
Top compression	0.014-0.022 (0.35-0.55)	0.0354 (0.90)
Bottom compression	0.012-0.014 (0.35-0.55)	0.0354 (0.90)
Oil control	0.010-0.016 (0.25-0.40)	0.0374 (0.95)
Ring side clearance, in. (mm)		
Top compression	0.0024-0.0035 (0.06-0.09)	0.005 (0.12)
Bottom compression	0.0016-0.0028 (0.04-0.07)	0.004 (0.10)
Oil control	0.0008-0.0020 (0.02-0.05)	0.004 (0.10)
PISTON PINS		
Diameter, in. (mm)	0.9447-0.9448 (23.996-24.000)	
Clearance in rod, in. (mm)	0.0004-0.0012 (0.01-0.03)	0.0016 (0.04)
CRANKSHAFT		
Number of main bearings	4	
Main bearing journal dia., in. (mm)		
Bearings 1-3	2.3610-2.3618 (59.97-59.99)	
Bearing 4	1.5740-1.5748 (39.98-40.00)	
Connecting rod journal dia., in. (mm)	1.968-1.969 (49.98-50.00)	

(continued)

2000 ENGINE SPECIFICATIONS (continued)

	Tolerance (new)	Wear limit
CRANKSHAFT (continued)		
Main bearing clearances, in. (mm)		
Bearings 1 and 3	0.002-0.004 (0.05-0.10)	0.0071 (0.18)
Bearing 2	0.0012-0.0035 (0.03-0.09)	0.0067 (0.17)
Bearing 4	0.002-0.004 (0.05-0.10)	0.0075 (0.19)
End play, in. (mm)	0.0028-0.005 (0.07-0.13)	0.0059 (0.15)
Permissible out-of-round		
Main bearing journal, in. (mm)		0.0012 (0.03)
Connecting rod journal, in. (mm)		0.0012 (0.03)
CONNECTING RODS		
Weight deviation in same engine, grams	6	
Weight (black), grams	791-794	
(white), grams	783-786	
Side clearance, in. (mm)	0.004-0.016 (0.1-0.4)	0.0276 (0.70)
Connecting rod bearing clearance, in. (mm)	0.0008-0.0028 (0.02-0.07)	0.0059 (0.15)
Piston pin bushing diameter in. (mm)	0.9455-0.9458 (24.015-24.024)	
CAMSHAFT		
Number of bearings	3	
Bearing diameter, in. (mm)	0.9837-0.9842 (24.99-25.00)	
Bearing clearance, in. (mm)	0.0008-0.0020 (0.02-0.05)	0.0047 (0.12)
End play, in. (mm)	0.0016-0.0051 (0.04-0.13)	0.0062 (0.16)
TIMING GEARS		
Backlash, in. (mm)	0.000-0.002 (0.00-0.05)	
VALVES—INTAKE		
Head diameter, in. (mm)	1.6535-1.6614 (42.0-42.2)	
Stem diameter, in. (mm)	0.3125-0.3179 (7.94-7.95)	
Valve guide inside diameter, in. (mm)	0.3150-0.3157 (8.00-8.02)	0.3173 (8.06)
Valve face angle	45°	
Valve seat angle	45°	
Valve seat width		
VALVES—EXHAUST		
Head diameter, in. (mm)	1.4173-1.4192 (36-36.2)	
Stem diameter, in. (mm)	0.3507-0.3511 (8.91-8.92)	
Valve guide inside diameter, in. (mm)	0.3543-0.3551 (9.00-9.02)	0.3576 (9.06)
Valve face angle	45°	
Valve seat angle	45°	
Valve seat width	0.0787-0.0984 (2.0-2.5)	
VALVE SPRINGS		
Length, in. (mm)	1.18 (30)	
@ load, lbs. (kg)	160-184 (72.5-83.5)	
OIL SYSTEM		
Oil pressure (SAE 30) @ 158°F. & 2,500 rpm	63 psi (4.5 kg/cm^2)	
Oil pressure relief valve spring		
Length, in. (mm)	1.54 (39.0)	
@ load, lbs. (kg)	15-19.4 (6.8-8.8)	

914/4 ALL MODELS - GENERAL SPECIFICATIONS

GENERAL DATA
Wheel base .... 2,450 mm (96.5")
Track width front (at dead weight acc.
  to DIN) .... 1,337 mm (52.7")
Track circle dia. .... approx. 10.35 mm (33.9 ft.)
Smallest turning circle dia. .... 11.0 m (36 ft.)
Center of tire contact .... 40.5 mm (1.594")
Front axle load at perm. total load .... 650 kp (1,433 lbs.)
Torsion bar: .... Length 611.5 mm (24.075")
                                                              Dia. 17.9 mm (0.705")
                                             Number of teeth 29
Total reduction of steering gear 17.78
Steering wheel turns from lock to lock .... Approx. 3.1

GENERAL SPECIFICATIONS
Rims .... 4½J x 15, optional 5½J x 15
Tires .... 155 SR 15; optional 165 SR 15 on either
                                                                4½J or 5½J x 15 rims (if subsequently installed,
                                                                speedometer must be replaced)
Wheelbase .... 96.5 in. (2450 mm)
Track (DIN curb weight) .... Front 52.40 in (1331 mm); with 5½J x 15 rims 52.87 in.
                                                                (1343 mm)
                                                          Rear 53.98 in. (1371 mm); with 5½J x 15 rims 54.45 in.
                                                                (1383 mm)
Overall length .... 156.8 in. (3985 mm)
Overall width .... 65.0 in. (1650 mm)
Overal height (car empty) .... 48.4 in. (120 mm)
Ground Clearance (car loaded) .... 4.7 in. (120 mm)
Turning circle .... Approx. 36 feet (11 m)

CAPACITIES
Engine .... Approx 3.7 US qts. without oil filter,
                                                               3.2 US qts. premium quality HD oil, acc. to API
                                                               specification SD or SE
                                                                 SAE 30 = 32°F (0°C)
                                                                 SAE 20 W 20 = from + 5° to 32°F (−15° to 0°C)
                                                                 SAE 10 W = below + 5°F (−15°C)
Transmission and differential .... Approx. 2.6 US qts, SAE 90
Torque convertor .... 6.3 US qts. HD oil SAE 20 W 20
Fuel tank .... 16.4 US gals. including approx. 1.6
                                                              US gals. reserve
                                                              Required octane rating: 98 octane
Brake fluid .... Approx. 12 fl. oz. J 1703

ENGINE
Type .... aircooled 4-stroke gasoline injection
                                                              engine
Number of cylinders 4
Cylinder arrangement .... 2 cylinders each opposed, flat flour

	1700	1800	2000
Bore	90 mm (3.543") dia.	93 mm. (3.661 in.)	94 mm. (3.701 in.)
Stroke	66 mm (2.598")		71 mm. (2.795 in.)
Total piston displacement	1,679 cc (102.5 cu. in.)	1,795 cc (109.6 cu. in.)	1,971 cc (120.2 cu. in.)
Compression ratio	8.2:1	7.3:1	7.6:1
Max. performance (SAE)	85 HP at 5,000 rpm	(DIN) 72 @ 5,000 rpm	(DIN) 95 @ 4,900 rpm
Max. torque (SAE)	99.45 ft. lb. at 3,500 rpm	(DIN) 99 @ 3,500 rpm	(DIN) 108 @ 3,500 rpm
Mean piston speed	10.8 m/s (35.4 ft/sec) at 4,900 rpm		(38.0 ft/sec) @ 4,900 rpm
Octane number	98 (Research Method)	91	91

IGNITION — battery ingntion
    Ignition coil — Bosch 022 905 115
    Ignition distributor — Bosch 022 905 205 Sportomatic: 022 905 205B
    Firing point — 27° BTDC at 3,500 rpm (vacuum hoses removed)
    Firing order — 1-4-3-2
    Ignition timing — by centrifugal governor and intake vacuum
    Timing angle — 44 - 50°
    Spark plugs — 14 mm (0.55") plug threads (long), thermal value 175
    Spark gap — 0.7 mm (0.0276")

COOLING — aircooled by radial blower on crankshaft
    Delivery volume — approx. 800 lits/sec (211 US gal.) at n (engine) = 4,600 rpm

LUBRICATION — forced feed by gear pump
    Oil cooling — oil cooler in blower air stream
    Oil filter — in main stream
    Oil pressure indic — by pilot lamp
    Oil capacity — 3.5 lits (0.92 US gal) with oil filter change
        3.0 lits (0.79 US gal) without oil filger change
    Oil consumption — 0.5-1.0 lits/1,000 km (0.13-0.26 US gal/6,214 miles)

CYLINDER HEAD — one each for 2 cylinders with cast-on cooling ribs, aluminum alloy
    Valve seat rings — shrunk-in, sintered steel
    Valve guides — shrunk-in, special brass
    Spark plug threads — cut into cylinder head

VALVES — 1 inlet and 1 exhaust valve per cylinder
    Exhaust valve — with hard-faced seat
    Arrangement — overhead

		1800cc	2000cc
Clearance with cold engine — Inlet	0.10 mm (0.004")	0.15mm (.006")	0.15mm (.006")
with cold engine — Exhaust	0.10 mm (0.004")	0.15mm (.006")	0.20mm (.008")

VALVE TIMING WITH .04" valve clearance:
    Intake opens — 12° BTDC
    Intake closes — 42° ABDC
    Exhaust opens — 43° BTDC
    Exhaust closes — 4° ATDC

CYLINDERS — individual cylinders, special grey iron casting with cooling ribs
    Center distance — 4.90"

PISTON — light metal alloy with steel insert
    Piston pin — floating, secured by circlips
    Piston rings — 2 compression rings / 1 oil scraper ring

CRANKCASE — split, with vertical center division by crankshaft and camshaft bearings, aluminum alloy

CAMSHAFT — grey casting, 3 plane bearings
    Camshaft bearings — thin-walled steel half shells with babbitt metal running surface
    Camshaft drive — spur gears, helical

CRANKSHAFT — forged, fine steel, 4 plane bearings
    Main bearings 1, 3 and 4 — aluminum sleeves with lead-coated running surface
    Main bearing 2 (center bearing) — half shells, three-component bearing
    Main bearings 1-3 — 60 mm dia. (2.36")
    Main bearing 4 — 40 mm dia. (1.87")
    Conrod bearing — 55 mm dia. (2.17") - 2000cc 50 mm (1.97")
    Flywheel — forged, with starter ring geear, one-piece

CONNECTING RODS . . . . forged, with I-shaped shank cross section
    Conrod bearings . . . . thin-walled half shells,
    three-component bearings
    Piston pin bearings . . . . pressed-in steel bushing with
    lead-bronze running surface

CLUTCH . . . . Diaphragm spring clutch
    Type . . . . single-plate dry clutch
    Total facing area . . . . 47.3 sq. in.

BRAKES
    Tandem main brake cylinder
      Bore . . . . 17.46 mm dia. (.6874")
      Stroke . . . . 18/13 mm (.7/.5")
      Play: actuating rod/Piston . . . . 1 mm (.04")
    Front wheel brake
      Brake disc (dia.) . . . . 281 mm (11.063")
      Min. thickness after refinishing . . . . 10.5 mm (.391")
      (The brake disc may be refinished
      only symmetrically, this is,
      uniformly from both sides.)
      Thickness tolerance . . . . max. 0.02 mm (.0008")
      Lateral wobble . . . . 0.2 mm (.008")
      Caliper piston dia. . . . . 42 mm (1.7")
      Thickness of lining . . . . 10 mm (.4")
      Release clearance . . . . .0020-.0079"
      Lining surface of four linings . . . . 16.4 sq. in.
    Rear wheel brake
      Brake disc (OD) . . . . 282 mm (11.102")
      Thickness, new . . . . 9.5 mm (.374")
      Lateral wobble . . . . 0.2 mm (.008")
      Caliper piston dia. . . . . 33 mm (1.3")
      Thickness of lining . . . . 10 mm (.4")
      Release clearance . . . . .008"
      Lining surface of four linings . . . . 12.4 sq. in.

SUSPENSION
    Total track of front wheels under pressure . . . . +20' ± 10'
    Size of force for front wheel pressure . . . . 15 kp (33 lbs.)
    Camber of front wheels . . . . 0 ± 20'
    Max. permissible difference in camber
      between both sides . . . . 20'
    Track difference angle at 20° lock . . . .
                                                to the left   0 + 30'
                                               to the right 0 + 30'
    Caster of front wheels . . . . 6° ± 30'
    Height adjustment of front axle . . . . 90 mm ± 5 mm
    (wheel center above torsion bar center—
    rear) . . . . (3.5 ± .2")
    Height difference left to right . . . . max. 5 mm (.2")
    Total Frictional torque (steering
      assembled) . . . . 6 — 8 cmkp
    Frame . . . . Welded pressed steel box section frame, welded to body
    Front suspension . . . . Independent, suspension struts and track control arm
    Front springs . . . . Round section longitudinal torsion bar for each wheel
    Rear suspension . . . . Independent, semi-trailing arms
    Rear springs . . . . Coil spring, double acting telescopic shock absorber
    and progressive rate hollow rubber spring for each wheel

ELECTRICAL SYSTEM
    Operating voltage . . . . 12 volts
    Battery capacity . . . . 45 Ah
    Alternator output . . . . 50 amps at 14 volts AC,
    700 watts capacity

5-SPEED TRANSMISSION

Transmission	Porsche, servo-lock synchronization
Number gears	5 forward, 1 reverse
Gearshift location	Floor-mounted, central
Final-drive	Spiral bevel pinion and differential – 4.43:1
Drive ratio	7:31 (4.429)
Rear axle drive	Over double joint half axles
Gear ratios	1st – 3.09:1
	2nd – 1.88:1
	3rd – 1.26:1
	4th – 0.93:1
	5th – 0.71:1
	Reverse – 3.13:1

(continued)

TOLERANCE (NEW) AND WEAR LIMITS

		Upon installation (new)	Wear limit
COOLING			
Thermostat	Opening temp.	65-70°C (149-158°F)	
Impeller/V-belt pulley	Unbalance	max. 5 cmg	
OIL CIRCUIT			
Oil pressure (for SAE 30 grades only) at 70°C (158°F) oil temp.: at 2,500 rpm	Pressure	approx. 3 kg/cm^2 (43 psi)	2 kg/cm^2 (28 psi)
Spring f. oil pressure relief valve Length under load: 23.4 mm (.921")	Load	11.1 kg (24.5 lbs)	
Spring f. oil pressure contr. valve Length under load: 16.8 mm (.661")	Load	4.35 kg (9.59 lbs)	
Oil pressure switch opens at	Pressure	0.15-0.45 kg/cm^2 (2.13-6.40 psi)	
CYLINDER HEAD WITH VALVES			
Depth of cylinder seat in cylinder head		5.4-6.5 mm (.213-.256")	
Combustion chamber capacity		51.1-52.6 cc (3.12-3.21 cu.in.)	
a) Rocker arm	ID	20.0-20.02 mm (.7874-.7882") dia.	20.04 mm (.7890") dia.
b) Rocker arm shaft	Dia	19.95-19.97 mm (.7854-.7862") dia.	19.93 mm (.7846") dia.
Valve spring Length under load 30.0 mm (1.18")	Load	72.5-83.5 kg (159.8-184.1 lbs)	
Valve seat a) Inlet	Width	1.8-2.2 mm (.0708-.0866")	
b) Exhaust	Width	2.0-2.5 mm (.0787-.0984")	
c) Inlet	Seat angle	30°	
d) Exhaust	Seat angle	45°	
e) External correction angle		15°	
f) Internal correction angle		75°	
Valve guides Inlet	ID	8.00-8.02 mm dia. (.3150-.3158")	8.06 mm dia. (.3173")
Exhaust	ID	9.00-9.02 mm dia. (.3543-.3551")	9.06 mm dia. (.3567")
Valve stem Intake	Dia.	7.94-7.95 mm dia. (.3126-.3130")	7.90 mm dia. (.3110")
Exhaust	Dia.	8.91-8.92 mm dia. (.3508-.3512")	8.87 mm dia. (.3492")
	out-of-round	max. 0.01 mm (.00039")	
Valve guide - valve stem Inlet and exhaust	Rocker play	max. 0.45 mm (.0177")	0.9 mm (.0354")
Valve disc Inlet	Dia.	39.0 mm dia (1.54")	
Exhaust	Dia	33.00 mm dia. (1.30")	
Valve clearance (cold) Inlet	Adjustment	0.10mm (.004")	
Exhaust	Adjustment	0.10mm (.004")	

	1800cc	2000cc
Inlet	0.15mm (.006")	0.15mm (.006")
Exhaust	0.15mm (.006")	0.20mm (.008")

		Upon installation (new)	Wear limit
Compression pressure (with throttle valve open and engine at operating temp., all plugs unscrewed, with practically no-loss pressure gauge in plug seat, cranking with starter)	Pressure	9.0-11.0 kp/cm^2 (128-156 psi)	7.0 kp/cm^2 (100 psi)
Pressure difference between individual cylinders		max. 1.5 kg/cm^2 (21.3 psi)	

CYLINDERS AND PISTONS

2 Excess sizes, each with 0.5 mm (.0197") higher dia.

Cylinder .... out-of-round	max. 0.01 mm (.0004)	
Cylinder/Piston .... Clearance	0.04-0.06 mm (.0016-.0024")	0.20 mm (.0079")
a) Upper piston ring .... Side clearance	0.06-0.09 mm (.0024-.0035")	0.12 mm (.0048")
b) Lower piston ring .... Side clearance	0.04-0.07 mm (.0016-.0028")	0.10 mm (.0039")
Oil scraper ring .... Side clearance	0.02-0.05 mm (.0008-.0020")	0.10 mm (.0039")
a) Upper piston ring .... Gap width	0.35-.055 mm (.0138-.0216")	0.90 mm (.0354")
b) Lower piston ring .... Gap width	0.30-0.35 mm (.0118-.0138")	0.90 mm (.0354")
Oil scraper ring .... Gap width	0.25-0.40 mm (.0098-.0157")	0.95 mm (.0374")
Piston weight		
- Weight (brown)	472-480 grams	
+ Weight (grey)	480-488 grams	
Weight difference of pistons of one engine	max. 4 grams	max. 10 grams*

*) In the event of repairs

CRANKCASE

Bore for crankshaft bearings		
a) Bearings 1-3 .... Dia.	70.00-70.02 mm dia. (2.7559-2.7567")	70.03 mm dia. (2.7571")
b) Bearing 4 .... Dia.	50.00-50.04 mm dia. (1.9685-1.9701")	50.04 mm dia. (1.9701")
Bore for sealing ring/flywheel end .... Dia.	95.00-95.05 mm dia (3.7402-3.7422")	
Bore for sealing ring/blower gear end .... Dia.	62.00-62.05 mm dia. (2.4409-2.4429")	
Bore for camshaft bearing .... Dia.	27.50-27.52 mm dia. (1.0827-1.0835")	
Bore for oil pump housing .... Dia.	70.00-70.03 mm dia. (2.7559-2.7571")	
Bore for tappet .... Dia.	24.00-24.02 mm dia. (.9449-.9457")	24.05 mm dia. (.9469")

CAMSHAFT

Bearings 1-3 .... Dia.	24.99-25.00 mm dia. (.9839-.9843")	
Measured on center bearing .... Out-of-true (1st and 3rd bearing point on V-blocks)	max. 0.02 mm (.008")	0.04 mm (.0016")
Camshaft/camshaft bearings (including bearing pressure through housing .... Radial play	0.02-0.05 mm (.0008-.0020")	0.12 mm (.0048")
Guide bearing .... Axial play	0.04-0.13 mm (.0016-.0051")	0.16 mm (.0063")
Camshaft gear .... Backlash	0.00-0.05 mm (.00-.0020")	
Tappet .... Dia.	23.96-23.98 mm dia (.9433-.9441")	23.93 mm dia. (.9421")
Housing bore/tappet .... Radial play	0.02-0.06 mm (.0008-.0024")	0.12 mm (.0047")
Push rod .... out-of true	max. 0.3 mm (.0118")	

CRANKSHAFT WITH CONNECTING RODS

3 Undersizes, with dia. reduced in 0.25 mm (.0098") steps

a) Bearings 1-3	Dia.	59.97-59.99 mm dia. (2.3610-2.3618")	
b) Bearing 4	Dia.	39.98-40.00 mm dia. (1.5740-1.5748")	
c) Connecting rod bearing	Dia.	54.98-55.00 mm dia. (2.1646-2.1654")	
Crankshaft on 2nd and 4th bearing point (1st and 3rd bearing point on V-blocks	Out-of true		0.02 mm (.008")
	Unbalance	max. 12 cmg	
Main bearing pin	Out-of-true		0.03 mm (.0012")
Conrod bearing pin	Out-of-true		0.03 mm (.0012")
Crankshaft/main bearing (including bearing pressure through housing)			
a) Bearings 1 and 3	Radial play	0.05-0.10 mm (.0020-.0039")	0.18 mm (.0071")
b) Bearing 2	Radial play	0.03-0.09 mm (.0012-.0035")	0.17 mm (.0067")
c) Bearing 4	Radial play	0.05-0.10 mm (.0020-.0039")	0.19 mm (.0075")
Crankshaft/main bearing 1	Axial play	0.07-0.13 mm (.0028-.0051")	0.15 mm (.0059")
Crank pin/conrod	Radial play	0.02-0.07 mm (.0008-.0029")	0.15 mm (.0059")
	Axial play	0.10-0.40 mm (.0039-.0157")	0.70 mm (.0276")
Conrod weight			
-Weight (white)		746-752 grams - 2000cc 783-786 grams	
+ Weight (black)		769-775 grams - 2000cc 791-794 grams	
Weight difference of conrods of one engine		max. 6 grams	
Piston pins	Dia.	23.996-24.000 mm dia. (.94472-.94488")	
Small end bushing	Dia.	24.015-24.024 mm dia. (.94547-.94582")	
Piston pin/small end bushing	Radial play	0.02-0.03 mm (.0008-.0012")	0.04 mm (.0016")
Fly wheel (measured in center of clutch area)	Lt. wobble	max. 0.4 mm (.0157")	
	Out-of-balance	max. 20 cmg	
Shoulder for sealing ring	OD	74.9-75.1 mm dia. (2.949-2.957")	74.4 mm dia. (2.929")
Refinishing of tooth width			max. 2 mm (.08")
Driven plate	Unbalance	max. 5 cmg	

CLUTCH

Total clutch pressure	Pressure	420-480 kg (926-1,058 lbs)	
Total clutch unbalance		max. 15 cmg	
Clutch pressure plate	Out-of-true		0.10 mm (.0039")
Clutch disc (measured at 210 mm dia. = 463")	Lat. wobble	max. 0.5 mm (.0197")	

TIGHTENING TORQUES

ENGINE ft. lb.
- Screws for universal shaft 32.5
- Nuts for transmission support 14.5
- Nuts for engine support (body) 21.7
- Screws for torque converter 21.7
- Nuts for engine attachment to transmission 21.7
- Spark plugs 25.3
- Nut for small pulley 43.4
- Screws for blower impeller 14.5
- Nuts for oil pump 14.5
- Oil drain plug 15.9
- Closing nut for oil strainer cover 9.4
- Nuts for rocker arm shaft 10.1
- Cylinder head nuts 23.1
- Screws for engine support (crankcase) 21.7
- Screw for blower wheel hub 23.1
- Screws for flywheel 79.6
- Screws for carrier plate 61.5
- Screws and nuts for crankcase halves 14.5
- Nuts for crankcase halves 23.9
- Conrod nuts 23.9
- Screws for clutch 14.5

BRAKES
- Tandem brake master cylinder on bulkhead nut ... 18
- Brake line to tandem master brake cylinder 11-14
- Bolt for clamp nut screw 11
- Hollow bolt on brake caliper 14
- Caliper on steering knuckle bolt 50
- Guard plate on steering knuckle bolt 18
- Bleed valve in caliper 1.5-2.5
- Wheel hub on brake disc nut .... (16.6)
- Housing bolt for front caliper 16
   (24.4-3.6)
- Caliper on rear axle steering arm bolt 50
- Brake disc on wheel hub bolt 3.6
- Guard plate on rear axle steering arm bolt 18
- Bleed valve in caliper 1.5-2.5
- Wheel on wheel hub bolt (25 mm), nut 108.5 (94)
- Wheel on wheel hub bolt (39 mm) 94

MANUAL TRANSMISSION ft.lb.
- Side and rear cover on transmission housing (studs) nut 16-18
- Fork piece on housing nut 15-17
- Guide tube for throwout bearing on housing nut . 7
- Transmission housing plug (oil filler hole) 15-18
- Transmission housing plug (oil drain hole) 15-18
- Transmission housing ball pin (bearing throwout fork) 15-17
- Transmission housing breather (breathing) 15-22
- Backup light switch on housing 25-29
- Holding plate on throwout fork screw 6-7
- Starter on transmission housing nut 33-35
- Clamping plate on intermediate plate screw 15-17
- Bolt for guide lever on intermediate plate 15-17
- Lock on intermediate plate screw (gear shift lock) 16-18
- Speedometer drive on rear housing cover bolt ... 12-13
- Miter drive in guide bushing screw 16-18
- Drive shaft nut 72-86
- Drive shaft nut 65-80
- Pinion shaft expansion bolt 80-87
- Shift forks on shift rods hex. screws (m 8 x 25) 18-19
- Ring gear on differential housing bolt 72-86
- Constant velocity flange on differential expansion bolt 25-29
- Shift rod bearings on rear nut transmission cover
  (914 only) 15-17
- Cover plate on rear transmission cover nut 6-7

19

TRANSMISSION – SPORTOMATIC

Hex. nuts on transmission housing M8	18.0
Hex. screw with trunnion (angle drive) M8	10.8
Closing screw on intermediate plate M12	21.7
Closing screw oil inlet M24	18.0
Magnetic plug oil drain M24	18.0
Hex. screws for intermediate plate clamping plate	18.0
Hex. nut on input shaft M24	80
Crown nut on input shaft M14	72
Expanding screw of pinion shaft M12	87
Hex. screws of shift forks M8	18.0
Hex. screws for ring gear attachment M 12	72
Expanding screws for universal flange of differential M10	25.3-18.9
Hex. nuts on converter housing and servo motor M 8	18.0
Hex. nuts on converter housing and starter M 10	32.5
Closing screw on front gearbox cover for parking lock M 12 x 1.5	34.0
Double hex. socket screws for clutch pressure plate M 6	10.8
Double hex. socket screws for freewheel support M 6	10.8
Double hex. screw for converter-drive plate M 8	17.4-18.8
Bridging switch M 18 x 1.5	25.3-28.9
Backup light switch M 18 x 1.5	25.3-28.9
Hollow screw of angle drive in guide bushing M 24 x 1.5	15.9-17.4

FRONT AXLE AND STEERING

	ft. lbs.
Fillister head bolt for clamp nut	11
Hollow bolt on caliper	14
Caliper on steering knuckle bolt	50
Wheel hub on brake disc nut	(17)
Guard plate on steering knuckle bolt	18
Shock absorber leg bottom on ball joint bolt	47
Shock absorber leg on supporting bearing nut	58
Supporting bearing on body socket	34.0
Protective clamp on body socket	32
Front wishbone bearing on body bolt	34
Ball joint on wishbone nut	108
Floor pan on body bolt	34
Floor pan on auxiliary support bolt	10.8
Auxiliary support on body bolt	65.1
Hub stud bolt, 25 mm	108
Hub stud bolt, 39 mm	94
Hub nut	(94)
Steering gear housing cover bolt	11
Steering gear housing filler bolt	11
Drive pinion coupling flange nut	34
Dust boot retainer for universal bushing nut	50
Fork on joint bushing bolt	34
Steering shaft on steering coupling bolt	18
Steering gear on auxiliary support bolt	34
Ball joint at tie rod end nut	32
Bottom universal joint on steering shaft lock nuts	18
Tie rod clamp nut	11
Steering wheel retaining nut	(54)
Steering and control switch components on body screw	7.2
Control switch components/steering post extension screw	7.2

REAR AXLE

Spring strut bottom nut on control arm	72-87
Spring strut top on body nut	36-43
Threaded bushing on piston rod	11-14
Castle nut on universal shaft	217-253
Synchronizing joint on universal flange screw	31
Control arm bearing on body bolt	50
Control arm bearing on control arm nut	108
Bearing cover on control arm bolt	18
Wheel bolt 914 bolt	108
Wheel nut 914/6 nut	94

914/6

2.0 MODELS

TECHNICAL

SPECIFICATIONS

DIMENSIONS

TOLERANCES

TORQUE SETTINGS

914/6 ENGINE SPECIFICATIONS 2.0L

	TOLERANCE (NEW)	WEAR LIMIT
GENERAL		
Number of cylinders	6	
Bore, inch (mm)	3.15 (80)	
Stroke, inch (mm)	2.60 (66)	
Displacement, cu. in. (cc)	121.5 (1991)	
Compression ratio	8.6	
Firing order	1-6-2-4-3-5	
Output (SAE) bhp @ rpm	125 @ 5800	
Torque (SAE) foot-pounds @ rpm	131 @ 4200	
CYLINDERS		
Bore, inch (mm)	See Table 3 (Chapter 5)	
Cylinder/piston clearance, inch (mm)	0.0021-0.0029 (0.055-0.075)	0.0007 (0.0180)
Out-of-round, inch (mm)		0.0008 (0.020)
PISTONS		
Material	light alloy	
Permissable weight deviation	3 grams	
Diameter	See Table 3 (Chapter 5)	
PISTON RINGS		
Number per piston		
Compression	2	
Oil control	1	
Ring end gap	0.0118-0.0177 (0.30-0.45)	0.394 (1.000)
Ring side clearance		
Top compression	0.0033-0.0037 (0.085-0.095)	0.0078 (0.20)
Bottom compression	0.0022-0.0024 (0.057-0.060)	0.0078 (0.20)
Oil control	0.0015-0.0016 (0.037-0.040)	0.0078 (0.20)
PISTON PINS		
Diameter	0.8659-0.8661 (21.994-22.000)	
Clearance in rod bushing, inch (mm)	0.0008-0.0015 (0.020-0.039)	0.0022 (0.055)

(continued)

914/6 ENGINE SPECIFICATIONS (continued)

	TOLERANCE (NEW)	WEAR LIMIT
CRANKSHAFT		
Number of main bearings	8	
Main bearing journal diameter		
Bearing journals 1-7	2.243-2.244 (56.971-56.990)	2.42 (56.960)
Bearing journal 8	1.219-1.220 (30.980-30.993)	1.218 (30.970)
Connecting rod journal diameter	2.243-2.244 (56.971-56.990)	2.242 (56.960)
Main bearing clearances		
Bearings 1-7	0.002-0.003 (0.049-0.069)	
Bearing 8	0.002-0.004 (0.061-0.091)	
End play	0.0043-0.0077 (0.110-0.195)	
CONNECTING RODS		
Weight deviation in same engine	9 grams	
Weight	551-659	
Side clearance	0.008-0.016 (0.200-0.400)	
Connecting rod bearing clearance	0.0012-0.0035 (0.030-0.088)	
Piston pin bushing inside diameter	0.8669-0.8674 (22.020-22.033)	
CAMSHAFT		
Number of camshafts	2	
Bearings per camshaft	3	
Journal diameter	1.8475-1.8481 (46.926-46.942)	
Bearing clearance	0.0010-0.0026 (0.025-0.066)	0.0039 (0.10)
End play	0.0059-0.0078 (0.150-0.200)	0.0157 (0.40)
Run-out		0.0008 (0.02)
VALVES — INTAKE		
Head diameter	1.654 (42)	
Stem diameter	0.3531 (8.97)	
Valve guide inside diameter	0.3543-0.3549 (9.000-9.015)	
Valve face angle	45°	
Valve seat angle	45°	
Valve seat width	0.0492±0.0059 (1.25±0.15)	
VALVES — EXHAUST		
Head diameter	1.496 (38)	
Stem diameter	0.3524 (8.95)	
Valve guide inside diameter	0.3519-0.3524 (8.938-8.950)	
Valve face angle	45°	
Valve seat angle	45°	
Valve seat width	0.0610±0.0059 (1.55±0.15)	
VALVE SPRINGS		
Installed length, intake	1.480±0.012 (63±0.3)	
Installed length, exhaust	1.480±0.012 (63±0.3)	

914/6 GENERAL SPECIFICATIONS

GENERAL DATA
Length	156.9 in.
Width	65.0 in.
Height	48.8 in.
Wheel base	96.5 in. (2450 mm)
Track width .... front	53.3 in (1352 mm)
rear	54.3 in. (1379 mm)
Minimum turning diameter	36 ft.
Front axle load @ perm. total load	1,433 lbs.
Tire size .... standard	16 HR 15
optional	185 HR 14
Rim size .... standard	5½J x 15
optional	5½J x 14
Weight .... empty	2072 lbs.
full, maximum	2778 lbs.
Speed maximum	122.5 mph @ 5650 rpm

CAPACITIES
Engine oil	9 liters (9½ qts.)
Gearbox and final drive	2.5 liters (5.3 pts.)
Torque converter	From engine oil circuit
Steering	25 grams
Brakes	3/4 pints
Windshield washer	6 pints
Fuel tank	16½ gallons

ENGINE
Number of cylinders	6
Cylinder arrangement	Horizontal, 3 cylinders each opposed (flat six)
Bore	80 mm dia. (3.15")
Stroke	66 mm (2.598")
Total piston displacement	1.991 cc (121.4 cu. in.)
Compression ratio	8.6:1
Performance ....SAE	125 HP at 5,800 rpm
Max. torque ....SAE	131 ft/lb
Max. rpm	6500

CARBURETOR
Type	Weber 40 IDT P1 36
Venturi dia.	27 mm
Preatomizer	4.5
Main jet	105
Air correction jet	170
Mixing tube	F1
Idle jet	45
Pump jet	50
Idle air jet	145
Pump suction valve	Closed
Float needle valve	1.75
Pump valve	Closed
Mixture outlet	5 mm (.97 in.)
Idle mixture outlet	1.0 mm (.039 in.)
Bypass holes	1 = 0.70 mm (.028 in.)
	2 = 1.30 mm (.051 in.)
	3 = 1.20 mm (.047 in.)
Fuel level	20.75 ± 1 mm (.81 ± .03 in.) from upper edge of housing
Float level adjustment	12.5 - 13.0 mm (.49 - .51 in.) from upper edge of float to upper edge of carburetor housing, without gasket.
CO level	4.0 ± 0.5% @ idle 900-950 rpm

IGNITION .... Heavy-duty battery ignition
   Ignition oil .... Bosch
   Ignition distributor .... to 4/70   Marelli S 112 BX
                                     from 4/70   Bosch 0 231 159 008 JFDR6 (R)
   Timing .... 35° BTDC at 6,000 rpm
   Firing order .... 1 - 6 - 2 - 4 - 3 - 5
   Ignition timing .... By centrifugal governor
   Dwell, point gap .... 40° ± 3° or 0.4 mm (.016")
   Spark plugs .... Beru 240/14/3, Bosch W 230 T 30
   Electrode gap .... 0.6 mm (.024 in.)

COOLING .... Air-cooled by axial blower on alternator
   Blower drive .... from crankshaft by V-belt transmission ration 1:1.3
   Delivered air volume .... 1.050 lits/sec. (277 US gal/sec) at 5,800 rpm

LUBRICATION .... Dry sump forced circulation
   Oil cooling .... Oil cooler on crankcase in blower air stream
   Oil filter .... in main stream
   Oil pressure indication .... Pilot lamp in combination instrument
   Oil capacity with filter .... 9 lits (2.4 US gal)
   Sportomatic .... Uses engine oil
   Oil consumption .... 1 liter/1,000 km (0.26 US gal/6,200 miles)

CYLINDER HEAD .... One each per cylinder with cast-on cooling ribs, aluminum alloy (Y-alloy)
   Valve seat ring .... Shrunk-in, alloyed grey casting
   Valve guide .... Shrunk-in, of special brass
   Spark plug threads .... Cut into cylinder head

VALVES .... 1 Intake and 1 exhaust valve per cylinder
   Exhaust valve .... Sodium-filled with hard-faced seat
   Arrangement .... Overhead in V-shape
   Valve clearance .... Intake & exhaust   0.10 mm (.004") with cold engine
   Valve springs .... 2 coil springs per valve
   Compression .... 128 - 156 psi @ cranking speed
                                                  Cable plug on switchgear removed.
   Intake valve head dia. .... 42.0 mm (1.654")
   Exhaust valve head dia. .... 38.0 mm (1.496")
   Timing adjustment .... Lift of intake valve at top center on valve overlap stroke = 2.3 - 2.7 mm (0.091 - 0.106 in.)

   Valve timing with 1 mm (.039") ....
                                  Intake opens   15° BTDC   Intake closes   29° ABDC
                                Exhaust opens   41° BBDC   Exhaust closes   5° BTDC

CYLINDERS .... Single cylinders, special grey casting with cooling ribs

PISTONS .... Light metal alloy with steel inserts
   Piston pins .... Floating, secured by circlips
   Piston rings .... 2 compression rings, 1 oil ring

CRANKCASE .... Split, with vertical center division by crankshaft and camshaft bearing

CAMSHAFT .... Grey casting, 3 plain bearings directly in camshaft housing
   Camshaft drive .... Chain drive
   Cam lift .... intake   1.4217 in.
                            exhaust   1.398 in.

CRANKSHAFT .... Forged
   Crankshaft bearings .... 8 Plain bearings
   Main bearings 1 - 7 .... Split, half shells, three-component bearings
   Main bearing 1 .... Guide bearing
   Main bearing 8 .... Aluminum bushing with hard lead running surface

CONNECTING RODS . . . . Forged, with I-shaped shank cross section

CONROD BEARINGS . . . . Split, half shells, three component bearings
    Piston pin bearings . . . . pressed-in bronze bushing

CLUTCH
    Type . . . . Single-plate dry clutch M 215 K - Fichtel a. Sachs
    Total contact area . . . . 203 sq. cm (31.5 sq. in.)

BRAKES
    Tandem main brake cylinder
    Bore . . . . 19.05 mm dia. (.7500")
    Stroke . . . . 18/13 mm (.7/.5")
    Reduction on brake foot lever 5.4:1
    Play: actuating rod/Piston . . . . 1 mm (.04")

    Front wheel brake
    Brake disk (dia.) . . . . 282.5 mm (11.122")
    Thickness, new . . . . 20 mm (.787")
    Min. thickness after refinishing . . . . 18.6 mm (.732")
    Wear limit . . . . 18.0 mm (.709")
    Thickness tolerance . . . . Max. 0.02 mm (.008")
    Lateral wobble, maximum . . . . 0.2 mm (.008")
    Caliper piston dia. . . . . 48 mm (1.9")
    Thickness of lining . . . . new 10 mm (.4")
                                                   minimum 2 mm (.08")
    Release clearance . . . . 0.05 - 0.2 mm (.0020 - .0079")
    Lining surface of four linings . . . . 106 cm^2 (16.4 sq. in.)

    Rear wheel brake
    Brake disk (OD) . . . . 286 mm (11.260")
    Thickness, new . . . . 105. mm (.591")
    Min. thickness after refinishing . . . . 9.5 mm (.374")
    Lateral wobble, maximum . . . . 0.2 mm (.008")
    Caliper piston dia. . . . . 38 mm (1.5")
    Thickness of lining . . . . new 10 mm (.4")
                                                   minimum 2 mm (.08")
    Release clearance . . . . 0.2 mm (.008")
    Lining surface of four linings . . . . 106 cm^2 (16.4 sq. in.)

STEERING
    Total reduction 17.78
    Turns, lock to lock . . . . 3.1 approx.
    Total functional torque, steering
       assembled . . . . 6 - 8 cmkp

SUSPENSION
    Front wheels
    Total toe-in under pressure . . . . +20' ± 10'
    Force . . . . 33 lbs.
    Camber . . . . 0° ± 20'
    Caster . . . . 6° ± 30'
    Height adjustment, wheel center
       above torsion bar center - rear . . . . 3.5 ± .2"
    Height difference, left to right . . . . .2"

    Rear wheels
    Total toe-in . . . . 0° + 15' (per wheel)
    Camber . . . . −30 ± 20'

    Torsion bar, length . . . . 24.075 in.
                                                        dia. 0.705 in.
                                                        teeth 30

Coil spring, free length . . . . 17.0 in.
                                                      dia. 3.7 in.
                                                Wire dia. 0.394 in.
                                           number of coils 11½
                                     number of active coils 10

ELECTRICAL
Alternator, Type . . . . Bosch K1 – 3 phase, 55 amp/770 watt

Battery, voltage . . . . 12 v – rating 45 A/hr

Regulator type . . . . Bosch ADN

Starter type . . . . Bosch 033 911 023A

5-SPEED TRANSMISSION
Type . . . . Porsche servo-lock synchronization
Gear ratios . . . . , 1 – 3.09:1
                                                                           2 – 1.78:1
                                                                           3 – 1.22:1
                                                                           4 – 0.93:1
                                                                           5 – 0.76:1
                                                                           Reverse – 3.13:1
Final drive ratio 4.429:1
Rear axle type . . . . Double joint half axles

TOLERANCE (NEW) AND WEAR LIMITS

CYLINDERS

Cylinder/piston clearance, inch (mm)	0.0021-0.0029 (0.055-0.075)	0.0007 (0.0180)
Out-of-round, inch (mm)		0.0008 (0.020)

PISTONS

Permissable weight deviation	3 grams

PISTON RINGS

Number per piston – Compression	2	
– Oil control	1	
Ring end gap	0.0118-0.0177 (0.30-0.45)	0.394 (1.000)
Ring side clearance		
Top compression	0.0033-0.0037 (0.085-0.095)	0.0078 (0.20)
Bottom compression	0.0022-0.0024 (0.057-0.060)	0.0078 (0.20)
Oil control	0.0015-0.0016 (0.037-0.040)	0.0078 (0.20)

PISTON PINS

Diameter	0.8659-0.8661 (21.994-22.000)	
Clearance in rod bushing, inch (mm)	0.0008-0.0015 (0.020-0.039)	0.0022 (0.055)

CRANKSHAFT

Main bearing journal diameter		
Bearing journals 1-7	2.243-2.244 (56.971-56.990)	2.42 (56.960)
Bearing journal 8	1.219-1.220 (30.980-30.993)	1.218 (30.970)
Connecting rod journal diameter	2.243-2.244 (56.971-56.990)	2.242 (56.960)
Main bearing clearances		
Bearings 1-7	0.002-0.003 (0.049-0.069)	
Bearing 8	0.002-0.004 (0.061-0.091)	
End play	0.0043-0.0077 (0.110-0.195)	

CONNECTING RODS
    Weight deviation in same engine   9 grams
    Weight   551-659
    Side clearance   0.008-0.016 (0.200-0.400)
    Connecting rod bearing clearance   0.0012-0.0035 (0.030-0.088)
    Piston pin bushing inside diameter   0.8669-0.8674 (22.020-22.033)

CAMSHAFT
    Number of camshafts   2
    Bearings per camshaft   3
    Journal diameter   1.8475-1.8481 (46.926-46.942)
    Bearing clearance   0.0010-0.0026 (0.025-0.066)   0.0039 (0.10)
    End play   0.0059-0.0078 (0.150-0.200)   0.0157 (0.40)
    Run-out   0.0008 (0.02)

VALVES — INTAKE
    Head diameter   1.654 (42)
    Stem diameter   0.3531 (8.97)
    Valve guide inside diameter   0.3543-0.3549 (9.000-9.015)
    Valve face angle   45°
    Valve seat angle   45°
    Valve seat width   0.0492±0.0059 (1.25±0.15)

VALVES — EXHAUST
    Head diameter   1.496 (38)
    Stem diameter   0.3524 (8.95)
    Valve guide inside diameter   0.3519-0.3524 (8.938-8.950)
    Valve face angle   45°
    Valve seat angle   45°
    Valve seat width   0.0610±0.0059 (1.55±0.15)

VALVE SPRINGS
    Installed length, intake   1.480±0.012 (63±0.3)
    Installed length, exhaust   1.480±0.012 (63±0.3)

TIGHTENING TORQUES

ENGINE   ft./lb.
    Screw bolts crankshaft half .... 15.9 - 18.1)
        Bearing points 25.3
    Connecting rod bolts 36.2
    Cylinder head .... 21.7 - 23.9
    Camshaft housing on cylinder heads 15.9
    Nut on camshaft 72.3
    Rocker arm shafts 13.0
    Flywheel attachment 108.5
    V-belt pulley on crankshaft 57.9
    V-belt pulley on alternator 28.9

MANUAL TRANSMISSION   ft.lb.
    Side and rear cover on transmission housing (studs) nut 16-18
    Fork piece on housing nut 15-17
    Guide tube for throwout bearing on housing nut 7
    Transmission housing plug (oil filler hole) 15-18
    Transmission housing plug (oil drain hole) 15-18
    Transmission housing ball pin (bearing throwout fork) 15-17
    Transmission housing breather (breathing) 15-22
    Backup light switch on housing 25-29
    Holding plate on throwout fork screw 6-7

Starter on transmission housing nut	33-35
Clamping plate on intermediate plate screw	15-17
Bolt for guide lever on intermediate plate	15-17
Lock on intermediate plate screw (gear shift lock)	16-18
Speedometer drive on rear housing cover bolt	12-13
Miter drive in guide bushing screw	16-18
Drive shaft nut	72-86
Drive shaft nut	65-80
Pinion shaft expansion bolt	80-87
Shift forks on shift rods hex. screws (m 8 x 25)	18-19
Ring gear on differential housing bolt	72-86
Constant velocity flange on differential expansion bolt	25-29
Shift rod bearings on rear nut transmission cover (914 only)	15-17
Cover plate on rear transmission cover nut	6-7

FRONT AXLE AND STEERING

	ft. lbs.
Fillister head bolt for clamp nut	11
Hollow bolt on caliper	14
Caliper on steering knuckle bolt	50
Wheel hub on brake disc nut	(17)
Guard plate on steering knuckle bolt	18
Shock absorber leg bottom on ball joint bolt	47
Shock absorber leg on supporting bearing nut	58
Supporting bearing on body socket	34.0
Protective clamp on body socket	32
Front wishbone bearing on body bolt	34
Ball joint on wishbone nut	108
Floor pan on body bolt	34
Floor pan on auxiliary support bolt	10.8
Auxiliary support on body bolt	65.1
Hub stud bolt, 25 mm	108
Wheel hub to brake disc	16.6
Hub nut	94
Steering gear housing cover bolt	11
Steering gear housing filler bolt	11
Drive pinion coupling flange nut	34
Dust boot retainer for universal bushing nut	50
Fork on joint bushing bolt	34
Steering shaft on steering coupling bolt	18
Steering gear on auxiliary support bolt	34
Ball joint at tie rod end nut	32
Bottom universal joint on steering shaft lock nuts	18
Tie rod clamp nut	11
Steering wheel retaining nut	54
Steering and control switch components on body screw	7.2
Control switch components/steering post extension screw	7.2

REAR AXLE

Spring strut bottom nut on control arm	72-87
Spring strut top on body nut	36-43
Threaded bushing on piston rod	11-14
Castle nut on universal shaft	217-253
Synchronizing joint on universal flange screw	31
Control arm bearing on body bolt	50
Control arm bearing on control arm nut	108
Bearing cover on control arm bolt	18
Wheel bolt 914 bolt	108
Wheel nut 914/6 nut	94

(continued)

BRAKES

Tandem brake master cylinder on bulkhead nut	18
Brake line to tandem master brake cylinder	11-14
Bolt for clamp nut screw	11
Hollow bolt on brake caliper	14
Caliper on steering knuckle bolt	50
Guard plate on steering knuckle bolt	18
Bleed valve in caliper	1.5-2.5
Wheel hub on brake disc nut	16.6
Housing bolt for front caliper	25
Caliper on rear axle steering arm bolt	50
Brake disc on wheel hub bolt	3.6
Guard plate on rear axle steering arm bolt	18
Bleed valve in caliper	1.5-2.5
Wheel on wheel hub bolt (25 mm) screw	**108.5**
Wheel on wheel hub bolt (39 mm)	**94**

NOTES

CHAPTER TWO

LUBRICATION AND MAINTENANCE

To ensure good performance, dependability and safety, regular preventive maintenance is necessary. This chapter outlines periodic lubrication and maintenance for a car driven by an average owner. One driven more than average will require more frequent attention, but even without use, rust, dirt, and corrosion cause unnecessary damage. Whether performed by the owner or a Porsche dealer, regular routine attention helps avoid expensive repairs.

The recommended schedule in this chapter includes routine checks which are easily performed at each fuel stop, periodic checks to be performed at each oil change, and periodic maintenance to prevent future trouble. The last part of this chapter suggests a systematic engine tune-up procedure which simplifies this important task. **Table 1** summarizes all periodic maintenance required in an easy-to-use form.

ROUTINE CHECKS

The following simple checks should be performed at each fueling stop.

1. Check engine oil. Oil should be checked with the engine warm and the car on level ground. The 914/6 engine must be idling. See **Figure 1** (914) or **Figure 2** (914/6). Level should be between the 2 marks on the dipstick; never below and never above. Top up if necessary.

2. Check battery electrolyte level. It should be even with the top of the vertical separators. Top up with distilled water.

Table 1　LUBRICATION AND MAINTENANCE SUMMARY

Interval	Item	Check Fluid Level	Replace	Lube	Inspect and/or Clean	Check and/or Adjust
Fuel stop	Engine oil	X				
	Battery electrolyte	X				
	Brake fluid	X				
	Fan belt tension					X
	Windshield washer	X				
	Tire pressure					X
3,000 miles	Engine oil		X			
	Air cleaner		X			
	Hinges & locks			X		
6,000 miles	Transaxle oil		X			
	Wheel bearings					X
	Front suspension			X		
	Engine oil filter		X			
	Distributor			X		
	Carburetor			X		
	Breaker points				X	X
	Spark plugs				X	X
	Ball-joint seals				X	
	Brake linings				X	
	Fuel filter				X	
	Valve clearance					X
	Compression					X
	Engine compartment				X	
	Exhaust system				X	
	Ball-joint play					X
	Front-end alignment					X
	Tires and wheels				X	
12,000 miles	Spark plugs		X			X
	Breaker points		X			X
	Crankcase ventilation system				X	
30,000 miles	Transmission oil		X			

3. Check that brake fluid level is at the top mark. See **Figure 3**. Use brake fluid clearly marked SAE 7OR3, SAE J1703 (which supersedes 7OR3), DOT 3, or DOT 4 only.

4. Check fan belt tension and condition. Tension is correct when the belt can be depressed ½ to ¾" (10-15mm) under slight thumb pressure.

5. Check tire pressure when tires are cold. Front tire pressure should be 26 psi; rear tire pressure, 29 psi. For speeds over 125 mph (200 kmh), increase pressures by 5 psi.

6. Check windshield washer container level. See **Figure 4**. The container holds about 2 quarts.

PERIODIC CHECKS

These checks are performed less frequently than routine checks. Recommended intervals

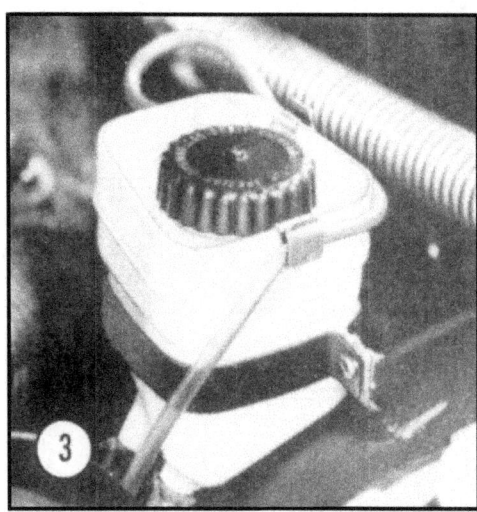

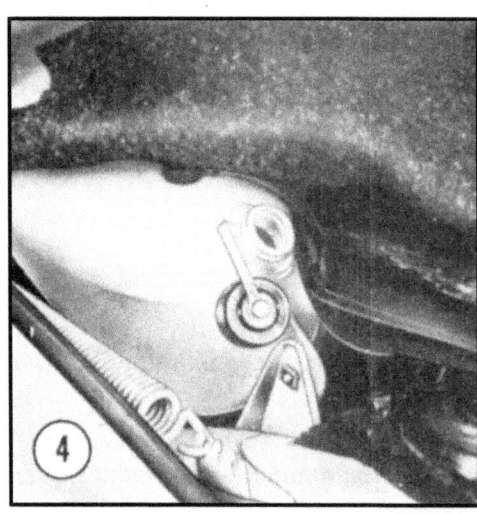

> **WARNING**
> *Do not use the tire jack when working under the car. Use only jackstands made specifically for this purpose.*

Cooling Fan Belt

Since cooling fan belt tension and condition affect engine cooling, it is important to check it frequently. When correct, the belt should deflect about ½-¾″ (10-15mm) under light thumb pressure. Check condition of the belt also; if worn or cracked, replace it.

To adjust or replace a belt on 914 engines, remove plastic insert in cover plate over alternator. Loosen Allen head and hex head bolts shown in **Figure 5**. If installing a new belt, move the alternator as far to the left as possible and slip the old belt off the pulleys. Install a new belt and tighten by moving alternator to the right.

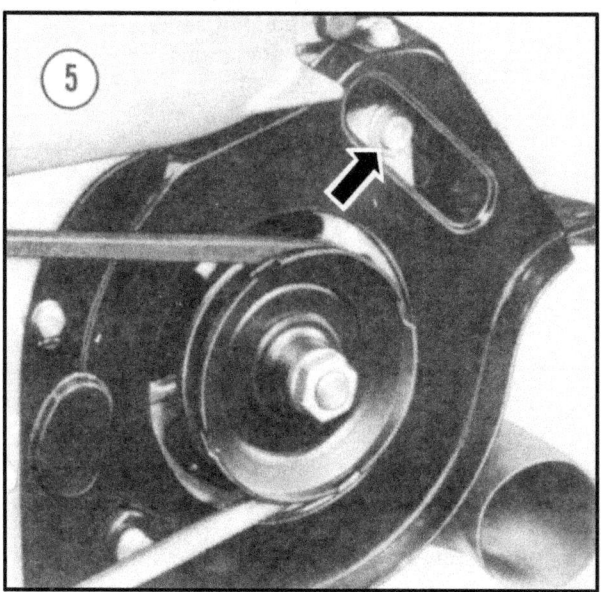

Belt tension is adjusted by pushing the alternator to the right until the belt can be deflected as described earlier. Tighten the bolts in this position.

To adjust or replace a belt on the 914/6 engine, hold the alternator pulley with the tool provided in the tool kit. See **Figure 6**. Remove pulley nut and defective belt. Install a new belt.

Adjust belt tension by varying the number of shims between pulley halves. Decreasing the

are discussed below and are summarized in Table 1. Many require that the automobile be on a hoist or jackstands.

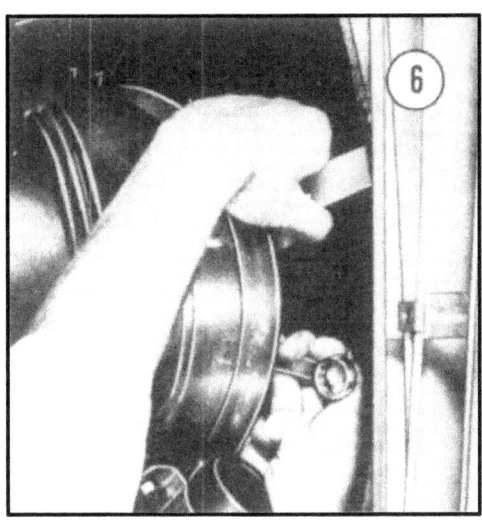

number tightens the belt; increasing the number loosens the belt. Store extra shims on the outer side of the pulley, under the concave washer. See **Figure 7**.

Compression Check

Every **6,000** miles, check cylinder compression. Record the results and compare them with the next 6,000 mile check. A running record will show trends in general deterioration so that corrective action can be taken before complete failure.

Engine Compartment Check

Every **6,000** miles, check entire engine compartment for leaking or deteriorated oil and fuel lines. Check wiring for breaks in insulation caused by deterioration or chafe. Check for loose or missing nuts, bolts, and screws.

Exhaust Emission Control Check

After every tune-up (see later section), check carbon monoxide (CO) content of exhaust gas. Use a good quality exhaust gas analyzer, following the manufacturer's instructions. With engine idling, CO content should be within the values shown in **Table 2**.

Table 2 EXHAUST EMISSION LEVELS

Year	(CO) Carbon Monoxide	(PPM) Hydrocarbons
1970-71	1.5-3%	400 maximum
1972-73	0.7% (914) 1.5% (914S)	400 maximum
1974-76	2.5%	400 maximum

Steering and Suspension

Every **6,000** miles, check entire steering and suspension systems. Check ball-joint and tie rod end dust seals. Check tie rods for tightness and damage. Check tire wear which may indicate damaged or worn suspension parts. Check shock absorbers for oil streaks indicating leaks; replace if necessary.

Jack up the front wheels. Move front wheels by hand; steering wheel should turn as soon as wheel turns; there should be no free-play. If free-play is present, adjust rack-and-pinion steering as described in Chapter Thirteen.

Wheel Bearings

Every **6,000** miles, check wheel bearing adjustment. See Chapter Thirteen.

Brakes

Every **6,000** miles, check brake pad thickness. The thickness shown in **Figure 8** should be at least 0.08" (2mm). If less, replace all 4 front or rear pads to keep brakes balanced. Never replace pads on one wheel only. Check handbrake and adjust if necessary; see Chapter Fourteen.

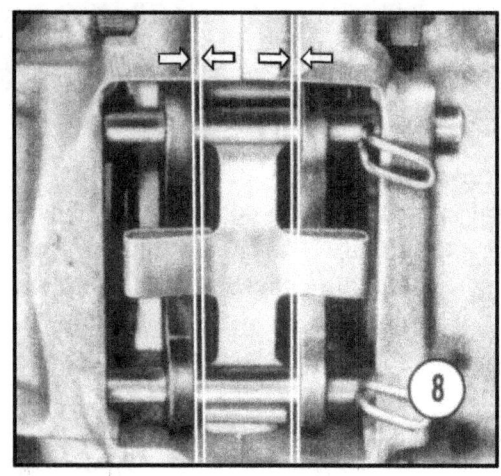

Windshield Wiper Blades

Long exposure to weather and road film hardens the rubber wiper blades and destroys their effectiveness. When blades smear or otherwise fail to clean the windshield, they should be replaced.

Tire and Wheel Inspection

Every **6,000** miles, check the condition of all tires. Check local traffic regulations concerning minimum tread depths. Most recommend replacing tires with tread less than 1/32" deep. Check lug nuts for tightness.

PERIODIC MAINTENANCE

Engine Oil Change

The oil change interval varies depending on the type of driving you do. For normal driving including some city traffic, change oil every **3,000** miles in a 914 and every **6,000** miles in a 914/6. If driving is primarily short distance with considerable stop-and-go city traffic, change oil more often, possibly even twice as often. Change oil at least twice a year if the car is driven only a few hundred miles a month.

Any oil used must be rated "FOR SERVICE MS" or with one of the newer designations, "FOR API SERVICE SD or SE." Non-detergent oils are *not recommended*. See **Table 3** for recommended oil grades.

To drain oil:

1. Warm engine to operating temperature.
2a. Remove drain plug from crankcase of 914 engine. See **Figure 9**.

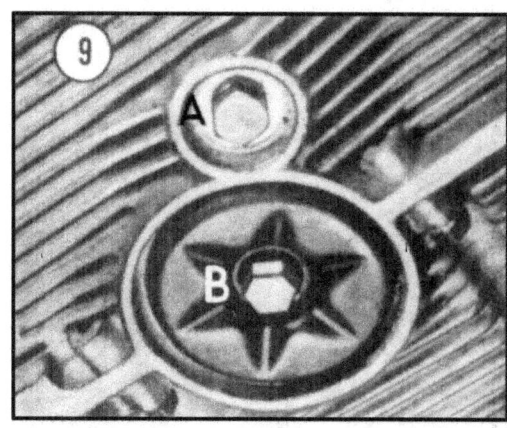

2b. On 914/6 engine, remove drain plug from center of oil strainer and disconnect oil line between oil tank and engine. See **Figures 10 and 11**.

Table 3 RECOMMENDED LUBRICANTS AND FUEL

	Temperature Range	Recommended Type	Capacity
Engine oil	Below 5°F (—15°C)	SAE 10W, 10W-30	3.2 qt. (3.0 liters)[1]
	5°F to 32°F (—15°C to 0°C)	SAE 20W-20, 10W-30	3.7 qt. (3.5 liters)[2]
	32°F (0°C) and above	SAE 30W, 10W-30	9.5 qt. (9.0 liters)[3]
Transaxle	All temperatures	SAE 90 hypoid gear oil[4]	2.6 qt. (2.5 liters)
		SAE 90 (MIL-L-2105B)[5]	3.17 qt. (3.0 liters)
Fuel	Non-applicable	98 octane[6]	16.4 gal. (62 liters)
		91 octane[7]	

1. 914/4 without filter change
2. 914/4 with filter change
3. 914/6 with filter change
4. Without limited slip differential
5. With limited slip differential
6. 1970 - 1971 cars
7. 1972 - 1976 cars

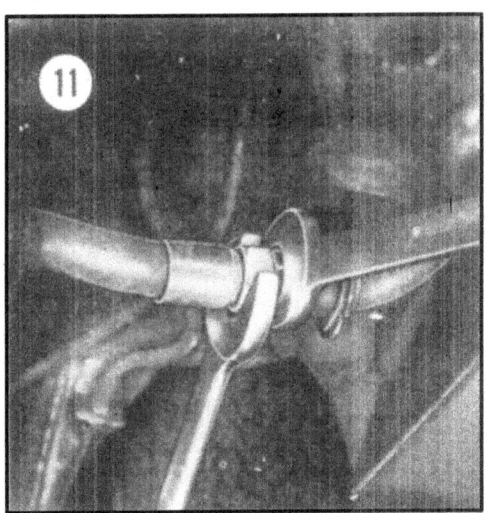

6. Change oil filter (**6,000**-mile intervals). See procedure below.

7. Remove oil filler cap. Refill with quantity specified in Table 3. See **Figure 12**. Refill the 914/6 with 9.5 U.S. pints (9 liters).

8. Check level on dipstick. See **Figure 13**.

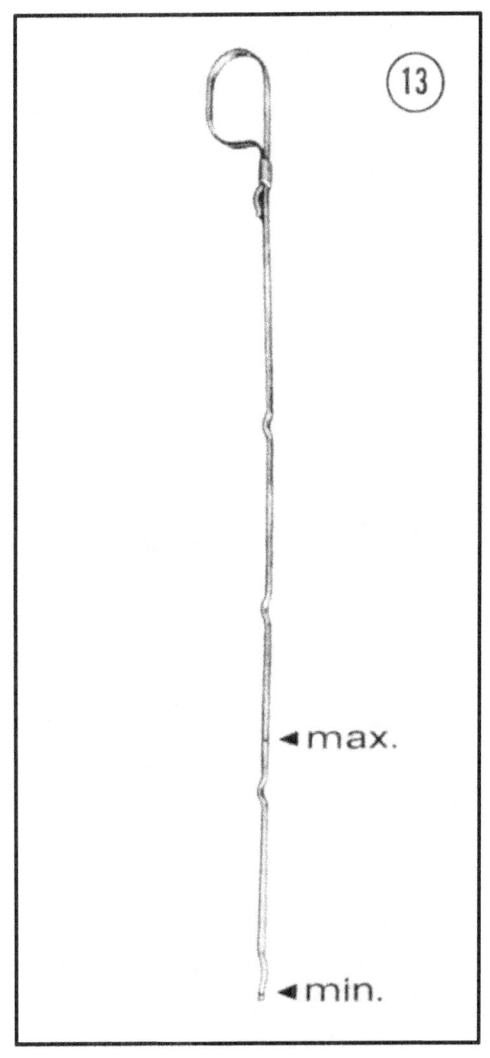

3. Let oil drain for at least 10 minutes.

4. Remove oil strainer and clean as described in Chapter Four (914) or Five (914/6). Install clean oil strainer with new gaskets.

5. Install the oil drain plug and reconnect the oil line (914/6).

Engine Oil Filter

Every **6,000** miles, replace the oil filter. This should be done after oil is drained and before new oil is poured in. All 914 models have a full flow spin-off filter. The 914 oil filter is mounted on the right front corner of the crankcase. The 914/6 oil filter is mounted on the oil tank in the engine compartment. See **Figure 14**.

To remove either filter, unscrew it by hand or use a filter wrench. See **Figure 15**. Wipe the gasket area of the base with a clean lint-free cloth. Coat the neoprene gasket on the new filter with clean oil. Screw the filter on by hand until the gasket just touches the base. Then tighten a half-turn by hand; do not use a filter wrench.

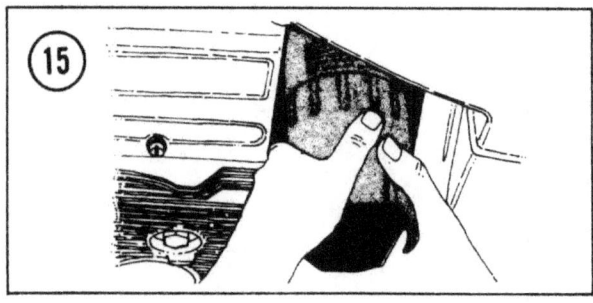

After adding engine oil, start the engine and check for leaks. Also check the oil level and adjust if necessary.

Air Cleaner

The 1970-1972 914 engine has an oil bath air cleaner. Later 914 and 914/6 engines have a disposable paper cartridge air cleaner. Air cleaners on 1970-1972 models should be serviced every **6,000** miles, later models every **12,000** miles.

To clean a 914 oil bath air cleaner, remove air cleaner and drain old oil. Clean thoroughly with solvent. Refill with same type oil used in the engine and install on engine.

Distributor Lubrication

Every **6,000** miles, apply a thin coat of high temperature grease to contact surfaces of breaker cam.

CAUTION
Do not get any grease on the breaker points. Dirty points pit and burn very rapidly.

Transaxle Oil Change

Change transaxle oil every **12,000** miles. Transaxle oil must be at normal operating temperature before draining. Remove drain plug from bottom of transaxle and let oil drain for at least 10-15 minutes. Clean and install drain plug. Wipe dirt away from filler plug and remove it. Fill transaxle slowly with 2½ U.S. quarts (approximately) of a lubricant specified in Table 3. It is good practice to fill with 2 or 3 pints, wait several minutes, then add the rest. Oil level should reach to the bottom of the oil filler hole.

CAUTION
Do not overfill. Before installing plug, let any excess drain out. Excess oil can damage seals.

The Sportomatic torque converter shares engine oil and need not be changed separately.

Clutch

Every **6,000** miles, check the clutch pedal free-play on manual shift cars. Depress the pedal by hand. Free-play should be 13/16-1 inch (20-25mm).

On Sportomatics, check clutch adjustment and gearshift switch adjustment as described in Chapter Eleven.

Exhaust System

Every **6,000** miles, examine the muffler, tailpipe(s), and heat exchangers for rust, holes, and other damage. Replace any damaged parts.

Carburetors (914/6 Only)

Every **6,000** miles, lubricate the carburetor controls and linkages. Use 1-2 drops of engine oil at all pivot points. Do not use too much oil; excessive oil attracts dirt which can cause dangerous throttle sticking. Disconnect and lubricate each ball-joint. Porsche recommends high temperature grease, but many mechanics prefer graphite powder to prevent possibility of throttle sticking.

Crankcase Ventilation System

Every **12,000** miles, clean the flame arrester in the air cleaner. To do this, disconnect the oil breather line and pull the flame arrester out. See **Figure 16**.

ENGINE TUNE-UP

In order to maintain a car in proper running condition, the engine must receive periodic tune-ups. Procedures outlined here are performed every **6,000** miles. However, every **12,000** miles, spark plugs and breaker points should be replaced, not merely cleaned.

Since different systems in an engine interact to affect overall performance, tune-up must be accomplished in the following order:

1. Valve clearance adjustment
2. Ignition adjustment and timing
3. Fuel system adjustment

Valve Clearance

This is a series of simple mechanical adjustments which are performed while the engine is *cold*. Valve clearance for your engine must be carefully determined. If the clearance is too small, the valves may be burned or distorted. Large clearance results in excessive noise. In either case, engine power is reduced.

Before adjusting valves, remove both rocker arm covers and all spark plugs. This makes the engine much easier to turn by hand; and plugs require cleaning or replacement at this time anyway.

Adjust all valves in the 914/6 to 0.004 in. (0.1mm) in the following order: 1-6-2-4-3-5. To begin, turn engine over until rotor points to notch on distributor housing and "Z1" mark on crankshaft pulley aligns with the blower housing notch. See **Figure 17**. This indicates cylinder No. 1 is at TDC on its compression stroke.

Adjust valve clearance for cylinder No. 1 valves; this is the left rear cylinder. See **Figure 18**. Loosen the locknut on the adjusting screw, insert a feeler gauge, and adjust until a slight drag is felt on the gauge. See **Figure 19**. Tighten locknut and recheck clearance to be sure it has not changed.

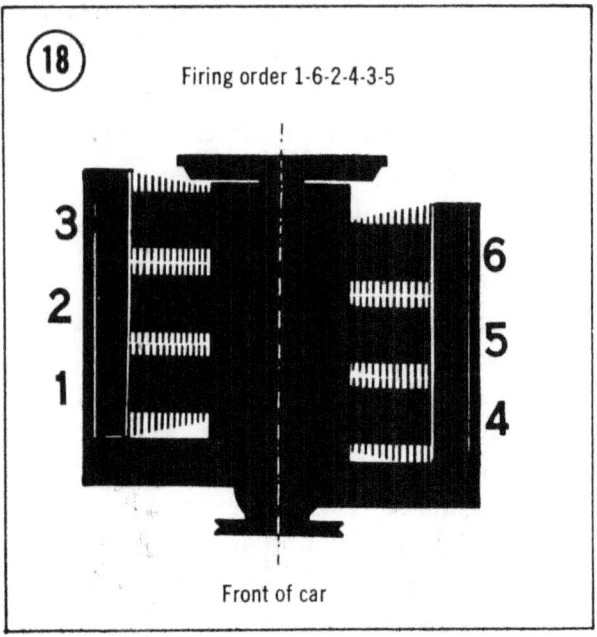

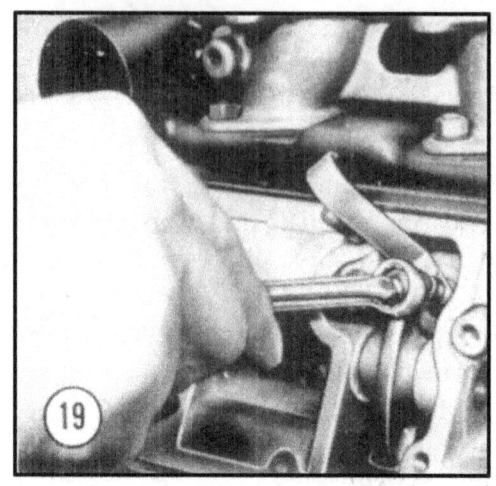

Rotate crankshaft pulley 120° clockwise until the next pulley mark aligns with the housing notch. Adjust valves for cylinder No. 6. Rotate pulley to next notch (120°) and adjust valves for cylinder No. 2. Repeat this procedure for cylinders 4, 3, and 5, each time turning pulley 120°.

When finished, install the rocker arm covers with new gaskets.

Adjust valves in the 914 in the following order: 1-2-3-4. Refer to **Table 4** for proper clearances.

Before adjusting valves in the 914, rotate the crankshaft until the distributor rotor moves counterclockwise *exactly* 90° from the notch on the distributor housing. See **Figure 20**. Examine the crankshaft pulley. There may be a paint mark exactly 180° from the TDC timing mark (OT). If not, make one.

To adjust the valves, turn the engine over so that piston No. 1 is at TDC on its compression stroke. This is evident when the timing mark on the pulley aligns with the timing pointer and the rotor points to the notch on the distributor. See **Figure 21**.

Table 4 TUNE-UP SPECIFICATIONS

	1700	1800	2000/4	2000/6
Valve Clearance[1]				
Intake in. (mm)	0.004 (0.1)	0.006 (0.15)	0.006 (0.15)	0.004 (0.1)
Exhaust in. (mm)	0.004 (0.1)	0.006 (0.15)	0.008 (0.20)	0.004 (0.1)
Ignition Timing[2]	27° BTDC	7.5° BTDC	27° BTDC	35° BTDC
	@ 3,500 rpm	@ 850 rpm	@ 3,500 rpm	@ 6,000 rpm
Spark Plugs				
Type	Bosch W175 T2	Bosch W175 T2	Bosch W175 T2	Bosch W230 T30
Gap in. (mm)	0.028 (0.7)	0.028 (0.7)	0.028 (0.7)	0.024 (0.55)
Breaker Gap in. (mm)	0.016 (0.4)	0.016 (0.4)	0.016 (0.4)	0.016 (0.4)
Dwell Angle	47 ± 3	47 ± 3	47 ± 3	40 ± 3
Firing Order	1-4-3-2	1-4-3-2	1-4-3-2	1-6-2-4-3-5
Idle Speed[3] (rpm)	850 - 900	850 - 900	850 - 900	900 - 950

1. Cold engine   2. Vacuum line(s) disconnected   3. Add 100 rpm for Sportomatic models

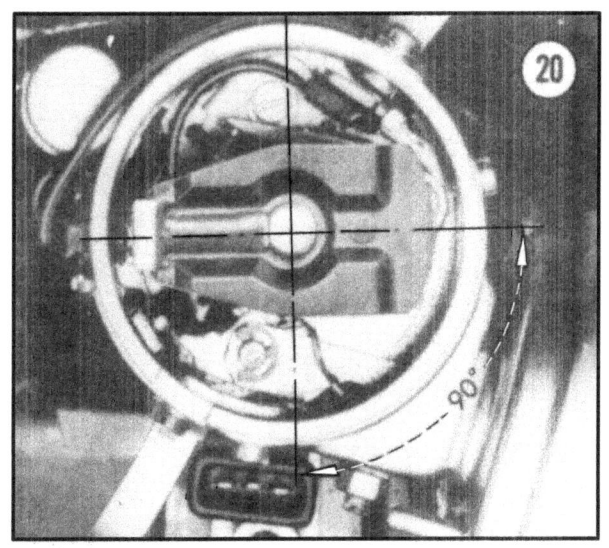

Loosen the locknut on the adjusting screw, insert a feeler gauge, and adjust to clearance given above. Tighten locknut and recheck the clearance to be sure it has not changed.

Rotate the crankshaft pulley 180° *counterclockwise* (backward) until the paint mark aligns with the crankcase seam. Adjust valves for cylinder No. 2. Rotate pulley another 180° counterclockwise and adjust cylinder No. 3. Rotate pulley another 180° counterclockwise and adjust cylinder No. 4.

When finished, install rocker arm covers with new gaskets.

Spark Plug Replacement

Once valve clearance is properly adjusted, work on the ignition system. Examine spark plugs and compare their appearance to **Figure 23**. Electrode appearance is a good indication of performance in each cylinder and permits early recognition of trouble. Clean the plugs, regap them, and reinstall, using new gaskets. Remove plugs in order. That way, you'll know which cylinder is malfunctioning, should such be the case.

> CAUTION
> *Ensure that the rubber seals on the spark plug wires are in good condition and seal properly. Replace them if necessary. These seals prevent loss of cooling air.*

Adjust valve clearance for cylinder No. 1, which is the left rear cylinder. See **Figure 22**.

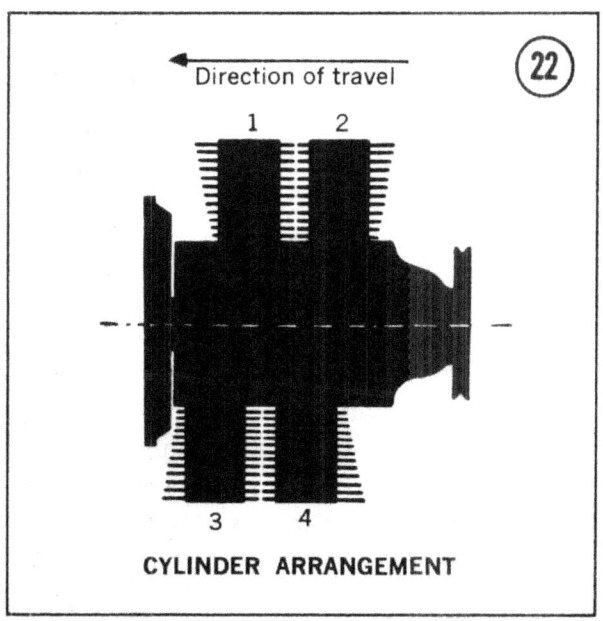

Breaker Point Replacement

Check breaker points for signs of pitting, discoloration, and misalignment. If this is a **12,000-mile** tune-up, replace the points and condenser.

The Marelli distributor used on the 914/6 is characterized by a very tall distributor cap. To replace the points, remove the distributor cap and mark the position of the rotor. Disconnect primary lead to distributor. Remove retaining nut at base of distributor (see **Figure 24**) and pull distributor out.

> NOTE: *Do not turn engine over with distributor removed. If you must turn it, refer to* Distributor Installation *procedure in Chapter Nine.*

Normal plug appearance noted by the brown to grayish-tan deposits and slight electrode wear. This plug indicates the correct plug heat range and proper air fuel ratio.

Red, brown, yellow and white coatings caused by fuel and oil additives. These deposits are not harmful if they remain in a powdery form.

Carbon fouling distinguished by dry, fluffy black carbon deposits which may be caused by an over-rich air/fuel mixture, excessive hand choking, clogged air filter or excessive idling.

Shiny yellow glaze on insulator cone is caused when the powdery deposits from fuel and oil additives melt. Melting occurs during hard acceleration after prolonged idling. This glaze conducts electricity and shorts out the plug.

Oil fouling indicated by wet, oily deposits caused by oil pumping past worn rings or down the intake valve guides. A hotter plug temporarily reduces oil deposits, but a plug that is too hot leads to pre-ignition and possible engine damage.

Overheated plug indicated by burned or blistered insulator tip and badly worn electrodes. This condition may be caused by pre-ignition, cooling system defects, lean air/fuel ratios, low octane fuel or over advanced ignition timing.

Spark plug condition photos courtesy of AC Spark Plug Division, General Motors Corporation.

Remove both breaker point retaining screws and loosen screw on wire lead terminal. See **Figure 25**. Install new points exactly like the old ones. Turn rotor until a cam lobe opens the points fully. Set points to 0.016 in. (0.4mm) by inserting a feeler gauge between the contacts and moving the fixed contact base. Tighten retaining screw to hold points in this position. See **Figure 26**. Position rotor according to mark made earlier. Install distributor and tighten retaining nut. Reconnect primary wire to distributor and install distributor cap.

Bosch distributors have a short distributor cap and are plainly marked. It is not necessary to remove distributor to change breaker points.

On later Bosch distributors, remove distributor cap and rotor. Remove the screw securing breaker points. Disconnect wire lead and lift out old points. Install new points. Turn engine over until a distributor cam lobe opens the contacts

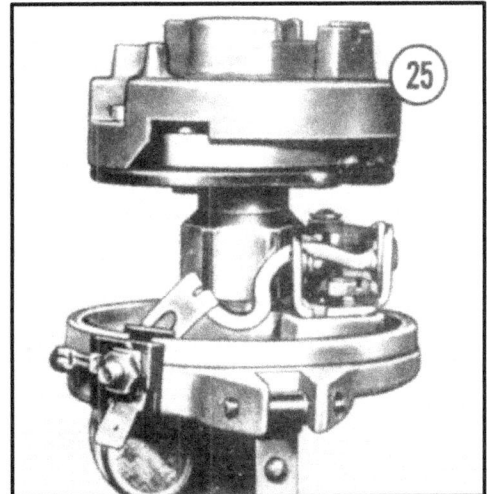

fully. Loosen retaining screw, insert 0.016 in. (0.4mm) feeler gauge and set point gap. Tighten screw. Install rotor and distributor cap.

More accurate measurement of breaker point gap is possible by measuring dwell angle at 2,000-2,500 rpm. Proper dwell angle depends on engine types as follows:

>914 —47° ± 3°
>914/6—40° ± 3°

Ignition Timing Adjustment

After adjusting breaker point gap, set the ignition timing. For most models, timing is set in 2 stages:

1. Static timing with test lamp
2. Dynamic timing with strobe

Static Timing

1. Remove distributor cap.

2a. On 914, remove plastic plug over crankshaft pulley. See **Figure 27**. Crank engine over by hand until black timing mark on pulley aligns with the blower housing notch.

2b. On 914/6, crank engine over by hand until TDC mark (Z1) on flywheel aligns with crankcase seam. See Figure 17.

3. Loosen distributor housing clamp nut.

4. Connect 12-volt test lamp from the primary lead on the distributor to ground.

5. Switch ignition on.

6. Rotate distributor body until the test lamp goes off (points close). Slowly rotate distributor in the opposite direction just until light goes on (points open). Tighten the distributor in this position.

7. Reinstall the distributor cap and disconnect the test lamp.

Stroboscopic Timing Adjustment

1. Connect timing light to spark plug No. 1 following manufacturer's instructions.

2. Warm engine to normal operating temperature (oil temperature 140-158°F).

3. Run 1.7 and 2.0 liter 914 engines at 3,500 rpm; 1.8 liter 914 engine at 800-900 rpm; and 914/6 engine at 6,000 rpm with vacuum advance disconnected.

4a. On 914, loosen distributor housing and turn it until red timing mark on the crankshaft pulley aligns with the blower housing notch when illuminated by timing light. See Figure 27.

4b. On 914/6, 35° mark on flywheel should align with the crankcase seam when illuminated by the strobe. Alignment may be off 2° (equivalent to 2mm on pulley rim) in either direction. If alignment is more than 2° off, go back to *Static Timing* procedure and reset it slightly to get total advance in specifications.

5. Tighten the distributor clamp and reconnect vacuum line when the adjustment is correct.

Fuel Injection Idle Speed Adjustment

1. Remove air cleaner and connect tachometer.

2. Loosen locknut (if any) on idle adjustment screw and back off screw until engine barely turns over. See **Figure 28**. Screw adjustment back in until engine speed is 850-900 rpm (manual transaxle) or 950-1,000 rpm (Sportomatic). If idle speed is above these figures, or you overshoot while adjusting, adjust idle below the desired idle, then come up to it again.

3. Look through air inlet and make certain that the throttle valve is fully closed.

4. Disconnect tachometer and install air cleaner.

CO Level Adjustment

To further reduce exhaust emissions, 1972-1976 models have an adjustment for CO (carbon monoxide) level. Previous models do not have any adjustment. To adjust the CO level:

1. Run the engine until thoroughly warm.

2. Connect a tachometer and an exhaust analyzer.

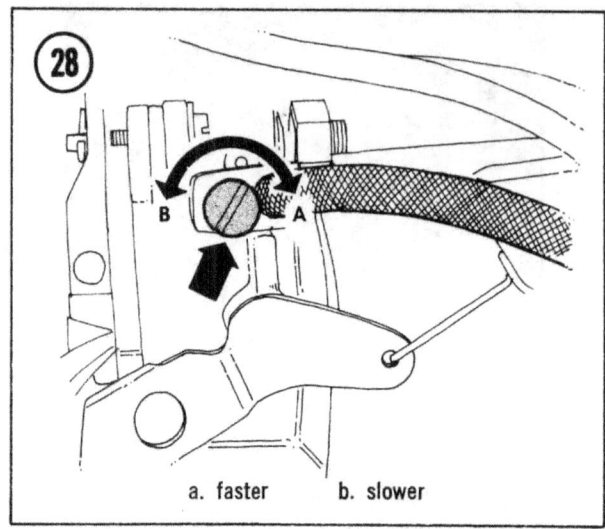

a. faster   b. slower

3. Test auxiliary air regulator as described in Chapter Seven.

4. Adjust idle speed as described in previous procedure.

5a. On 1972-1973 models, adjust CO to level in Table 2 with the adjustment screw on the control unit. See **Figure 29**.

5b. On 1974 and later models, adjust CO to level in Table 2 with the adjustment screw on the intake sensor. See **Figure 30**.

Carburetor Adjustment (914/6)

1. Bring engine to operating temperature, i.e., oil temperature should be about 140°F (60°C).

2. Remove the air cleaner assembly. See Chapter Eight.

3. Disconnect throttle rod on each side shown in **Figure 31**.

4. Turn 2 idle speed stop screws (one on each side) equally until engine idles between 1,000 and 1,200 rpm. See (a), **Figure 32**.

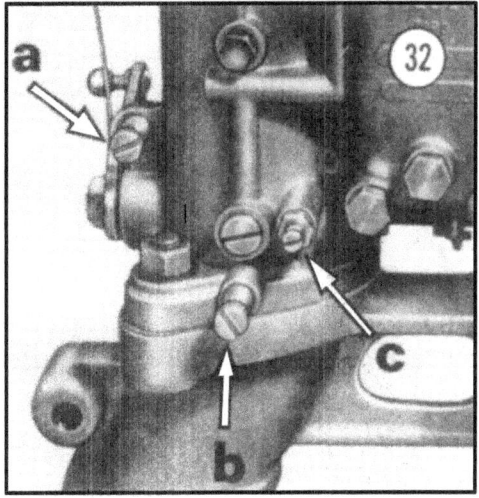

a. Idle stop screw   c. Idle air adjusting screw
b. Idle mixture adjusting screw

10. Recheck idle mixture settings.
11. Reconnect throttle linkage.
12. Reinstall air cleaner assembly.
13. Recheck idle mixture settings.

Throttle Valve Compensator Adjustment (914/6)

After carefully adjusting the carburetors, adjust the throttle valve compensator on cars equipped with exhaust emission control.

The compensator is correctly adjusted when the engine speed drops from 3,000 rpm to about 1,000 rpm 4-6 seconds after quickly releasing the throttle. If adjustment is incorrect:

1. Disconnect wire from insulated terminal on throttle positioner. Connect this terminal to +12 volts with a small jumper cable. See **Figure 33**.

5. Place a Unisyn or other carburetor synchronization tool over the left rear throat. Adjust Unisyn so that ball is about halfway up the tube.

6. Place Unisyn on each remaining throat. If Unisyn ball does not return to same point, the throat must be adjusted. Adjust air adjusting screw for that throat. See (c), Figure 32.

7. Reduce idle speed to 900-950 rpm with idle speed stop screws. See Figure 32.

8. Adjust idle mixture screw at each throat (6 in all) until engine runs smoothly.

9. Recheck synchronization.

2. Accelerate the engine to 3,000-4,000 rpm. Slowly decelerate. Engine speed should drop to 1,250-1,300 rpm; if not, shorten or lengthen the throttle positioner connecting rod.

3. Disconnect jumper and reconnect wire to throttle positioner. Accelerate briefly to 3,000-4,000 rpm. Quickly decelerate and note engine speed drops to 900-950 rpm.

4. Connect 12-volt test lamp across throttle positioner terminals. See **Figure 34**. Ensure that the light goes on at 2,000-3,000 rpm, and goes off at 1,450-1,550 rpm. Replace throttle positioner if the light stays on.

EMISSION CONTROL SYSTEMS

Harmful emissions are minimized by 3 systems:

a. Crankcase ventilation

b. Exhaust emission control

c. Fuel evaporation control

The crankcase ventilation system scavenges emissions (e.g., piston blow-by) from the crankcase and directs them to the air intake. Eventually they can be returned in the normal combustion process. Chapter Seven includes a detailed description of the system.

Exhaust emission control is more complex. Harmful exhaust emissions consists mainly of carbon monoxide and unburned hydrocarbons. The relative amounts of these emissions depends on the carburetor air/fuel mixture ratio, ignition timing, engine temperature, and condition. Exhaust emission control, therefore, depends largely on proper ignition and carburetor adjustment.

Even with a properly tuned engine, excessive emissions are produced when the rear wheels drive the engine, e.g., when coasting downhill or decelerating. Special throttle positioners and air injection techniques described in Chapter Seven ensure adequate air/fuel mixture to minimize unburned fuel in the exhaust.

The fuel evaporation control eliminates emission of fuel vapor into the atmosphere. Fuel vapor forms in the fuel tank of a car parked in the hot sun. This vapor is stored until the engine is started and the vapor can be burned in the engine. Chapter Seven describes the system in detail.

TUNE-UP SPECIFICATIONS 914/4 AND 914/6

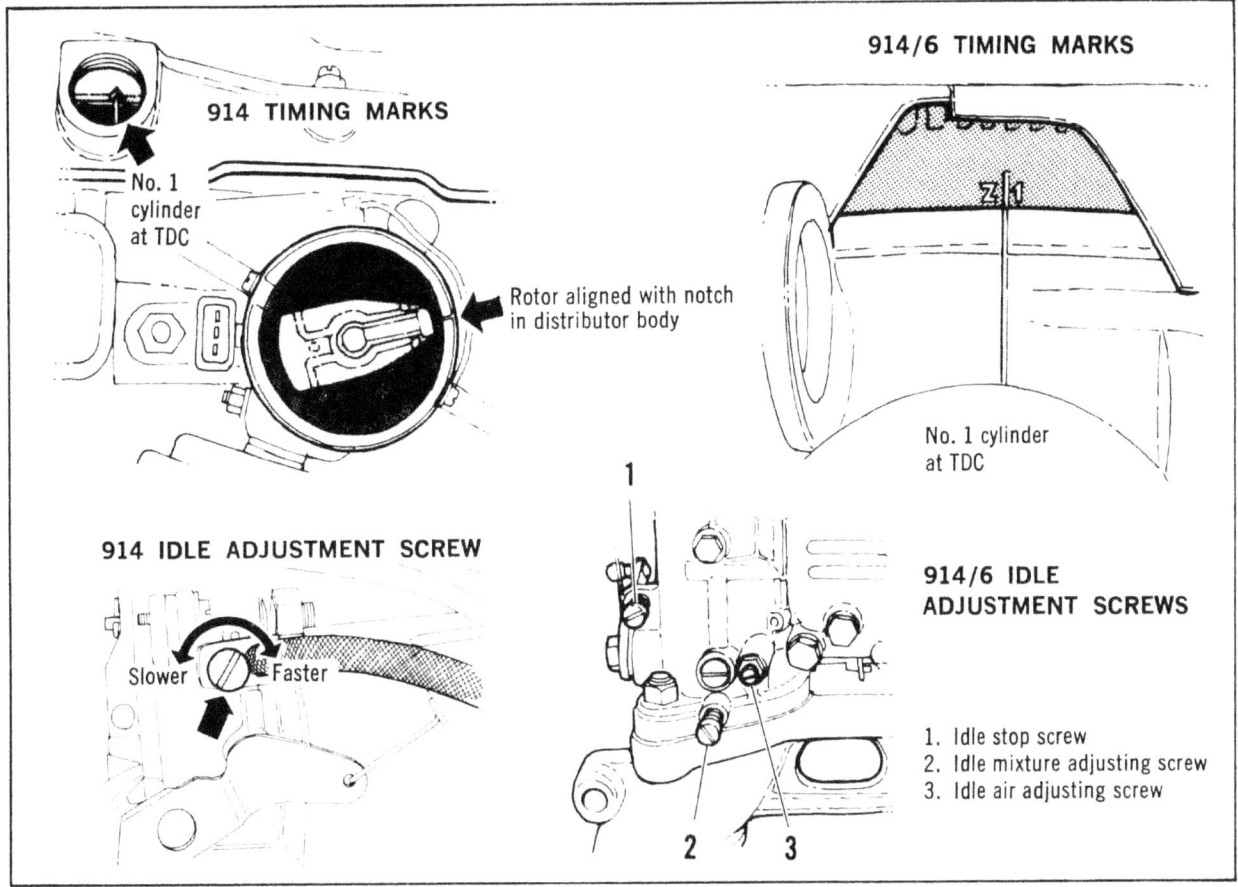

TUNE-UP SPECIFICATIONS — 2000cc ENGINES 914/4 AND 914/6

	2000 (4-Cylinder)	2000 (6-Cylinder)
Valve clearance ①		
Intake	0.006 in. (0.15mm)	0.004 in. (0.1mm)
Exhaust	0.008 in. (0.20mm)	0.004 in. (0.1mm)
Ignition timing ②	27° BTDC @ 3,500 rpm	35° BTDC @ 6,000 rpm
Spark plugs	Bosch W175T2, Autolite AG3, Autolite AG3X, AC 43XL, AC S43XL, Champion N7, Champion N6, NGK B-6ES	Bosch W230T30, Autolite AG12, AC 41XLS, Champion 7Y, NGK BP-7ES
Gap	0.028 in. (0.7mm)	0.024 in. (55mm)
Breaker point gap	0.016 in. (0.4mm)	0.016 in. (0.4mm)
Dwell angle	47° ± 3°	40° ± 3°
Firing order	1-4-3-2	1-6-2-4-3-5
Idle speed ③	850-900 rpm	900-950 rpm

① Checked with engine cold. ② Vacuum line(s) disconnected. ③ Add 100 rpm for Sportomatic models.

TUNE-UP SPECIFICATIONS — 1700 AND 1800cc ENGINES

	1700	1800
Valve clearance ①		
Intake	0.004 in. (0.1mm)	0.006 in. (0.15mm)
Exhaust	0.004 in. (0.1mm)	0.006 in. (0.15mm)
Ignition timing ②	27° BTDC @ 3,500 rpm	7.5° BTDC @ 850 rpm
Spark plugs	Bosch W175T2, Autolite AG3, Autolite AG3X, AC 43XL, AC S43XL, Champion N7, Champion N6, NGK B-6ES	Bosch W175T2, Autolite AG3, Autolite AG3X, AC 43XL, AC S43XL, Champion N7, Champion N6, NGK B-6ES
Gap	0.028 in. (0.7mm)	0.028 in. (0.7mm)
Breaker point gap	0.016 in. (0.4mm)	0.016 in. (0.4mm)
Dwell angle	47° ± 3°	47° ± 3°
Firing order	1-4-3-2	1-4-3-2
Idle speed ③	850-900 rpm	850-900 rpm

① Checked with engine cold.   ② Vacuum lines disconnected.   ③ Add 100 rpm for Sportomatic models.

RECOMMENDED LUBRICANTS AND FUEL

	Temperature Range	Recommended Type	Capacity
Engine oil	Below 5°F (—15°C)	SAE 10W, 10W-30	3.2 qt. (3.0 liters)[1]
	5°F to 32°F (—15°C to 0°C)	SAE 20W-20, 10W-30	3.7 qt. (3.5 liters)[2]
	32°F (0°C) and above	SAE 30W, 10W-30	9.5 qt. (9.0 liters)[3]
Transaxle	All temperatures	SAE 90 hypoid gear oil[4]	2.6 qt. (2.5 liters)
		SAE 90 (MIL-L-2105B)[5]	3.17 qt. (3.0 liters)
Fuel	Non-applicable	98 octane[6]	16.4 gal. (62 liters)
		91 octane[7]	

1. 914/4 without filter change
2. 914/4 with filter change
3. 914/6 with filter change
4. Without limited slip differential
5. With limited slip differential
6. 1970 - 1971 cars
7. 1972 - 1976 cars

EXHAUST EMISSION LEVELS

Year	(CO) Carbon Monoxide	(PPM) Hydrocarbons
1970-1971	1.5-3%	400 maximum
1972-1973	0.7% (914) 1.5% (914S)	400 maximum
1974-1976	2.5%	400 maximum

CHAPTER THREE

TROUBLESHOOTING

Troubleshooting can be a relatively simple matter if it is done logically. The first step in any troubleshooting procedure must be defining the symptoms as closely as possible. Subsequent steps involve testing and analyzing areas which could cause the symptoms. A haphazard approach may eventually find the trouble, but in terms of wasted time and unnecessary parts replacement, it can be very costly.

The troubleshooting procedures in this chapter analyze typical symptoms and show logical methods of isolation. These are not the only methods. There may be several approaches to a problem, but all methods must have one thing in common—a logical, systematic approach.

FUEL SYSTEM - SEE SUPPLEMENT AT END OF CHAPTER FOR 914/6 FUEL SYSTEM

Condition	Possible Cause	Correction
ENGINE DOES NOT START; FUEL PUMP NOT WORKING	(a) Wires to pump or relay defective (b) Fuse to pump relay defective (c) Pump relay defective.	(a) Check and repair or replace wires. (b) Replace 8A fuse. (c) Check with voltmeter; replace if necessary.
ENGINE DOES NOT START; FUEL PUMP WORKING	(a) Plug at pressure sensor disconnected, causing flooding. (b) Open circuit to cylinder head temp. sensor. (c) Pinched fuel line or defective pressure regulator.	(a) Replace plug. Crank engine with injector plug disconnected to clear engine. (b) Check and correct. Check all plugs and connections. (c) Check fuel loop for 28 psi pressure with starter turning engine.
ENGINE STARTS BUT STALLS	(a) Plug at distributor loose or defective wiring. (b) Trigger contacts defective.	(a) Check and replace contacts if necessary. (b) Replace.
ENGINE MISFIRES AND STALLS	(a) Trigger contacts dirty or worn.	(a) Check, clean and replace if necessary.

Condition	Possible Cause	Correction
	(b) Plugs loose	(b) Check and press on securely.
	(c) No fuel pressure	(c) Check pressure.
ENGINE MISSES ON ONE CYLINDER. WHITE EXHAUST SMOKE	(a) One fuel injector sticking or windings defective.	(a) Replace.
	(b) Plug connection loose	(b) Press plug on securely.
ENGINE MISFIRES	(a) Loose connections. Poor ground at injectors.	(a) Check connections and tighten ground screws.
ENGINE LACKS POWER	(a) Low fuel pressure.	(a) Check pressure and correct.
	(b) Pressure sensor defective	(b) Replace sensor
	(c) Throttle valve does not open fully.	(c) Check and adjust.
	(d) Pressure switch not working.	(d) Check switch and wiring for open circuits.
EXCESSIVE FUEL CONSUMPTION	(a) Sensors not operating or voltage leaks in wiring.	(a) Check hose connections and sensors. Check wiring.
	(b) Throttle valve switch	(b) Check and adjust.
	(c) Excessive fuel pressure.	(c) Check regulator; replace if necessary.
RPM RISES AND FALLS (1000–2000 rpm)	(a) Hose between auxiliary air regulator and intake air distributor loose or broken.	(a) Connect securely or replace.
	(b) Throttle valve stays open too wide.	(b) Check and adjust
	(c) Idle speed too high.	(c) Adjust to correct speed.
ENGINE BACKFIRES DURING ACCELERATION	(a) Mixture enrichment in throttle valve switch not operating.	(a) Check with tester.
HIGH IDLE SPEED	(a) Leak in idle air system.	(a) Check and correct
	(b) Rubber seals of injectors leaking.	(b) Replace seals.
	(c) Throttle valve needs adjusting.	(c) Adjust.

IGNITION SYSTEM

Condition	Possible Cause	Correction
BURNED OR PITTED DISTRIBUTOR CONTACTS	(a) Dirt or oil on contacts.	(a) If oil is on contact face, determine cause and correct condition. Clean distributor cam of dirt and grease, apply a light film of distributor cam lubricant to cam lobes; wipe off excess. See "Distributor Lubrication." Replace contact set and adjust as necessary.
	(b) Alternator voltage regulator setting too high.	(b) Test alternator voltage regulator setting, adjust as necessary. Replace contact set and adjust as necessary.
	(c) Contacts misaligned or gap too small.	(c) Align and adjust contacts.
	(d) Faulty coil.	(d) Test and replace coil if necessary. Replace and adjust contacts.
	(e) Ballast resistor not in circuit.	(e) Inspect conditions, and correctly connect the coil.
	(f) Wrong condenser or faulty condenser.	(f) Test condenser and replace if necessary. Replace and adjust contacts.
	(g) Faulty ignition switch.	(g) Replace ignition switch.
	(h) Bushings worn.	(h) Replace housing.

Condition	Possible Cause	Correction
IGNITION COIL FAILURE	(i) Touching contacts with the hands during installation. (a) Coil damaged by excessive heat from engine. (b) Coil tower carbon-tracked. (c) Oil leak at tower.	(i) Replace and adjust contacts. (a) Replace coil. Inspect condition of the distributor contacts. (b) Replace the coil. (c) Replace the coil.

ACCESSORY DRIVE BELTS

Condition	Possible Cause	Correction
INSUFFICIENT ACCESSORY OUTPUT DUE TO BELT SLIPPAGE	(a) Belt too loose. (b) Belt excessively glazed or worn.	(a) Adjust belt tension. (b) Replace and tighten as specified.
BELT SQUEAL WHEN ACCELERATING ENGINE	(a) Belts too loose. (b) Belts glazed.	(a) Adjust belt tension. (b) Replace belts.
BELT SQUEAK AT IDLE	(a) Belt too loose. (b) Dirt and paint imbedded in belt. (c) Non-uniform belt. (d) Misaligned pulleys. (e) Non-uniform groove or eccentric pulley.	(a) Adjust belt tension. (b) Replace belt. (c) Replace belt. (d) Align accessories (file brackets or use spacers as required). (e) Replace pulley.

ENGINE

Condition	Possible Cause	Correction
ENGINE WILL NOT START	(a) Weak battery. (b) Corroded or loose battery connections. (c) Faulty starter. (d) Moisture on ignition wires and distributor cap. (e) Faulty ignition cables. (f) Faulty coil or condenser. (g) Dirty or corroded distributor contacts. (h) Incorrect spark plug gap. (i) Incorrect ignition timing. (j) Dirt or water in fuel line	(a) Test battery specific gravity. Recharge or replace as necessary. (b) Clean and tighten battery connections. Apply a coat of petroleum to terminals. (c) Refer to "Starting Motor". (d) Wipe wires and cap clean and dry. (e) Replace any cracked or shorted cables. (f) Test and replace if necessary. (g) Clean or replace as necessary. (h) Set gap (i) Refer to "Ignition Timing." (j) Clean lines
ENGINE STALLS	(a) Idle speed set too low. (b) Incorrect choke adjustment. (c) Idle mixture too lean or too rich. (d) Incorrect carburetor float setting. (e) Leak in intake manifold. (f) Dirty, burned or incorrectly gapped distributor contacts. (g) Worn or burned distributor rotor. (h) Incorrect ignition wiring.	(a) Adjust carburetor. (b) Adjust choke. (c) Adjust carburetor. (d) Adjust float setting. (e) Inspect intake manifold gasket and replace if necessary. (f) Replace contacts and adjust. (g) Install new rotor. (h) Install correct wiring.

Condition	Possible Cause	Correction
	(i) Faulty coil or condenser.	(i) Test and replace if necessary.
	(j) Incorrect tappet lash.	(j) Adjust to specifications.
ENGINE LOSS OF POWER	(a) Incorrect ignition timing.	(a) Refer to "Ignition Timing."
	(b) Worn or burned distributor rotor.	(b) Install new rotor.
	(c) Worn distributor shaft or cam.	(c) Remove and repair distributor.
	(d) Dirty or incorrectly gapped spark plugs.	(d) Clean plugs and set gap
	(e) Dirt or water in fuel line, carburetor or filter.	(e) Clean lines, carburetor and replace filter.
	(h) Incorrect valve timing.	(h) Refer to "Checking Valve Timing."
	(j) Low compression.	(j) Test compression of each cylinder.
	(k) Burned, warped or pitted valves.	(k) Install new valves.
	(l) Plugged or restricted exhaust system.	(l) Install new parts as necessary.
	(m) Faulty ignition cables.	(m) Replace any cracked or shorted cables.
	(n) Faulty coil or condenser.	(n) Test and replace as necessary.
ENGINE MISSES ON ACCELERATION	(a) Dirty, burned, or incorrectly gapped distributor contacts.	(a) Replace contacts and adjust.
	(b) Dirty, or gap too wide in spark plugs.	(b) Clean spark plugs and set gap
	(c) Incorrect ignition timing.	(c) Refer to "Ignition Timing."
	(e) Acceleration pump in carburetor.	(e) Install new pump.
	(f) Burned, warped or pitted valves.	(f) Install new valves.
	(g) Faulty coil or condenser.	(g) Test and replace if necessary.
ENGINE MISSES AT HIGH SPEED	(a) Dirty or incorrectly gapped distributor contacts.	(a) Clean or replace as necessary.
	(b) Dirty or gap set too wide in spark plug.	(b) Clean spark plugs and set gap
	(c) Worn distributor shaft or cam.	(c) Remove and repair distributor.
	(d) Worn or burned distributor rotor.	(d) Install new rotor.
	(e) Faulty coil or condenser.	(e) Test and replace if necessary.
	(f) Incorrect ignition timing.	(f) Refer to "Ignition Timing."
	(h) Dirt or water in fuel line.	(h) Clean lines.
NOISY VALVES	(a) High or low oil level in crankcase.	(a) Check for correct oil level.
	(b) Thin or diluted oil.	(b) Change oil.
	(c) Low oil pressure.	(c) Check engine oil level.
	(d) Dirt in tappets.	(d) Clean tappets.
	(e) Bent push rods.	(e) Install new push rods.
	(f) Worn rocker arms.	(f) Inspect oil supply to rockers.
	(g) Worn tappets.	(g) Install new tappets.
	(h) Worn valve guides.	(h) Ream and install new valves with O/S stems.
	(i) Excessive run-out of valve seats or valve faces.	(i) Grind valve seats and valves.
	(j) Incorrect tappet lash.	(j) Adjust to specifications.

Condition	Possible Cause	Correction
CONNECTING ROD NOISE	(a) Insufficient oil supply. (b) Low oil pressure. (c) Thin or diluted oil. (d) Excessive bearing clearance. (e) Connecting rod journals out-of-round. (f) Misaligned connecting rods.	(a) Check engine oil level. (b) Check engine oil level. Inspect oil pump relief valve and spring. (c) Change oil to correct viscosity. (d) Measure bearings for correct (e) Replace crankshaft or regrind journals. (f) Replace bent connecting rods.
MAIN BEARING NOISE	(a) Insufficient oil supply. (b) Low oil pressure. (c) Thin or diluted oil. (d) Excessive bearing clearance. (e) Excessive end play (f) Crankshaft journal out-of-round or worn. (g) Loose flywheel or torque converter.	(a) Check engine oil level. (b) Check engine oil level. Inspect oil pump relief valve and spring. (c) Change oil to correct viscosity. (d) Measure bearings for correct clearance. (e) Check thrust bearing for wear on flanges. (f) Replace crankshaft or regrind journals. (g) Tighten to correct torque.
OIL PUMPING AT RINGS	(a) Worn, scuffed, or broken rings. (b) Carbon in oil rings slots. (c) Rings fitted too tight in	(a) Hone cylinder bores and install new rings. (b) Install new rings. (c) Remove the rings. Check

CLUTCH

Condition	Possible Cause	Correction
CLUTCH CHATTER	(a) Worn or damaged disc assembly. (b) Grease or oil on disc facings. (c) Improperly adjusted cover assembly. (d) Broken or loose engine mounts (e) Misaligned clutch housing	(a) Replace disc assembly. (b) Replace disc assembly and correct cause of contamination. (c) Replace cover assembly. (d) Replace or tighten mounts (e) Align clutch housing
CLUTCH SLIPPING	(a) Burned, worn, or oil soaked facings. (b) Insufficient pedal free play. (c) Weak or broken pressure springs.	(a) Replace disc assembly and correct cause of contamination. (b) Adjust release fork rod. (c) Replace cover assembly.
DIFFICULT GEAR SHIFTING	(a) Excessive pedal free play. (b) Excessive deflection in linkage or firewall. (c) Worn or damaged disc assembly. (d) Improperly adjusted cover assembly. (e) Clutch disc splines sticking. (f) Worn or dry pilot bushing. (g) Clutch housing misaligned.	(a) Adjust release fork rod. (b) Repair or replace linkage. (c) Replace disc assembly. (d) Replace cover assembly. (e) Remove disc assembly and free up splines or replace disc. (f) Lubricate or replace bushing. (g) Align clutch housing.
CLUTCH NOISY	(a) Dry clutch linkage. (b) Worn release bearing. (c) Worn disc assembly. (d) Worn release levers. (e) Worn or dry pilot bushing. (f) Dry contact-pressure plate lugs in cover.	(a) Lubricate where necessary. (b) Replace release bearing. (c) Replace disc assembly. (d) Replace cover assembly. (e) Lubricate or replace bushing. (f) Lubricate very lightly.

MANUAL—TRANSMISSION

Condition	Possible Cause	Correction
HARD SHIFTING	(a) Incorrect clutch adjustment.	(a) Refer to Clutch Group for corrections.
	(b) Improper linkage adjustment.	(b) Perform linkage adjustment
	(c) Synchronizer clutch sleeve damaged.	(c-d-e) Causes noted can only be corrected by disassembling transmission and replacing damaged or worn parts.
	(d) Synchronizer spring improperly installed.	
	(e) Broken or worn synchronizer stop rings.	
TRANSMISSION SLIPS OUT OF GEAR	(a) Linkage interference.	(a) Inspect and remove all linkage interferences.
	(b) Gearshift rods out of adjustment.	(b) Adjust gearshift rods
	(c) Synchronizer clutch teeth worn.	(c) Disassemble transmission and replace parts as necessary.
	(d) Clutch housing bore or face out of alignment.	(d) Refer to Clutch Group for correction procedure.
TRANSMISSION NOISES	(a) Excessive end play in countershaft gear.	(a) Replace thrust washers.
	(b) Loose synchronizer hub spline fit on mainshaft.	(b) Inspect mainshaft and synchronizer hub and replace parts as necessary.
	(c) Damaged, broken or excessively worn gear teeth.	(c) Replace worn gears.
	(d) Rough or pitted bearing races or balls.	(d) Replace worn bearing.

REAR AXLE

Condition	Possible Cause	Correction
REAR WHEEL NOISE	(a) Wheel loose.	(a) Tighten loose wheel nuts.
	(b) Spalled wheel bearing cup or cone.	(b) Check rear wheel bearings. If spalled or worn, replace.
	(c) Defective, brinelled wheel bearing.	(c) Defective or brinelled bearings must be replaced. Check rear axle shaft end play.
	(d) Excessive axle shaft end play.	(d) Readjust axle shaft end play.
	(e) Bent or sprung axle shaft flange.	(e) Replace bent or sprung axle shaft.
SCORING OF DIFFERENTIAL GEARS AND PINIONS	(a) Insufficient lubrication.	(a) Replace scored gears. Scoring marks on the pressure face of gear teeth or in the bore are caused by instantaneous fusing of the mating surfaces. Scored gears should be replaced. Fill rear axle to required capacity with proper lubricant. See Specification Section.
	(b) Improper grade of lubricant.	(b) Replace scored gears. Inspect all gears and bearings for possible damage. Clean out and refill axle to required capacity with proper lubricant. See Lubrication section.
	(c) Excessive spinning of one wheel.	(c) Replace scored gears. Inspect all gears, pinion bores and shaft for scoring, or bearings for possible damage. Service as necessary.

Condition	Possible Cause	Correction
TOOTH BREAKAGE (RING GEAR AND PINION)	(a) Overloading.	(a) Replace gears. Examine other gears and bearings for possible damage. Replace parts as needed. Avoid Overloading.
	(b) Erratic clutch operation.	(b) Replace gears, and examine remaining parts for possible damage. Avoid erratic clutch operation.
	(c) Ice-spotted pavements.	(c) Replace gears. Examine remaining parts for possible damage. Replace parts as required.
	(d) Improper adjustment.	(d) Replace gears. Examine other parts for possible damage. Make sure ring gear and pinion backlash is correct.
REAR AXLE NOISE	(a) Insufficient lubricant.	(a) Refill rear axle with correct amount of the proper lubricant. See Specification section. Also check for leaks and correct as necessary.
	(b) Improper ring gear and pinion adjustment.	(b) Check ring gear and pinion tooth contact.
	(c) Unmatched ring gear and pinion.	(c) Remove unmatched ring gear and pinion. Replace with a new matched gear and pinion set.
	(d) Worn teeth on ring gear or pinion.	(d) Check teeth on ring gear and pinion for contact. If necessary, replace with new matched set.
	(e) End play in drive pinion bearings.	(e) Adjust drive pinion bearing preload.
	(f) Side play in differential bearings.	(f) Adjust differential bearing preload.
	(g) Incorrect drive gearlash.	(g) Correct drive gearlash.
LOSS OF LUBRICANT	(a) Lubricant level too high.	(a) Drain excess lubricant by removing filler plug and allow lubricant to level at lower edge of filler plug hole.
	(b) Worn axle shaft oil seals.	(b) Replace worn oil seals with new ones. Prepare new seals before replacement.
	(c) Cracked rear axle housing.	(c) Repair or replace housing as required.
	(d) Worn drive pinion oil seal.	(d) Replace worn drive pinion oil seal with a new one.
	(e) Scored and worn companion flange.	(e) Replace worn or scored companion flange and oil seal.
	(f) Clogged vent.	(f) Remove obstructions.
	(g) Loose carrier housing bolts or housing cover screws.	(g) Tighten bolts or cover screws to specifications and fill to correct level with proper lubricant.
OVERHEATING OF UNIT	(a) Lubricant level too low.	(a) Refill rear axle.
	(b) Incorrect grade of lubricant.	(b) Drain, flush and refill rear axle with correct amount of the proper lubricant. See Specification Section.
	(c) Bearings adjusted too tightly.	(c) Readjust bearings.
	(d) Excessive wear in gears.	(d) Check gears for excessive wear or scoring. Replace as necessary.
	(e) Insufficient ring gear to pinion clearance.	(e) Readjust ring gear and pinion backlash and check gears for possible scoring.

Condition	Possible Cause	Correction
DRIVE SHAFT VIBRATION	(a) Undercoating or other foreign matter on shaft.	(a) Clean exterior of shaft and wash with solvent.
	(b) Loose universal joint flange bolts.	(b) Tighten bolt nuts to specific torque.
	(c) Loose or bent universal joint flange or high runout.	(c) Install new flange. Tighten to specifications.
	(d) Improper drive line angularity.	(d) Correct angularity. See "Propeller Shaft Angularity."
	(f) Worn universal joint bearings or missing rollers.	(f) Recondition universal joint.
	(g) Shaft damaged (bent tube) or out of balance.	(g) Install new shaft.
	(h) Broken rear spring.	(h) Replace rear spring.
	(i) Excessive runout or unbalance condition.	(i) Reindex propeller shaft 180 degrees, reride and correct as necessary.
UNIVERSAL JOINT NOISE	(a) Shaft flange bolts nuts loose.	(a) Tighten nuts to specified torque.
	(b) Lack of lubrication	(b) Recondition universal joint.

SHOCK ABSORBERS

Condition	Possible Cause	Correction
SHOCK ABSORBER NOISY	(a) Loose bolt or stud.	(a) Tighten to specifications.
	(b) Undercoating on shock absorber reservoir.	(b) Clean undercoating off shock absorber.
	(c) Bushing excessively worn.	(c) Replace bushing.
	(d) Air trapped in system.	(d) Purge shock absorber.
SHOCK ABSORBER DRIPPING OIL	(a) Worn seal.	(a) Replace shock absorber.
	(b) Damaged crimp or reservoir.	(b) Replace shock absorber.

STEERING

Condition	Possible Cause	Correction
HARD STEERING	(a) Low or uneven tire pressure.	(a) Inflate tires to recommended pressures.
	(b) Insufficient lubricant in the steering gear housing or in steering linkage.	(b) Lubricate as necessary.
	(c) Steering gear shaft adjusted too tight.	(c) Adjust according to instructions.
	(d) Front wheels out of line.	(d) Align the wheels. See "Front Suspension."
PULL TO ONE SIDE (Tendency of the Vehicle to veer in one direction only)	(a) Incorrect tire pressure.	(a) Inflate tires to recommended pressures.
	(b) Wheel bearings improperly adjusted.	(b) See "Front Wheel Bearing Adjustment."
	(c) Dragging brakes.	(c) Inspect for weak, or broken brake shoe spring, binding pedal.
	(d) Improper caster and camber.	(d) See "Front Wheel Alignment Group."
	(e) Incorrect toe-in.	(e) See "Front Wheel Alignment Group."
	(f) Grease, dirt, oil or brake fluid in brake linings.	(f) Inspect, replace and adjust as necessary.
	(g) Front and rear wheels out of alignment.	(g) Align the front wheels. See "Front Suspension Group"

Condition	Possible Cause	Correction
	(h) Broken or sagging rear springs.	(h) Replace rear springs.
	(i) Bent suspension parts.	(i) Replace parts necessary.
WHEEL TRAMP (Excessive Vertical Motion of Wheels)	(a) Incorrect tire pressure.	(a) Inflate tires to recommended pressures.
	(b) Improper balance of wheels, tires and brake drums.	(b) Lubricate as necessary.
	(c) Loose tie rod ends or steering connections.	(c) Inspect and repair as necessary.
	(d) Worn or inoperative shock absorbers.	(d) Replace shock absorbers as necessary.
EXCESSIVE PLAY OR LOOSENESS IN THE STEERING WHEEL	(a) Steering gearshaft adjusted too loose or badly worn.	(a) Replace worn parts and adjust according to instructions.
	(b) Steering linkage loose or worn	(b) Replace worn parts. See "Front Wheel Alignment."
	(c) Front wheel bearings improperly adjusted.	(c) Adjust according to instructions.
	(d) Steering arm loose on steering gear shaft.	(d) Inspect for damage to gear shaft and steering arm, replace parts as necessary.
	(e) Steering gear housing attaching bolts loose.	(e) Tighten attaching bolts according to tigntening reference.
	(f) Steering arms loose at steering knuckles.	(f) Tighten according to tightening reference.
	(g) Worn ball joints.	(g) Replace ball joints as necessary. See "Front Suspension."
	(h) Steering gear adjustment too loose.	(h) Adjust

BRAKES

Condition	Possible Cause	Correction
DRAGGING BRAKES (ALL WHEELS)	(a) Brake shoes improperly adjusted.	(a) Adjust brakes.
	(b) Brake pedal linkage binding.	(b) Free up linkage.
	(c) Excessive hydraulic seal friction.	(c) Lubricate seal.
	(d) Compensator port plugged.	(d) Clean out master cylinder.
	(e) Fluid cannot return to master cylinder.	(e) Inspect pedal return.
	(f) Parking brake not returning.	(f) Free up as required.
	(g) Disc brake metering valve malfunction.	(g) Replace metering valve.
	(h) Contaminated brake fluid.	(h) Drain and flush system-replace all rubber parts in hydraulic system.
GRABBING BRAKES	(a) Grease or brake fluid on linings.	(a) Inspect for a leak and replace lining as required.
PEDAL GOES TO FLOOR (OR ALMOST TO FLOOR)	(a) Self-adjusters not operating.	(a) Inspect self-adjuster operations.
	(b) Air in hydraulic system.	(b) Bleed brakes.
	(c) Hydraulic leak.	(c) Locate and correct leak.
	(d) Fluid low in master cylinder.	(d) Add brake fluid.
	(e) Shoe hanging up on rough platform.	(e) Smooth and lubricate platforms.
	(f) Loose disc brake rotor	(f) Check wheel bearing adjustment.
HARD PEDAL (POWER UNIT TROUBLE)	(a) Faulty vacuum check valve.	(a) Replace check valve.
	(b) Collapsed or leaking vacuum hose.	(b) Replace hose.
	(c) Plugged vacuum fittings.	(c) Clean out fittings.
	(d) Leaking vacuum chamber.	(d) Replace unit.

Condition	Possible Cause	Correction
	(e) Diaphragm assembly out of place in housing.	(e) Replace unit.
	(f) Vacuum leak in forward vacuum housing.	(f) Replace unit.
EXCESSIVE PEDAL TRAVEL	(a) Rear brake adjustment required.	(a) Check and adjust rear brakes.
	(b) Air leak, or insufficient fluid in system or caliper.	(b) Check system for leaks.
	(c) Warped or excessively tapered shoe and lining assembly.	(c) Install new shoe and linings.
	(d) Excessive disc runout.	(d) Check disc for runout with dial indicator. Install new disc.
	(e) Loose wheel bearing adjustment.	(e) Readjust wheel bearings to specified torque.
	(f) Improper brake fluid (boil).	(f) Drain and install correct fluid.
	(g) Damaged caliper piston seal.	(g) Install new piston seal.
BRAKE ROUGHNESS OR CHATTER (Pedal Pulsating)	(a) Excessive out-of-parallelism of braking disc.	(a) Check disc for runout with dial indicator. Install new disc.
	(c) Excessive lateral runout of braking disc.	(c) Check disc for lateral runout with dial indicator. Install new disc.
	(d) Excessive front bearing clearance.	(d) Readjust wheel bearings to specified torque.
	(e) Rear brake drums distorted by improper tightening of nuts.	(e) Check drums for out-of-round and reface if necessary.
EXCESSIVE PEDAL EFFORT	(a) Power brake malfunction.	(a) Replace
	(b) Frozen or seized pistons.	(b) Disassemble caliper and free up pistons. Clean parts.
	(c) Shoe and lining worn below .180 in. (Lining only— .30 in.)	(c) Install new shoe and linings.
	(d) Brake fluid, oil or grease on linings.	(d) Install new shoe linings as required.
	(e) Incorrect lining.	(e) Remove lining and install correct lining.
PULL	(a) Loose calipers.	(a) Tighten caliper mounting bolts from 45 to 60 ft. pounds.
	(b) Frozen or seized pistons.	(b) Disassemble caliper and free up pistons.
	(c) Rear brake pistons sticking.	(c) Free up rear brake pistons.
	(d) Front end out of alignment.	(d) Check and align front end.
	(e) Broken rear spring.	(e) Install new rear spring.
	(f) Out-of-round rear drums.	(f) Check and reface drums if necessary.
	(g) Incorrect tire pressure.	(g) Inflate tires to recommended presures.
	(h) Brake fluid, oil or grease on linings.	(h) Install new shoe and linings.
	(i) Restricted hose or line.	(i) Check hoses and lines and correct as necessary.
	(j) Rear brakes out of adjustment.	(j) Adjust rear brakes.
	(k) Unmatched linings.	(k) Install correct lining.
	(l) Distorted brake shoes.	(l) Install new brake shoes.
NOISE Groan—Brake noise emanating when slowly releasing brakes (creep—groan)	(a) Not detrimental to function of disc brakes—no corrective action required. (Indicate to operator this noise may be eliminated by slightly increasing or decreasing brake pedal efforts).	
Rattle-Brake noise or rattle emanating at low speeds on rough roads, (front wheels only).	(a) Excessive clearance between shoe and caliper.	(a) Install new shoe and lining assemblies.
Scraping—	(a) Loose wheel bearings.	(a) Readjust wheel bearings to correct specifications.

Condition	Possible Cause	Correction
	(b) Braking disc rubbing housing.	(b) Check for rust or mud buildup on caliper mounting and bridge bolt tightness.
	(c) Mounting bolts too long.	(c) Install mounting bolts of correct length.
FRONT BRAKES HEAT UP DURING DRIVING AND FAIL TO RELEASE	(a) Residual pressure valve in master cylinder.	(a) Remove valve from cylinder.
	(b) Frozen or seized piston.	(b) Disassemble caliper, hone cylinder bore, clean seal groove and install new pistons, seals and boots.
	(c) Operator riding brake pedal.	(c) Instruct owner how to drive with disc brakes.
	(d) Sticking pedal linkage.	(d) Free up sticking pedal linkage.
	(e) Power brake malfunction.	(e) Replace
LEAKY WHEEL CYLINDER	(a) Corroded bore.	(a) Hone bore and replace boots and cups.
	(b) Damaged or worn caliper piston seal.	(b) Disassemble caliper and install new seal.
	(c) Scores or corrosion on surface of piston.	(c) Disassemble caliper and hone cylinder bore. If neccessary, install new pistons.
GRABBING OR UNEVEN BRAKING ACTION	(a) Causes listed under "Pull."	(a) Corrections listed under "Pull."
	(b) Power brake malfunction.	(b) Replace unit.
BRAKE PEDAL CAN BE DEPRESSED WITHOUT BRAKING EFFECT	(a) Air in hydraulic system or improper bleeding procedure.	(a) Bleed system.
	(b) Leak in system or caliper.	(b) Check for leak and repair as required.
	(c) Pistons pushed back in cylinder bores during servicing of caliper (shoe and lining not properly positioned).	(c) Reposition brake shoe and lining assemblies. Depress pedal a second time and if condition persists, check following causes:
	(d) Leak past piston cups in master cylinder.	(d) Recondition master cylinder.
	(e) Damaged piston seal in one or more of cylinders.	(e) Disassemble caliper and replace piston seals as required.
	(f) Leak in rear brake cylinder.	(f) Hone cylinder bore. Install new piston cylinder cups.
	(g) Rear brakes out of adjustment.	(g) Adjust rear brakes.
	(h) Bleeder screw open.	(h) Close bleeder screw and bleed entire system.

PARKING BRAKES

Condition	Possible Cause	Correction
DRAGGING BRAKE	(a) Improper cable or brake shoe adjustment.	(a) Properly adjust the service brakes, then adjust the parking brake cable.
	(b) Broken brake shoe return spring.	(b) Replace any broken return spring.
	(c) Broken brake shoe retainer spring.	(c) Replace the broken retainer spring.
	(d) Grease or brake fluid soaked lining.	(d) Replace the grease seal or recondition the wheel cylinders and replace both brake shoes.
	(e) Improper stop light switch adjustment	(e) Adjust stop light switch
	(f) Sticking or frozen brake cable.	(f) Replace cable.
	(g) Broken rear spring.	(g) Replace the broken rear spring.
	(h) Bent or rusted cable equalizer.	(h) Straighten, or replace and lubricate the equalizer.

Condition	Possible Cause	Correction
BRAKE WILL NOT HOLD	(h) Heat set parking brake cable spring. (a) Broken or rusted brake cable. (b) Improperly adjusted brake or cable. (c) Soaked brake lining. (d) Ratchet or pedal mechanism worn.	(h) Replace parking brake cable. (a) Replace cable. (b) Adjust brakes and cable as necessary. (c) Replace the brake lining. (d) Replace pedal assembly.

FRONT SUSPENSION AND STEERING LINKAGE

Condition	Possible Cause	Correction
FRONT END NOISE	(a) Ball joint needs lubrication. (b) Loose shock absorber mounting. Shock absorber inoperative or bushings worn. (c) Worn strut bushings. (d) Loose struts—Lower control arm bolts and nuts. (e) Loose steering gear on frame. (f) Worn upper control arm bushings. (g) Worn lower control arm shaft bushings. (h) Worn upper or lower ball joint. (i) Worn tie rod ends. (j) Loose or worn front wheel bearings. (k) Steering knuckle arm contacting the lower control arm wheel stop.	(a) Lubricate ball joint. (b) Tighten shock absorber mounting nuts. Replace bushings or shock absorber. (c) Replace bushing. (d) Tighten all bolts and nuts. (e) Tighten the steering gear mounting bolts. (f) Replace worn bushings. (g) Replace worn bushings. (h) Replace ball joint. (i) Replace tie rod end. (j) Adjust or replace bearings as necessary. (k) Smooth off the contacting area and lubricate with a water resistant grease.
INSTABILITY	(a) Low or uneven tire pressure. (b) Loose wheel bearings. (c) Improper steering cross shaft adjustment. (d) Steering gear not centered. (e) Worn idler arm bushing. (f) Loose or excessively worn front strut bushings. (g) Weak or broken rear spring. (h) Incorrect front wheel alignment. (i) Shock absorber inoperative.	(a) Inflate tires to correct pressure. (b) Adjust wheel bearing. (c) Adjust steering cross shaft. (d) Adjust steering gear. (e) Replace bushing. (f) Replace bushings. (g) Replace spring. (h) Measure and adjust front wheel alignment. (i) Replace shock absorber.
HARD STEERING	(a) Ball joints-require lubrication. (b) Low or uneven tire pressure. (e) Incorrect front wheel alignment (particularly caster) resulting from a bent control arm, steering knuckle or steering knuckle arm. (f) Steering gear low on lubricant. (g) Steering gear not adjusted. (h) Idler arm binding.	(a) Lubricate ball joints. (b) Inflate tires to recommended pressures. (e) Replace bent parts and adjust the front wheel alignment. (f) Fill gear to correct level. (g) Adjust steering gear. (h) Replace idler arm.
CAR PULLS TO ONE SIDE	(a) Low or uneven tire pressure. (b) Front brake dragging. (c) Grease, lubricant or brake fluid leaking onto brake lining. (d) Loose or excessively worn strut bushings. (e) Power steering control valve out of adjustment.	(a) Inflate tires to recommended pressure. (b) Adjust brakes. (c) Replace brake shoe and lining as necessary and stop all leaks. (d) Tighten or replace strut bushings. (e) Adjust steering gear control valve.

Condition	Possible Cause	Correction
EXCESSIVE PLAY IN STEERING	(f) Incorrect front wheel alignment (particularly camber).	(f) Adjust front wheel alignment.
	(g) Broken or weak rear spring.	(g) Replace spring.
	(a) Worn or loose front wheel bearings.	(a) Adjust or replace wheel bearings as necessary.
	(b) Incorrect steering gear adjustment.	(b) Adjust steering gear.
	(c) Loose steering gear to frame mounting bolts.	(c) Tighten steering gear to frame bolts.
	(d) Worn ball joints or tie rod.	(d) Replace ball joints or tie rods as necessary.
	(e) Worn steering gear parts.	(e) Replace worn steering gear parts and adjust as necessary.
	(f) Worn upper or lower ball joints.	(f) Replace ball joints.
	(g) Worn idler arm bushing.	(g) Replace bushing.
FRONT WHEEL SHIMMY	(a) Tire, wheel out of balance.	(a) Balance wheel and tire assembly.
	(b) Uneven tire wear, or excessively worn tires.	(b) Rotate or replace tires as necessary.
	(c) Worn or loose wheel bearings.	(c) Replace or adjust wheel bearings as necessary.
	(d) Worn tie rod ends.	(d) Replace tie rod ends.
	(e) Strut mounting bushings loose or worn.	(e) Replace strut mounting bushings.
	(f) Incorrect front wheel alignment (particularly caster).	(f) Adjust front wheel alignment.
	(g) Worn or loose upper control arm ball joints.	(g) Inspect ball joints and replace where required.

STARTER—ELECTRICAL

Condition	Possible Cause	Correction
STARTER FAILS TO OPERATE	(a) Weak battery or dead cell in battery.	(a) Test specific gravity. Recharge or replace battery as required.
	(b) Ignition switch faulty.	(b) Test and replace switch if necessary.
	(c) Loose or corroded battery cable terminals.	(c) Clean terminals and clamps, replace if necessary. Apply a light film of petrolatum to terminals after tightening.
	(d) Open circuit, wire between the ignition — starter switch and ignition terminal on starter relay.	(d) Inspect and test all the wiring.
	(e) Starter relay defective.	(e) Test relay and replace if necessary.
	(f) Faulty starter.	(f) Test and repair as necessary.
	(g) Armature shaft sheared.	(g) Test and repair.
	(h) Open solenoid pull-in wire.	(h) Test and replace solenoid if necessary.
STARTER FAILS AND LIGHTS DIM	(a) Weak battery or dead cell in battery.	(a) Test for specified gravity. Recharge or replace battery as required.
	(b) Loose or corroded battery cable terminals.	(b) Clean terminals and clamps, replace if necessary. Apply a light film of petrolatum to terminals after tightening.
	(c) Internal ground in windings.	(c) Test and repair starter.
	(d) Grounded starter fields.	(d) Test and repair starter.
	(e) Armature rubbing on pole shoes.	(e) Test and repair starter.
STARTER TURNS, BUT ENGINE DOES NOT ENGAGE	(a) Starter clutch slipping.	(a) Replace clutch unit.

Condition	Possible Cause	Correction
	(b) Broken clutch housing.	(b) Test and repair starter.
	(c) Pinion shaft rusted, dirty or dry, due to lack of lubrication.	(c) Clean, test and lubricate.
	(d) Engine basic timing wrong.	(d) check engine basic timing and condition of distributor rotor and cap.
	(e) Broken teeth on engine ring gear.	(e) Replace ring gear. Inspect teeth on starter clutch pinion.
STARTER RELAY DOES NOT CLOSE	(a) Battery discharged.	(a) Recharge or replace battery.
	(b) Faulty wiring.	(b) Test for open circuit, wire between starter relay ground terminal post and neutral starter switch (automatic transmission only). Also test for open circuit; wire between ignition-starter switch and ignition terminal and starter relay.
	(c) Clutch start switch or neutral starter switch on automatic transmission faulty.	(c) Test and replace the switch if necessary.
	(d) Starter relay faulty.	(d) Test and replace if necessary.
RELAY OPERATES BUT SOLENOID DOES NOT	(a) Faulty wiring.	(a) Test for open circuit wire between starter-relay solenoid terminal and solenoid terminal post.

ALTERNATOR-REGULATOR—ELECTRICAL

Condition	Possible Cause	Correction
ALTERNATOR FAILS TO CHARGE (No Output or Low Output)	(a) Alternator drive belt loose.	(a) Adjust drive belt to specifications.
	(b) Regulator Base improperly grounded.	(b) Connect regulator to a good ground.
	(c) Worn brushes and/or slip rings.	(c) Install new brushes and/or slip rings.
	(d) Sticking brushes.	(d) Clean slip rings and brush holders. Install new brushes if necessary.
	(e) Open field circuit.	(e) Test all the field circuit connections, and correct as required.
	(f) Open charging circuit.	(f) Inspect all connections in charging circuit, and correct as required.
	(g) Open circuit in stator windings.	(g) Remove alternator and disassemble. Test stator windings. Install new stator if necessary.
	(h) Open recitfiers.	(h) Remove alternator and disassemble. Test the recitfiers. Install new recitfiers if necessary.
LOW, UNSTEADY CHARGING RATE	(a) High resistance in body to engine ground lead.	(a) Tighten ground lead connections. Install new ground lead if necessary.
	(b) Alternator drive belt loose.	(b) Adjust alternator drive belt.
	(c) High resistance at battery terminals.	(c) Clean and tighten battery terminals.
	(d) High resistance in charging circuit.	(d) Test charging circuit resistance. Correct as required.

Condition	Possible Cause	Correction
	(e) Open stator winding.	(e) Remove and disassemble alternator. Test stator windings. Install new stator if necessary.
LOW OUTPUT AND A LOW BATTERY	(a) High resistance in charging circuit.	(a) Test charging circuit resistance and correct as required.
	(b) Shorted rectifier. Open recitfier.	(b) Perform current output test. Test the rectifiers and install new rectifiers as required. Remove and disassemble the alternator.
	(c) Grounded stator windings.	(c) Remove and disassemble alternator. Test stator windings. Install new stator if necessary.
	(d) Faulty voltage regulator.	(d) Test voltage regulator.
EXCESSIVE CHARGING RATE TO A FULLY CHARGED BATTERY	(a) Faulty ignition switch.	(a) Install new ignition switch.
	(b) Faulty voltage regulator.	(b) Test voltage regulator. Replace as necessary.
NOISY ALTERNATOR	(a) Alternator mounting loose.	(a) Properly install and tighten alternator mounting.
	(b) Worn or frayed drive belt.	(b) Install a new drive belt and adjust to specifications.
	(c) Worn bearings.	(c) Remove and disassemble alternator. Install new bearings as required.
	(d) Interference between rotor fan and stator leads or rectifiers.	(d) Remove and disassemble alternator. Correct interference as required.
	(e) Rotor or rotor fan damaged.	(e) Remove and disassemble alternator. Install new rotor.
	(f) Open or shorted rectifier.	(f) Remove and disassemble alternator. Test rectifiers. Install new recitfiers as required.
	(g) Open or shorted winding in stator.	(g) Remove and disassemble alternator. Test stator windings. Install new stator if necessary.
EXCESSIVE AMMETER FLUCTUATION	(a) High resistance in the alternator and voltage regulator circuit.	(a) Clean and tighten all connections as necessary.

SUPPLEMENT - 914/6

NOTE:
FOR ALL OTHER TROUBLESHOOTING PROCEDURES REFER TO PREVIOUS SECTION

FUEL SYSTEM 914/6 ONLY

Condition	Possible Cause	Correction
POOR IDLING	(a) Idle air bleed carbonized or of incorrect size.	(a) Disassemble carburetor. Then, use compressed to clear idle bleed after soaking it in a suitable solvent.
	(b) Idle discharge holes plugged or gummed.	(b) Disassemble carburetor. Then, use compressed air to clear idle discharge holes after soaking main and throttle bodies in a suitable solvent.
	(c) Throttle body carbonized or worn throttle shaft.	(c) Disassemble carburetor. Check throttle valve shaft for wear. If excessive wear is apparent, replace throttle body assembly.
	(d) Damaged or worn idle mixture needle.	(d) Replace throttle body assembly.
	(e) Low grade fuel or incorrect float level.	(e) Test fuel level in carburetor. Adjust as necessary to obtain correct float level.
	(f) Loose main body to throttle body screws.	(f) Tighten main body to throttle body screws securely to prevent air leaks.
	(g) Worn or worroded needle valve and seat.	(g) Clean and inspect needle valve and seat. If found to be in questionable condition, replace assembly. Then, test fuel pump pressure.
	(h) Incorrect valve lash.	(h) Adjust valves.
	(i) Engine miss (ignition.)	(i) Check ignition system.
POOR ACCELERATION	(a) Accelerator pump diaphragm too hard, worn, or loose on stem.	(a) Disassemble carburetor. Replace accelerator pump assembly. Test follow-up spring for compression.
	(b) Faulty accelerator pump discharge ball.	(b) Disassemble carburetor. Use compressed air to clean discharge nozzle and channels after soaking main body in a suitable solvent. Test fuel pump capacity.
	(c) Faulty accelerator pump inlet check ball.	(c) Disassemble carburetor. Check accelerator pump inlet, check ball for poor seat or release. If part is faulty, replace.
	(d) Incorrect fuel or float level.	(d) Test fuel or float level in carburetor. Adjust as necessary to obtain correct float level.
	(e) Worn accelerator pump and throttle linkage.	(e) Disassemble carburetor. Replace worn accelerator pump and throttle linkage and measure for correct position.
	(f) Incorrect pump setting.	(f) Reset pump.
CARBURETOR FLOODS OR LEAKS	(a) Cracked body.	(a) Disassemble carburetor. Replace cracked body. Make sure main to throttle body screws are tight.

Condition	Possible Cause	Correction
	(b) Faulty body gaskets.	(b) Disassemble carburetor. Replace defective gaskets and test for leakage. Be sure screws are tightened securely.
	(c) High float level.	(c) Test fuel level in carburetor. Make necessary adjustment to obtain correct float level.
	(d) Worn needle valve and seat.	(d) Clean and inspect needle valve and seat. If found to be in a questionable condition, replace complete assembly and test fuel pump pressure.
	(e) Excessive fuel pump pressure.	(e) Test fuel pump pressure. If pressure is in excess of recommended pressure replace fuel pump.
POOR PERFORMANCE MIXTURE TOO RICH	(a) Restricted air cleaner.	(a) Remove and clean air cleaner or replace element.
	(b) Leaking float.	(b) Disassemble carburetor. Replace leaking float. Test float level and correct as necessary, to proper level.
	(c) High float level.	(c) Adjust float level as necessary to secure proper level.
	(d) Excessive fuel pump pressure.	(d) Test fuel pump pressure. If pressure is in excess of recommended pressure, replace fuel pump assembly.
	(e) Worn metering jet.	(e) Disassemble carburetor. Replace worn metering jet, using a new jet of the correct size and type.
	(b) Choke adjustment lean.	(b) Adjust to specifications.
ENGINE OUTPUT LOW	(a) Fast idle speed low.	(a) Adjust to specification.
	(b) Fast idle cam position adjustment incorrect.	(b) Adjust to specifications.
	(c) Engine lubrication oil of incorrect viscosity.	(c) Recommend proper grade oil for ambient temperature.
CARBURETOR LEAN	(a) Curb idle set very lean.	(a) Adjust to specifications.
	(b) Air leak bypassing the carburetor.	(b) Repair.
INCORRECT PROCEDURE	(a) (See Owners Manual.)	(a) Instruct owner.
CHOKE VALVE FAILS TO CLOSE	(a) Choke thermostat adjustment leaner than specified.	(a) Adjust.
	(b) Choke thermostat corroded such that it has cracked and distorted lean.	(b) Replace assembly.
	(c) Choke linkage, shaft or related parts corroded, bent or dirty such that the system is not entirely free to move from the open to the closed position.	(c) Repair, clean or replace.
	(d) Choke valve improperly seated.	(d) Reseat valve.
	(e) Air cleaner gasket interferes with choke valve or linkage.	(e) Reinstall gasket properly.

CHAPTER FOUR

ENGINE—914/4

The 914 engine is a 4-cylinder horizontally opposed air-cooled design. See **Figure 1**. Each cylinder has its own finned barrel. Two cylinders on each bank share a common head with pushrod-operated overhead valves.

The cylinders mount on an aluminum crankcase manufactured in 2 halves. Four main bearings support the crankshaft and 3 bearings support the camshaft. Those familiar with VW engines will find this engine easy to work on.

This chapter includes repair procedures for all 914 engines.

ENGINE REMOVAL/INSTALLATION

1. Mark engine compartment lid near hinges to aid installation, then remove lid. See Chapter Fifteen.
2. Disconnect battery ground cable.
3. Remove air cleaner (see Chapter Seven or Eight).
4. Remove the heater blower and hoses (see Chapter Six).
5. Disconnect cables from fuel injection components (see **Figure 2**).
6. Disconnect throttle valve cable and push through engine cover plate.
7. Disconnect fuel lines shown in **Figure 3**.
8. Disconnect starter cables.

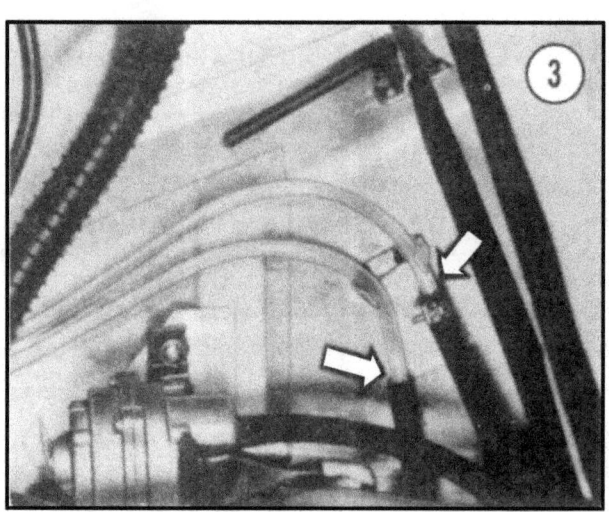

9. Raise rear of vehicle.
10. Disconnect heater hoses from bottom of engine.
11. Unscrew shift rod holder (see **Figure 4**).
12. Remove bolts shown in **Figure 5** and remove rear shift rod.
13. Remove heat control box with hoses and cables.
14. Loosen adjusting nut and mounting nut on clutch cable guide roller. See **Figure 6**. Disconnect clutch cable.

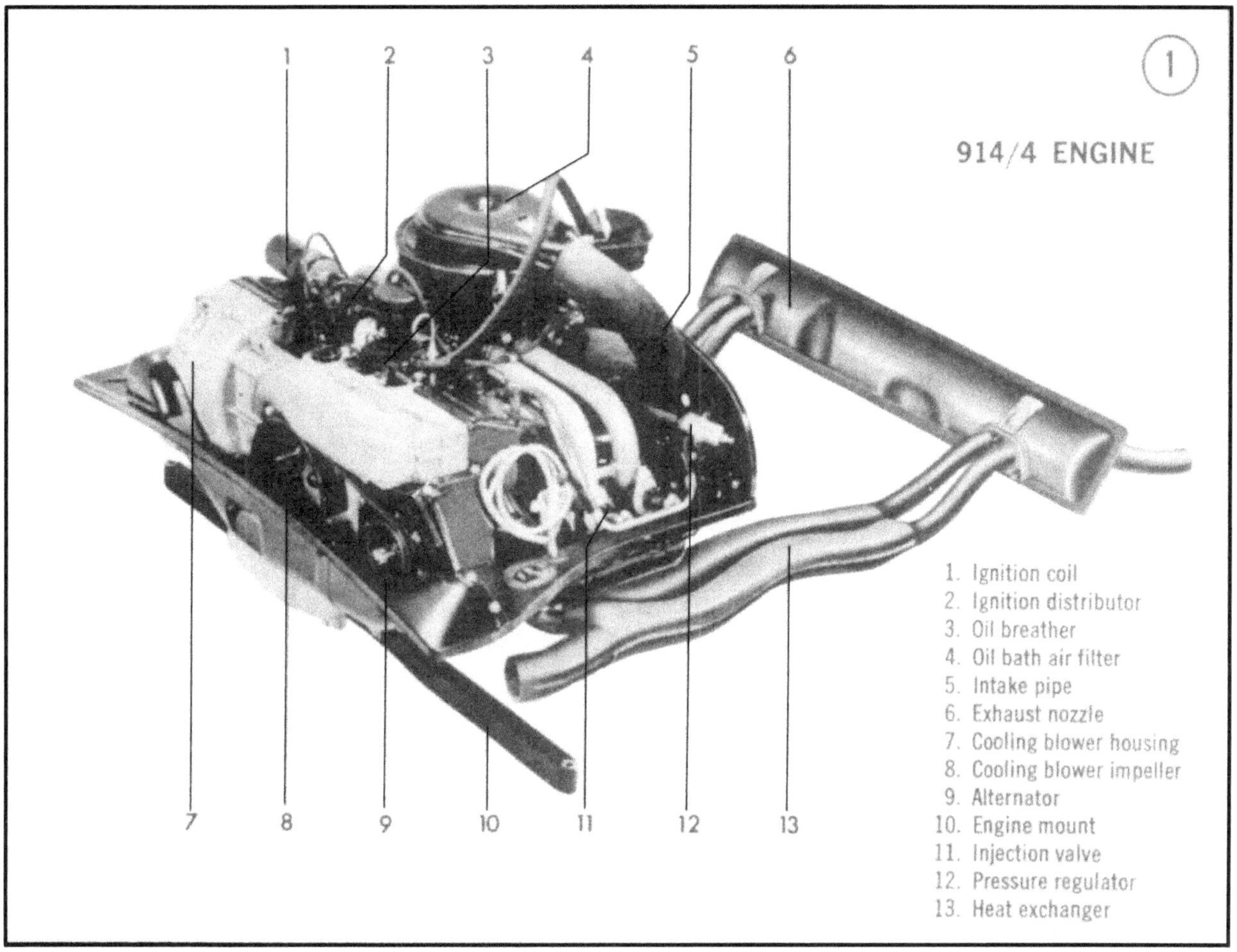

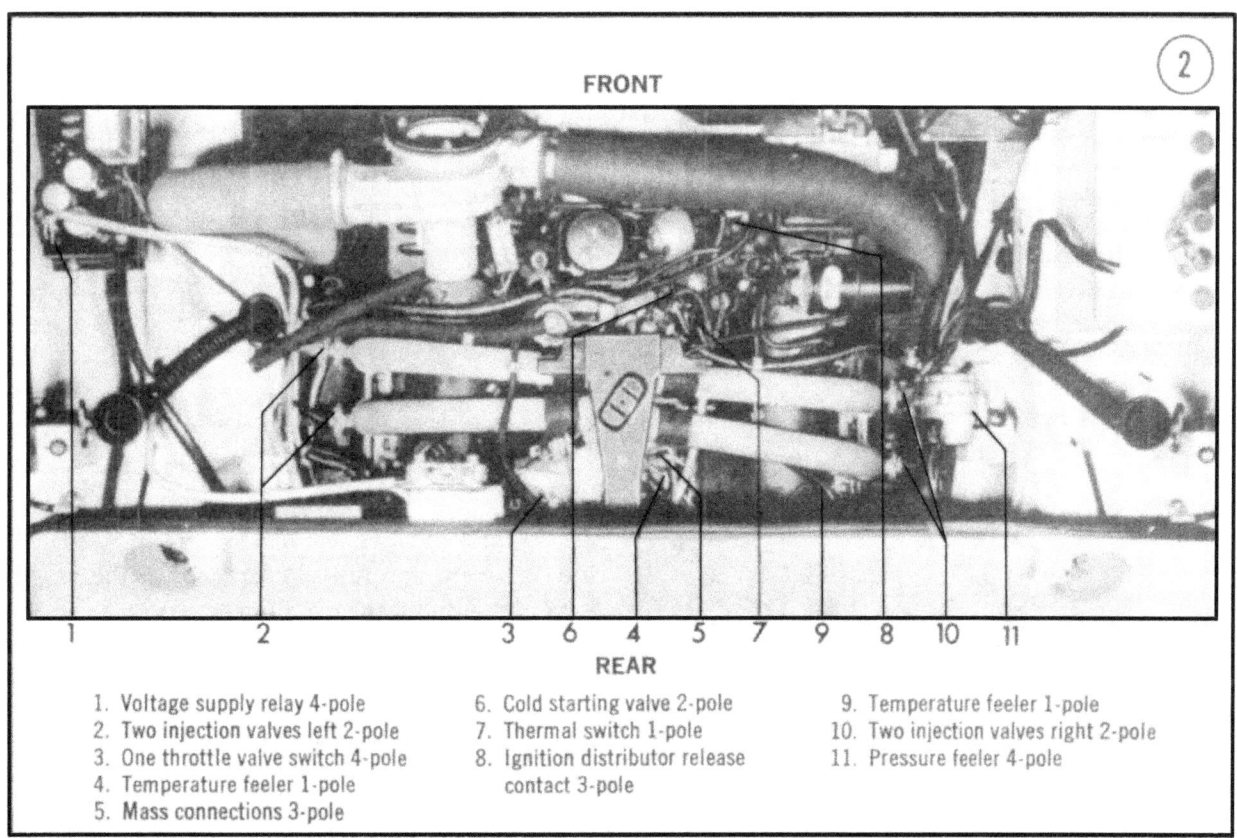

1
2
3
4
5
6
1
914/4 ENGINE
7
8
9
10
11
12
13
1. Ignition coil
2. Ignition distributor
3. Oil breather
4. Oil bath air filter
5. Intake pipe
6. Exhaust nozzle
7. Cooling blower housing
8. Cooling blower impeller
9. Alternator
10. Engine mount
11. Injection valve
12. Pressure regulator
13. Heat exchanger

2
FRONT
1
2
3
6
4
5
7
9
8
10
11
REAR
1. Voltage supply relay 4-pole
2. Two injection valves left 2-pole
3. One throttle valve switch 4-pole
4. Temperature feeler 1-pole
5. Mass connections 3-pole
6. Cold starting valve 2-pole
7. Thermal switch 1-pole
8. Ignition distributor release contact 3-pole
9. Temperature feeler 1-pole
10. Two injection valves right 2-pole
11. Pressure feeler 4-pole

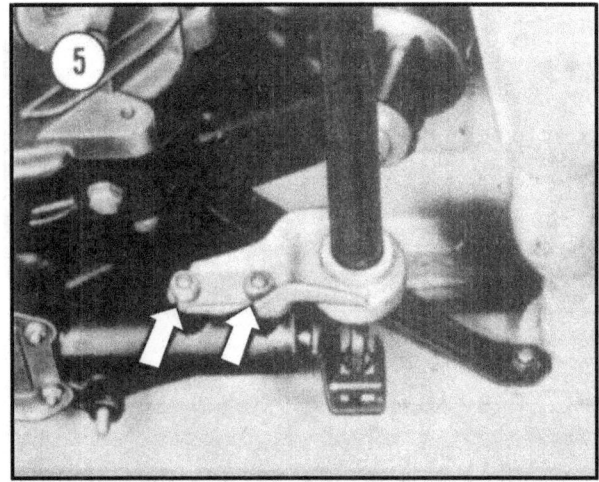

15. Disconnect speedometer drive cable.
16. Remove starter and ground strap.

17. Disconnect axle shafts from transaxle (see Chapter Twelve). Suspend from body with wire.
18. Place garage-type jack under center of engine/transaxle assembly and raise the jack just far enough to take weight of assembly.
19. Remove 4 nuts on transaxle support. See **Figure 7**.

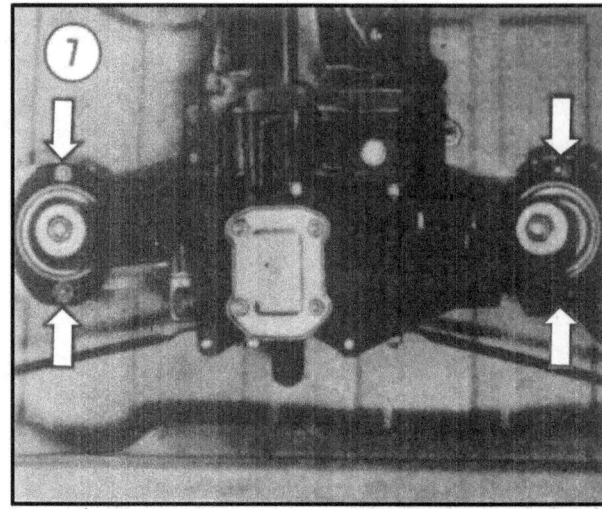

20. Remove the engine mounting bolts. See **Figure 8**.

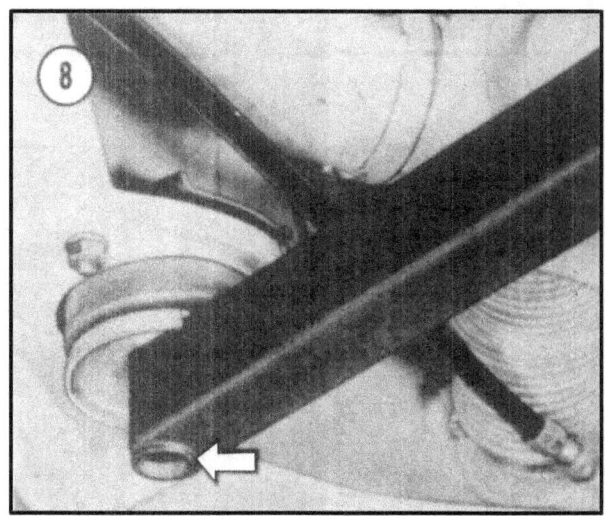

21. While a helper steadies the engine/transaxle on the jack, carefully lower it until the engine clears the body, then pull it out.
22. Installation is the reverse of these steps.

NOTE: *Be sure you do not pinch fuel lines to injectors and that the handbrake cables are above the engine mount.*

23. Tighten the engine mounting bolts to 22 foot-pounds (3.0 mkg) and the transaxle support nuts to 14.5 foot-pounds (2.0 mkg).

ENGINE/TRANSAXLE SEPARATION (MANUAL)

1. Remove 2 lower engine mounting nuts. Remove 2 upper engine mounting nuts.
2. Pull engine straight back until clutch release plate clears the main shaft.

CAUTION
Do not let engine tilt or let engine weight put any load on shaft or clutch parts.

ENGINE/TRANSAXLE JOINING (MANUAL)

1. Clean transaxle case and engine flange thoroughly.
2. Ensure that clutch disc is properly centered (see Chapter Ten). Inspect clutch release bearing for wear and cracks. Replace if necessary.
3. Lubricate starter shaft bushing with graphite grease. Put 2-3cc in flywheel gland nut.
4. Apply molybdenum disulphide powder or graphite grease to main shaft spline and pilot journal. Apply same lubricant to starter pinion gear teeth and ring gear teeth (on flywheel).
5. Put transmission in gear to steady mainshaft.
6. Rotate engine crankshaft with fan belt so that the clutch plate hub lines up with the main shaft splines. Take care that gland nut needle bearing, clutch release bearing, and main shaft are not damaged when pushing engine forward.

CAUTION
Do not let engine tilt or let engine weight put any load on drive shaft or clutch parts.

7. Guide lower engine mounting studs into position, then push engine firmly against transaxle until it is flush all the way around.
8. Install upper mounting bolts and nuts and tighten slightly. Then tighten all bolts and nuts to 34 foot-pounds (4.7 mkg).

ENGINE/TRANSAXLE SEPARATION (SPORTOMATIC)

1. Disconnect oil hose and pressure line from temperature sensor housing. See **Figure 9**.

2. Loosen oil hose clamp at transmission.
3. Disconnect vacuum hose from vacuum servo.
4. Remove 12-point bolts which hold the torque converter to the drive plate. See **Figure 10**.

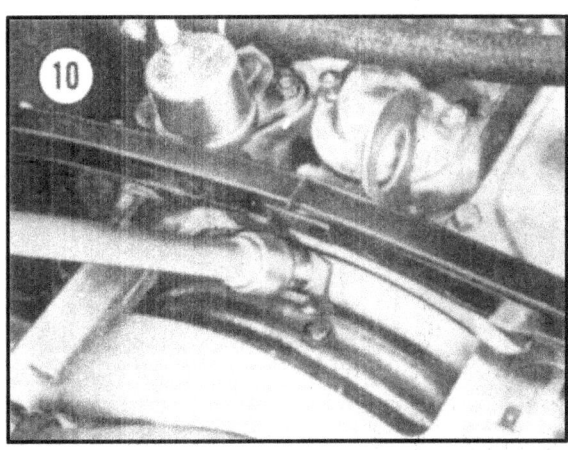

5. Remove 2 lower mounting nuts.
6. Remove 2 upper engine mounting nuts.
7. Separate engine and transaxle. Leave torque converter in transaxle and secure with a strap. See **Figure 11**.

ENGINE/TRANSAXLE JOINING (SPORTOMATIC)

1. Clean the transaxle case and engine flanges thoroughly.
2. Lubricate starter shaft bushing with graphite grease.

69

3. Remove strap from torque converter.

4. Join engine and transaxle and bolt them together. Tighten to 34 foot-pounds (4.7 mkg).

5. Rotate crankshaft so that drive plate-to-torque converter bolts can be installed. Tighten them to 17-19 foot-pounds (2.4-2.6 mkg).

6. Connect vacuum hose to vacuum servo.

7. Connect oil hose and pressure line to temperature sensor housing.

8. Adjust cluch free-play as described in Chapter Eleven.

ENGINE DISASSEMBLY/ASSEMBLY

The following sequences are designed so that the engine need not be disassembled any further than necessary. Each step includes chapter numbers of detailed procedures required to complete the step. Unless otherwise indicated, procedures for major assemblies in these sequences are included in this chapter. The procedures are arranged in the approximate order in which they are performed.

To perform a step, turn to the procedure for the major assembly indicated, e.g., cylinder head, and perform the removal and inspection procedures, etc., until the engine is disassembled. To reassemble, reverse the disassembly sequence order and perform the installation procedure for the major assembly involved.

Decarbonizing or Valve Service

1. Remove cover plates.
2. Remove valve rocker assemblies.
3. Remove cylinder heads.
4. Remove and inspect valves, guides, and seats.
5. Assembly is the reverse of these steps.

Valve and Ring Service

1. Perform Steps 1-4 for valve service.
2. Remove cylinders.
3. Remove rings. It is not necessary to remove the pistons unless they are damaged.
4. Assembly is the reverse of these steps.

General Overhaul Sequence

1. Remove cover plates and fan housing.
2. Remove engine carrier.
3. Remove oil cooler.
4. Remove distributor (Chapter Nine) and distributor drive gear.
5. Remove clutch assembly (Chapter Ten) and flywheel.
6. Remove valve rocker assemblies.
7. Remove cylinder heads.
8. Remove cylinders and pistons.
9. Remove oil pump and oil strainer.
10. Disassemble crankcase.
11. Remove camshaft, crankshaft, and connecting rods.
12. Assembly is the reverse of these steps.

OIL COOLER

If the oil cooler has been leaking, check the oil pressure relief valve(s) for damage possibly causing high oil pressure.

> NOTE: *Oil cooler fins often bulge due to high oil pressure. Since this may restrict air cooling, replace bulging oil coolers.*

If non-detergent oil has been used and you wish to change to detergent oil, clean the oil cooler thoroughly to remove all foreign particles and blow out with compressed air. If cleaning is not effective, replace with a new oil cooler.

Removal

Refer to **Figure 12** for the following procedure.

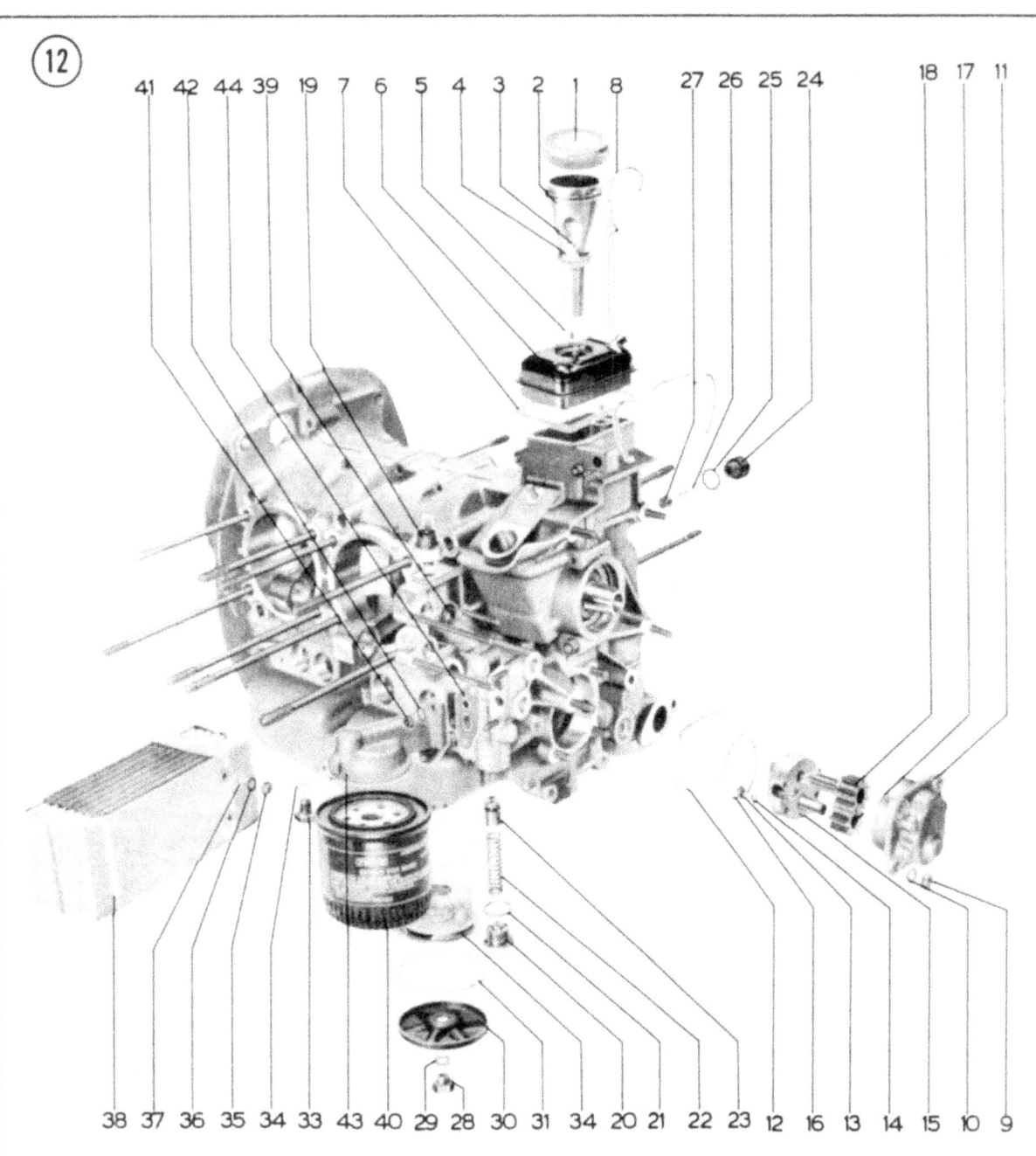

OIL COOLER

1. Oil filler cover
2. Oil filler
3. Nut
4. Lockwasher
5. Seal
6. Oil vent
7. Seal
8. Dipstick
9. Nut
10. Lockwasher
11. Oil pump housing
12. Seal
13. Nut
14. Lockwasher
15. Oil pump cover
16. Sealing ring
17. Oil pump gear
18. Drive shaft
19. Oil pressure switch
20. Plug
21. Sealing ring
22. Spring
23. Piston
24. Plug
25. Sealing ring
26. Spring
27. Piston
28. Plug
29. Sealing ring
30. Oil strainer cover
31. Seal
32. Oil strainer
33. Closing screw
34. Sealing ring
35. Hex nut
36. Lockwasher
37. Washer
38. Oil cooler
39. Sealing ring for oil cooler
40. Oil filter
41. Hex nut
42. Lockwasher
43. Intermediate flange for oil filter
44. Seal

1. Remove the oil cooler retaining nuts.
2. Pull oil cooler off and remove rubber seals.
3. Pour solvent into the cooler and let it soak upside down. Pour the solvent out and flush with clean solvent.
4. Check that no ribs are touching and no parts are loose.

Installation

Refer to Figure 12 for the following procedure.
1. Install new seals on the bracket.
2. Install the oil cooler and nuts. Tighten all nuts evenly. The oil cooler must be horizontal or the seals may leak.

DISTRIBUTOR DRIVE SHAFT

Removal

The distributor drive shaft may be removed with the engine installed.

1. If the engine will not be disassembled, remove the distributor cap and turn the engine so the rotor points toward the notch on the distributor housing rim. This puts piston #1 at TDC of its compression stroke.

> NOTE: Do not turn the crankshaft after removing the distributor. If you do, see Chapter Two (Valve Adjustment) to position piston #1 at TDC.

2. Remove the distributor (see Chapter Nine).
3. Remove the spring on top of the distributor drive shaft.
4. Extract the drive shaft with a special tool by rotating it to the left and lifting up simultaneously. One method which works well is shown in **Figure 13**.
5. Reach down into the crankcase through the distributor drive shaft hole, using a magnet, and lift out the thrust washer.

> CAUTION
> Do not drop the washer into the crankcase if you do not intend to disassemble the crankcase. Occasionally it is possible to fish it out if dropped; usually it means splitting the crankcase.

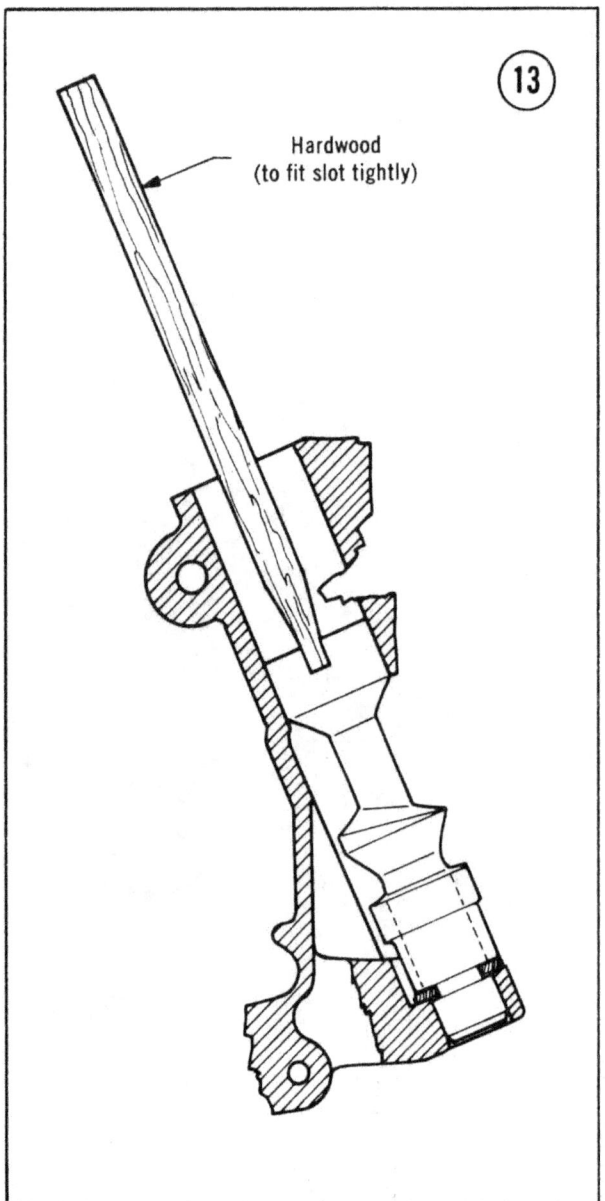

Inspection

Check the distributor drive gear for wear. If the distributor drive gear is worn you should also check the crankshaft gear. This means completely disassembling the engine.

Installation

This procedure should be performed after the engine is completely assembled, with the exception of the distributor and fuel pump.

1. Ensure that piston #1 is at TDC on its compression stroke. If you have not disassembled the engine or turned the crankshaft since distributor removal, it should be correct. Otherwise, see Chapter Two (*Valve Adjustment*) to set piston #1 correctly.

2. Insert a small wire rod (coathanger wire) to the bottom of the distributor shaft hole.

3. Apply universal grease to the thrust washer and slide it down the wire (see **Figure 14**). Do not move the rod until the washer is in place; the rod keeps the washer from dropping into the crankcase. Look into the hole and check that the washer is all the way down and centered, then remove the rod. Grease holds the washer in place.

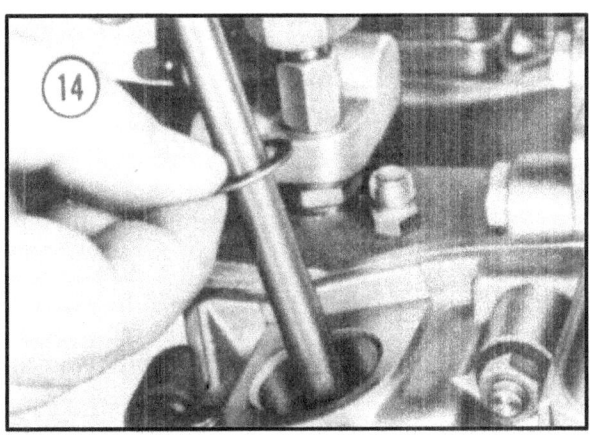

4. Oil the distributor drive shaft and insert it. The slot must be at a 12° angle to the crankcase seam with the small segment towards the oil cooler. See **Figure 15**. Push the shaft down with a large screwdriver until you are certain it is seated in the thrust washer.

5. Turn the crankshaft by hand and watch the distributor drive shaft. If the shaft turns, it is seated properly.

6. Insert the wire rod into the hole in the distributor drive shaft. Slide the small spring over the rod into the shaft. See **Figure 16**. Remove the rod.

7. Install the distributor.

FLYWHEEL

Removal

1. Remove the clutch pressure plate and clutch disc. See Chapter Ten.

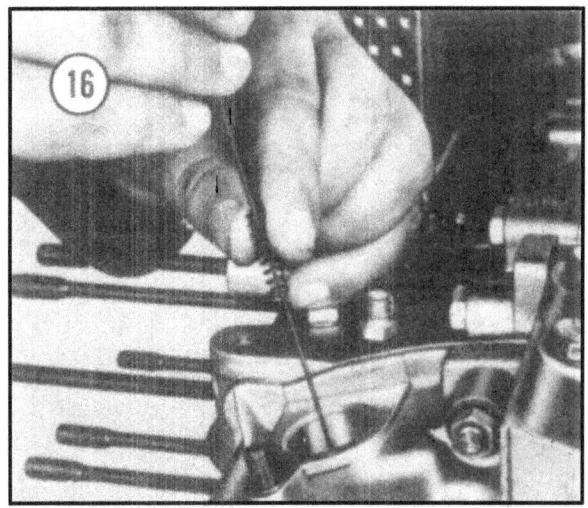

2. Mark the relationship between the flywheel and crankshaft.

3. Hold the flywheel in a special retainer. Remove 5 bolts holding the flywheel to the crankshaft. If a special retainer is unobtainable, use the equipment shown in **Figure 17A**.

4. Pull the flywheel off.

Inspection

1. Check the flywheel teeth for wear or damage. If teeth are damaged only slightly, up to 0.08″ may be machined off the clutch side. Rechamfer the edges of the teeth.

2. Check the drive shaft bushing in the flywheel. If worn, have your dealer replace it.

3. Check flywheel friction surface. If worn excessively, replace the flywheel.

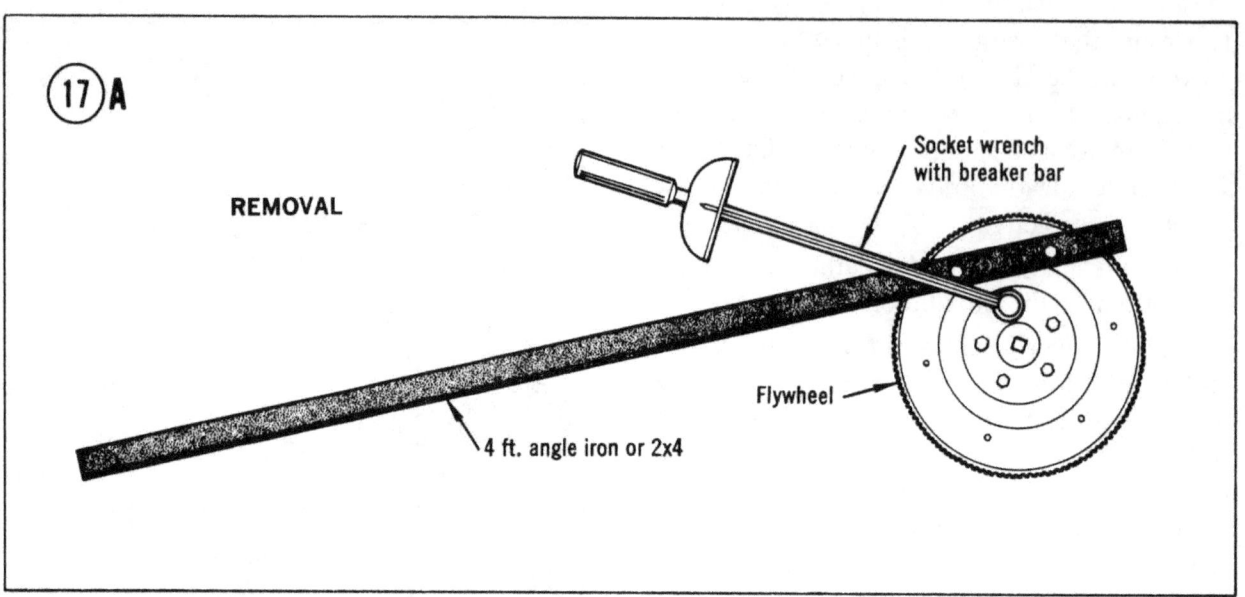

Installation

1. Lubricate the outer surfaces of the front crankcase oil seal.

2. Reinstall the flywheel on the crankshaft using the roll pin and a new rubber seal. If the crankshaft, flywheel, or clutch is new, note that the heaviest points are marked. The crankshaft is marked with a spot of paint and a 5mm hole on the flywheel end. The flywheel and clutch may be marked with a painted line on the outer edge. If all 3 parts have a mark, install them so the marks are positioned 120° from each other. If only 2 have a mark, install them so the marks are 180° from each other.

3. Install 5 bolts with new outer plate. See **Figure 17B**.

4. Check crankcase end-play using a procedure applicable to your engine (see *Crankshaft End-Play*).

5. Check flywheel runout. The easiest method is to attach a dial indicator as in **Figure 18**, rotate the flywheel and note the reading variation or runout. A more tedious method requires the threaded stock and flat bar used for end-play measurement (see **Figure 19**). Set the bar 0.012" from the face of the flywheel. Mark off the rim of the flywheel so each segment is near the flat bar and measure the gap. When all 6 gaps are

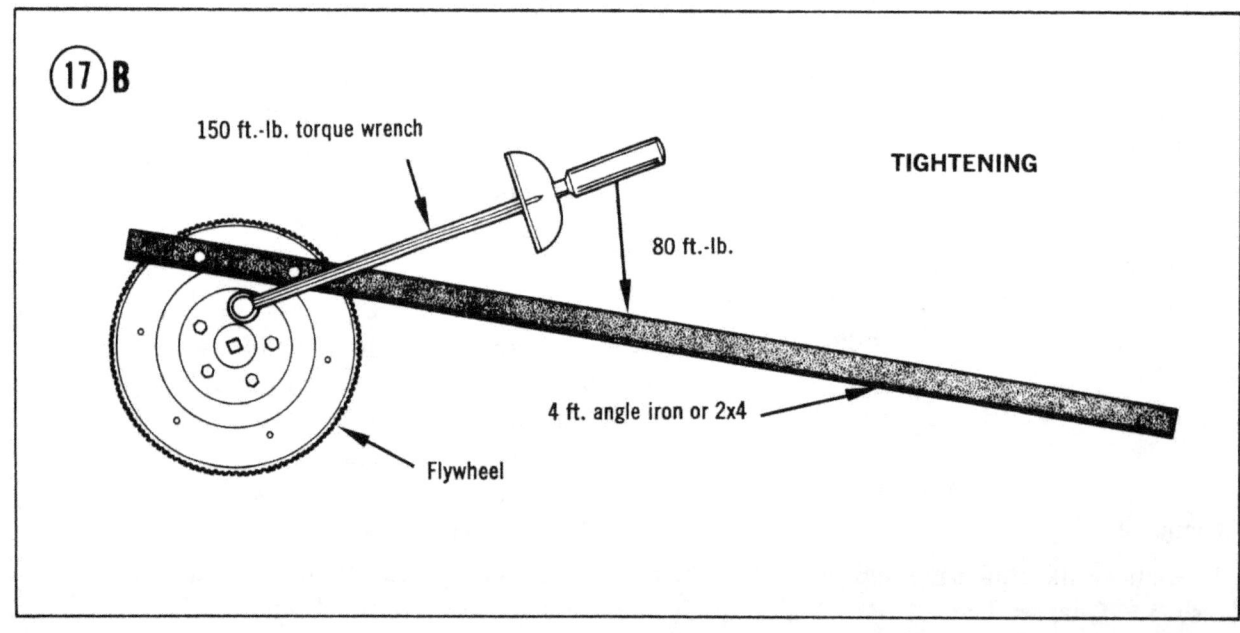

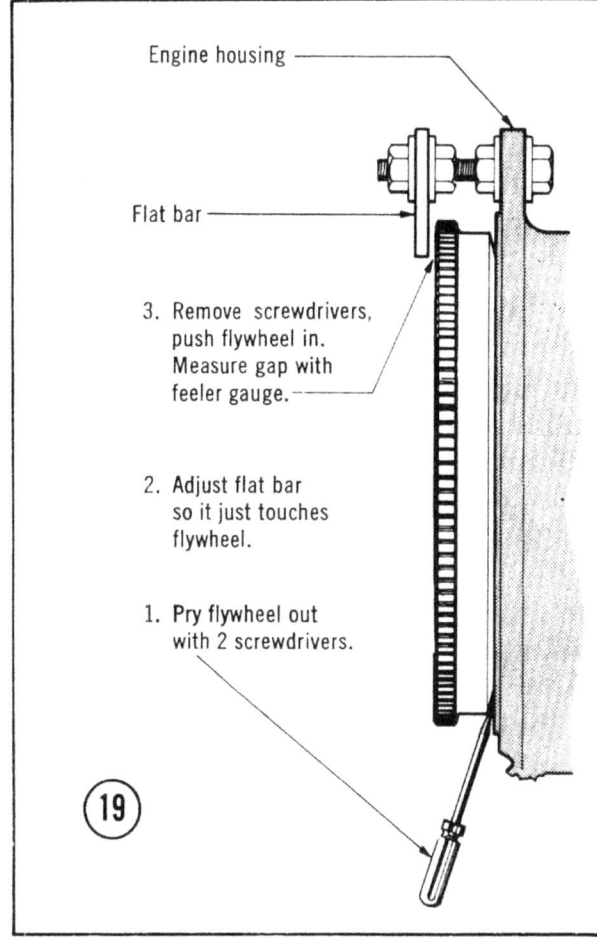

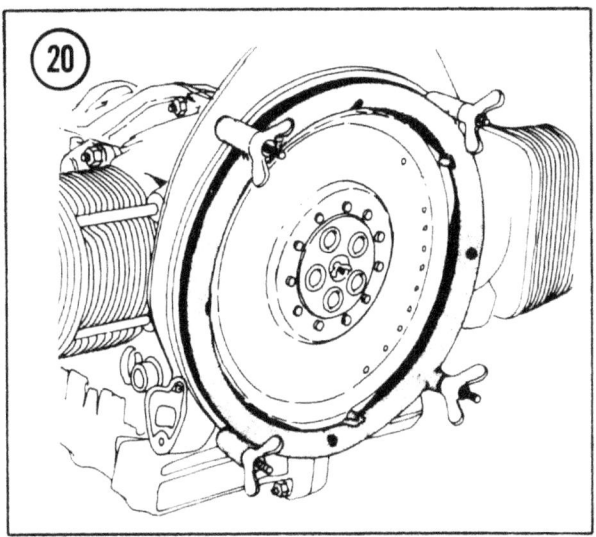

recorded, determine that no 2 gaps vary more than 0.012". If any do, the flywheel must be machined true or replaced.

DRIVE PLATE

The drive plate for the Sportomatic is attached to the crankshaft with 5 cap screws in the same manner as the flywheel.

A special retaining ring shown in **Figure 20** is required to hold the drive plate while removing the cap screws. Rather than improvise a ring and risk warping the drive plate, take the entire engine to a Porsche dealer and let him remove it. Later when the engine is reassembled, let Porsche reinstall the drive plate.

CRANKSHAFT END-PLAY

Crankshaft end-play must be adjusted any time the engine is completely disassembled, and should be checked any time the engine is removed for whatever purpose.

Two methods are used to check end-play. By far the easiest is the dial indicator method. But dial indicators are expensive. Those who do not wish to purchase one may use the second method.

Dial Indicator Method

1. If not done previously, remove rear oil seal.
2. Install the flywheel with 2 shims, but without the rubber seal.
3. Attach a dial indicator as shown in Figure 18.
4. Move the crankshaft back and forth. Read the end-play on dial indicator. Record this figure.
5. Calculate the thickness of the 3rd shim by subtracting desired end-play, 0.0028-0.0051" (0.07-0.13mm), from the figure recorded in the previous step.
6. Remove the flywheel, install a 3rd shim as

calculated above, and reinstall the flywheel. Use a new rubber seal.

7. Remeasure the end-play. If it is correct, remove the flywheel, and install the rear oil seal (see procedure later in this chapter). Reinstall the flywheel. If end-play is not correct, change one of the shims and remeasure.

Without Dial Indicator

1. Install the flywheel as described in Step 2 of the dial indicator method.

2. Attach a 5" length of ⅜" threaded stock to the crankcase with 2 nuts. See Figure 19.

3. Attach a piece of flat bar stock to the threaded stock with 2 nuts. Leave the nuts loose.

4. With a large screwdriver, carefully pry between the flywheel and crankcase to move the crankshaft all the way forward. Have someone hold the screwdriver in this position.

5. Adjust the flat bar stock on the threaded rod until it just touches the surface of the flywheel. Tighten the nuts in this position.

6. Remove the screwdriver and push the flywheel back.

7. Insert a feeler gauge between the flat bar stock and the flywheel. This is end-play; record this figure.

8. Calculate the thickness of the 3rd shim and install it and the flywheel as described in Steps 4-6 of the dial indicator method.

REAR OIL SEAL

The oil seal normally leaks a small amount of oil which lubricates the seal lips and prevents them from burning. This leaking causes a thin smear of oil to coat the transmission case, and does not indicate a defective seal. Replace the seal if leaking appears excessive or if the seal is removed for any reason; never reuse a seal.

Removal

1. Remove flywheel using the procedure given previously.

2. Carefully pry the old seal out with a screwdriver or other sharp object. See **Figure 21**. Don't nick crankcase surface. Discard oil seal.

3. Leave all end-play shims in the crankcase.

Installation

1. If oil seal replacement is part of an engine overhaul, adjust the crankshaft end-play as described earlier before installing the oil seal. Otherwise, end-play adjustment is desirable, but not necessary.

2. Clean the recess between the crankcase and crankshaft. If necessary, chamfer the edges of the crankcase opening slightly so that the oil seal seats without damage. Carefully clean any metal flakes out.

3. Ensure that proper end-play shims are in place and install oil seal with the closed side out. One method is to put the seal in place and gently tap it with a hammer via a small block of wood, working slowly and evenly around the seal until it is flush with the bottom of the crankcase recess. Another method requires a special tool shown in **Figure 22** which presses the seal in evenly. This is easily improvised with a metal plate, large nut, and bolt to fit the hole in the end of the crankshaft.

4. Reinstall flywheel as described previously.

FRONT OIL SEAL

Removal

1. Pull the fan hub with a special puller as shown in **Figure 23**.

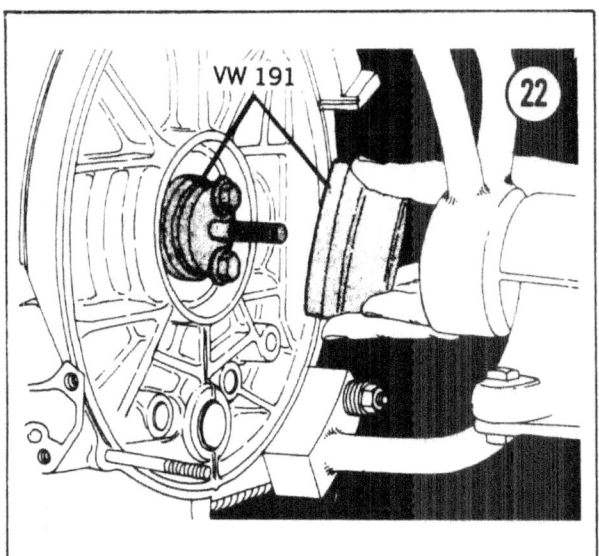

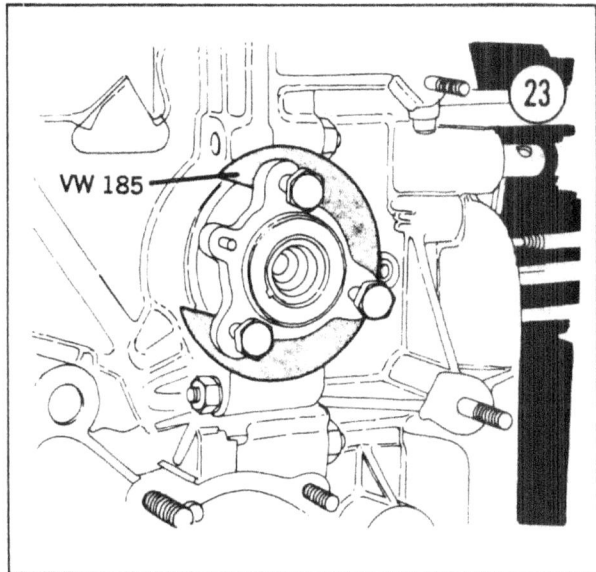

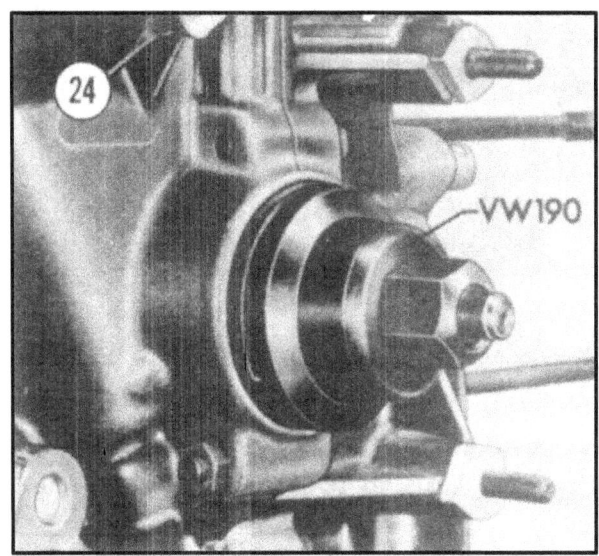

2. Carefully pry the old seal out with a screwdriver or other sharp object. Don't nick the crankcase. Discard the oil seal.

Installation

1. Clean the recess between crankcase and crankshaft. If necessary, chamfer the edges of the crankcase opening slightly so that the oil seal seats without damage. Carefully clean out any metal flakes.

2. Install oil seal with the closed side out. One method is to put the seal in place and gently tap it with a hammer via a small block of wood. Work slowly and evenly around the seal until it is flush with the bottom of the crankcase recess. Another method requires a special tool shown in **Figure 24** which presses the seal in evenly. This is easily improvised with a metal plate, large nut, and bolt to fit the hole in the end of the crankshaft.

3. Install the fan hub with Woodruff key and new seal.

VALVE ROCKER ASSEMBLY

Removal

1. Clean away road dirt around the valve covers.

2. Pry the valve cover holder down and remove the valve cover.

3. Remove pushrod tube retainer wires. See **Figure 25**.

4. Remove rocker shaft support nuts and keep them separate from other hardware. These are copper-plated and must be used to reinstall the rocker shaft.

5. Pull off rocker shafts with rocker arms.

6. Remove all 4 pushrods and store them so that they may be reinstalled in exactly the same place. See **Figure 26**.

Rocker Shaft Disassembly/Assembly

1. Mark the rocker arms so they may be reinstalled in the same position.

2. Slide all the parts off the shaft.

3. Clean all parts in solvent. Examine the bearing surfaces of the shaft and rocker arms. Small

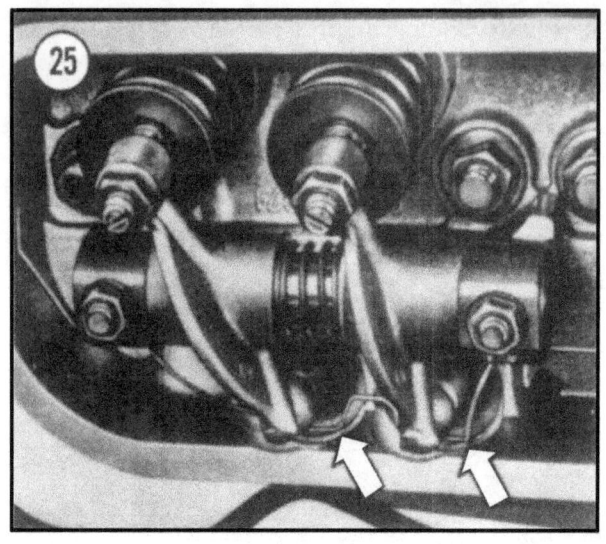

irregularities may be removed with crocus cloth. Check rocker arm seats and ball sockets for wear.

4. Coat all parts with assembly lubricant and reassemble as shown in **Figure 27**.

Installation

1. Roll each pushrod on a flat surface to check for bends.

2. Install pushrods in the cylinder head.

3. Install the rocker shaft assemblies. The chamfered edge of the support points outward and the slot points downward. See Figure 27.

4. Ensure that the pushrod ball ends are centered in the rocker arm sockets. In addition, ensure that the rocker arm adjusting screws contact the valves slightly off center as shown in **Figure 28**.

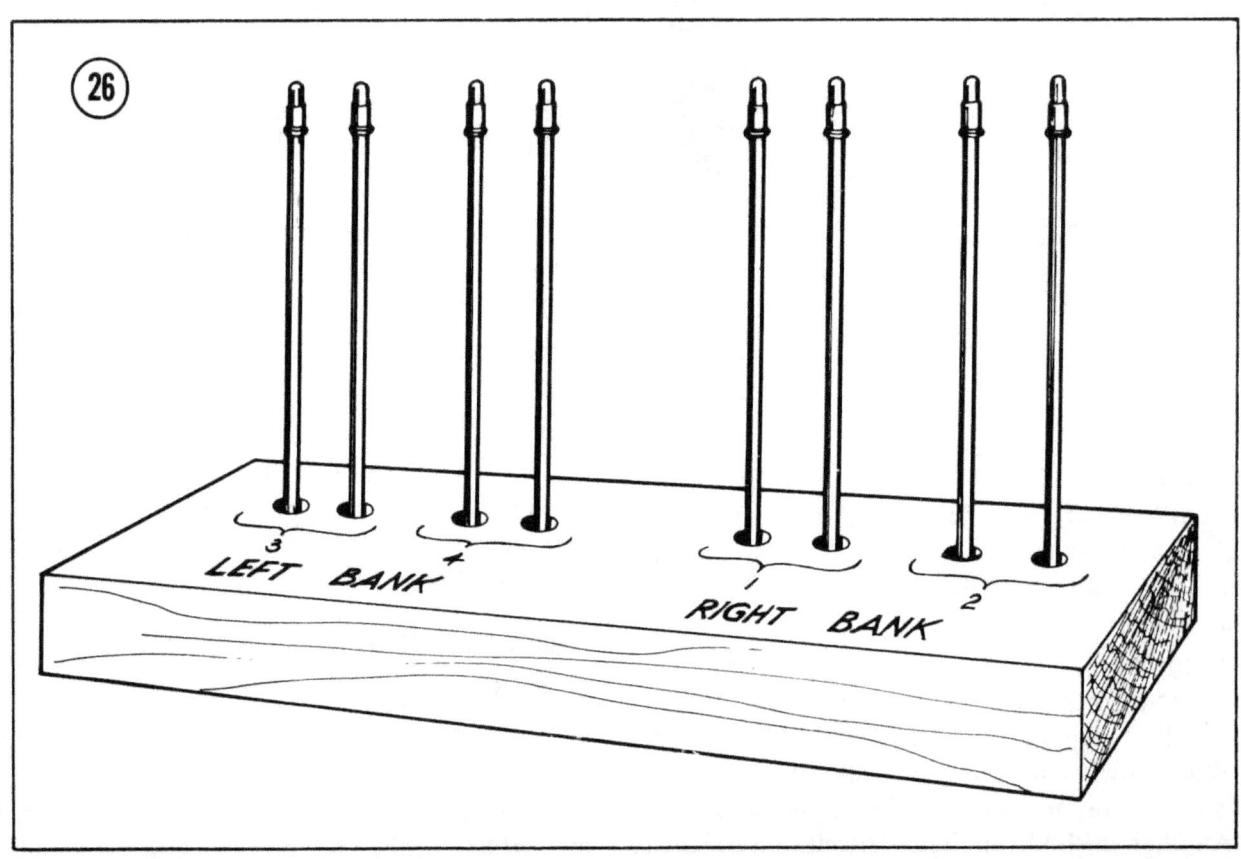

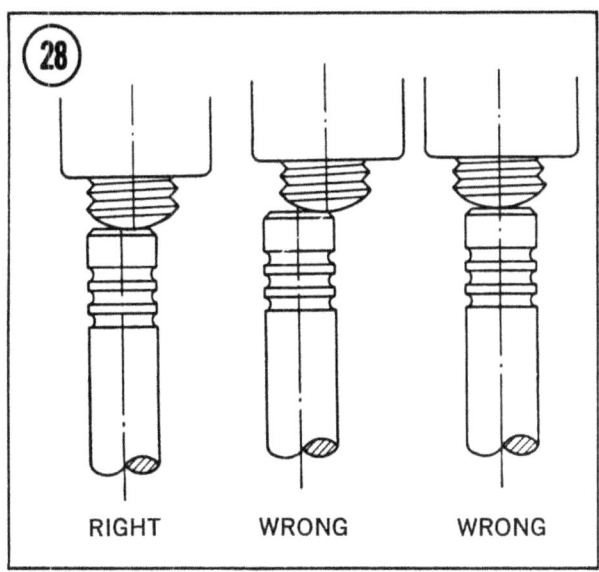

RIGHT — WRONG — WRONG

5. Tighten rocker arm shaft nuts to 10 foot-pounds (1.4 mkg).

6. Adjust intake and exhaust valves. See Chapter Two.

7. Clean all traces of old gasket from the valve covers.

8. Hold new gaskets in place on the valve covers with grease. Install covers.

CYLINDER HEADS

Cylinder heads for various models and years differ in many ways. The cooling rib design may differ. Spark plugs are angled differently on some heads and project farther into the combustion chambers. In addition, larger engines have larger valve seats.

Removal

1. Remove the valve rocker assemblies as described.

2. Loosen all 8 cylinder head nuts (see **Figure 29** for location). Remove the nuts and washers. Keep all head washers separate from other hardware. They are special and available only from Porsche if lost.

3. Pull the cylinder head off. If it is stuck, carefully pry the head and cylinders apart. In particularly tough cases, tap on the exhaust manifold studs with a hammer and block of wood. Never hammer on the fragile fins.

4. Remove the copper sealing rings from the shoulder of the cylinders.

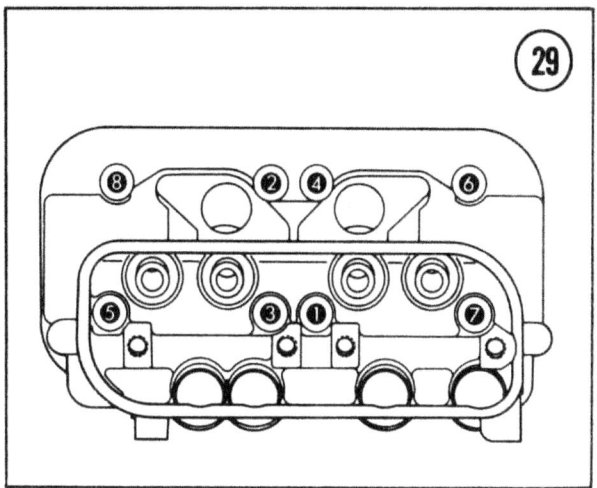

5. If performing a valve job, it is unnecessary to remove the cylinders. Tie them on with soft wire.

Inspection

1. Without removing valves, remove all carbon deposits from the combustion chambers with a wire brush. A blunt screwdriver or chisel may be used if care is taken not to damage the head or valves.

2. After all carbon is removed from combustion chamber, both valves, and intake and exhaust ports, clean the entire head with solvent.

3. Clean away all carbon on the piston crown. DO NOT remove the carbon ridge at the top of the cylinder bore.

4. Check for cracks in the combustion chamber and exhaust ports. Cracked heads must be replaced.

5. Check all studs for tightness. If a stud can't be tightened, have a machinist drill the hole out and and install a Heli-coil threaded insert.

6. Push the valve stem ends sideways with your thumb. If there is any play, the valve guides are probably worn. Replace them as described later if in doubt.

Installation

1. Install new rubber seals on both ends of all pushrod tubes. The white seal goes on the cylinder head end of the tube; the black seal goes on the crankcase end.

2. Install new sealing rings on the cylinder shoulders. The narrow edge faces out.

3. Place the head on the studs and push it in slightly.

4. Install at least one head nut with washer. If the washer won't fit at this time, install nut without it. Tighten the nut until the other washers and nuts can be installed. Then be sure to install a washer under the first nut. Remember, these are special thick washers available only from Porsche.

5. Tighten the nuts to 7 foot-pounds (1 mkg).

6. Tighten nuts to 22-23 ft.-lbs. (3-3.2 mkg) in the order shown in **Figure 29**.

7. Insert pushrod tubes from top of cylinder head as far as they will go. Do not damage seals. Install retaining wire so it engages in the rocker shaft support slots and rests on the lower edges of the tubes. See **Figure 25**.

VALVES AND VALVE SEATS

See **Figure 30** for valve specifications.

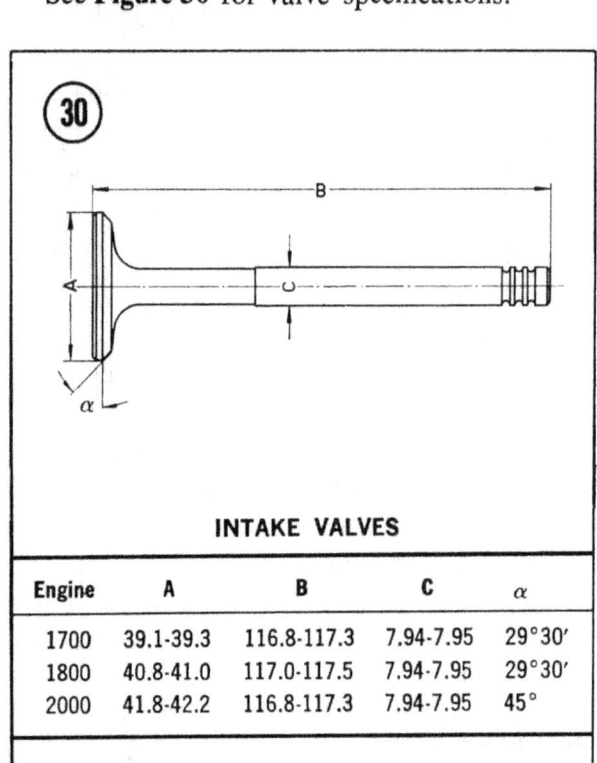

INTAKE VALVES

Engine	A	B	C	α
1700	39.1-39.3	116.8-117.3	7.94-7.95	29°30'
1800	40.8-41.0	117.0-117.5	7.94-7.95	29°30'
2000	41.8-42.2	116.8-117.3	7.94-7.95	45°

EXHAUST VALVES

Engine	A	B	C	α
1700	32.7-33.0	117.0-117.5	8.91-8.92	45°
1800	33.7-34.0	116.8-117.5	8.91-8.92	45°
2000	35.8-36.2	117.0-117.5	8.91-8.92	45°

Removal

1. Remove cylinder head.

2. Compress springs with a valve spring compression tool, remove the valve keepers, and release compression. See **Figure 31**.

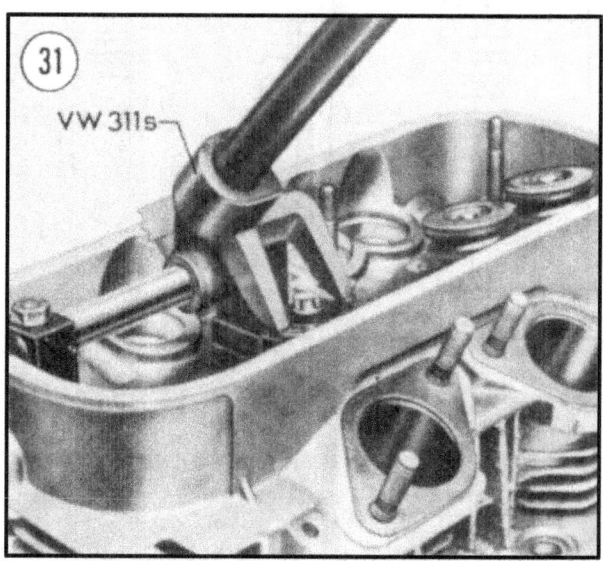

3. Remove the valve spring caps, springs, oil deflector rings, and valves.

CAUTION
Remove any burrs from valve stem grooves before removing valve. Otherwise valve guides will be damaged.

Inspection

1. Clean valves with a wire brush and solvent. Discard burned, warped, or cracked valves. If any valves are to be refaced, refer to Figure 30 for critical dimensions.

2. Measure the valve stems for wear.

3. Remove all carbon and varnish from valve guides with a stiff spiral wire brush.

4. Insert the valves in the corresponding valve guides. Hold the valve just slightly off its seat and rock it sideways. If it rocks more than slightly, the guide is worn and should be replaced. See *Valve Guide Replacement* later in this section.

5. Measure the valve spring heights. All should be of equal length with no bends or other distortion. Replace defective springs.

6. Test valve springs under load. Compare to specifications. Replace any which fail this test.

7. Check the valve keepers. If they are reusable, grind the joining faces until it is still possible to turn the valve while holding the keeper halves pressed together. New keepers must be ground in the same manner.

8. Inspect valve seats. If worn or burned, they must be reconditioned. This should be performed by the dealer or local machine shop, although the procedure is described later in this section. Seats and valves in near perfect condition can be reconditioned by lapping with fine carborundum paste. However, lapping is always inferior to precision grinding.

Installation

Refer to **Figure 32** for the following procedures.

1. Coat the valve stems with molybdenum disulphide paste and insert them into the cylinder head.

2. Install oil deflector rings with sleeves.

3. Install valve springs with close-pitched coils next to cylinder head.

4. Install valve spring caps, compress springs, and install valve keepers.

Valve Guide Replacement

When the valve guides are worn so that there is excessive stem-to-guide clearance or valve tipping, the valve guides must be replaced. Replace all valve guides even if only one is worn. Porsche recommends dealer replacement since he has special equipment using liquid gas to do the job. If you would rather do it yourself, the following procedure may be used.

1. Measure exact distance valve guides extend above cylinder head. See **Figure 33**.

2. Place punch with a pilot in the guide. The punch diameter should be a few thousandths of an inch smaller than the guide diameter so that the punch does not bind in the guide hole. Hold the punch firmly, and drive the valve guide out (see Figure 33).

3. To make insertion of the new guides easier, put the cylinder head in an oven set at 300°F. Clean all grease and oil away to avoid fire. Put the valve guides in the freezer section of a refrigerator.

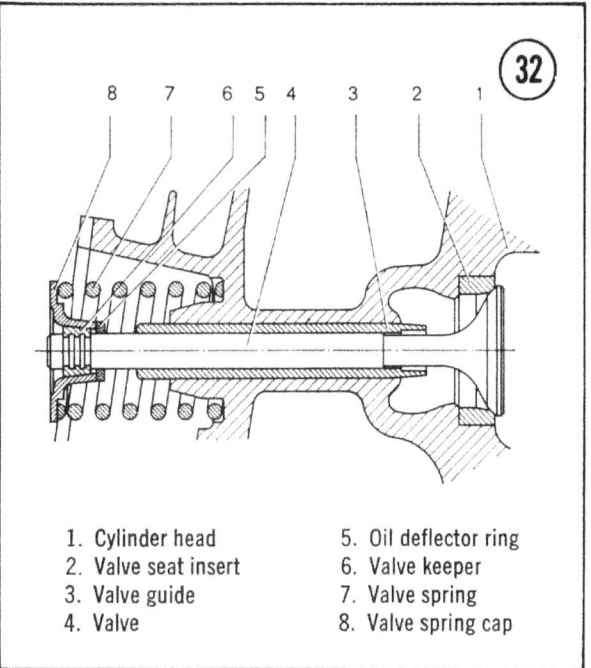

1. Cylinder head
2. Valve seat insert
3. Valve guide
4. Valve
5. Oil deflector ring
6. Valve keeper
7. Valve spring
8. Valve spring cap

4. When ready to install the guides, take the cylinder head out of the oven.

WARNING
The cylinder head will be very hot. Handle carefully to avoid serious burns.

5. Take one valve guide from the freezer and drive it into the head with the same punch used to remove it. Drive it in to the *exact depth measured in Step 1*.

6. Repeat Step 5 for each valve guide. Don't take all the guides out of the freezer at the same time or they will warm up, making insertion difficult.

Valve Seat Reconditioning

This job is best left to your dealer or local machine shop. They have the special equipment and knowledge required for this exacting job. The following procedure is provided in the event you are not near a dealer and the local machine shop is not familiar with Porsches.

Valve seats are shrunk into the cylinder heads. Damaged or burned seats may be reconditioned until the edge of the top 15° chamfer reaches the outer edge of the valve seat. After this point is reached, the cylinder head must be replaced.

1. On 1700 and 1800cc engines, use a 30° cutter or stone to cut the 30° surface on the intake

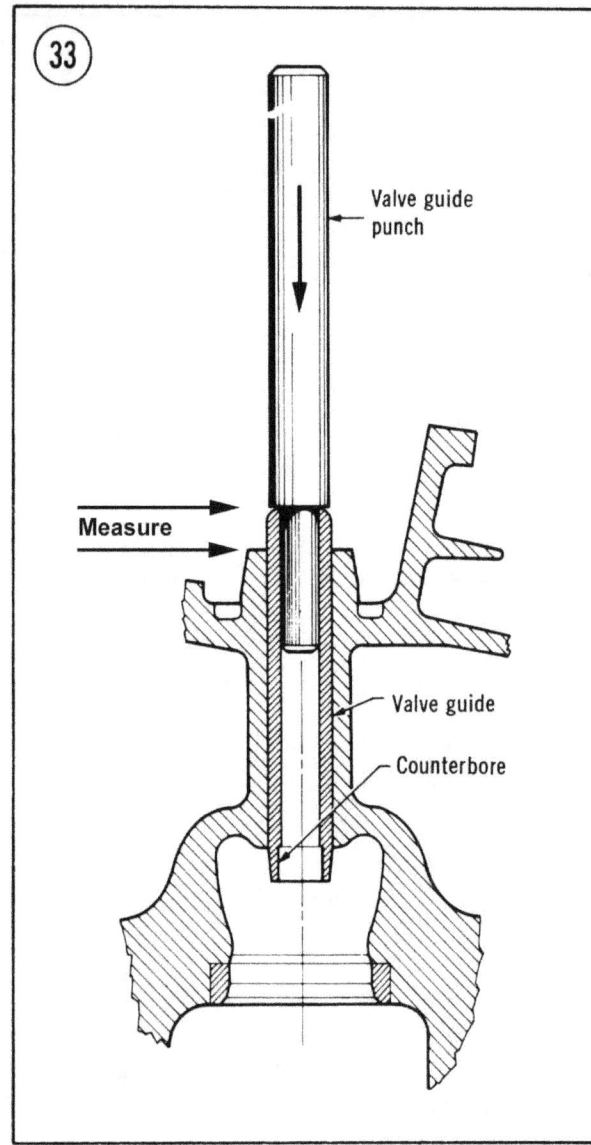

2. Use a 45° cutter or stone to cut the 45° surface on the exhaust valve seats. See **Figure 35**.

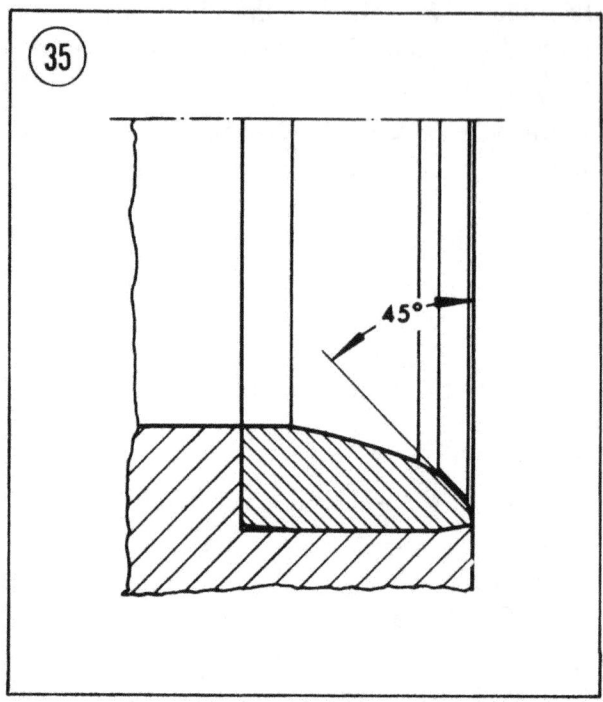

3. Slightly chamfer the bottom of the 45° or 30° seat with a 75° cutter or stone (**Figure 36**).

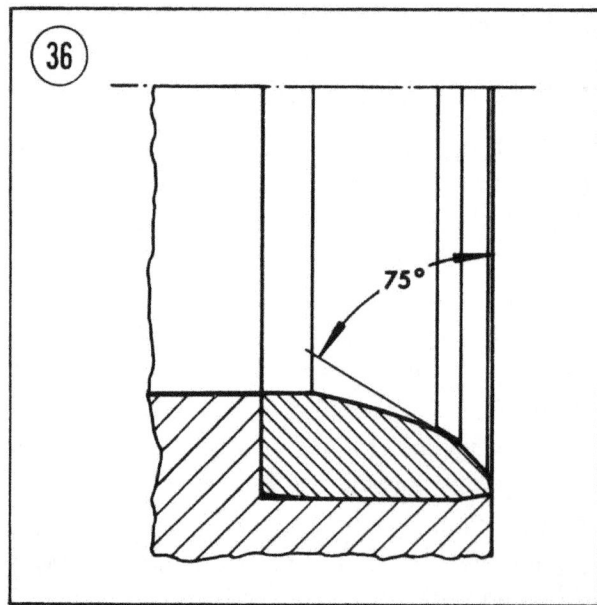

valve seats. See **Figure 34**. On 2000cc engines, cut a 45° surface.

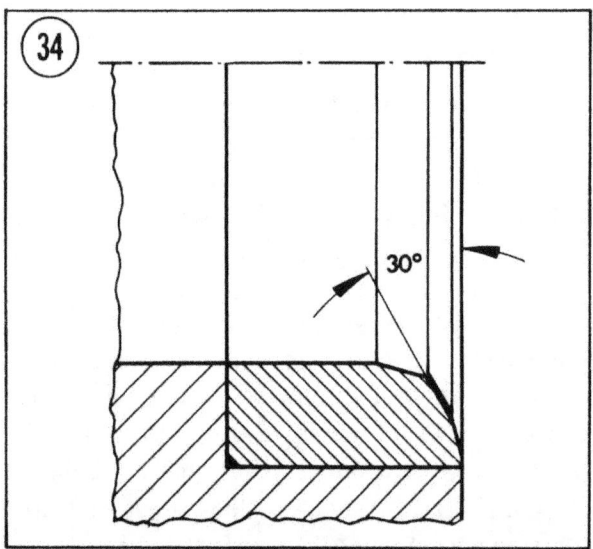

4. Narrow the width of the 45° or 30° seat by cutting the top with a 15° cutter or stone. See **Figure 37**. Intake seat and exhaust seat widths are shown in *Specifications*.

5. Coat the corresponding valve face with Prussian blue.

6. Insert the valve into the guide.

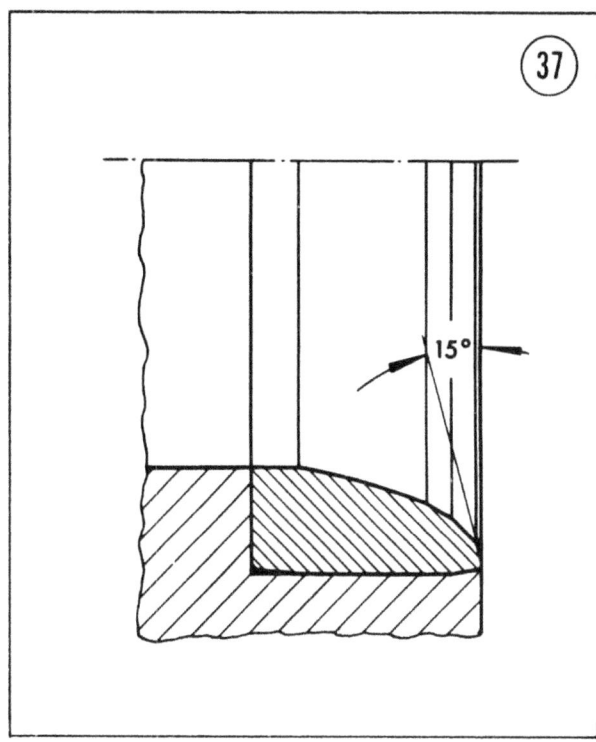

7. Rotate the valve under light pressure about ¼ turn.

8. Lift the valve out. If the valve seats properly, the blue will transfer to the valve seat face evenly.

CYLINDERS

Removal

1. Remove the valve rocker assembly, pushrods, and cylinder head using the procedures described earlier.

2. Remove deflector plate below cylinders.

3. Mark the cylinder number on each cylinder and carefully lift it off.

Inspection and Cleaning

1. Check the bore for wear. If worn, replace with a matched cylinder and piston of the same displacement.

2. Carefully clean the cylinder inside and out. Brush out all dirt from between the fins. Clean away any dirt on the cylinder sealing surfaces and remove the old gasket on the crankcase end.

Installation

1. Install a new gasket on the crankcase end of the cylinder.

2. Rotate the crankshaft until the desired piston is out as far as possible.

CAUTION
While rotating the crankshaft, watch that skirts of any exposed pistons do not catch on the crankcase. This will crack the piston.

3. Apply a heavy coat of assembly lubricant to the piston.

4. Make sure the oil ring gap is straight up. The other two ring gaps should be evenly spaced 120° apart. See **Figure 38**. Compress the rings with a ring compressor. The compressor must be a 2 piece breakaway type so it can be removed.

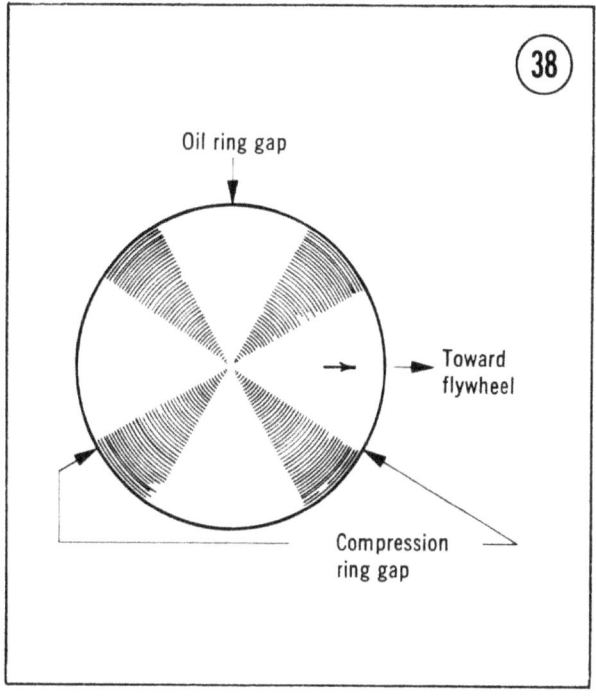

5. Liberally oil the cylinder bore and slide the cylinder over the piston. See **Figure 39**. Be careful not to break any cooling fins on the studs.

6. Install the cylinder head as described previously.

PISTONS, PINS, AND RINGS

Removal

1. Remove the cylinder head and cylinders as described previously.

2. Mark the piston to make sure it is installed in the same place. See **Figure 40**. Counting from

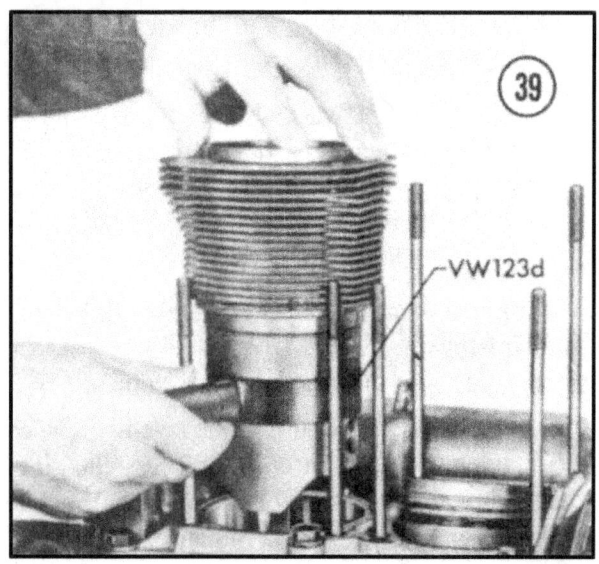

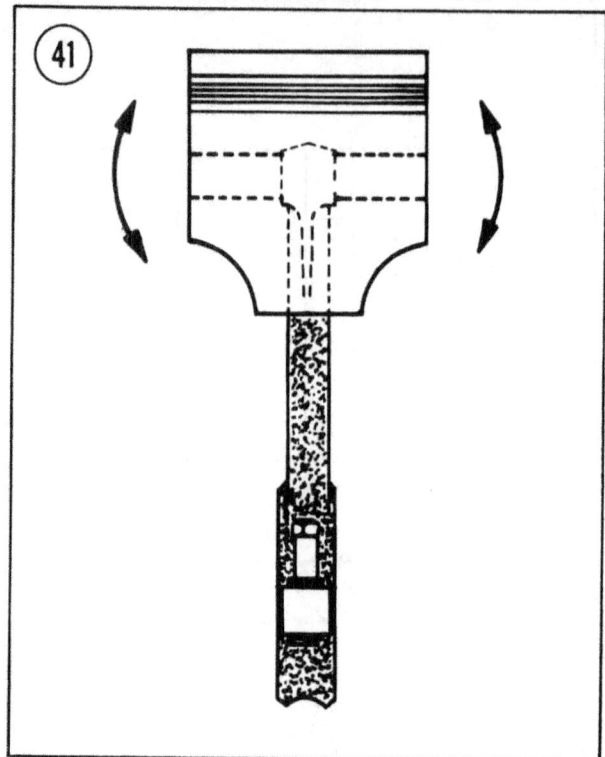

the flywheel, pistons are numbered 1, 2 on the right bank and 3, 4 on the left bank.

3. Rotate the crankshaft until the desired piston is out as far as it goes.

CAUTION
While rotating the crankshaft, watch that skirts of any exposed pistons do not catch on the crankcase. This will crack the piston.

4. Before removing the piston pin, hold the connecting rod tightly and rock the piston as shown in **Figure 41**. Any rocking movement (do not confuse with sliding motion) indicates wear in the piston pin, rod bushing, piston pin bore, or more likely, a combination of all three. Mark the piston, pin, and rod for further examination later.

5. Remove the snap rings at each end of the piston pin.

6. Turn the engine so that the crankshaft is vertical and place wet rags around the oily areas of the crankcase.

7. Heat the piston and pin with a small butane torch. The piston pin will probably drop right out, but may need coaxing with a metal rod. Heat the piston to 176°F (80°C), i.e., until it is too warm to touch but not too hot.

Inspection

1. Clean the piston thoroughly in solvent. Scrape carbon deposits from the top of the piston and ring grooves. Don't damage the piston.

2. Examine each ring groove for burrs, dented edges, and side wear. Pay particular attention to the top compression ring, since it usually wears more than the others.

3. Weigh each piston. The difference in weight between any 2 pistons in the same engine must not exceed 10 grams.

4. If damage, wear, or weight of a piston suggests replacement, replace it with a size and

weight comparable to others in the engine. **Figure 42** shows markings on the top of each VW piston used to identify its size, weight range, and assembly orientation.

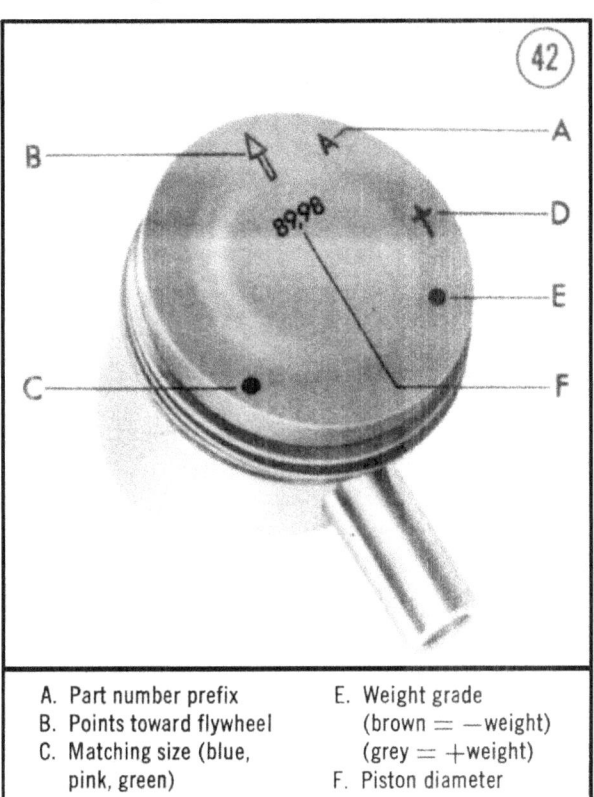

A. Part number prefix
B. Points toward flywheel
C. Matching size (blue, pink, green)
D. Weight grade (+ or —)
E. Weight grade
   (brown = —weight)
   (grey = +weight)
F. Piston diameter

NOTE: Matching size cylinders have the same color dot to the top cooling fin.

5. Measure any parts marked in Step 4, *Piston Removal*, with a micrometer to determine which part or parts are worn. Any machinist can do this for you if you don't have micrometers.

6. When replacing a piston pin, select a size compatible with the piston pin bore. Piston pin bore is stamped on the top of the piston (see Figure 42). Piston pins are painted black or white to match piston markings (S=black, W=White).

Piston Clearance

Porsche discourages using a feeler gauge to check piston clearance and therefore does not provide specifications to do so. The following procedure is the "hard way", but certainly adequate.

1. Make sure the piston and cylinder walls are clean and dry.

2. Measure the inside diameter of the cylinder bore at a point 0.4-0.6" (10-15mm) from the upper edge. See **Figure 43**.

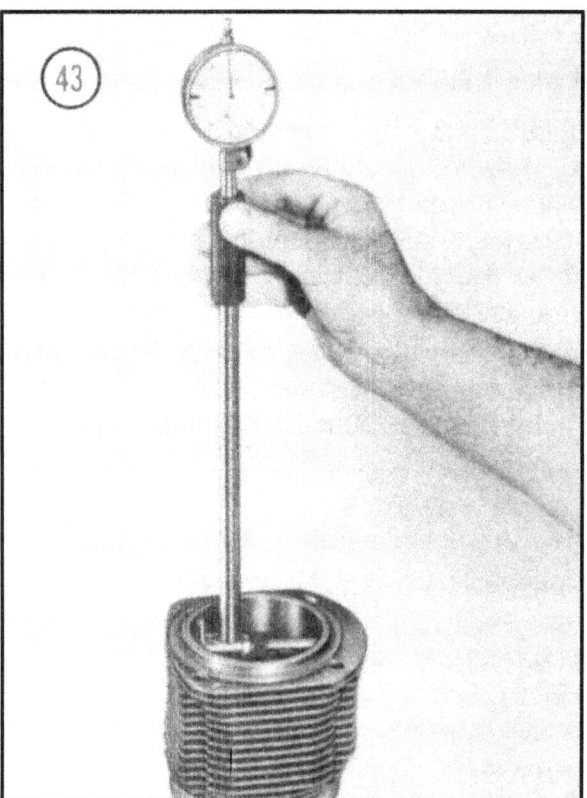

3. Measure the outside diameter of the piston at the bottom of the skirt. See **Figure 44**.

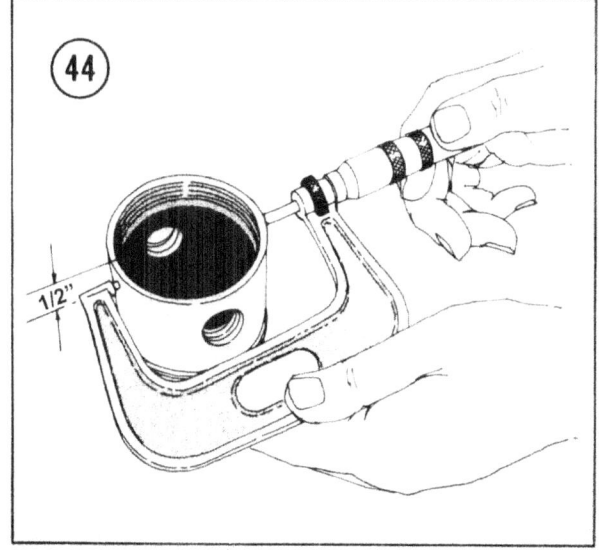

4. If the difference in the 2 readings is near 0.008" (0.2mm) or the engine oil consumption is greater than 1 quart in 600 miles (1 liter/ 1,000 km), the piston/cylinder combination requires overhaul. If cylinder bore is excessive, replace the cylinder and piston. If the piston is

worn or damaged, you may replace the piston only. Choose one which is the correct size and weight.

Piston Ring Fit and Installation

1. Check the gap of each ring. To check a ring, insert it in the bottom of the cylinder bore and square it with the wall by tapping with a piston. The ring should be in about 0.2". Insert a feeler gauge as shown in **Figure 45**. Compare ring gaps to specifications for your engine. If the gap is smaller than specified, hold a small file in a vise, grip the ends of the ring with your hands and enlarge the gap. See **Figure 46**.

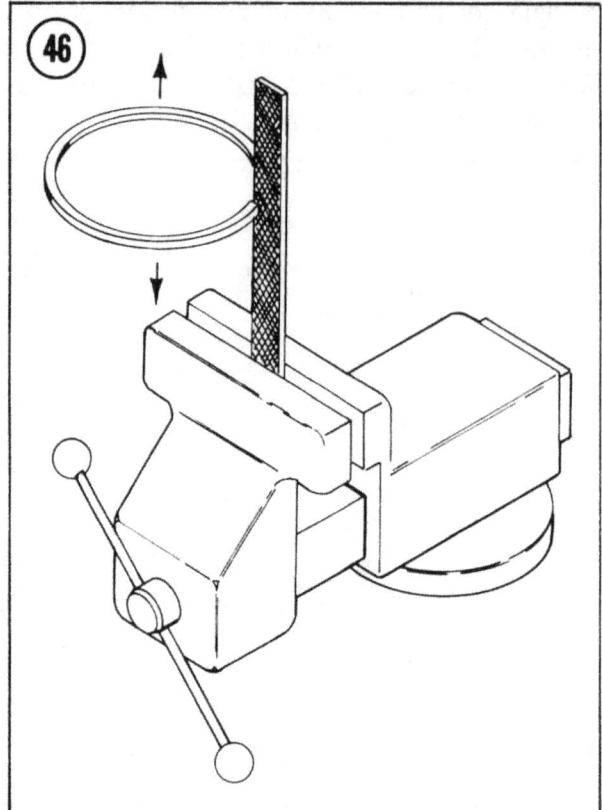

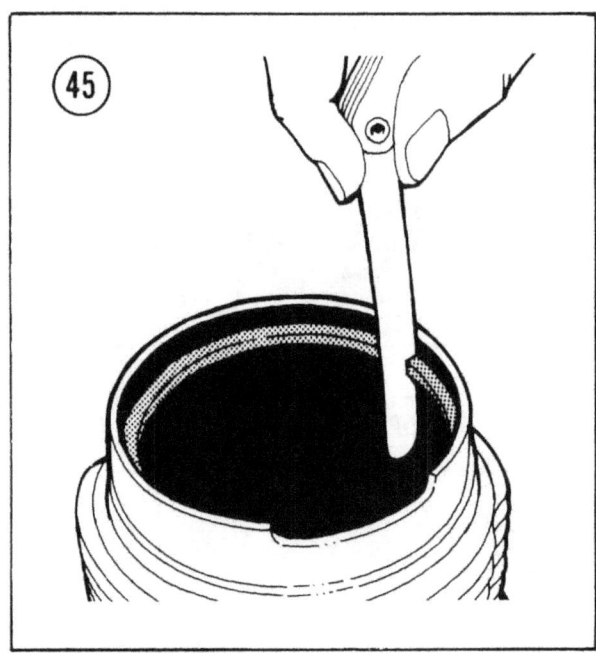

2. Roll each ring around its piston groove as shown in **Figure 47** to check for binding.

3. With a ring expander tool, carefully install the oil ring, then 2 compression rings (see **Figure 48**). The compression ring side marked TOP *must* be up. See **Figure 49**.

4. Check the side clearance of the ring as shown in **Figure 50**. Compare with specifications.

Piston Installation

1. Install the rings on all 4 pistons, following the procedures outlined above.

2. Rotate crankshaft until connecting rod #1 is out as far as possible. Counting from the flywheel, rods are numbered 1, 2 on the right bank and 3, 4 on the left bank.

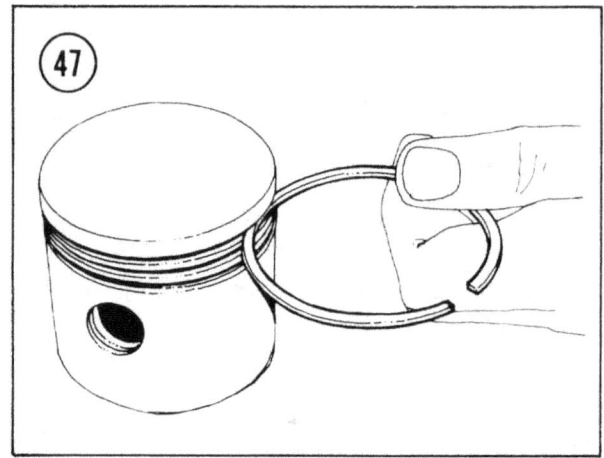

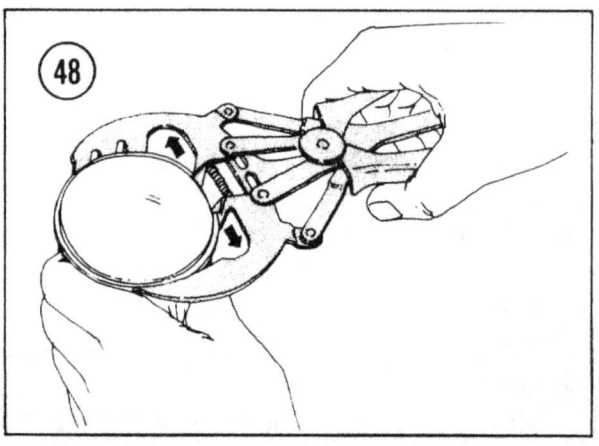

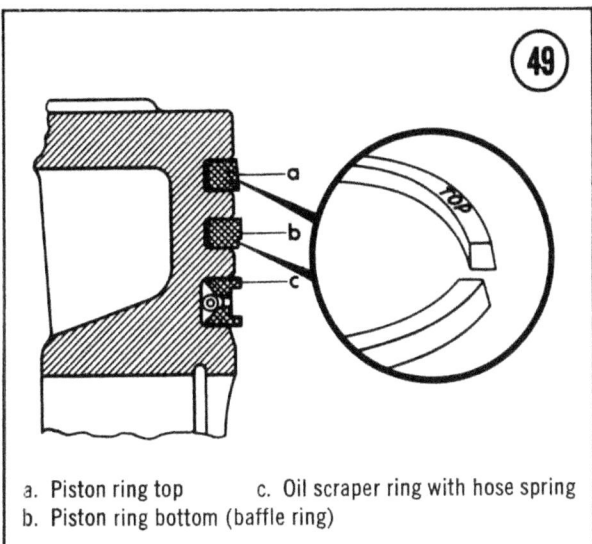

a. Piston ring top
b. Piston ring bottom (baffle ring)
c. Oil scraper ring with hose spring

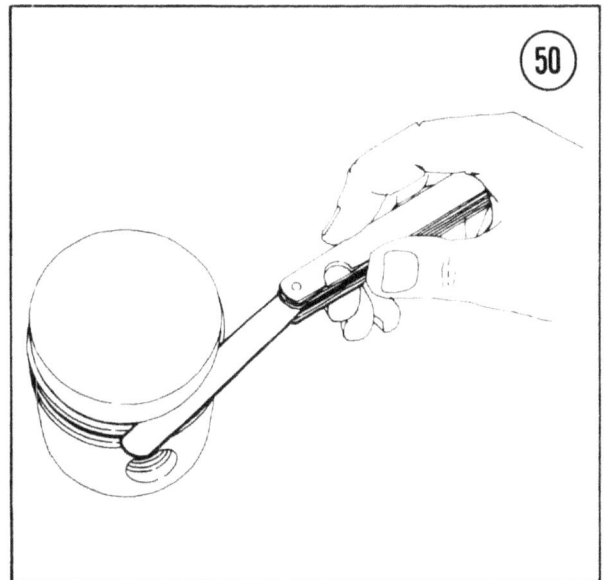

3. Starting with piston #1, install an end lock (snap ring) on the piston pin hole nearest the alignment arrow.

4. Coat the connecting rod bushing, piston pin, and piston holes with assembly lubricant.

5. Place the piston over the connecting rod *with the top arrow pointing toward the flywheel*. Insert the piston pin and tap it with a plastic hammer until it starts into the connecting rod bushing. If it doesn't slide in easily, heat the piston until it is warm to the touch but not too hot. Continue to drive the piston pin in. While hammering, hold the piston so that the rod does not have to take any shock. Otherwise, it may be bent. Drive the pin in until it touches the end lock.

6. Insert the other end lock.

7. Rotate crankshaft until connecting rod #2 is out as far as it will go.

CAUTION
While rotating the crankshaft, watch that skirts of any exposed pistons do not catch on the crankcase. This will crack the piston.

8. Repeat Steps 3-7 for piston #2, #3, and #4. When all are installed, check that all arrows on the pistons point toward the flywheel.

SINGLE OIL PUMP
Removal
1. Remove oil pump retaining nuts.
2. Pry out oil pump with levers as shown in **Figure 51**.

3. Remove 4 nuts securing oil pump cover and pull cover with a special tool. See **Figure 52**.
4. Remove 2 gears.

Inspection
1. Clean all parts thoroughly in solvent.
2. Check oil pump housing and cover for scoring and wear, particularly where gears contact cover.
3. Check gear shafts and gears for scoring and wear. See specifications.
4. Ensure that gears turn freely, then install the oil pump in the crankcase with a new gasket. Drive gear shaft must fit in the slot in the crankshaft.

Removal

1. Remove oil pump cover nuts. Remove cover and gasket.
2. Remove the transmission oil pump gears (7 & 8), plate (10), engine oil gears (13 & 14), and gasket (15). See **Figure 53**.
3. Mark the crankcase and oil pump body on the outside edge to aid reassembly. Do not mark on the sealing surface of the pump body.
4. Remove the oil pump body with an extractor. See **Figure 54**.

Inspection

1. Clean all parts thoroughly in solvent.
2. Check oil pump cover and plate for excessive wear or scoring. Replace if necessary.
3. Check gear seats in oil pump body for wear which can lower oil pressure to dangerous levels.
4. Check the engine oil pump idler gear shaft for tightness. If necessary, peen the oil pump body lightly or replace it.
5. Check the transmission oil pump idler gear shaft for tightness. Replace it if the shaft is loose.

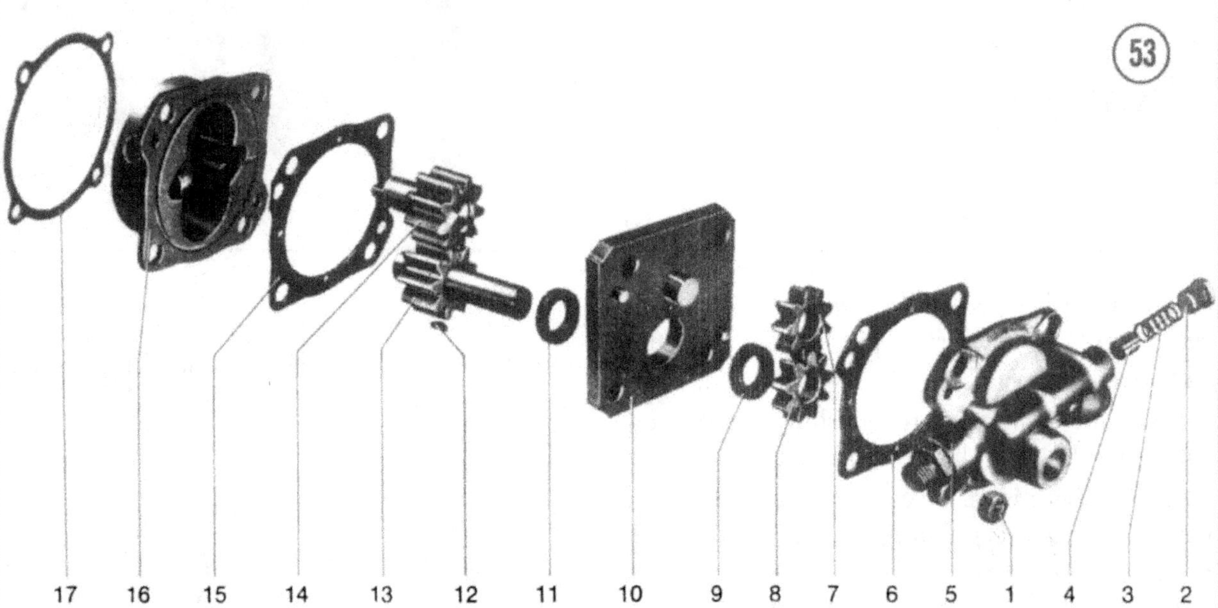

5. Turn the crankshaft 2-3 revolutions to center the pump and tighten the retaining nuts to 14 foot-pounds (2 mkg).

DUAL OIL PUMP

Sportomatic models have a transmission oil pump mounted on the engine oil pump.

DUAL OIL PUMP

1. Sealing nut
2. Plug
3. Spring
4. Piston
5. Cover
6. Gasket for plate and cover
7. Outer, upper gear
8. Outer, lower gear
9. Oil seal for plate
10. Plate
11. Oil seal for plate
12. Woodruff key
13. Lower shaft with inner gear
14. Upper shaft with inner gear
15. Gasket for plate and cover
16. Oil pump housing
17. Gasket for housing

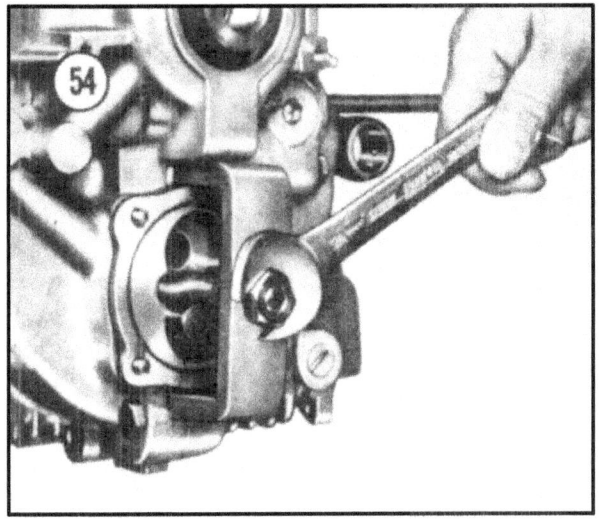

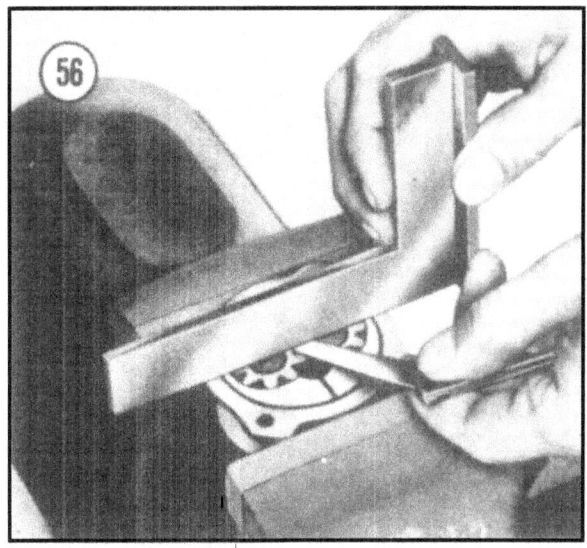

6. Install engine oil gears in pump body. Check backlash by inserting a feeler gauge between gear teeth as shown in **Figure 55**; backlash should be 0.0012-0.0031" (0.03-0.08mm). Place a square over the oil pump body and insert a feeler gauge as shown in **Figure 56**. Maximum end-play without the cover gasket is 0.004" (0.1mm).

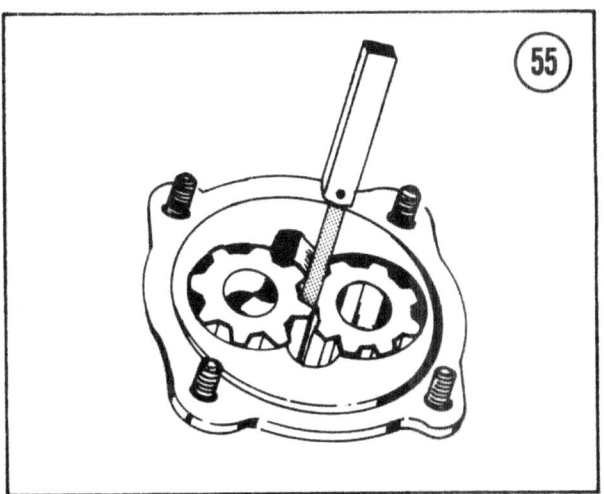

7. Leave the engine oil gears in place as in Step 5. Install plate (10) and gears (7 & 8). Check backlash with a feeler gauge.

8. Remove the oil pressure relief valve plug, spring, and piston in the transmission oil pump cover. Check for piston wear and scoring. Examine the spring for distortion. Replace questionable parts.

9. Check the mating surfaces on the pump body and crankcase for dirt and damage.

Installation

1. Clean all parts in solvent just prior to installation, even though they were thoroughly cleaned for inspection.

2. Install the pump body in the crankcase using a new gasket. Line up the marks made during removal.

3. Coat all internal parts with assembly lubricant and assemble the pump as shown in Figure 53.

4. Install the transmission oil pump pressure relief valve parts (2, 3, & 4).

OIL PRESSURE RELIEF VALVES

There is an oil pressure relief valve located on the bottom rear of the engine near the oil pump. There is an additional oil pressure relief valve on the crankcase between cylinder #1 pushrod tubes.

Removal

Refer to Figure 12 and **Figure 57** for the following procedure.

1. Remove the plug and gasket.

2. Remove the spring and piston. If the piston is stuck, thread a 10mm tap lightly into it and pull it out.

Inspection

1. Check the crankcase bore and piston for signs of scoring or seizure. Dress up the bore

1. Plunger 3. Gasket
2. Spring 4. Plug

with crocus cloth and replace the piston if necessary.

2. Measure the spring length. Unloaded length should compare with specifications for your engine.

Installation

Install the piston, spring, new gasket, and plug in the order shown in Figure 57.

OIL STRAINER

The oil strainer can be removed with the engine installed. See Figure 12 and **Figure 58** for the following procedures.

Removal

1. Drain engine oil.
2. Remove bolt in center of cover plate and remove plate.
3. Remove oil strainer and 2 gaskets.

Inspection

1. Check that the oil suction pipe is tight and centered in the large hole. If not, the engine must be dismantled and the right crankcase half peened. See *Crankcase Inspection*.
2. Clean all parts in solvent and remove all traces of old gasket.

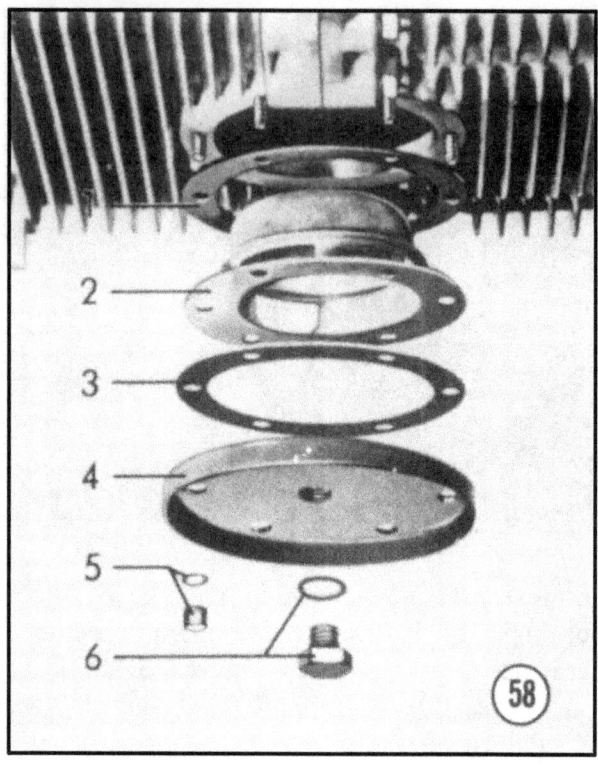

1. Gasket 4. Cover plate
2. Oil strainer 5. Cap nut with washer
3. Gasket 6. Plug with washer

3. Check that the cover plate is not bent. Straighten or replace if necessary.

Installation

1. Install all parts in the order shown in Figure 58.
2. Secure cover plate with center bolt and new seal. Do not overtighten as severe engine damage may result.

CRANKCASE

Disassembly

1. Remove the oil pressure switch near the distributor.
2. Unbolt filler tube at bottom flange. See **Figure 59**.
3. Remove oil strainer on the bottom of the crankcase. Pull off the cover, 2 gaskets, and strainer (see Figure 58).
4. Tip crankcase so that it leans on left half cylinder studs. Remove all 13mm nuts around crankcase seam. Loosen 6 large nuts (17mm).
5. Pull the oil pump out and remove all 6 large nuts. Leave bolts in place.

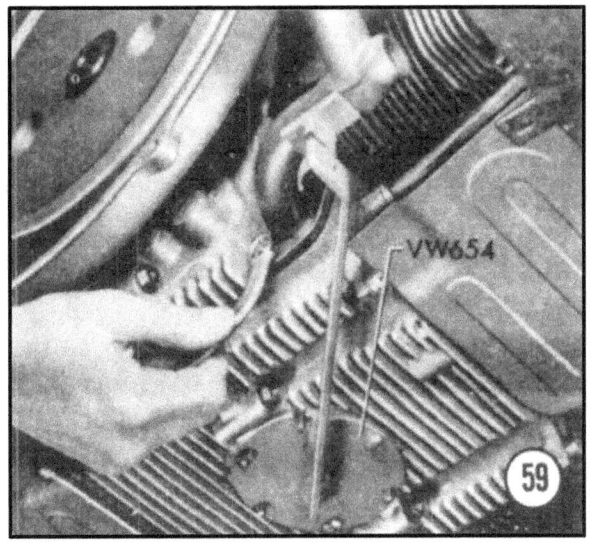

6. Check carefully all around the crankcase for any remaining nuts.

7. Loosen the right half of the crankcase by tapping with a rubber hammer or block of wood. Keep pulling upward on the crankcase half and tapping with the hammer until the right half is free. See **Figure 60**.

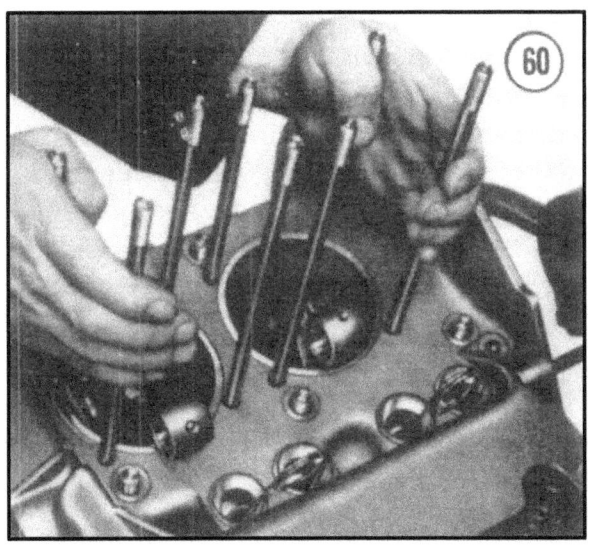

CAUTION
Never try to pry the crankcase halves apart with a screwdriver or similar object or you will damage the sealing surfaces.

8. Remove camshaft end seal (see **Figure 61**) and lift the camshaft out.

9. Lift the crankshaft out.

10. Remove the center crankshaft bearing inserts and camshaft bearing inserts.

11. Remove the oil pressure relief valves as described in an earlier procedure.

12. Withdraw the long crankcase bolts.

Inspection

1. Clean and flush both halves of the crankcase with solvent. Blow out oil passages with air. Remove all traces of old sealing compound on mating faces.

2. Check both crankcase halves for cracks and other damage. Mating and sealing surfaces should be free of nicks and scratches or they will leak.

3. Check all studs in the crankcase for looseness. If any cannot be tightened, have a machinist install a Heli-coil insert.

4. Inspect all bearing bores (crankshaft and camshaft) for burrs. Remove with a file. Flush out any metal particles.

Assembly

1. Insert crankshaft bearing dowel pins in the left case half. See **Figure 62**.

2. Install crankshaft bearing inserts for #2 bearing in crankcase halves. Ensure that the inserts fit properly on the dowels. Coat the bearings with assembly lubricant.

3. Install camshaft bearing inserts in the crankcase halves. Make sure the tangs on the bearings fit in the notches. Note that bearing #3, which fits in the left crankcase half, has shoulders to support axial loads from the camshaft. See **Figure 63**.

should drop into place. Do this for each bearing, making sure each bearing seats in its dowel. Keep checking until none of the bearings rotate or move back and forth.

9. Turn the crankshaft until the centerpunched marks on the timing gear face towards the camshaft bearings.

10. Coat camshaft journals and bearings surfaces with assembly lubricant.

11. Install the camshaft so that the camshaft gear tooth marked "O" fits between the crankshaft gear teeth marked with centerpunches. See **Figure 65**. This alignment is *very important* as it establishes the valve timing.

4. Coat the inside of #1 and #4 main bearings and crankshaft journals with assembly lubricant.

5. Slide #1 bearing (with thrust flanges) onto the flywheel end of the crankshaft with the dowel pin hole closest to the flywheel end.

6. Slide #4 bearing onto the timing gear end of the crankshaft with slot inside the bearing facing toward the timing gear end.

7. Lift the crankshaft assembly by connecting rods #1 and #2. Place the crankshaft on the main bearing holders as shown in **Figure 64**. Connecting rods #3 and #4 must protrude through the corresponding cylinder holes.

8. Take the weight off one bearing at a time, rotate it until the bearing lines up with its dowel. There will be a slight click and the crankshaft

12. Install the camshaft end seal using VW sealing compound. The open end must face the camshaft.

13. Make a final check that the main bearings and cam bearings are seated. Lubricate all exposed crankshaft and camshaft journals and bearings.

14. Spread VW sealing compound on the crankcase mating surfaces. Do not get any on the bearings.

15. Hold connecting rods #1 and #2 up. Tip the right case half over the left and slide it down on the studs.

16. Insert long crankcase bolts, washers, and nuts finger-tight. Sealing rings on these special nuts must face out.

17. Install the rest of the washers and nuts finger-tight.

CAUTION
The tightening sequence described in the next 4 steps is very important. Throughout the process, turn the crankshaft occasionally. If there is any binding, STOP. Take the case apart and find the trouble. Usually it is a main bearing off its dowel pin.

18. Torque the 2 large center nuts to 20 foot-pounds, then to 25 foot-pounds.

19. Torque all other large nuts to 20 foot-pounds, then to 25 foot-pounds.

20. Torque all the rest of small nuts to 10 foot-pounds, then to 14 foot-pounds.

21. Coat cam followers with assembly lubricant and insert them in the crankcase.

CRANKSHAFT

In order to increase stroke on the 2000cc engine, the connecting rod journals are 5mm smaller. Therefore, the crankshafts cannot be interchanged.

Removal

1. When the right half of the crankcase has been removed, lift the crankshaft out.

2. Remove the bearing inserts from the crankcase halves. Mark each with a pencil on its back as it is removed so that it may be reinstalled in the same position.

Gear and Bearing Disassembly

Refer to **Figure 66** for following procedure.

1. Slide #4 main bearing off the crankshaft.
2. Slide #1 main bearing off the crankshaft.
3. Remove snap ring on front of crankshaft.
4. With a large gear puller, pull on the bottom of the innermost (timing) gear. Remove the distributor drive and timing gears. Save the Woodruff key(s).
5. Slide #3 main bearing off.

Inspection

1. Check connecting rod end-play, then remove all connecting rods. Both procedures are described under *Connecting Rod Removal* later in this chapter.

2. Clean the crankshaft thoroughly with solvent. Clean the oil holes with rifle type brushes. Flush thoroughly and blow dry with air. Lightly oil all journal surfaces immediately to prevent rust.

3. Carefully inspect each journal for scratches, ridges, scoring, nicks, etc. Very small nicks and scratches may be removed by grinding; a job for a machine shop.

4. Even if the surface finish on all journals is undamaged, take the crankshaft to your dealer or local machine shop. They can check for out-of-roundness, taper, and wear on the journals. They will also check crankshaft alignment and inspect for cracks.

Gear and Bearing Assembly

Refer to Figure 66 for the following procedure.

1. Fit #1, #3, and #4 main bearings in the left crankcase half. Make sure the bearings fit properly in the dowels. Mark their depth on the bearings to help position the bearings correctly on the crankshaft.

2. Wipe #3 crankshaft bearing journal. Coat journal and #3 bearing with assembly lubricant. Note the hole in #3 bearing is offset. Slide #3 bearing on the crankshaft so the hole is close to the flywheel end of the crankshaft.

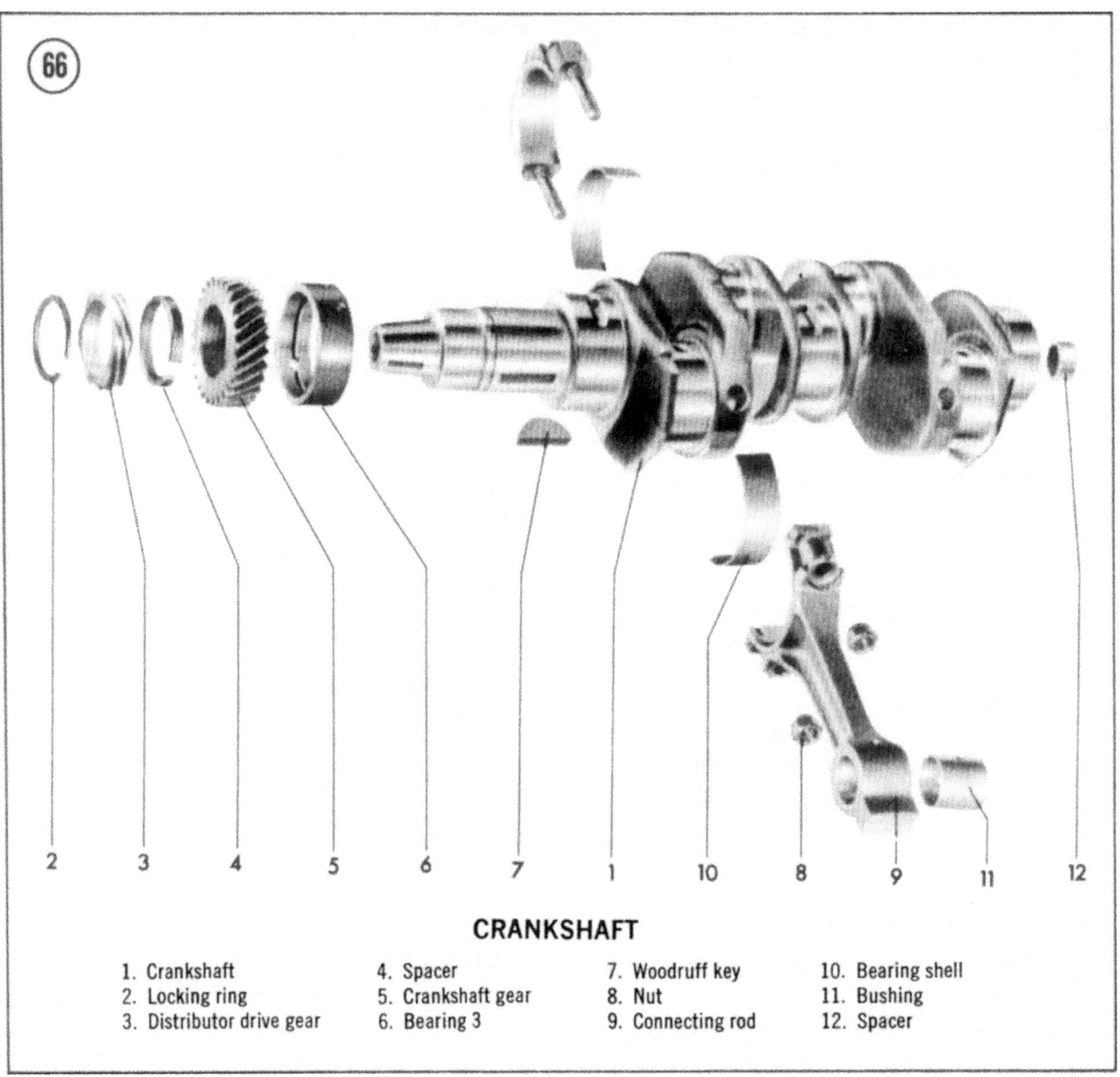

CRANKSHAFT

1. Crankshaft
2. Locking ring
3. Distributor drive gear
4. Spacer
5. Crankshaft gear
6. Bearing 3
7. Woodruff key
8. Nut
9. Connecting rod
10. Bearing shell
11. Bushing
12. Spacer

3. Lay the crankshaft vertically on a piece of wood with the flywheel end down.

4. Insert the large Woodruff key in the crankshaft slot. Fit the timing gear over the crankshaft with the centerpunched timing marks facing up (towards the rear of the shaft). Align the timing gear slot with the Woodruff key.

5. Tap lightly around the gear with a hammer and dull punch until the gear engages the Woodruff key. The key must be flat, not canted in the slot.

6. Heat the timing gear with a small butane torch for a few minutes. Do not heat the bearing or the crankshaft. After 3 or 4 minutes, fit a length of 2″ pipe over the crankshaft and drive the gear into position.

7. Slide the spacer ring in place and align its slot with the Woodruff key slot.

8. Slide the brass distributor drive gear over the crankshaft and align it with the Woodruff key Tap the gear down slightly over the Woodruff key in the same manner as the timing gear.

9. Heat the distributor drive gear about one minute, then drive it down with a length of pipe until it is against the spacer ring.

10. Spread the snap ring with snap ring pliers and slide it over the crankshaft into the groove cut for it. Don't nick or scratch the #4 bearing journal.

11. Leave the #1 and #4 bearings off until ready to install the crankshaft. See *Crankcase Assembly*.

Installation

Installation is simply a matter of setting the crankshaft in place after the crankcase is prepared. See *Crankcase Assembly*.

CONNECTING RODS

The 1700/1800cc and 2000cc connecting rods differ. The 2000cc rods are 4mm longer and have a 5mm larger big-end bore.

Removal

1. Remove the crankshaft from the engine. Clamp it down or have someone hold it.
2. File very small marks on each of the rods to indicate its position for reassembly. For example, make one mark on rod #1, 2 marks on rod #2, etc. The rods are numbered 3, 1, 4, 2 from the flywheel end of the crankshaft.
3. Insert a feeler gauge between the side of the rod and the crank throw (see **Figure 67**). If this gap (connecting rod end-play) is greater than 0.026", mark the rod for replacement.

4. Remove the connecting rod nuts ONLY and pull off the rod caps. DO NOT remove the bolts from the rod caps.
5. Remove the bearing inserts from the rod and cap. Mark the back of the insert with rod number for later inspection and reassembly. Do not mix up the bearings.
6. Install the caps on the rods to keep them together.

Inspection

1. Discard any rods which show excessive end play (see Step 3 above).
2. Check each rod for such obvious damage as cracks and burns. If either bolt on a rod cap is damaged, the entire rod must be replaced.
3. Check the piston pin bushing for wear or scoring. At room temperature, a piston pin should slide through with light finger pressure.
4. Take the rods to a machine shop and have alignment checked for twisting and bending.
5. Weigh each rod on a scale. Rods should be within 6 grams of each other. If not, find the lightest rod and lighten the others as required to match it. You can remove as much as 8 grams total by filing or grinding metal away from the points indicated in **Figure 68**.

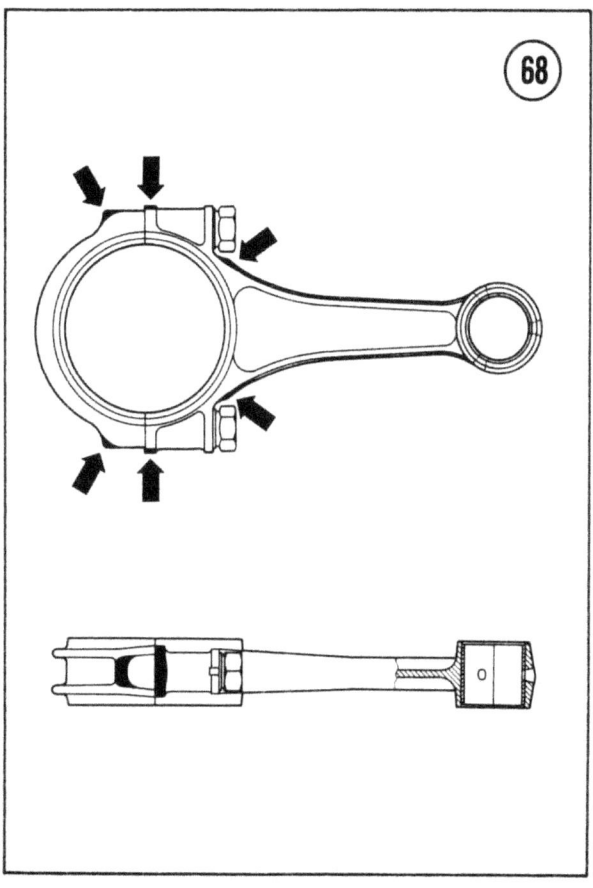

6. Examine the bearing inserts for wear, scoring, or burning. They are reusable if in good condition. Make a note of the bearing size (if any) stamped on the back of the insert if the bearing is to be discarded; a previous owner may have used undersize bearings.

Installation

1. Remove the rod cap from the rod and *discard the nuts*. You must use new nuts. Do not remove the rod bolts.

2. Carefully match the number on the side of each rod to its associated rod cap.

3. Install the bearing inserts in the rods and caps. Press the bearings in with your thumbs on the ends of the bearings. Be sure the tang on the bearings fit into the notches on the rods and caps.

CAUTION
The bearing ends will extend slightly above the cap or rod. See **Figure 69**. *Do not file any part of the rod, cap, or bearing for a different fit.*

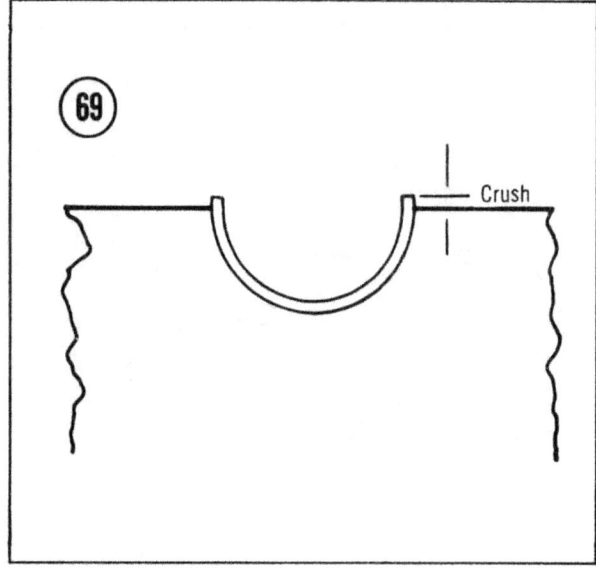

4. Oil the nuts and rod cap bolts lightly.

5. Cut a piece of Plastigage the width of the rod bearing. Assemble the rod cap on the crank throw for cylinder #3 (the one closest to the flywheel) with the Plastigage inserted between the rod cap and the crank throw. Tighten the nuts to 22-25 foot-pounds.

6. Remove the bearing cap and measure the width of the flattened Plastigage following the manufacturer's instructions. This is the bearing clearance. Compare it to the specifications for your engine. If it is not right, ensure that you have installed the proper bearings.

7. Wipe out the strip of Plastigage, coat the bearing and crank throw with assembly lubricant, and reassemble the rod on the corresponding crank throw.

8. Check that the rod rotates freely 180° as a result of its own weight.

9. Measure the rod end-play with a feeler gauge (see *Removal*, Step 3). Compare with the specifications.

10. Repeat Steps 5-9 for each rod. Be sure you assemble each rod on the crank throw originally used for that rod. Also ensure that the rod and cap number are aligned.

11. Peen the nuts into the slots in the rods to lock them in place. See **Figure 70**.

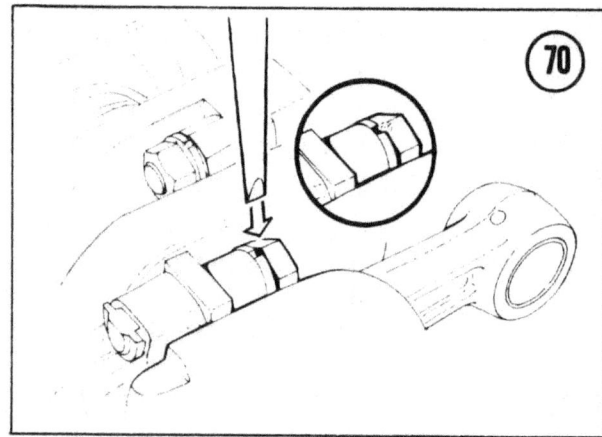

CAMSHAFT

Removal

1. When the right half of the crankcase has been removed, lift the camshaft out.

2. Remove the camshaft bearing inserts from crankcase halves and pencil a mark on the back of each as it is removed so that it may be reinstalled in the same position.

Inspection

1. Check bearing journals and cam lobes for wear. The cam lobes should not be scored and the edges should be square. Slight damage may be removed with a silicon carbide oilstone. Use 100-200 grit initially, then polish with a 280-320 grit.

2. Check camshaft runout at center bearing (**Figure 71**). Not to exceed 0.0016" (0.04mm).

3. Examine timing gear rivets and check for gear looseness.

4. Check the timing gear teeth for wear and proper tooth contact.

5. Chamfer all edges of the bearing bores slightly to prevent seizure due to bearing pressure.

6. Check the bearing inserts for wear, scoring, or burns. Replace if necessary.

7. Check the cam followers for wear and scoring.

Installation

Installation is simply a matter of setting the camshaft in place after the crankcase is prepared. See *Crankcase Assembly*.

Table 1   TIGHTENING TORQUES

	foot-pounds	mkg
Connecting rods	22-25	3-3.5
Crankcase halves (large nuts)	25	3.5
Crankcase halves (small nuts)	14	2.0
Cylinder head nuts	23	3.2
Rocker shaft nuts	10	1.4
Oil pump cover nuts	14	2.0
Oil drain plug	16	2.2
Flywheel cap screws	80	11.0
Pressure plate bolts	18	2.5
Torque converter to drive plate	22	3.0
Crankshaft pulley	43	6.0
Spark plugs	22-29	3-4
Engine-to-transaxle	22	3.0
Engine-to-body	22	3.0
Transaxle-to-body	18	2.5

CHAPTER FIVE

ENGINE—914/6

The 914/6 engine is a 6-cylinder horizontally opposed air-cooled engine. See **Figures 1 and 2**. Each cylinder has its own finned cylinder barrel and alumnium head. Three heads in a bank bolt to a housing containing an overhead camshaft and rocker arms to operate the valves.

The cylinders mount on an aluminum crankcase manufactured in 2 halves. Eight main bearings support the crankshaft. The crankcase contains a twin oil pump driven by the crankshaft through gears and an intermediate shaft. The intermediate shaft also drives 2 camshafts through chains. A system of tensioners and guides keep the chain under proper tension and control.

ENGINE REMOVAL/INSTALLATION

The engine/transaxle must be removed as a single unit.

1. Prop the engine compartment lid open or remove it.
2. Drain engine oil. See Chapter Two.
3. Drain transaxle oil. See Chapter Two.
4. Put transmission in neutral and chock the front tires.
5. Disconnect battery cables.
6. Remove air cleaner.
7. Disconnect multiple connectors from relay plate (1, **Figure 3**).
8. Disconnect wires from terminals 1 and center voltage terminal of ignition coil.
9. Disconnect fuel lines from carburetor float chambers. See 3, Figure 3.
10. Disconnect throttle linkage from bellcrank (left arrow, **Figure 4**).

11. Disconnect the oil breather hose from the oil filler (6, Figure 3).
12. Disconnect wire from oil pressure sender.

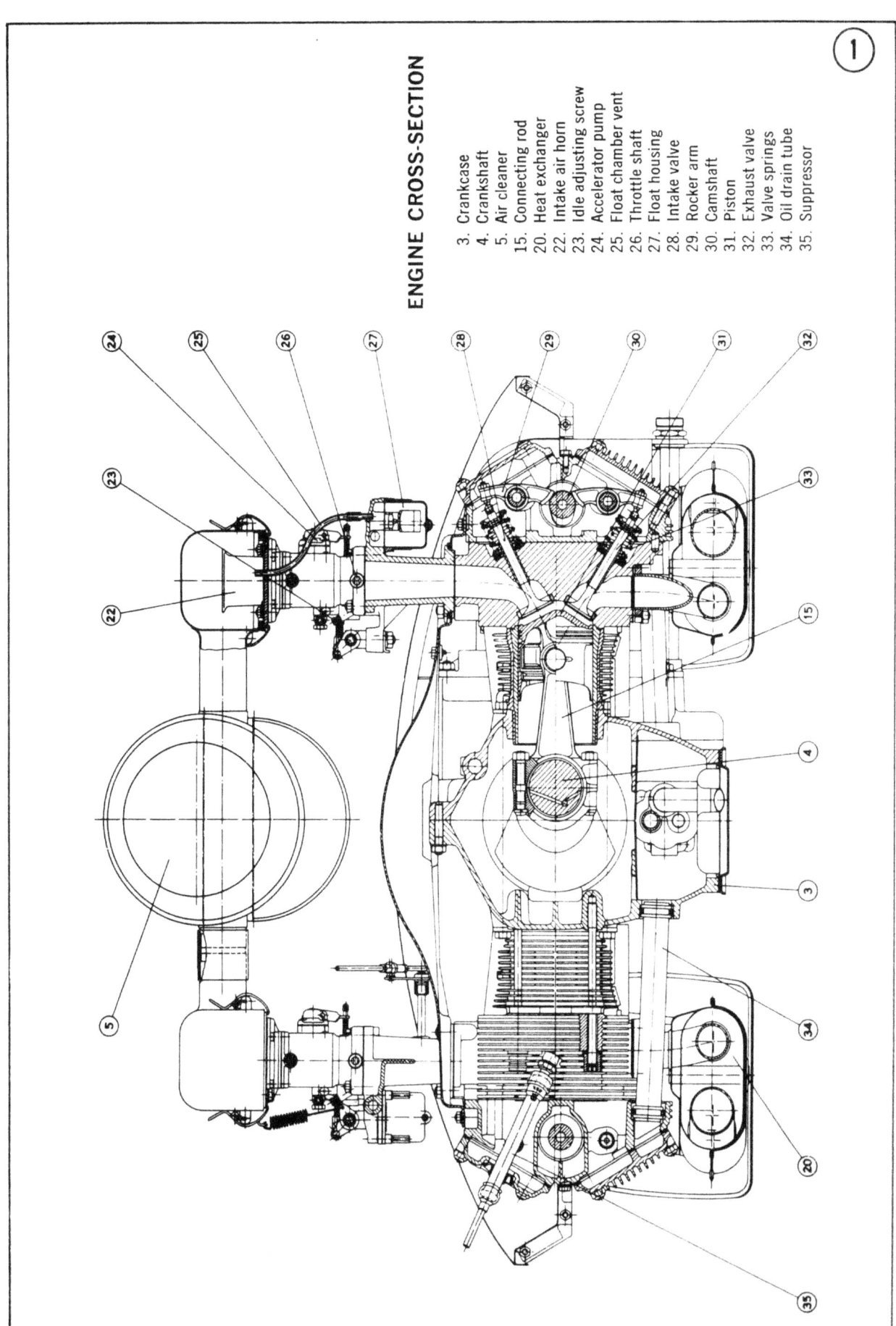

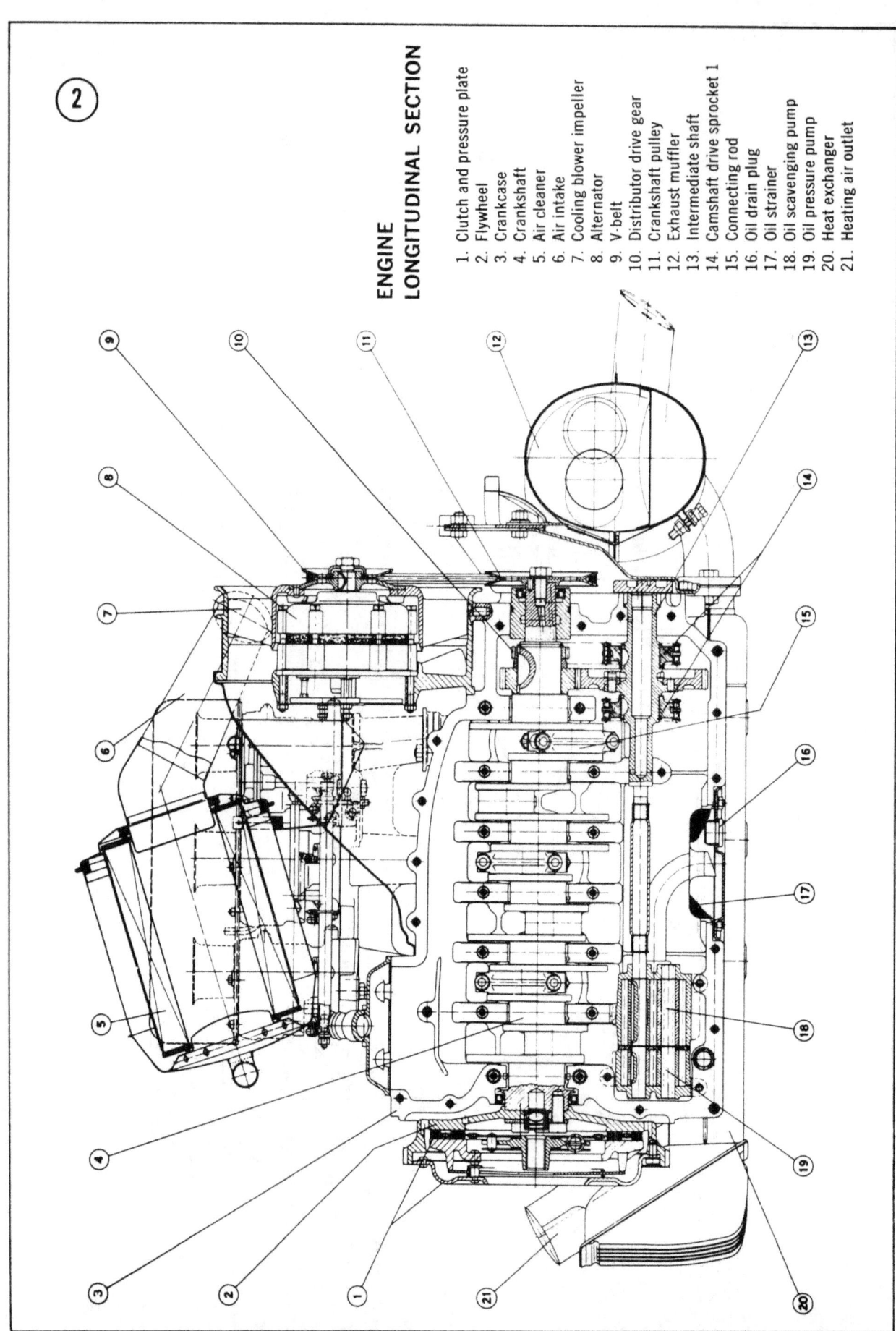

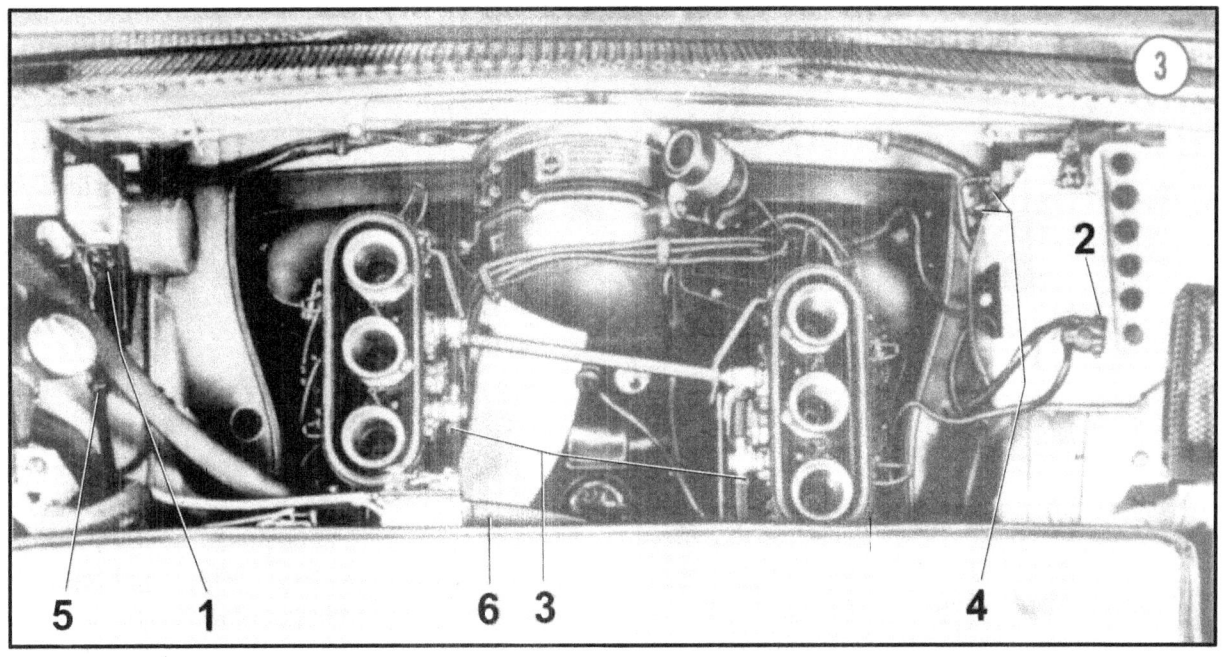

1. Multiple connector
2. Allen-head screw
3. Carburetor fuel inlet line
4. Multiple connector at trigger unit
5. Wire retainer
6. Oil breather hose

NOTE: *The following 3 steps apply to the Sportomatic only.*

13. Disconnect oil lines from torque converter oil pump. See **Figure 5**.

14. Disconnect vacuum hoses from vacuum reservoir. See **Figure 6**.

15. Pull rubber cap off control valve. Remove cotter pin and disconnect cable. See **Figure 7**.

NOTE: *Remaining steps apply to all models unless otherwise specified.*

16. Disconnect oil hoses from engine oil tank. See **Figure 8**.

17. Raise rear of car on jackstands.

18. Unscrew the shift rod holder. See **Figures 9 and 10**.

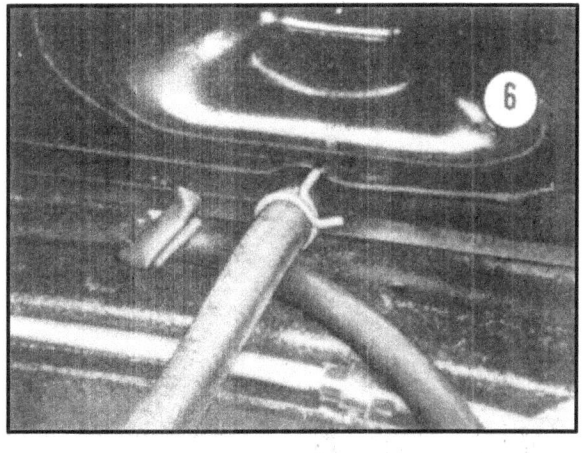

19. Remove nuts shown in Figure 10 and remove rear shift rod.

20. Disconnect speedometer cable from transaxle. See 6, Figure 10.

21. Remove axle halfshafts as described in Chapter Twelve.

22. Disconnect starter cables.

23. Disconnect hot air ducts from front of heat exchangers.

24. Loosen and withdraw clutch cable at clutch release lever. See Chapter Ten.

25. Disconnect ground strap from luggage pan. Disconnect wire from back-up light switch at transaxle.

26. Disconnect throttle cable ball-joint (3, Figure 10). Disconnect throttle pushrod (8, Figure 10).

27. Place garage-type floor jack at center of engine/transaxle assembly and raise it to take the weight of the assembly.

28. Remove bolts securing rear engine support to body. See **Figure 11**.

29. Remove 4 nuts securing transaxle support to body. See **Figure 12**.

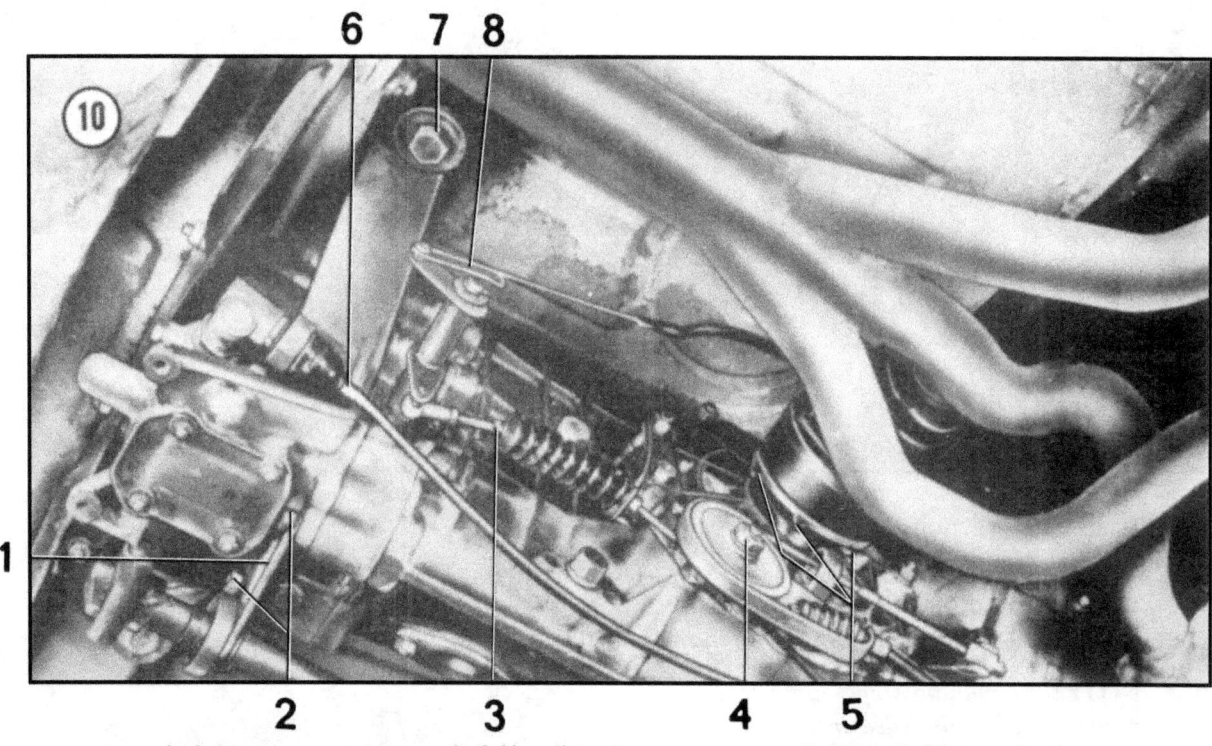

1. Support
2. Nut
3. Throttle cable
4. Cable pulley nut
5. Allen-head bolt
6. Speedometer drive cable
7. Transmission support nut
8. Throttle push rod

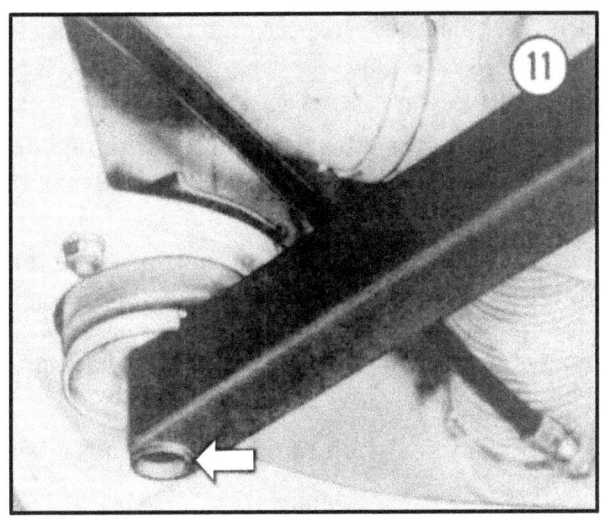

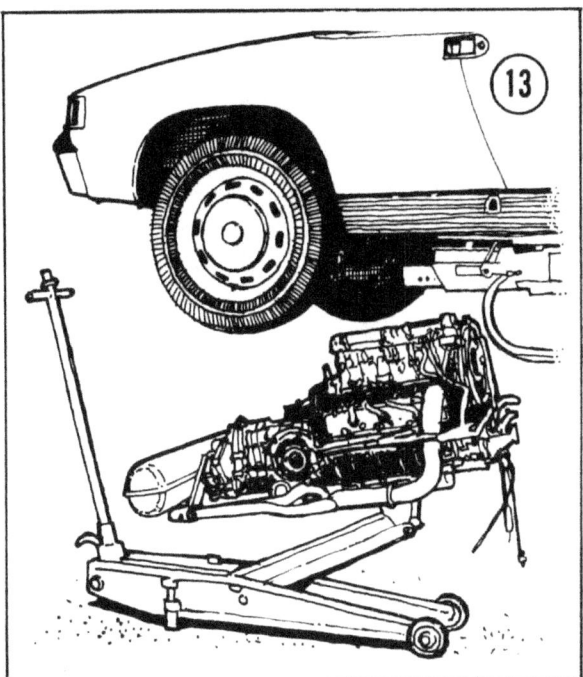

30. Lower engine/transaxle carefully while a helper balances it on jack. See **Figure 13**. On Sportomatic models, disconnect electrical cables to temperature switch and sensor as soon as they are accessible. See **Figure 14**.

31. Pull jack to rear.

32. Installation is the reverse of these steps. Tighten engine mounting bolts to 22 foot-pounds (3.0 mkg) and the transaxle support nuts to 14.5 foot-pounds (2.0 mkg).

ENGINE/TRANSAXLE SEPARATION (MANUAL)

1. Disconnect rear throttle rod.

2. Remove starter. Install a spacer and Allen head screw in each of the 3 holes in the pressure plate. See **Figures 15 and 16**. These parts are available from your Porsche dealer. Tighten the screws alternately and evenly to relieve spring

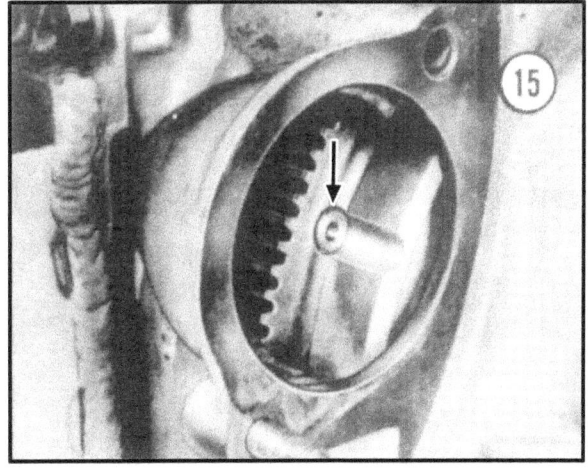

tension on release bearing. Turn release bearing 90° through access hole as shown in **Figure 17**.

103

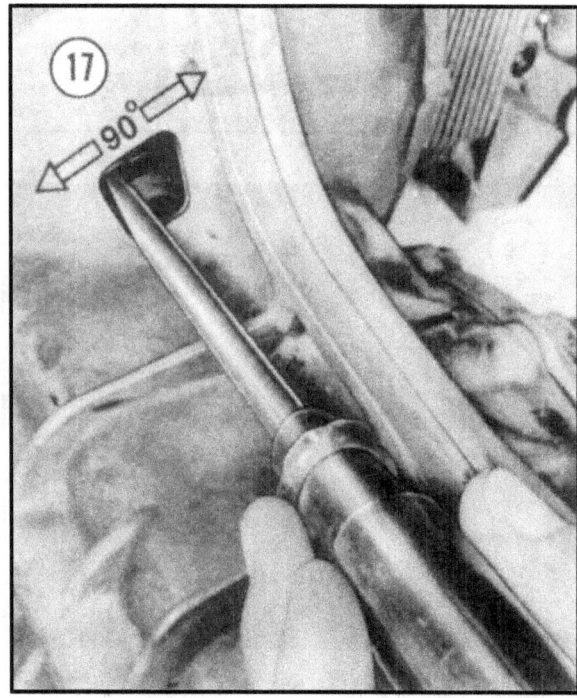

3. Remove 2 lower engine mounting nuts. Remove 2 upper engine mounting nuts. Pull engine straight back until clutch release plate clears the main drive shaft.

> **CAUTION**
> *Do not let engine tilt or let engine weight put any load on driveshaft or clutch parts.*

ENGINE/TRANSAXLE JOINING (MANUAL)

1. Clean transaxle case and engine flange thoroughly.

2. Ensure that clutch disc is properly centered (see Chapter Ten). Inspect clutch release bearing and release plate for wear and cracks. Replace if necessary.

3. Lubricate starter shaft bushing with graphite grease. Put 2-3cc graphite grease in flywheel gland nut.

4. Apply molybdenum disulphide powder or graphite grease to main drive shaft spline and pilot journal. Apply same lubricant to starter pinion gear teeth and ring gear teeth (on flywheel).

5. Put transmission in gear to steady main drive shaft.

6. Rotate engine crankshaft with the fan belt so that the clutch plate hub lines up with the main drive shaft splines. Take care that gland nut needle bearing, clutch release bearing, and drive shaft are not damaged when pushing engine forward.

> **CAUTION**
> *Do not let engine tilt or let engine weight put any load on driveshaft or clutch parts.*

7. Guide lower engine mounting studs into position, then push engine firmly against transaxle until it is flush all the way around.

8. Install upper engine mounting bolts and nuts and tighten slightly. Install the lower mounting nuts and tighten slightly. Then tighten all bolts and nuts.

9. Rotate release bearing through opening in case until it engages with release fork. See **Figure 17**. Remove Allen bolts and spacers from pressure plate.

ENGINE/TRANSAXLE SEPARATION (SPORTOMATIC)

1. Disconnect oil hose and pressure line from temperature sensor housing. See **Figure 18**.

2. Loosen oil hose clamp at transmission.

3. Disconnect vacuum hose from vacuum servo.

4. Unhook and remove rear throttle control rod.

5. Remove 12-point bolts which hold the torque converter to the drive plate. See **Figure 19**.

6. Remove 2 lower engine mounting nuts.

7. Remove 2 upper engine mounting nuts.

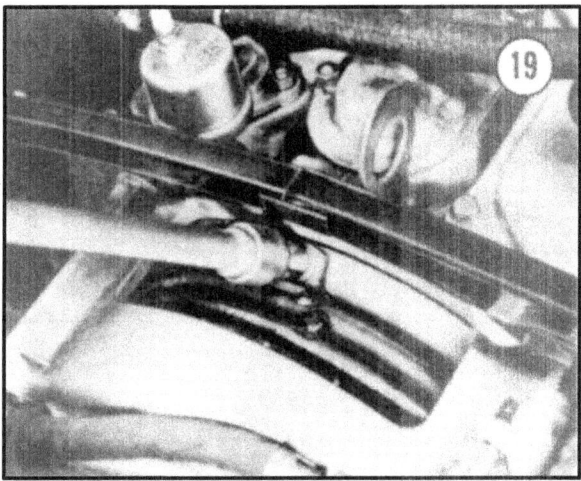

8. Separate engine and transaxle. Leave torque converter in transaxle and secure with a strap. See **Figure 20**.

ENGINE/TRANSAXLE JOINING (SPORTOMATIC)

1. Clean transaxle case and engine flanges thoroughly.

2. Lubricate starter shaft bushing with graphite grease.

3. Remove strap from torque converter.

4. Join engine and transaxle and bolt them together. Tighten to 34 foot-pounds (4.7 mkg).

5. Rotate engine crankshaft so that drive plate-to-torque converter bolts can be installed. Tighten them to 17-19 foot-pounds (2.4-2.6 mkg).

6. Connect rear throttle control rod.

7. Connect vacuum hose to vacuum servo.

8. Connect oil hose and pressure line to temperature sensor housing.

9. Adjust clutch free-play as described in Chapter Eleven.

ENGINE DISASSEMBLY/ASSEMBLY

The following sequences are designed so that the engine need not be disassembled any further than necessary. Unless otherwise indicated, procedures for major assemblies in these sequences are included in this chapter. The procedures are arranged in the approximate order in which they are performed.

To perform a step, turn to the procedure for the major assembly indicated, e.g., cylinder head, and perform the removal and inspection procedures, etc., until the engine is disassembled. To reassemble, reverse the disassembly sequence and perform the installation procedure for the major assembly involved.

Decarbonizing or Valve Service

1. Remove cover plates and fan.
2. Remove valve rocker assemblies.
3. Remove camshaft housing.
4. Remove cylinder heads.
5. Remove and inspect valves, guides, and seats.
6. Assembly is the reverse of these steps.

Valve and Ring Service

1. Perform Steps 1-4 for valve service.
2. Remove cylinders.
3. Remove rings. It is not necessary to remove the pistons unless they are damaged.
4. Assembly is the reverse of these steps.

General Overhaul Sequence

1. Remove carburetors (see Chapter Eight).
2. Remove distributor.
3. Remove cooling air ducts and cover plates.
4. Remove rear engine mount.
5. Remove fuel pump.
6. Remove muffler.
7. Remove crankshaft pulley and blower housing (see Chapter Six).
8. Remove heat exchangers (see Chapter Six).
9. Remove camshafts.
10. Remove oil cooler.
11. Remove cylinder heads.
12. Remove cylinders and pistons.
13. Remove breather stack.
14. Remove thermostat and oil pressure sender.
15. Remove flywheel.
16. Disassemble crankcase.
17. Remove crankshaft and connecting rods.
18. Remove oil pump and intermediate shaft.
19. Assembly is the reverse of these steps.

OIL PRESSURE RELIEF AND BYPASS VALVES

The oil pressure relief valve is located on the bottom front edge of the crankcase. The bypass valve is slightly above the oil pressure relief valve on the left side. See **Figure 21**. Both are serviced in the same manner.

Relief Valve (Bottom) By-Pass Valve (Top)

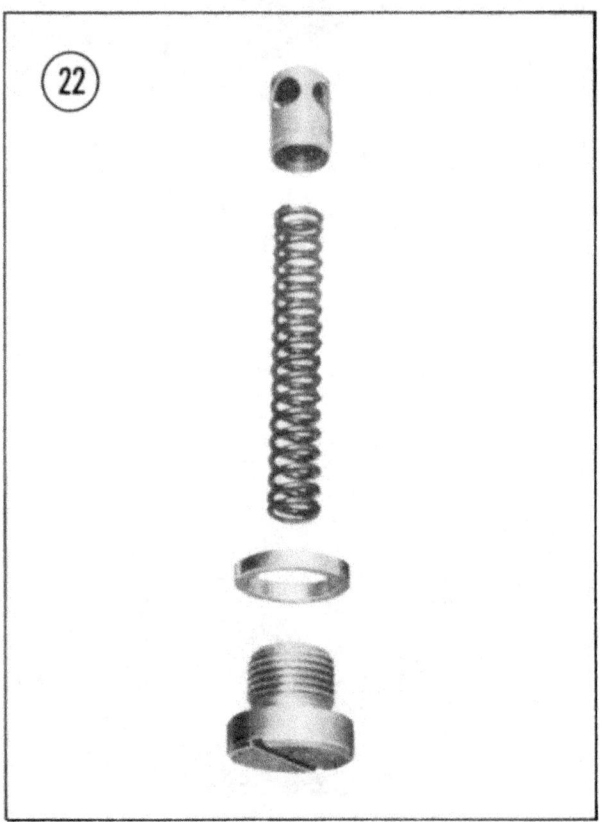

Removal

1. Remove slotted plug and sealing ring. See Figure 21.
2. Withdraw spring and valve piston. See **Figure 22**.

Inspection

1. Check the crankcase bore and piston for signs of scoring or seizure. Dress the bore with crocus cloth and replace the piston if necessary.
2. Measure spring length. Unloaded length should be 2.75" (70mm). Ensure that the spring ends cannot scratch the bore when installed.

Installation

1. Insert piston and spring in bore.
2. Install slotted cap with metal sealing ring. See Figure 21.

OIL STRAINER

The oil strainer can be removed for cleaning with the engine installed. Refer to **Figure 23** for the following procedures.

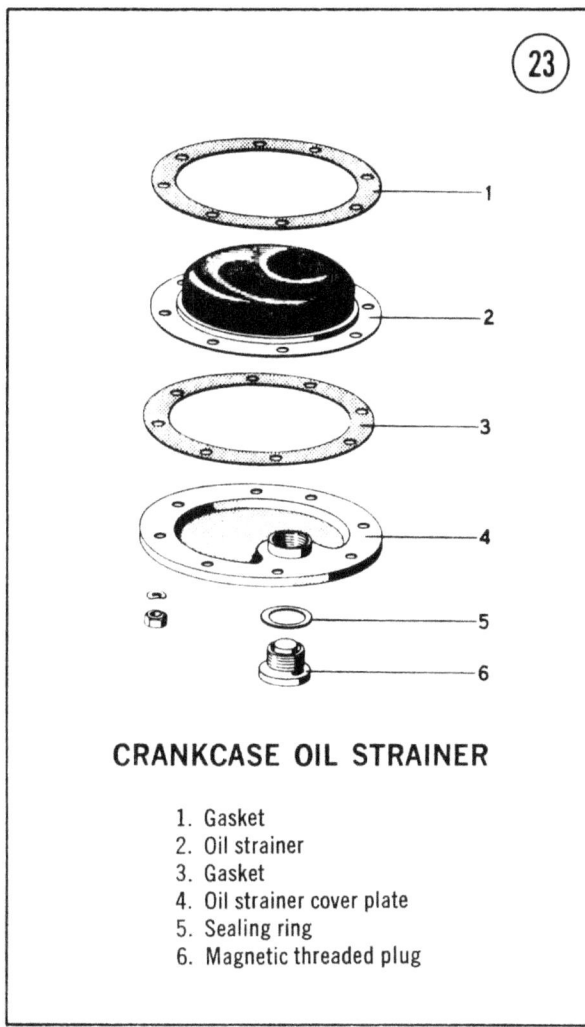

CRANKCASE OIL STRAINER

1. Gasket
2. Oil strainer
3. Gasket
4. Oil strainer cover plate
5. Sealing ring
6. Magnetic threaded plug

Removal

1. Remove nuts securing cover plate to crankcase and remove cover plate.
2. Remove oil strainer and gaskets.

Inspection

1. Check that the oil suction pipe is tight and not bent to one side of the large opening. If not, the engine must be dismantled and crankcase peened around the pipe. See *Crankcase Inspection* procedure.
2. Clean all parts in solvent and remove all traces of old gasket.
3. Ensure that the cover plate is not bent. Straighten or replace if necessary.

Installation

1. Install all of the parts in the order shown in Figure 23. Use 2 new gaskets and be sure that the oil suction pipe fits the opening in the oil strainer exactly.
2. Secure cover plate. Do not overtighten nuts or the plate will bend and cause leaks.

REAR OIL SEAL

The rear oil seal is a simple O-ring. Engine must be removed to replace it.

Replacement

1. Remove crankshaft pulley as described elsewhere in this chapter.
2. Pry out the O-ring with a screwdriver as shown in **Figure 24**.

> CAUTION
> *Do not damage the crankshaft with the screwdriver.*

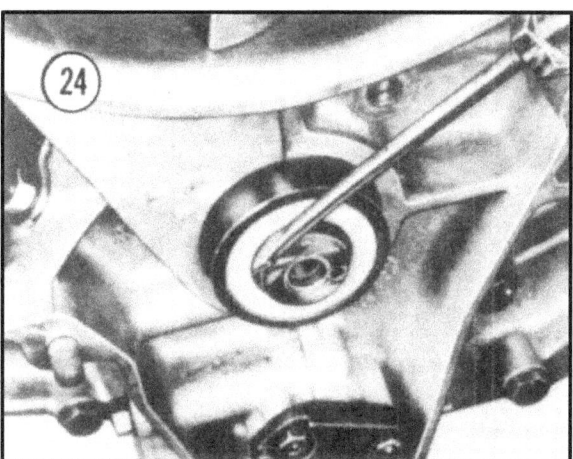

3. Lightly coat a new O-ring with oil.
4. Install the O-ring as shown in **Figure 25**. Although a special Porsche tool (Tool #P216) is shown, other methods may be easily improvised.
5. Install crankshaft pulley.

FRONT OIL SEAL

Engine must be removed to replace the front oil seal.

Removal

1. Remove flywheel or drive plate (Sportomatic) as described previously.

2. Deform old seal by striking it with a punch and hammer through the slot in the crankcase. See **Figure 26**.

3. Pry seal out with a screwdriver or similar tool.

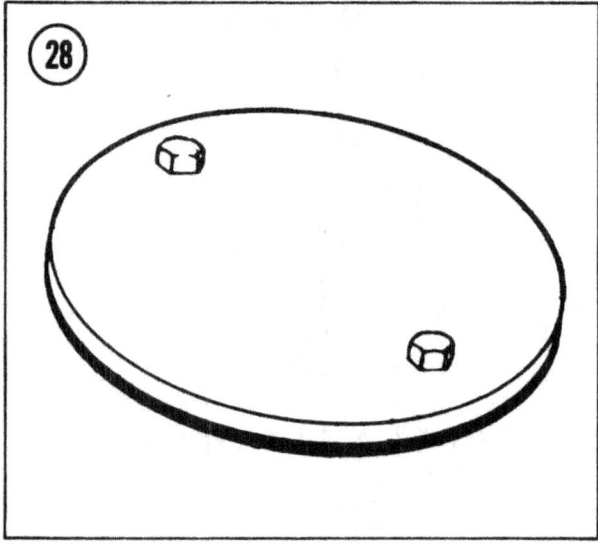

3. Oil inner lips of seal at crankshaft.

4. Reinstall flywheel as described earlier.

Installation

1. Clean recess between crankcase and crankshaft thoroughly. Remove any burrs from oil seal seat. If necessary, chamfer edges of crankcase opening slightly so that oil seal seats without damage. Clean out metal flakes carefully.

2. Install oil seal with closed side out. One method is to put the seal in place and gently tap it with a hammer and block of wood. Work slowly and evenly around the seal until it is flush with the bottom of the crankcase recess. Another method requires a special tool (Porsche P215) shown in **Figure 27** which presses the seal in evenly. This is easily improvised with a metal plate and 2 bolts to fit flywheel mounting holes. See **Figure 28**. Tighten bolts alternately and evenly a few turns at a time.

VALVE ROCKER ASSEMBLY

Refer to **Figure 29** for the following procedures.

Removal

1. Clean away road dirt around valve covers.
2. Disconnect spark plug wires.
3. Remove nuts and lockwashers and remove valve covers.
4. Mark rocker arms so that they may be reinstalled in the same place.
5. Loosen Allen bolt in center of each rocker shaft that is to be removed. See **Figure 30**.
6. Push rocker shaft out and lift out the rocker arm. Mark rocker shafts as they are removed to aid reassembly.

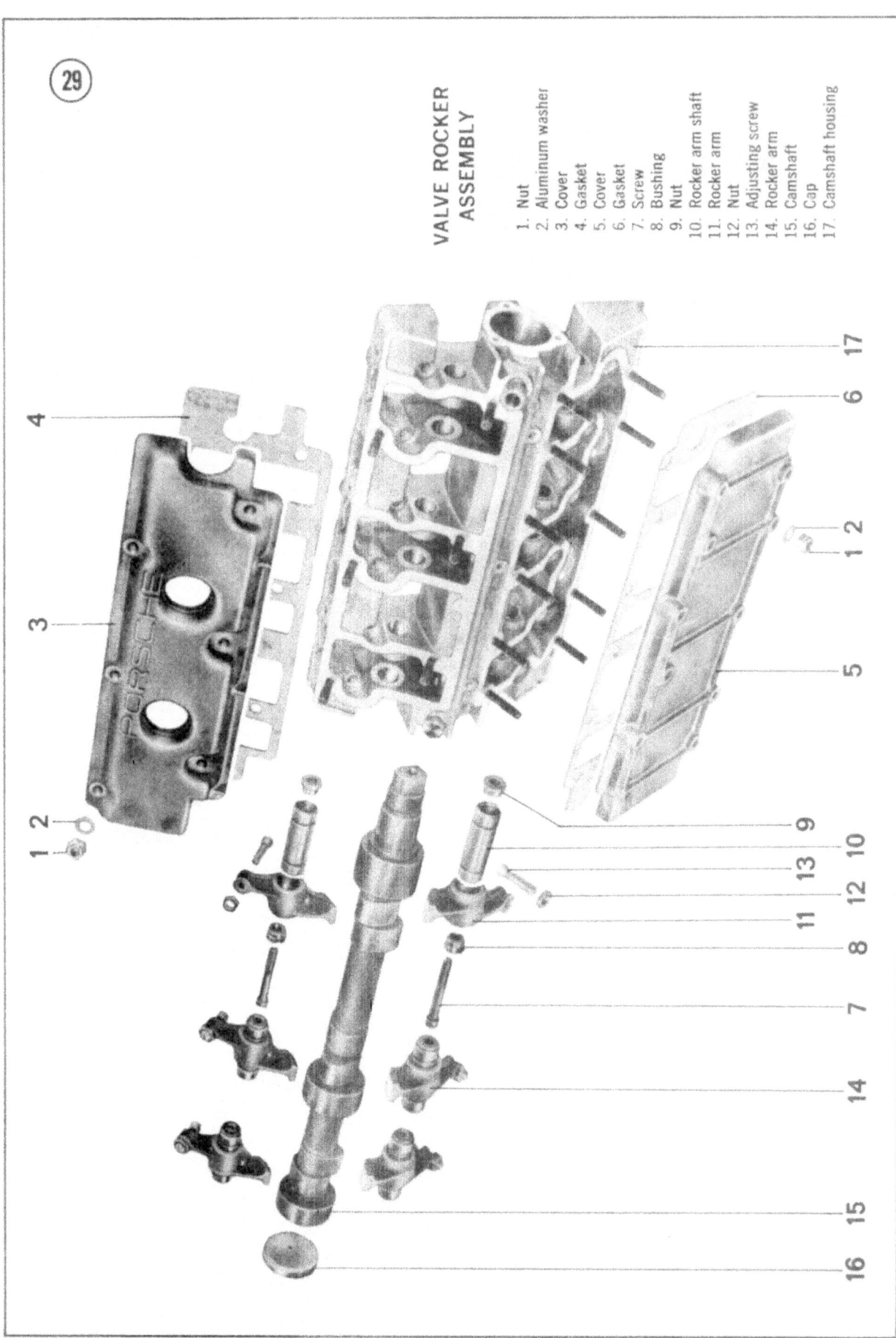

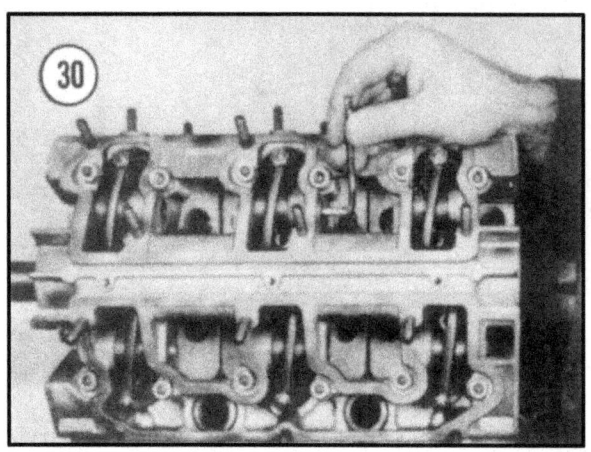

CAUTION
Depending on camshaft position, some rocker arms will be under tension. Do not force the rocker shaft out. Rotate crankshaft to relieve the tension, then remove the shaft.

Inspection

1. Clean all parts in solvent.
2. Check rocker shafts for wear, scoring, and signs of seizure. Replace if necessary.
3. Check rocker arm inside bore and at each end where it bears on the valve and camshaft.

Installation

1. Assemble cones and Allen bolts on rocker shafts. Do not tighten Allen bolt. See **Figure 31**.
2. Hold rocker arm in position in head and insert rocker shaft.

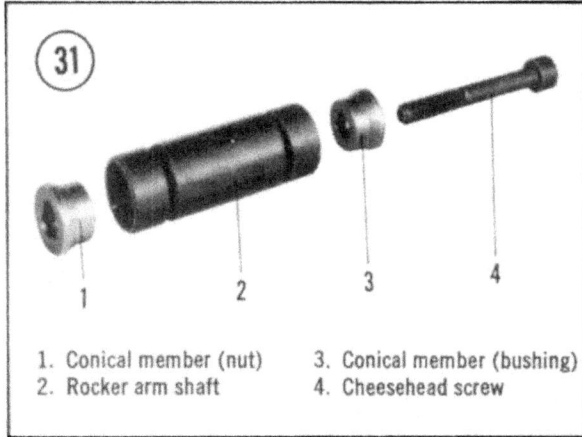

1. Conical member (nut)
2. Rocker arm shaft
3. Conical member (bushing)
4. Cheesehead screw

CAUTION
Insert rocker shafts for cylinders 1, 3, 4, and 6 so that the Allen bolt head faces towards the center rocker arms.

3. The rocker shaft must be centered in its bore. To do this, insert a feeler gauge between the rocker arm and the camshaft housing. Push the rocker shaft into its bore until the feeler gauge slips into the rocker shaft groove. See **Figure 32**. Push the shaft additionally until the feeler gauge is held firmly.

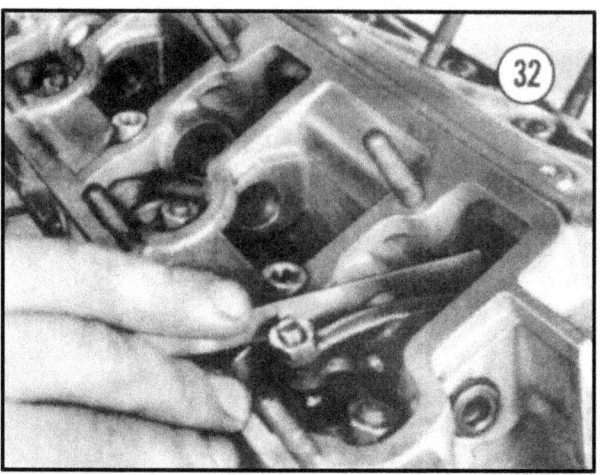

4. Withdraw the feeler gauge.
5. Push shaft in approximately 0.060″ (1.5mm) more in the same direction as in Step 3. This will center the shaft as shown in **Figure 33**.

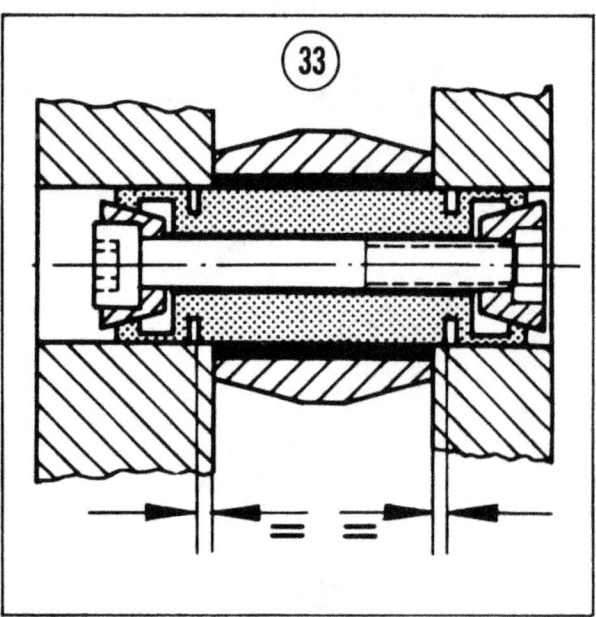

6. Install valve covers and reconnect spark plug wires.

CAMSHAFT

Refer to **Figure 34** for the following procedures.

110

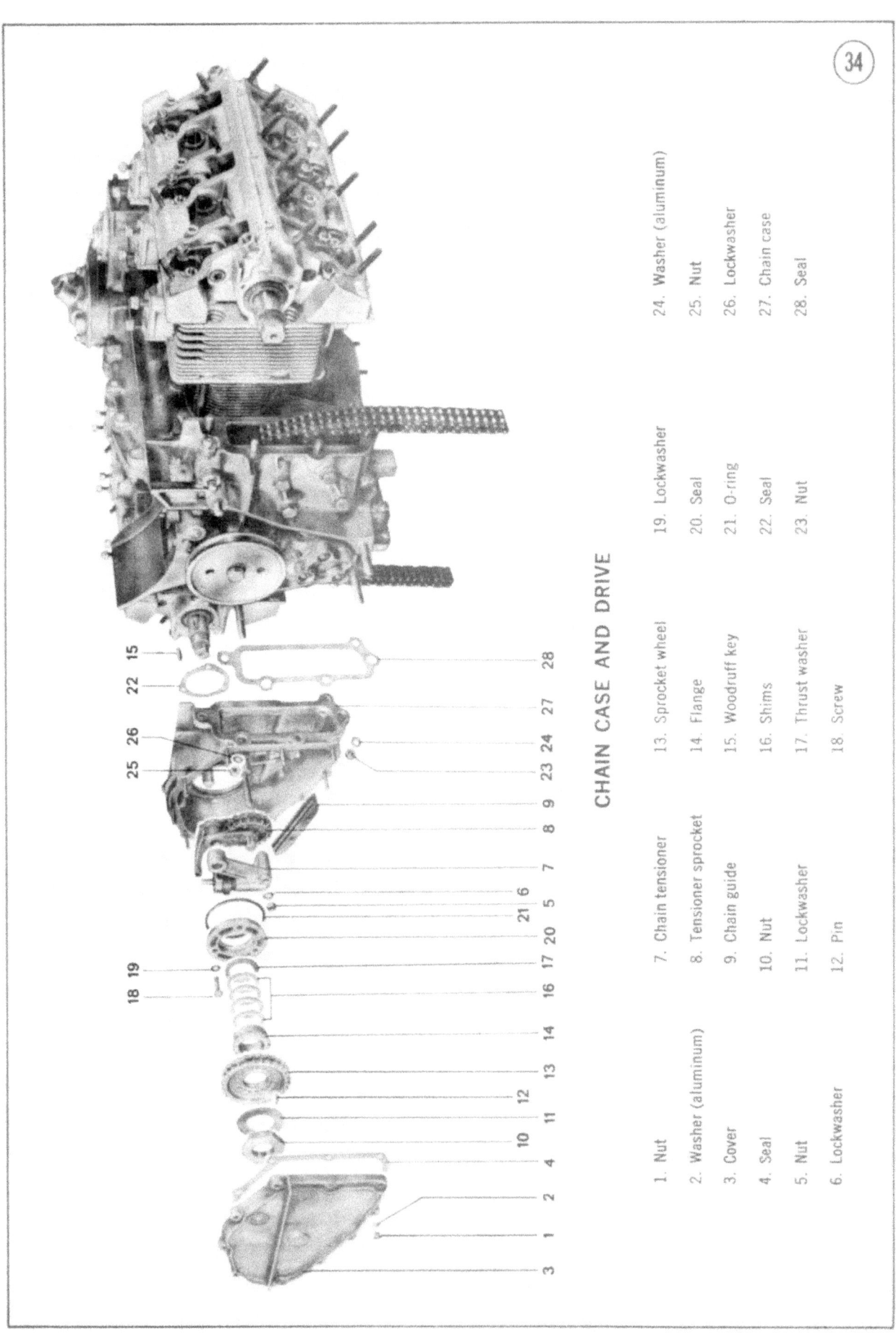

CHAIN CASE AND DRIVE

1. Nut
2. Washer (aluminum)
3. Cover
4. Seal
5. Nut
6. Lockwasher
7. Chain tensioner
8. Tensioner sprocket
9. Chain guide
10. Nut
11. Lockwasher
12. Pin
13. Sprocket wheel
14. Flange
15. Woodruff key
16. Shims
17. Thrust washer
18. Screw
19. Lockwasher
20. Seal
21. O-ring
22. Seal
23. Nut
24. Washer (aluminum)
25. Nut
26. Lockwasher
27. Chain case
28. Seal

Removal

1. Remove rocker arms and shafts as described previously.

2. Remove muffler.

3. Remove oil connecting hose from crankcase to chain housing cover at cover. See **Figure 35**.

4. Remove chain housing cover.

5. Remove chain tensioner and chain tensioning sprocket. See procedure later in this chapter.

6. Remove large nut securing camshaft sprocket. See **Figure 36**.

7. Pull out dowel pin securing camshaft sprocket. Porsche dealers use a special threaded rod (Porsche tool P212) for this (**Figure 37**). The tool has metric threads.

8. Remove chain guide as shown in **Figure 38**.

9. Pull off camshaft sprocket, sprocket mounting flange, and small Woodruff key.

10. Remove 3 bolts securing sealing ring, O-ring, and gasket. Remove parts from end of camshaft. See **Figure 39**. Count the number of

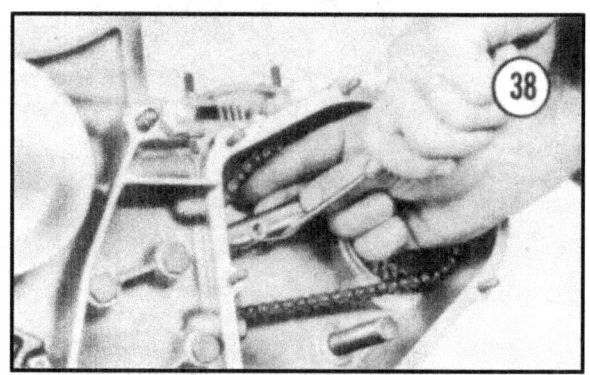

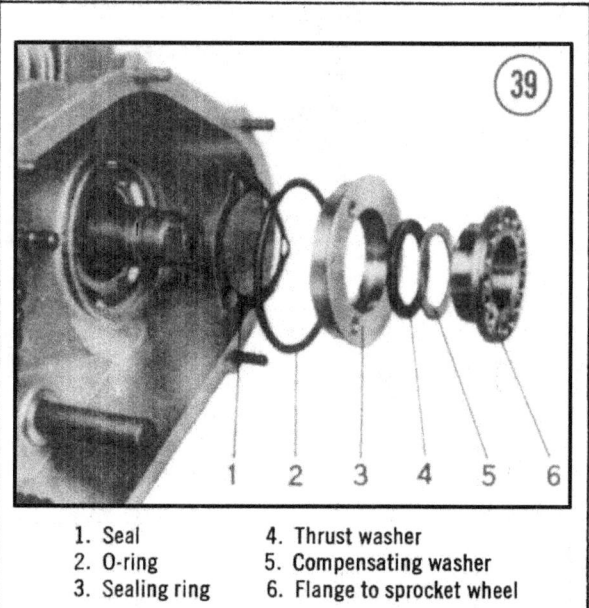

1. Seal
2. O-ring
3. Sealing ring
4. Thrust washer
5. Compensating washer
6. Flange to sprocket wheel

shim washers so that the same number are reinstalled.

11. Pull camshaft out of housing.

Inspection

1. Clean all parts thoroughly in solvent.

112

2. Inspect bearing journals and cam lobes for wear. Cam lobes should not be scored and the edges should be square. Slight damage may be removed with a silicon carbide oilstone. Use 100-120 grit initially, then polish with a 280-320 grit.

3. Clean oilways with compressed air.

4. Check camshaft runout at the center bearing journal. See **Figure 40**.

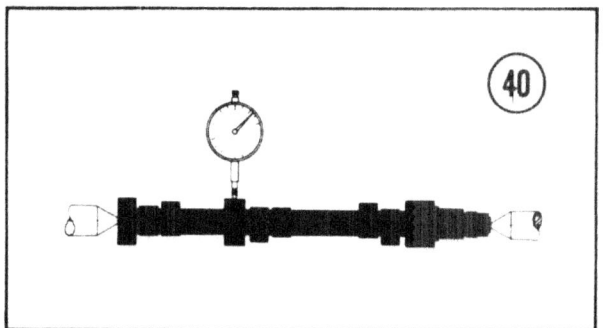

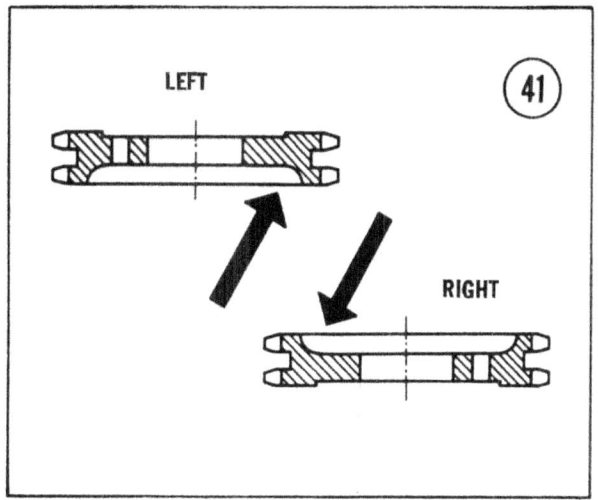

Installation

1. Slide camshaft into housing. Ensure that it rotates smoothly and freely.

2. Install new gasket over camshaft.

3. Fit new O-ring over aluminum sealing ring. Hold in place with grease.

4. Install sealing ring and secure with 3 bolts.

5. Attach dial indicator to end of camshaft and move the camshaft back and forth. End-play with all new parts is 0.006-0.0078" (0.15-0.20mm). Replace sealing ring if end-play exceeds 0.0157" (0.4mm).

6. Install thrust washer and shim washers (see Figure 39). Install the same number of shim washers removed in Step 10, *Removal*.

7. Install sprocket flange with Woodruff key.

8. Fit sprocket on camshaft large nut. Do not install dowel pin or large nut yet.

> NOTE: *Sprockets used on left and right banks are identical. However, when installed on the left bank (cylinders 1-3), the deep recess shown in* **Figure 41** *faces out (toward the rear of the engine). When the sprocket is mounted on the right bank (cylinders 4-6), the deep recess faces inward (towards the front of the engine).*

9. Push the intermediate shaft and right bank camshaft towards the front of the engine as far as they will go.

10. With a straightedge and depth gauge, measure distance A from the rear face of the drive sprocket to the crankcase edge. **See Figures 42 and 43**. Note the hole below the intermediate shaft which permits access to the drive sprocket face.

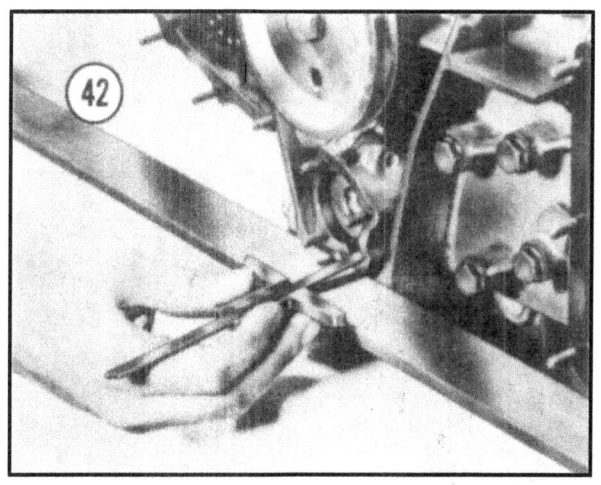

11. Measure distance B, the depth of the right camshaft sprocket face in the same way. See **Figure 44** and Figure 43.

12. Compare measurements A and B. If the difference exceeds 0.01" (0.25mm), remove the camshaft sprocket and flange and adjust the number of shim washers to correct the difference. Reinstall flange and sprocket.

13. Measure distance C as shown in **Figure 45** and Figure 43.

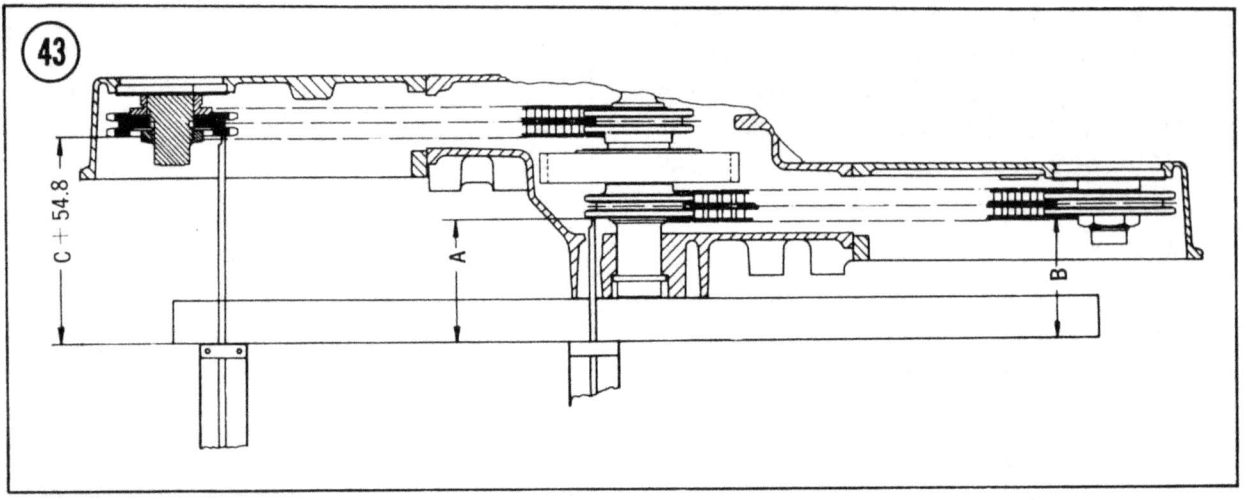

14. Add 2.157" (54.8mm) to measurement A (see Step 10). Compare this new figure to measurement C. If the difference exceeds 0.01" (0.25mm), remove left sprocket and flange and adjust number of shims to correct difference. Reinstall flange and sprocket.

15. Install heat exchangers if removed.

16. Lift retaining spring away from chain guide and slide chain guide onto crankcase studs. See **Figure 46**.

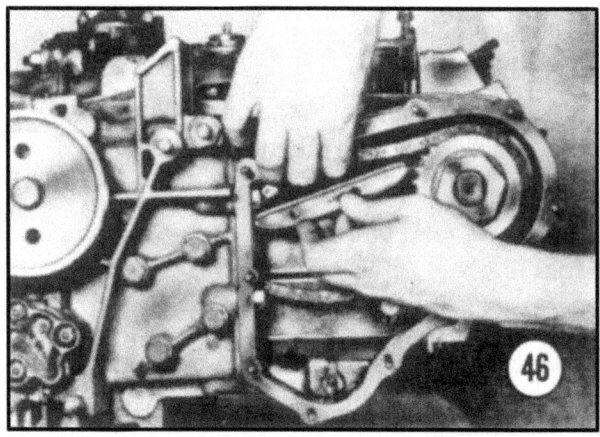

17. Install chain tensioner as described later.

18. Rotate crankshaft until the "Z1" marked on the crankshaft pulley aligns with the crankcase seam. See **Figure 47**.

19. Rotate camshafts until punch marks point straight up. See Figure 47.

20. Fit the dowel pin through whichever sprocket lines up with a flange hole.

21. Install large sprocket nut and tighten to 72 foot-pounds (10 mkg).

22. Install rocker arms and shafts.

CAUTION
Valve timing is not correct at this point. Rotating either the crankshaft or camshaft could cause valves and pistons to collide and damage each other. To prevent damage, rotate the crankshaft very slowly and carefully. When the slightest resistance is felt, STOP, back off a little, then rotate either or both camshafts to move the valves out of the way.

23. Adjust valve timing as described later in this chapter.

CYLINDER HEADS

Each cylinder has its own cylinder head. The 3 cylinder heads for one bank are joined by a camshaft housing containing the camshaft and rocker arms for that bank.

The cylinder heads may be removed individually or all 3 cylinders on one bank may be removed simultaneously. Both procedures are described below.

Cylinder Head Bank Removal

Only parts associated with the desired bank need be removed.

1. Remove front engine support shown in **Figure 48**.

2. Remove muffler and heat exchanger as described in Chapter Six.

3. Perform Steps 3-10, *Camshaft Removal*.

4. Remove nuts securing chain housing to crankcase and remove housing.

5. Loosen cylinder head nuts with Allen wrench. See **Figure 49**.

6. Remove cylinder head nuts and lift off complete assembly as shown in **Figure 50**.

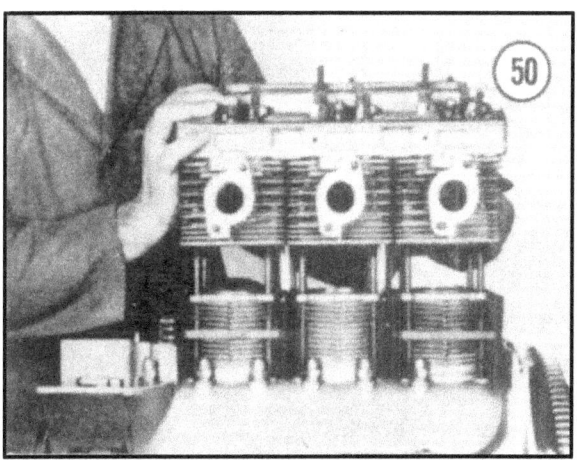

Cylinder Head Inspection

1. Without removing the valves, remove all carbon deposits from the combustion chambers with a wire brush. A blunt screwdriver or chisel may be used if care is taken not to damage the head or valves.

2. After all carbon is removed from the combustion chamber, both valves, intake and exhaust ports, clean the entire head with solvent.

3. Clean away all carbon on the piston crown. Do not remove the carbon ridge at the top of the cylinder bore.

4. Check for cracks in the combustion chamber and exhaust ports. Cracked heads must be replaced.

5. Check all studs for tightness. If a stud can't be tightened, have a machinist drill the hole out and install a Heli-coil threaded insert.

6. Push the valve stem ends sideways with your thumb. If there is any play, the valve guides are probably worn. Replace them as described later if there is any doubt.

Cylinder Head Bank Inspection

Before installing cylinder heads, see *Inspection* procedure above.

1. Remove rocker arms and shafts as described in an earlier section to prevent camshaft bearing damage during installation.

2. Ensure that sealing surfaces on cylinder heads and cylinders are clean and in good condition.

3. Install new gaskets on cylinders. Perforations face towards the cylinders.

4. Install new rubber O-rings on oil return pipes and install the pipes in the crankcase.

5. Lower cylinder head/camshaft housing assembly into position. Make sure that oil return pipes seat properly in the camshaft housing and crankcase.

6. Install washers and cylinder head nuts. Tighten finger-tight.

7. Install chain housing on crankcase. Tighten nuts shown in **Figure 51** and loop chain over camshaft as shown.

8. Tighten diagonally opposite cylinder head nuts evenly and progressively until all are tightened to 22-24 foot-pounds (3.0-3.3 mkg).

9. Perform Steps 2-23, *Camshaft Installation*.

10. Install heat exchangers, muffler, and rear engine support.

Individual Cylinder Head Removal

Only parts associated with the desired cylinder head need be removed.

1. Remove front engine support shown in Figure 48.

2. Remove muffler and heat exchanger.

3. Perform Steps 3-11, *Camshaft Removal* procedure.

4. Remove nuts securing chain housing to crankcase and remove housing.

5. Remove rocker arms and shafts as described in another section.

6. Remove 12 nuts securing camshaft housing to cylinder heads. Three of them shown in **Figure 52** require an 8mm Allen wrench.

7. Remove nuts securing desired cylinder head(s) and lift head(s) off. See **Figure 53**.

Individual Cylinder Head Installation

Before installing a cylinder head, see *Inspection* procedure above.

1. Ensure sealing surfaces on cylinder head and cylinders are clean and in good condition.

2. Install new gasket on cylinder. Perforations face toward the cylinder. See **Figure 54**.

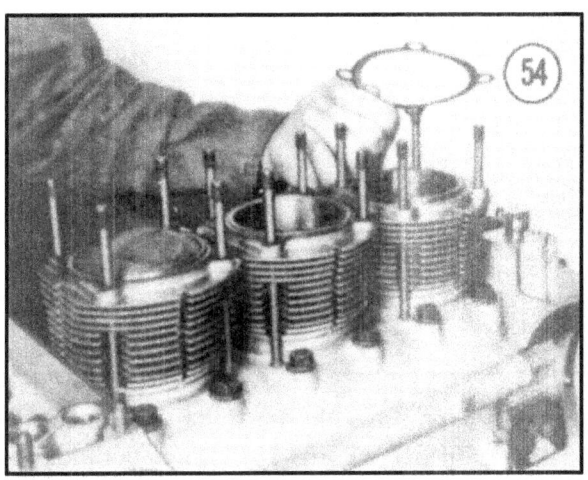

3. Install cylinder head.

4. Install washers and cylinder head nuts. Tighten finger-tight.

5. Install new rubber O-rings on oil return pipes and install the pipes in the crankcase.

6. Ensure that camshaft housing and cylinder head surfaces are clean and in good condition. Coat these surfaces with sealing compound (Permatex Aviation Form-a-Gasket No. 3 or equivalent).

7. Install camshaft housing in place. Make sure that oil return pipes seat in camshaft housing and crankcase properly. Install washers and housing nuts finger-tight.

8. Tighten diagonally opposite cyinder head nuts evenly and progressively until all are tightened 22-24 foot-pounds (3.0-3.3 mkg).

9. Tighten diagonally opposite camshaft housing nuts evenly and progressively until all are tightened 16-18 foot-pounds (2.2-2.5 mkg).

CAUTION
Periodically while tightening these nuts, insert camshaft and make certain that it turns freely. If there is any binding, remove the camshaft housing and find out the reason.

10. Install chain housing on crankcase. Tighten nuts shown in Figure 51 and loop chain over camshaft.

11. Install camshaft as described in another procedure.

12. Install heat exchanger, muffler, and rear engine support.

CHAIN AND CHAIN TENSION SYSTEM

Several chain guides and 2 oil-operated tensioners keep the chains running smoothly. These parts are shown in **Figure 55**. While it is possible to perform some of these procedures with the engine installed, it is actually easier to remove the engine/transaxle first.

Chain Housing Cover Removal

1. Disconnect oil lines to chain housing cover. See **Figure 56**.

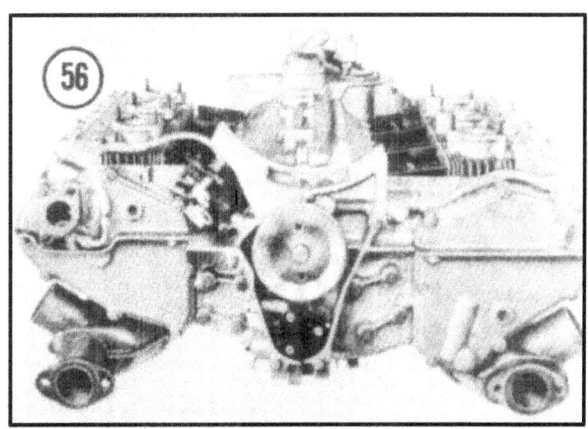

2. Remove nuts securing chain housing cover and remove the cover.

3. Installation is the reverse of these steps.

Chain Guide Replacement

Each chain housing contains one guide.

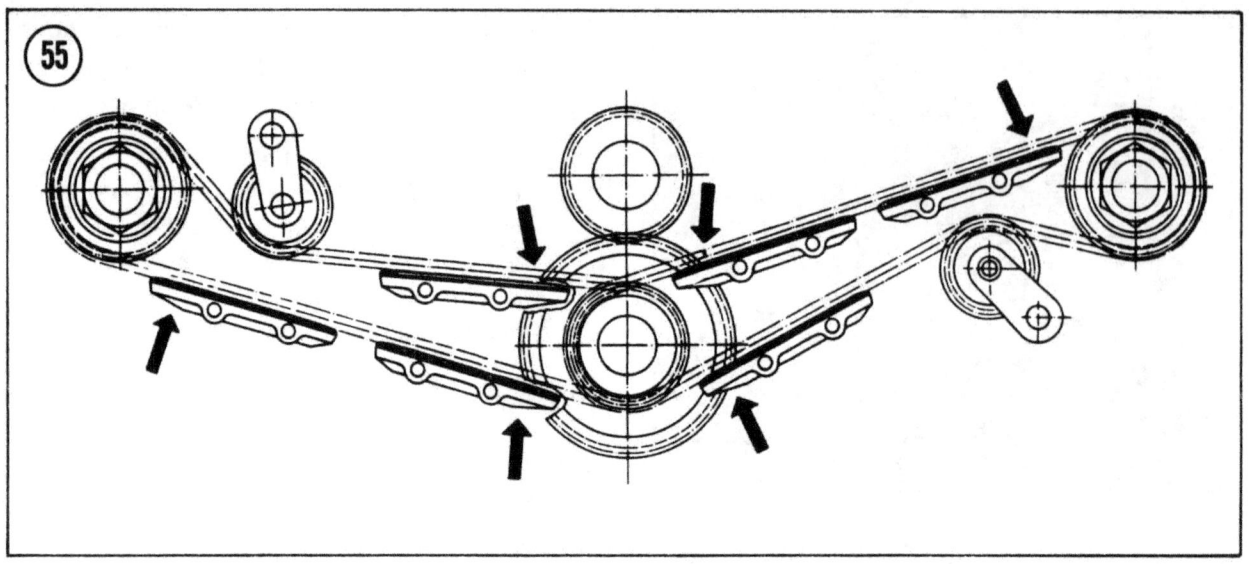

The crankcase contains 4 additional guides held in place by studs.

To replace crankcase chain guides:

1. Remove chain housing cover.

2. Remove camshaft(s) as described in this chapter.

3. Remove chain housing nuts shown in **Figure 51** and lift housing off.

4. Pry retainer spring down and unscrew 2 stud bolts holding chain guide. Lift guide out.

> NOTE: *Do not drop chain guide into crankcase or you may have to disassemble the crankcase to retrieve it.*

5. Installation is the reverse of these steps.

Chain Tensioner Removal/Installation

1. Remove chain housing covers.

2. Remove distributor cap. Turn crankshaft over until rotor points to notch on distributor housing and "Z1" on crankshaft pulley aligns wtih the crankcase seam. This indicates piston No. 1 is at TDC on compression stroke.

3. Wedge the chain tension wheels so that they maintain tension after chain tensioner has been removed. It is also possible to tie them to a cover stud with strong wire to maintain tension.

4. Remove nut securing chain tensioner and remove tensioner. See **Figure 57**.

5. Installation is the reverse of these steps. Porsche mechanics use a special tool (Porsche

P214) to compress the tensioner piston during installation. See **Figure 58**. Other methods are easily devised.

Chain Tensioner Disassembly/Assembly

Refer to **Figure 59** for the following procedure.

> WARNING
> *Internal parts are under considerable spring tension. Do not allow them to fly out.*

1. Depress spring retainer and pry out C-ring.

2. Remove oil retainer with long nose pliers.

3. Depress piston and pry out C-ring. See **Figure 60**.

4. Remove remaining internal parts. Do not lose small ball.

5. Clean all parts in solvent.

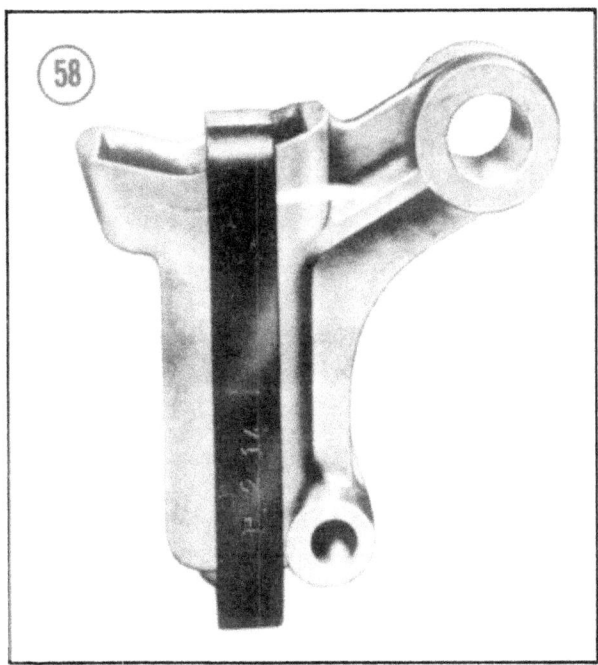

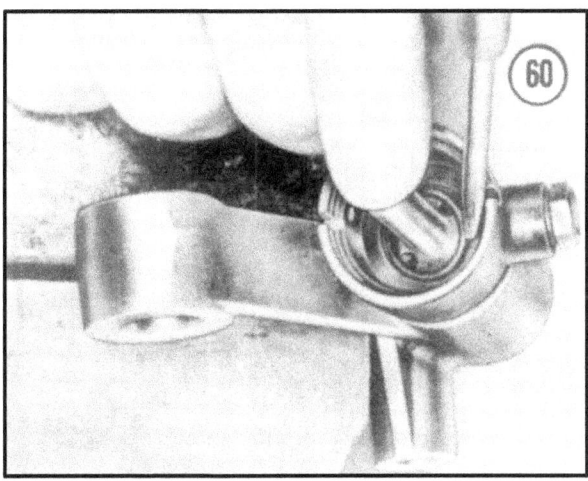

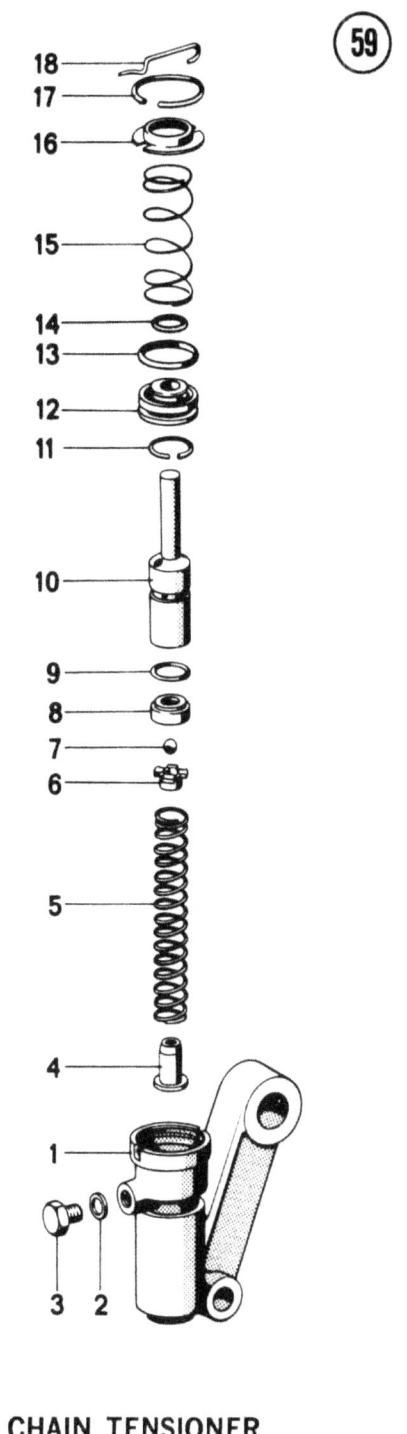

6. Examine all parts for wear and scoring. Replace questionable parts.

7. Install intermediate piece with O-ring, ball, and ball retainer in piston.

8. Fill tensioner body with SAE 30 engine oil.

9. Install spring guide, spring, and piston assembly in body. Secure piston with C-ring.

10. Insert a 0.039" (1mm) diameter steel wire through the hole in the piston. See **Figures 61 and 62**.

11. Depress the ball valve and pump the piston up and down until no more air bubbles are visible. Remove wire.

12. Take tensioners to dealer. Have him install remaining parts (12-17 in Figure 59) and bleed the upper reservoir with Porsche tool P214v.

CHAIN TENSIONER

1. Housing
2. Copper washer
3. Bleeder screw
4. Spring guide
5. Piston spring
6. Ball retainer
7. Ball (5mm dia.)
8. Intermediate piece
9. O-ring
10. Piston
11. C-ring
12. Oil retainer
13. O-ring
14. O-ring
15. Oil retainer spring
16. Spring retainer
17. C-ring
18. Clamp (supplied only with new chain tensioners to help installation)

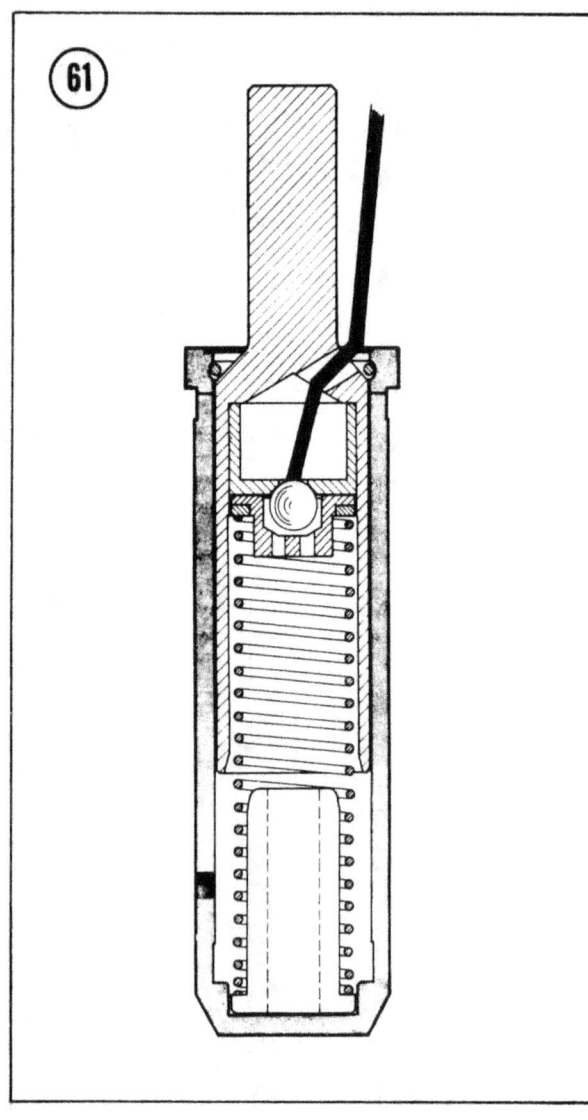

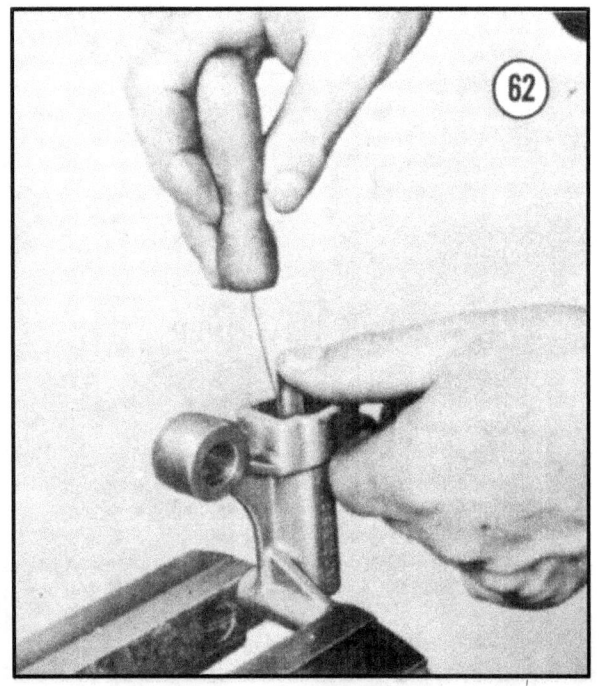

Camshaft Chain Replacement

1. Disassemble crankcase as described in this chapter.
2. Reassemble crankcase with new chain(s).

VALVE AND VALVE SEATS

Valve Removal

Refer to **Figure 63** for the following procedure.

1. Remove cylinder head.
2. Compress springs with a valve spring compression tool, remove valve cotters and release compressions.
3. Remove valve spring caps, springs, and valves.

> CAUTION
> *Remove any burrs from valve stem grooves before removing valves. Otherwise, valve guides will be damaged.*

4. Remove valve guide seals from valve guides.
5. Remove spacer washers and spring supports under springs.

Inspection

1. Clean valves with a wire brush and solvent. Discard burned, warped, or cracked valves. If any valves are to be refaced, refer to **Figure 64** for critical dimensions.
2. Check valve stems for wear, bends, and traces of seizure. Check end for excessive wear (ridge formation). Valves with stem damage must be replaced; valve stems cannot be reground or straightened.
3. Remove all carbon and varnish from valve guides with a stiff wire brush.
4. Insert valves in guides.
5. Rig a dial indicator so that it bears on the valve stem just above the valve guide See **Figure 65**.
6. Lift the valve about 1/16" off its seat and rock the valve stem back and forth. Play indicated on the dial indicator should be 0.0012-0.0022" (0.030-0.057mm) on the inlet valve and 0.002-0.003" (0.050-0.077mm) on the exhaust valve. If play is excessive, the valve guide

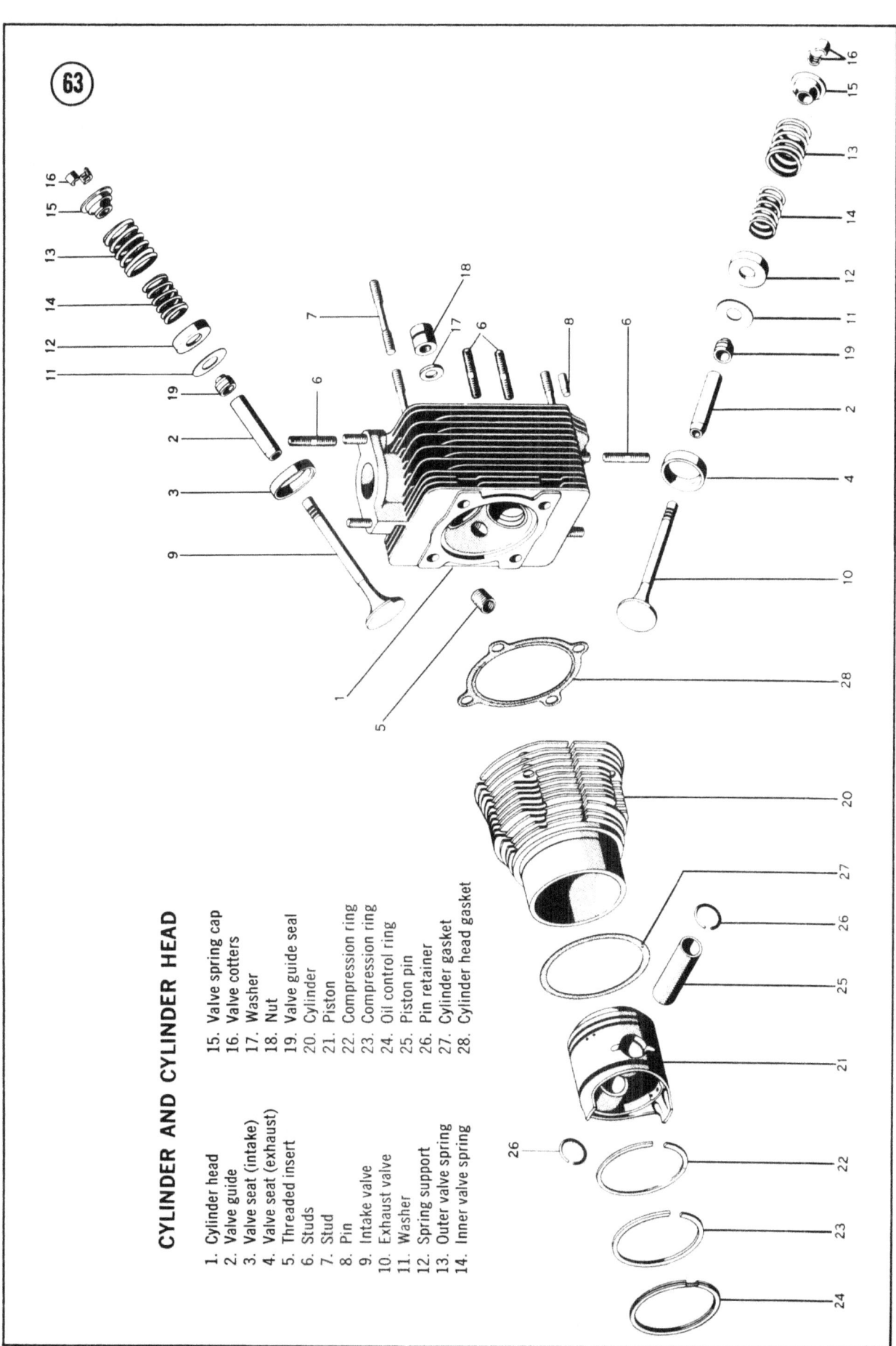

CYLINDER AND CYLINDER HEAD

1. Cylinder head
2. Valve guide
3. Valve seat (intake)
4. Valve seat (exhaust)
5. Threaded insert
6. Studs
7. Stud
8. Pin
9. Intake valve
10. Exhaust valve
11. Washer
12. Spring support
13. Outer valve spring
14. Inner valve spring
15. Valve spring cap
16. Valve cotters
17. Washer
18. Nut
19. Valve guide seal
20. Cylinder
21. Piston
22. Compression ring
23. Compression ring
24. Oil control ring
25. Piston pin
26. Pin retainer
27. Cylinder gasket
28. Cylinder head gasket

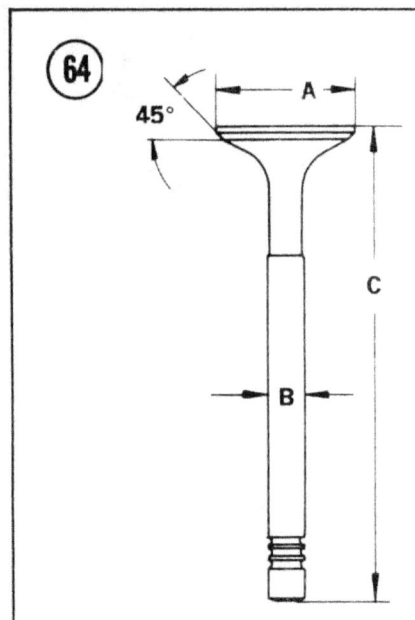

VALVE DIMENSIONS

	A	B	C
Intake valves	1.654±0.004″ (42±0.1mm)	0.3531-0.0005″ (8.77-0.012mm)	4.4882±0.008″ (114±0.2mm)
Exhaust valves	1.496±0.004″ (38±0.1mm)	0.3524-0.0005″ (8.95-0.012mm)	4.4685±0.008″ (113.5±0.2mm)

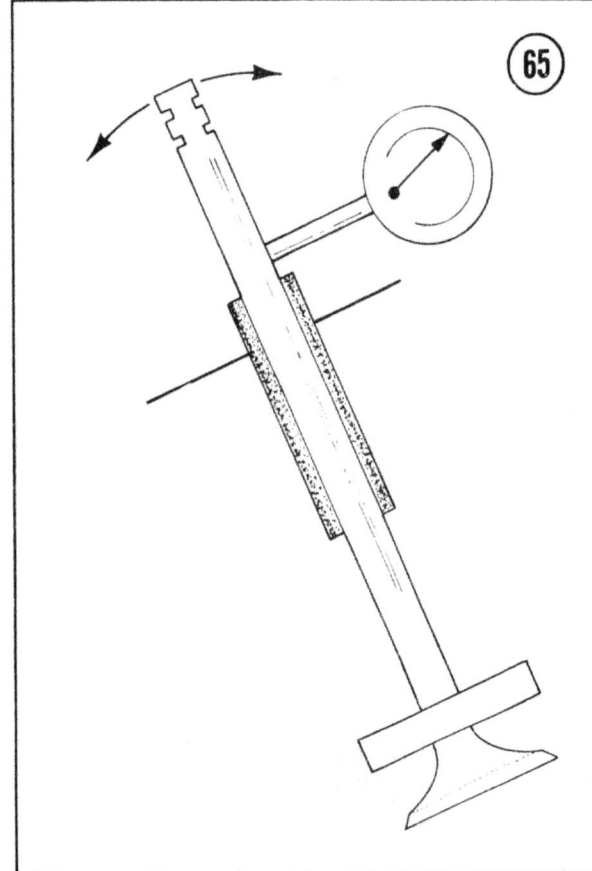

and/or valve stem is worn. See *Valve Guide Replacement* later in this section.

7. Measure valve spring heights. All should be of equal height (up to 5% variation permissible), with no bends or other distortion. Replace defective springs. Inner and outer spring must be replaced as a set.

NOTE: *Intake and exhaust springs are identical.*

8. Test inner/outer spring combination with spring support and valve spring cap on a spring tester. Compare dimensions B in **Figure 66** with specifications in the figure.

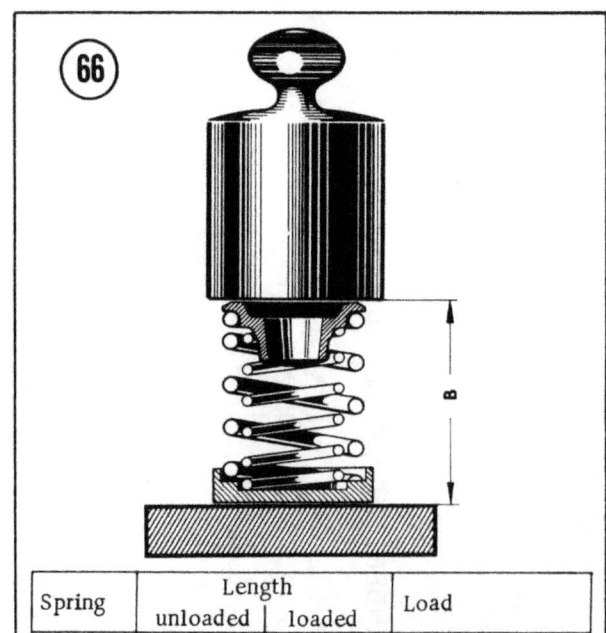

Spring	Length unloaded	Length loaded	Load
external	41.8 mm (1.65″)	35 mm (1.38″)	17.5 ± 1 kp (38.6 ± 2.2 lbs.)
internal	38.4 mm (1.51″)	35.5 mm (1.40″)	6.5 ± 0.8 kp (14.3 ± 1.8 lbs.)

9. Check valve cotters. Press them together on the end of the valve. The valve should turn freely within the cotters.

10. Inspect valve seats. If worn, burned, or loose, they must be reconditioned by a dealer or other competent machine shop. The procedure is provided later in this section. Seats and valves in near perfect condition can be reconditioned by lapping with fine carborundum paste. Lapping, however, is always inferior to precision grinding.

11. Check valve seating with Prussian (machinist's) blue as described in Step 4-7, *Valve Seat Reconditioning*.

Installation

1. Coat valve stems with molybdenum disulphide paste and insert them into cylinder head.

2. Fit valve guide seals over end of valves and push seals down until the base contacts the top of the guide.

3. Install 2 washers and spring support over each valve guide. See **Figure 67**.

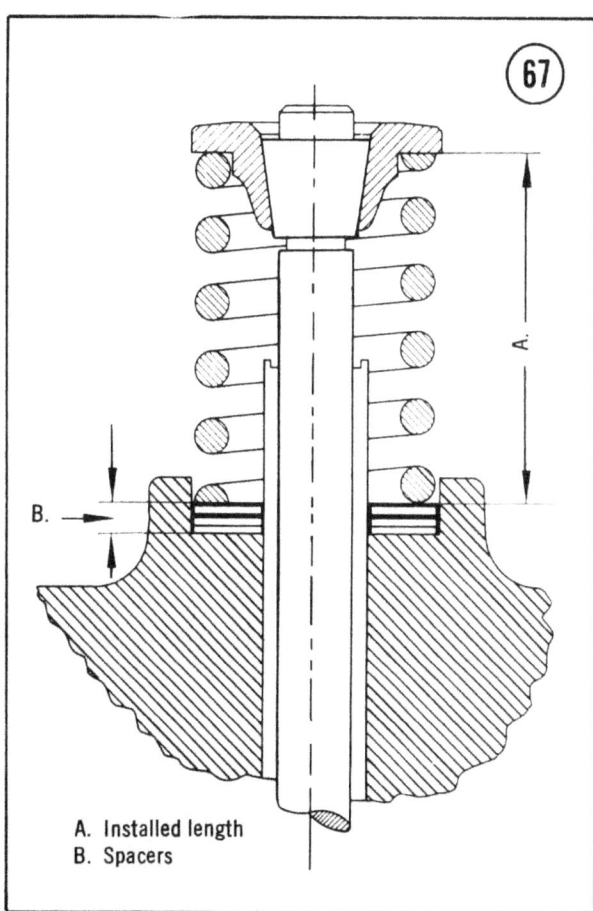

A. Installed length
B. Spacers

4. Install springs with close-pitched coils next to the cylinder head.

5. Install valve spring caps, compress springs with compression tool and install valve cotters.

6. Measure installed length of all valve springs (A, **Figure 68**). Disassemble and adjust number of washers if necessary so installed length is 1.417 ± 0.012" (36 ± 0.3mm).

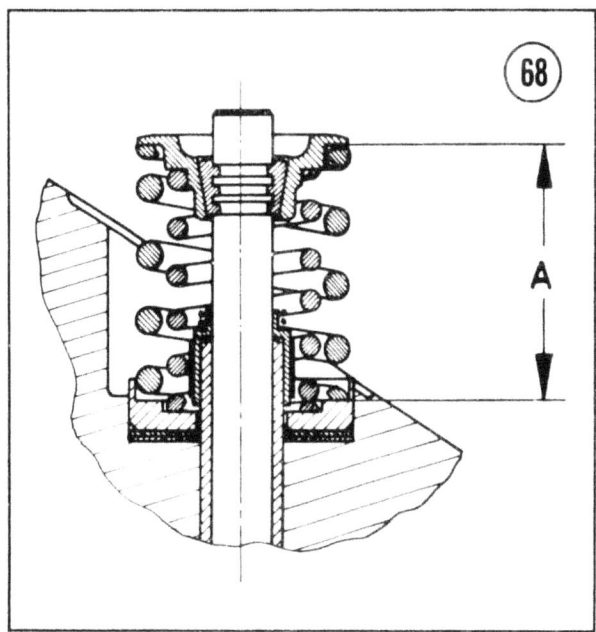

Valve Guide Replacement

Valve guide replacement is a very exacting job requiring several special tools and skills. Inexperienced and/or poorly equipped mechanics can quickly ruin these very expensive cylinder heads. Take the job to your dealer or competent machine shop. The following procedure is for use by properly equipped machine shops unfamiliar with Porsches.

1. Drill out the old guide from the camshaft side with an 11mm drill. See **Figure 69**. Be sure the head is firmly clamped at the proper angle.

2. Hammer the guide out with a drift from the camshaft side.

3. Accurately measure the valve guide bore.

> NOTE: *Driving the old guide out increases the bore.*

4. **Turn** oversize valve guide down to 0.001-0.002" (0.03-0.06mm) larger than the measured bore. **Table 2** shows oversizes available.

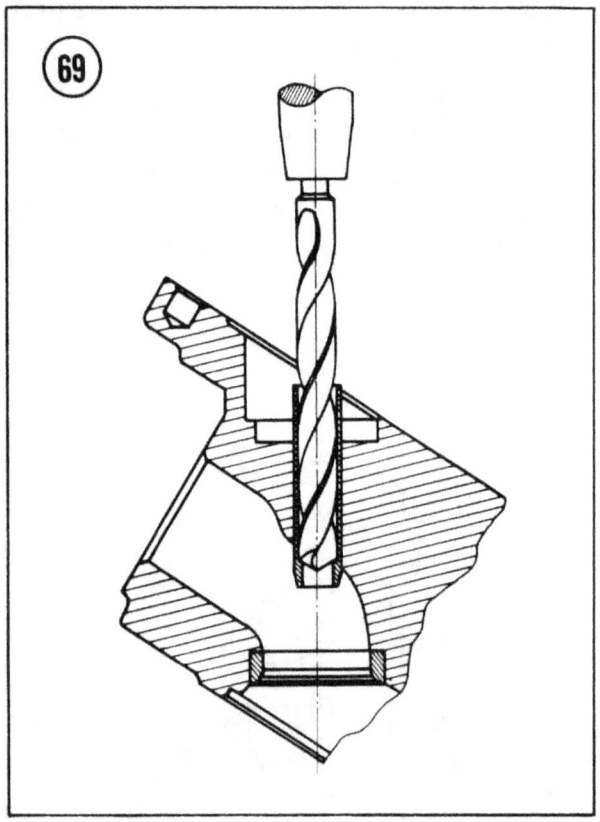

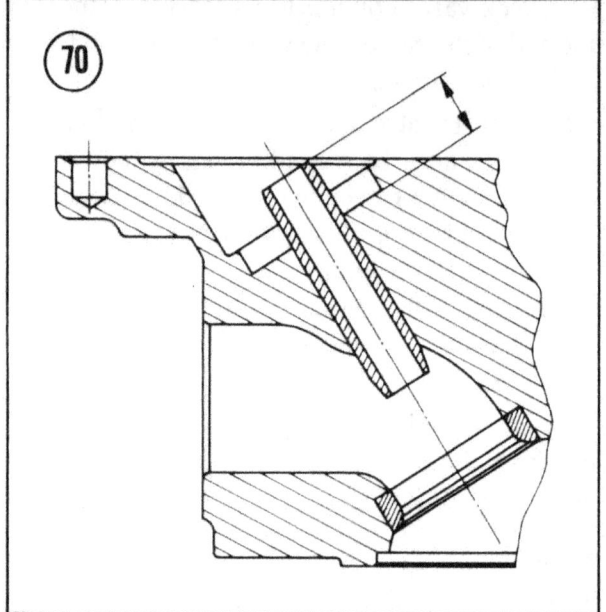

5. Lubricate valve guide with Lubriplate and press it into cylinder head from camshaft side. Guide should protrude *exactly* 0.515 ± 0.012" (13.2 ± 0.3mm) above recess in head. See **Figure 70**.

> NOTE: *Chill valve guides in a freezer if possible to shrink them and make insertion easier.*

6. Ream the guides with a broach or fine boring mill to 0.3543-0.3549" (9.000-9.015mm).

Valve Seat Reconditioning

This job is best left to your dealer or local machine shop. They have the special equipment and knowledge required for this exacting job. The following procedure is provided in the event you are not near a dealer and the local machine shop is not familiar with Porsches.

Valve seats are shrunk into the cylinder heads. Damaged or burned seats may be reconditioned as long as the proper 45° seat width can be maintained (see *Specifications*) and dimension A, **Figure 71**, is within specifications.

When the valve seats can no longer be reconditioned, replace the cylinder heads; seats cannot be replaced with the standard machine shop tools.

Table 2   VALVE GUIDES AND SEATS

	Standard	1st Oversize	2nd Oversize
Valve seat, d_1			
Intake	1.66-1.6599" (42.180-42.164mm)	1.6732-1.6726" (42.500-42.484mm)	—
Exhaust	1.5039-1.5033" (38.200-38.184mm)	1.5260-1.5254" (38.760-38.744mm)	—
Valve seat bore, D_1			
Intake	1.6535-1.6545" (42.000-42.025mm)	1.6661-1.6671" (42.320-42.345mm)	—
Exhaust	1.4960-1.4970" (38.000-38.025mm)	1.5181-1.5191" (38.560-38.585mm)	—
Valve Guide, d_2	0.5142-0.5137" (13.060-13.049mm)	0.5220-0.5216" (13.260-13.249mm)	0.5299-0.5295" (13.460-13.449mm)
Valve guide bore, D_2	0.5118-0.5125" (13.000-13.018mm)	0.5196-0.5203" (13.200-13.218mm)	0.5276-0.4889" (13.400-12.418mm)
Valve guide bore, g	0.3543-0.3549" (9.000-9.015mm)		

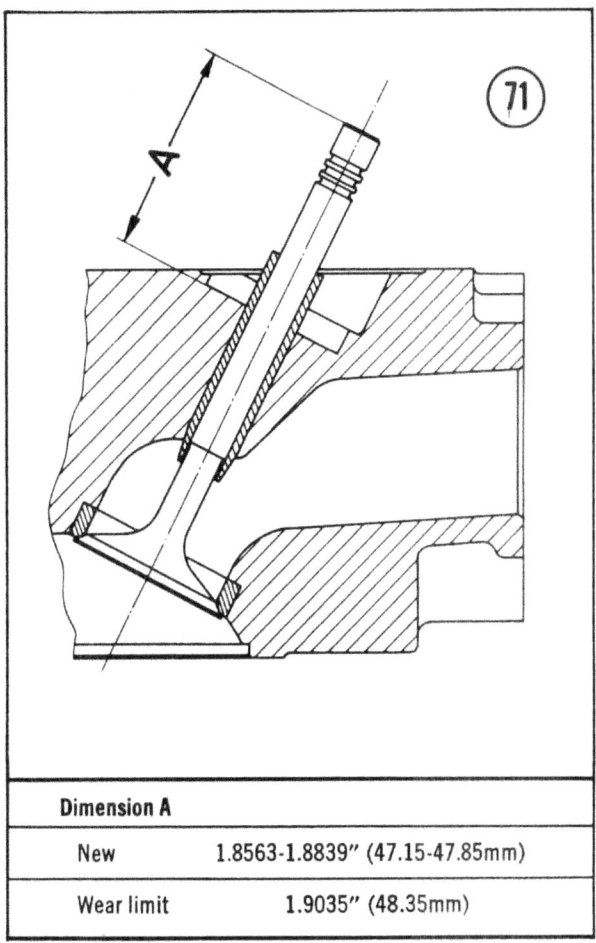

Dimension A	
New	1.8563-1.8839" (47.15-47.85mm)
Wear limit	1.9035" (48.35mm)

1. Using a 45° valve seat cutter or special stone, cut the 45° face. Don't take off any more metal than necessary to provide a clean, concentric seat. See **Figure 72**.

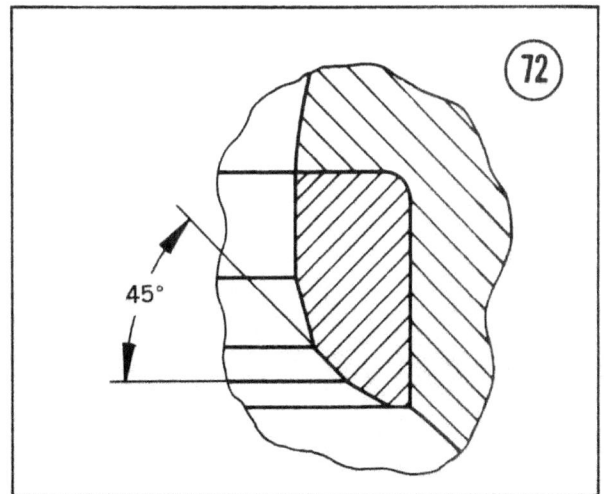

2. Slightly chamfer the bottom of the 45° seat with a 75° cutter or stone. See **Figure 73**.

3. Narrow the width of the 45° seat by cutting

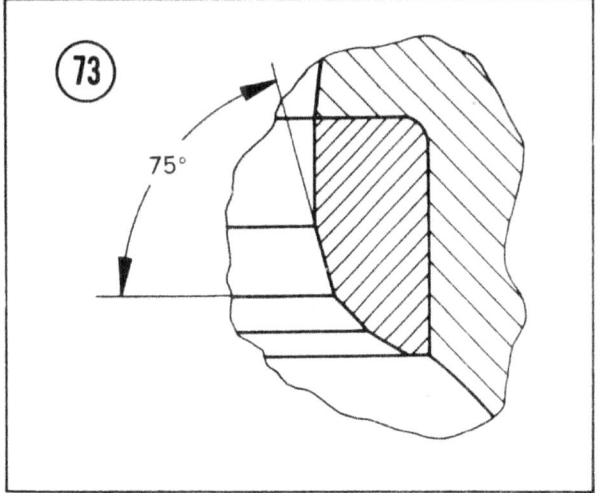

the top of the seat with a 25° cutter or stone. See **Figure 74**. (see *Specifications* for proper intake and exhaust valve seat widths.)

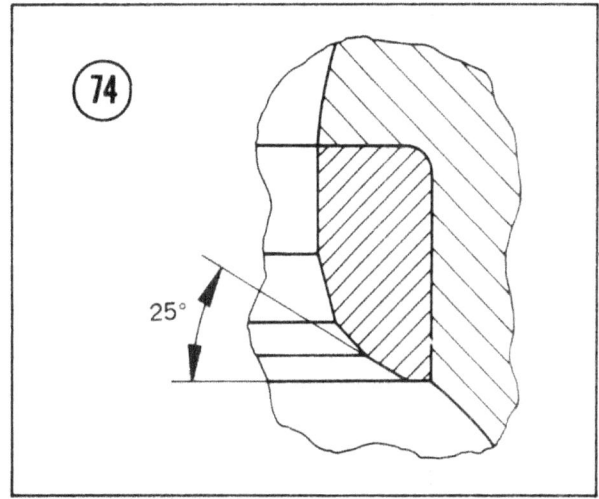

4. Coat the corresponding valve face with Prussian blue.

5. Insert the valve into the guide.

6. Rotate the valve under light pressure about ¼ turn.

7. Lift the valve out. If the valve seats properly, the blue will transfer to the valve seat evenly.

VALVE TIMING

Whenever a chain has been removed from either camshaft sprocket, such as when removing the camshaft, valve timing must be checked and adjusted. Penalty for failing to do so ranges from a rough running engine to very expensive destruction.

This procedure is very important. Read through it several times if necessary before you start. Look for the following points while reading. The relation between camshafts and crankshaft is set roughly in Steps 1-4. Steps 5-10 permit fine adjustment of valve timing for the left camshaft, using cylinder No. 1. The remainder of the procedure permits fine adjustment of the right camshaft using cylinder No. 4.

1. Turn crankshaft very slowly until "Z1" mark on pulley aligns with crankcase joint. See Figure 47.

CAUTION
Since the camshaft and crankshaft are not synchronized, it is possible for the pistons to collide with the valves. If any resistance is felt while turning the crankshaft, STOP and back off a little. Turn the camshaft(s) to move the valves out of the way, then continue turning the crankshaft.

2. Turn both camshafts until punch marks stamped on the camshafts point straight up. See Figure 47.

3. Find the hole (only one) in each camshaft sprocket which lines up with a hole in each sprocket flange. Insert dowel pin into each hole.

4. Install lockwashers and sprocket retaining nuts. Tighten to 72 foot-pounds (10 mkg).

5. Adjust cylinder No. 1 intake valve clearance to 0.004" (0.1mm).

6. Install dial gauge so it bears on the edge of the valve spring retaining collar. Adjust dial gauge for a preload of 0.3937" (10mm). See **Figure 75**.

7. Depress chain tensioner with a screwdriver (see **Figure 76**), and block it in this position. Turn crankshaft 360° so that "Z1" again aligns with crankcase seam. Dial gauge should read 0.09-0.11" (2.3-2.7mm).

8. If dial gauge reading is higher or lower than specified, remove camshaft sprocket nut and remove dowel pin (see **Figure 77**). Turn camshaft (see **Figure 78**) until dial gauge reading is proper. One and only one hole in the sprocket will align with the sprocket flange hole. Reinsert dowel pin in this hole. Install lockwasher and

sprocket retaining nut. Torque to 72 foot-pounds (10 mkg).

9. Turn crankshaft 2 complete turns (720°)

clockwise and observe dial gauge again. If reading agrees with Step 7, go to next step. If reading does not agree, repeat entire procedure.

10. If you have followed the procedure exactly to this point, piston No. 4 is at TDC on its compression stroke. Repeat Steps 5-10 for cylinder No. 4.

11. When the valve timing is correct, remove blocks used on chain tensioners. See Step 7.

CYLINDERS

Removal

1. Remove cylinder heads either individually or in groups of 3 as described earlier.
2. Remove air deflector plates below cylinders.
3. Mark cylinder numbers on each cylinder (see **Figure 79**) and carefully lift them off.

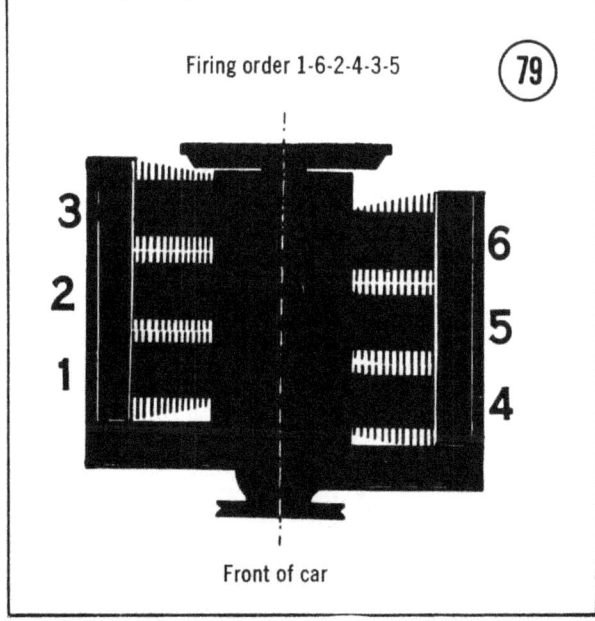

Inspection and Cleaning

1. Carefully clean the cylinder inside and out. Brush out all dirt between the fins. Clean away dirt on the cylinder sealing surfaces, and remove old gasket on the crankcase end.
2. Check wear pattern in cylinder bore. If uneven, the corresponding connecting rod/piston may be out of alignment. Remove and inspect connecting rods as described later in this chapter.
3. Check cylinder bore for excessive wear. See *Piston Clearance*. If worn, replace with a *matched* cylinder and piston of the same diameter, piston weight, and cylinder height. See **Table 3**.
4. Check cylinder inside and out for cracks. Replace cylinder and piston if necessary.

Installation

1. Install a new gasket on the crankcase end of each cylinder.
2. Rotate the crankshaft slowly until the desired piston is out as far as possible.

CAUTION
While rotating the crankshaft, watch that skirts of exposed pistons do not catch on the crankcase. This will crack the piston.

3. Apply a heavy coat of assembly lubricant to the piston.
4. Make sure that the oil ring gap is straight up. The other 2 ring gaps should be evenly spaced 120° apart. See **Figure 80**. Compress the rings with a 2-piece breakaway type ring compressor.
5. Liberally oil the cylinder bore and slide the cylinder over the piston. See **Figure 81**. Be careful not to break any cooling fins against the studs.
6. Repeat Steps 2-5 for remaining cylinders.
7. Rotate the cylinder back and forth to ensure that there is clearance between the studs and the holes in the cylinder. Position the cylinders so that the studs do not touch the cylinders. If this is not possible, check for bent studs and straighten or replace them.

Table 3 CYLINDER AND PISTON DIAMETERS

	NORMAL		
	0	1	2
Cylinders	80.00 - 80.010	80.010 - 80.020	80.020 - 80.030
Pistons			
Mahle	79.965 - 79.975	79.975 - 79.985	79.985 - 79.995
Schmidt	79.955 - 79.965	79.965 - 79.975	79.975 - 79.985
	OVERSIZE		
	0KD1	1KD1	2KD1
Cylinders	80.500 - 80.510	80.510 - 80.520	80.520 - 80.530
Pistons			
Mahle & Schmidt	80.455 - 80.465	80.465 - 80.475	80.475 - 80.485

1. All measurements in millimeters

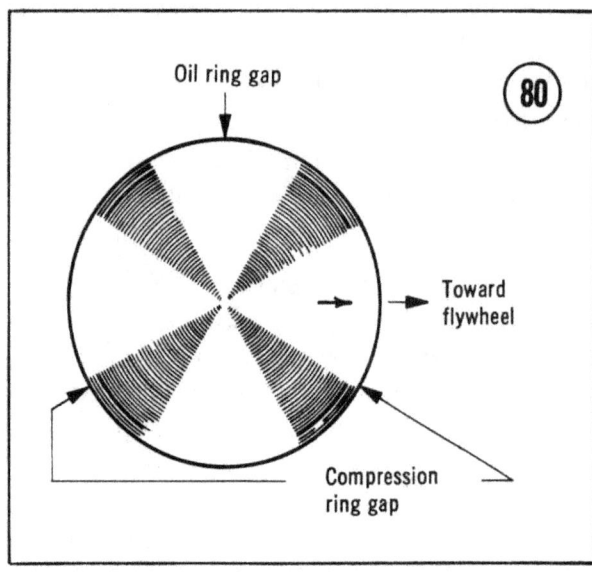

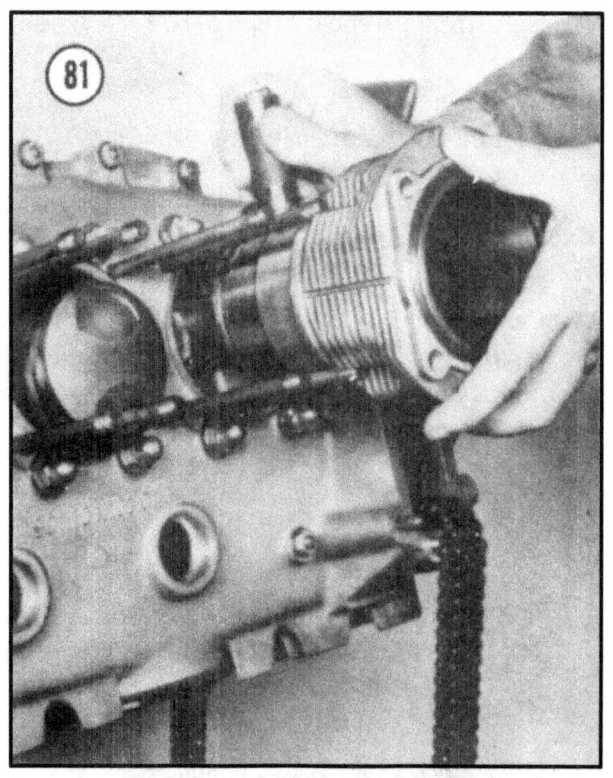

8. Install air deflectors around cylinders and secure with clips. See **Figure 82**.

9. Install cylinder heads as described previously.

PISTONS, PINS, AND RINGS

Piston Removal

1. Remove cylinder heads and cylinders as described previously.

2. Mark piston crown to make sure it is reinstalled in the direction and in the same cylinder. See Figure 79 for numbering.

3. Rotate crankshaft slowly until desired piston is out as far as it goes.

CAUTION
While rotating the crankshaft, watch that skirts of any exposed pistons do not catch on the crankcase. This will damage the piston.

4. Before removing the piston pin, hold the connecting rod tightly and rock the piston as shown in **Figure 83**. Any rocking movement (do not

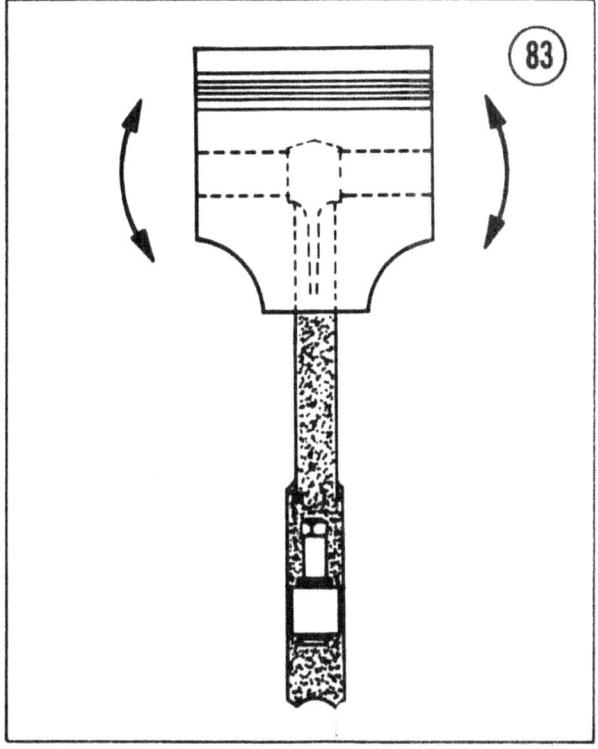

confuse with sliding motion) indicates wear in the piston rod, rod bushing, piston pin bore, or more likely, a combination of all three. Mark the piston, pin, and rod for further examination later.

5. Remove the snap rings at each end of the piston pin.

6. Turn the engine so that the crankshaft is vertical, and place wet rags around the oily area of the crankcase.

7. Heat the piston and pin with a small butane torch. The piston pin will probably drop right out, but may need coaxing with a metal rod. Heat the piston to 176°F (80°C), i.e., until it is too warm to touch, but not excessively hot.

Inspection

1. Clean the piston thoroughly in solvent. Scrape carbon deposits from the top of the piston and ring grooves. Don't damage the piston.

2. Examine each ring groove for burrs, dented edges, and side wear. Pay particular attention to the top compression ring groove as it usually wears more than the others.

3. Weigh each piston. The difference in weight between any two pistons in the same engine must not exceed 10 grams.

4. If damage, wear, or weight suggest replacement, replace with a size and weight comparable to others in the engine. If the associated cylinder shows no wear or damage, it may be possible to replace the piston alone with one in the same size group. See **Table 3**. Otherwise, replace piston and cylinder.

5. Measure any parts marked in Step 4, *Piston Removal*, with a micrometer to determine which part or parts are worn. Any machinist can do this for you if you do not have micrometers.

6. When replacing a piston pin, select a size compatible with the piston pin bore. Proper piston pin size is indicated by a color code marking inside the piston on the piston pin boss. Match new piston pin color code (see **Table 4**) with the piston color code.

Piston Clearance

Porsche discourages using a feeler gauge to check piston clearance and therefore does not provide specifications to do so. The following procedure is the "hard way," but certainly adequate.

1. Make sure that the piston and cylinder walls are clean and dry.

2. Measure the inside diameter of the cylinder bore at a point 1.2" (30mm) from the bottom edge. See **Figure 84**.

3. Measure outside diameter of piston skirt at the bottom of the skirt. See **Figure 85**.

4. If the difference in the 2 readings is near 0.004" (0.1mm), the piston/cylinder combination requires overhaul. If the cylinder bore is excessive, replace the cylinder *and* piston. If the piston is worn or damaged, you may replace the piston only. Choose one which is the correct

Table 4 PISTON PIN SIZES

Color Code	Piston Pin Diameter	Bushing Diameter
White	21.997-22.000	21.997-22.000
Black	21.997-22.006	21.997-22.006
NOTE: All measurements in millimeters		

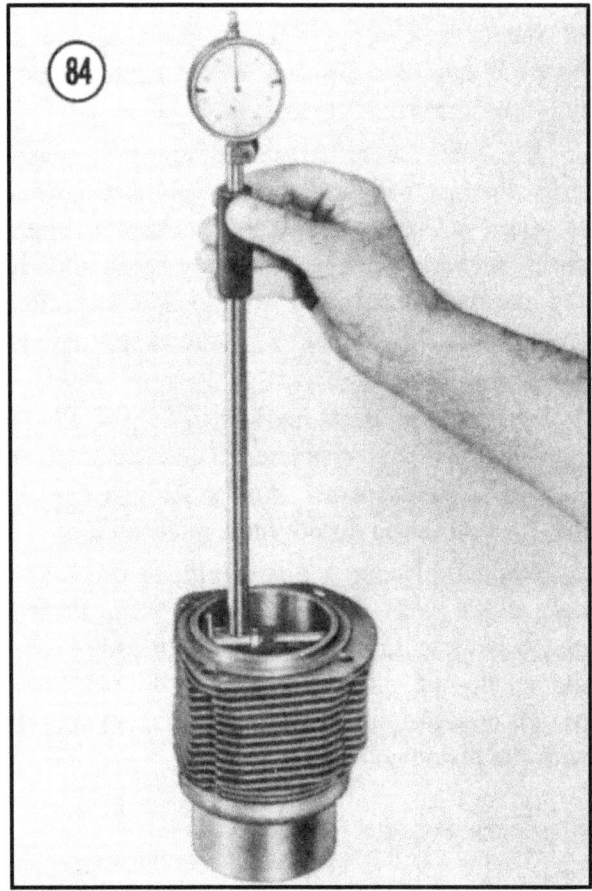

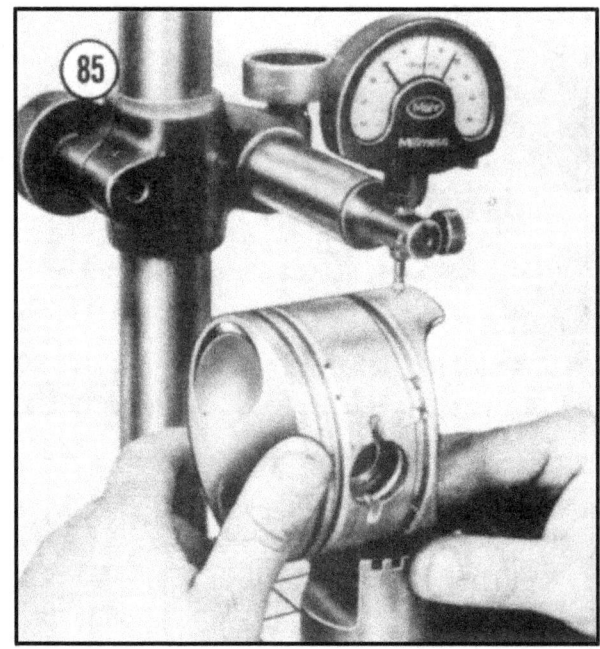

size and weight. See Table 3 to select correct components. Also see *Cylinder Inspection* procedure earlier in this chapter.

Piston Ring Fit and Installation

1. Check ring gap of each ring. To check a ring, insert it in the bottom of a cylinder bore and square it with the wall by tapping with a piston. The ring should be in about 0.2″. Insert a feeler gauge as shown in **Figure 86**. The gap should be 0.012-0.018″ (0.30-0.45mm). If the gap is smaller, hold a small flat file in a vise, grip the ends of the ring with your fingers, and enlarge the gap. See **Figure 87**.

2. Roll each ring around its piston groove as shown in **Figure 88** to check for binding.

3. With a ring expander tool, carefully install oil ring, then 2 compression rings (**Figure 89**). The compression ring side marked TOP *must* be up.

4. Check the side clearance of the ring as shown in **Figure 90**. Compare with the specifications for your engine.

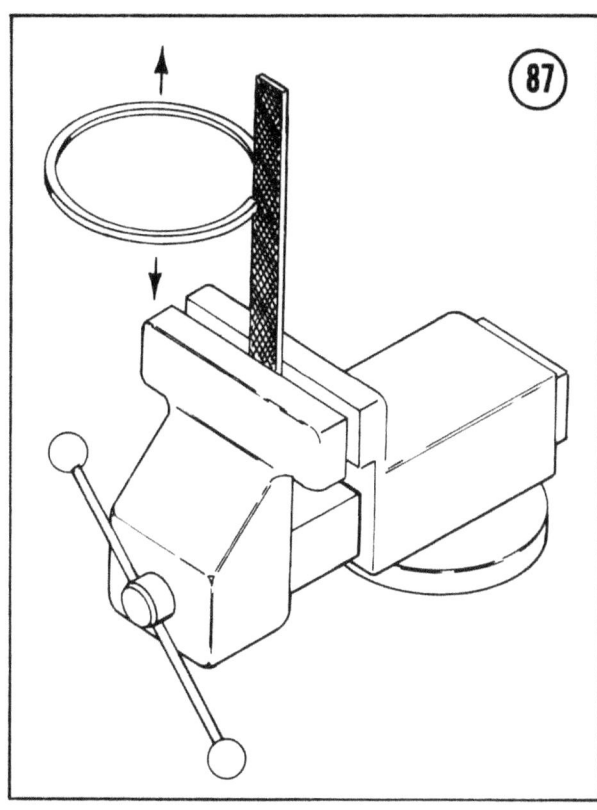

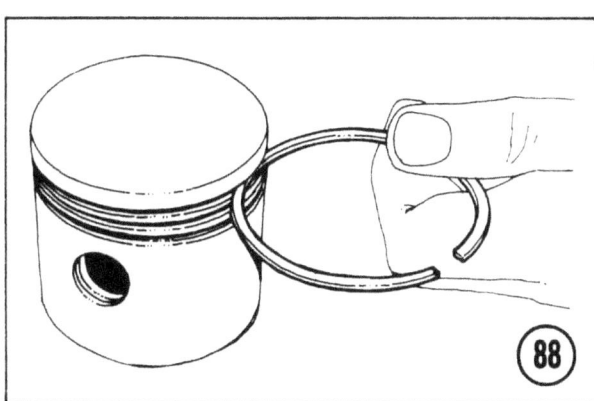

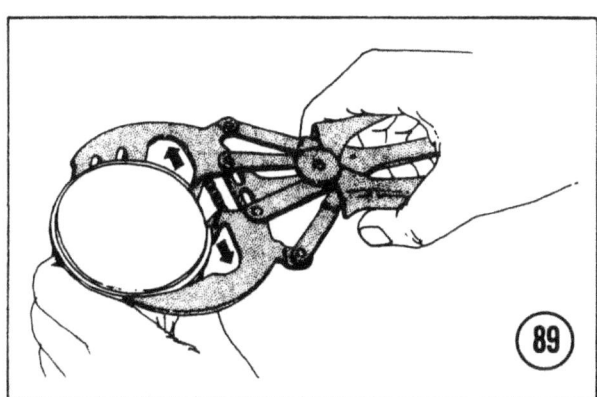

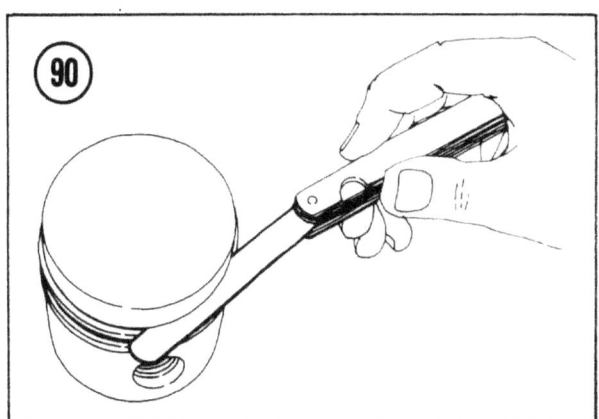

2. Rotate crankshaft until connecting rod #1 is out as far as possible. See Figure 79 for numbering.

CAUTION
While rotating crankshaft, watch that skirts of any exposed pistons do not catch on the crankcase. This will crack the piston.

3. Install a snap ring in one end of piston #1.

4. Coat the connecting rod bushing, piston pin, and piston holes with assembly lubricant.

5. Place the piston over the connecting rod so that it is aligned in the direction marked in Step 2, *Piston Removal*. New pistons are symmetrical and may be installed in either direction on the rod.

6. Heat the piston to about 176°F (80°C) as in Step 7, *Removal*. Push the piston pin through the piston and connecting rod until it touches the snap ring.

7. Install the other snap ring.

8. Rotate the crankshaft slowly until connecting rod #2 is out as far as possible.

CAUTION
While rotating crankshaft, watch that skirts of any exposed pistons do not catch on the crankcase. This will crack the piston.

9. Repeat Steps 3-8 for the remaining piston.

FLYWHEEL

Removal

1. Remove clutch pressure plate and disc as described in Chapter Ten.

Piston Installation

1. Install rings on all 6 pistons using the preceding procedure.

2. Remove 6 Allen bolts securing flywheel to crankshaft. See **Figure 91**.

3. Remove flywheel and washer.

Inspection

1. Check flywheel teeth for wear or damage. If teeth are damaged only slightly, remachine and rechamfer as described in procedure below.

2. Check surface which contacts clutch disc. Slight refacing is possible. See procedure below.

3. Check drive shaft bushing in flywheel for wear. See specifications. Replace bushing if necessary.

Remachining

Figure 92 shows critical flywheel dimensions and tolerances. Only dimension "b" can be remachined to any extent and should be done in stages as shown in the figures. Dimensions "a" and "c" may be slightly refaced (use extra hard tool steel), but neither dimension should be reduced below that shown in the figures.

Drive Shaft Bushing Replacement

1. Drive out old bushing with a press as shown in **Figure 93**.

2. Press in new bushing as shown in **Figure 94**.

Installation

1. Ensure that flywheel washer and crankshaft mating surfaces are smooth and absolutely clean.

2. Lightly oil threads of mounting bolts. Fit

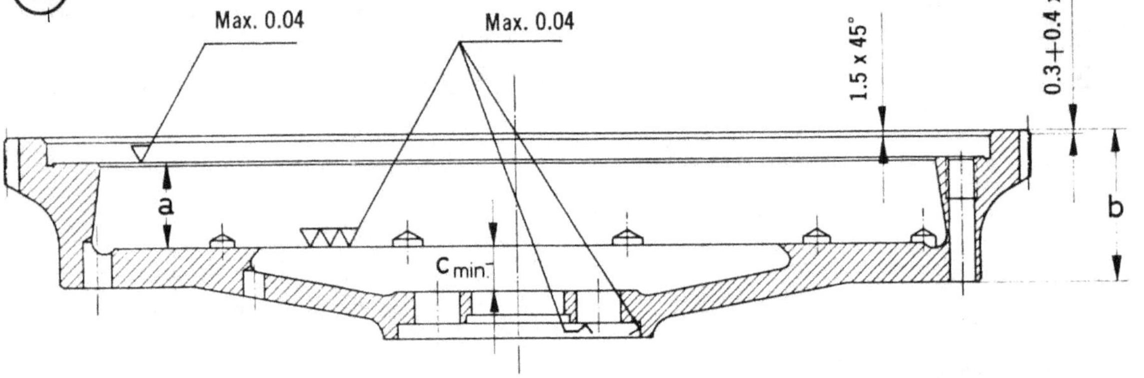

Measurement point	Dimensions when new	Re-machining stages inch (mm)				Tolerances
		1	2	3	4	
a	.886" (22.5mm)	.886 (22.5)	—	—	—	.0078" (+ 0.2)
b	1.5354" (39.0mm)	1.5197 (38.6)	1.5039 (38.2)	1.4882 (37.8)	1.4724 (37.4)	.0078" (+ 0.2)
c	Wear (reject) .4330" (11.000mm)					

flywheel and washer over crankshaft. Insert mounting bolts and tighten finger-tight.

> NOTE: *The original crankshaft and flywheel are balanced as a unit. Mounting holes for flywheel are staggered so that the flywheel can be installed only one way. Replacement crankshafts and flywheels are perfectly balanced so they are individually replaceable.*

3. Tighten diagonally opposite bolts evenly and progressively until all are tightened to 108.5 foot-pounds (15 mkg).

SPORTOMATIC

The drive plate is attached to the crankshaft in the same manner as a flywheel except that much shorter bolts are required.

A special retaining ring shown in **Figure 95** is required to hold the drive plate while removing the mounting bolts. Rather than improvise a retaining ring and risk warping the drive plate, take the entire engine to a Porsche dealer and let him remove it. Later, when the engine is reassembled, let the dealer reinstall the drive plate.

CRANKSHAFT

Removal

1. When the right half of the crankcase has been removed (see *Crankcase Disassembly*), lift the crankshaft out.

2. Remove bearing inserts from crankcase halves. Mark each on its back as it is removed so that it may be reinstalled in the same position. Set them aside where they won't be damaged.

Inspection

1. Check connecting rod play, then remove all connecting rods. Both procedures are described under *Connecting Rod Removal* later in this chapter.

2. Clean the crankshaft thoroughly with solvent. Clean the oil holes with rifle cleaning brushes; flush thoroughly and blow dry with air. Lightly oil all journal surfaces immediately to prevent rust.

3. Carefully inspect each journal for scratches, ridges, scoring, nicks, etc. Very small nicks and scratches may be removed with crocus cloth. More serious damage must be removed by grinding; a job for a machine shop.

4. If the surface finish on all journals is satisfactory, take the crankshaft to your dealer or local machine shop. They can check for out-of-roundness, taper, and wear on the journals. They will also check crankshaft alignment and inspect for cracks. See **Figure 96** for crankshaft specifications.

5. Check condition of distributor drive and timing gears. Replace if worn.

Gear and Bearing Disassembly

Refer to **Figure 97** (next page) for the following procedure.

1. Remove snap ring on rear of crankshaft. See **Figure 98**.

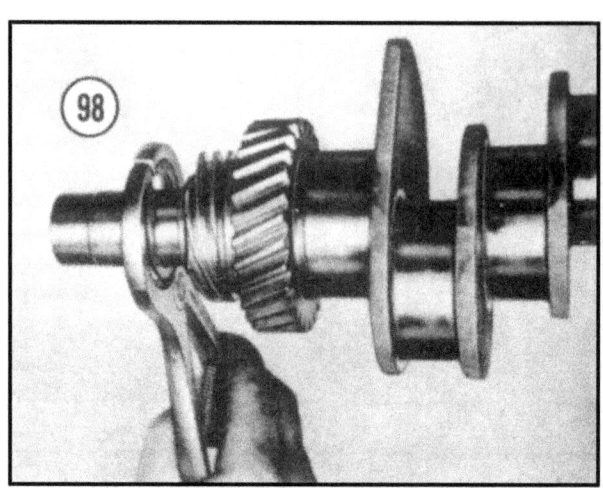

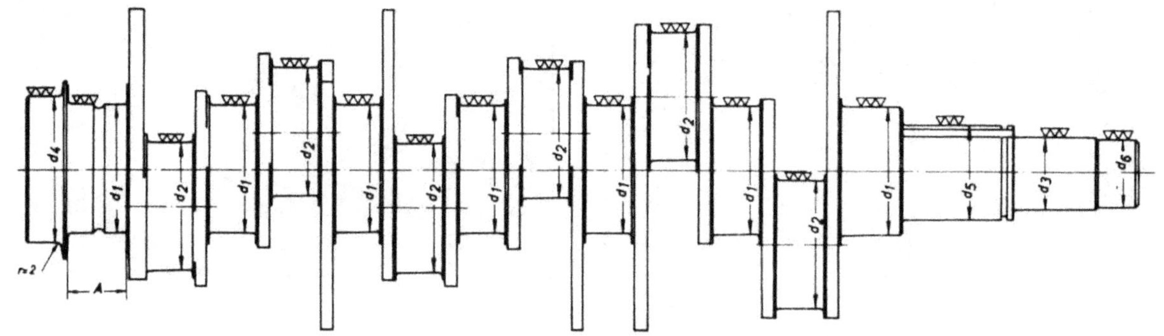

Degree of wear	Crankcase bore diameter (bearings 1-8)		All main bearings d_1 and connecting rod bearings d_2 on crankshaft	Main bearing diameter d_3 on crankshaft bearing 8	Shoulder diameter	Timing gear seat diameter d_5	Bearing surface diameter d_6	Guide bearing width A
Std.	Normal 2.4409-2.4417" (62.000-62.019mm)	Oversize 2.4515-2.4508" (62.269-62.250mm)	2.2437-2.2429" (56.990-56.971mm)	1.2202-1.2197" (30.993-30.980mm)	2.5591-2.5583" (65.000-64.981mm)	1.6540-1.6536" (42.013-42.002mm)	1.1808-1.1795" (29.993-29.960mm)	1.1024-1.1044" (28.000-28.052mm)
0.25			2.2338-2.2331" (56.740-56.721mm)	1.2104-1.2098" (30.743-30.730mm)				
0.50			2.2240-2.2232" (56.490-56.471mm)	1.2005-1.1999" (30.493-30.480mm)				
0.75			2.2141-2.2134" (56.240-56.221mm)	1.1906-1.1901" (30.243-30.230mm)				

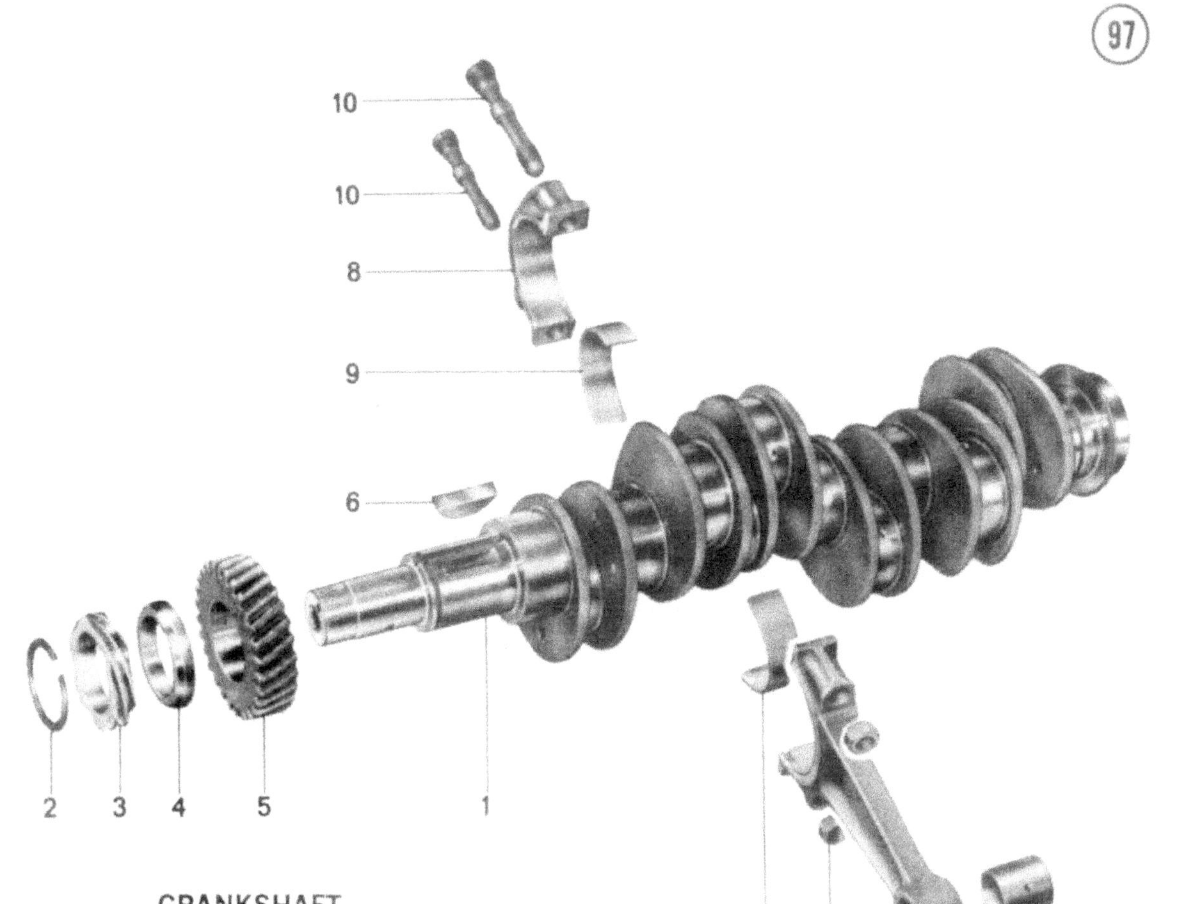

CRANKSHAFT

1. Crankshaft
2. Locking ring
3. Distributor drive gear
4. Spacer
5. Timing gear
6. Woodruff key
7. Connecting rod nut
8. Connecting rod
9. Bearing shell
10. Connecting rod bolts
11. Piston pin bushing

2. With a large gear puller, pull on the bottom of the innermost (timing) gear. See **Figure 99**. Remove the distributor drive spacer and timing gears. Save the Woodruff key.

Gear and Bearing Assembly

Refer to Figure 97 for the following procedure.

1. Lay the crankshaft vertically on a piece of wood with the flywheel end down.

2. Insert Woodruff key in crankshaft slot. It must be flat, not canted in the slot.

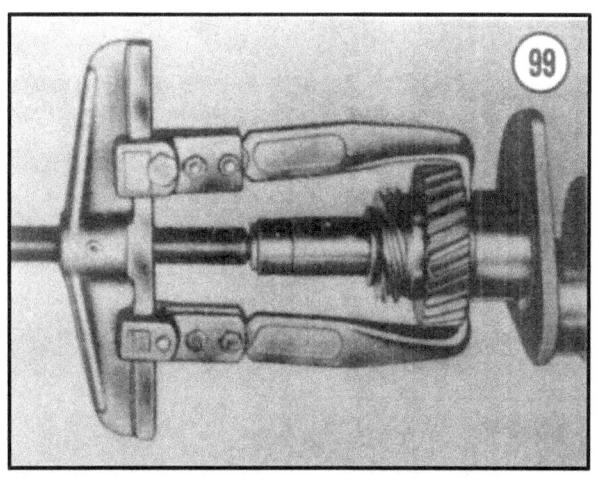

3. Heat timing gear to approximately 300°F in an oven. Push it onto the crankshaft with the shoulder facing toward the flywheel. See **Figure 100**.

WARNING
Handle gear very carefully with asbestos gloves or cloth. It is hot enough to cause severe burns.

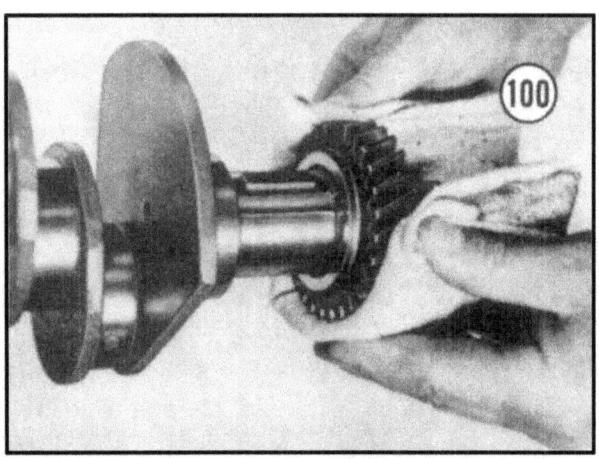

4. Install spacer over Woodruff key.
5. Heat distributor drive gear to about 212°F and push it onto the crankshaft.
6. Install snap ring.

Installation
Installation is simply a matter of setting the crankshaft into place while assembling the crankcase. See *Crankcase Assembly* procedure.

CONNECTING RODS
Removal
1. Remove crankshaft from engine. Clamp it down or have someone hold it.
2. File very small marks on each rod to indicate its position for reassembly. For example, make one mark on rod #1, 2 marks on rod #2, etc. Rods are numbered as shown in **Figure 101**.
3. Insert a feeler gauge between side of each rod and the crank throw. See **Figure 102**. If the gap of the connecting rod end-play is greater than 0.016″ (0.4mm), mark the rod for replacement.
4. Remove connecting rod bolts and pull off rod caps and rod.
5. Remove bearing inserts from rods and caps. Mark inserts with rod numbers for later inspection and reassembly. Do not mix up bearings.
6. Loosely install caps on rods to keep them together.

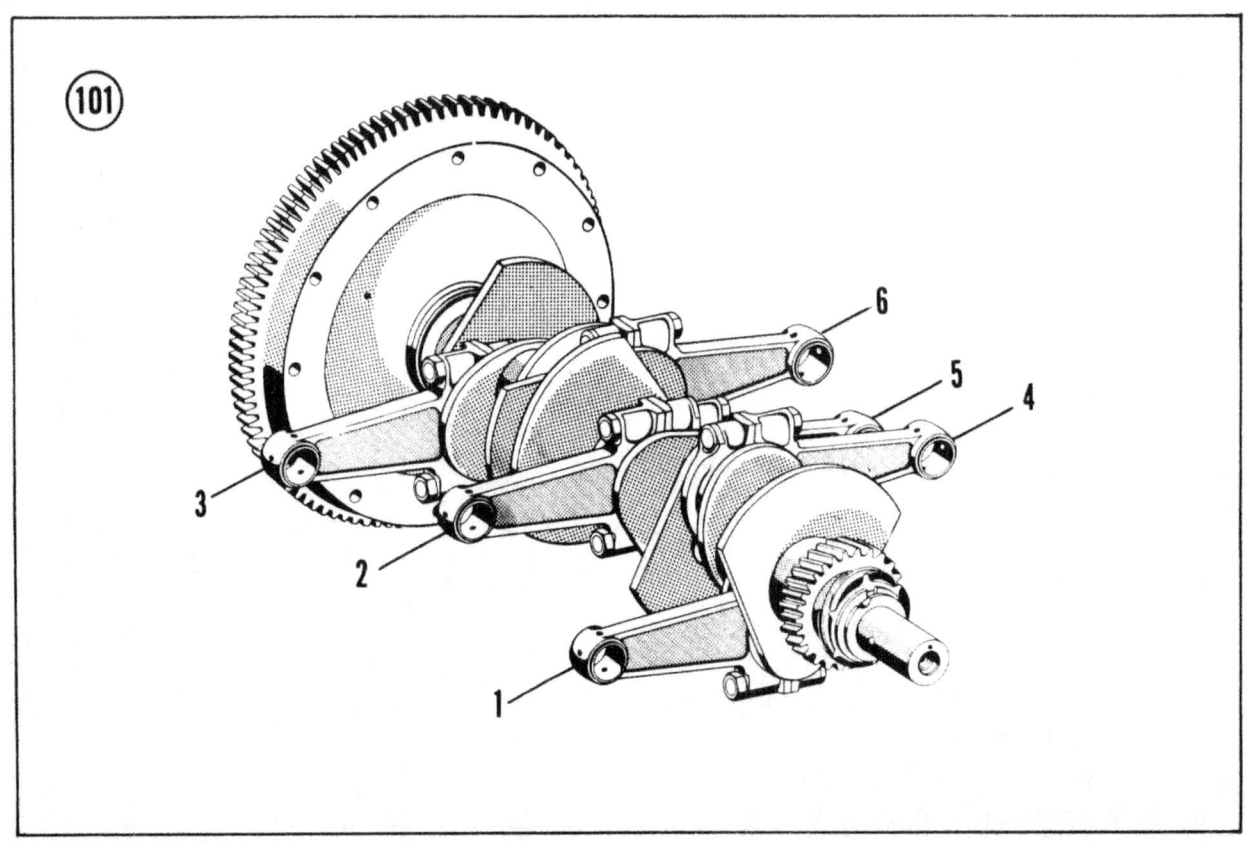

Inspection

1. Discard any rods with excessive end-play. See Step 3, above.

2. Clean all parts thoroughly in solvent.

3. Check each rod for obvious damage such as cracks or burns.

4. Check piston pin bushing for wear or scoring. At room temperature, a piston pin should slide through with light finger pressure.

5. Discard all rod bolts and nuts. Replace with new ones.

6. Take rods to a machine shop and have their alignment checked for twisting and bending.

7. Weigh each rod with new nuts and bolts, but without bearing inserts, on a scale. They should be within 9 grams of each other. Replacement rods are available in weights from 551 to 659 grams in 9 gram increments.

8. Examine bearing inserts for wear, scoring, or burning. They are reusable if in good condition. Make a note of bearing size (if any) stamped on the back if a bearing is to be discarded; a previous owner may have used undersize bearings.

Installation

1. Carefully match the number on the side of each rod to its associated rod cap.

2. Install bearings inserts in the rods and caps. Press the bearings in with your thumbs on the ends of the bearing. Don't press down on the middle of the bearing. Be sure that the tangs on the bearings fit into the notches on the caps.

CAUTION
Bearing ends will extend slightly above the cap or rod. Do not file any part of the rod, cap, or bearing for a different fit.

3. Oil the nuts and rod cap bolts lightly.

4. Cut a piece of Plastigage the width of the rod bearing. Assemble the rod cap on the crank throw for cylinder #3 (the one closest to the flywheel) with the Plastigage inserted between the rod cap and the crank throw. Tighten the nuts to 36 foot-pounds (5 mkg).

5. Remove the bearing cap and measure the width of the flattened Plastigage wire following the manufacturer's instructions. This is the bearing clearance. Compare it to the specifications for your engine. If it is not right, make sure that you have installed the proper bearings.

6. Remove the strip of Plastigage, coat the bearing and crank throw with assembly lubricant and reassemble the rod on the corresponding crank throw.

7. Check that the rod rotates freely 180° through its own weight alone.

8. Measure the rod end-play with a feeler gauge (see *Removal*, Step 3). Compare with the specifications.

9. Repeat Steps 4-9 for each rod. Be sure you assemble each rod on the crank throw originally used for that rod. Also ensure that the rod and cap number are aligned.

10. Peen nuts around rod bolts with a center punch to lock them in place. See **Figure 103**.

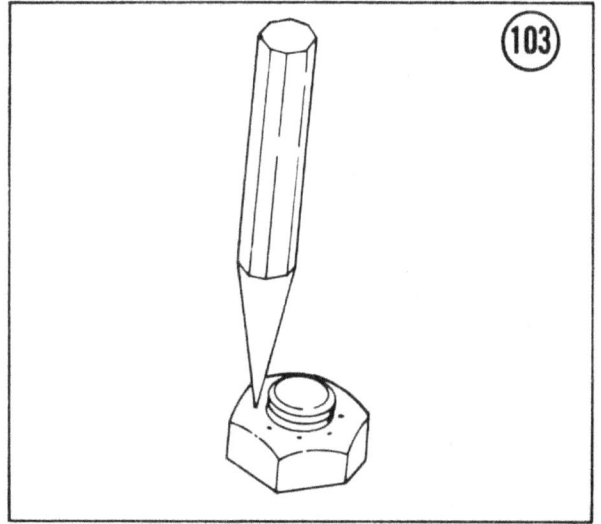

OIL PUMP (ENGINE)

Engine must be removed to perform this procedure.

Removal

1. Separate crankcase halves as described under *Crankcase Disassembly*.
2. Remove bolts securing oil pump. See **Figure 104**.

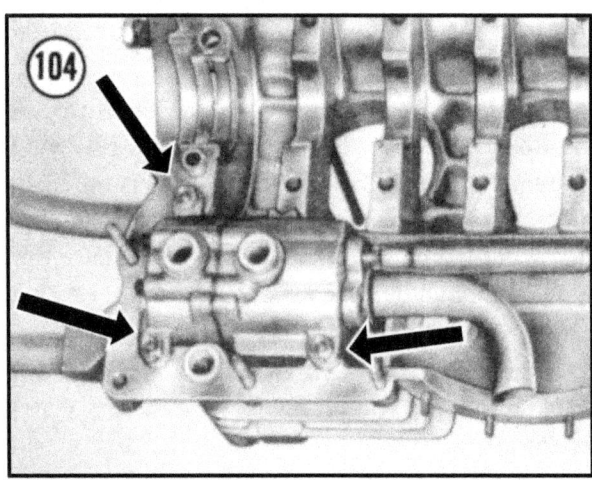

3. Lift out oil pump, intermediate shaft, and connecting shaft.
4. Separate pump from shafts.

Inspection

The oil pump cannot be disassembled or repaired. When defective, replace the entire pump.
1. Clean pump in solvent and blow dry with compressed air.
2. Turn shaft. Pump gears should turn smoothly and quietly.
3. Examine sealing surfaces at all oil inlets and outlets.

Installation

1. Insert new seal in right crankcase half oil passage. See **Figure 105**.
2. Insert oil pump intermediate shaft, connecting shaft, and drive chains in right crankcase half. Make sure that seals remain in place.
3. Secure pump with new tabbed lockwashers and nuts. Bend tabs up.
4. Reassemble crankcase.

OIL PUMP (TORQUE CONVERTER)

The left camshaft drives the Sportomatic torque converter oil pump. The oil pump can be removed and installed with the engine in the car.

Removal/Installation

1. Raise rear of car on jackstands and remove left rear wheel.
2. Remove left heat exchanger. See Chapter Six for this procedure.
3. Disconnect oil pressure and suction lines from oil pump. See **Figure 106**.

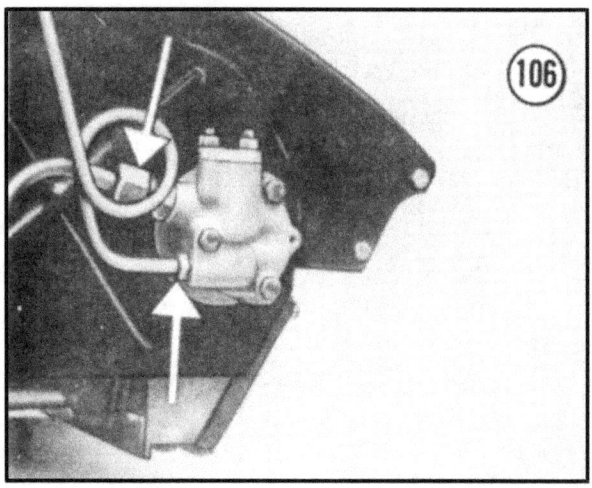

4. Remove 3 bolts securing pump to engine and remove pump.
5. Installation is the reverse of these steps. Use a new paper gasket. Make sure that the roll pins in the end of the crankshaft are oriented as in **Figure 107** so that the oil pump dowel pin does not contact the slot in either roll pin. See **Figure 108**.

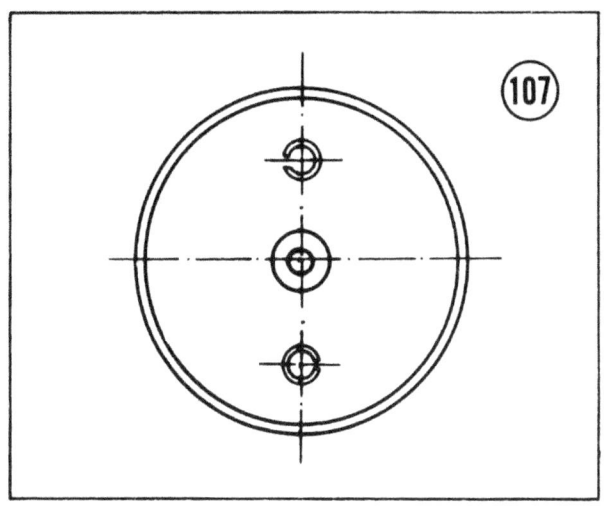

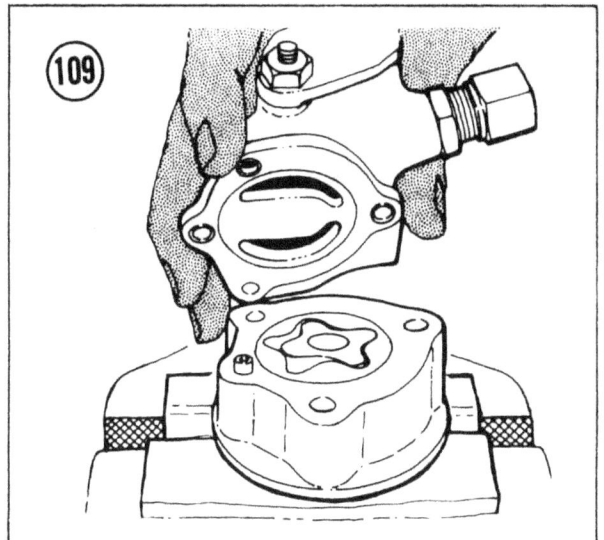

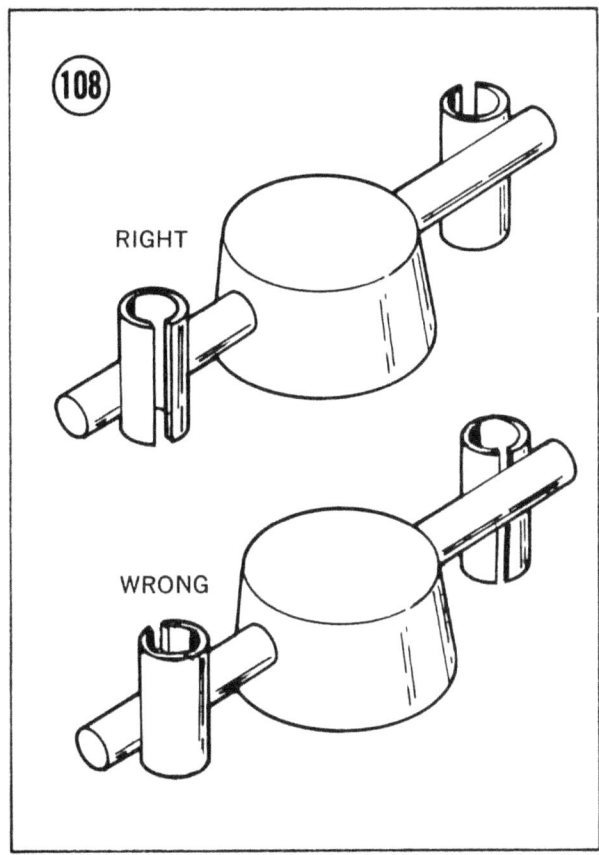

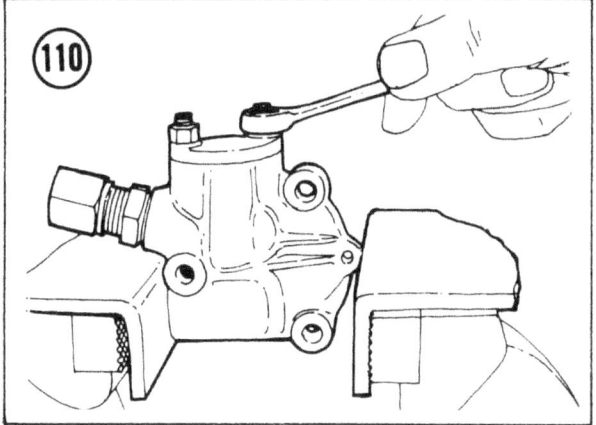

NOTE: *Inner and outer rotor with shaft must be replaced as a unit.*

6. Lubricate oil pressure relief piston and insert it in pump body. Install spring and cover with new O-ring. Tighten nuts equally.

7. Lubricate inner and outer rotors thoroughly with SAE 30 engine oil.

8. Install inner rotor in rotor housing.

9. Install rotor shaft drive pin so that it is centered in shaft. See **Figure 111**.

10. Install outer rotor with beveled edge toward rotor housing. See **Figure 112**.

11. Fit oil pump cover to rotor housing with new paper gasket.

INTERMEDIATE SHAFT

Removal

1. Separate crankcase halves as described under *Crankcase Disassembly*.

Disassembly/Assembly

1. Lift off oil pump cover. See **Figure 109**.

2. Remove drive pin out of rotor shaft and remove rotors.

3. Remove nuts from pressure relief valve cover. See **Figure 110**. Remove cover, spring, and control piston.

4. Clean all parts in solvent.

5. Inspect all parts for wear or damage. Replace if necessary.

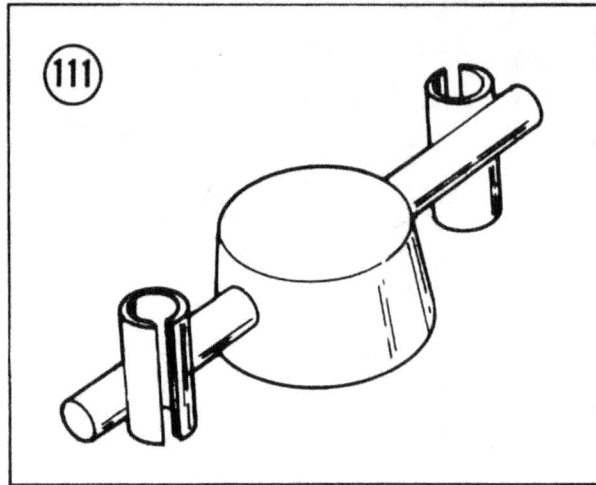

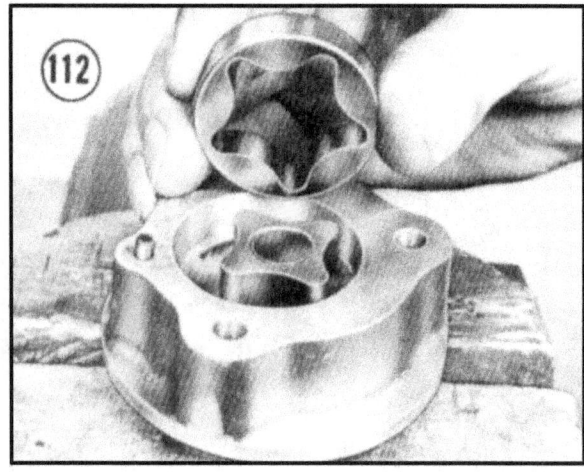

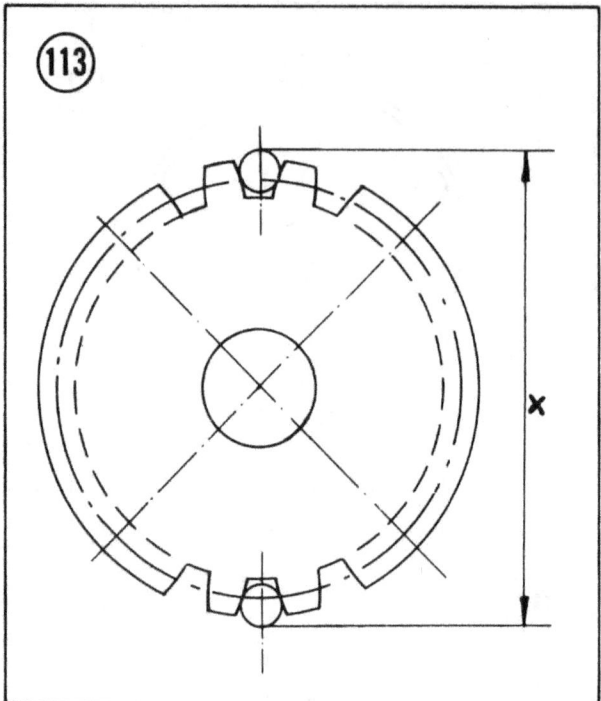

2. Remove the nuts securing the oil pump. See Figure 104.

3. Lift out oil pump, intermediate shaft, and connecting shaft.

4. Separate pump from shafts.

Inspection

1. Clean shaft thoroughly in solvent.

2. Check shaft bearing surfaces for wear or scoring.

3. Check chain sprockets and gear for wear and broken or cracked teeth.

4. Insert 2 steel balls 4.5mm diameter between teeth 180° from each other. See **Figure 113**. Measure dimension X which should be 136.5mm for gears marked "O" and 136.55mm for gears marked "1". If X is smaller, gear is worn; replace it.

5. If engine was torn down for general overhaul and/or bearing replacement, the aluminum plug in the intermediate shaft should be removed so that the oilway can be thoroughly cleaned. Drill and tap the plug for a 5/16x2" bolt. Cut a 1" length of pipe to bear on end of shaft with an inside diameter large enough to clear the plug. Fit a steel washer over the pipe and install the bolt. The finished puller is shown in **Figure 114**. Tighten the bolt and pull the plug out.

6. Clean oilway in shaft when aluminum plug is out. Press in a new plug.

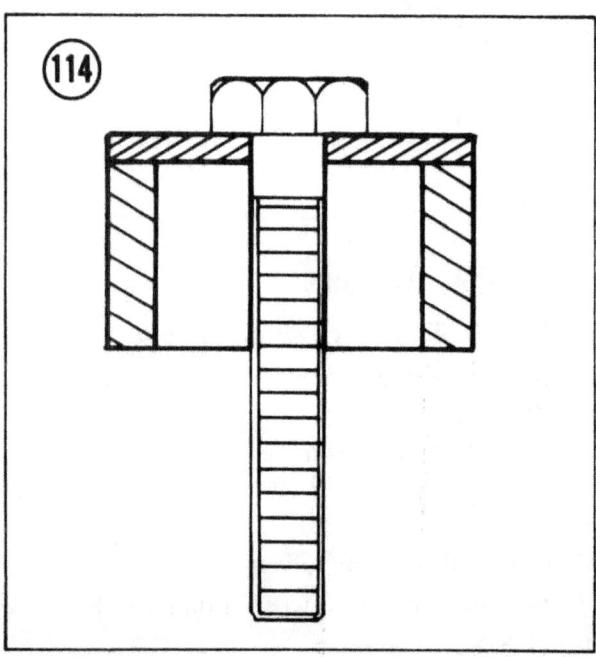

Installation

Crankcases have been manufactured with 2 different distances between crankshaft and intermediate shaft centers. A number (0 or 1) is stamped on the left crankcase half below the alternator mounting point (see **Figure 115**) identifying the crankcase size. A similar number is stamped onto the intermediate shaft gear and the crankshaft gear.

Table 5 CRANKCASE SIZES

Crankcase Number	Crankshaft Gear Number	Intermediate Gear Number	Gear Backlash
0	0	0	0.00114-0.00193" (0.029-0.049mm)
	1	0	0.00063-0.00165" (0.016-0.042mm)
	0	1	0.00067-0.00169" (0.017-0.043mm)
	1	1	Not possible
1	0	0	Not possible
	1	1	0.00047-0.00161" (0.012-0.041mm)
	0	1	0.00098-0.00193" (0.025-0.049mm)
	1	0	0.00098-0.00189" (0.025-0.048mm)

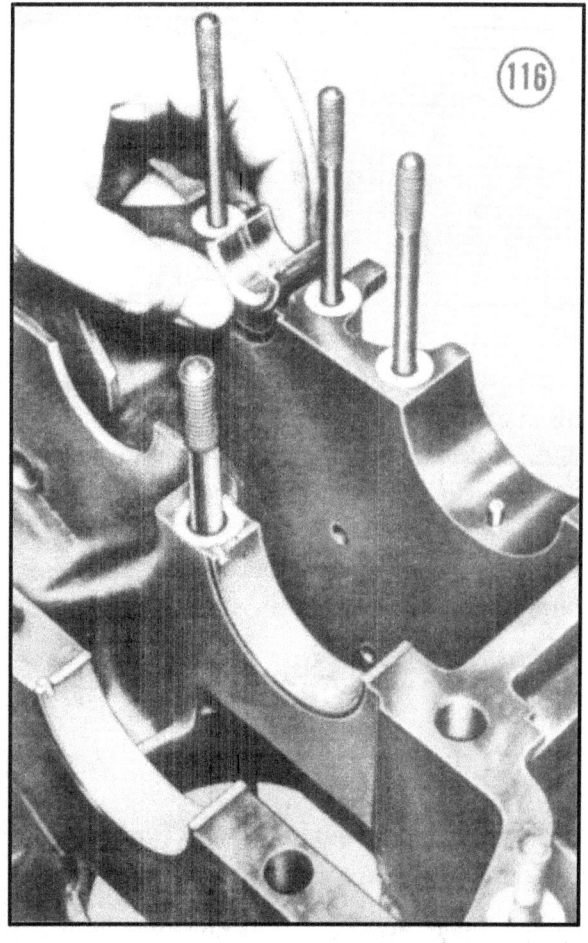

The numbers on the crankcase and gears must be matched according to **Table 5**. For example, if you have a crankcase stamped "0", you may use gears marked "0", or one marked "0" and the other "1". You cannot use two gears marked "1". The last column indicates the gear backlash you will get by using each gear/crankcase combination.

1. Install intermediate shaft bearing shells in crankcase halves. See **Figure 116**.

2. Coat bearing surfaces of connecting shaft and intermediate shaft with assembly lubricant.

3. Install intermediate shaft, connecting shaft, and oil pump without camshaft chains. See **Figure 117**.

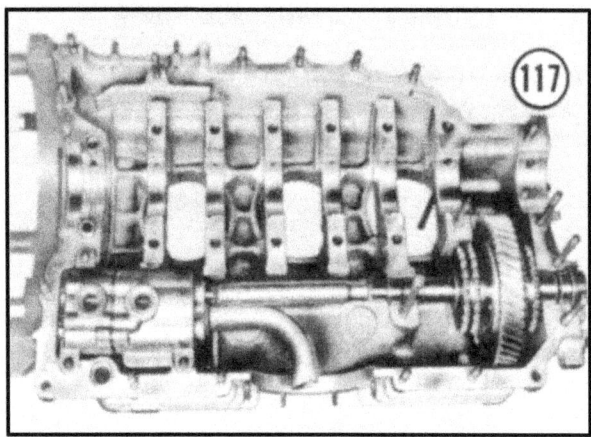

4. Turn intermediate shaft and ensure that it runs smoothly.

5. Lift intermediate shaft, connecting shaft, and oil pump out.

6. Insert new seals in right crankcase half oil passage. See **Figure 118**.

7. Insert oil pump, intermediate shaft, connecting shaft, and camshaft chains in right crankcase half. Make sure that seals remain in place.

8. Secure pump with new lock tabs and nuts. Bend tabs up.

9. Reassemble crankcase as described in *Crankcase Assembly*.

CRANKCASE

Disassembly

1. Perform Steps 1-15 of *General Overhaul Sequence* earlier in this chapter.

2. Remove oil pressure relief and bypass valves.

3. Remove crankcase breather outlet. See **Figure 119**.

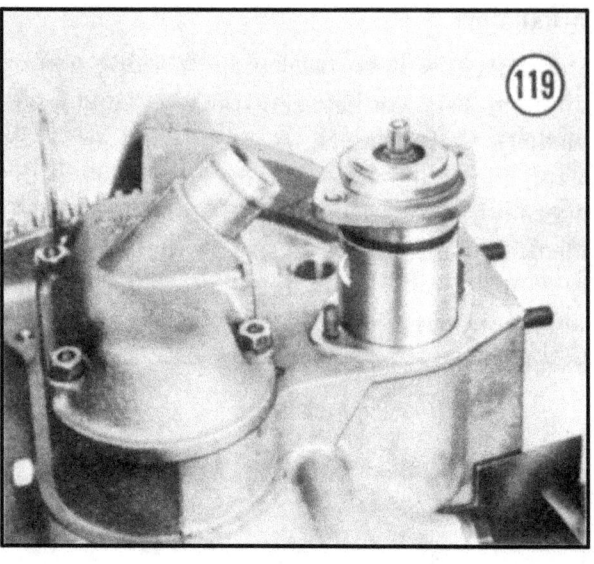

4. Remove cover over intermediate shaft. See **Figure 120**.

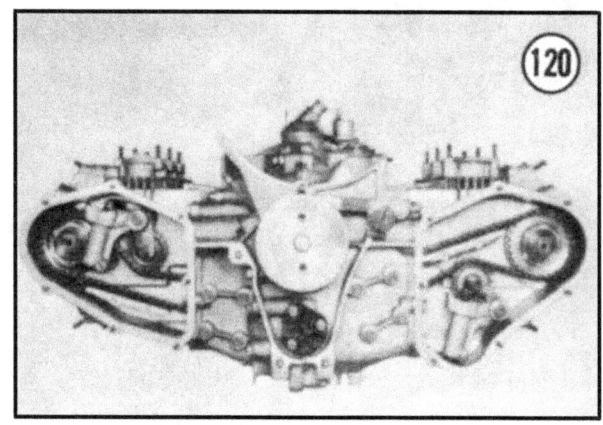

5. Remove all M8 nuts around outer edges of crankcase.

6. Remove acorn nuts shown in **Figure 121**.

7. Remove large thru-bolts.

8. Remove nut shown in **Figure 122**.

9. Check very carefully all around crankcase for any remaining nuts and bolts.

10. Loosen the left crankcase half by tapping with a rubber mallet or block of wood. Keep pulling upward on the crankcase half and tapping until the left half is free.

11. Lift out crankshaft.

12. Remove engine oil pump with intermediate shaft and chains as described in *Intermediate Shaft Removal*.

13. Bend up tabs on oil screens and remove them. See **Figure 123**.

14. Remove bearing inserts from crankshaft and intermediate shaft.

Inspection

1. Clean and flush both halves of crankcase with solvent. Blow out oil passages with air. Remove all traces of old sealing compound on mating surfaces.

2. Check both crankcase halves for cracks and other damage. Mating and sealing surfaces should be free of nicks and scratches or they will leak.

3. Check all studs in the crankcase for looseness. If any cannot be tightened, have a machinist install a Heli-coil insert.

4. Inspect all bearings bores for burrs. Remove very carefully with a file. Flush out any metal particles.

Assembly

1. Install oil screens and bend tabs over. See Figure 123.

2. Install intermediate shaft, oil pump, and camshaft chains exactly as described in *Intermediate Shaft Installation* in this chapter.

3. Install main bearing 2-7 shells in both crankcase halves. See **Figure 124**.

4. Install main bearing 1 shells. See **Figure 125**.

5. Install O-ring and oil seal on main bearing. Mark position of dowel hole with a pencil. See **Figure 126**. Coat inside of bearing with assembly lubricant and slide onto rear of crankshaft.

6. Coat main bearings and crankshaft journals with assembly lubricant.

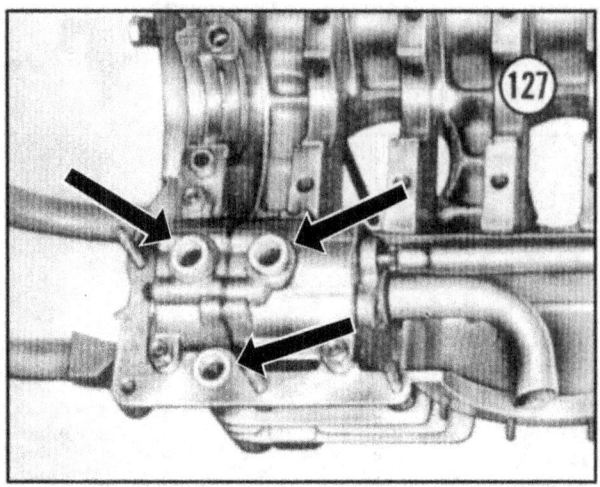

CAUTION
Do not get any gasket compound on bearings or in oil passages.

11. Hold connecting rods #1, #2, and #3 up. Place left crankcase half over right.

12. Fit a double chamfered washer over each long thru-bolt. The smoothest side of the washer should face the crankcase. Slide a rubber O-ring in place over each bolt.

13. Install thru-bolts. Slide a rubber O-ring over the threaded end of each bolt. Install a double chamfered washer over each bolt with smoothest side next to crankcase. Install cap nuts finger-tight. Completed assembly of each bolt should look like **Figure 128**.

14. Slide on O-ring and double chamfered washer (smooth side down) over the 2 studs shown in **Figure 129**. Install the cap nuts finger-tight.

7. Lift the crankshaft assembly by connecting rods #1 and #3. Hold #2 up. Place crankshaft on the main bearings. Make absolutely certain that dowel hole (indicated by pencil mark) fits over dowel. If the oil hole fits over the dowel instead, the bearing will appear to be properly seated, but will not receive any oil when the engine is run. Also connecting rods #4, #5, and #6 must protrude through corresponding cylinder holes.

8. Install 2 oil seal rings in oil pump and one oil seal ring in the right crankcase half. See **Figure 127**.

9. Coat outer perimeter of front oil seal with gasket compound and install it in the right crankcase half.

10. Spread a thin layer of gasket compound on crankcase and mating surfaces.

15. Install a steel washer and nut on stud shown in **Figure 130**. Tighten finger-tight.

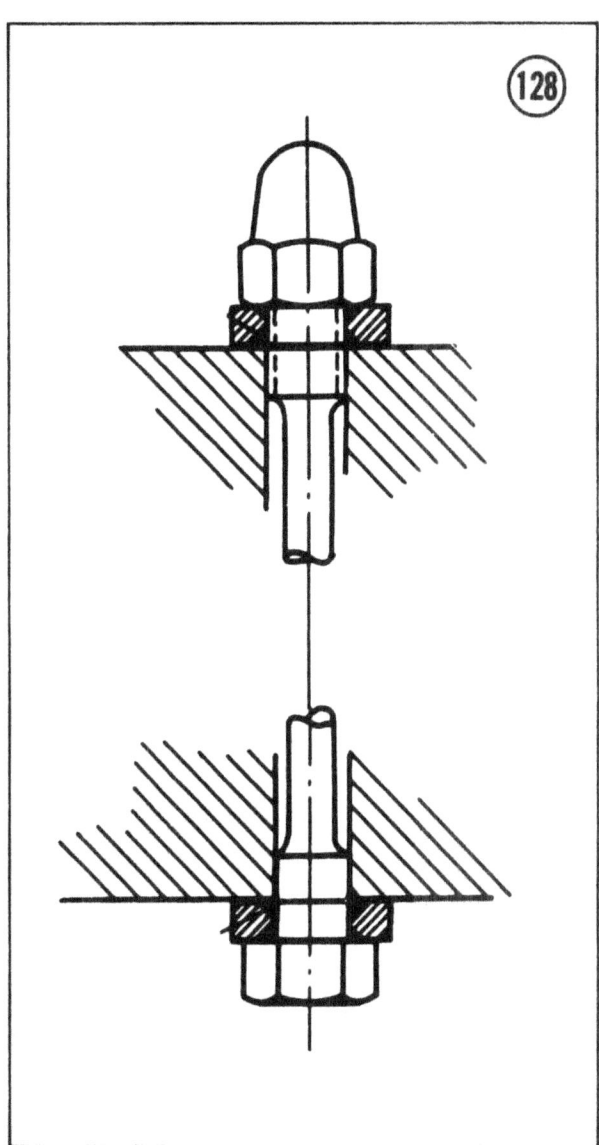

CAUTION
Throughout the tightening process in the next 2 steps, turn the crankshaft occasionally. If there is any binding, STOP, take the case apart and find the trouble.

16. Tighten all through bolts and 3 studs to 25 foot-pounds (3.5 mkg). Tighten finger-tight.

17. Tighten lockwashers and nuts on remaining crankcase studs to 16-18 ft.-lbs. (2.2-2.5 mkg).

18. Install cover over intermediate shaft. See *Intermediate Shaft* procedure.

19. Install oil pressure relief and bypass valves.

20. Perform Steps 1-15 of *General Overhaul Sequence* in reverse order.

CHAPTER SIX

COOLING, HEATING, AND EXHAUST

The engine cooling, heating, and exhaust systems on a Porsche are closely related. A large fan directs fresh air to the engine for cooling. In addition, fresh air from the fan passes through heat exchangers where it is heated by the engine exhaust for use in the passenger area.

Figure 1 shows the complete passenger compartment heating system. The cooling fan draws fresh outside air into the engine compartment to cool the engine. A duct (3) directs a portion of the fan output to the heat exchangers (4). Exhaust gases from the cylinders pass through the heat exchangers to the muffler and heat the fresh air. The heated air from the heat exchangers passes through heater control hoses (8), sound mufflers (9), and into the passenger area.

A steady fresh air flow passes through the heat exchangers. Varying the heater control lever in the passenger area directs either more or less of this air flow into the passenger area.

The exhaust system on all models is straightforward. Exhaust gases from the engine pass through the heat exchangers to the muffler.

COOLING SYSTEM (914)

Fan Housing Removal

1. Remove 3 Allen bolts (see **Figure 2**) and remove fan/pulley assembly.

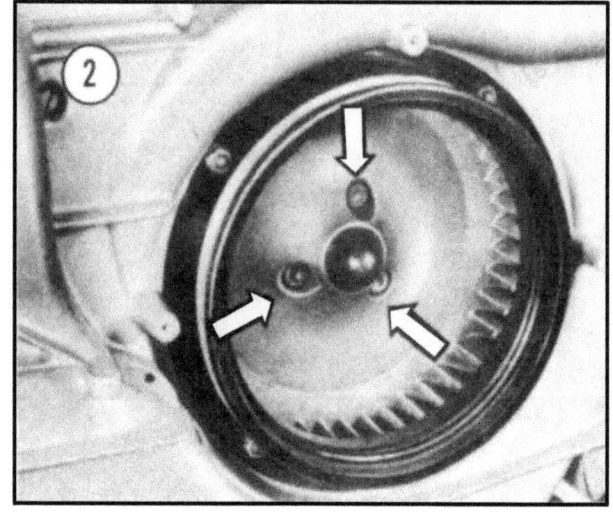

2. Remove spacer from end of crankshaft.
3. Remove cover plate over alternator.
4. Disconnect cooling air regulator cable from shaft. See **Figure 3**.
5. Remove 4 nuts. Remove front and rear halves of fan housing as an assembly. See **Figure 4**.

Fan Housing Installation

1. Assemble front and rear halves of fan housing if they have been separated.
2. Mount fan housing on engine with 4 nuts.

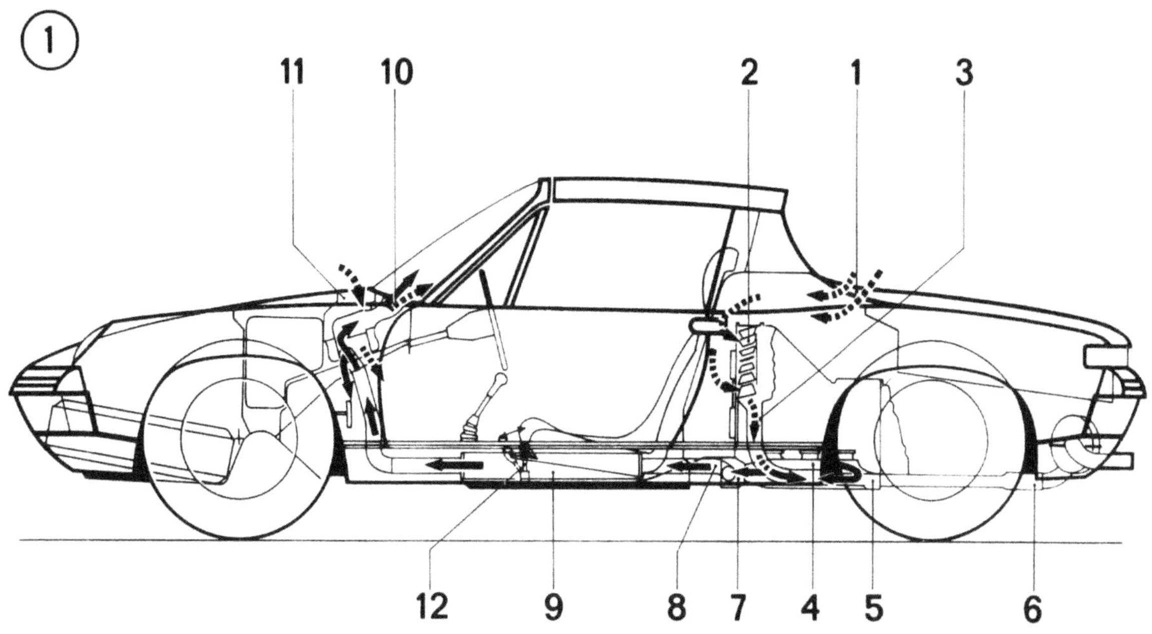

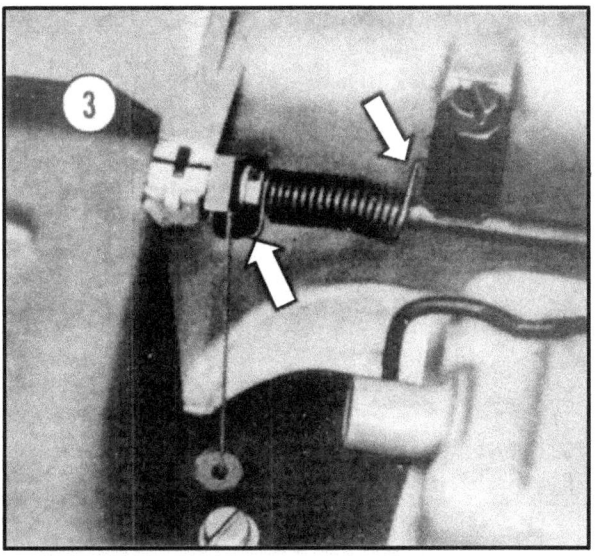

HEATING AND VENTILATING SYSTEM

1. Grill
2. Cooling air blower
3. Air duct
4. Heat exchanger
5. Exhaust pipes
6. Muffler
7. Heat control flap
8. Hot air duct
9. Sound muffler
10. Defroster outlet
11. Fresh air vent
12. Heat control lever

3. Ensure that the dipstick boot fits tightly on both ends of tubes. See **Figure 5**.

4. Install connecting elbow for cooling air between the alternator and the front half of the fan housing. See **Figure 6**.

5. Install cover plate over alternator.

6. Install fan on end of crankshaft, using a split and flat washer between the hub, otherwise the bolt will protrude too far into the hub and may damage the oil seal.

7. Install fan belt and adjust belt tension as described in Chapter Two.

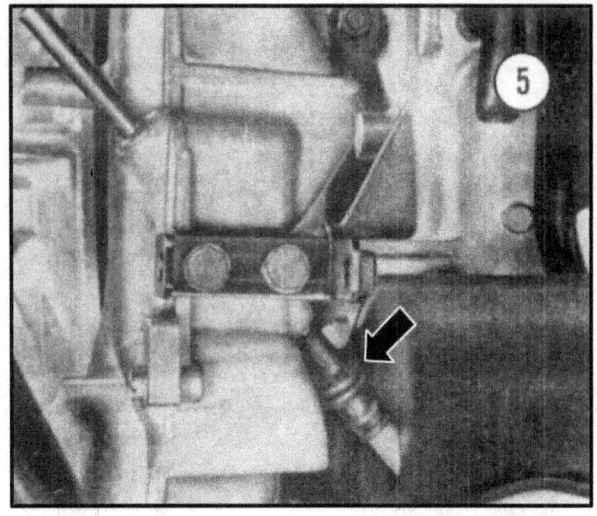

8. Connect cooling air regulator cable to shaft and adjust as described below.

Cooling Air Control Adjustment

1. Lubricate bearing surfaces on shaft.
2. Press flaps closed and hold them.
3. Loosen cable clamp screw. See Figure 3. Pull gently on cable to remove slack and tighten the clamp screw.

COOLING SYSTEM (914/6)

Cooling Fan Removal/Installation

The cooling fan and alternator must be removed as an assembly. To do so, follow the alternator removal procedure in Chapter Nine. Once this is done, remove 6 nuts securing the alternator/fan to the fan housing and remove the fan housing. Installation is the reverse. Be sure that you adjust the fan belt tension as described in Chapter Two.

Cover Plate Removal/Installation

This procedure assumes the engine has been removed. Refer to **Figure 7**.

1. Remove carburetors and intake manifolds.
2. Remove rear cover plate. See **Figure 8**(1).

3. Disconnect fuel lines passing over fan housing. See Figure 8(2).
4. Disconnect both air hoses to heat exchangers.
5. Remove all screws attaching fiberglass upper air channel.
6. Remove left and right heater ducts.
7. Remove front cover plates.
8. Remove side cover plate.
9. Installation is the reverse of these steps.

HEATING SYSTEM

Heat Exchanger Removal/Installation

Refer to **Figure 9** (914) or **Figure 10** (914/6).

1. Remove muffler as described later.
2. Disconnect hot air outlet hose from front of heat exchanger.
3. Disconnect fresh air hose from side of heat exchanger.
4. Remove exhaust flange nuts.
5. Check carefully for leaks in the exhaust pipe running through the exchanger.

COOLING SYSTEM (914/6)

1. Nut
2. Clamp
3. Pulley half
4. Shims
5. Impeller
6. Key
7. Engine cover
8. Engine cover plate
9. Engine cover plate
10. Heating air scoop
11. Heating air scoop
12. Engine cover plate
13. Engine cover plate
14. Upper air guide
15. Blower housing
16. Lock nut
17. Lockwasher
18. Hub extension
19. Alternator
20. Leaf spring
21. Baffle plate

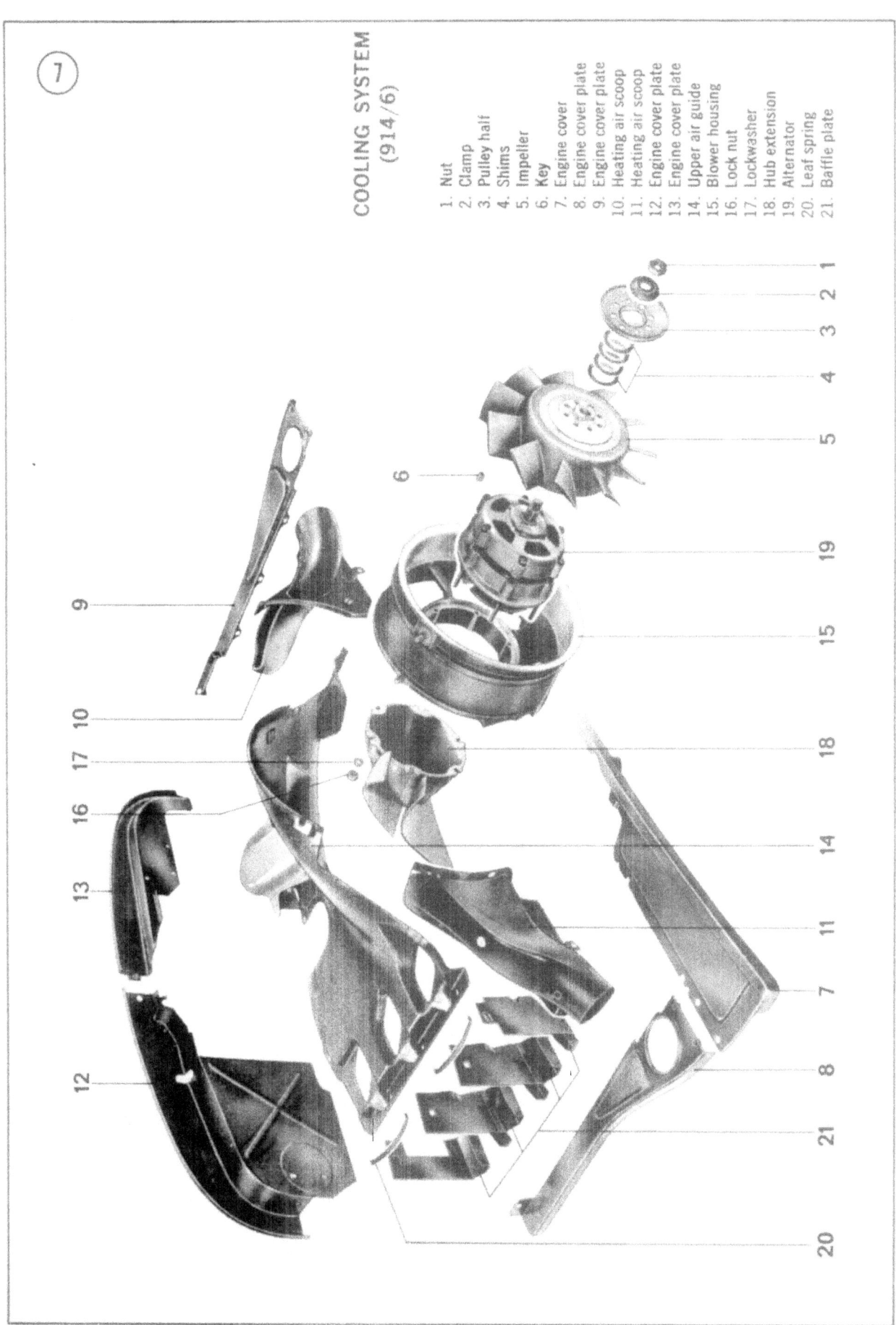

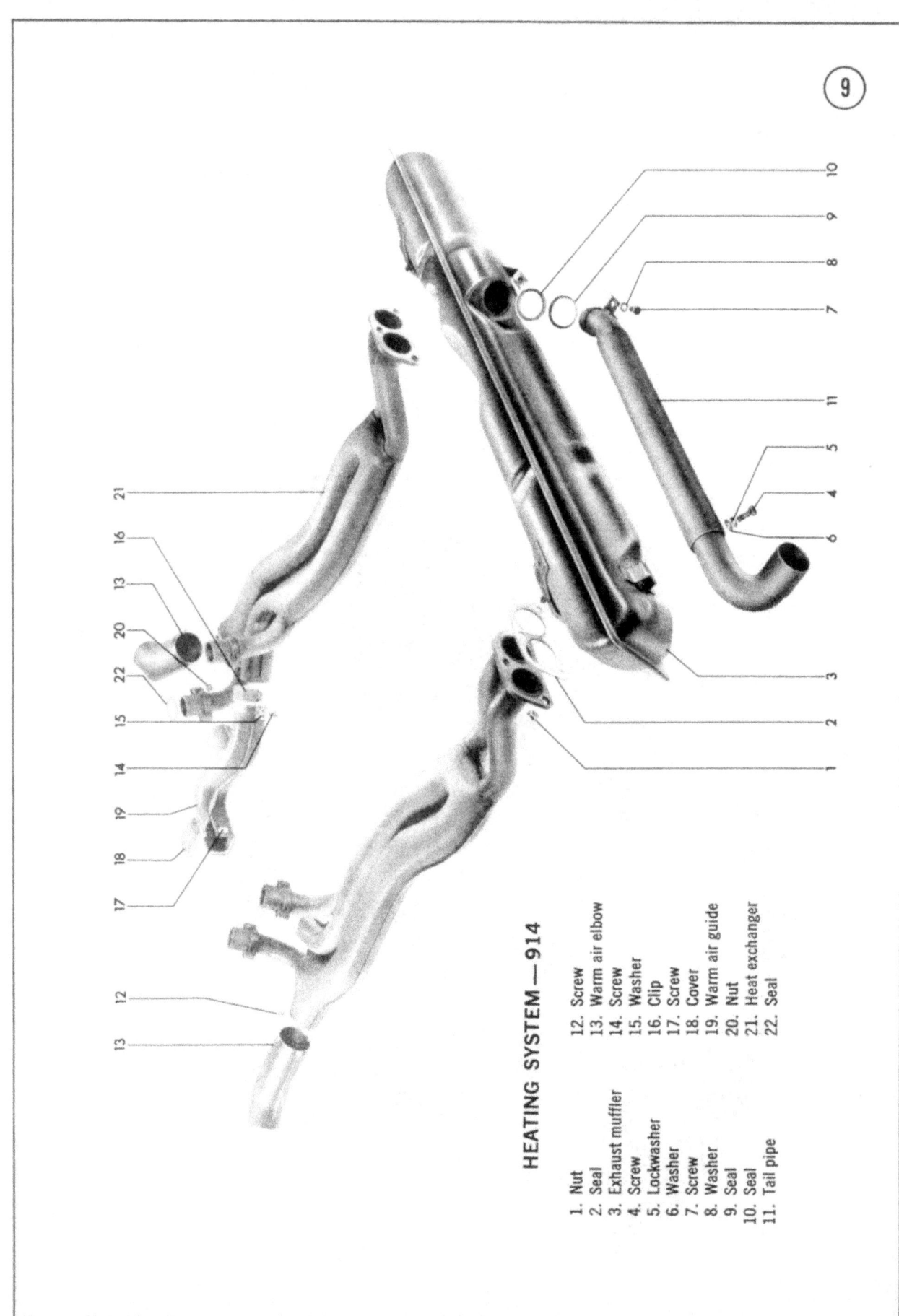

HEATING SYSTEM — 914

1. Nut
2. Seal
3. Exhaust muffler
4. Screw
5. Lockwasher
6. Washer
7. Screw
8. Washer
9. Seal
10. Seal
11. Tail pipe
12. Screw
13. Warm air elbow
14. Screw
15. Washer
16. Clip
17. Screw
18. Cover
19. Warm air guide
20. Nut
21. Heat exchanger
22. Seal

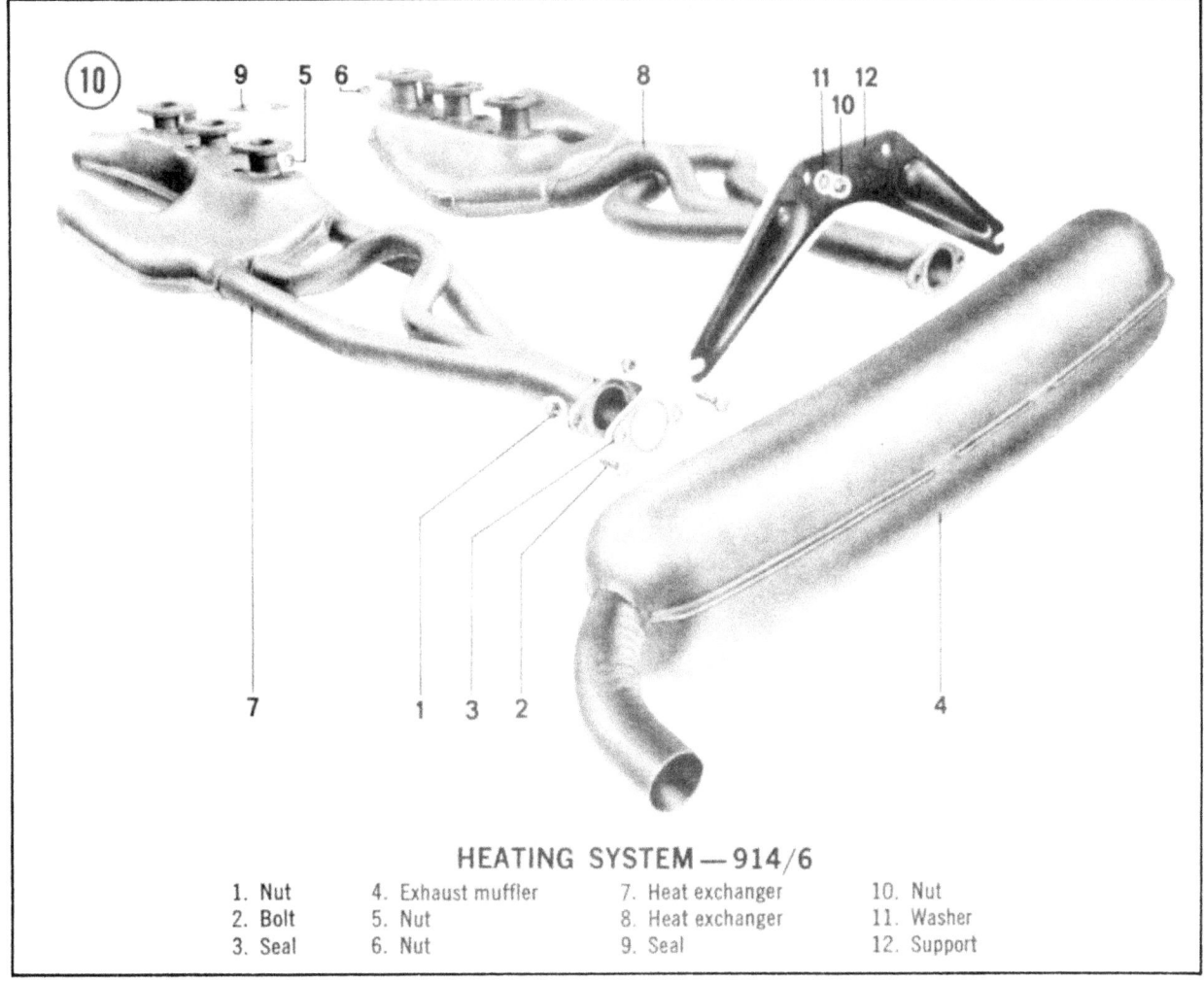

HEATING SYSTEM — 914/6

1. Nut	4. Exhaust muffler	7. Heat exchanger	10. Nut
2. Bolt	5. Nut	8. Heat exchanger	11. Washer
3. Seal	6. Nut	9. Seal	12. Support

WARNING
Exhaust leaks can cause poisonous exhaust fumes to enter the passenger area. Replace defective heat exchangers immediately.

6. Installation is the reverse of these steps. Use new gaskets.

Heater Control Cable Replacement

1. Disconnect cable ends from heat control boxes.
2. Remove tunnel cover in passenger area.
3. Remove screws securing heater control lever assembly. Lift assembly slightly and disconnect cable.
4. Pull cable out of tunnel from either end.
5. Connect end of new cable to lever.
6. Insert heater control box ends into guide tube. Make sure that the ends do not tangle together.
7. Secure heater control lever assembly to tunnel.
8. Push heat control lever all the way forward.
9. Connect cables to heater control boxes.
10. Operate the lever and ensure that both control boxes work smoothly.
11. Install tunnel cover.

EXHAUST SYSTEM

Muffler Replacement

Figure 9 shows the 914 engine exhaust system; Figure 10 shows the 914/6 system.

1. Remove bolts and/or nuts joining muffler to heat exchangers.
2. Remove muffler.
3. Installation is the reverse of these steps. Use new gaskets.

CHAPTER SEVEN

FUEL INJECTION—914/4

Two different electronic fuel injection systems are used on the 4-cylinder engines. From 1970-1973 the system uses intake manifold pressure to control the duration of injection. Later systems use the amount of air drawn into the system to control the injection duration. The early system is called MPC (manifold pressure controlled) injection and the later system is called AFC (air flow controlled) injection.

> NOTE: *All 914 2.0 liter engines use the MPC injection system, regardless of year.*

Complete service information for the fuel injection systems are beyond the scope of this manual. Because of special knowledge and electronic test fixtures required, some services cannot be performed by the home mechanic. The procedures in this chapter permit you to isolate and repair a majority of mechanical troubles, but some mechanical and all electrical unit procedures should be performed by the dealer.

PRINCIPLES OF MPC INJECTION

The heart of the fuel injection system is the control unit, a small electronic "computer." Various sensors transmit information concerning air temperature, engine temperature, engine speed, and engine load to the control unit. The control unit uses the information to determine the exact amount of fuel to be distributed to the cylinders. **Figure 1** is a simplified diagram of the entire fuel injection system; refer to it for the following descriptions. **Figures 2 and 3** are electrical diagrams which may be helpful when troubleshooting. **Figure 4** shows location of major components.

Air System

Components of the air system are shown in **Figure 5**. Clean air from the oil bath air cleaner enters the intake air distributor past a throttle valve to the combustion chambers. The throttle valve controls the flow of air.

During idle, the throttle valve is completely closed. A bypass around the throttle valve permits a small amount of air, controlled by the idle speed screw, to pass. When the engine is cold (below 122°F), the auxiliary air regulator bypasses a larger amount of air around the throttle valve. This extra air mixes with extra fuel injected for cold starts. As the engine warms

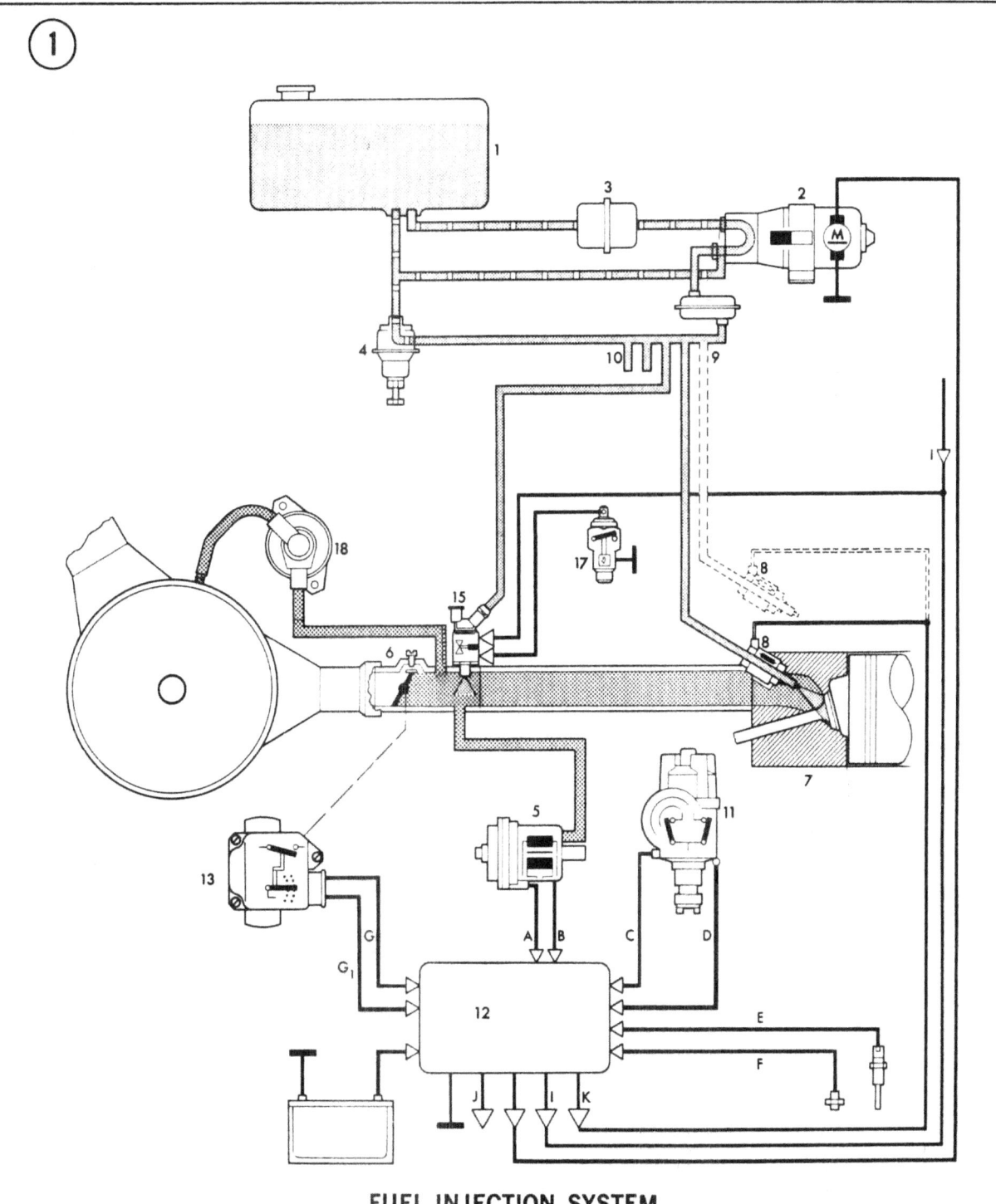

FUEL INJECTION SYSTEM

1. Fuel tank
2. Electric fuel pump
3. Fuel filter
4. Fuel pressure regulator
5. Pressure sensor
6. Air intake distributor
7. Cylinder head
8. Fuel injectors
9. Fuel loop line
10. Connection for fuel line (cold starting)
11. Ignition distributor with trigger contacts
12. Electronic control unit
13. Throttle valve switch with power mixture enrichment
15. Cold starting jet
16. Electro-magnetic valve (cold starting)
17. Temperature switch (cold starting)
18. Auxiliary air regulator

A and B. Signals from pressure sensor
C and D. Signals from trigger contacts
E and F. Signals from temperature sensors (warming up phase)
G. Signal from throttle valve switch (fuel shut off on overrun)
G1. Power mixture enrichment
I. Signal from starter (term 50)
J. Signal to injectors 1 and 4
K. Signal to injectors 2 and 3

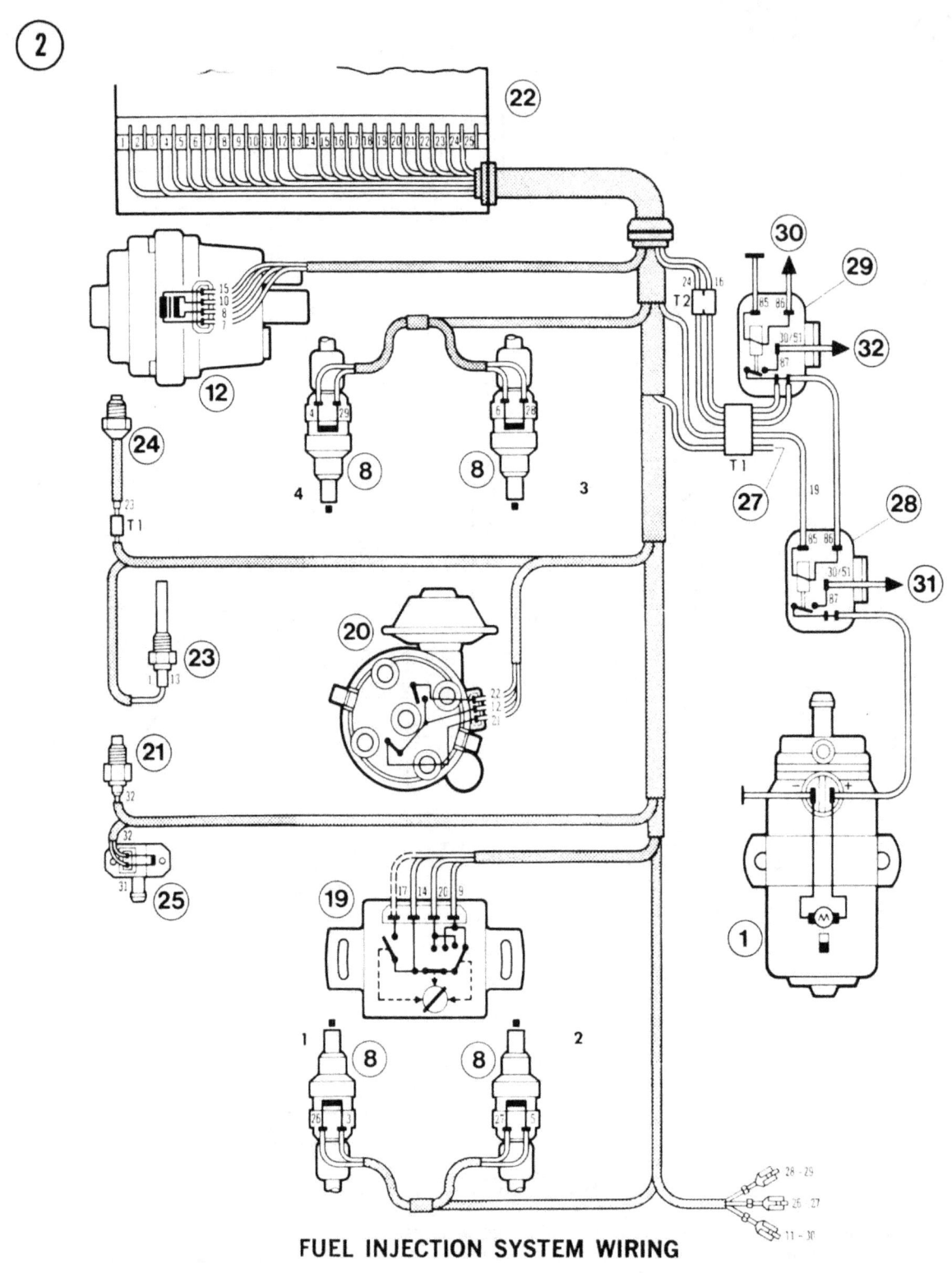

FUEL INJECTION SYSTEM WIRING

1. Electric fuel pump
8. Injector
12. Pressure sensor
19. Throttle valve switch with mixture enrichment
20. Ignition distributor with trigger contacts
21. Thermo (temp.) switch
22. Control unit
23. Temperature sensor in air intake distributor
24. Temperature sensor in cylinder head
25. Cold start valve
27. Wire 18 and 31 from terminal 50
28. Pump relay
29. Main relay
30. To ignition terminal 15 (fuse box)
31. To terminal 30 (fuse box)
32. To battery + terminal
T1. Wire plug connection
T2. Wire connector

Wire Number	From	To
1.	Control unit	Temperature sensor in air intake distributor
2.	Not connected	
3.	Control unit	No. 1 injector
4.	Control unit	No. 4 injector
5.	Control unit	No. 2 injector
6.	Control unit	No. 3 injector
7.	Control unit	Pressure sensor
8.	Control unit	Pressure sensor
9.	Control unit	Throttle valve switch
10.	Control unit	Pressure sensor
11.	Control unit	Engine crankcase (ground wire)
12.	Control unit	Trigger contacts in ignition distributor
13.	Control unit	Temperature sensor in air intake distributor
14.	Not connected	
15.	Control unit	Pressure sensor
16.	Control unit	Terminal 87 main relay (voltage) (via wire connector T 1)
17.	Control unit	Throttle valve switch (only with fuel shut off)
18.	Control unit	Terminal 50 of starter motor
19.	Control unit	Terminal 85 of pump relay (via wire connector T 1)
20.	Control unit	Throttle valve switch
21.	Control unit	Ignition distributor (trigger contacts)
22.	Control unit	Ignition distributor (trigger contacts)
23.	Control unit	Temperature sensor in cylinder head
24.	Control unit	Terminal 87 main relay (via wire connector T 1)
25.	Not connected	
26.	No. 1 injector	Engine ground
27.	No. 2 injector	Engine ground
28.	No. 3 injector	Engine ground
29.	No. 4 injector	Engine ground
30.	Terminal 14 throttle valve switch	Engine ground
31.	Terminal 50 starter	Cold start valve (via wire connector T 1)
32.	Cold start valve	Temperature switch

up, the air regulator gradually closes; when the engine is fully warmed up (above 122°F), the regulator closes completely.

A pressure sensor connects to the intake air distributor to sample manifold pressure and determine engine load.

Fuel System

Figure 6 is a simplified drawing of the fuel system. The fuel pump draws fuel from the front-mounted fuel tank through a filter and delivers it to 4 injectors. A pressure regulator on the return line maintains fuel pressure at 28 psi. Excess fuel from the regulator returns to the fuel tank.

The control unit controls the fuel pump through a relay, not shown in Figure 1 or Figure 6. When the ignition switch is turned on, the control unit turns the fuel pump on for 1-2 seconds; this prevents flooding the engine if an injector or the cold start valve is defective. The control unit turns the fuel pump back on when the starter is on or the engine is running.

The control unit also controls the electromagnetic fuel injectors. The injectors are turned on in pairs. The control unit sends an electrical pulse to injectors 1 and 4 simultaneously, and then another pulse to injectors 2 and 3 simultaneously. On 1970-1971 models, injectors 1 and 3 inject when the respective intake valve is open, while injectors 2 and 4 inject when the respective intake valve is closed. On 1972 and 1973 models, all injection takes place behind closed intake valves. Fuel is effectively stored in the intake ports of cylinders until the intake valve opens.

Figure 7 shows a cutaway of an injector. The control unit sends an electrical pulse to the magnetic winding in the injector. The pulse causes the needle to move off its seat and inject fuel. Then the return spring reseats the needle at the end of the pulse. The time the injector is open varies from about 2-10 milliseconds (0.002-0.010 seconds).

The duration of the electrical pulses to the injectors depends mainly on engine speed and engine load. Special contacts in the ignition distributor provide electrical signals to the control

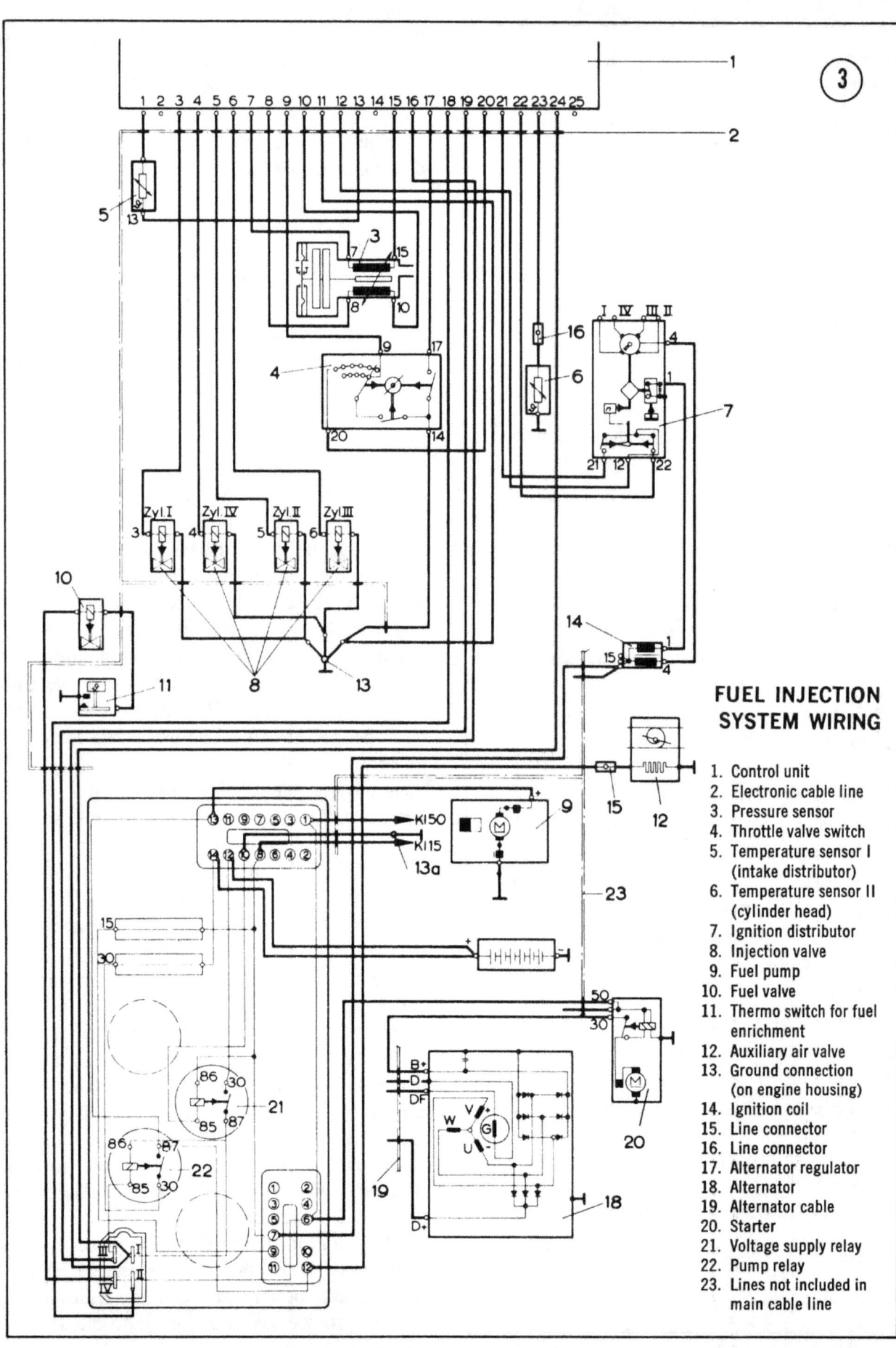

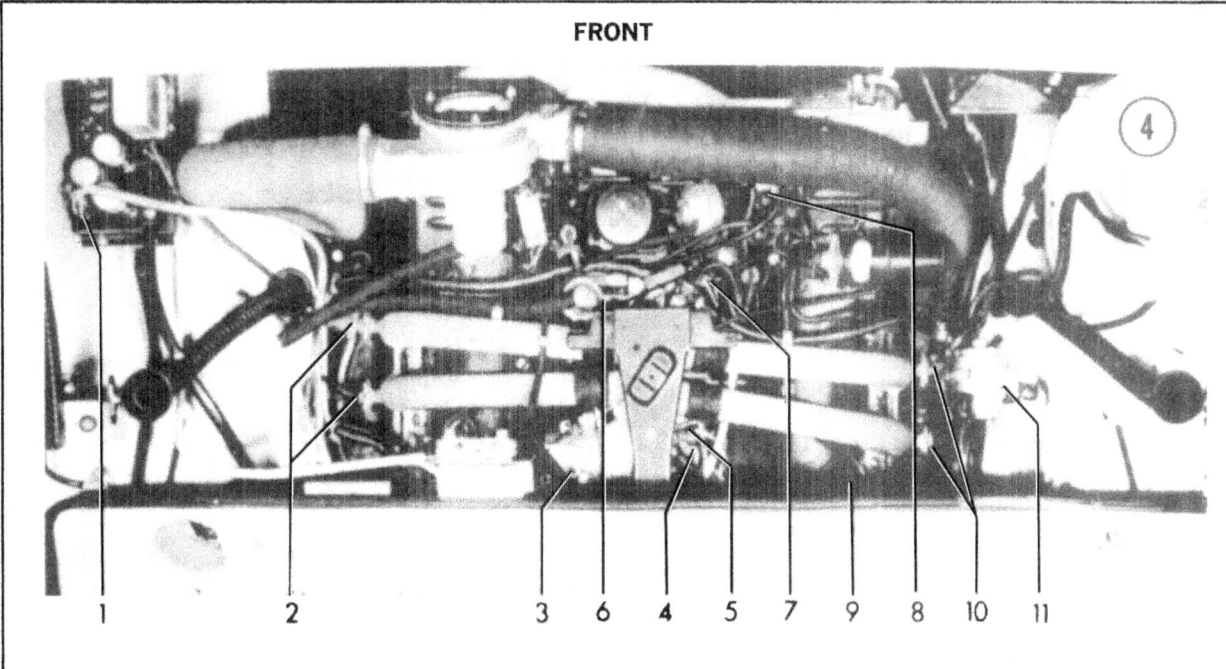

FRONT / REAR

1. Voltage supply relay 4-pole
2. Two injection valves left 2-pole
3. One throttle valve switch 4-pole
4. Temperature feeler 1-pole
5. Mass connections 3-pole
6. Cold starting valve 2-pole
7. Thermal switch 1-pole
8. Ignition distributor release contact 3-pole
9. Temperature feeler 1-pole
10. Two injection valves right 2-pole
11. Pressure feeler 4-pole

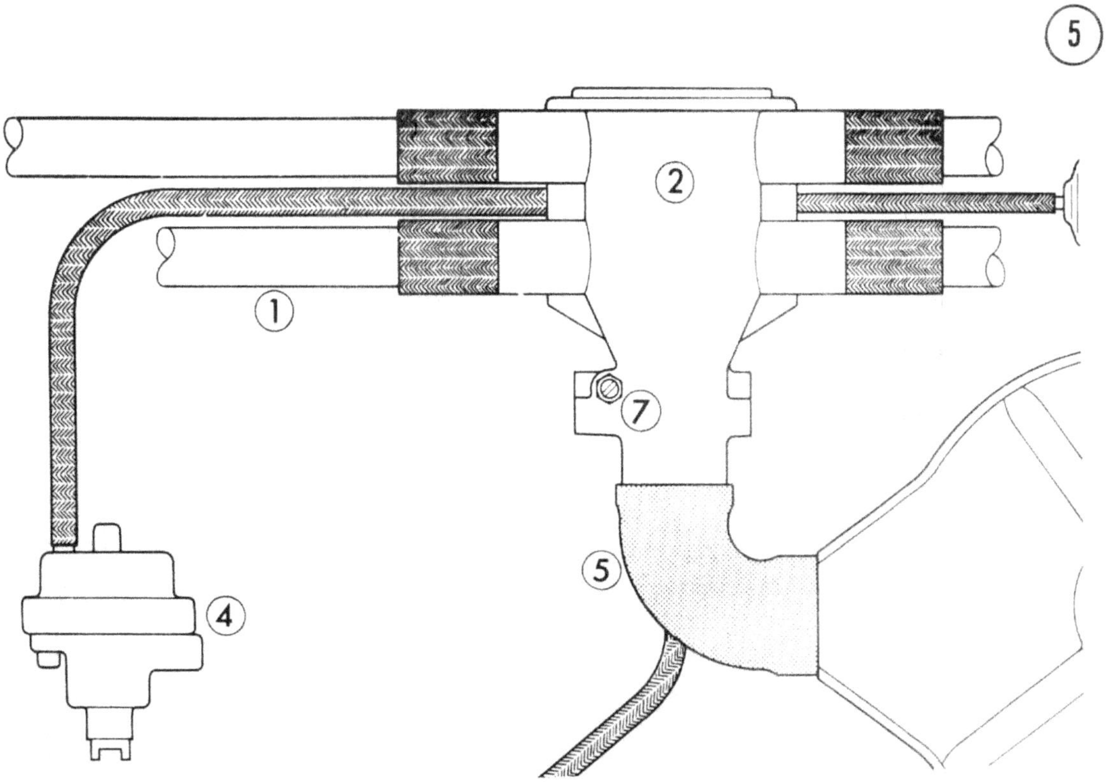

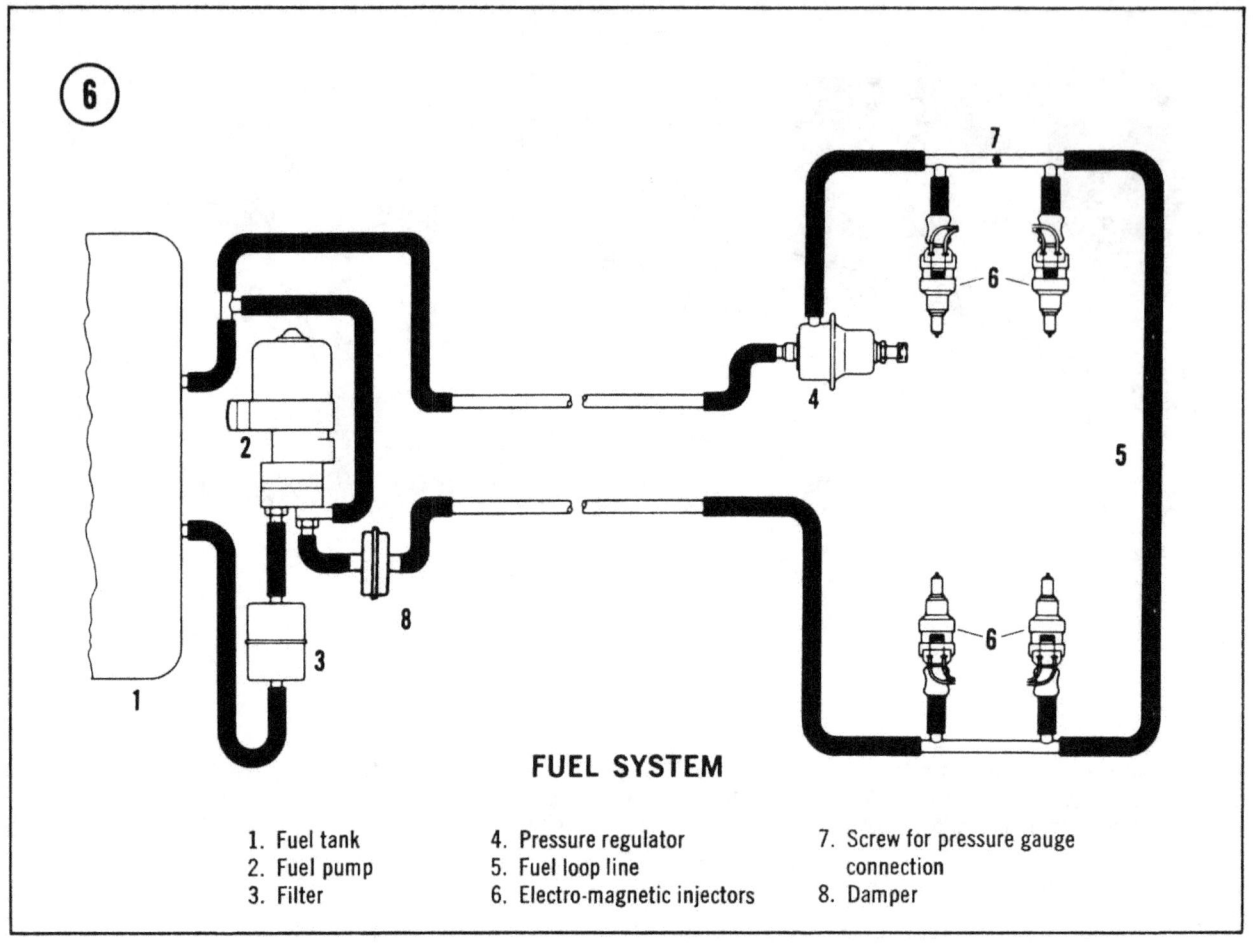

FUEL SYSTEM

1. Fuel tank
2. Fuel pump
3. Filter
4. Pressure regulator
5. Fuel loop line
6. Electro-magnetic injectors
7. Screw for pressure gauge connection
8. Damper

unit indicating the engine speed. The pressure sensor generates electrical signals which indicate pressure (vacuum) in the intake air distributor and therefore the engine load. The control unit processes the 2 electrical signals and determines the duration of electrical pulses to the injectors.

The rate of acceleration and deceleration have an effect on fuel delivery. When the driver depresses the accelerator, the throttle valve switch transmits an electrical signal to the control unit indicating how fast the pedal is being depressed. The control unit uses this information to comput how many extra injections are needed and how long injection duration should be.

When the driver eases up on the accelerator pedal, the throttle valve switch transmits another signal to the control unit. On 1970 and 1971 models, if engine speed is above 1,800 rpm, the control unit actually shuts off all injection until the speed drops to about 1,250 rpm. At this point, injection begins again, permitting a smooth transition to idle speed if the car continues to decelerate. Naturally, if the driver depresses the accelerator below 1,800 rpm and before reaching 1,250 rpm, the control unit resumes injection immediately. This method of leaning mixtures has been discontinued in favor of an air injection system on 1972 and 1973 models. Air injection is described in a later section in this chapter.

Different means are used to signal enrichment for full throttle acceleration. A switch included in the pressure sensor signals when pressure approaches atmospheric pressure (wide open throttle valve). In 1972, Porsche installed a new throttle valve switch with extra contacts to signal full throttle.

In addition to engine speed and engine load signals, the control unit receives signals from temperature sensors. One sensor monitors temperature of incoming air while another monitors cylinder head temperature. The control unit "computes" the effect these sensors should have on the injectors. When the sensors detect cold temperatures, the control unit increases injection duration.

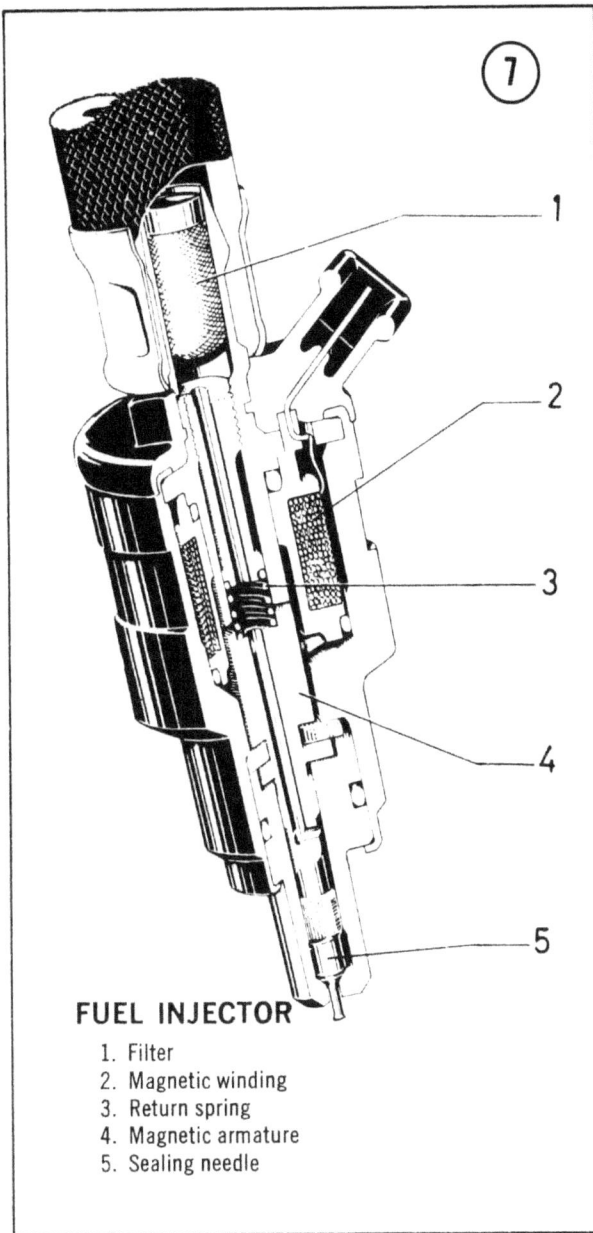

FUEL INJECTOR
1. Filter
2. Magnetic winding
3. Return spring
4. Magnetic armature
5. Sealing needle

Cold Start System

When the engine is cold, but above 5°F (—15°C), even more fuel must be injected. A special cold start system provides this additional fuel. See Figure 1. The cold start thermostat operates the cold start valve through a relay. The cold start valve injects extra fuel through a jet fitted in the intake air distributor.

PRINCIPLES OF AFC INJECTION

The electronic control unit is the central component in the air flow controlled (AFC) injection system. Sensors located at various points on the engine transmit information concerning intake air flow, engine temperature, and engine speed to the control unit. The control unit uses the information to control the flow of fuel from the injectors into the combustion chambers.

Figure 8 shows a simplified diagram of the entire system; refer to it for the discussion which follows. **Figure 9** is a wiring diagram of the system which may be helpful when troubleshooting. **Figure 10** shows the location of major components in the system.

Air System

The air system consists of the:

a. Air filter and housing
b. Intake air sensor
c. Throttle valve housing
d. Air distributor

Clean fresh air enters the intake air distributor, past the intake air sensor and the throttle valve. The throttle valve position determines the amount of air entering the system.

The intake air sensor produces an electrical signal proportional to the amount of air entering and passes this information to the control unit. The control unit in turn opens the injectors to inject the precise amount of fuel required for the amount of air entering the system.

During idle, the throttle valve is closed. A bypass around the valve permits a small amount of air, controlled by the idle speed screw, to pass.

Fuel System

The fuel system consists of the:

a. Fuel tank
b. Fuel pump
c. Filter
d. Regulator
e. Injectors

The fuel pump draws fuel from the front-mounted tank and delivers it through a filter to the 4 injectors. A pressure regulator varies fuel pressure to suit engine load. When the engine load is light, manifold vacuum is high and fuel pressure is low. As engine load increases, manifold vacuum drops and fuel pressure rises. Ex-

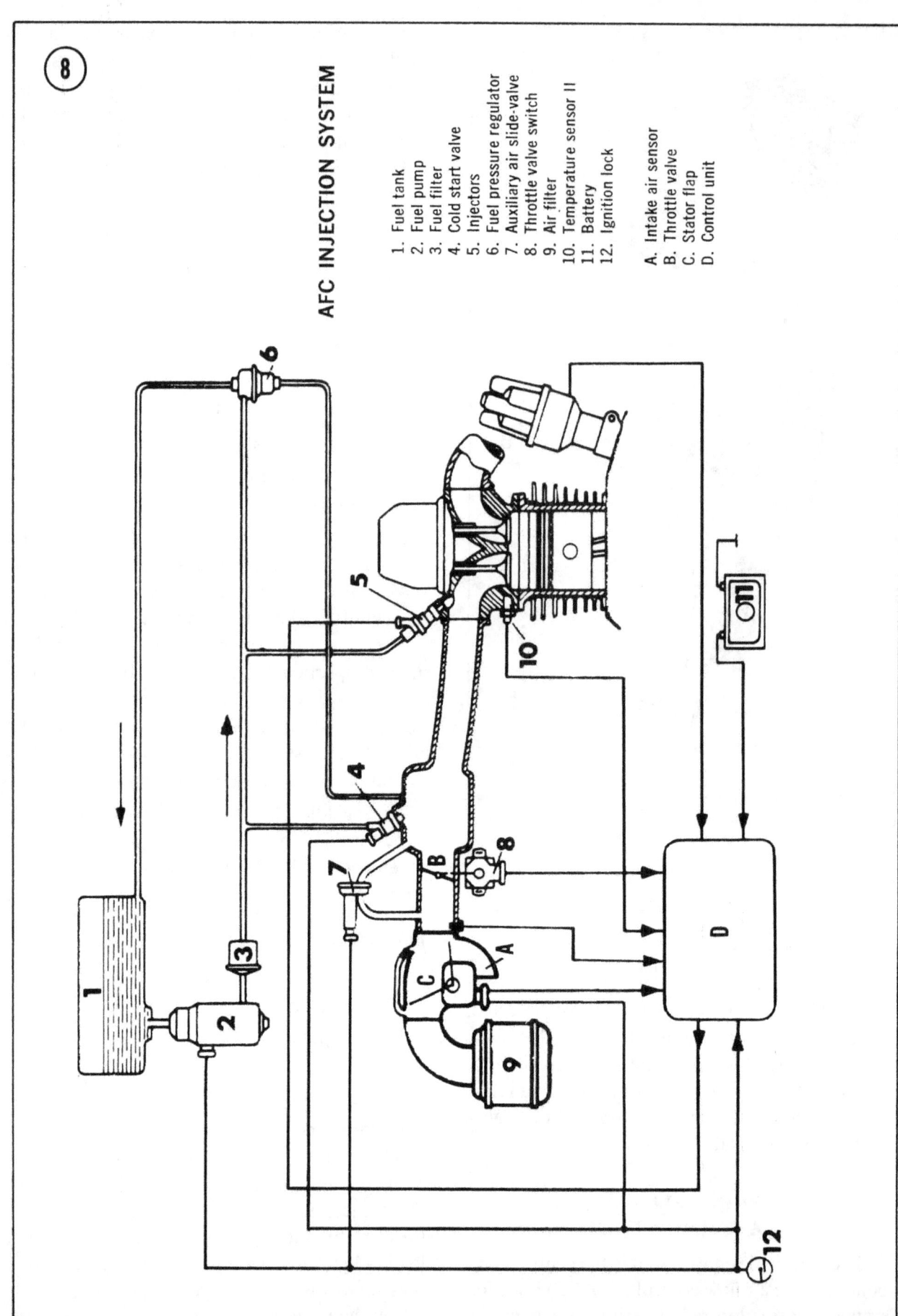

WIRING DIAGRAM
AFC INJECTION

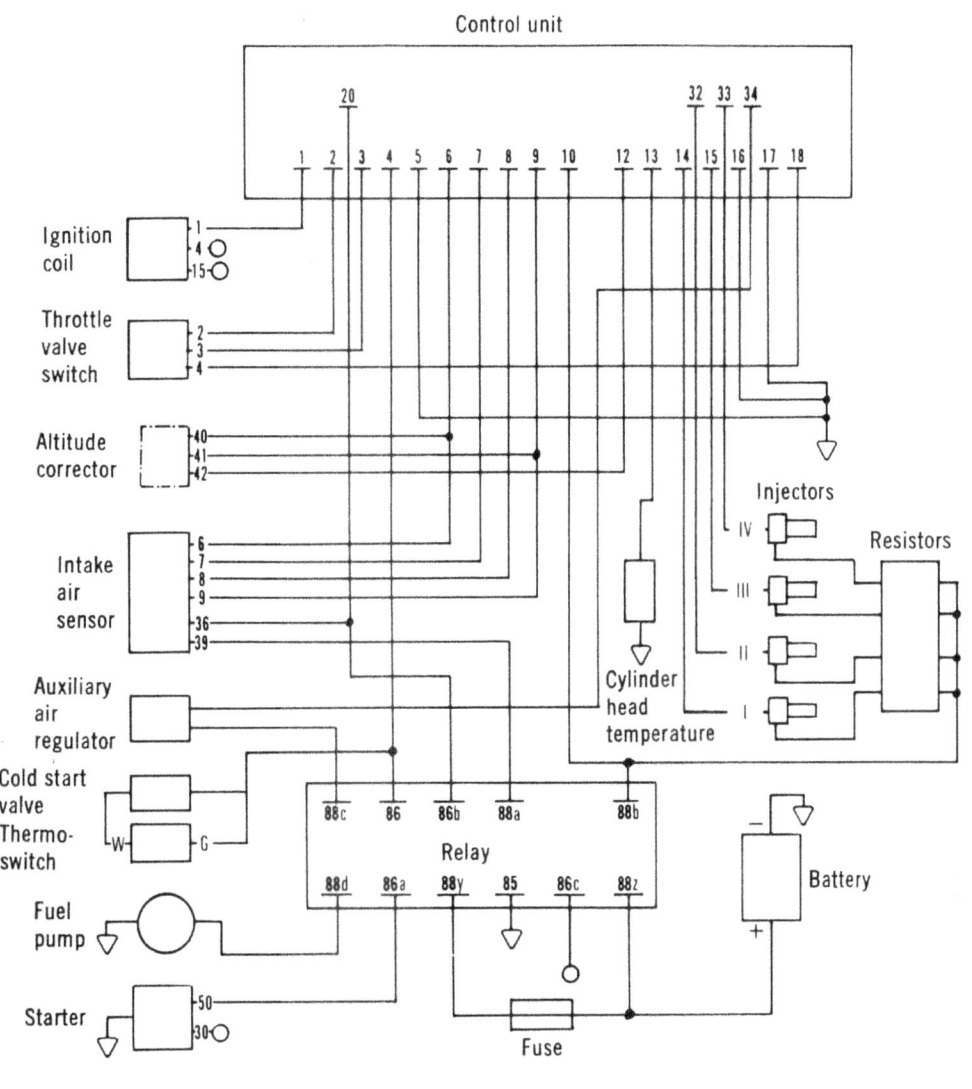

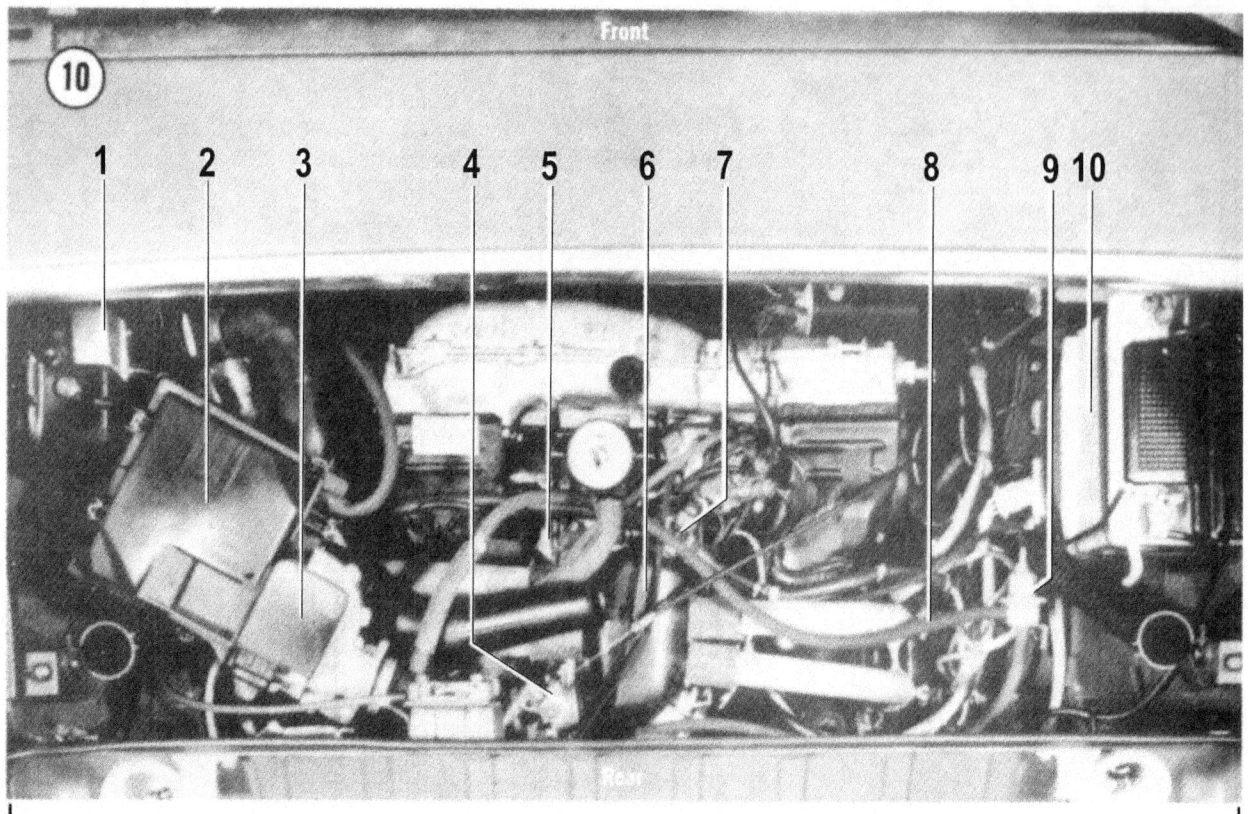

AFC INJECTION

1. Relay
2. Air filter
3. Intake air sensor
4. Throttle valve
5. Auxiliary air regulator
6. Intake air distributor
7. Cold start valve
8. Injector
9. Fuel pressure regulator
10. Control unit

cess fuel from regulator returns to the fuel tank.

Special contacts in the intake air sensor turn the fuel pump on when the stator flap moves from its closed position.

The control unit controls the timing and duration of fuel delivery by the injectors. The unit measures impulses from the distributor breaker points to determine engine speed and triggers all 4 injectors once for every 2 impulses, that is, once for each crankshaft revolution. Injection does not necessarily coincide with the period that any given intake valve is open. Fuel is effectively stored in the intake ports until the intake valve opens.

The duration of injection depends primarily on the amount of air entering the system as measured by the intake air sensor. The duration is longest for large amounts of air and shorter for lesser amounts of air.

Other factors influence the duration of injection. These are:

a. Intake air temperature
b. Cylinder head temperature
c. Throttle valve position

Sensors in the intake air stream and on one cylinder head, provide temperature information for the control unit. The control unit increases injection duration for low temperatures and decreases duration as temperature increases.

The throttle valve contains switch contacts which signal full throttle operation to the control unit. When these contacts close, injection duration increases. Another set of contacts indicate closed throttle operation, but these are not used.

Cold Start System

The cold start system consists of:

a. Auxiliary air regulator
b. Cold start valve
c. Thermo-time switch

The auxiliary air regulator bypasses air around the throttle valve when the engine is cold. When the ignition switch is turned on, a heating element warms a bimetallic strip in the regulator. See **Figure 11**. As the strip warms, the rotary valve in the regulator closes off the air passage.

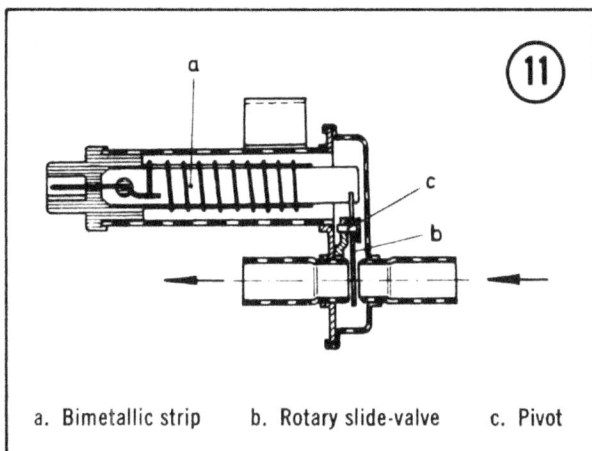

a. Bimetallic strip   b. Rotary slide-valve   c. Pivot

When engine temperature is above 50°F, but not fully warmed, the intake air and cylinder head temperature sensors cause the control unit to inject enough extra fuel. However, for colder engine temperatures, a cold start valve provides additional fuel to the engine. A thermo-time switch turns on the valve for about 11 seconds after you turn the ignition switch on. The control unit does not control the cold start valve. The cold start valve injects fuel into the intake air distributor.

SERVICE PRECAUTIONS

The same precautions which apply to carburetor fuel systems apply to fuel injected systems, only more so. Before suspecting any trouble in the fuel system, thoroughly check out the ignition system, including spark plugs. Whenever disconnecting any fuel lines, clean away all traces of dirt from the end of the line before disconnecting it. When the line is reconnected, examine it for dirt. Even very small dust particles can jam the injectors.

There are a few more precautions which should be observed when working on the fuel injected engine. Never run the engine with the battery disconnected. And do not use a battery charger to start the car when the battery is dead. Furthermore, if you want to charge the dead battery, disconnect it first. If these precautions are ignored, the voltage to the control unit can rise high enough to cause expensive damage.

AIR CLEANER

Removal/Installation

1. Disconnect all small hoses from air cleaner. The number of hoses varies with year. Mark them permanently so they may be removed and reconnected easily.
2. Open clamp securing intake boot to air cleaner. Pull boot off air cleaner.
3. Loosen clamp securing rubber boot to intake air distributor. Pull boot off air distributor.
4. Unscrew wing nut on top of air cleaner.
5. Lift air cleaner off.

  NOTE: *1970-1972 air cleaner contains oil. Do not tip or oil will spill.*

6. Clean the air cleaner if necessary. See Chapter Two.
7. Installation is the reverse of these steps.

ACCELERATOR CABLE REPLACEMENT

The accelerator cable connects the accelerator, through the frame tunnel and front engine cover plate, to the throttle valve in the intake air distributor.

1. Loosen clamp bolt on throttle lever and disconnect cable.
2. Fold accelerator cable forward. Unhook cable from lever and pull the cable out through the front.
3. Ensure that the plastic tubing and rubber boot are securely in place and that the tubing is routed alongside the transaxle.
4. Grease the cable with universal grease and install it through guide tube in frame tunnel. The cable must lay straight with no kinks.
5. Insert cable end into throttle link.
6. Have an assistant fully depress the accelerator pedal. Open throttle valve until there is about 0.04" (1mm) clearance between throttle lever and stop. Tighten cable clamp screw.

CONTROL UNIT

The control unit is a complex electronic device requiring very specialized knowledge and equipment to check and repair. At the present time, no U.S. dealers are equipped to service these units. Instead, an exchange is made and the defective unit returned to Germany.

Removal/Installation

The control unit is located in the engine compartment behind the battery.

1. Remove 2 Allen screws on bracket and loosen slotted screw. See **Figure 12**.

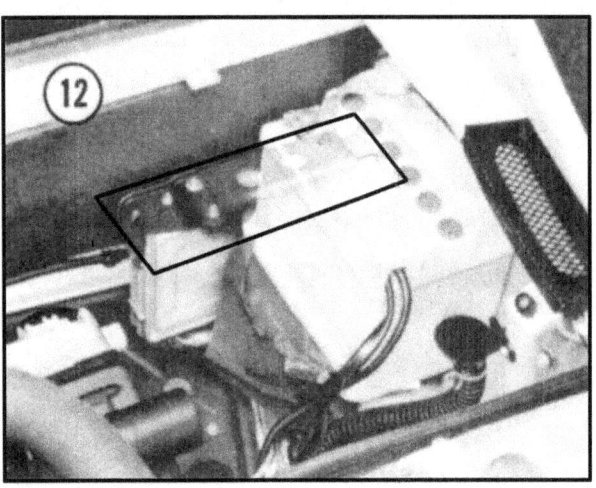

2. Pull control unit to left with bracket and lift out.

3. Open cable clamp and remove end cover. See **Figure 13**.

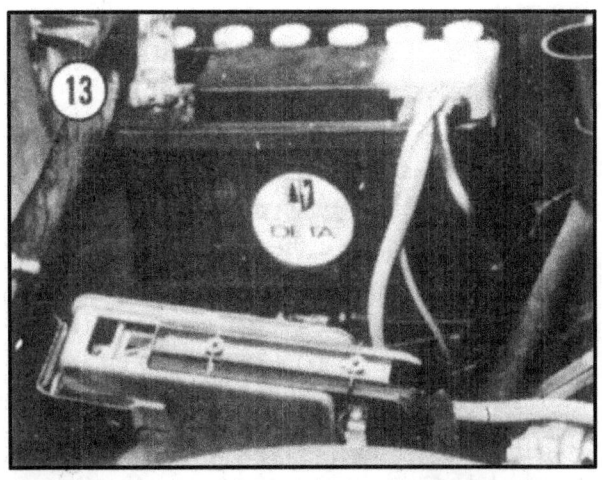

4. Disconnect multiple plug from control unit. Use a wire hook. See **Figures 14 and 15**.

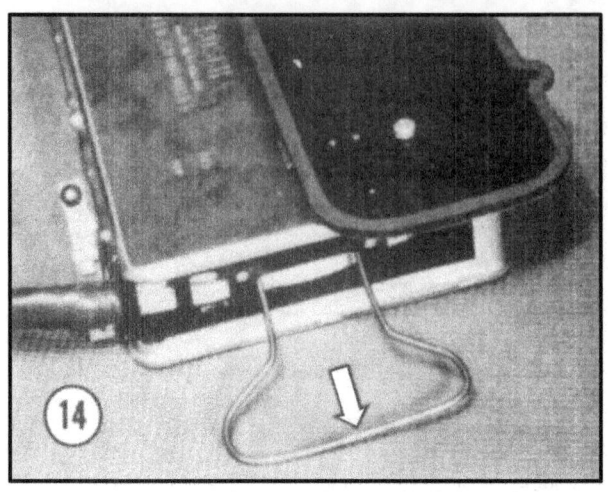

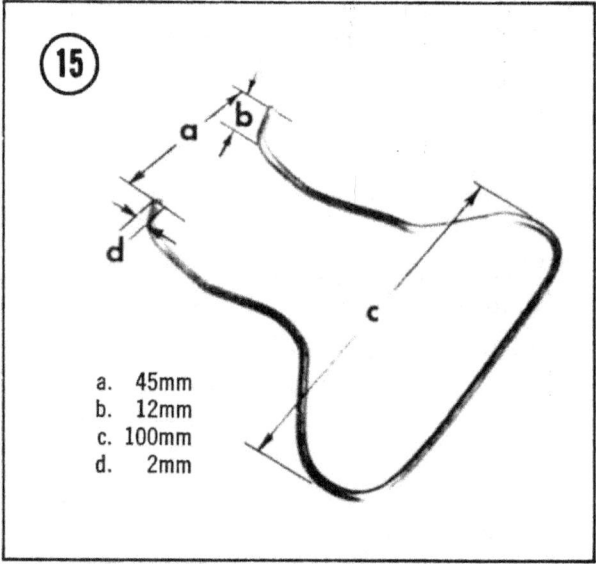

a. 45mm
b. 12mm
c. 100mm
d. 2mm

5. Installation is the reverse of these steps. Always clean contacts of multiple plug and socket with contact cleaner before reconnecting.

RELAYS

Relays for the fuel injection are located on the relay plate at the left side of the engine compartment. See **Figure 16**.

Testing (MPC Injection)

Failure of either relay will prevent starting the engine. When relays are suspected, always check the main power relay first. To do this:

1. Remove screws and retaining clips securing relay plate and lift it up.

2. Turn ignition switch on.

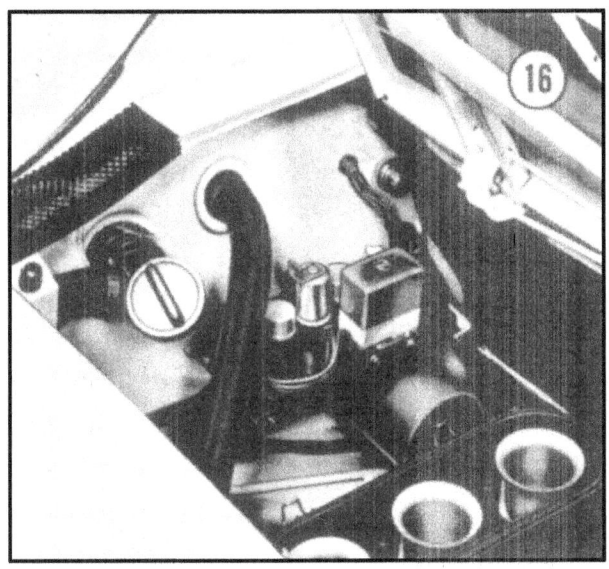

3. Measure voltage at pin 87. See **Figure 17**. The voltage should be 12 volts.

4. If pin 87 measures 12 volts, the main power relay is good, but the fuel pump relay may be at fault.

5. If pin 87 does not measure 12 volts, check pin 86. If 12 volts are present at pin 86, the relay is defective; replace it. If 12 volts are not present at pin 86, check wiring back to ignition switch.

If the main power relay is good, check the fuel pump relay. To do this:

1. Turn ignition switch on to operate main power relay.

2. Measure pin 87 on fuel pump relay. See Figure 17. If it measures 12 volts, the relay is good; the fuel pump may be defective.

3. If pin 87 measures 0 volts, check pins 86 and 30. Both should be 12 volts. If they are, replace the relay. If either pin is 0 volts, check wiring to that pin.

Testing (AFC Injection)

The best way to test the AFC relay is direct substitution. If you purchase a new relay to test the system, make sure the dealer will let you return the new relay if the old one proves to be good. Many dealers will not accept returns of electrical components.

The following procedure is more tedious, but works well. You will need 3 small jumper wires, a 12 volt battery, and an ohmmeter or other continuity tester.

1. Remove relay from system.

2. Measure with tester between terminals 88d and 88y, then between 88b and 88z. Both measurements must shown an open-circuit.

3. With jumper wires, connect terminal 85 to —12 volts and terminal 86c and 86 to +12 volts. See **Figure 18**.

4. With battery connected, measure with tester between terminals 88d and 88y, then between 88b and 88z. Both measurements must show a short-circuit now.

5. If relay fails Step 2 or 4, replace it.

Relay Replacement

1. Disconnect battery ground cable.

2. Pull defective relay out of socket in relay plate.

3. Plug new relay in.

4. Reconnect battery and check operation of fuel system.

FUEL PUMP

The fuel pump is located on the right-hand side in front of the engine. It is accessible only from underneath.

Testing (MPC Injection)

The fuel pump only operates for about 1½ seconds when the ignition switch is turned on. To operate the fuel pump longer for testing, disconnect T1/19 in the wire to pin 85 of the fuel pump relay. See Figure 2 or 3. Ground the wire to pin 85. The pump should run as long as the wire is grounded.

If the pump doesn't run at all, check electrical connectors to pump. Check voltage on pin 87 when 85 is grounded. If it measures 12 volts, the pump is bad; if it measures 0 volts, the pump relay is bad. If fuel pump runs, check its delivery capacity as described below.

Testing (AFC Injection)

The fuel pump operates when the intake air sensor flap opens. To operate the fuel pump for testing, connect a jumper wire from terminal 88d

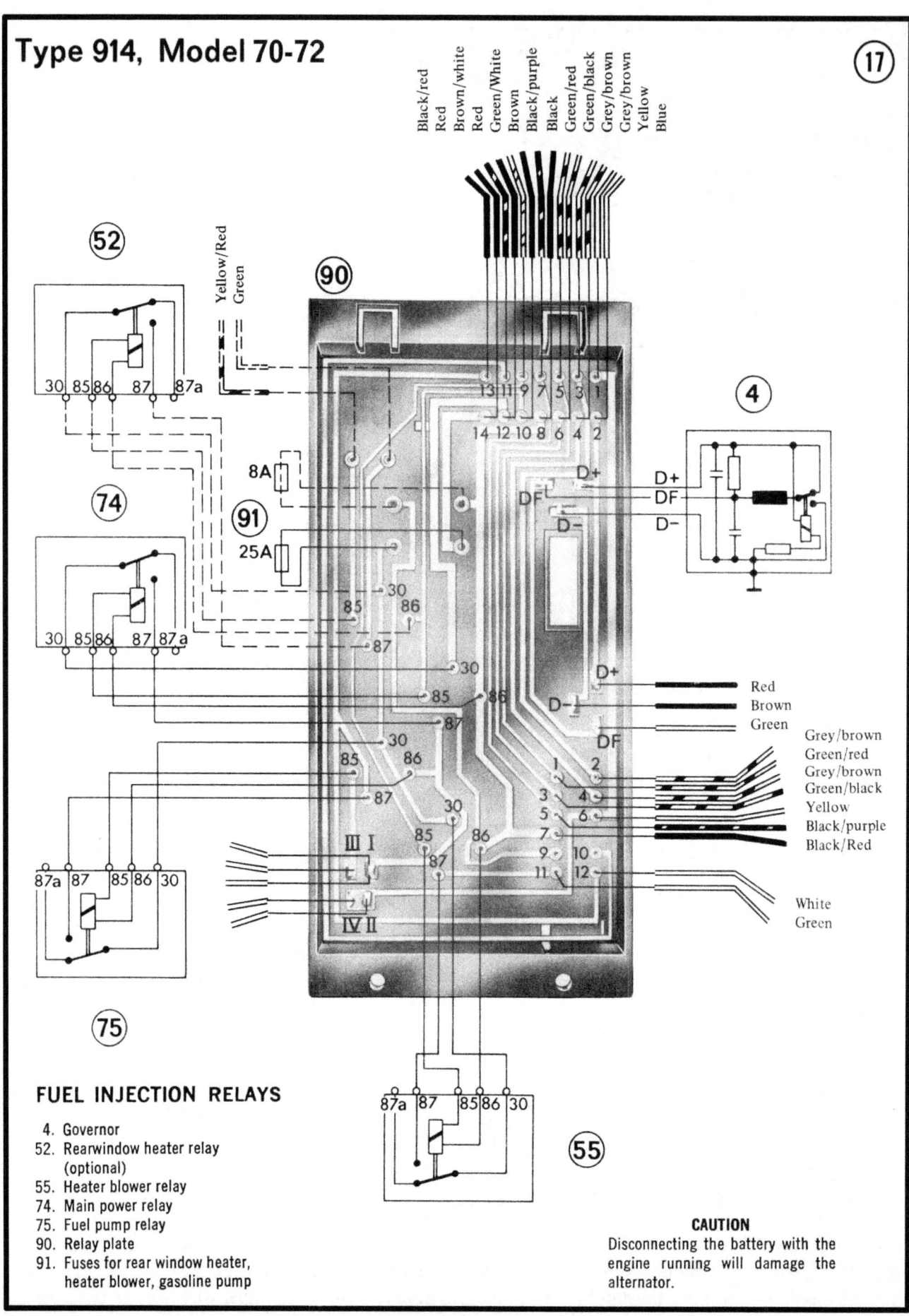

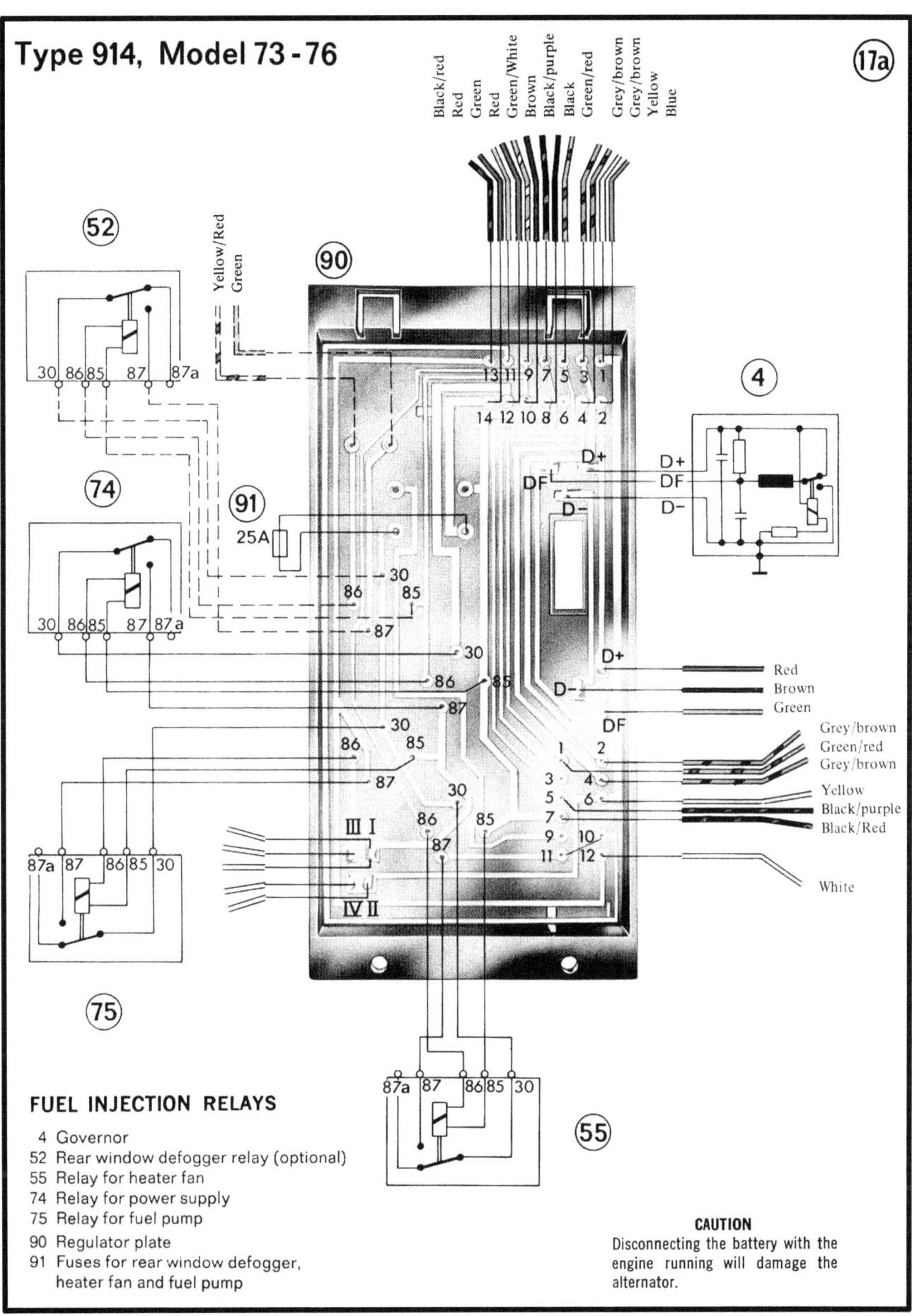

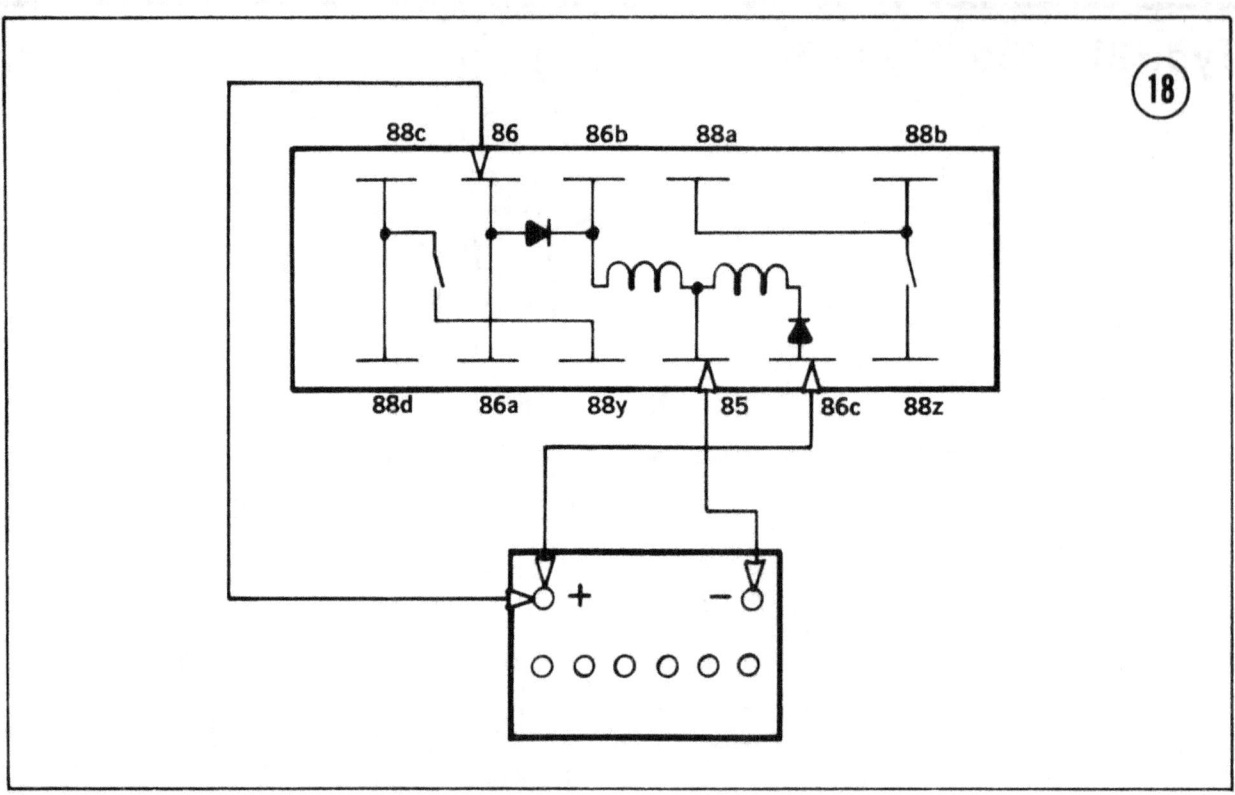

to 88y of the relay. See Figure 10. The pump will run as long as the jumper is in place.

If the pump does not run at all, check the fuse between terminals 88y and 88z of the relay. If the fuse is good, measure from terminal 88d to ground (jumper connected). Terminal 88d should measure 12 volts. If not, the pump is defective and must be replaced.

If the pump runs, yet a fuel delivery problem still exists, check the fuel pump delivery capacity as described below.

Fuel Pump Capacity

1. Disconnect fuel line between right fuel distributor pipe and fuel pressure regulator at the distributor pipe.

2. Connect a long hose to the right fuel distributor pipe. Put the other end in a gallon container.

3. Force the pump to run as described above.

4. Let the pump run for exactly 30 seconds. The container should contain 1½ quarts or more of fuel.

5. If the pump delivers less than specified, the trouble could be a restricted tank vent, restricted fuel filter or line, or a defective fuel pump.

Removal/Installation

1. Clamp all fuel lines to the pump.

2. Disconnect electrical wires to pump.

3. Cut off crimped hose clamp(s) on fuel lines. Some models have just one clamp, other have 3.

4. Remove nuts securing pump to frame and remove pump.

5. Installation is the reverse of these steps. Use new hose clamps at fuel pump.

FUEL PRESSURE REGULATOR

Testing and Adjustment
(MPC Injection)

This is not a routine maintenance procedure. Do not adjust unless trouble is suspected or a new regulator has been installed.

1. Remove air cleaner.

2. Remove screw plug in right fuel distribution pipe. Connect fuel pressure gauge capable of measuring about 40 psi. See **Figure 19**.

3. Start engine. Check for leaks around pressure gauge connection.

4. Fuel pressure should be 28 psi (2.0 kg/cm^2). If the pressure is not correct, loosen the locknut

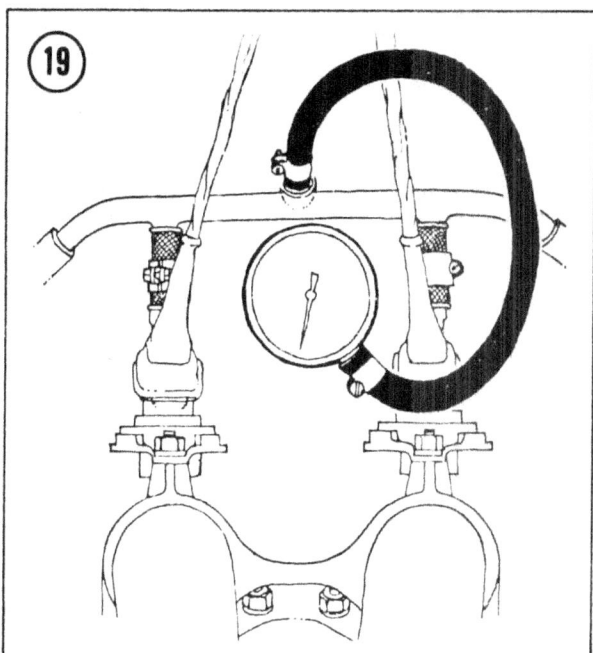

on the regulator (see **Figure 20**) and adjust pressure. Retighten the locknut.

> NOTE: *In hot climates, it is permissible to increase fuel pressure to 31 psi. This helps prevent vapor lock. Consult your dealer before doing this, however; there may be other troubles that should be repaired.*

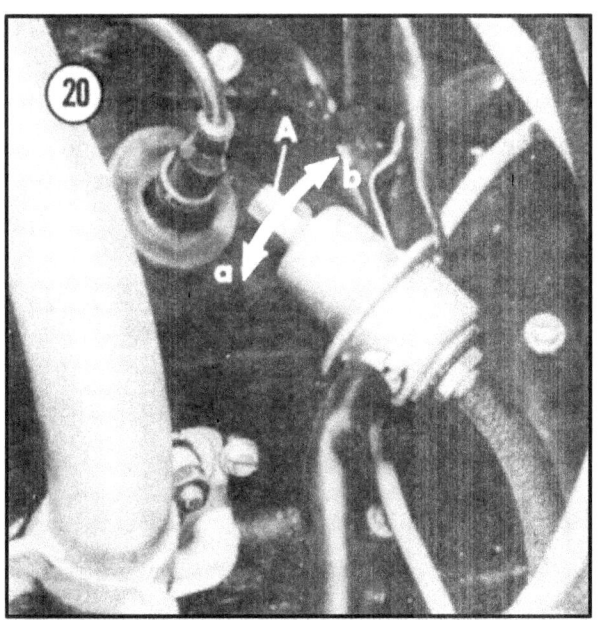

A. Adjusting screw
 a. more
 b. less pressure

5. If fuel pressure cannot be adjusted to 28 psi, replace pressure regulator as described below.

Removal/Installation (MPC Injection)

Fuel pressure regulator is located near spark plug No. 1. See Figure 20.

1. Clamp fuel line on front of pressure regulator.
2. Remove air cleaner as described previously.
3. Disconnect fuel line from regulator.
4. Remove the bolt securing the regulator to cover plate.
5. Remove regulator and disconnect other fuel line from it.
6. Installation is the reverse of these steps.

> NOTE: *1972 and 1973 vehicles destined for California have a special fuel regulator. This unit must not be interchanged with other regulators.*

Testing (AFC Injection)

1. Remove screw plug in right fuel distribution pipe. See **Figure 21**.

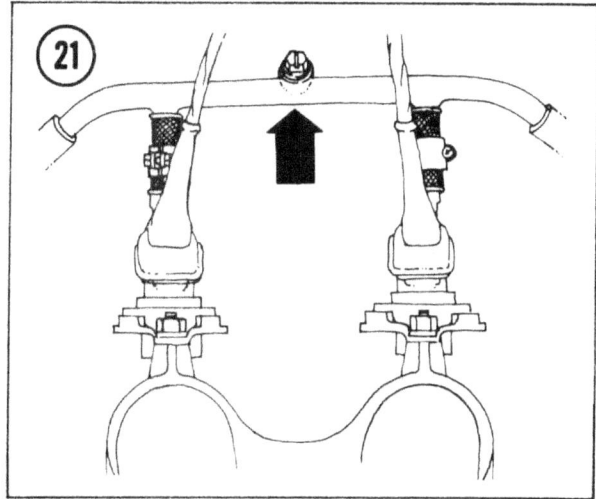

2. Connect fuel pressure gauge to a distribution pipe capable of measuring about 40 psi.
3. Start engine. Check for leaks around pressure gauge connection. Fuel pressure should be about 28 psi (2.0 kg/cm^2).
4. Disconnect vacuum hose from pressure regulator. Fuel pressure should rise to about 35 psi (2.5 kg/cm^2).
5. Reconnect vacuum hose. Fuel pressure should drop to 28 psi again.

> NOTE: *Fuel pressure is not adjustable. If it is incorrect, replace the pressure regulator.*

Removal/Installation (AFC Injection)

The fuel pressure regulator is located on the right side of the engine compartment near the battery. See **Figure 22**.

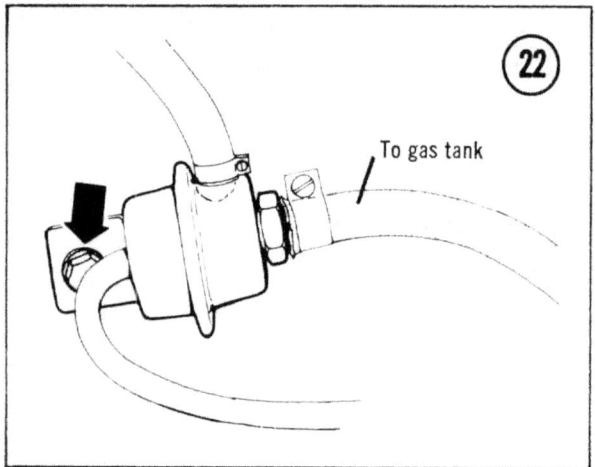

1. Clamp fuel line at rear of regulator leading to fuel tank.
2. Disconnect clamped line from regulator.
3. Remove bolt securing regulator to body.
4. Remove regulator and disconnect other fuel line and vacuum line from regulator.
5. Installation is the reverse of these steps.

NOTE: *When replacing the fuel pressure regulator, make sure the new one has the same part number as the old one.*

INJECTORS

Testing

This test assumes that the engine misfires or runs erratically and the ignition system has been checked out.

1. Disconnect one spark plug wire at a time while the engine is running. When the spark plug wire of a faulty cylinder is removed, the engine misfiring will not increase. Removing the plug wire from a good cylinder will increase roughness and misfiring.
2a. On MPC injected engines, to determine if the injector or the control unit is at fault, remove the suspected injector and interchange it with the adjacent injector. Be extremely careful not to get any dirt in the system.
2b. On AFC injected engines, to determine if the injector or the control unit is at fault, simply interchange the electrical plugs between adjacent injectors. If the trouble is in the same cylinder, the injector in the bad cylinder is at fault.

NOTE: *The electrical cables on AFC injected engines can be interchanged without affecting engine performance, because all injectors operate at the same time.*

3. Test the 2 injectors as in Step 1. If the trouble has moved to the adjacent cylinder, the suspected injector is at fault. If the trouble is in the same cylinder, the control unit is at fault.

Sometimes a mixture trouble is indicated in a single cylinder by spark plug appearance. The following procedure provides a quick check of injector performance.

1. Disconnect the high voltage output of the ignition coil so the engine will not start when the key is engaged.
2. Remove the suspected injector, following Steps 1-3 of removal procedure.
3. Reconnect electrical cable to injector.
4. Hold a small container under injector to collect fuel.
5. Turn the ignition switch on, but do not crank the engine.
6. When fuel pressure builds up, the end of the injector may be wet with fuel but should not leak more than 2 drops per minute. A larger leak may cause an overly rich mixture to one cylinder.
7. Crank the engine and note if the injector squirts fuel. If it works at all, it is probably good. To be certain, reinstall it in a different cylinder and examine the plugs again after driving several miles.

Removal/Installation

Refer to **Figure 23** for the following procedure. Injectors for the 914 and 914S are *not interchangeable*.

1. Disconnect electrical cable from injector.
2. Remove nut securing injector retainer.
3. Carefully lift out injector with all mounting hardware. Ensure that inner seal is on end of

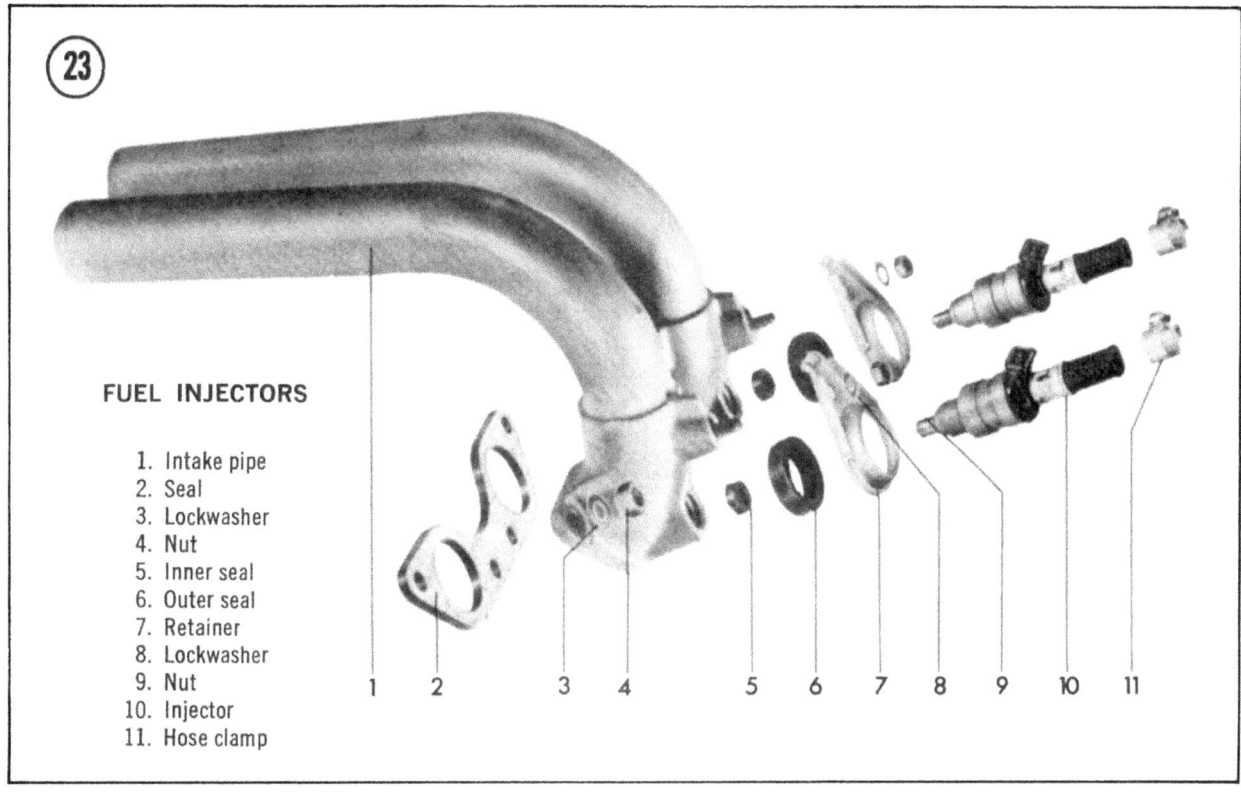

FUEL INJECTORS

1. Intake pipe
2. Seal
3. Lockwasher
4. Nut
5. Inner seal
6. Outer seal
7. Retainer
8. Lockwasher
9. Nut
10. Injector
11. Hose clamp

injector. See **Figure 23**. If not, carefully pry seal out of intake manifold seat.

> **CAUTION**
> *Keep the ends of the injectors clean. Even very small dust particles can jam injectors.*

4. Pull retainer plate and rubber bushing off injector.

5. Loosen hose clamp on injector and pull injector off.

6. Installation is the reverse of these steps. Use new seals, and torque the nuts to 4.3 foot-pounds (0.6 mkg).

7. Start engine, check for leaks, and check engine performance.

THROTTLE VALVE SWITCH

The throttle valve is located on the side of the intake air distributor. See **Figure 24**.

Testing (MPC Injection)

Because of the complex interaction among components in the fuel injection system, it is difficult to trace a throttle valve switch malfunction with a single test. If the following test is

performed satisfactorily, the throttle valve must be working; however, if the test fails, there are many other potential causes outside of a defective throttle valve switch.

1. Switch on the ignition switch but do not start the engine.

2. Open and close the throttle valve slowly. Listen for small clicks from the injectors indicating extra fuel for acceleration being supplied.

3. Start the engine and let it warm up.

4. Temporarily disconnect the hose between the

intake duct and the side of the air regulator. There are 2 hoses here; one comes out of the top of the regulator and one comes out the side. Be sure to get the right one.

5. The engine speed should slowly fluctuate between approximately 900 rpm and 1,700 rpm. This indicates the throttle valve contacts and that portion of the control unit which meters fuel during deceleration are working properly.

Testing (AFC Injection)

The contacts in the throttle valve switch control full throttle enrichment. To test the switch, disconnect the electrical plug, and connect an ohmmeter or other continuity tester between pins 3 and 18 of the switch. With the throttle valve closed, the circuit should measure "open" or infinity. With the valve fully open, the circuit must be a short-circuit or zero.

Removal/Installation

1. Remove air cleaner as described earlier.
2. Disconnect electrical cable to switch.
3. Disconnect throttle valve return spring.
4. Remove 2 screws securing intake air horn and remove with switch. See **Figure 25**.

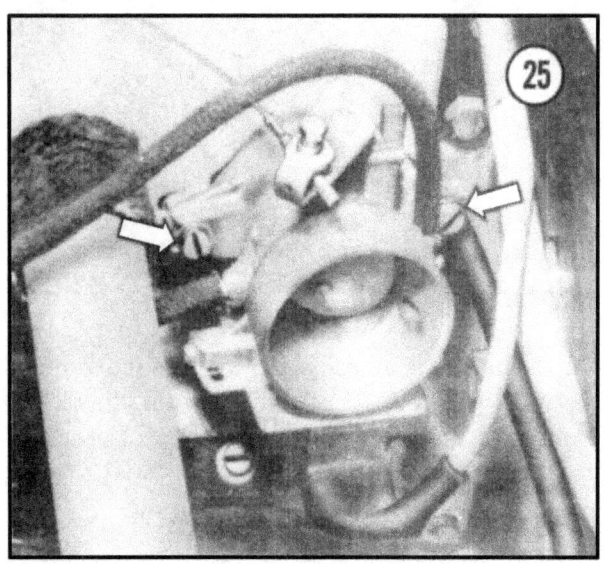

5. Remove switch from intake air horn.
6. Installation is the reverse of this procedure.
7. Adjust switch position before installing intake air horn.

Adjustment (MPC Only)

NOTE: *Only the MPC injected version is adjustable.*

1. Loosen mounting screws on throttle valve switch.
2. Look inside intake air distributor and ensure that the throttle valve is completely closed.
3. Connect an ohmmeter (set to R x 10) across the contacts 14 and 17 on the switch plug. See **Figures 26 and 27**.

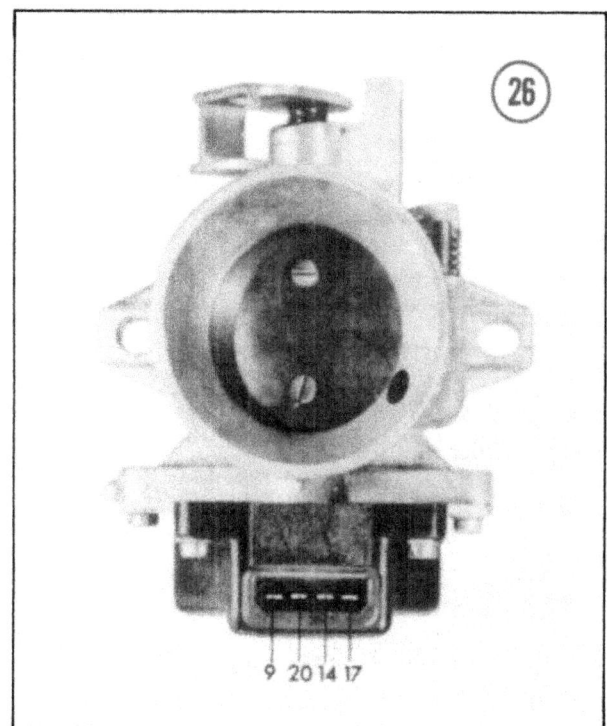

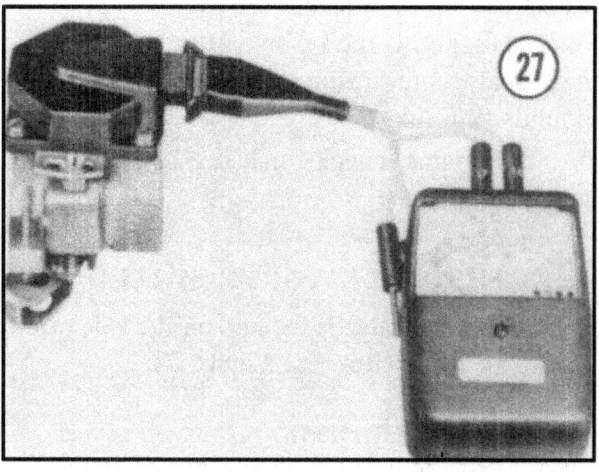

4. Rotate the switch slowly in the slotted mounting holes until the switch just closes, i.e., the ohmmeter reads zero.

5. Turn the switch counterclockwise one major graduation (2°). See **Figure 28**. Tighten mounting screws.

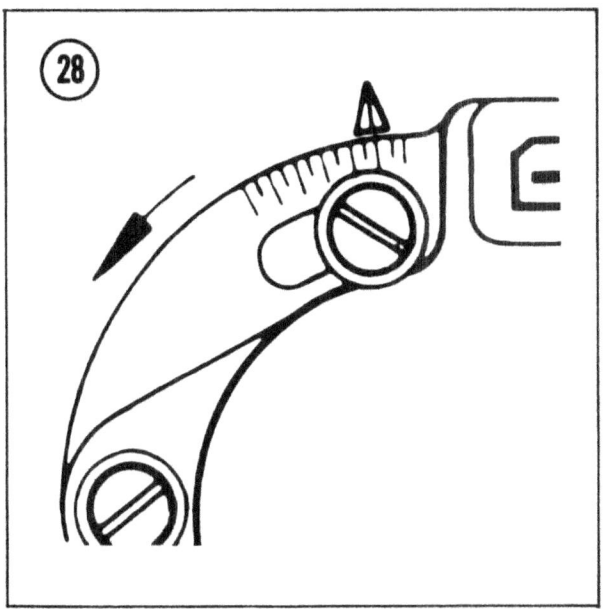

AUXILIARY AIR REGULATOR

The auxiliary air regulator is located at the left front edge of the intake air distributor. See **Figure 29**.

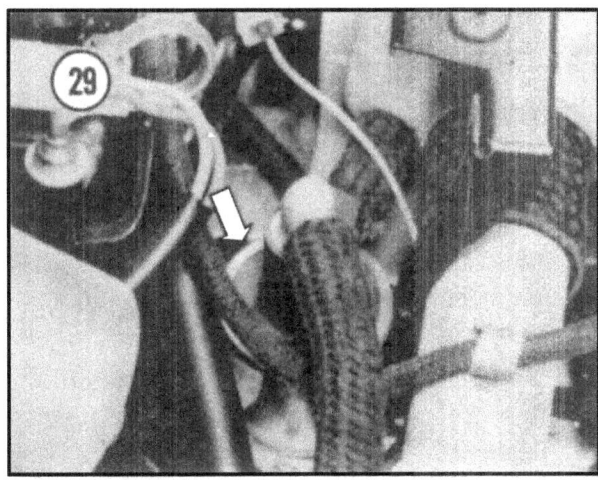

Testing

1. Disconnect the electrical plug from the regulator.
2. Measure resistance across the terminals on the regulator. Resistance should be approximately 30 ohms. If resistance differs considerably, replace the regulator.
3. Reconnect the electrical plug.

NOTE: *The following tests must be performed on a cold engine.*

4. Disconnect hoses from the intake air distributor and throttle valve housing. Blow through one of the hoses. With a cold engine, the air passage should be unrestricted. If not, replace the regulator.
5. Switch on the ignition without starting the engine.
6. Continue to blow through the regulator. As the regulator heats up electrically, the passage will become more and more restricted and finally close. If not, replace the regulator.

Removal/Installation

1. Disconnect air hoses and electrical cable from air regulator.
2. Remove 2 mounting bolts.
3. Lift regulator out.
4. Installation is the reverse of these steps.

PRESSURE SENSOR (MPC ONLY)

The pressure sensor is located on the right side of the engine compartment. See **Figure 30**.

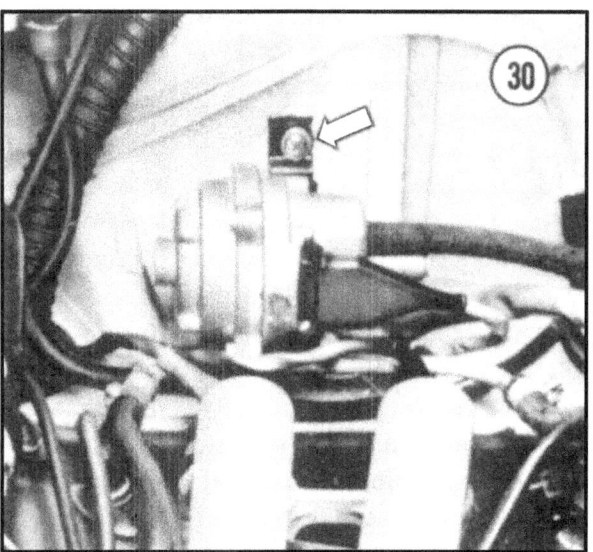

Removal/Installation

1. Disconnect electrical cable from sensor. Disconnect ground wire on 1972 sensors.
2. Loosen mounting screws.
3. Slide sensor toward the front and remove it.
4. Disconnect vacuum hose.

5. Installation is the reverse of these steps.

   NOTE: *Several different sensors are used for VW and Porsche systems. They are NOT interchangeable even though they look similar.*

HEAD TEMPERATURE SENSOR

The head temperature sensor is located on top and is accessible from the engine compartment through an access hole. Use a long 13mm socket. See **Figure 31**.

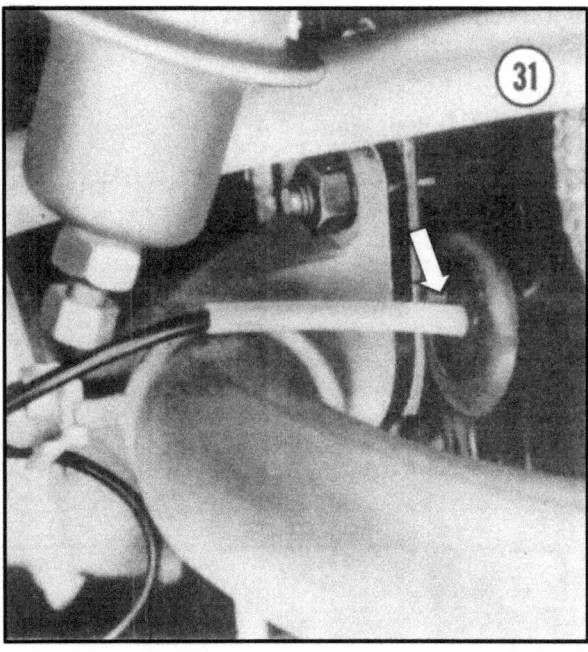

Testing

An open sensor prevents the engine from running. To test the sensor, turn the ignition switch on and connect a voltmeter across it. A 12 volt reading indicates an open sensor which must be replaced. A good sensor measures 0.2-0.4 volts with the engine idling and fully warmed up.

The sensor may also be tested with an ohmmeter. It should measure 1,500-2,500 ohms when cold and less than 300 ohms when hot; disconnect wire to measure.

Removal/Installation

1. Disconnect cable connector on temperature sensor cable. See Figure 31.
2. Unscrew temperature sensor.
3. Installation is the reverse of these steps. Do not overtighten sensor.

INTAKE AIR TEMPERATURE SENSOR

The MPC intake air temperature sensor is mounted on the right side of the intake air distributor. See **Figure 32**. The AFC sensor is part of the intake air sensor; it cannot be replaced separately.

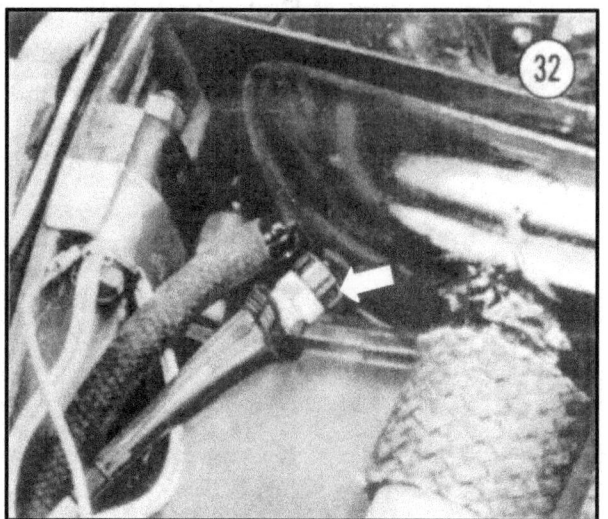

Removal/Installation (MPC Only)

1. Disconnect electrical cable on sensor.
2. Unscrew sensor from intake air distributor.
3. Installation is the reverse of these steps.

DISTRIBUTOR TRIGGER CONTACTS (MPC ONLY)

Testing

Faulty triggering contacts can cause misfiring or complete failure to start. This procedure will verify that the contacts work.

1. Disconnect the high voltage output of the ignition coil so the engine won't start when cranked.
2. Disconnect the electrical plug to the distributor triggering contacts.
3. Connect an ohmmeter between the center terminal on the distributor contact plug and one of the other terminals.
4. Crank the engine over. The ohmmeter will fluctuate between zero and infinity, indicating the contact is opening and closing properly.
5. Connect the ohmmeter between the center terminal and the other end terminal.

6. Crank the engine and look for the same indications as in Step 4.

7. If either contact fails, replace the contacts. The procedure for changing is included in the *Electrical System* chapter.

INTAKE MANIFOLDS

Removal

1. Remove air cleaner.

2. Remove injectors but leave them on their mounting plates.

3. Remove 4 nuts and washers securing manifold and remove it from hoses. See **Figure 33**.

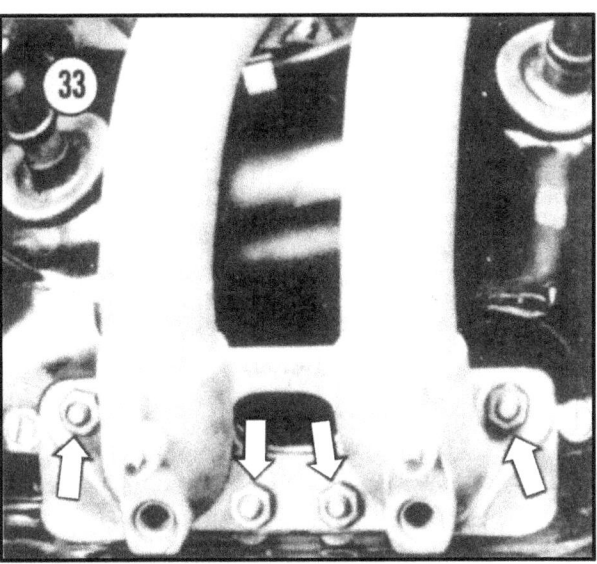

Installation

1. Install manifold with new gasket.

2. Install injectors.

3. Install air cleaner.

INTAKE AIR DISTRIBUTOR

Removal/Installation

1. Remove air cleaner.

2. Make a special tool with dimensions shown in **Figure 34**.

3. Use special tool to slide 4 hoses off intake air distributor and onto intake manifold. See **Figure 35**.

4. Remove throttle valve switch and air horn.

5. Disconnect accelerator cable.

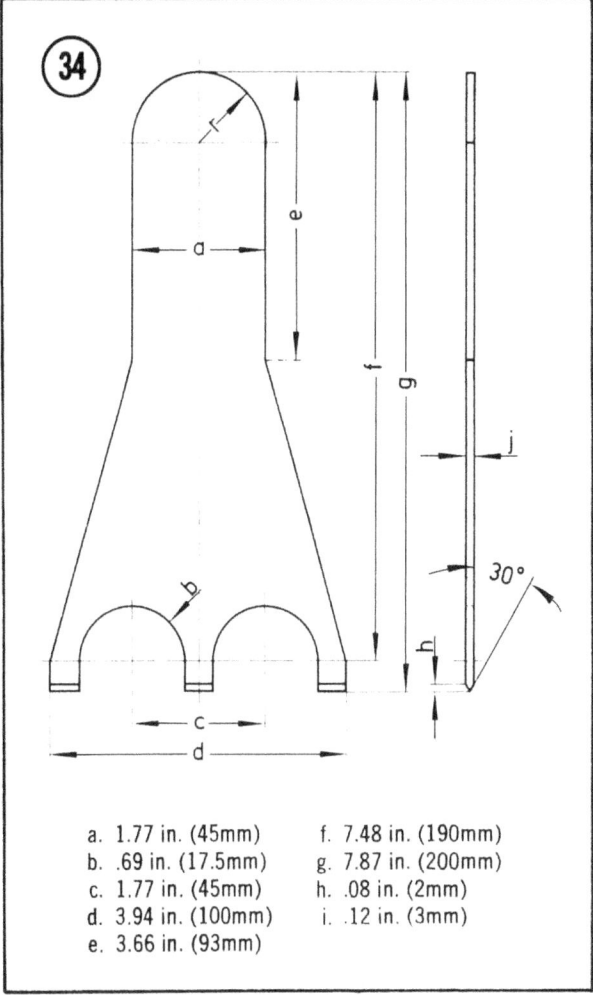

a. 1.77 in. (45mm)
b. .69 in. (17.5mm)
c. 1.77 in. (45mm)
d. 3.94 in. (100mm)
e. 3.66 in. (93mm)
f. 7.48 in. (190mm)
g. 7.87 in. (200mm)
h. .08 in. (2mm)
i. .12 in. (3mm)

6. Disconnect vacuum hose between intake air distributor and ignition distributor.

7. Disconnect wires to cold start valve and temperature sensor.

8. Disconnect air hose to auxiliary air regulator.

175

9. Loosen bolts securing intake air distributor and remove it.

10. Installation is the reverse of these steps.

COLD START SYSTEM

The cold start system consists of a cold start valve, thermostat, and fuel line.

Cold Start Valve Removal/Installation

1. Disconnect fuel line from valve.

2. Disconnect electrical wires from valve.

3. Remove screws attaching valve to intake air distributor.

4. Installation is the reverse of these steps.

Thermostat Removal/Installation

1. Disconnect wire from thermostat.

2. Unscrew from bracket with 24mm wrench. See **Figure 36**.

3. Installation is the reverse of these steps.

EXHAUST EMISSION CONTROL

Crankcase Ventilation

Two different ventilation systems are used. On 1970-1971 models, crankcase vapors enter the oil breather through an integral valve and are routed through a hose to the air cleaner.

Ventilation on later models is more sophisticated and thorough. See **Figure 37**. Fresh air from the air cleaner passes through hoses to the valve covers. This air circulates through the crankcase and is drawn out through the oil breather and introduced into the intake air distributor.

Fuel Cutoff (1970-1971)

In order to lean out the air/fuel mixture during coasting and reduce emissions, 1970-1971 models shut off the fuel supply. Special contacts in the throttle valve switch signal when the throttle valve is closed. This is explained in the *Basic Principles* section.

Air Injection (1972-1973)

Additional air is injected to lean the mixture during coasting rather than cutting off the fuel supply. **Figure 38** shows the system used on models equipped with a manual transaxle. When coasting, the throttle valve closes and a high depression (vacuum) exists in the intake air distributor. This vacuum operates a valve which opens and admits air from the air cleaner around the throttle valve to lean the mixture.

CO Adjustments (1972-1973)

Different control units are used in 1972 and 1973 models. These have an adjustable potentiometer to adjust carbon monoxide levels. See Chapter Two for adjustment procedure. No adjustment is possible on earlier models.

All 1974 and later models have an adjustment screw on the intake air sensor. The screw is sealed and should not be adjusted until all other systems affecting CO emissions are in perfect working order, yet the CO content is still above $2.5 \pm 0.5\%$.

> **CAUTION**
> *Do not attempt adjustment without a properly calibrated exhaust gas analyzer.*

FUEL EVAPORATIVE CONTROL SYSTEM

All 1970 and later Porsches sold in California are equipped with a fuel evaporative control system to prevent the release of fuel vapor into the atmosphere.

Refer to **Figure 39**. Fuel vapor from the fuel tank passes through the expansion tank to the

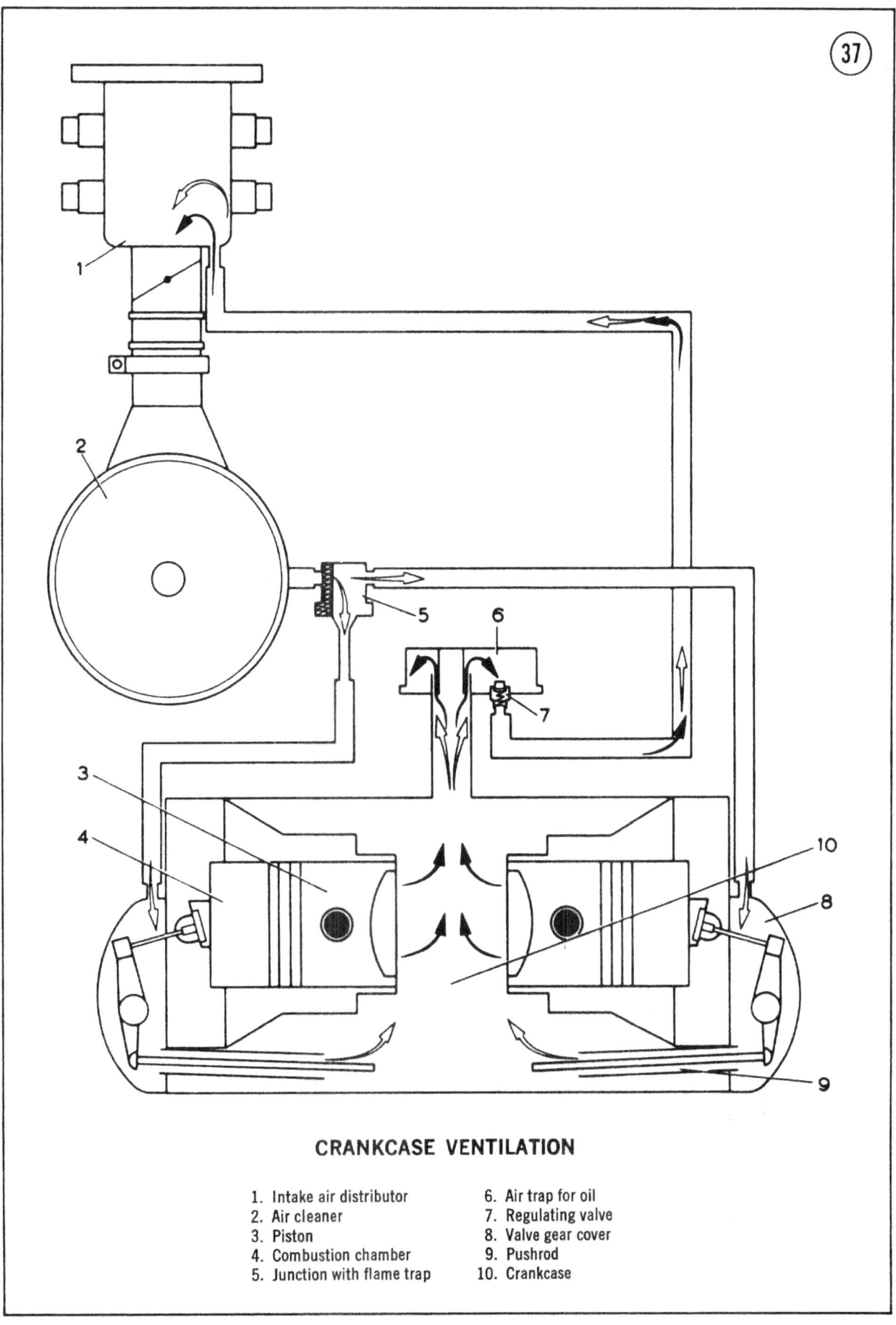

CRANKCASE VENTILATION

1. Intake air distributor
2. Air cleaner
3. Piston
4. Combustion chamber
5. Junction with flame trap
6. Air trap for oil
7. Regulating valve
8. Valve gear cover
9. Pushrod
10. Crankcase

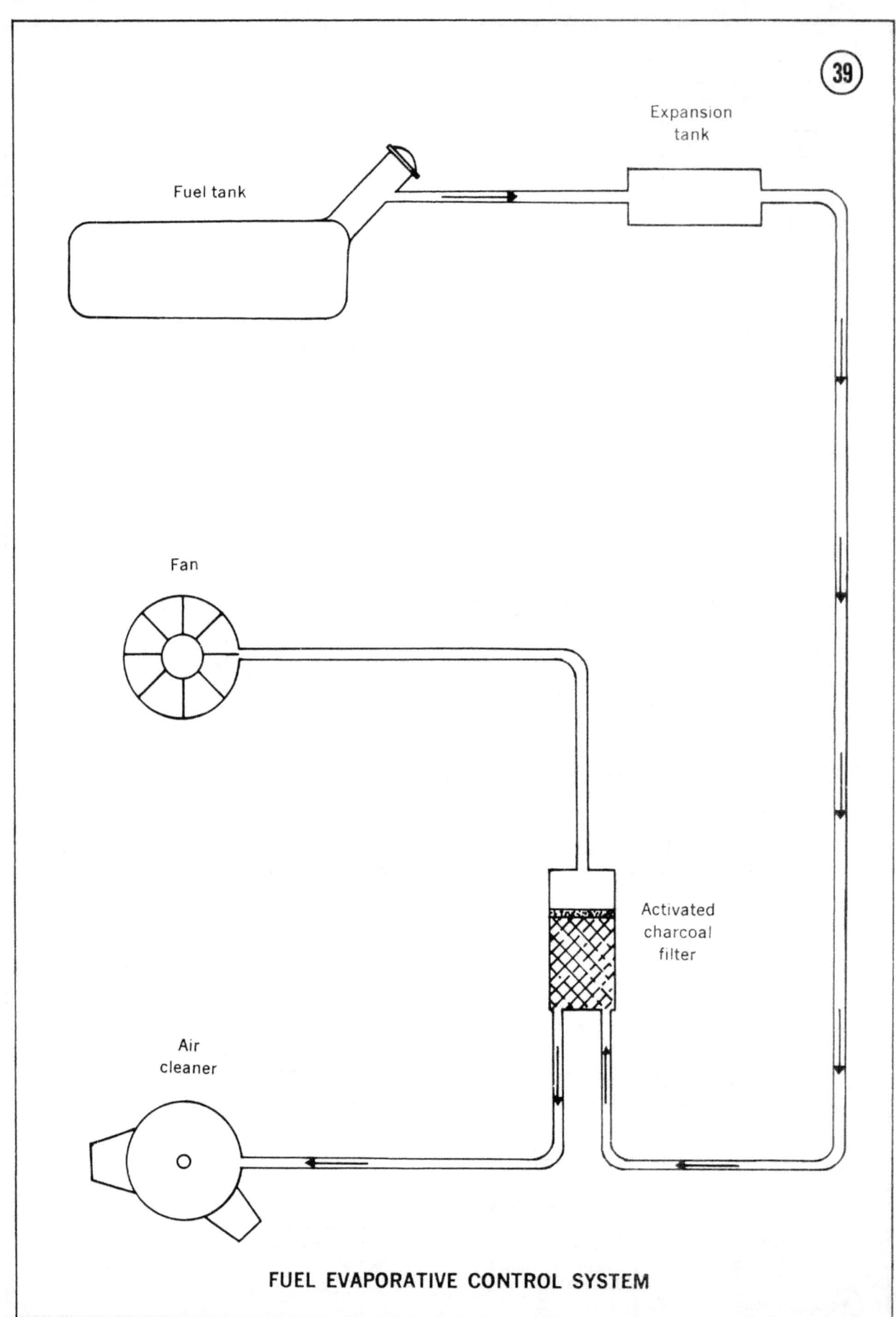

FUEL EVAPORATIVE CONTROL SYSTEM

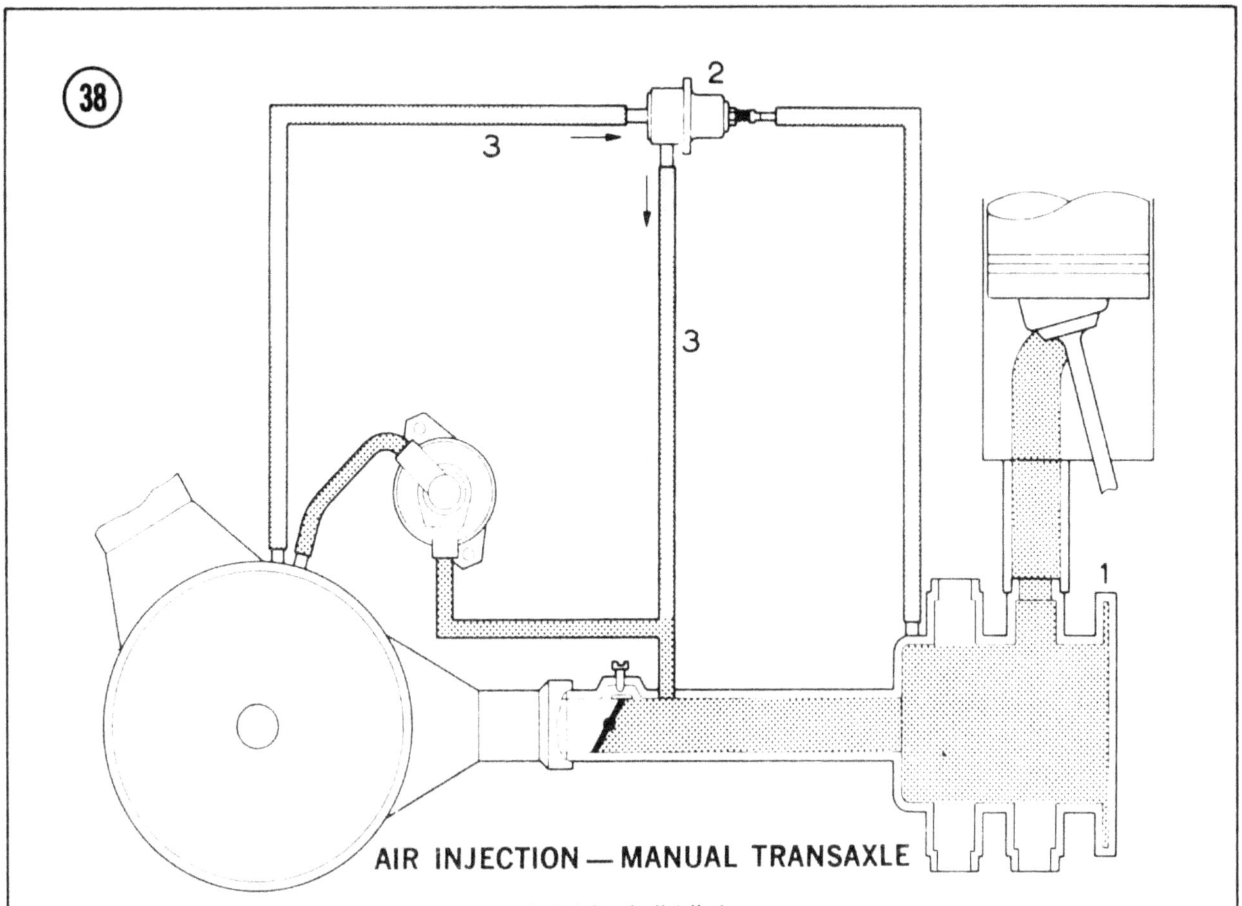

AIR INJECTION — MANUAL TRANSAXLE

1. Intake air distributor
2. Valve
3. Bypass line

activated charcoal filter. When the engine runs, cool air from the fan housing forces the fuel vapor into the air cleaner. Instead of being released into the atmosphere, the fuel vapor takes part in the normal combustion process.

There is no preventive maintenance other than checking the tightness and condition of the lines connecting parts of the system. The expansion tank and activated charcoal filter are located in the front luggage compartment. See **Figure 40**.

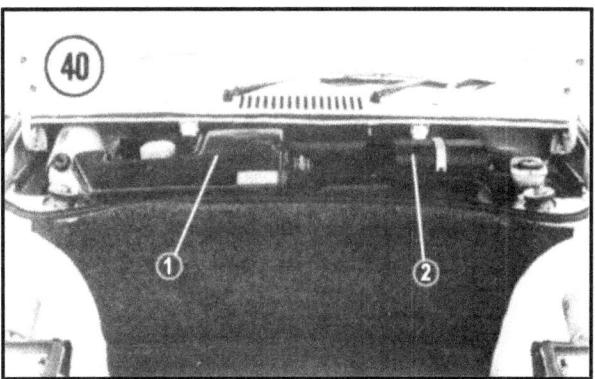

1. Expansion tank   2. Activated charcoal filter

NOTES

CHAPTER EIGHT

FUEL SYSTEM—914/6

A single Hardi electric fuel pump delivers fuel from the fuel tank to 2 triple-throat Weber carburetors. See **Figure 1**. This system is nearly identical to that used on the late 1966-1969 Porsche 911's. **Table 1** (end of chapter) provides specifications.

AIR CLEANER

All 914/6 models use a disposable type paper cartridge. Replacement is described in Chapter Two.

Removal/Installation

This procedure describes removal/installation of the entire air cleaner housing.

1. Disconnect preheater hose from air cleaner. See **Figure 2**.

2. Disconnect crankcase breather hose from back of air cleaner. See **Figure 3**. Clean flame arrestor as described in Chapter Two.

3. Unsnap 4 clips at each carburetor and lift air cleaner off.

4. Remove nuts securing air cleaner bases to carburetors. Lift bases off.

5. Installation is the reverse of these steps. Ensure that gaskets are in good condition.

WEBER CARBURETORS

Removal/Installation

1. Disconnect condensation hose from air cleaner. See **Figure 4**.

2. Unsnap air cleaner cover and remove air cleaner element.

3. Unsnap air cleaner ducts from top of carburetors.

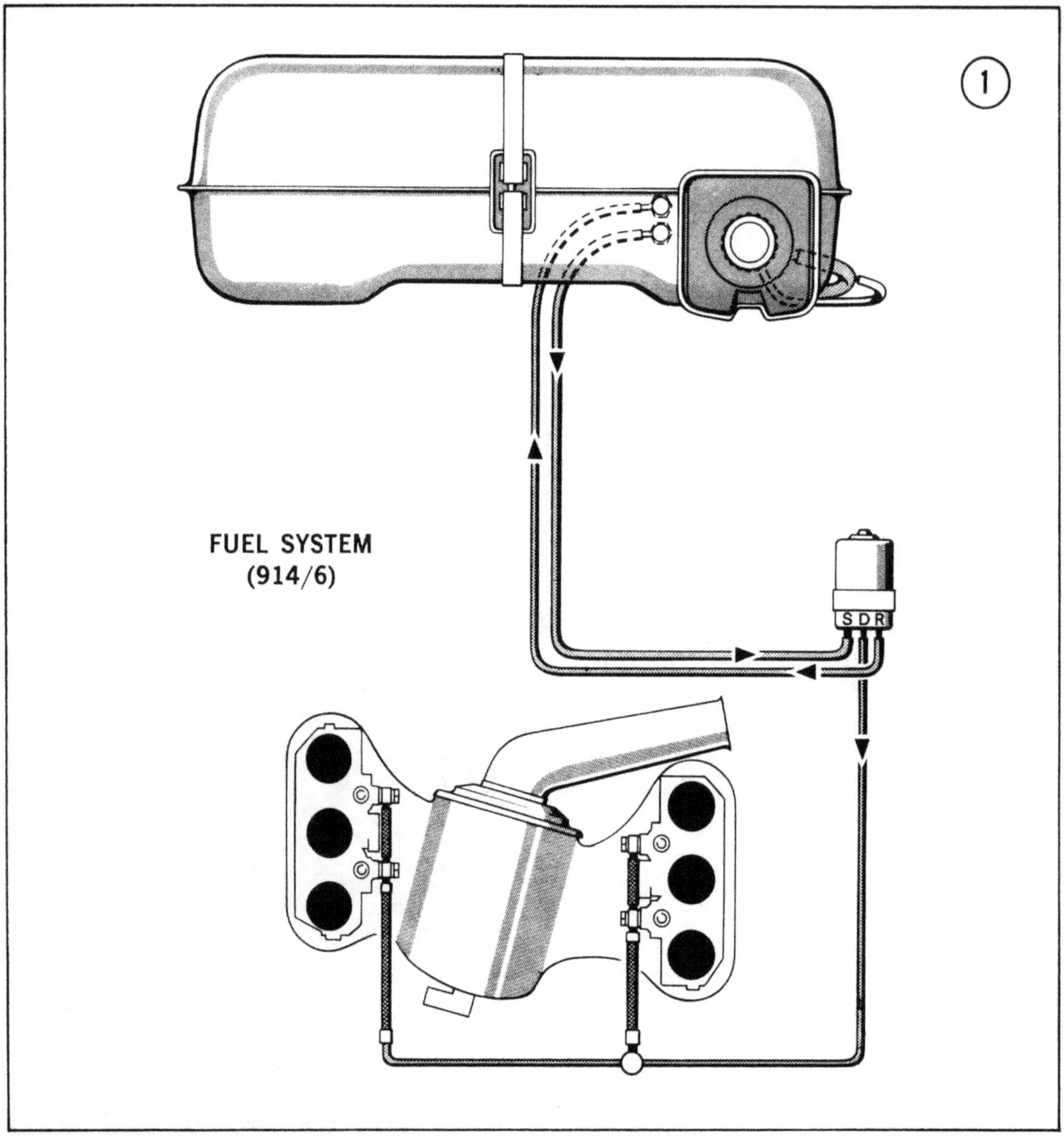

**FUEL SYSTEM
(914/6)**

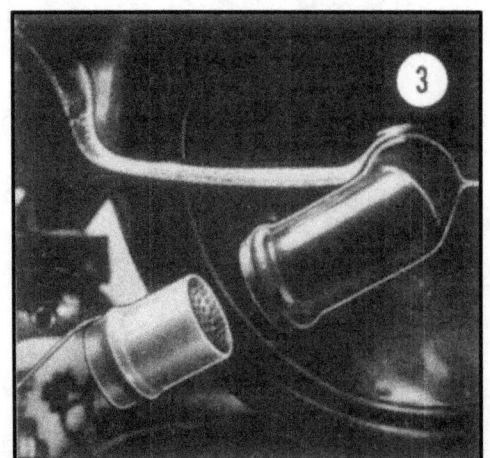

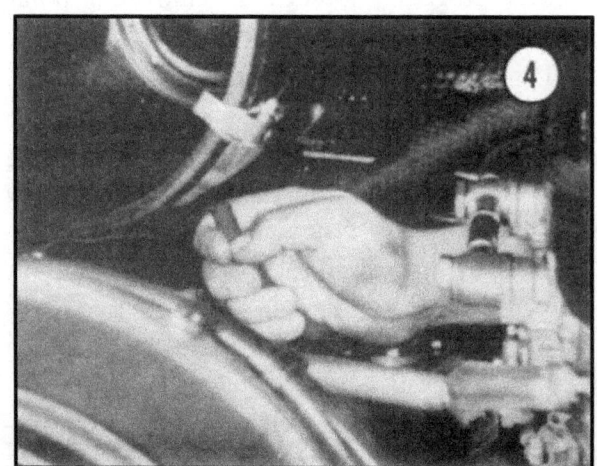

4. Disconnect fuel lines from carburetors.

5. Disconnect throttle linkage from carburetors. See **Figure 5**.

6. Remove the retaining nuts and lift the carburetor(s) off.

CAUTION
Do not let lockwashers or other loose parts fall into intake manifolds.

7. Cover intake manifolds (see **Figure 6**) to prevent entry of dirt and loose parts.

8. Installation is the reverse of these steps. Clean carburetor base and manifold surfaces and use new gaskets. Adjust idle speed.

Disassembly

Each Weber carburetor consists of 3 nearly identical throats. To aid reassembly, keep parts from the 3 throats in 3 separate containers. Keep parts common to all throats in a fourth container.

Refer to **Figure 7** for the following procedure.

1. Remove 10 nuts securing top of carburetor and lift top off. See **Figure 8**.

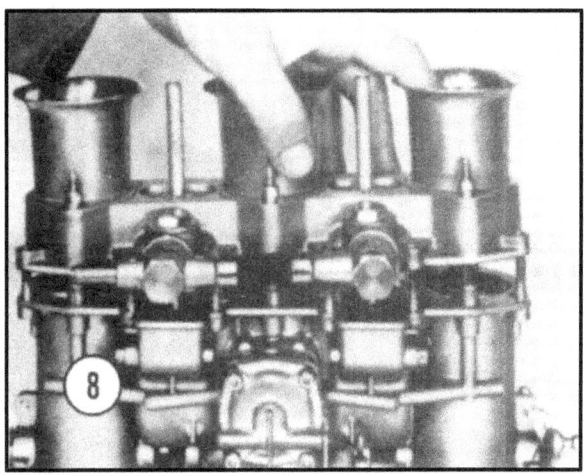

2. Remove hollow bolts securing fuel line to top of carburetor. See **Figure 9**.

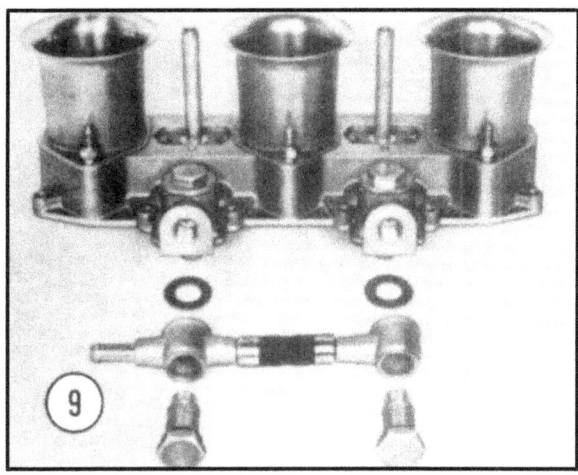

3. Remove needle valve plugs and float needle valves. See **Figure 10**.

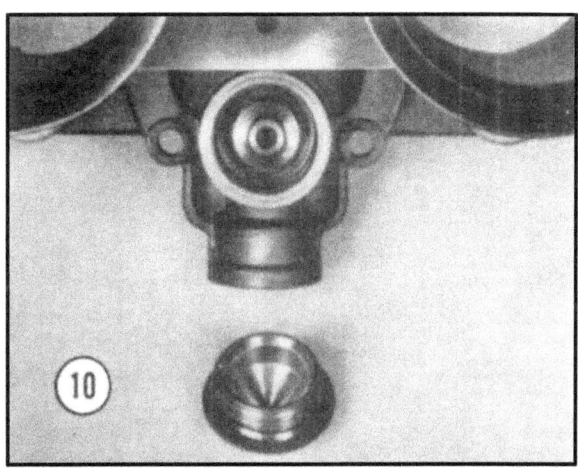

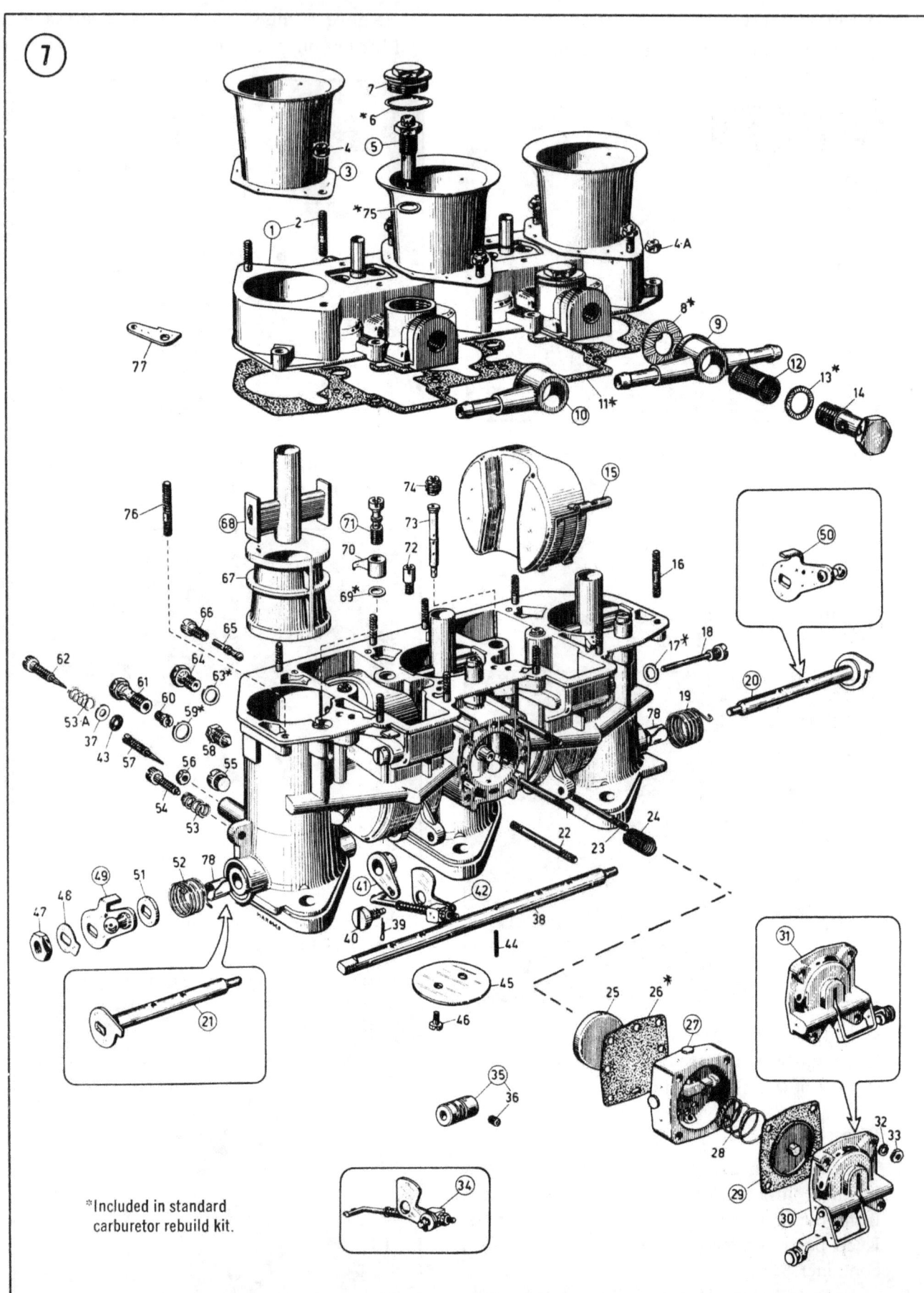

*Included in standard carburetor rebuild kit.

WEBER CARBURETOR

1. Cover
2. Stud
3. Velocity Stack
4. Nut
5. Needle valve
6. Seal
7. Plug
8. Seal
9. T-fitting
10. Banjo
11. Seal
12. Filter
13. Seal
14. Plug
15. Float
16. Stud
17. Seal
18. Screw
19. Spring
20. Throttle shaft (40 IDT)
21. Throttle shaft (40 IDT)
22. Stud
23. Stud
24. Spring
25. Valve
26. Diaphragm
27. Pump body
28. Spring
29. Diaphragm
30. Pump cover (left)
31. Pump cover (right)
32. Lockwasher
33. Nut
34. Linkage
35. U-joint
36. Screw
37. Spacer
38. Shaft
39. Cotter pin
40. Screw
41. Lever
42. Linkage
43. O-ring
44. Shear pin
45. Butterfly
46. Screw
47. Nut
48. Spacer
49. Lever (left)
50. Lever (right)
51. Spacer
52. Spring
53. Spring
54. Adjustment screw
55. Inspection screw
56. Nut
57. Adjustment screw
58. Setscrew
59. Seal
60. Main jet
61. Jet support
62. Idle screw
63. Gasket
64. Plug
65. Idle jet
66. Jet support
67. Venturi
68. Pre-atomizer
69. Gasket
70. Pump jet
71. Pressure valve
72. Suction valve
73. Emulsion tube
74. Air correction jet
75. Gasket
76. Stud
77. Bracket
78. Bushing

4. Remove main jet carrier. See **Figure 11**. Unscrew main jet from back of each jet carrier. See **Figure 12**.

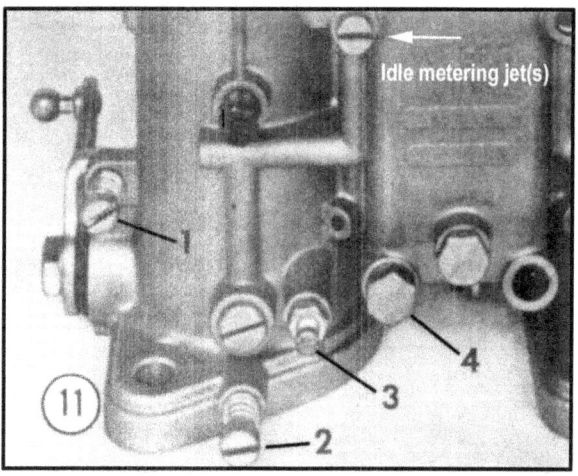

1. Idle speed adjustment screw
2. Idle mixture screw
3. Air adjusting screw
4. Main jet carrier

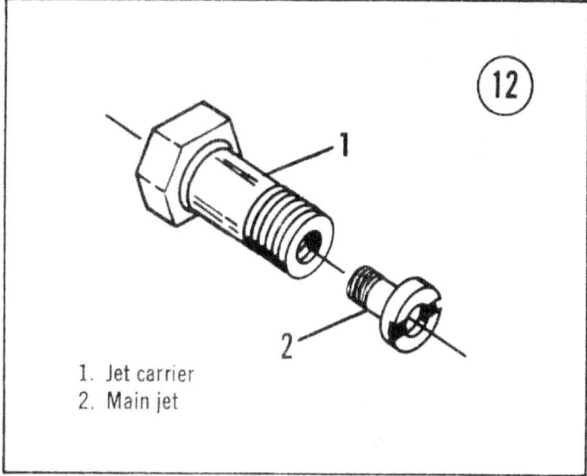

1. Jet carrier
2. Main jet

5. Remove air adjustment locknuts and screws. See Figure 11.

6. Remove idle metering jets. See Figure 11.

7. Remove idle speed adjustment screw. See Figure 11.

8. Remove idle mixture screws. See Figure 11.

9. Remove air correction jets and shake out emulsion tubes.

10. Remove check valves and accelerator pump nozzles. See **Figure 13**.

11. Remove preatomizers; if stuck, tap very lightly to loosen. See Figure 13.

12. Loosen venturi setscrews and remove venturis.

13. Unscrew float pins (see **Figure 14**) and lift out floats.

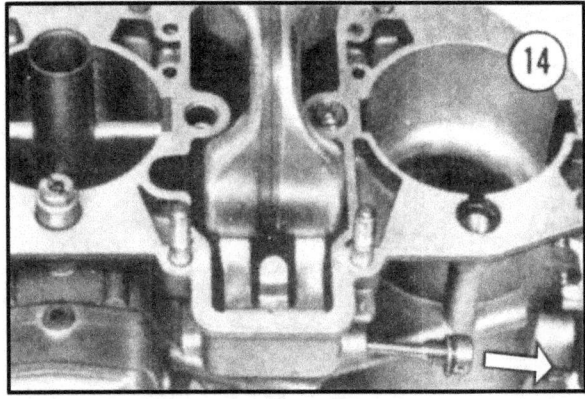

14. Remove nuts securing accelerator pump cover and remove cover. (See Figure 7).

15. Remove accelerator pump, outer diaphragm, spring, pump body, inner diaphragm, valve, and spring.

Cleaning

1. Clean all parts in solvent.

2. Clean jets and drillings in the carburetor body with compressed air. Do not clean them with pins or pieces of wire; you might enlarge the holes.

Inspection/Reassembly

Refer to Figure 7 for the following procedure.

> NOTE: *Use all new parts included in a standard Porsche rebuild kit; asterisks identify these parts on Figure 7.*

1. Check throttle shaft for wear.

2. Hold carburetor up to light and close throttle. No light should be visible around any of the throttle valves.

3. Install accelerator pump parts in order shown in Figure 7.

4. Immerse float in hot water. If it is leaking, bubbles will appear and the float must be replaced. Do not attempt to solder the hole. This increases float weight and causes high fuel level.

5. Install floats and secure with float pins.

6. Install venturis and secure with setscrews. Safety-wire the setscrews.

7. Install preatomizers.

8. Install check valves and accelerator pump nozzles.

9. Install emulsion tubes and air correction jets.

10. Install idle mixture screws. Make sure they are not bent or scored; replace if necessary.

11. Install idle speed adjustment screw.

12. Install idle metering jets.

13. Install air adjustment locknuts and screws.

14. Install main jets in jet carriers. Install carriers in carburetor.

15. Install top of carburetor on body.

16. Install float needle valves and plugs.

17. Check float needle valve and seat for wear. To do this, install it in top cover, hold the valve in lightly with your finger and blow in the fuel inlet. If it leaks, install a new needle valve.

18. Install fuel lines with hollow bolts and fuel screens.

INTAKE MANIFOLD

Removal/Installation

1. Remove air cleaner assembly.

2. Disconnect throttle linkage.

3. Disconnect fuel lines from carburetors.

4. Remove intake manifold retaining nuts. Lift intake manifold off complete with carburetors.

> **CAUTION**
> *Keep intake parts covered to prevent entry of dirt and other foreign material.*

5. Remove carburetor from intake manifold.

6. Installation is the reverse of these steps. Use new gaskets.

ELECTRIC FUEL PUMP

Removal

1. Disconnect battery ground cable.
2. Disconnect fuel lines at pump. Clamp them to prevent fuel leakage.
3. Remove bolts securing pump and disconnect ground cable.
4. Disconnect positive lead from pump terminal.
5. Installation is the reverse of these steps. Use new seals at banjo fittings and replace mounting grommets if deteriorated.

Diaphragm Replacement

Refer to **Figure 15** for the following procedure.

1. Remove 6 screws securing valve housing to magnetic housing.
2. Unscrew diaphragm assembly from magnetic housing.
3. Install tapered spring over pressure rod on diaphragm assembly. Small end goes toward diaphragm. Do not change spring length.
4. Screw diaphragm assembly (clockwise) into magnetic housing. Occasionally press the center of the diaphragm in and determine that breaker points still open and close. Continue screwing diaphragm in until breaker points no longer open when diaphragm is pressed.
5. Unscrew diaphragm (counterclockwise) just to the point where the points can be opened. Now turn the diaphragm an additional 300° (5 screws on the pump body mark off 300°).
6. Install valve housing on magnetic housing and tighten 6 screws evenly.

FUEL TANK

The fuel tank is accessible through the front luggage compartment.

Removal

> **WARNING**
> *Always disconnect battery before starting tank removal. Tank can brush against electrical connections during removal. If power is connected, sparks can cause a gasoline fire. It has happened more than once.*

1. Set a fire extinguisher nearby.
2. Disconnect battery ground cable.

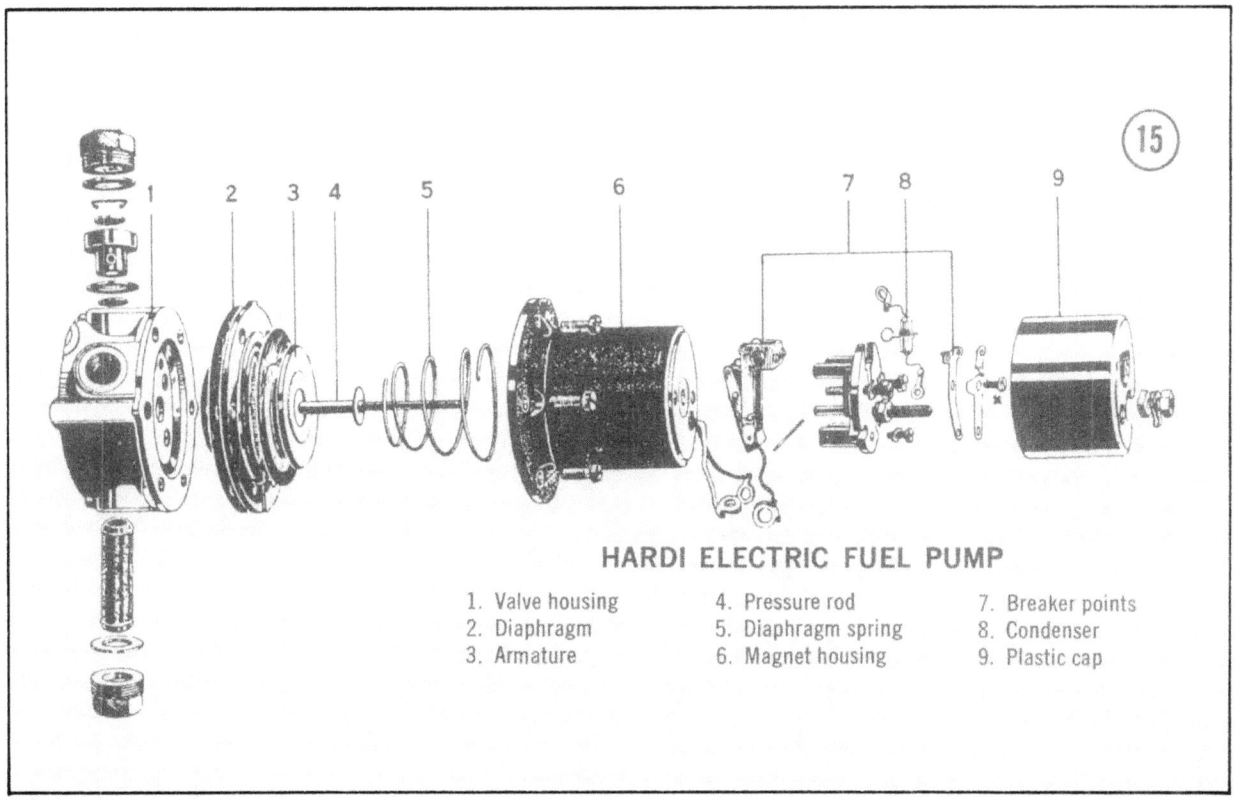

HARDI ELECTRIC FUEL PUMP

1. Valve housing
2. Diaphragm
3. Armature
4. Pressure rod
5. Diaphragm spring
6. Magnet housing
7. Breaker points
8. Condenser
9. Plastic cap

3. Warn others nearby not to smoke or use any open flames while you are working.

4. Remove drain plug and drain fuel into container.

5. Disconnect both fuel lines from tank.

6. Open front luggage compartment. Remove compartment padding, spare tire, and spare tire pad.

7. Disconnect vent hose.

8. Disconnect fuel gauge wire from sender.

9. Disconnect mounting strap securing tank.

10. Lift fuel tank out through the luggage compartment.

11. Installation is the reverse of these steps. Replace the rubber tank supports if damaged.

Table 1 SPECIFICATIONS

Carburetor	
Type	(2) Weber triple throat
Venturi	30
Main jet	125
Air correction jet	180
Idle metering jet	52
Idle air bleed	110
Accelerator pump jet	50
Emulsion tube	F26
Float needle valve	1.75
Float weights (grams)	25.5
Fuel Pump	
Type	Hardi electric
Delivery pressure	3.6-4.3 psi (0.25-0.30 atm)
Delivery capacity	30 oz. (900cc)/minute

CHAPTER NINE

ELECTRICAL SYSTEM

Electrical layout for all models is quite similar. All are alternator-based 12-volt systems. Differences occur mainly as small design changes in the alternator, regulator, starter, distributor, and fuse arrangements.

This chapter includes service procedures for the battery, starter, charging system, lighting system, fuses, instruments, and windshield wipers. **Table 1**, which is found at the end of the chapter, provides specifications for all electrical systems.

BATTERY

Care and Inspection

1. Open the engine compartment.
2. Remove battery hold down clamps. Disconnect battery cables and remove the battery.
3. Clean the top of the battery with baking soda solution. Scrub with a stiff bristle brush. Wipe battery clean with a cloth moistened in ammonia or baking soda solution.

CAUTION
Keep cleaning solution out of battery cells or the electrolyte will be seriously weakened.

4. Clean battery terminals with a stiff wire brush or one of the many tools made for this purpose.
5. Examine entire battery case for cracks.
6. Install the battery and reconnect battery cables. Observe battery polarity.
7. Coat the battery connections with light mineral grease or Vaseline after tightening.
8. Check electrolyte level and top up if necessary.

Testing

Hydrometer testing is the best way to check battery condition. Use a hydrometer with numbered graduations from 1.100 to 1.300 rather than one with color coded bands. To use the hydrometer, squeeze the rubber ball, insert the tip in the cell and release the ball (see **Figure 1**). Draw enough electrolyte to float the weighted float inside the hydrometer. Note the number in line with surface of the electrolyte; this is the specific gravity for this cell. Return the electrolyte to the cell from which it came.

The specific gravity of the electrolyte in each battery cell is an excellent indication of that cell's condition. A fully charged cell will read 1.275-1.380, while a cell in good condition may read from 1.250-1.280. A cell in fair condition reads from 1.225-1.250, and anything below 1.225 is practically dead.

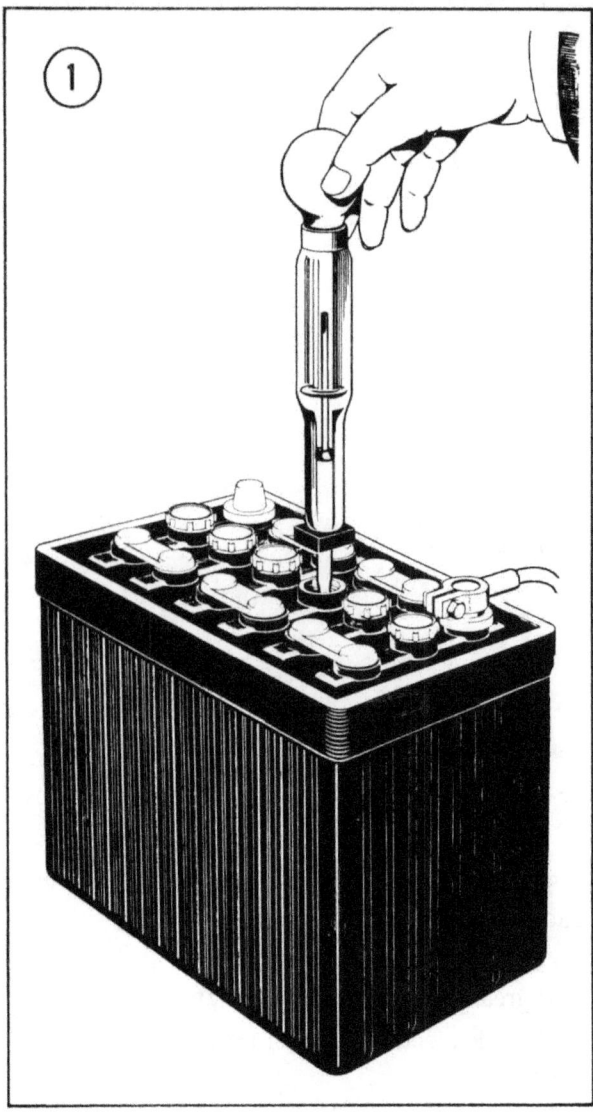

If the cells test in the poor range, the battery requires recharging. The hydrometer is useful for checking the progress of the charging operation. A reading from 1.200 to about 1.225 indicates a half charge; 1.275-1.380 indicates a full charge.

CAUTION
Always disconnect BOTH battery connections before connecting charging equipment.

ALTERNATOR (914)

The alternator generates alternating current (AC) which is converted to direct current (DC) by 6 internal silicon diodes. The alternator consists of the rotor, stator, end plate, housing, and drive pulley. Refer to Table 1 at the end of the chapter for specifications.

Removal/Installation

1. Open engine compartment lid.
2. Remove plastic insert in cover over alternator and remove Allen head bolt.
3. Move alternator as far to the left as possible and slip belt off alternator pulley.
4. Remove right heat exchanger as described in Chapter Six.
5. From underneath, remove nut on bottom alternator mounting bolt. Have an assistant remove bolt from inside engine compartment while supporting alternator from underneath.
6. Lower alternator. See **Figure 2**.

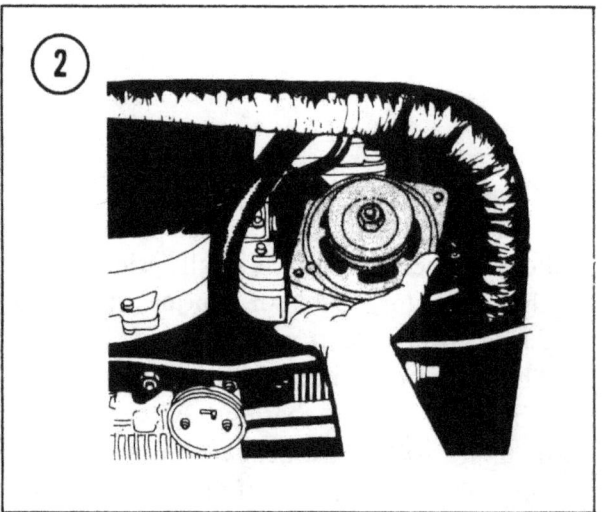

7. Mark air intake cover and alternator housing to make reassembly easier.
8. Remove screws securing intake cover to alternator and remove cover and gasket.
9. Disconnect wires from alternator.
10. Installation is the reverse of these steps. Use a new intake cover gasket. Ensure that rubber air intake seats properly on the fan housing cooling air outlet.
11. Adjust fan belt tension as described in Chapter Two.

Disassembly

Refer to **Figure 3** for the following procedure.

1. Mark the end plate and housing to make reassembly easier. Also mark the air intake cover and housing.
2. Remove screws securing intake cover and

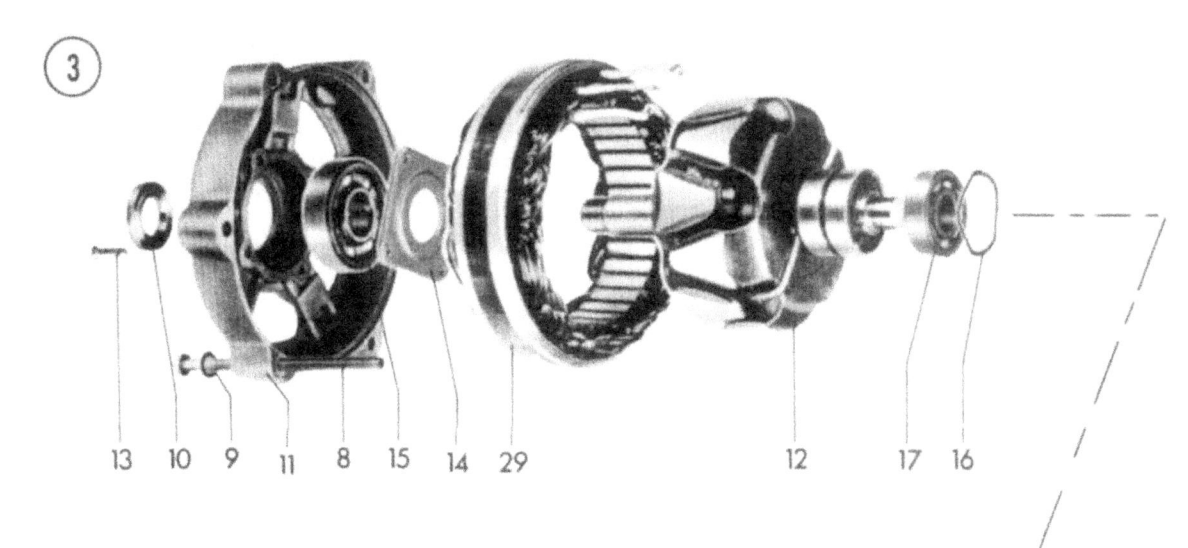

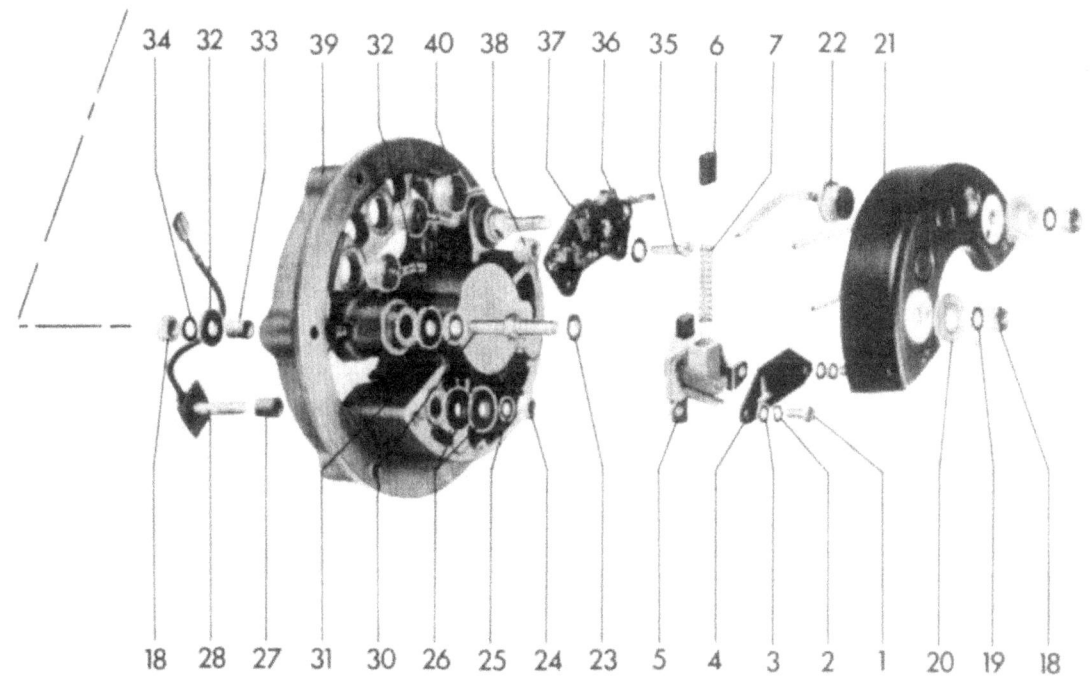

ALTERNATOR

1. Screw
2. Lockwasher
3. Washer
4. Fibre plate
5. Brush holder plate
6. Brush
7. Spring
8. Bolt
9. Lockwasher
10. Intermediate ring
11. End plate
12. Rotor
13. Screw
14. Bearing cover
15. Ball bearing
16. Shim
17. Ball bearing
18. Nut
19. Washer
20. Washer
21. Positive diode carrier
22. Positive diodes
23. Washer
24. Nut
25. Washer
26. Insulating washer
27. Insulating sleeve
28. D+ terminal
29. Stator
30. Stud
31. Washer
32. Insulating washer
33. Insulating sleeve
34. Lockwasher
35. Bolt
36. Washer
37. Exciter diode carrier
38. Spacer
39. Alternator housing
40. Negative diodes

plate to housing. Remove cover and gasket. Disconnect wires from alternator.

3. Hold pulley in a vise with soft jaws as shown in **Figure 4**. Remove pulley nut and pulley. Remove Woodruff key.

4. Pull carbon brushes away from slip rings. If pulled far enough, brush springs may be used to hold the brushes out.

5. Carefully separate end plate/rotor assembly from the stator/housing assembly. If necessary, pry them apart carefully with a screwdriver.

CAUTION
Do not insert screwdriver blade more than 1/16" (2mm) or the stator windings may be damaged.

6. Press the rotor out of the end plate as shown in **Figure 5**.

7. Remove screws holding bearing retainer plate. Remove plate and press bearing out.

8. Pull bearing off rotor. Use a puller which grips the inner race. If you must use a puller which grips only the outer race, discard the bearing and reassemble with a new bearing.

9. Remove nuts and washers securing positive diode carrier. Lift carrier up and carefully bend it aside.

10. Disconnect B+ cable from brush holder at the exciter diode carrier. Remove 2 screws securing brush holder and remove it.

11. Unsolder positive diodes, negative diodes, and stator wires from exciter diode carrier terminal strip. See **Figure 6**. Mark the leads and make a rough sketch to facilitate reassembly. Note long nose pliers used as a heat sink to draw away excessive heat.

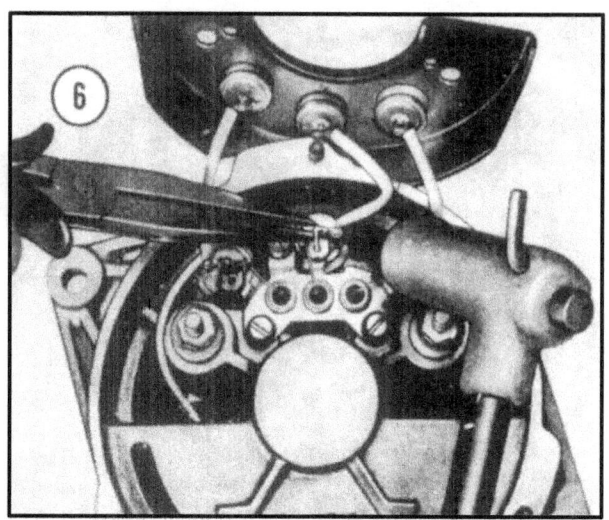

Testing the Alternator (Disassembled)

For the following tests use an ohmmeter powered by a 3.0-volt battery (no more), or make a small continuity tester wired as shown in **Figure 7**.

1. Test for a grounded rotor by touching one test lead of the ohmmeter or continuity tester to the rotor shaft and the other test lead to each of the slip rings (see **Figure 8**). If the ohmmeter reads a low resistance or the lamp lights, the winding is grounded and rotor must be replaced.

2. Test for an open-circuited rotor by touching one test lead to one slip ring. See **Figure 9**. The lamp should light if using the continuity tester. If using an ohmmeter, the resistance should be

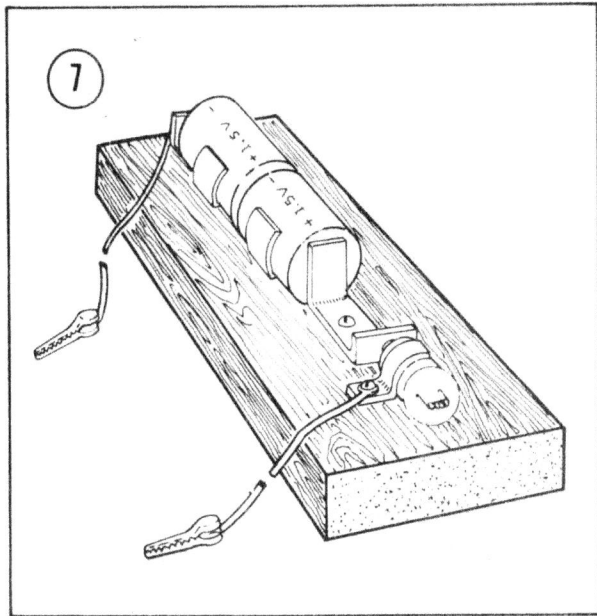

CAUTION
Do NOT use 110 volts to test the stator as recommended for some other alternator makes.

4. Test for open stator winding by measuring resistance between successive pairs of stator leads. Resistance should be about 1.26 ohms.

5. Check the slip rings. If the Bosch slip rings are scored or otherwise damaged, they must be turned down on a lathe. Do not turn down to less than 1.24" (31.5mm) in diameter.

6. Test diodes for opens and shorts. Proceed as follows. Connect one test lead of the ohmmeter to the positive diode plate and the other test lead to the diode terminal. Note the reading, then reverse the test leads and note the reading again. A high resistance (lamp out) in one direction, but a low resistance (lamp lit) in the other indicates a good diode. A low resistance or a high resistance in both directions indicates a shorted or open diode, respectively, and it must be replaced.

about 4 ohms. If it reads "00", the winding is open. If it reads less than 4 ohms, the winding is shorted. In the latter 2 cases, replace the rotor.

3. Test for a grounded stator by connecting one test lead of an ohmmeter to the frame and the other test lead to any stator lead (see **Figure 10**). A low resistance indicates a grounded stator. Replace the stator.

7. Check the negative diodes in the same manner, i.e., connect one test lead to the slip ring end shield and the other test lead to the diode

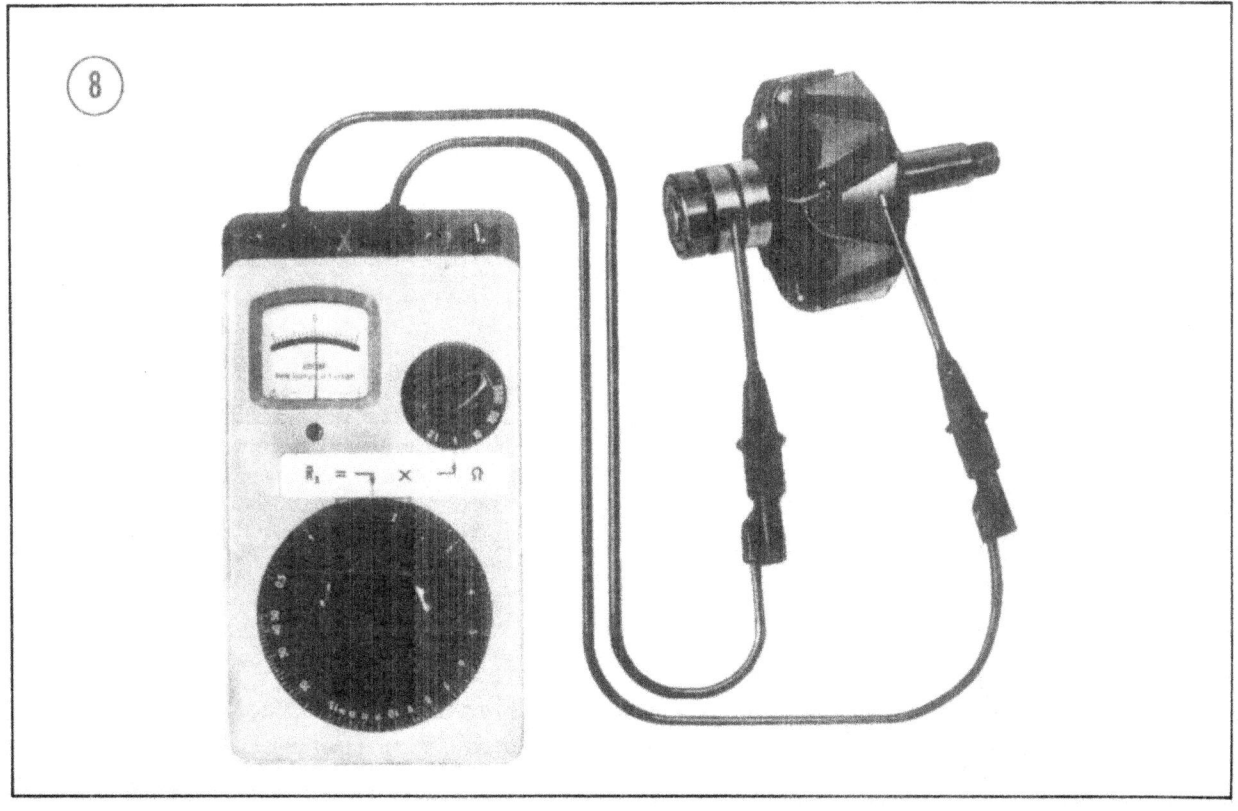

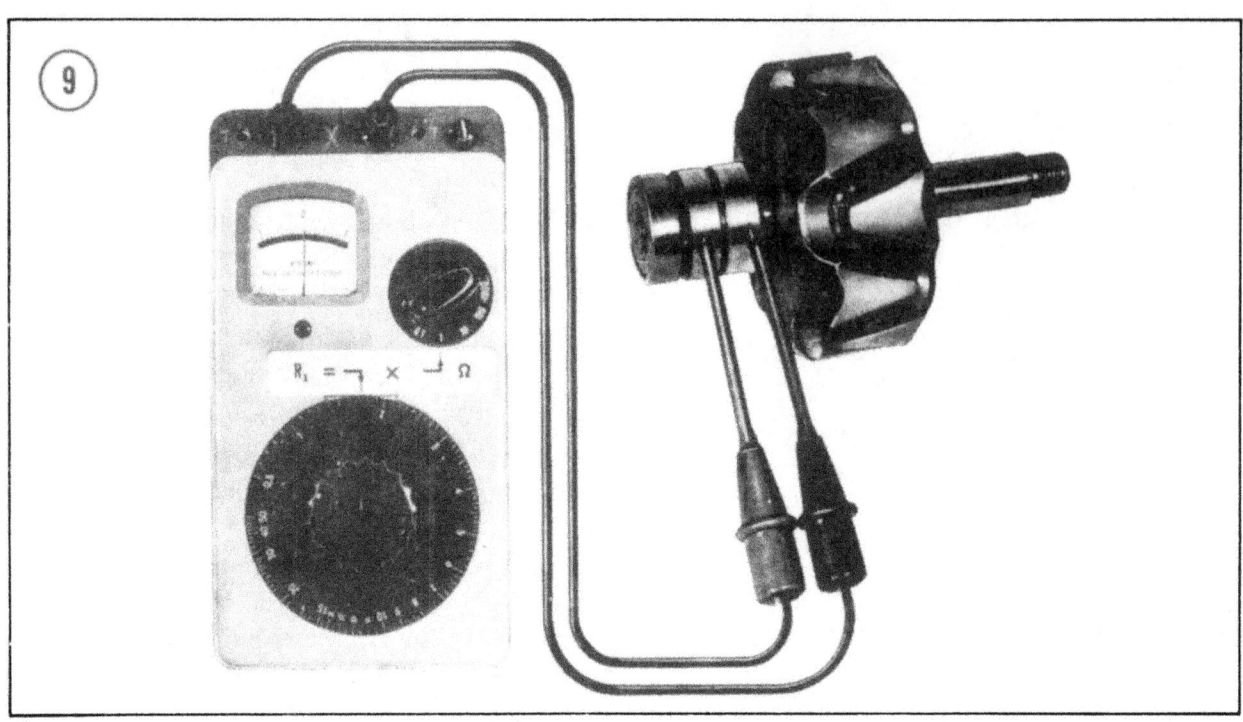

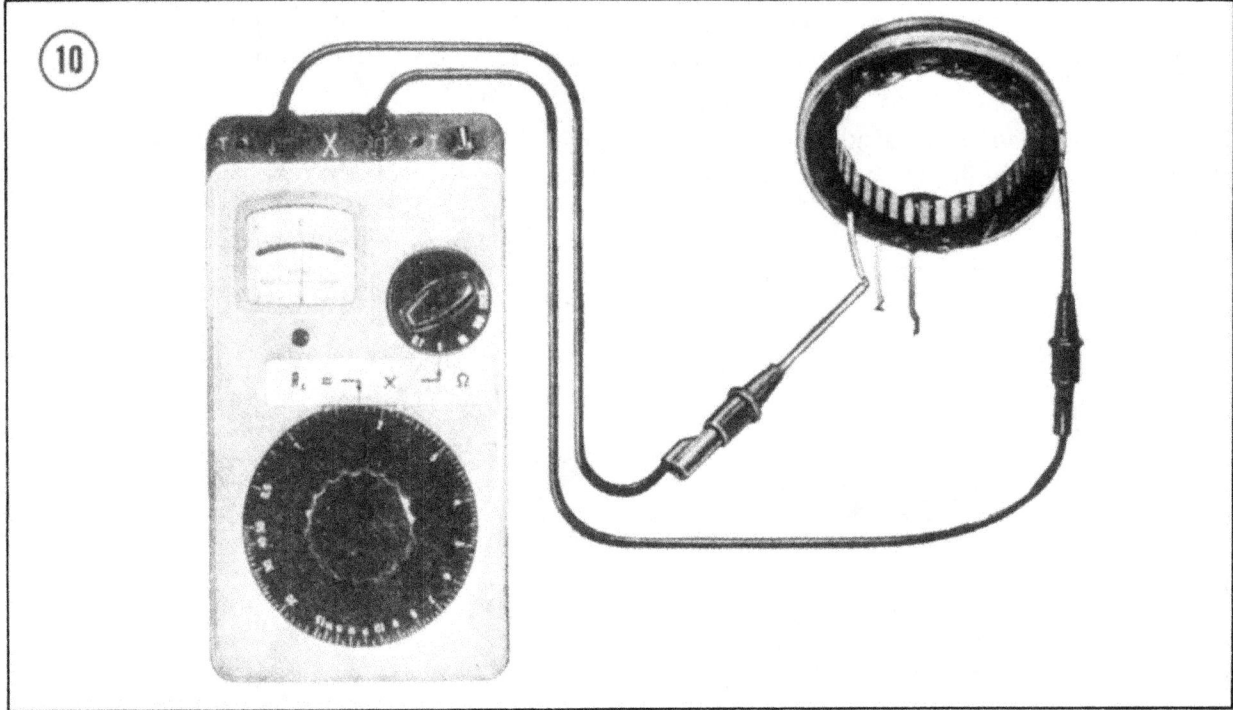

terminal. Note the readings in this direction and with the leads reversed.

Replacing Diodes

The following steps are not easily performed without proper tools and it might be advisable to let your dealer or automotive electrical shop perform them.

1. Press out the faulty diode.

CAUTION
Do not hammer the defective diode out as the shock may internally damage other diodes.

2. Apply a thin coat of silicone grease (available at automotive or electronic supply houses) to the new diode and press the new diode in place.

Assembly

Refer to Figure 3 for the following procedure.
1. Place the stator in the alternator housing.
2. Solder the leads from the positive diodes to the correct terminals on the exciter diode carrier terminals. See rough sketch made during Step 11, *Disassembly*.
3. Install exciter diode carrier in housing. Solder negative diode leads and stator leads to carrier terminals according to rough sketch.
4. Ensure that the brushes are retracted in the holder. Route the D+ wire from the holder as shown in **Figure 11**. Connect it to exciter diode carrier.

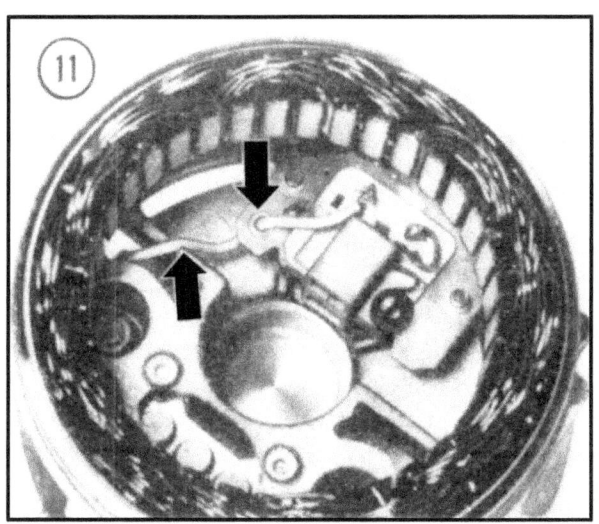

5. Bend positive diode carrier down so it can be installed on its mounting studs. Install an insulating washer (with tab in holder), lockwasher, and nut on each stud to hold the carrier.
6. Grease the bearing for the slip ring end of the rotor and press it on.
7. Grease the end plate bearing, and press it in. Install bearing retainer with screws.
8. Press the end plate onto the rotor.
9. Assemble the end plate/rotor and stator housing. Do not install thru-bolts yet.
10. Pull back brush springs and drop brushes down to contact slip ring.
11. Connect B+ wire to positive diode carrier stud with 2 washers and a nut. Connect 3-wire connector to brush holder.
12. Install thru-bolts and air intake cover with new gasket.

ALTERNATOR VOLTAGE REGULATOR

Adjusting the alternator voltage regulator requires special equipment not ordinarily available to a home mechanic. If a trouble appears to be in the voltage regulator, take the job to your dealer or competent garage.

You might also consider replacing the regulator with a new one. The cost of adjusting an old regulator may be many times that of buying a replacement. There is even a chance the old regulator cannot be adjusted; so you'll end up buying a new one anyway.

Removal/Installation

The alternator voltage regulator is located in the engine compartment.
1. Disconnect the battery ground cable.
2. Remove cover over electrical junction box.
3. Unbolt regulator.
4. Disconnect electrical cable.
5. Install a new regulator by reversing these steps.

ALTERNATOR (914/6)

The alternator generates alternating current (AC) which is converted to direct current (DC) by 6 internal silicone diodes. The alternator consists of the rotor, stator, end plate, housing, and drive pulley. **Table 1** (end of chapter) provides specifications.

Removal/Installation

1. Open engine compartment lid.
2. Disconnect battery ground cable.
3. Remove air cleaner.
4. Remove upper shroud bolts. See **Figure 12**.
5. Remove alternator pulley nut while holding fan with special tool included with owner's tool kit. See **Figure 13**. Remove fan belt.
6. Remove blower housing strap bolts. See **Figure 14**.
7. Pull blower/alternator assembly out towards the rear. See **Figure 15**.
8. Disconnect and mark alternator wires.

9. Installation is the reverse of these steps. **Figure 16** shows proper wire connections to alternator.

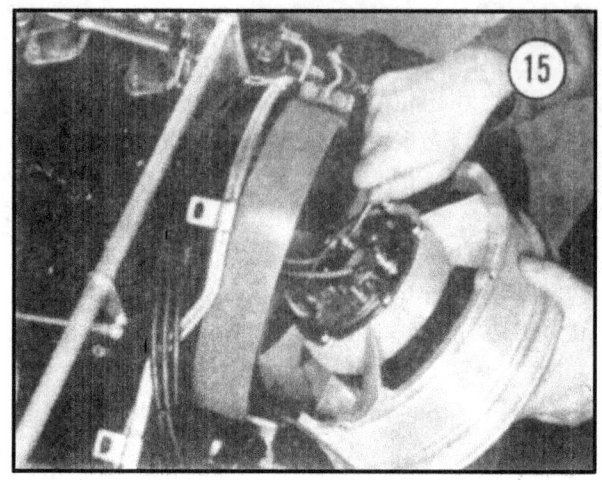

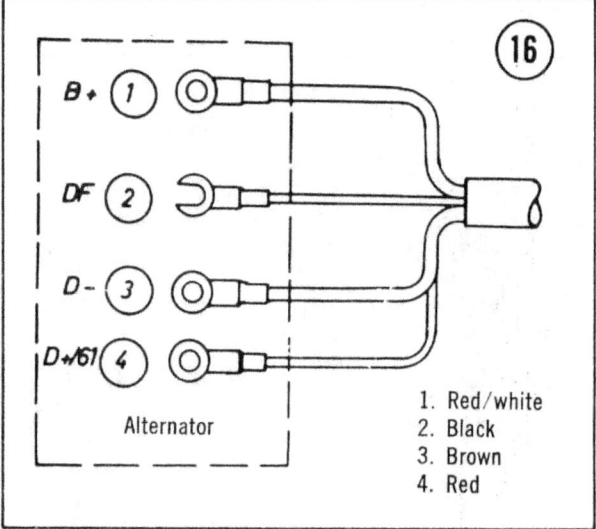

1. Red/white
2. Black
3. Brown
4. Red

10. Adjust fan belt tension as described in Chapter Two.

Brush Replacement

1. Remove 4 screws securing brush plate assembly. See **Figure 17**.

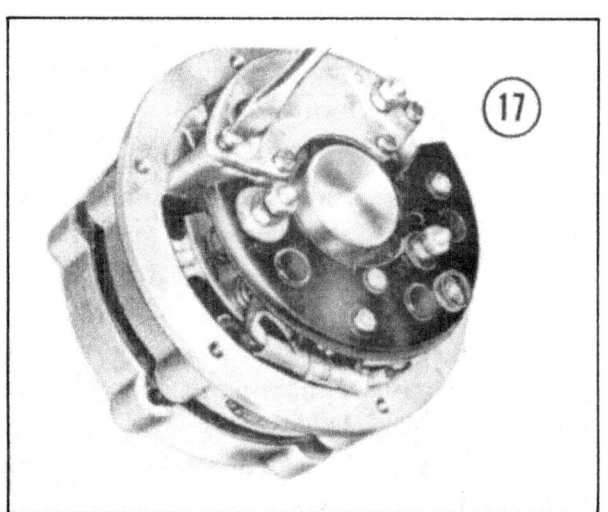

2. Measure brush length as shown in **Figure 18**. Minimum length should be 0.55" (14mm).

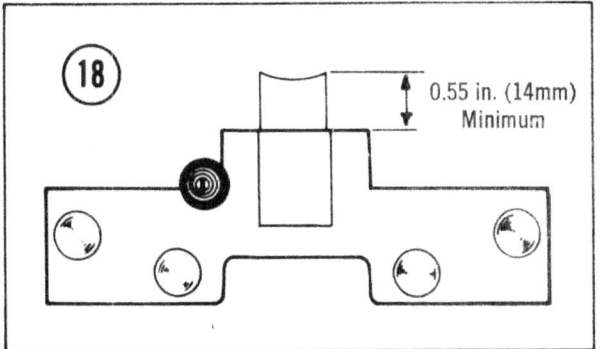

3. If brushes are too short, unsolder them (see **Figure 19**) and insert new ones. When soldering, do not allow solder to flow up braided lead; the lead will lose its flexibility.

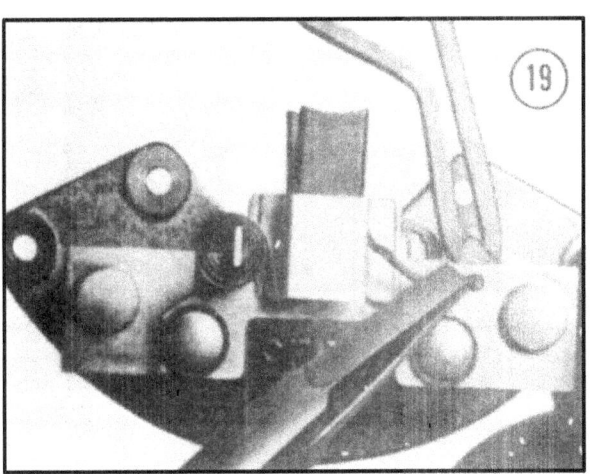

Disassembly

1. Remove brush plate assembly with brushes. See Figure 17.
2. Remove 6 retaining bolts and separate alternator halves. See **Figure 20**.

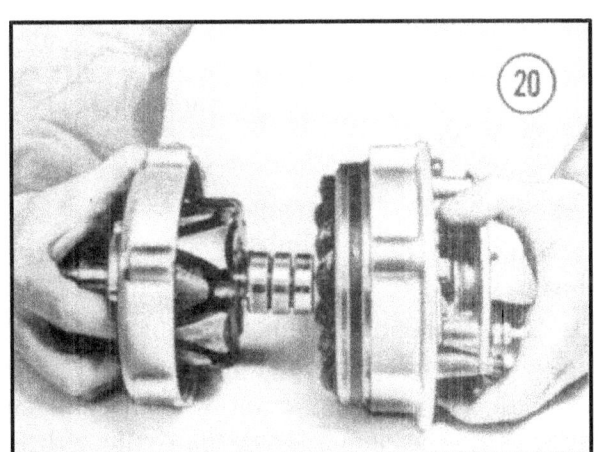

3. Press rotor out of front housing as shown in **Figure 21**.

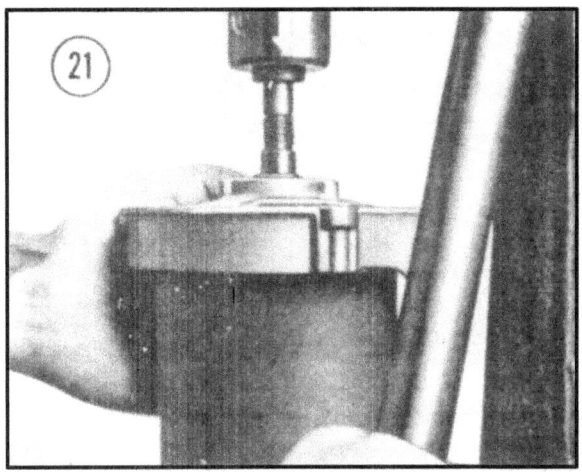

4. Press bearing off rotor on slip ring end. See **Figure 22**. It is also possible to remove the bearing with a puller which bears on the inner race only. If the outer race is subjected to any force, replace the bearing.

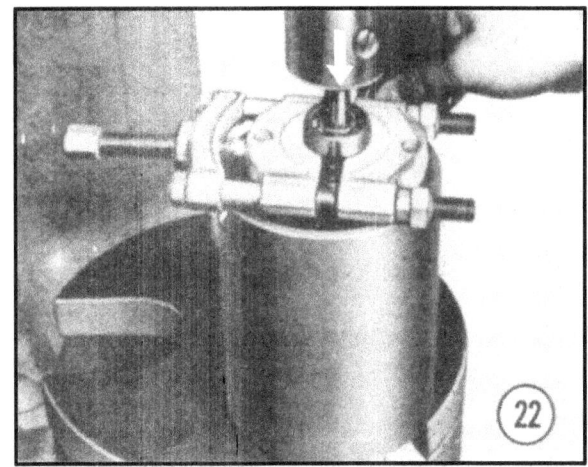

5. Open 3 retaining clamps as shown in **Figure 23**. Remove insulating sleeve from end of all 3 wire bundles. Cut each wire bundle as close to solder joint as possible. See **Figure 24**.

> NOTE: *Each wire bundle consists of one stator lead, one negative diode lead, one positive diode lead, and one isolation diode lead. The diodes cannot be tested until these leads are separated.*

6. Lift stator out.

Testing Diodes

For the following tests, use an ohmmeter powered by 24 volts (maximum) or less, or make a small continuity tester as shown in Figure 7. **Figure 25** shows location of various diodes.

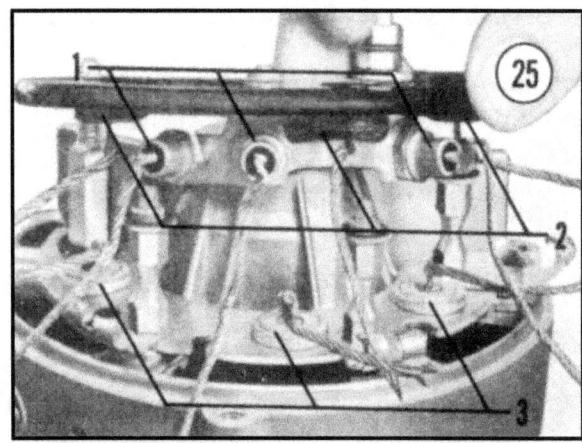

1. Isolation diodes
2. Positive diodes
3. Negative diodes

1. Disassemble alternator as described above.

2. Connect one test lead of an ohmmeter or other continuity tester to negative diode heat sink. Touch the other test lead to each negative diode lead. See **Figure 26**. If all diodes indicate a low resistance, reverse the leads and ensure that all diodes indicate a very high resistance.

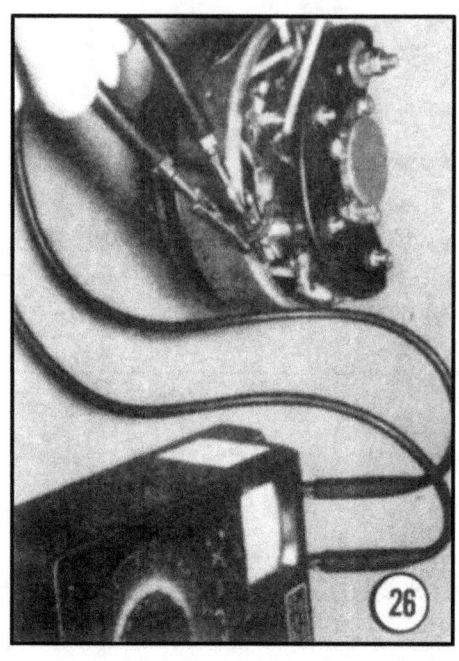

3. Test positive diodes in the same manner.

NOTE: *Positive diodes conduct electricity in the opposite direction from negative diodes; whatever test lead connection indicated a low resistance for negative diodes will indicate a high resistance for positive diodes. The important thing is to ensure that all 6 diodes indicate low resistance (a few ohms) in one direction and high resistance (several kilohms) in the other direction.*

4. Test isolation diodes in same manner as positive diodes.

Testing Stator

See *Testing Diodes* for suitable test instruments.

1. Examine stator winding for evidence of burning. If present, replace stator.

2. Test for a grounded stator by connecting one test lead of an ohmmeter to the frame and the

other test lead to any stator lead (see **Figure 27**). A low resistance indicates a grounded stator. Replace the stator.

CAUTION
Do NOT use 110 volts to test the stator as recommended for some other alternator makes.

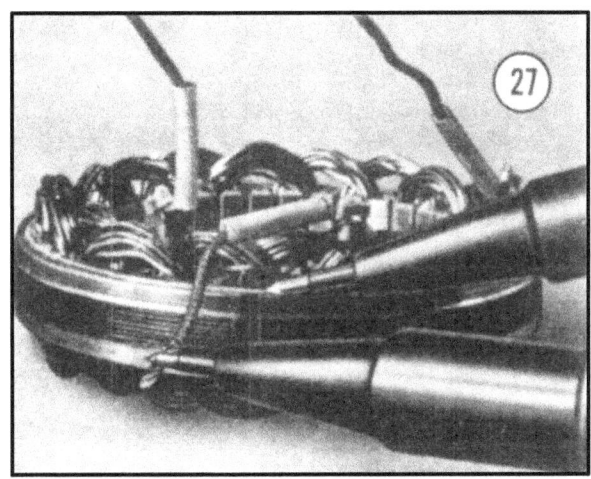

3. Test for open stator winding by measuring resistance between successive pairs of stator leads. Resistance should be about 0.26 ohms. See **Figure 28**.

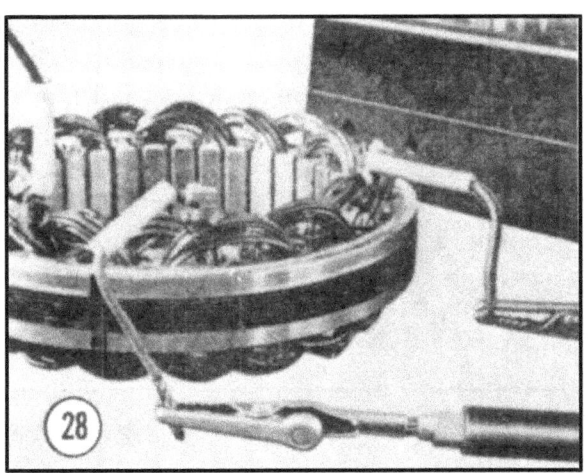

Testing Rotor

See *Testing Diodes* for suitable test instruments.

1. Test for a grounded rotor by touching one test lead of the ohmmeter or continuity tester to the rotor and the other test lead to each of the slip rings (see **Figure 29**). If the ohmmeter reads a low resistance or the lamp lights, the winding is grounded and rotor must be replaced.

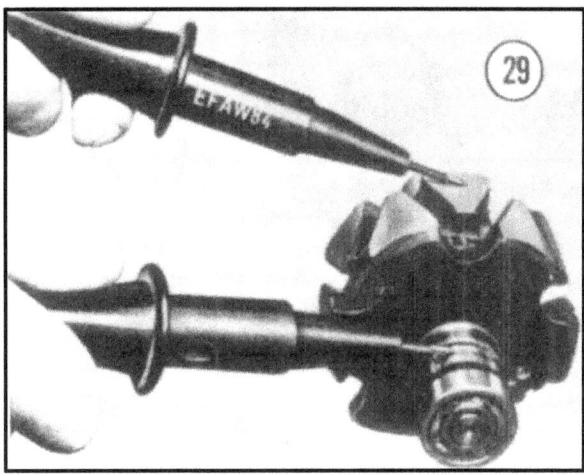

2. Test for an open-circuited rotor by touching one test lead to one slip ring, the other test lead to the other slip ring. See **Figure 30**. The lamp should light if using the continuity tester. If using an ohmmeter, the resistance should be about 4 ohms. If it reads "infinity," the winding is shorted. In the latter 2 cases, replace the rotor.

3. Check the slip rings. If the slip rings are scored or otherwise damaged, they may be turned down on a lathe. Do not turn down to less than 1.24" (31.5mm) in diameter.

Diode Replacement

Diodes are very fragile and must be carefully pressed in and out of the heat sink. If you find a defective diode, take the heat sink to your dealer or shop specializing in alternator rebuilding. They will install a new diode for you.

NOTE: *Porsche recommends replacing all 3 diodes on a heat sink if one is defective.*

To remove/install positive diode heat sink:

1. Remove nuts on B+ stud and 3 smaller studs. See **Figure 31**.

2. Lift heat sink off. See **Figure 32**. Do not lose insulating washers on studs.

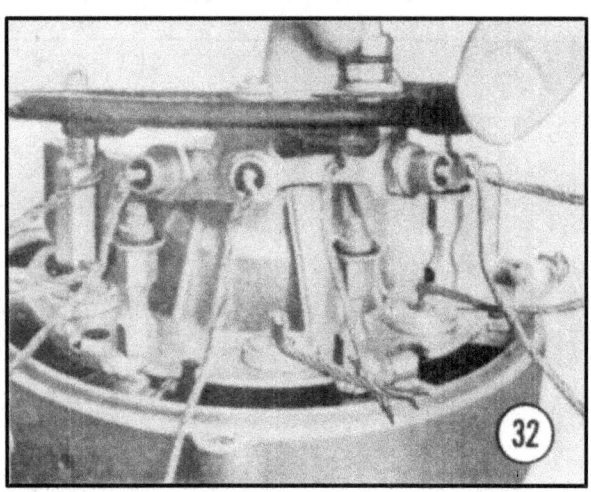

3. Installation is the reverse of these steps. Use insulating washer on studs shown in Figure 32.

To remove/install isolation diodes:

1. Unscrew 3 isolation diodes with socket wrench from positive heat sink.
2. Install 3 new diodes.

To remove/install negative diode heat sink:

1. Remove positive diode heat sink.
2. Remove B+ stud and 3 small studs (**Figure 33**).
3. Installation is the reverse of these steps. Note location of longest clip (arrow, Figure 33).

Assembly

1. Install negative diode heat sink with 3 small studs and B+ stud. See Figure 33. Note location of longest clip and the insulator under the B+ stud.

2. With an ohmmeter or other continuity tester, ensure that B+ stud is not shorted to ground.

3. Install positive diode heat sink. Use insulating washers on small studs. See Figure 32. Install nuts on studs.

4. Set stator in place.

5. Bundle one positive diode and the negative diode lead just below it in a piece of insulating tubing. Slide another piece of insulating tubing over the nearest isolation diode lead and another over the nearest stator lead. Tape all 3 pieces of tubing together as shown in **Figure 34**. Clamp together with a small metal ring or piece of stiff wire (see Figure 34). Solder the end and cut off excess wire beyond the metal ring. Remove tape and slip large insulating sleeve over the solder joint.

6. Repeat Step 5 for the remaining 2 sets of diodes and stator leads.

7. Fit wire bundles into fastening clips and bend clips over. See **Figure 35**.

8. Press bearing onto slip ring end of rotor if removed.

9. Press rotor into front housing.

10. Join front and rear housings with 6 bolts.

11. Install brush plate assembly.

STARTER (914)

See Table 1 at the end of the chapter for starter specifications.

Removal/Installation

1. Disconnect the battery ground cable.

2. Disconnect battery cable from starter solenoid terminal 30, and the small wire from terminal 50.

3. Remove bolts securing the starter to the transmission case. Withdraw the starter.

4. Installation is the reverse of these steps. Before installing, apply universal grease to the starter shaft bushing. Use VW D1a Sealing Compound between the starter and the transmission case.

Brush Replacement

Brushes should be checked every 6,000 miles. Starters must be partially disassembled as described below. Pull on the brush leads to ensure that they slide freely in their holders. Also make sure that the brushes are not worn; if the flexible lead is nearly touching the metal holder, all 4 brushes should be replaced.

After removing the starter as described earlier, perform Steps 2-6 of the disassembly procedure to expose the brushes. Unsolder all 4 brushes and solder in a set of new ones. Examine the commutator before reassembling. If it is dirty or oily, clean it with a cloth moistened in solvent. If it is scored, burned, or worn down to the mica strips, overhaul the starter. Reassembly is by reversing Steps 2-6 of the disassembly procedure.

Solenoid Replacement

1. Disconnect the large connecting wire between starter and solenoid. See **Figure 36**.

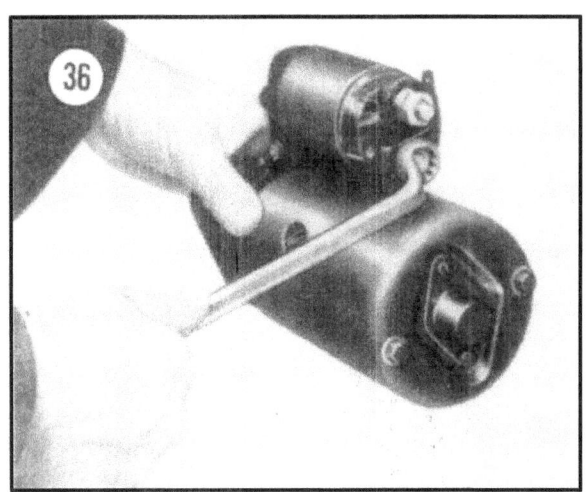

2. Remove 2 screws securing solenoid to the mounting bracket. See **Figure 37**.

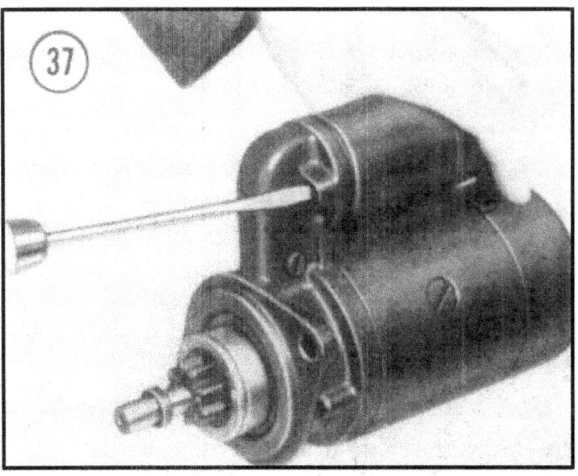

3. Lift solenoid pull rod free of the operating lever and remove solenoid (**Figure 38**).

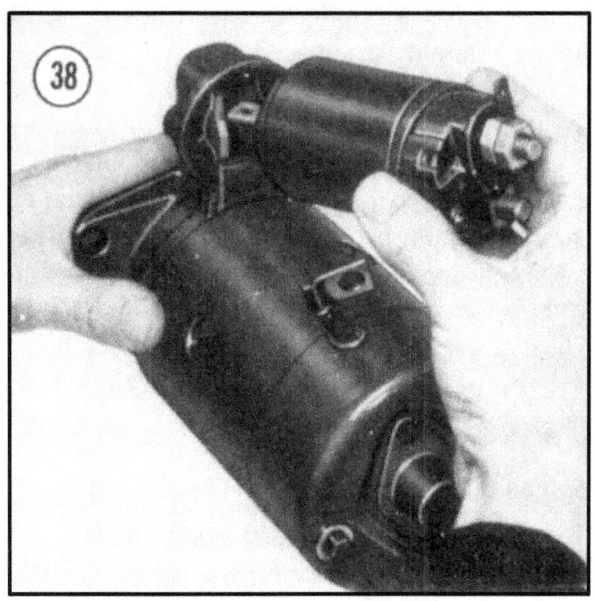

4. Do not change pull rod adjustment if old solenoid is to be reinstalled. On new solenoids, loosen the locknut and adjust dimension (a) shown in **Figure 39** to 0.748 ± 0.004" (19 ± 0.1mm). Tighten locknut.

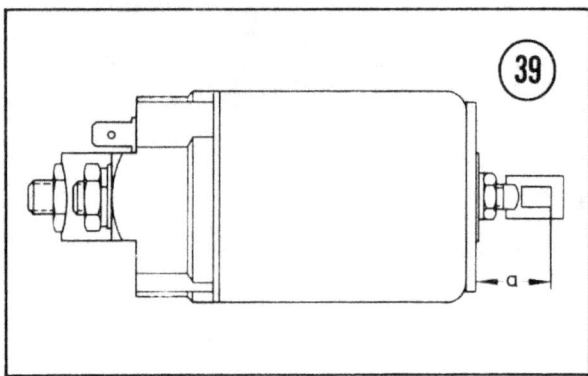

5. Place a strip of VW D14 Plastic Sealer on the outer edge of solenoid face.

6. Pull the drive pinion to bring the operating lever back towards solenoid opening. Connect the pull rod to the operating lever.

7. Secure solenoid with mounting screws and reconnect large wire from starter.

Disassembly

Refer to **Figure 40** for following procedure.

1. Remove solenoid as described earlier.
2. Remove end cap (10) and seal (11).
3. Pry out the lock ring (12) and remove the shims (13).

STARTER

1. Nut
2. Lockwasher
3. Screw
4. Molded rubber
5. Disc
6. Solenoid
7. Spring
8. Screw
9. Washer
10. End cap
11. Seal
12. C-ring
13. Shim
14. Screws
15. Washer
16. End plate
17. Brush holder
18. Negative brush
19. Positive brush
20. Retaining spring
21. Rubber grommet
22. Housing
23. Field winding
24. Insulating washer
25. Thrust washer
26. Armature
27. Operating sleeve
28. Engaging lever
29. Engaging spring
30. Detent balls
31. Drive pinion
32. Pin
33. Lockwasher
34. Nut
35. Drive end plate

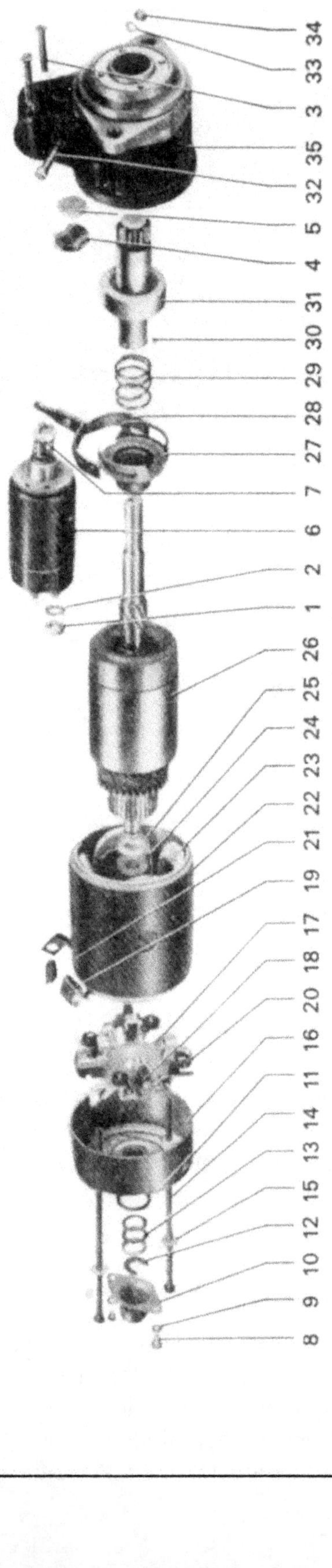

4. Remove cover bolts (14) and cover (16).
5. Lift brushes out of brush holder.
6. Remove brush holder.
7. Remove housing (22) from the armature/mounting bracket assembly.
8. Hold the armature in a vise with soft jaws (copper, or wood blocks), commutator end down. Pull operating sleeve against drive pinion to release locking balls. Slide pinion assembly off the armature. Don't lose any of the balls.

Cleaning

Do not immerse starter parts in cleaning solvent. Solvent can permanently damage insulation on the field housing or armature; wipe these parts with a clean cloth. Other parts not containing insulated wiring may be cleaned with a brush moistened in solvent, then wiped dry with a clean cloth.

Inspection

1. Examine the armature for obvious mechanical damage such as damaged windings, bent or worn shaft, or scored commutator. Scored or unevenly worn commutators may be turned on a lathe to a diameter not less than 1.292" (32.8mm). After turning, undercut the mica strips separating the brass segments about 1/64" (0.4mm). **Figure 41** shows right and wrong undercuts. Use a short piece of hacksaw blade or a special tool made for this purpose.

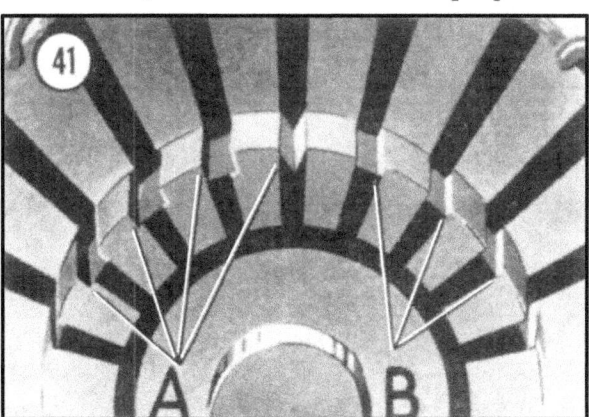

A. Incorrect   B. Correct

2. Check armature for shorts to ground with an ohmmeter or other continuity tester. Connect one test prod to the armature core. Connect the other test prod to each commutator bar. See **Figure 42**. If continuity occurs on any bar, replace the armature.

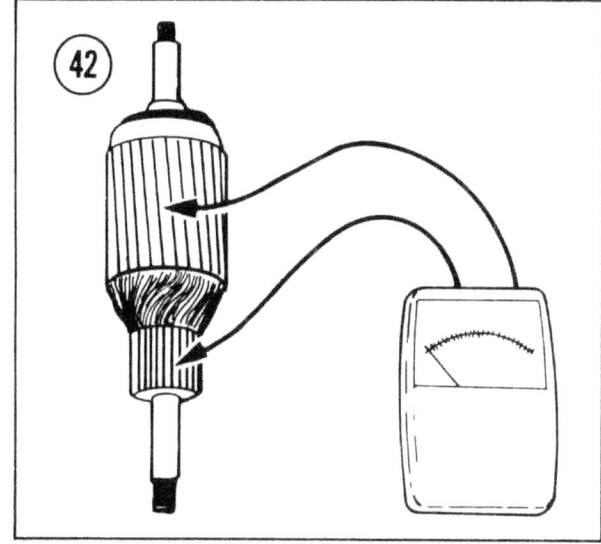

3. Check armature for opens. Usually these are evidenced by burn marks between commutator bars caused by the brushes bridging the open circuit.

4. Check armature for winding shorts. To do this, insert the armature in a growler. Turn the growler on and hold a hacksaw blade slightly above, but not touching the armature. See **Figure 43**. Rotate the armature slowly; if the blade vibrates and is attracted to the armature, a winding is shorted. If visual inspection does not reveal a short, replace the armature.

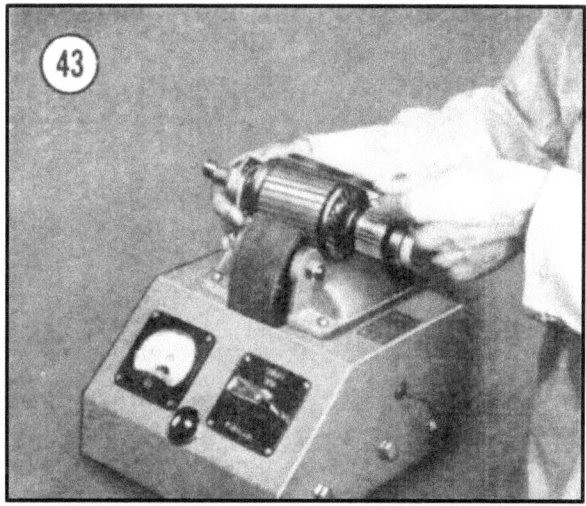

5. Check field winding for shorts to ground. To do this, connect an ohmmeter or other continuity tester between a field winding lead (coil

end) and the field housing. See **Figure 44**. If continuity occurs, a field winding is shorted. Unsolder the connecting wires and test each field coil separately until the ground is traced. Replace the grounded winding.

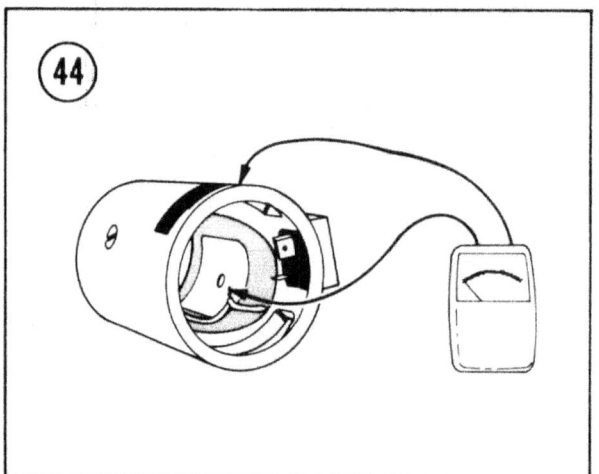

6. Check field winding for open circuit. Connect an ohmmeter between the field terminal and the field coil lead going to the armature terminal. See **Figure 45**. Continuity should be measured; if not, a field winding is open and must be replaced.

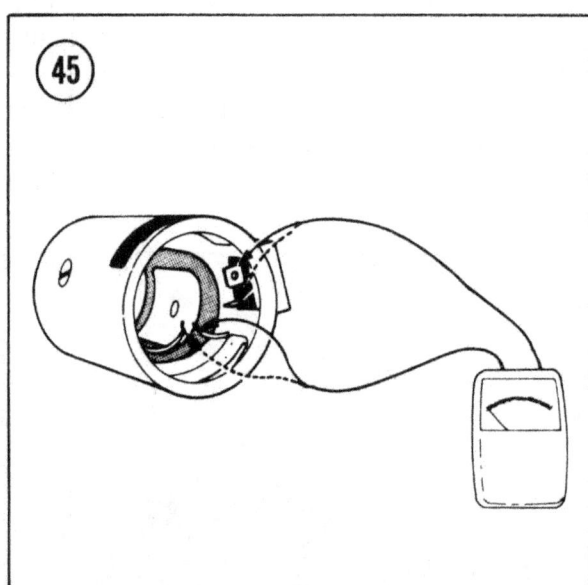

7. Examine all other parts for wear, particularly bushings. Replace any that are worn or questionable.

Bushing Replacement

1. If either the mounting bracket bushing or end cover bushing is scored or worn, drive out the old bushing with a suitable drift.

2. Clean out the bushing hole and remove any burrs.

3. Soak new bushings in hot light oil for at least an hour.

4. Install bushings with a suitable drift.

Assembly

Refer to Figure 40 for the following procedure.

1. Place balls in locking ring. Hold in place with grease. See **Figure 46**.

2. Hold armature in a vise with soft jaws.

3. Push pinion assembly onto armature shaft until balls lock in place. See **Figure 47**.

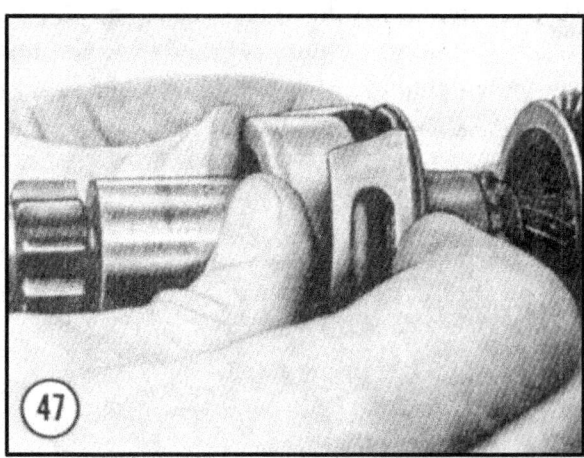

4. Install activating lever on pinion assembly.

5. Install armature into drive housing. Secure lever with pin.

6. Install rubber seal in mounting bracket and fit the starter housing. Ensure that the tab on the housing locates in the mounting bracket slot. Use sealing compound at D in **Figure 48**.

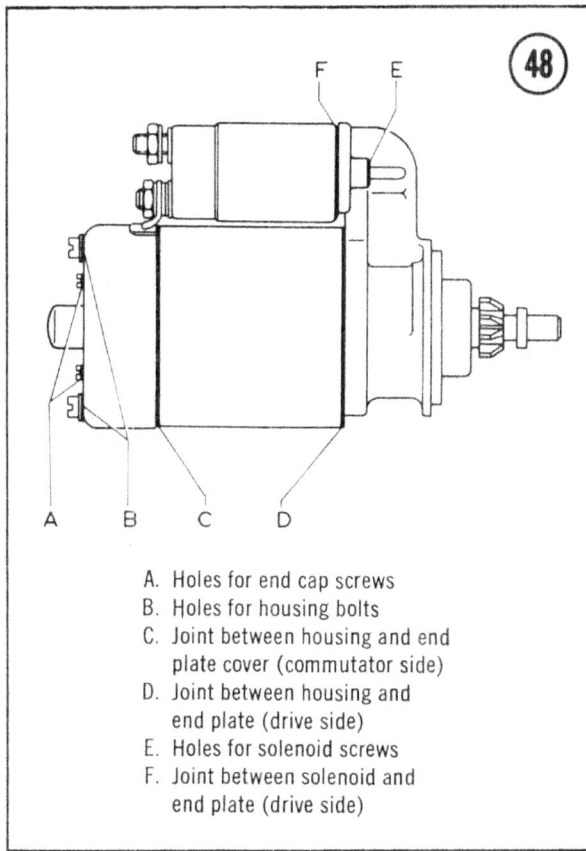

A. Holes for end cap screws
B. Holes for housing bolts
C. Joint between housing and end plate cover (commutator side)
D. Joint between housing and end plate (drive side)
E. Holes for solenoid screws
F. Joint between solenoid and end plate (drive side)

7. Slide steel washer (25) and fiber washer (24) on the armature shaft.

8. Install the brush holder on the commutator and insert the brushes.

9. Lubricate the bushing in end cover (16) with oil. Install the end cover on the housing and secure with long screws to the mounting bracket. Use sealing compound at B and C in Figure 48. Ensure that the rubber grommet on the wire to the solenoid fits properly in the cover.

10. Install shims (13) and lock ring (12). Check shaft end-play, which should be 0.004-0.012" (0.1-0.3mm). Adjust by adding or removing shims (13).

11. Install a new seal (11) and install the end cap. Use sealing compound at A to E in Fig. 48.

12. Install the solenoid as described earlier.

STARTER (914/6)

Removal/Installation

1. Disconnect battery ground cable(s).

2. Disconnect battery cable from starter solenoid terminal 30 and the small wire from terminal 50.

3. Remove bolts securing the starter to the transmission case. Withdraw the starter.

4. Installation is the reverse of these steps. Before installing, apply universal grease to the starter shaft bushing. Use VW D1a Sealing Compound between the starter and transmission case.

Brush Replacement

Brushes should be checked every 6,000 miles. Starters must be partially disassembled as described below. Pull on the brush leads to check that they slide freely in their holders. Make sure the brushes are not worn; if the flexible lead is nearly touching the metal holder, all 4 brushes should be replaced.

After removing the starter as described earlier, perform Steps 2-6 of the disassembly procedure to expose the brushes. Unsolder commutator before reassembling. If it is dirty or oily, clean it with a cloth moistened in solvent. If it is scored, burned, or worn down to the mica strips, overhaul the starter. Reassemble by reversing Steps 2-6 of the disassembly procedure.

Solenoid Replacement

1. Disconnect the large connecting wire between starter and solenoid. See **Figure 49**.

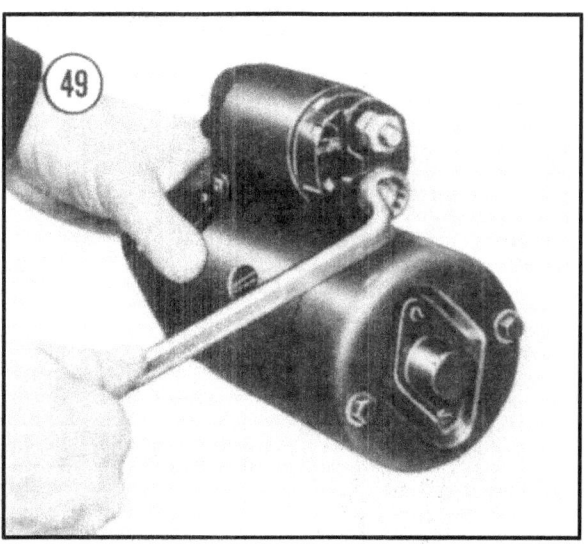

2. Remove 2 screws securing solenoid to the mounting bracket. See **Figure 50**.

3. Lift solenoid pull rod free of the operating lever and remove solenoid (**Figure 51**).

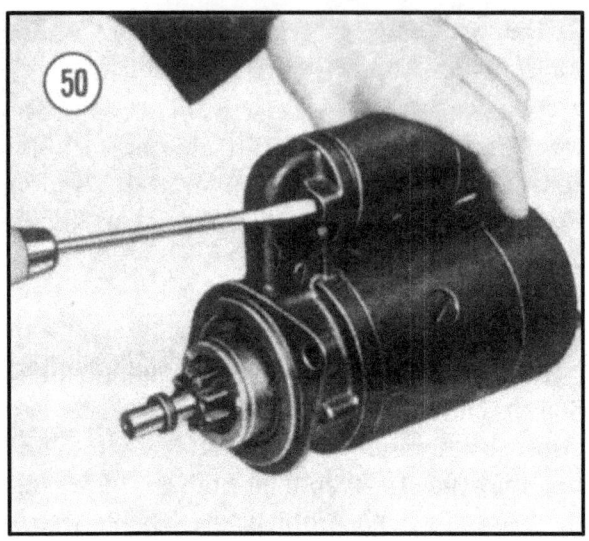

6. Pull the drive pinion to bring the operating lever back towards solenoid opening. Connect the pull rod to the operating lever.

7. Secure solenoid with mounting screws and reconnect large wire from starter. Ensure that the rubber grommet on the wire to the solenoid fits properly in the cover.

8. Install shims and lock ring. Check shaft endplay, which should be 0.004-0.006" (0.1-0.15mm). Adjust by adding or removing shims.

9. Install a new seal and install the end cap. Use sealing compound at A to E in Figure 48.

10. Install solenoid as described earlier.

Disassembly

Refer to **Figure 53** for the starter disassembly procedure.

1. Remove solenoid as described earlier.
2. Remove end cap (23) and seal (22).
3. Pry out the lock ring (21) and remove the shims (20).
4. Remove cover bolts (15) and cover (19).
5. Lift brushes out of brush holder.
6. Remove brush holder. See **Figure 54A**.

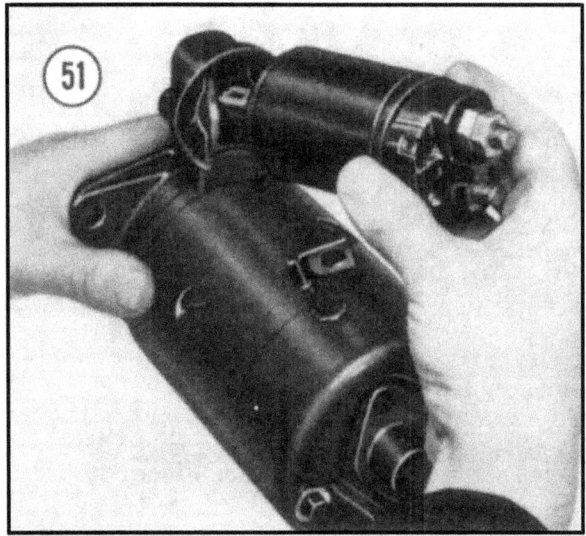

4. Do not change pull rod adjustment if old solenoid is to be reinstalled. On new solenoids, loosen the locknut and adjust dimension (a) shown in **Figure 52** to 0.748 ± 0.004" (19 ± 0.1mm). Tighten locknut.

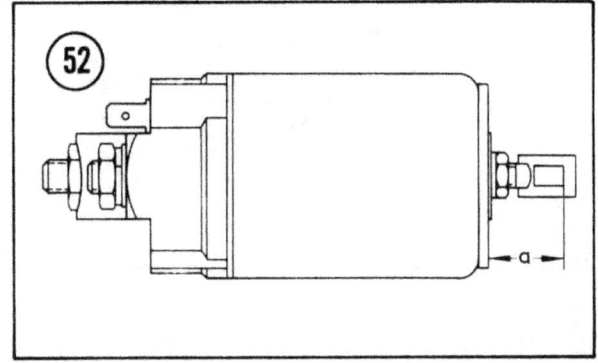

7. Remove housing (16) from the armature/mounting bracket assembly. See **Figure 54B**.

8. Remove actuating lever pin (1) and remove lever/armature assembly from housing.

9. Hold armature in a vise with soft jaws.

10. Pull actuating sleeve against overrunning clutch to release locking balls. Slide pinion assembly off the armature. Don't lose any of the small locking balls. See **Figure 55**.

5. Place a strip of VW D14 Plastic Sealer on the outer edge of solenoid face.

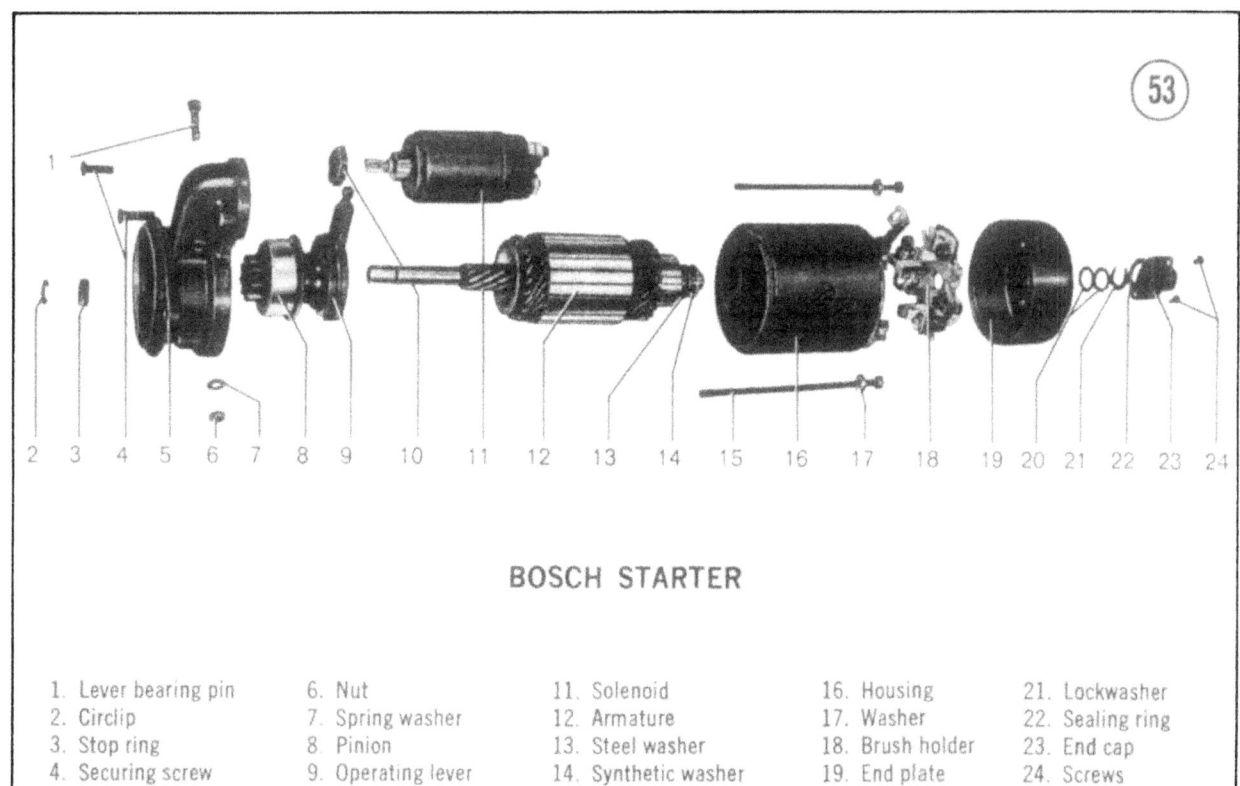

BOSCH STARTER

1. Lever bearing pin
2. Circlip
3. Stop ring
4. Securing screw
5. Mounting bracket
6. Nut
7. Spring washer
8. Pinion
9. Operating lever
10. Rubber seal
11. Solenoid
12. Armature
13. Steel washer
14. Synthetic washer
15. Housing screw
16. Housing
17. Washer
18. Brush holder
19. End plate
20. Shims
21. Lockwasher
22. Sealing ring
23. End cap
24. Screws

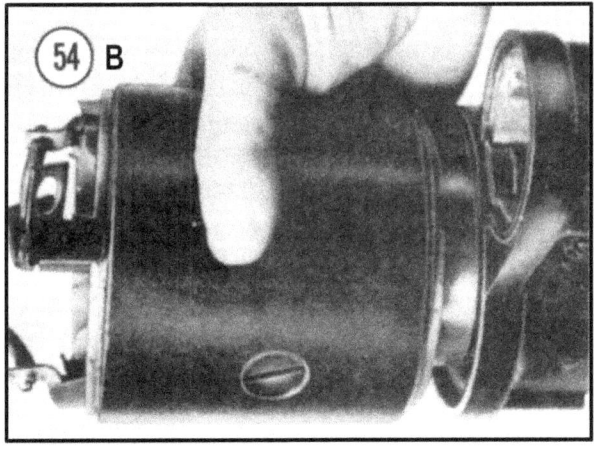

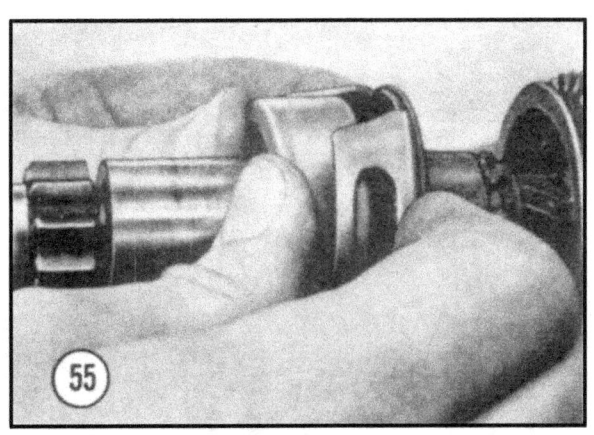

Cleaning and Inspection

Clean all parts, carefully following the same procedure provided for the 914 starter. Inspection is also identical to the 914 starter inspection procedure.

Bushing Replacement

1. If either the mounting bracket bushing or end cover bushing is scored or worn, drive out the old bushing with a suitable drift.

2. Clean out the bushing hole and remove any burrs.

3. Soak new bushings in hot light oil for at least an hour.

4. Install bushings with a suitable drift.

Assembly

1. Place balls in locking ring. Hold in place with grease. See **Figure 56**.

2. Hold armature in a vise with soft jaws.

3. Push pinion assembly onto armature shaft until balls lock in place. See **Figure 57**.

4. Install actuating lever on pinion assembly.

⑤⑥

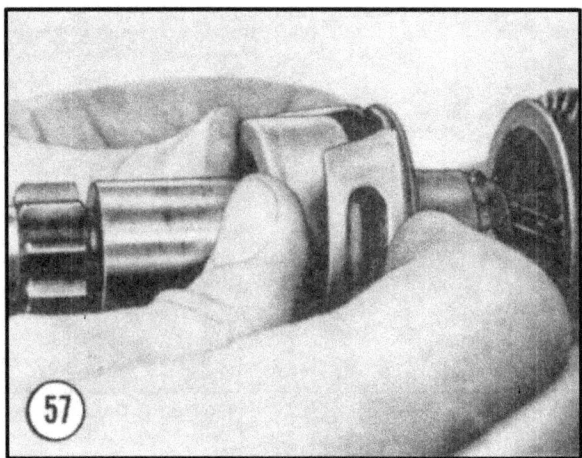

㊺

5. Install armature into drive housing. Secure lever with pin.

6. Install rubber seal into drive housing. See **Figure 58**.

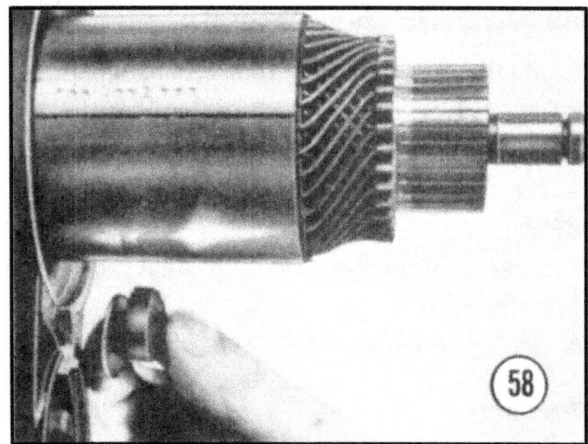

㊽

7. Install field housing over armature.

8. Slide steel shim(s) (13) and fiber washer (14) onto armature shaft.

9. Install brush holder on the commutator and insert brushes.

10. Lubricate bushing in end cover (19) with oil. Install end cover on the housing with long screws. Use sealing compound at A to E in Figure 48.

LIGHTING SYSTEM

The following procedures describe replacement of lamps and relays associated with the lighting system. Refer to **Table 2** for bulb type used for each function.

Table 2 BULBS

Function	U.S. Replacement	Porsche Part No.
Headlight	6014	
Front turn signals	1141 ①	900.631.115.90
Front parking	1891	900.631.104.90
Side marker	—	999.631.104.91
Stop/tail	1034	999.631.115.90
Rear turn signal	1141 ①	999.631.114.90
License plate	—	900.631.103.90
Back-up	1141	999.631.114.90
Interior light	—	900.631.106.90
Instrument	—	900.631.102.90
Warning	—	900.631.102.90
Luggage compartment	—	900.631.103.90

① 1972 on. Earlier models use 1034.

Headlight Replacement

1. Turn headlights on to raise them.

2. Disconnect battery ground cable.

3. Loosen Phillips screw and lift off headlight casing. See **Figure 59**.

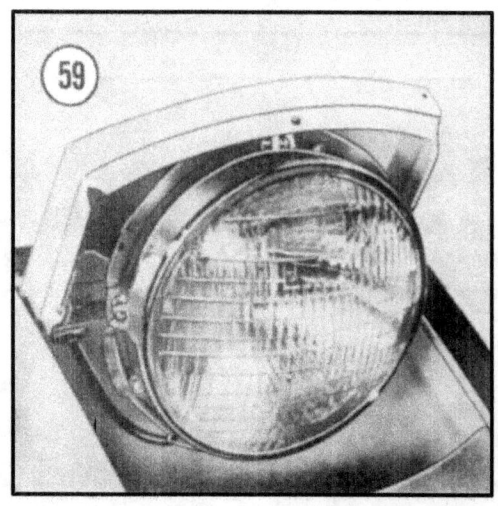

㊾

4. Remove retaining ring, lift sealed beam lamp out, and unplug it.

5. Installation is the reverse of these steps. Adjust headlights according to local traffic regulations. Adjusting screws are shown in **Figure 60**.

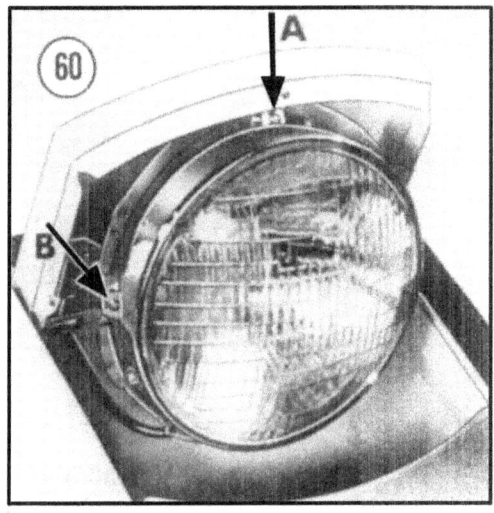

A. Vertical aim   B. Lateral aim

Headlight Switch Replacement

1. Disconnect the battery ground cable.

2. Unscrew the instrument panel knob. Unscrew the retaining ring with a special tool shown in **Figure 61**. Pull switch out.

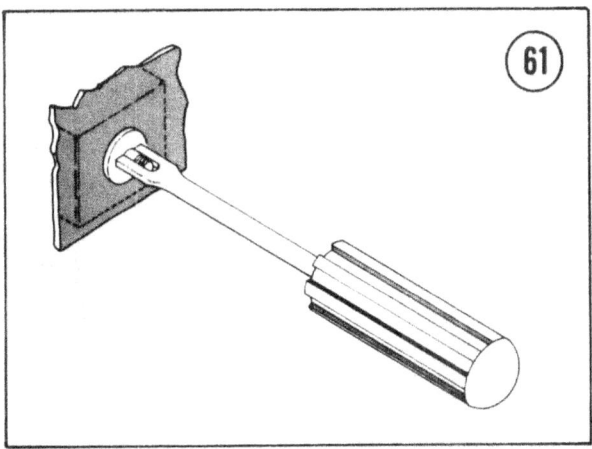

3. Sketch the switch terminals indicating wire color. Mark wires with terminal number. Remove wires from the switch.

4. Installation is the reverse of these steps. Connect wires correctly according to your sketch.

Front Parking, Turn Signal Lights

Front parking and turn signal lamps are located in the same fender-mounted assembly. To replace any of the lamps, remove 2 screws securing the lens and lift it off. Replace the lamp and secure the lens. See **Figure 62**.

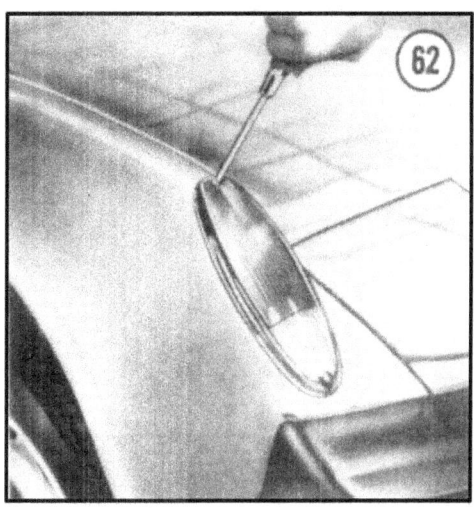

Front side marker lights are separate assemblies. Remove 2 screws securing lens (see **Figure 63**), replace lamp and reinstall lens.

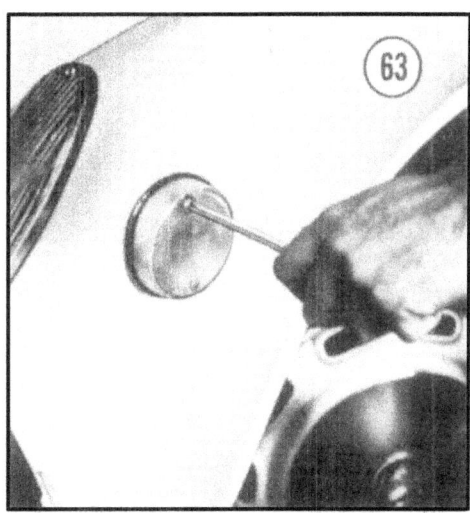

Taillights

To replace the rear turn signal, brake, or back-up lamps, unscrew 3 knurled knobs on back of taillight assembly and lift off lens. See **Figures 64 and 65**.

License Plate Light

Remove 2 screws securing light assembly to bumper. See **Figure 66**. Replace lamp and reinstall assembly.

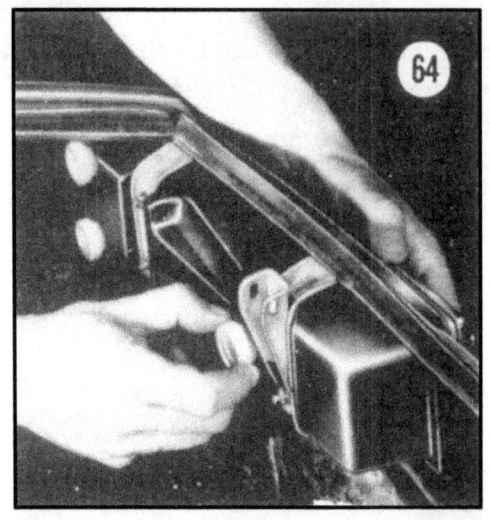

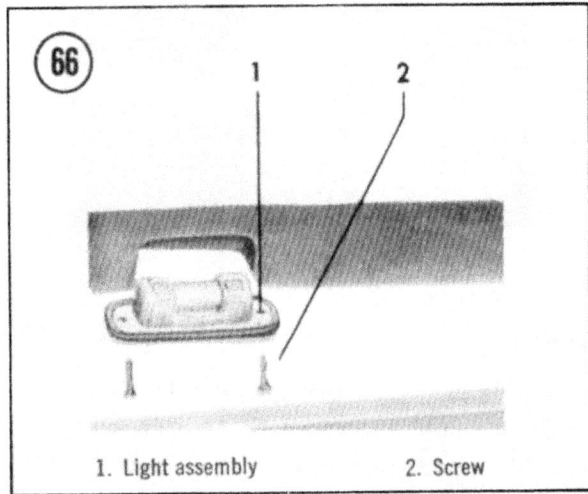

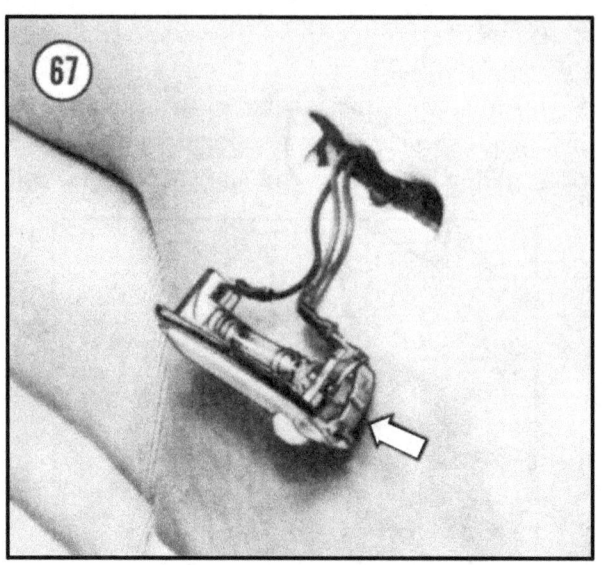

Interior Light

The interior light is mounted between the seats. To replace the lamp, *carefully* pry assembly out of backrest (see **Figure 67**), replace bulb, and snap assembly back in place.

INSTRUMENTS

Dash Panel Insert—Removal/Installation

1. Disconnect battery ground cable.

2. Remove steering wheel as described in Chapter Thirteen.

3. Remove 4 screws securing insert. See **Figure 68**.

4. Pull insert forward slightly. Disconnect speedometer and tachometer cables. See **Figure 69**.

5. Sketch back of instruments and mark all wires to aid in installation. Disconnect wires and instrument lights from instruments.

6. Installation is the reverse of these steps. **Figure 70** shows connections.

Instrument Removal/Installation

1. Perform Steps 1-4 of *Dash Panel Insert Removal*.

2. Sketch back of instrument to be removed and mark wires. Disconnect wires from instrument.

3. Push instrument out through the front of the insert.

4. Installation is the reverse of these steps.

DIRECTIONAL SIGNAL SYSTEMS

The directional signal system consists of the steering column-mounted switch, flasher, and indicator lamps.

Switch Removal/Installation

1. Disconnect battery ground cable.

2. Remove steering wheel. See Chapter Thirteen.

3. Remove 2 screws from horn contact ring. See **Figure 71**. Disconnect wire and remove ring.

4. Remove screws holding upper and lower halves of switch housing.

5. Disconnect wires from combination switch.

6. Remove switch mounting screws and lift switch out.

Flasher Relay Replacement

The flasher relay is located under the instrument panel near the steering column. Unplug old relay and install new one.

Lamp Replacement

Front directional signal lamps are behind same lens as parking lamps and side markers. See *Front Parking, Turn Signal Lights* and *Front Side Marker Lights* procedures in this chapter.

Rear directional signal lamps are part of brake lamps. See *Taillight* procedure in this chapter.

FUSES

The main fuse box is located under the instrument panel to the left of the steering column. The function of each fuse is clearly marked inside the protective cover. See **Figure 72**.

Two additional fuses for the rear window defogger and fuel pump are located on the relay panel at the left side of the engine compartment. See **Figure 73**.

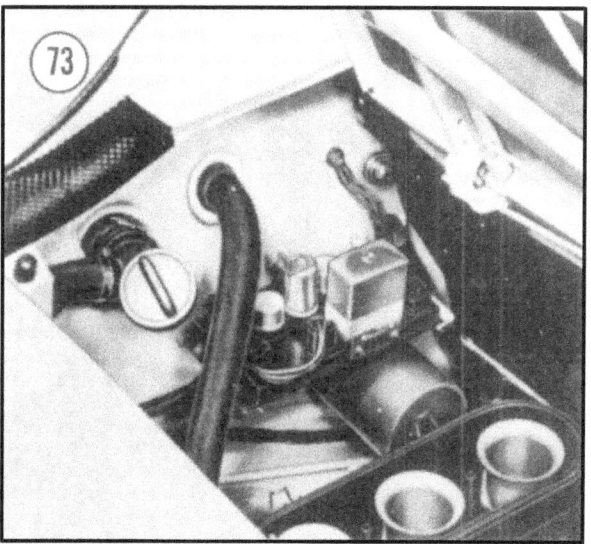

Whenever a fuse blows, ascertain the reason for the failure before replacing the fuse. Usually the trouble is a short circuit in the wiring. This may be caused by worn-through insulation or a

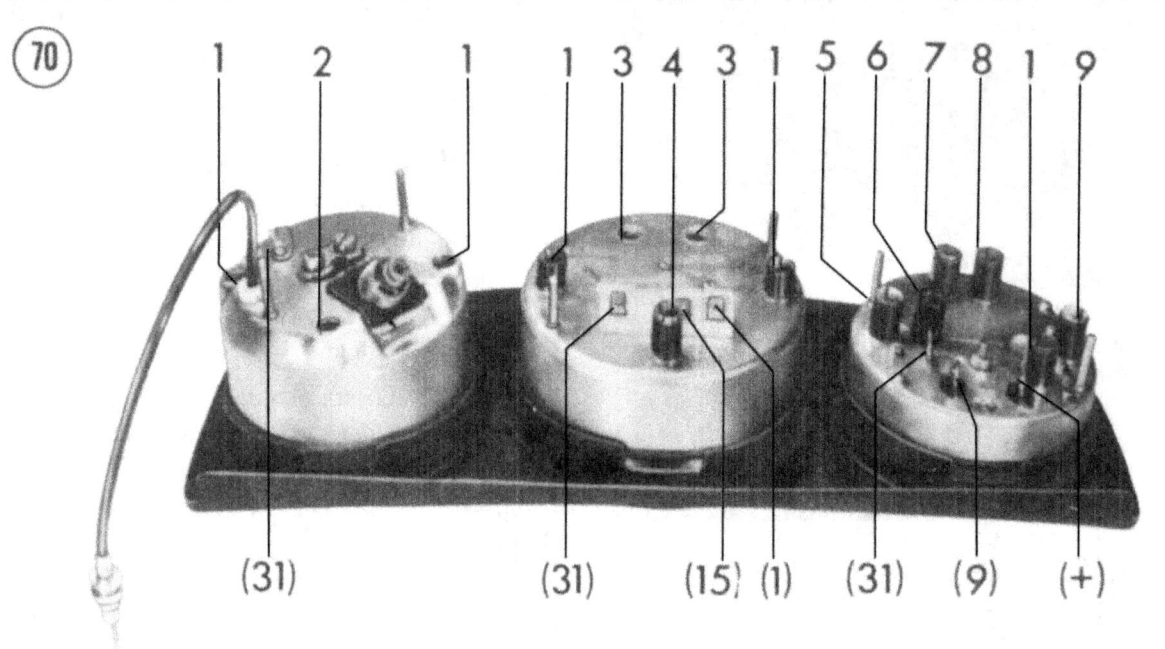

914 INSTRUMENTS

Numbers in parentheses indicate actual terminal designations.

0. Not used
1. Instrument illumination
2. Parking light indicator—green
3. Turn signal indicator—green
4. High beam indicator—blue
5. Generator warning light—red
6. Low fuel indicator—red
7. Oil temperature indicator light
8. Brake warning light—red
9. Oil pressure warning light—green
10. Terminal #15
11. To oil temperature sensor
12. To fuel level sensor
13. To tachometer ballast unit
14. To ground
15. Flex shaft for trip mileage reset
16. Washer
17. Round nut
18. Knurled knob

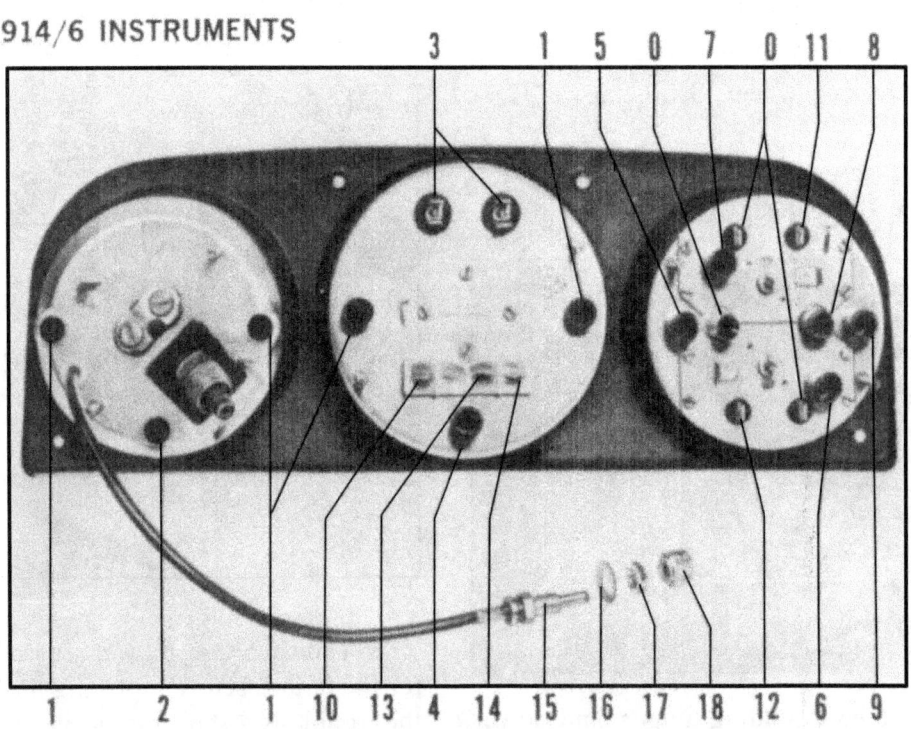

914/6 INSTRUMENTS

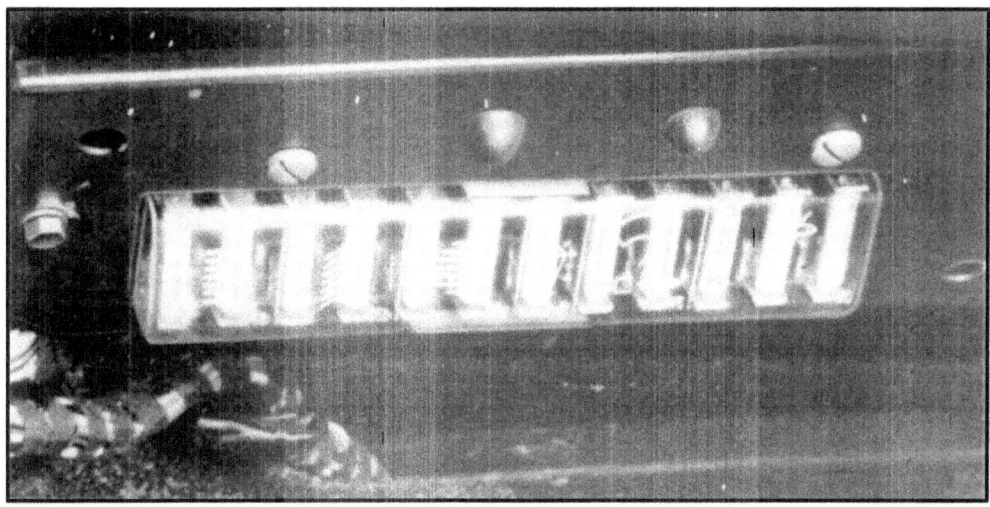

FUSES

Fuse No.	Amps Through 1973	Amps 1974 and Later	Function	Fuse No.	Amps Through 1973	Amps 1974 and Later	Function
1	8	8	Left headlight high beam	7	8	8	License plate lights
2	8	8	Right headlight high beam	8	25	16	Windshield wipers, Ventilator, horn cigarette lighter
3	8	8	Left headlight	9	8	8	Turn signals, stop lights, back-up light
4	8	8	Right headlight	10	8	16	Additional headlights, horn (1974 on)
5	8	8	Left parking lights	11	8	8	Emergency flashers
6	8	8	Right parking lights	12	25	16	Headlight raising and lowering, interior light

wire which works its way loose and shorts to ground. Carry several spare fuses in the glove compartment.

CAUTION
Never substitute tinfoil or wire for a fuse. An overload could result in fire and complete loss of the automobile.

HORN

If the horn works, but not loudly or not at the correct pitch, make sure it is not touching the body. Horn pitch and loudness can be adjusted by removing the seal on the rear of the horn and turning the adjusting screw.

When the horn does not work at all, check the wiring to the horn and check the horn switch. To service the switch:

1. Disconnect battery ground cable.

2. Turn horn button to left and lift off. See **Figure 74**.

3. Remove contact pin.

4. Remove the steering wheel as described in Chapter Thirteen.

5. Remove 2 screws securing contact ring. Disconnect wire from ring.

6. Clean contact points with fine crocus cloth.

7. Installation is the reverse of these steps.

Horn Replacement

The horn is located behind the left grill in the bumper. An additional horn is behind the right bumper grill on the 914/6 only.

1. Remove grill.

2. Remove nut securing horn to bracket. See **Figure 75**.

3. Disconnect wire from horn.

4. Installation is the reverse of these steps. Make sure the horn does not touch the body.

FRESH AIR SYSTEM

Fresh Air Blower Removal/Installation

1. Remove fuel tank. See Chapter 8.

2. Remove the bolt from each end of the blower box.

3. Disconnect the air ducts from the blower. See **Figure 76**.

4. Disconnect water drain hoses from blower. See **Figure 77**.

5. Disconnect Belden cable. See **Figure 78**.

6. Pull off electrical plug.

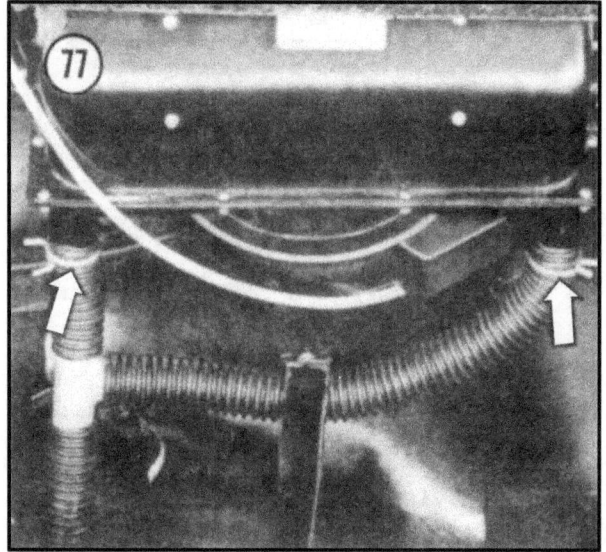

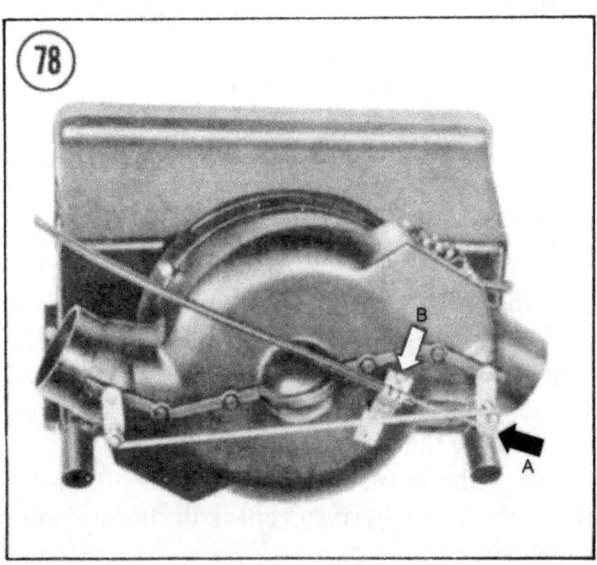

214

7. Remove blower.

8. Installation is the reverse of these steps. Adjust cable length so that both air flaps on blower are open when control is on position III.

Fresh Air Control Removal/Installation

1. Disconnect battery ground cable.
2. Disconnect Belden cables from fresh air flaps.
3. Remove bolt (see **Figure 79**) and pull control assembly out slightly.

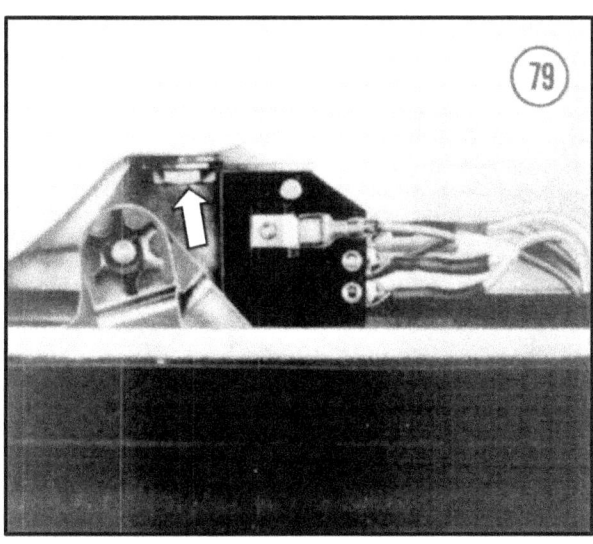

4. Disconnect electrical connections (see **Figure 80**).

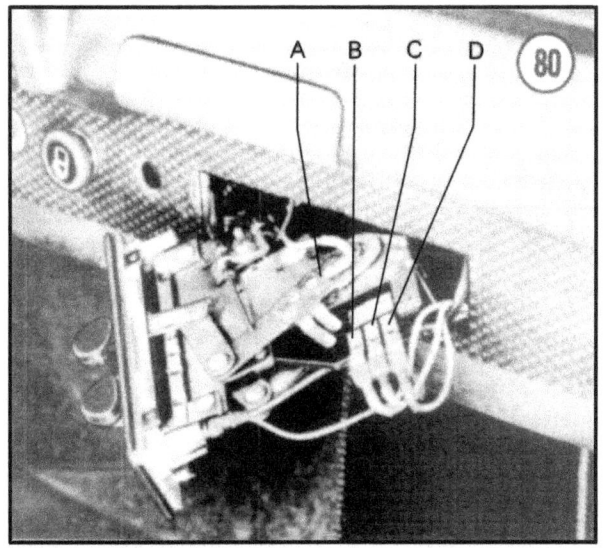

A. Ground
B. Slow speed (white/green wire)
C. Medium speed (white/yellow wire)
D. Fast speed (white wire)

5. Pull control assembly out complete with control cables.
6. Installation is the reverse of these steps.

WINDSHIELD WIPER

Wiper Motor Removal/Installation

Refer to **Figure 81** for the following procedure.

1. Disconnect battery ground cable.
2. Remove cap nuts from wiper arms, and remove arms.
3. Remove bearing cap, nut, washer, and seal from each wiper arm shaft.
4. Remove activated charcoal filter.
5. Remove fuel tank. See Chapter 8.
6. Remove fresh air blower housing (see procedure in this chapter).
7. Loosen nut securing wiper frame to body under instrument panel. See **Figure 82**.

8. Pull the wiper frame and the motor downward and out.
9. Disconnect wires from motor. Make a small sketch to aid reassembly.
10. Remove nuts securing motor shaft to drive crank.
11. Pull the drive crank off the motor shaft with a suitable puller.
12. Remove 3 bolts securing motor to frame and remove motor.
13. Before remounting the motor on the frame,

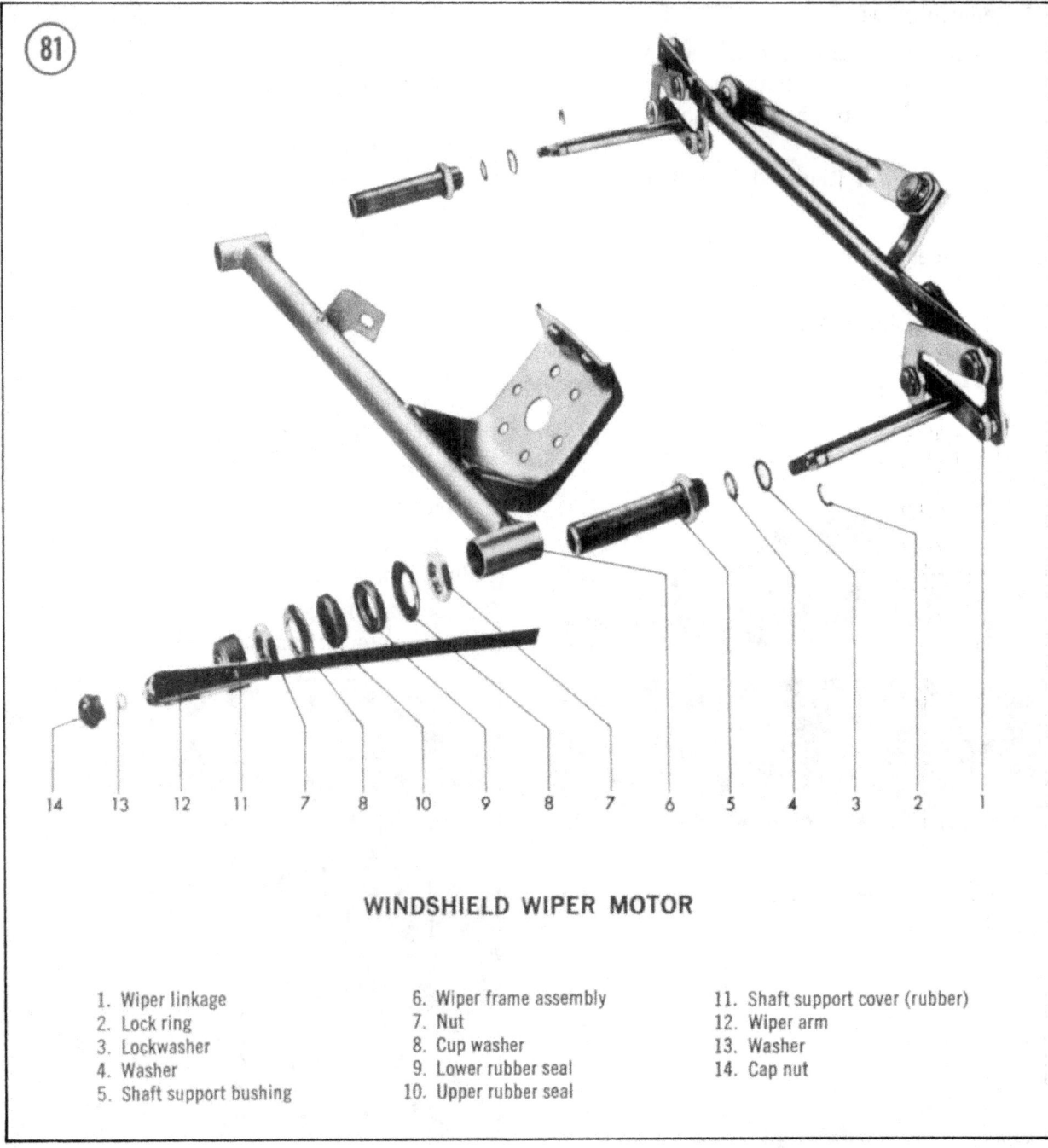

WINDSHIELD WIPER MOTOR

1. Wiper linkage
2. Lock ring
3. Lockwasher
4. Washer
5. Shaft support bushing
6. Wiper frame assembly
7. Nut
8. Cup washer
9. Lower rubber seal
10. Upper rubber seal
11. Shaft support cover (rubber)
12. Wiper arm
13. Washer
14. Cap nut

connect the battery ground cable. Connect proper wires from motor to terminals 53 and 53a on switch. Let motor run for about 30 seconds, then disconnect the wire to terminal 53. The motor will stop at its "park" position. Disconnect terminal 53a, then the battery ground cable.

14. Mount motor in frame and connect drive crank.

15. Reinstall motor/frame assembly by reversing Steps 1-7.

Wiper Switch Removal/Installation

Perform *Directional Switch Removal* procedure, except remove the right-hand switch instead of the left.

IGNITION SYSTEM

The ignition system consists of the battery, ignition switch, ignition coil, distributor, spark plugs, and associated wiring. The following steps describe replacement procedures.

Ignition Switch Replacement

1. Remove fuse box.
2. Remove headlight and emergency flasher switches from instrument panel. See **Figure 83**.

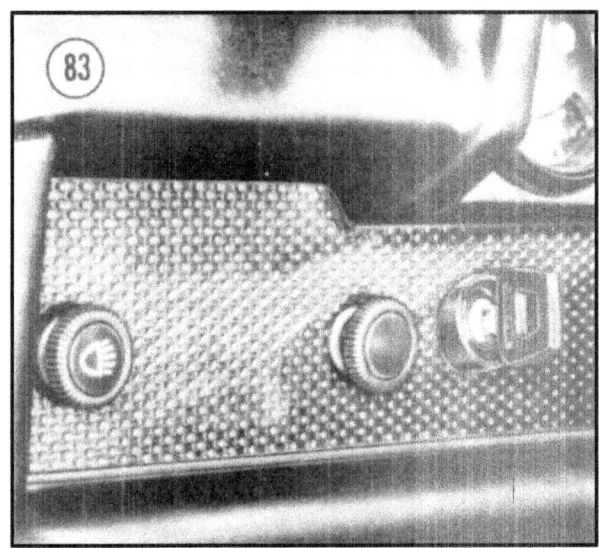

3. Remove connector from ignition switch. Unscrew trim ring around switch. Remove instrument panel from dash.
4. Remove screw shown in **Figure 84** which secures the switch.

5. Drill out shear bolts securing ignition switch. See **Figure 85**. Remove switch and support plate.
6. Install new ignition switch and tighten *new* shear bolts lightly. Install Phillips screw also.
7. Insert key and turn switch "ON". Turn steering wheel from lock to lock to ensure the lock pin does not touch locking grooves on steering shaft. Tighten shear bolts until the heads break off.
8. Glue instrument panel on.
9. Install ignition switch trim ring and headlight and emergency flasher switches.
10. Connect plug to ignition switch.
11. Install fuse box.
12. Check for proper operation.

Ignition Coil Replacement

A defective ignition coil must be replaced. Disconnect primary and secondary wires from coil and remove it from bracket. Install new coil; connect wires.

Distributor Removal

1. Turn engine crankshaft over until piston No. 1 is at TDC on a compression stroke. See Chapter Two, *Valve Adjustment*.
2. Remove distributor cap. Leave wires connected.
3. Disconnect primary lead from ignition coil terminal 1.
4. Disconnect the vacuum line to the advance unit, if any.
5. Remove the distributor clamp nut. See **Figure 86**.
6. Lift distributor out.

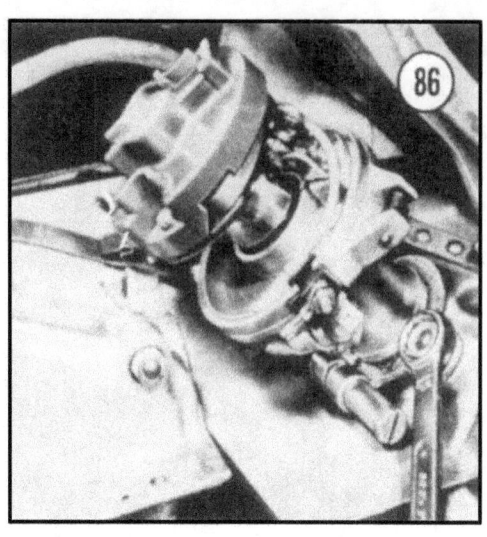

Distributor Installation

1. Ensure that piston No. 1 is still at TDC on a compression stroke.

2. Insert distributor. Rotor must point in approximate direction shown in **Figure 87** (914, 914S) or **Figure 88** (914/6). Rotate distributor housing until notch lines up with rotor.

3. Tighten clamp nut.

4. Install distributor cap and adjust ignition timing as described in Chapter Two.

Table 1   SPECIFICATIONS

	914	914/6
BATTERY		
Voltage	12	12
Capacity	45aH	45aH
ALTERNATOR		
Part No.	022 903 023	911.603.118.00
Regulator	021 903 803A	901.603.206.02
Maximum current	50A	55A
Mean regulating voltage	14V	14V
Nominal output speed	2,000 rpm	2,000 rpm
STARTER		
Type	003 911 023A	003 911 023A
Voltage	12	12
Output	0.8 hp	0.8 hp
Solenoid cut-in voltage	7	7
DISTRIBUTOR		
Breaker point gap	0.016" (0.4mm)	0.016" (0.4mm)
Dwell angle	44-50°	35-41°
Total advance @ 3,500 rpm	27°	—
Total advance @ 6,000 rpm	—	35°

WIRING DIAGRAMS

914/4 1970

914/4 1971

914/4 1972 & 1973

914/4 AFC 1974, 1975 & 1976

914/4 MPC 1974, 1975 & 1976

914/6

914/6 (German Language w/ English Key)

1970 914/4

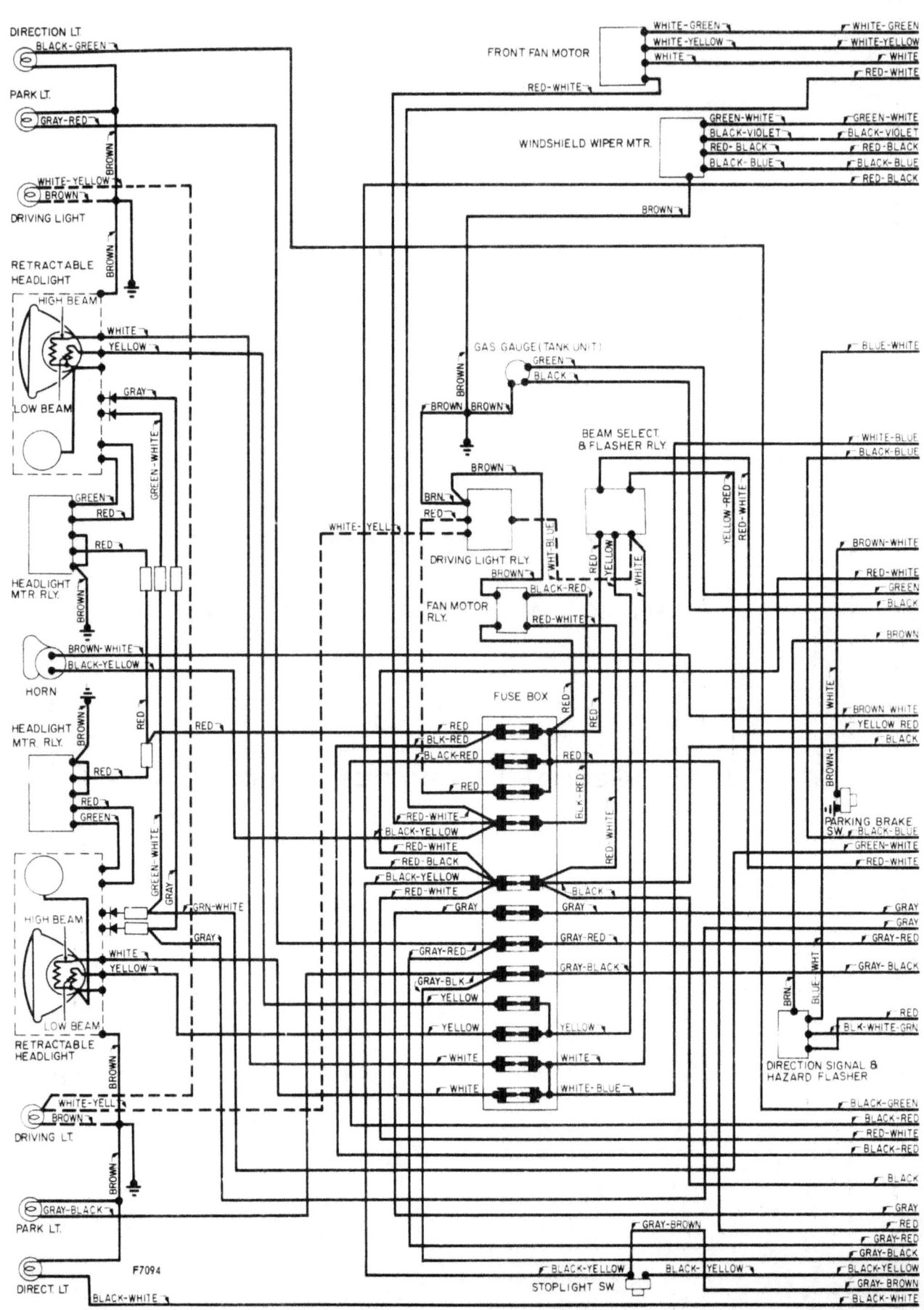

1970 914/4

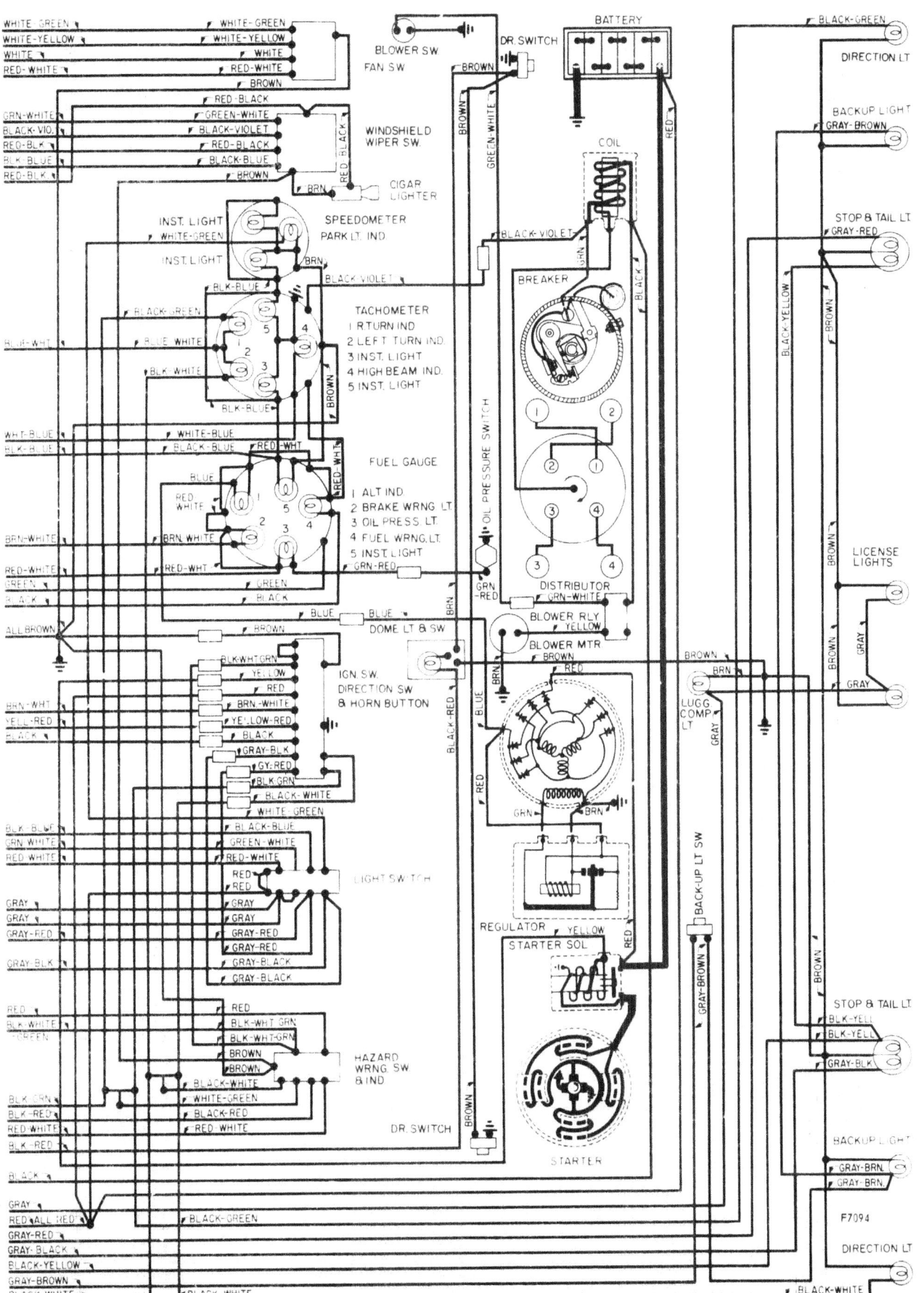

1971 914/4

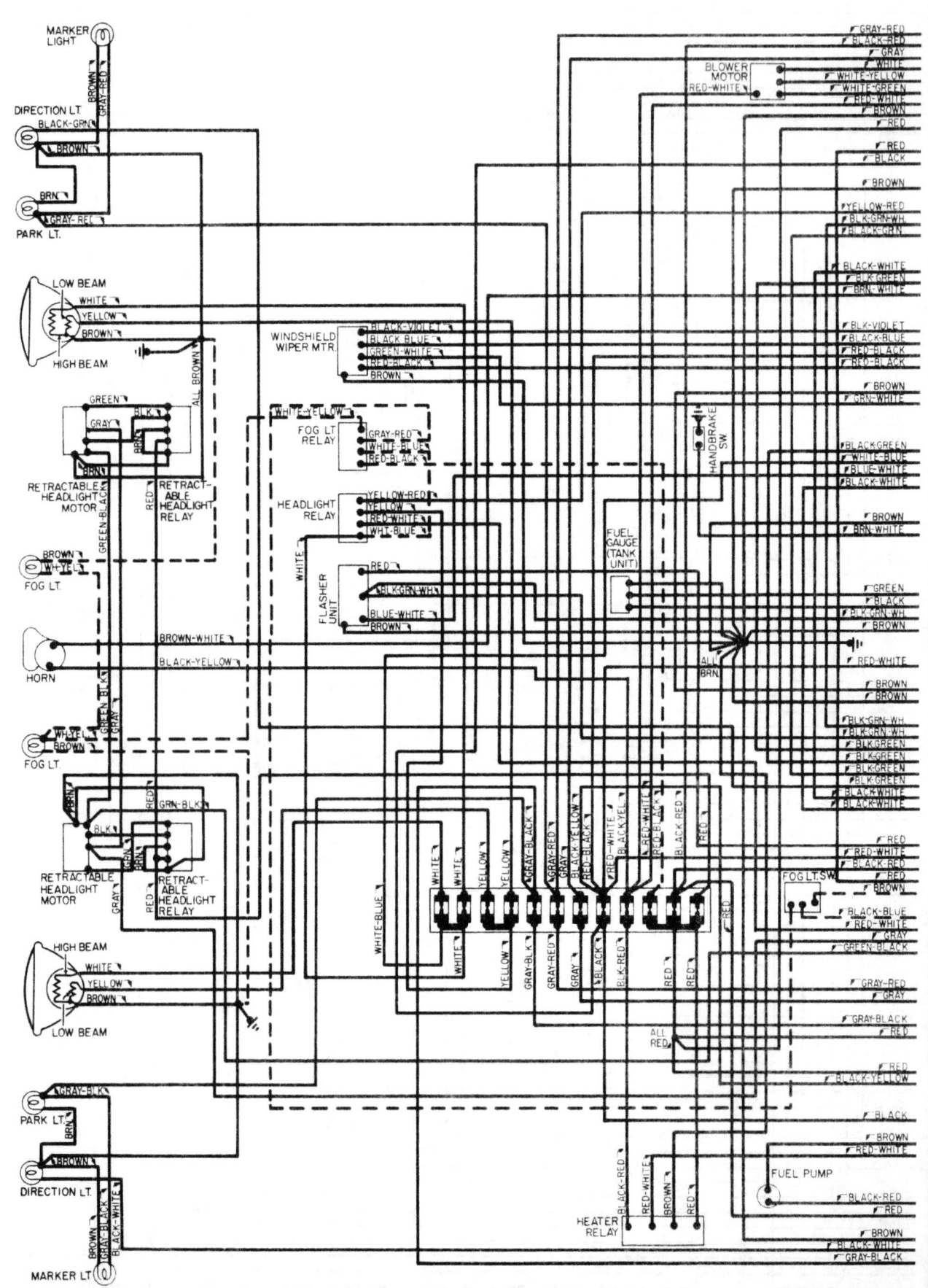

1971 914/4

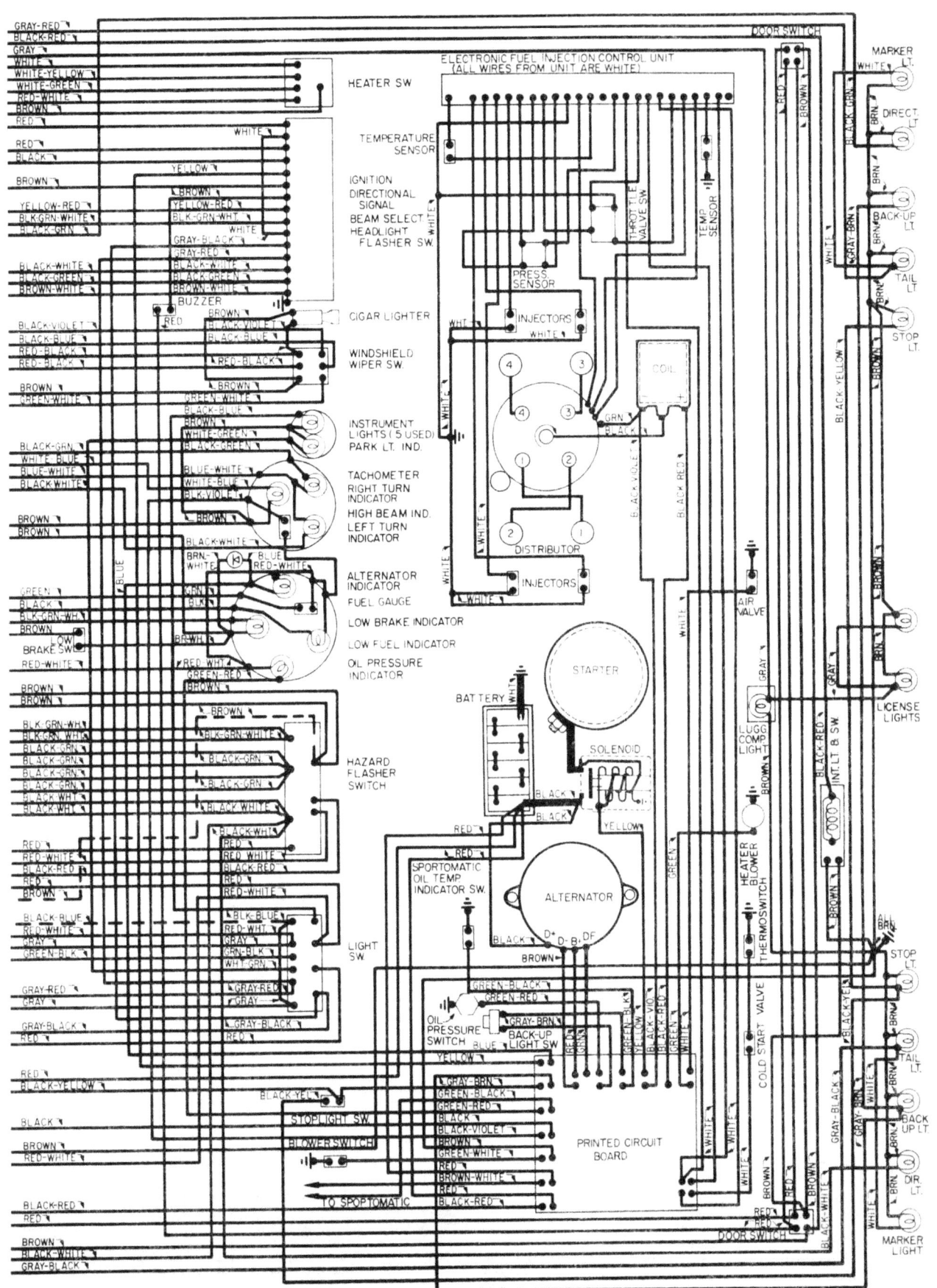

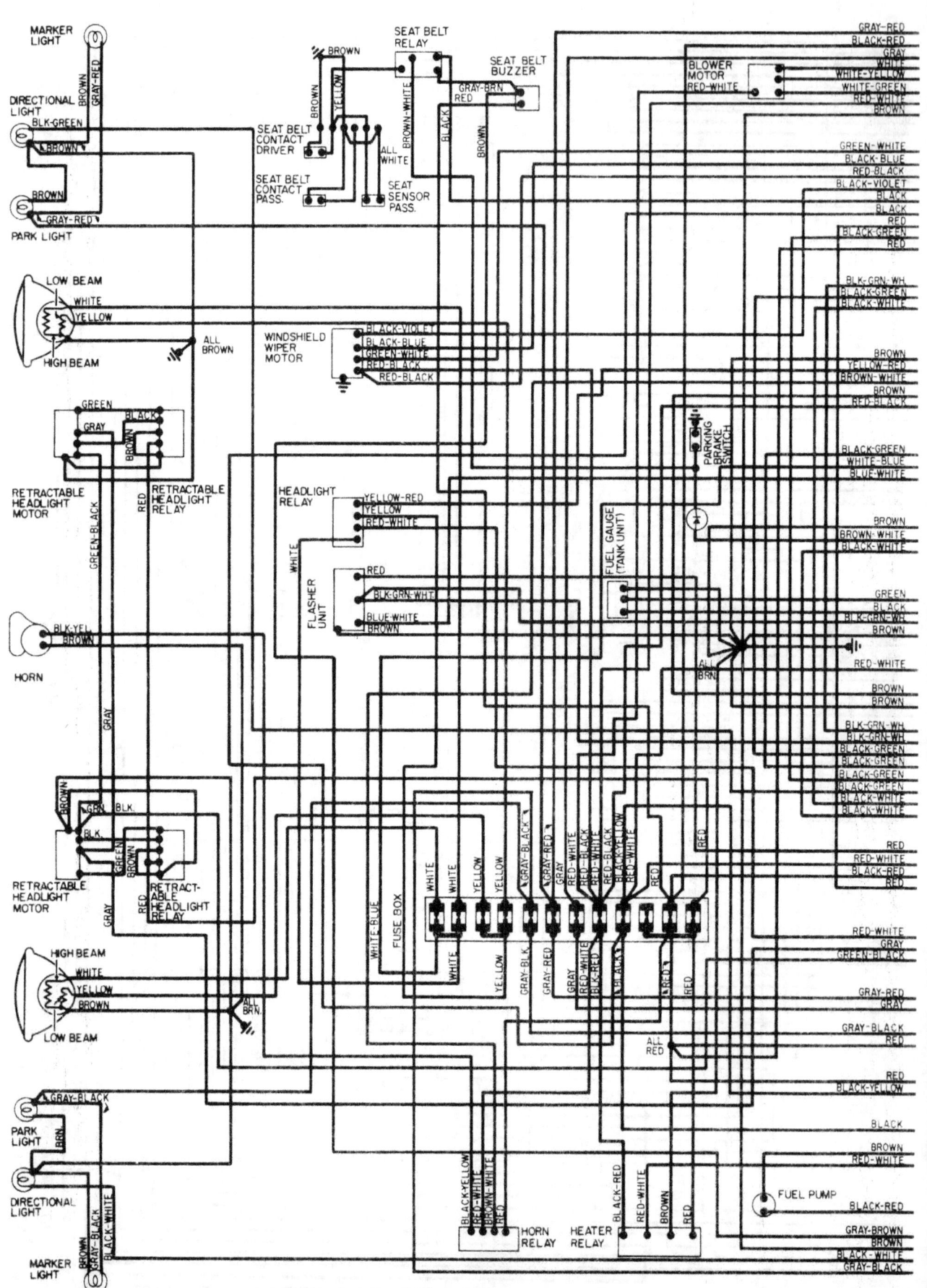

1972-1973 914/4

1972 - 1973 914/4

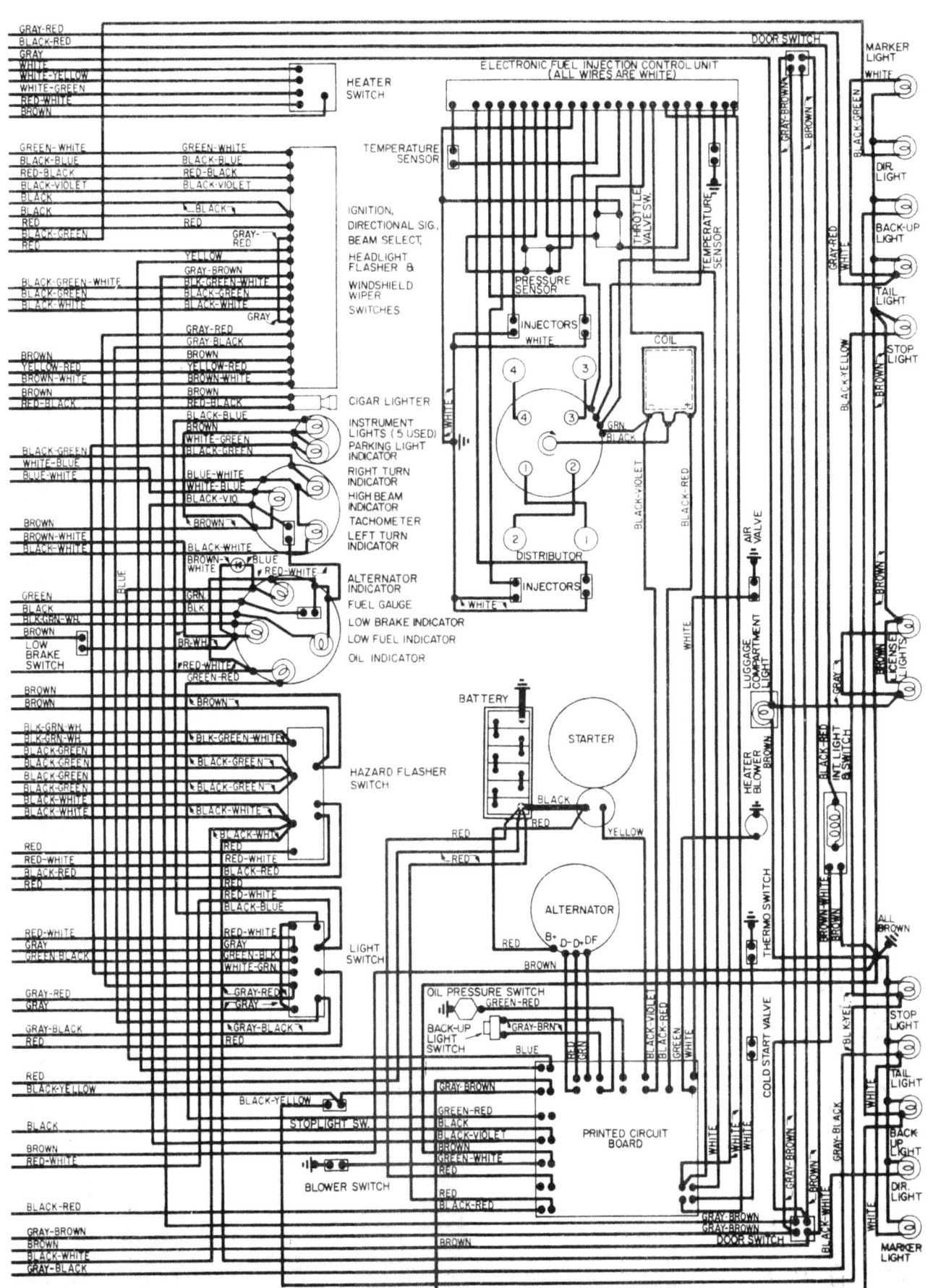

1974-1975-1976 914/4 AFC

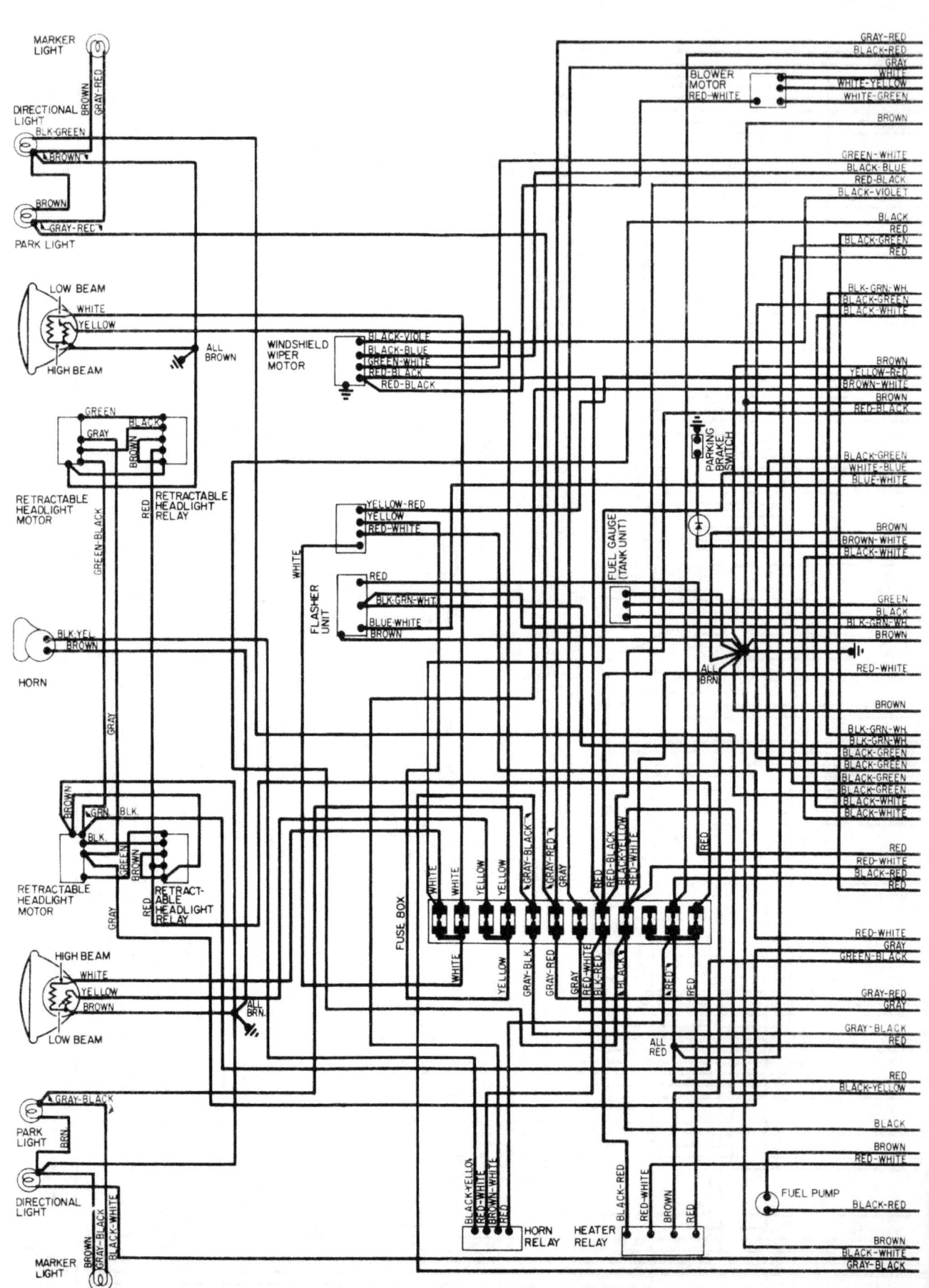

1974-1975-1976 914/4 AFC

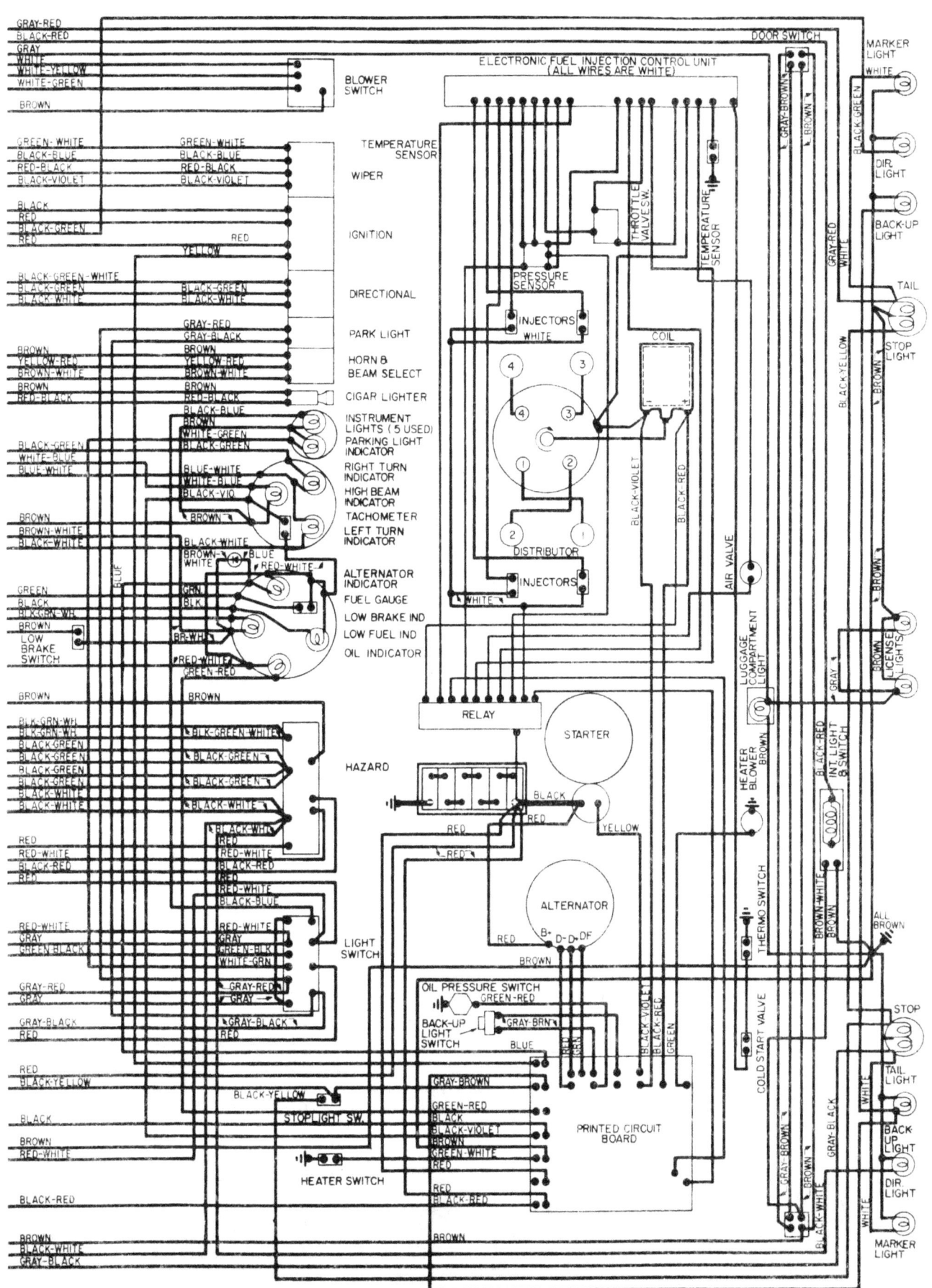

227

1974-1975-1976 914/4 MPC

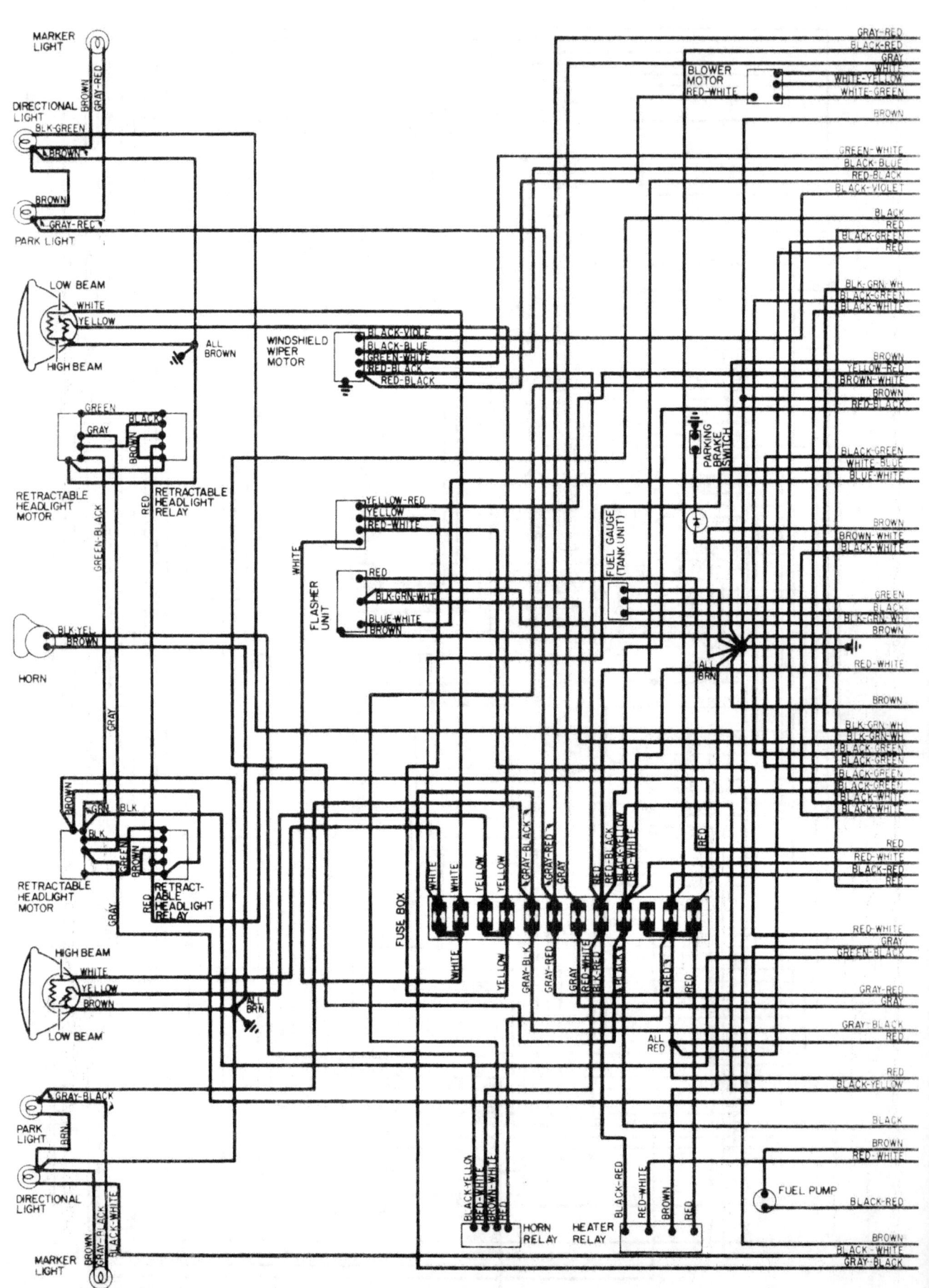

1974 - 1975 - 1976 914/4 MPC

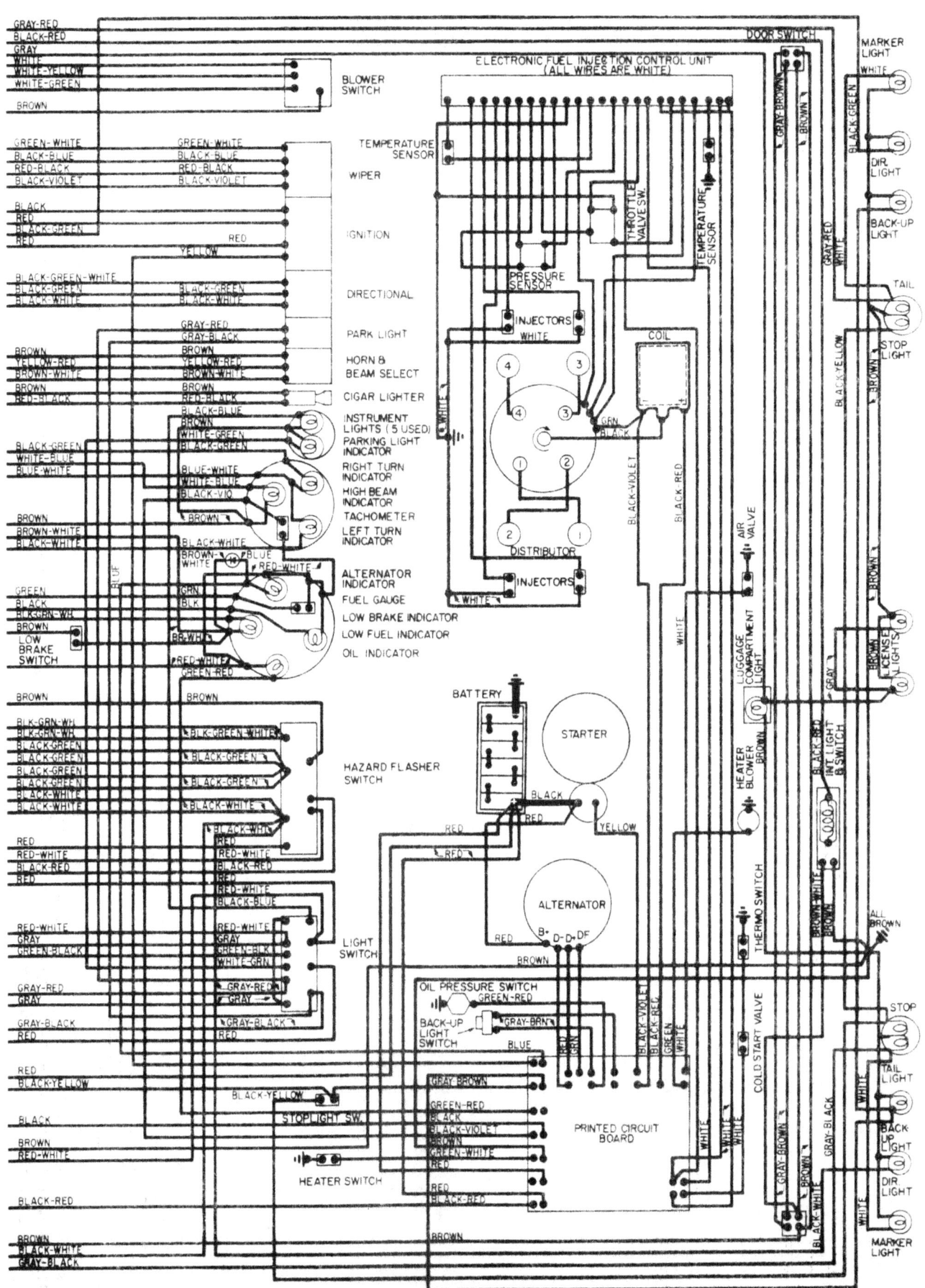

914/6

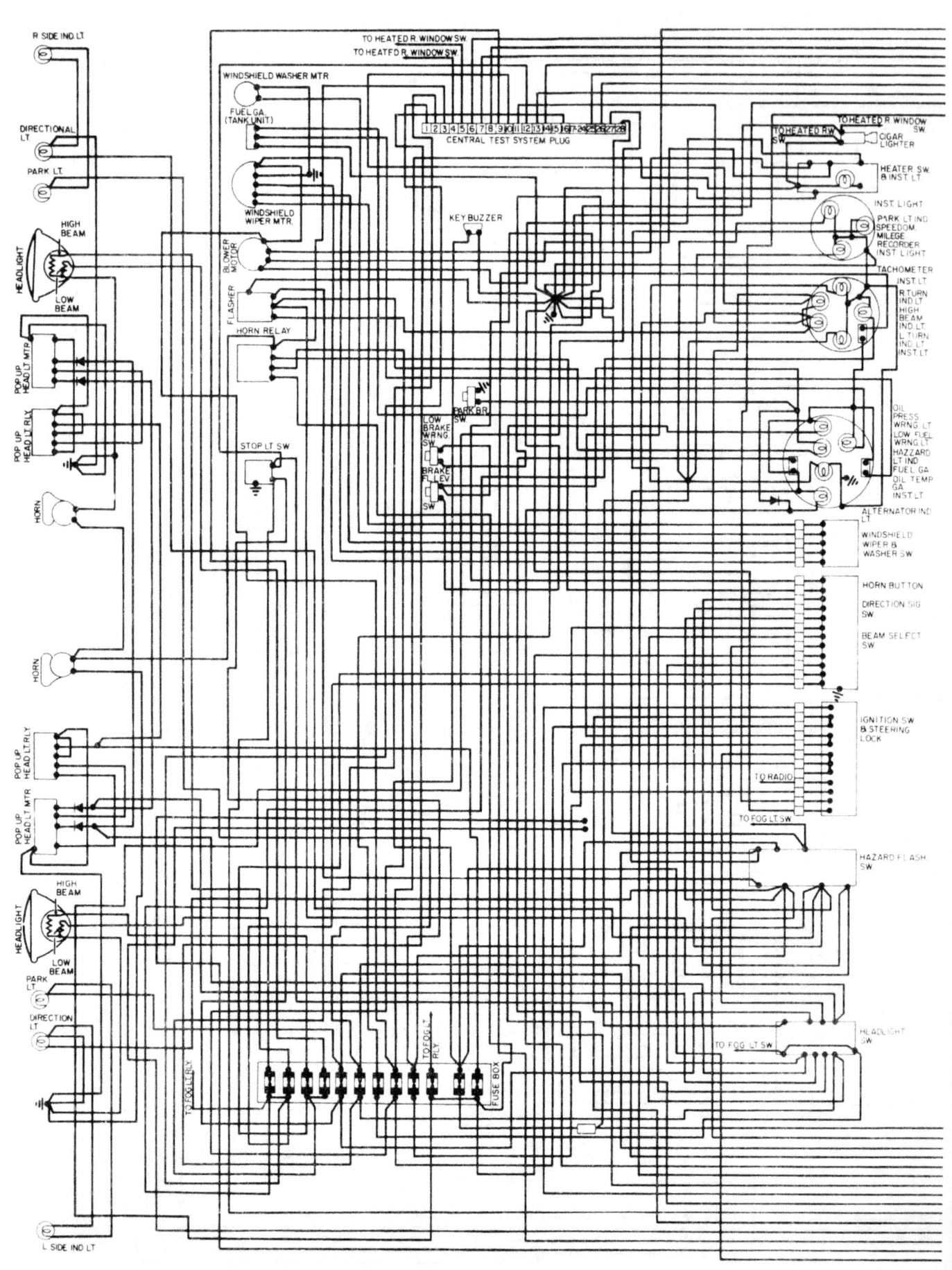

914/6

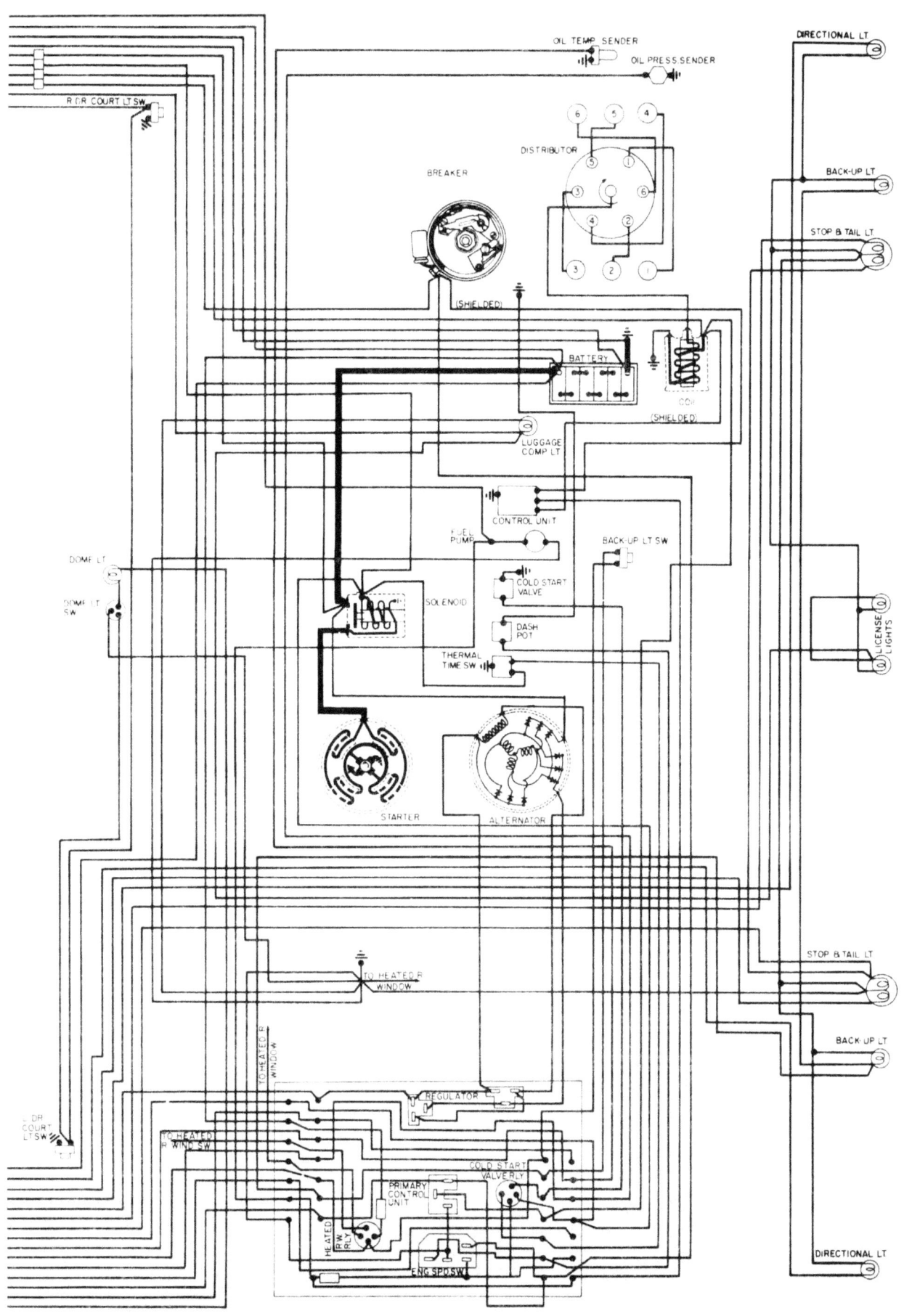

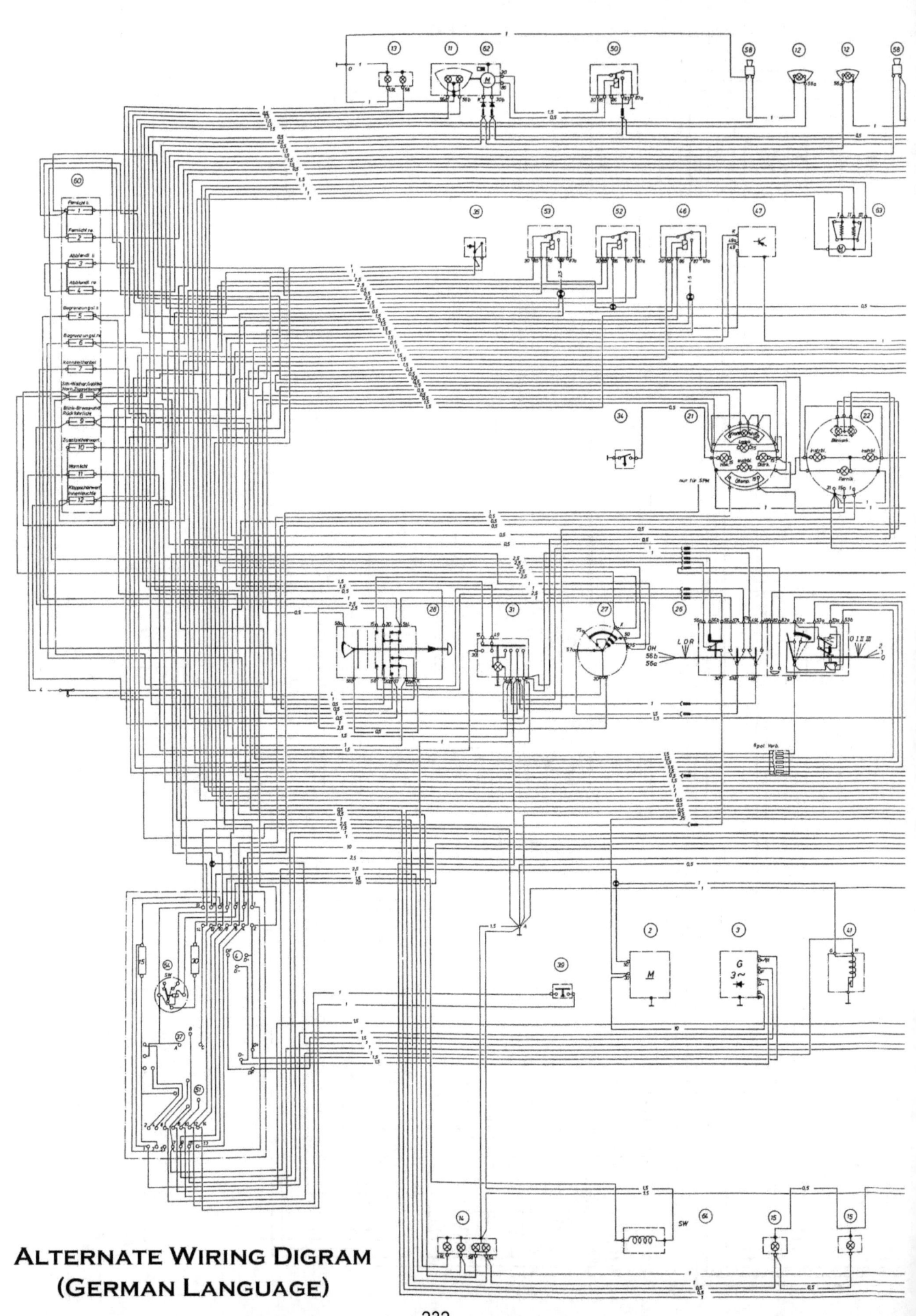

ALTERNATE WIRING DIGRAM (GERMAN LANGUAGE)

914/6

ELECTRICAL WIRING DIAGRAM

No.	Description	Remarks
	Engine	
1	Battery	
2	Starter	
3	Alternator	
4	Regulator	
5	Ignition distributor	
6	Coil (ignition transformer)	
7	Spark plugs	
9	Fuel pump	
10	Cold start valve	
	Lights	
11	Headlamps	
12	Additional high beam headlamps	
13	Turn indicator and side lights	
14	Rear, stop, turn indicator and backup lights	
15	Licence plate light	
16	Interior light	
18	Luggage compartment light, rear	
	Instruments	
21	Small combined instrument with oil temperature and fuel gauges, fuel level, charge, handbrake and oil pressure warning lights	
22	Revolution counter with turn indicator and high beam warning lights	
23	Speedometer with trip mileage recorder and sidelight telltale	
	Switches	
26	Combined turn indicator, low beam wiper and washer switch with horn push in steering wheel	
27	Ignition/starter switch with steering lock	
28	Main light switch	
30	Switch for blower and auxiliary heater	
31	Hazard warning flasher switch	
33	Door operated light switches	
34	Handbrake contact	
35	Stop light switch	
36	Control unit	
37	Primary control unit	
39	Back up light switch	
40	Oil pressure contact	
41	Thermal time switch	
42	Heated rear window switch	Optional

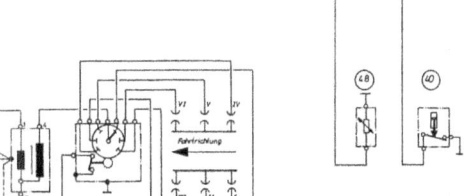

Fuses
1. Headlight (LH) - main beam
2. Headlight (RH) - main beam
3. Headlight (LH) - low beam
4. Headlight (RH) - low beam
5. Side/tail lights (LH)
6. Side/tail lights (RH)
7. Rear boot and license plate light
8. Windshield wiper, ventilation and heater blower, horn and cigarette lighter
9. Brake/indicator/reversing lights
10. Additional headlights
11. Emergency warning flasher
12. Headlight motor and interior light.

No.	Description	Remarks
	Contacts and relays	
46	Horn relay	
47	Turn indicator and hazard warner flasher unit	
48	Oil temperature sensor	
49	Fuel tank float, electric	
50	Pop-up headlamp relay	
51	Cold start valve relay	
52	Headlamp flasher	
53	Additional headlamp relay	
54	Heated rear window relay	Optional
	Equipment	
56	Windshield wiper motor	
57	Washer pump	
58	Standard horn	
59	Cigar lighter	
60	Fuse box	
62	Motor for pop-up headlamps	
63	Blower	
64	Heated rear window	Optional

NOTES

CHAPTER TEN

CLUTCH

All Porsche clutches are single plate, dry disc types mounted on the flywheel and incorporating a diaphragm spring. All are mechanically operated through an adjustable wire cable. **Figure 1** is typical.

CLUTCH PEDAL ADJUSTMENTS

Two adjustments are required—clutch pedal travel and free-play. Both should be checked occasionally and adjusted if necessary, particularly after engine/transaxle removal, clutch replacement, or clutch cable replacement.

Pedal Free-Play Adjustment

Pedal free-play adjustment involves taking up cable slack caused by cable stretch or lining wear. To check, depress clutch by hand until resistance is felt. Free-play should be ½-¾″ (15-20mm). See **Figure 2**.

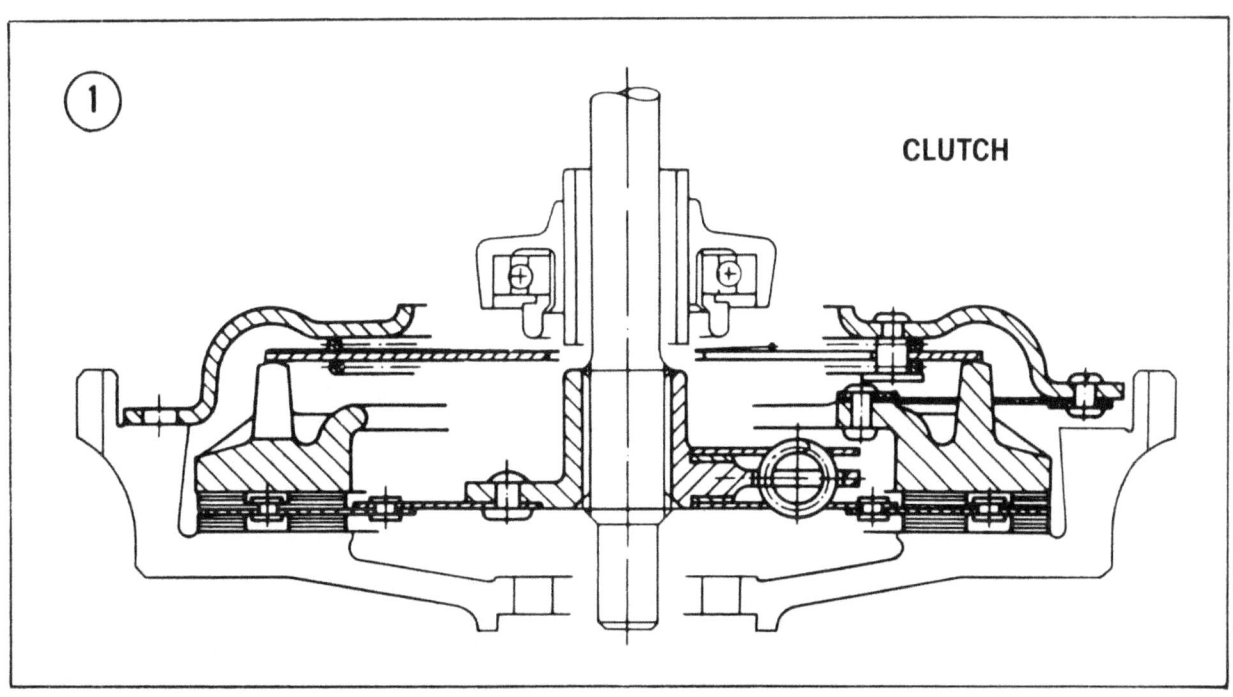

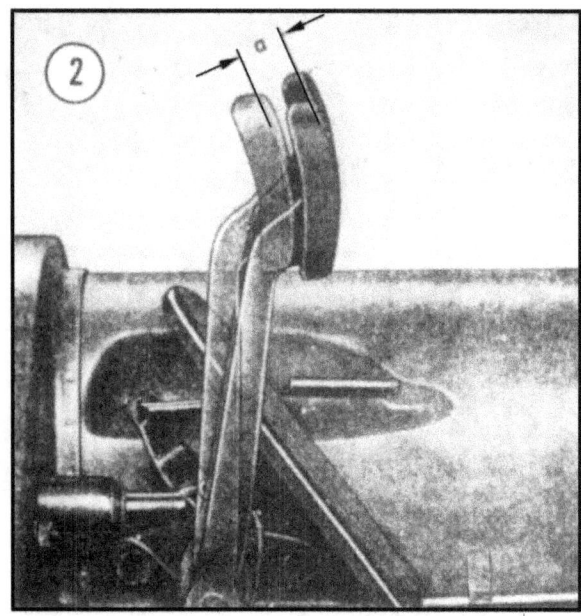

1. Jack up car on jackstands.
2. Loosen locknut at end of cable. See **Figure 3**.

3. Adjust free-play with adjusting nut. When free-play is correct, tighten locknut.
4. Lower car.

Pedal Travel

1. Warm up transmission by driving about 5 miles.
2. Depress clutch pedal against the stop.
3. Ensure that reverse gear can be engaged silently.
4. If gear clash should occur, fold back the front floor mat.
5. Loosen bolts securing stop and slide stop up or down as required (**Figure 4**). Tighten bolts.
6. Retest by performing Steps 2 and 3.

7. Check that cable length is correct as described in next procedure.

CLUTCH CABLE

Replacement

1. Fold back front floor mat and tunnel cover.
2. Loosen locknut on clevis. See **Figure 5**.

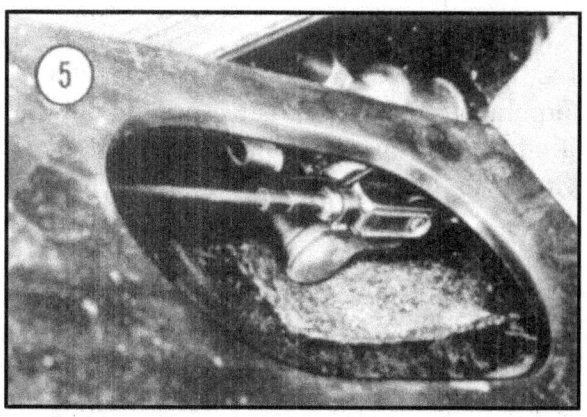

3. Snap retaining spring upward and remove clevis pin to disengage cable from pedal lever.
4. Screw clevis and locknut off cable.
5. Remove locknut and adjusting nut from rear end of cable.
6. Remove retaining nut and remove pulley from shaft (Figure 3). Remove cable from pulley and pull out cable from the rear.
7. Lubricate cable with universal grease and thread forward end into tunnel from the rear. Thread rear end of cable through grommet in engine support.
8. Install clevis with locknut to front end of cable. Measure from the face of the threaded insert to the face of the locknut; adjust clevis position so that this measurement is 0.67-0.87" (17-2mm).

9. Connect cable to clutch lever with clevis pin and retaining spring.

10. Install rubber boot on cable and install cable around rear pulley. Install pulley with retaining nut. Install adjusting nut and locknut on the cable and connect it to the release fork.

11. Adjust pedal free play and travel as described earlier.

CLUTCH MECHANISM

Removal

1. Remove engine/transaxle and separate them as described in **Chapter Four** (914) or **Chapter Five** (914/6).

2. Using a sharp punch, mark the flywheel and clutch cover for later reassembly.

3. Unscrew bolts securing the clutch cover, one turn at a time. Unscrew bolts diagonally opposite one another rather than working directly around the clutch cover. This ensures that heavy spring pressure will not warp the clutch cover.

4. Once spring pressure is relieved, unscrew each bolt and remove clutch from flywheel.

Inspection

Never replace clutch parts without giving thought to the reason for failure. To do so only invites repeated troubles.

1. Clean the flywheel face and pressure plate assembly in a non-petroleum base cleaner such as trichlorethylene.

2. Check the friction surface of the flywheel for cracks and grooves. Attach a dial indicator and check runout. Compare with specifications for your engine. If necessary, have the flywheel reground; replace it in cases of severe damage.

3. Check the pressure plate for cracked or broken springs, evidence of heat, cracked or scored friction surface, and looseness. Check release lever ends for wear. On diaphragm spring clutches, check the spring fingers for wear. If there is any damage, replace with a new pressure plate assembly.

4. Check the clutch disc lining for wear, cracks, oil, and burns. The assembled thickness of the disc should be at least 0.36″ (9mm); see **Figure 6**. Check for loose rivets and cracks in

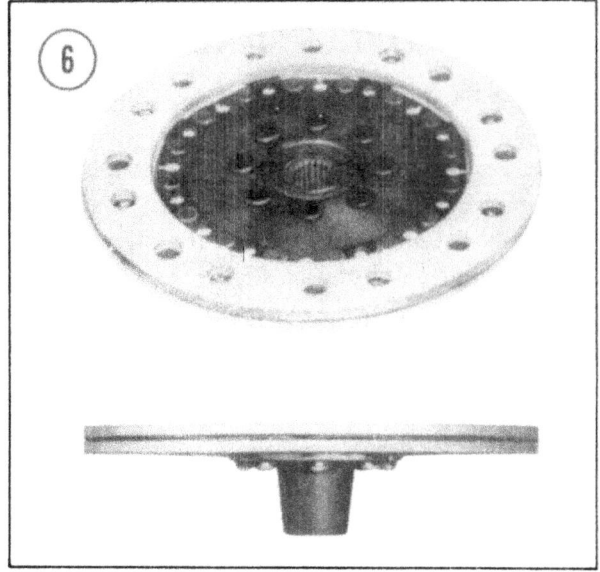

the spring leaves or carrier plate. Ensure that the disc slides freely on the transmission spline without excessive radial play. If the disc is defective, replace it with a new one.

5. Check the release bearing for wear to determine if it caused the original trouble. Never reuse a release bearing unless necessary. When other clutch parts are worn, the bearing is probably worn. If it is necessary to reinstall the old bearing, do not wash it in solvent; wipe it with a clean cloth.

Installation

1. Wash your hands *clean* before proceeding.

2. Sand the friction surface of the flywheel and pressure plate with a medium-fine emery cloth. Sand lightly across the surfaces (not around) until they are covered with fine scratches. This breaks the glaze and aids seating a new clutch disc.

3. Clean the flywheel and pressure plate with trichlorethylene or equivalent.

4. Insert clutch disc.

5. Center the clutch disc over the gland nut hole with a pilot. An excellent pilot is an old transmission main shaft available from a wrecking yard.

6. Start all pressure plate bolts. Tighten diagonally opposite bolts a few turns at a time until all are tight. Torque to 18 foot-pounds (2.5 mkg).

7. Remove the centering pilot.

RELEASE BEARING REPLACEMENT

The release bearing is mounted in the transaxle case and is accessible after removing the engine. In addition to checking a suspect release bearing, always remove clutch assembly from the flywheel and check for damage as described earlier. Refer to **Figure 7**.

1. Loosen Allen bolt securing release fork. See **Figure 8**.

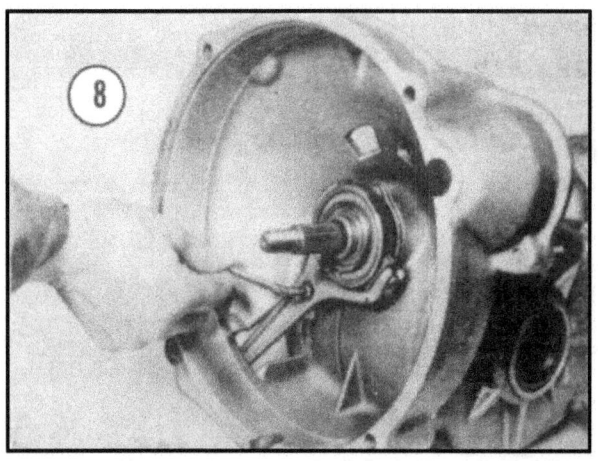

2. Withdraw release bearing and fork.

3. Hold the inner race of the bearing. Lightly press the outer race against the inner race and rotate the outer race. If there is any noise or roughness, the bearing is defective and must be replaced.

CAUTION
The release bearing is prelubricated and sealed. Do not wash it in solvent or it will be ruined. Wipe the bearing with a clean cloth.

4. Install the release bearing with plastic guides in the release fork. Ensure that the bearing moves freely in the fork without binding. Dress the plastic guides with fine crocus cloth if necessary.

5. Lubricate all bearing surfaces of the release bearing and fork with molybdenum disulphide paste.

6. Install bearing and fork in transaxle and secure with Allen bolt. Tighten bolt to 7 foot-pounds (1 mkg).

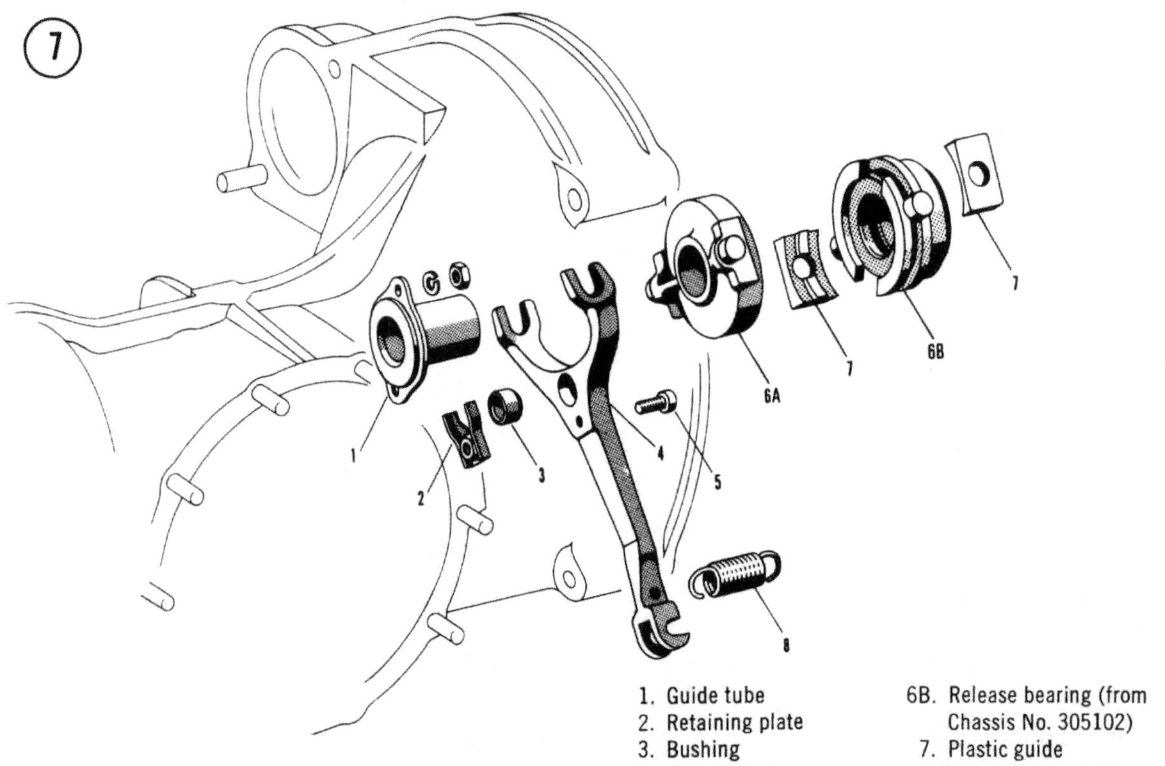

CLUTCH RELEASE MECHANISM

1. Guide tube
2. Retaining plate
3. Bushing
4. Release fork
5. Allen bolt
6A. Release bearing (up to Chassis No. 305101)
6B. Release bearing (from Chassis No. 305102)
7. Plastic guide
8. Return spring (up to Chassis No. 305101)

CHAPTER ELEVEN

MANUAL AND AUTOMATIC TRANSAXLES

Porsche transaxles bolt to the rear of the engine and the entire assembly is supported by several rubber mounts. A single housing contains a 4- or 5-speed transmission and differential gears. Each transaxle is described below.

Repairs requiring disassembly of either transaxle are not possible for home mechanics or garage mechanics without special skills and a large assortment of special Porsche tools.

Considerable money can be saved by removing the old transmission and installing a new or rebuilt one yourself. This chapter includes removal and installation procedures, plus other simple repairs. Specifications and tightening torques are included at the rear of the chapter in **Tables 1 and 2**, respectively. See Chapter Two for lubrication and preventive maintenance.

MANUAL TRANSAXLES

The manual transaxle is a 5-speed. The gears are in constant mesh and all forward speeds are fully synchronized. **Figure 1** shows a cutaway view of the entire transaxle.

Basic Operation (Transmission)

Refer to **Figure 2**(A). Gears for 1st/reverse, 2nd, and 3rd are fixed on the main shaft. In addition, the synchronizer hub for 4th/5th gears is fixed on the main shaft. Main shaft 4th and 5th gears are free to rotate on needle bearings. On the pinion shaft, the reverse is true. Gears for 4th and 5th and the synchronizer for 2nd and 3rd are fixed on the pinion shaft, while 1st, 2nd, and 3rd gears are free to rotate. The reverse gear on the pinion shaft is fixed, but slides back and forth on the shaft.

In neutral, Figure 2(A), engine rotation transmitted through the clutch turns the main shaft. Main shaft gears 1st/reverse, 2nd, and 3rd rotate since they are fixed to the shaft. Drive pinion gears for 1st/reverse, 2nd, and 3rd, however, are not engaged by the synchronizer and turn freely. No power is transmitted to the pinion gear.

When the gearshift lever moves to 1st, Figure 2(B), a fork moves the sliding 1st/reverse gear toward 1st gear on the pinion shaft and these gears lock together. Power is transmitted from the main shaft to the pinion shaft which drives the differential.

In 2nd gear, Figure 2(C), a fork moves the 2nd/3rd gear synchronizer toward 2nd gear. Power is transmitted from the main shaft to the pinion.

Power transfer in the 3rd-5th gears is similar. A fork moves the appropriate synchronizer toward the desired gears. See Figure 2, (D-F).

Reverse gear is different. See Figure 2(G). The 1st/reverse gear on the main shaft drives a

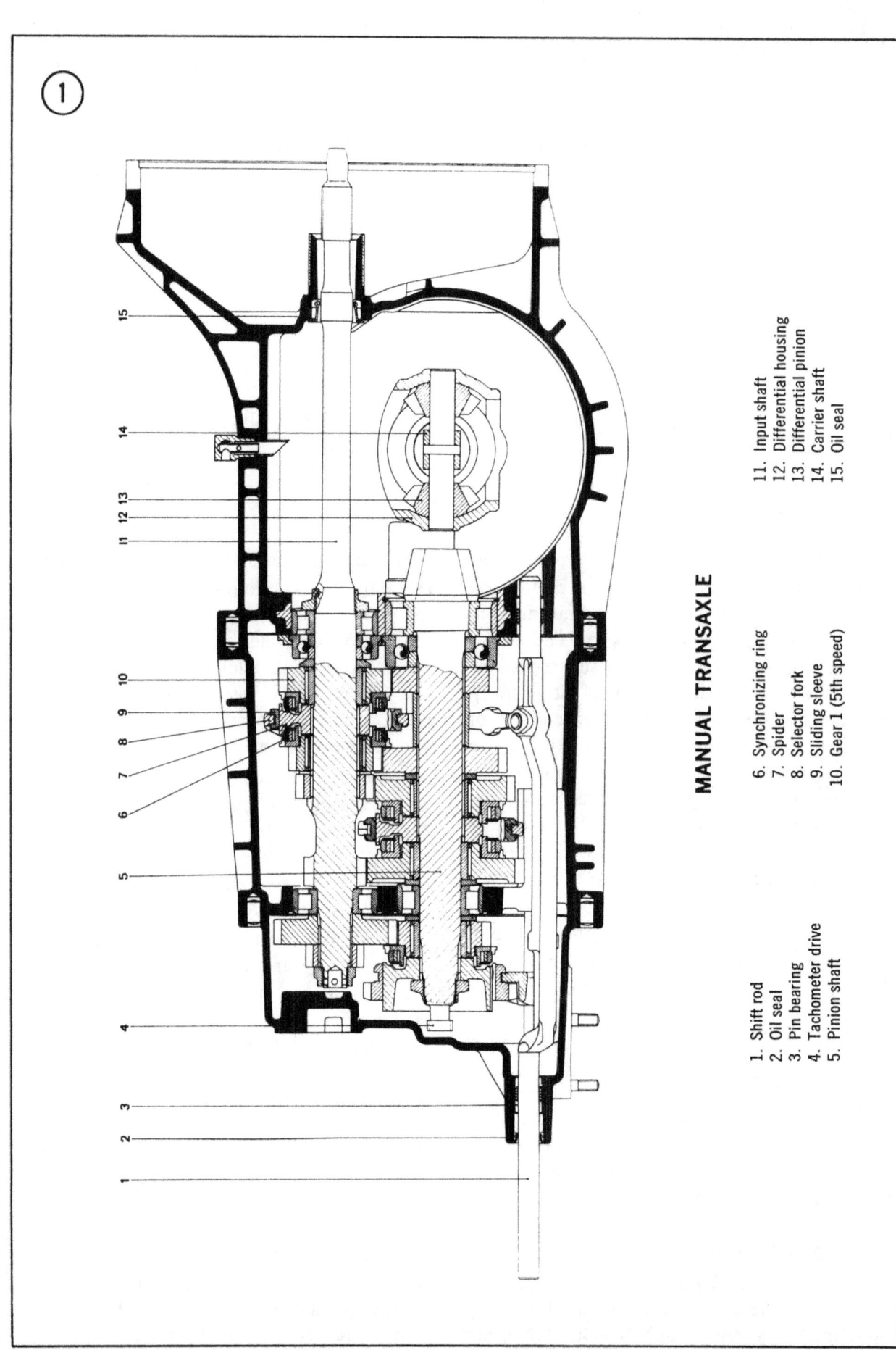

similar gear on the reverse shaft. When the gearshift lever moves to reverse, the sliding gear on the pinion shaft meshes with a gear on the reverse shaft. This sliding gear is fixed on the pinion shaft which rotates in reverse.

Basic Operation (Differential)

Conventional and limited-slip differentials are available on the Porsche. Both types permit the rear wheels to rotate at different speeds; for example, while turning the car. There is one notable difference, however. A conventional differential transfers most power to the wheel with the *least* traction, causing that wheel to spin uselessly. A limited-slip differential transfers most power to the wheel with the *most* traction; power is taken from the wheel with least traction, preventing it from spinning.

The conventional differential is very simple. The pinion gear, driven by the transmission, drives a large ring gear. See **Figure 3**. The ring gear in turn drives a differential case containing differential pinion gears. The differential pinion gears mesh with side gears splined to the axle shaft.

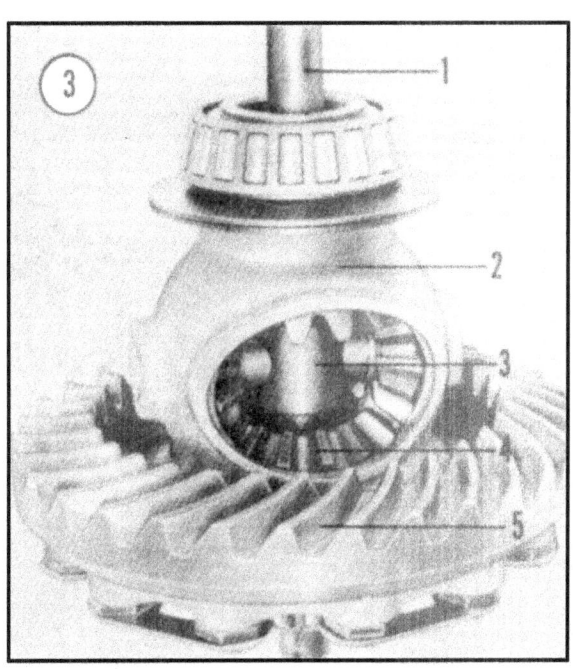

1. Axle shaft
2. Differential case
3. Differential pinion gears
4. Differential side gears
5. Ring gear

When driving straight ahead on a level surface, there is no tendency for the wheels to rotate at different speeds. The ring gear rotates the differential case. The pinion gears rotate with the differential case, but do not rotate about their own axis. Instead, they apply equal force to each of the differential side gears and axle shafts.

When turning the car, the inside wheel must slow down. The inside axle shaft and side gear resist the force from the pinion gears and the pinion gears rotate about their own axis while rolling around the differential side gears. This permits the inside wheel to slow down and the outside wheel to speed up. In fact, if the rear of the car is jacked up in gear with the engine running, stopping one wheel will cause the other wheel to rotate at twice its normal speed.

The limited-slip differential operates in a similar manner, except that the ring gear cannot drive the differential case and pinion gears directly. Instead, the ring gear drives the case through friction discs.

See **Figure 4**. The degree of coupling through the friction discs depends on the traction at each wheel.

The pinion shaft ends are beveled and fit similarly shaped openings in the differential case halves. The pinion shafts and pinions, therefore, float between the side gears and the differential case. The wheel forces on the pinion gears and shafts force the side gears apart. This increases the pressure on the friction discs which couple more power to the wheel with the most traction.

Gearshift Housing Removal/Installation

1. Remove both front seats.
2. Remove heater knob, dust boot, and tunnel cover.
3. Remove 5 bolts securing lever housing to tunnel. See **Figure 5**.
4. Lift lever housing off.
5. Installation is the reverse of these steps.

Gearshift Housing Disassembly/Assembly

See **Figure 6** for the following procedure.

1. Pull plastic ball socket off bottom of lever.
2. Hold housing in a vise.
3. Remove C-rings on spring pins. See **Figure 7**.
4. Push one pin about half way out.

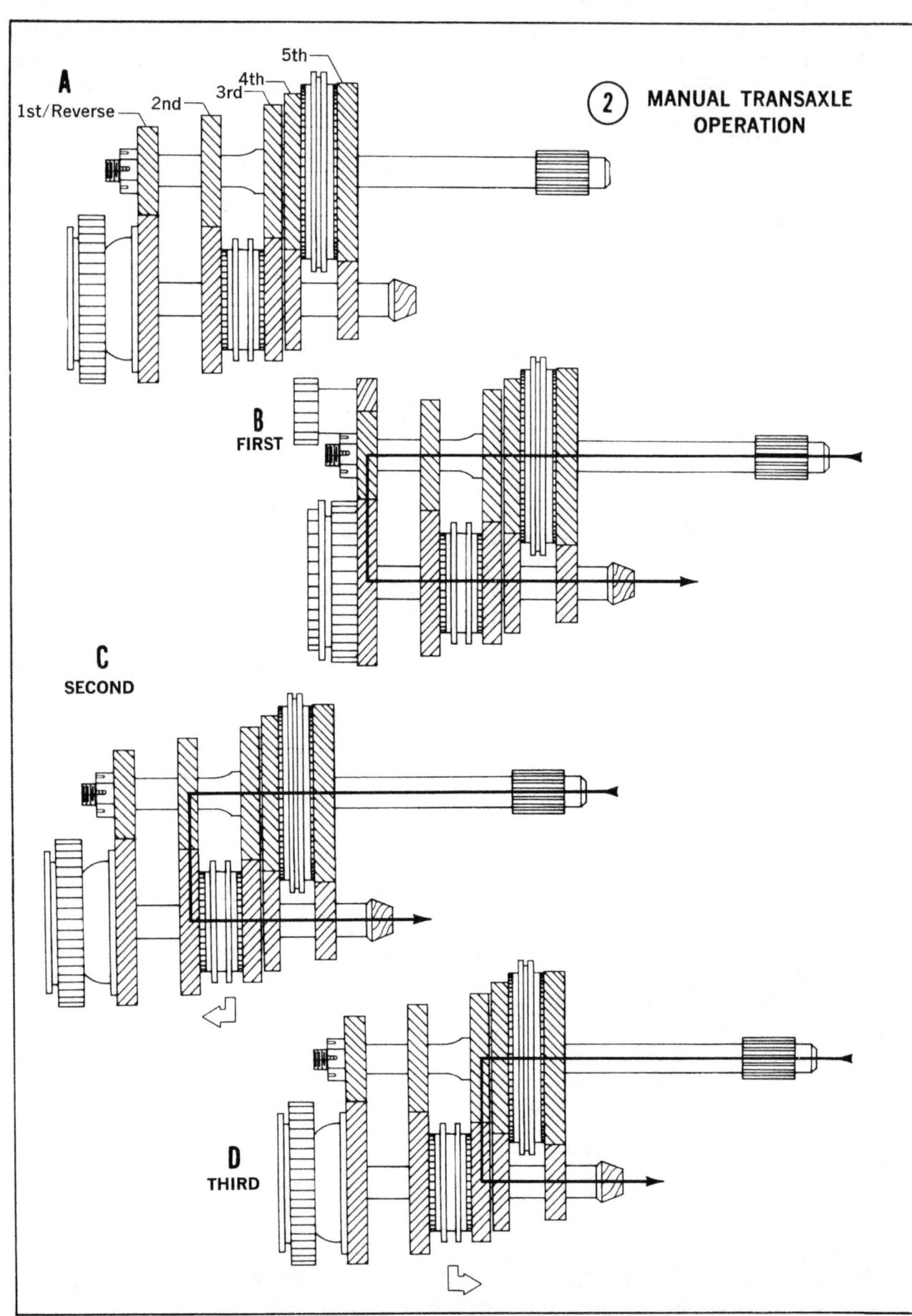

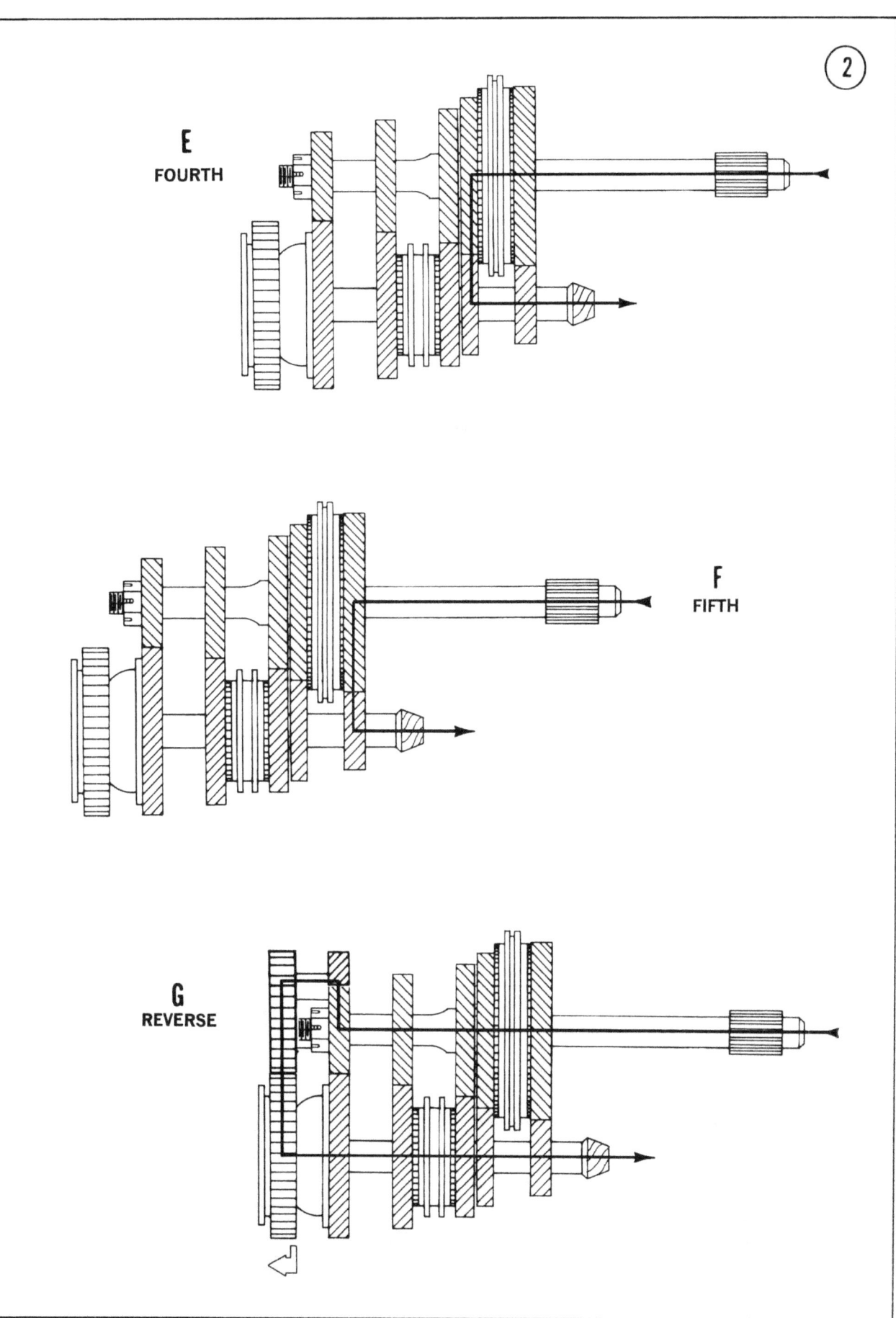

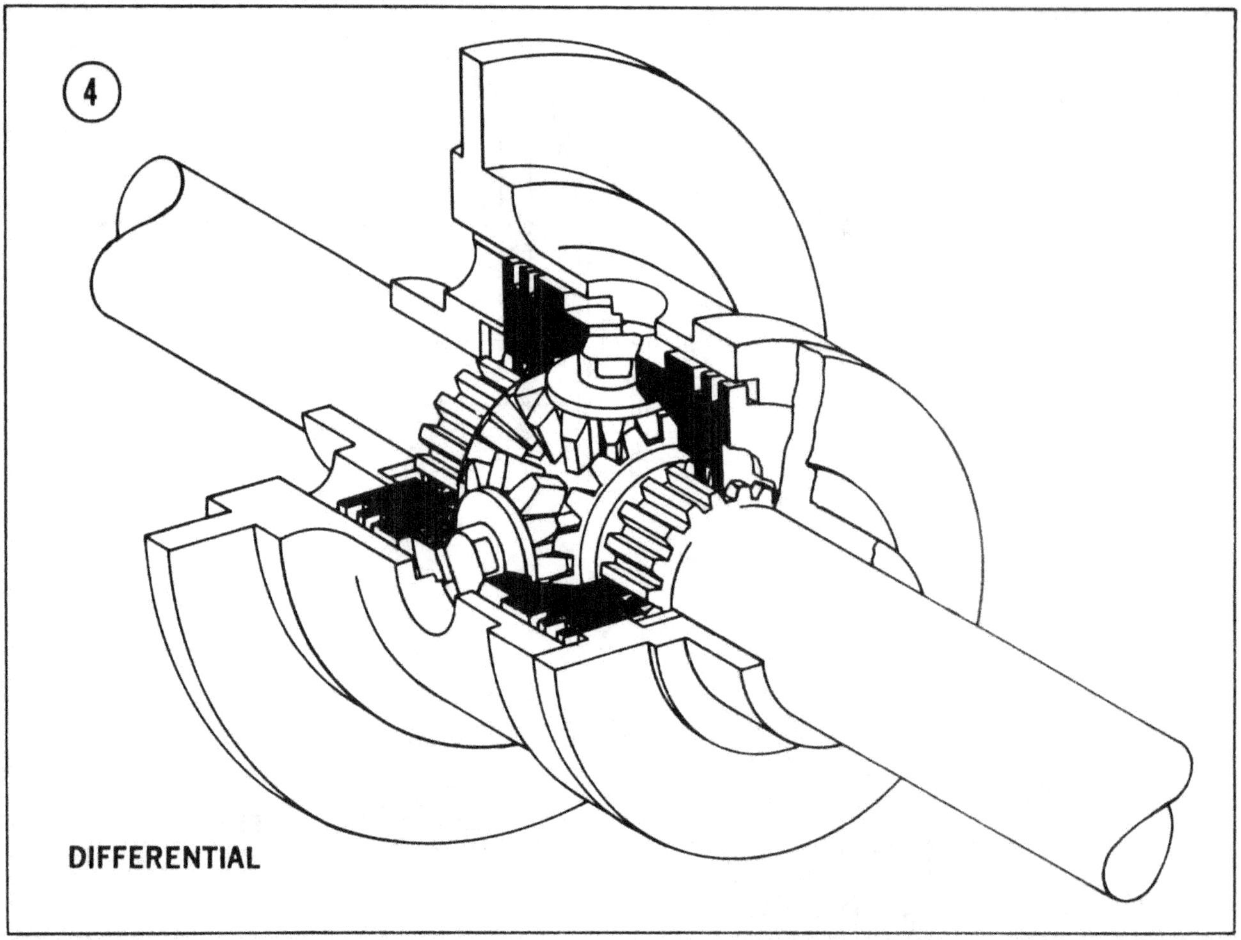

DIFFERENTIAL

WARNING
The spring could fly out of the housing. Hold a rag around the housing to prevent injury.

5. Keep the rag in place and pry the loose spring out. See **Figure 8**.

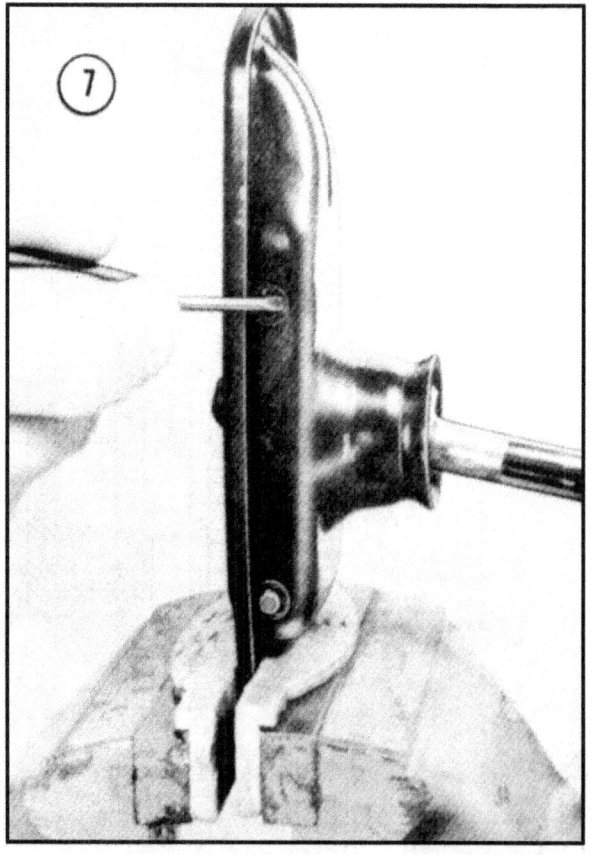

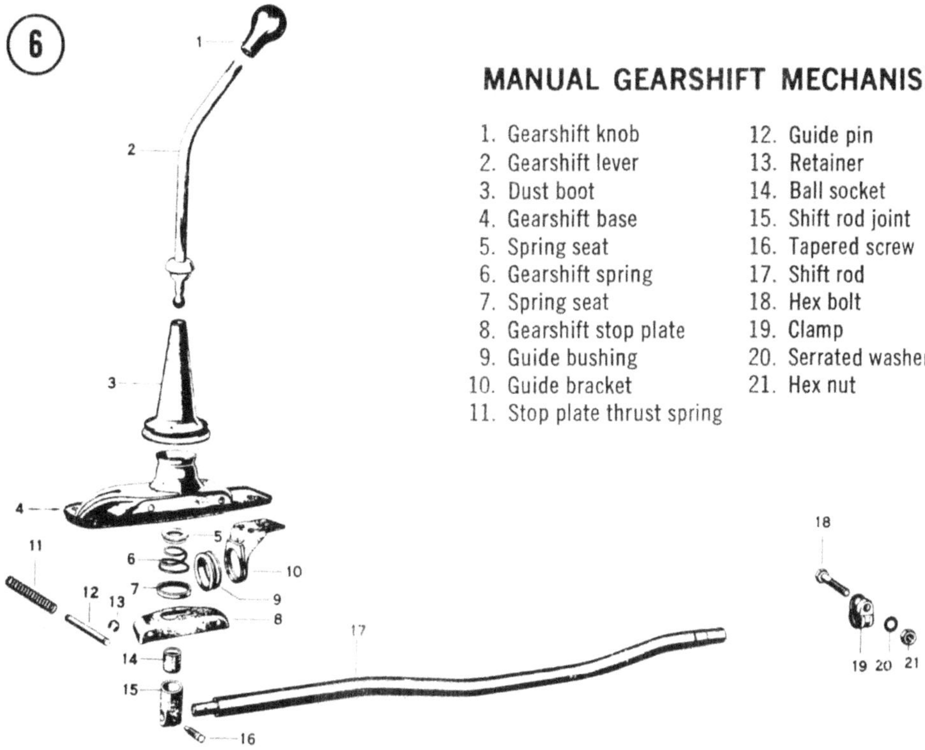

MANUAL GEARSHIFT MECHANISM

1. Gearshift knob
2. Gearshift lever
3. Dust boot
4. Gearshift base
5. Spring seat
6. Gearshift spring
7. Spring seat
8. Gearshift stop plate
9. Guide bushing
10. Guide bracket
11. Stop plate thrust spring
12. Guide pin
13. Retainer
14. Ball socket
15. Shift rod joint
16. Tapered screw
17. Shift rod
18. Hex bolt
19. Clamp
20. Serrated washer
21. Hex nut

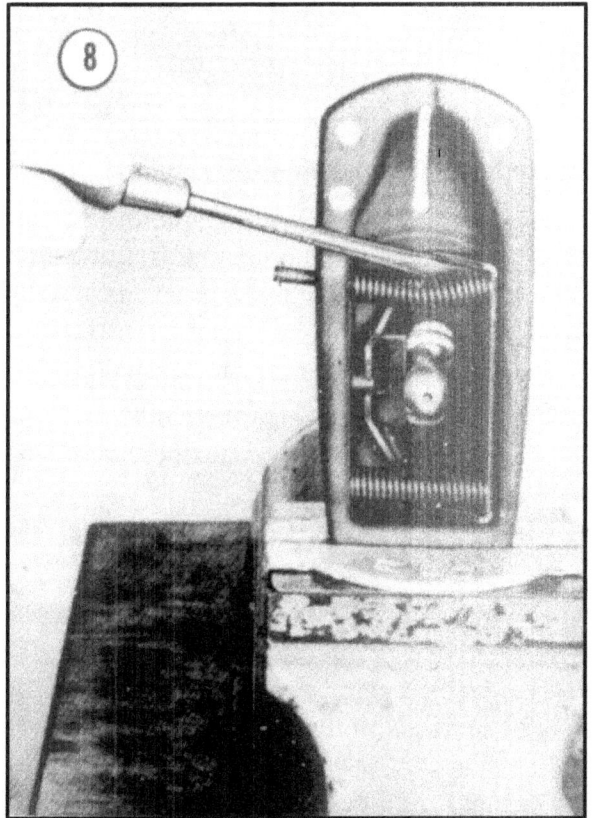

NOTE: *The rag is not shown as it would hide the operation.*

6. Remove the other spring in the same way.

7. Pull stop plate, spring, and spring seat out.

8. Remove gearshift lever.

9. Clean all parts in solvent.

10. Inspect stop plate and lever for wear. Replace if necessary.

11. Assembly is the reverse of these steps. Lubricate the bottom end of the lever with multipurpose (lithium) grease. When installing the springs, slip the pin about half way, then compress the spring with a modified screwdriver. See **Figures 9 and 10**.

Main Shaft Oil Seal Replacement

1. Remove engine/transaxle as described in Chapters Four and Five.

2. Remove the clutch release bearing. See Chapter Ten.

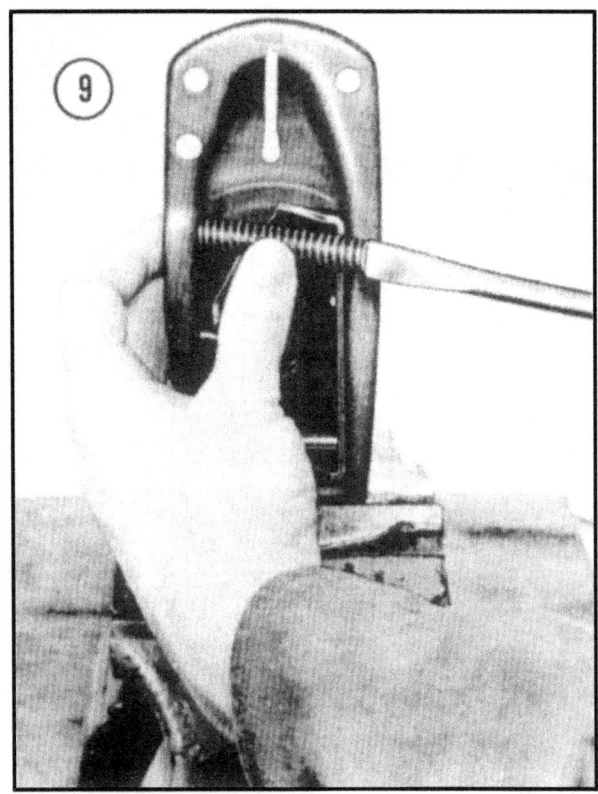

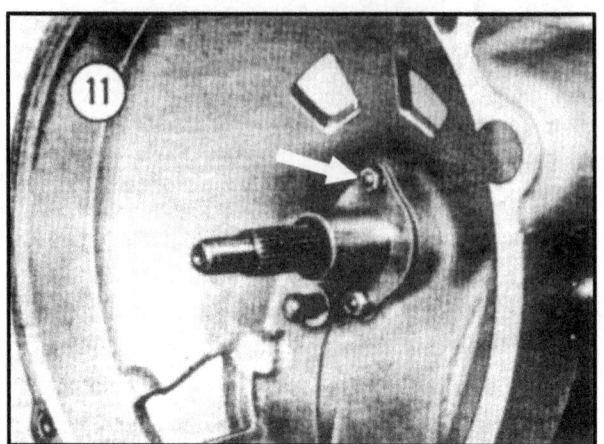

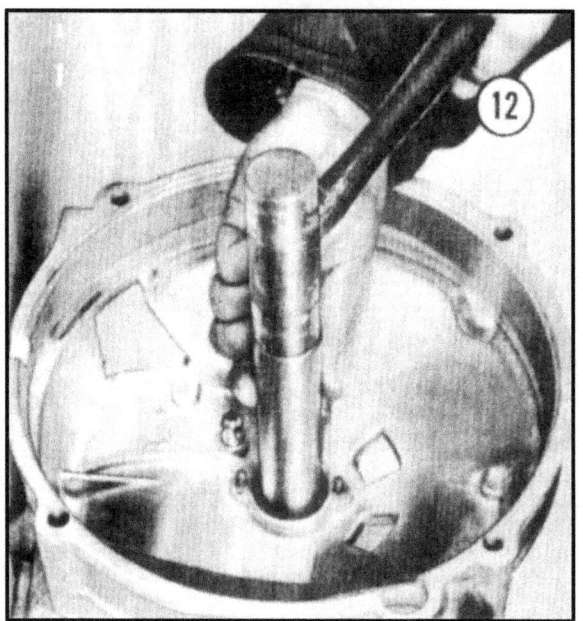

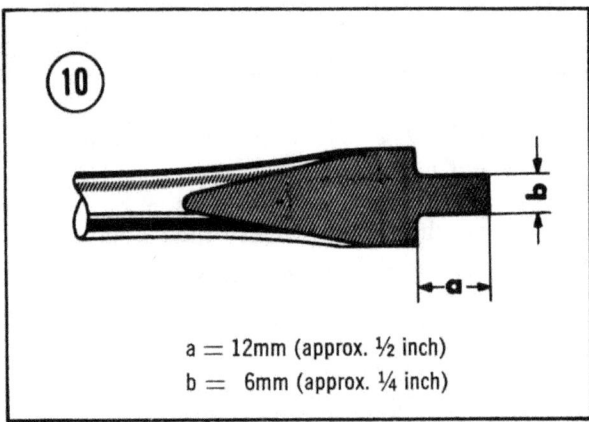

a = 12mm (approx. ½ inch)
b = 6mm (approx. ¼ inch)

3. Remove clutch release bearing guide. See **Figure 11**.

4. Clean dirt from outside of oil seal.

5. Pry oil seal out with a screwdriver.

CAUTION
Do not nick any metal surface.

6. Clean opening around main shaft.

7. Coat outer edge of seal with gasket compound. Oil main shaft and seal lip.

8. Slide oil seal on the main shaft and drive it into place. Use a special hollow drift or length of pipe as shown in **Figure 12**.

Determining Transmission Gear Ratios

Porsche offers a staggering number of optional gear ratios for the manual transmission. The safest way to determine gear ratios is by actual measurement.

1. Raise the rear of the car on jackstands.

2. Disconnect output of ignition coil.

3. Move the gearshift lever to the gear to be measured.

4. Make a chalk reference mark on one rear tire.

5. Count the number of crankshaft revolutions necessary to rotate the tire exactly one full turn.

6. Divide the engine revolutions in Step 5 by 4.429 (final drive ratio). The result is the gear ratio of the gear selected.

7. Repeat for all gears if desired.

SPORTOMATIC

The Sportomatic consists of a torque converter, servo operated mechanical clutch, and 4-speed transmission. **Figure 13** is a detailed cutaway view of the transmission. **Figure 14** shows the hydraulic circuits and **Figure 15** shows the vacuum circuits in simplified form.

The Sportomatic has a conventional torque converter to provide smooth application of power over a wide range. But unlike full automatics, the Sportomatic requires a mechanical clutch to interrupt power flow for gear changes. Gear changes are entirely manual, not automatic.

The torque converter is capable of multiplying engine torque over 2:1 when the car moves from a complete stop. At this point, torque is maximum and slippage within the torque converter is also maximum. As slippage decreases, i.e., the speed difference between the turbine and impeller in the torque converter decreases, torque multiplication also decreases. When slippage decreases so that turbine speed is 84% of the impeller speed, there is no multiplication and coupling is direct. The turbine can reach 96% of the impeller speed—the maximum coupling efficiency possible.

The torque converter uses the engine oil supply independent of the rear axle and transmission oil. See Figure 14. Half of the dual oil pump driven by the engine camshaft delivers engine oil from the oil tank to the torque converter and back through a return line to the oil tank.

The torque converter drives a conventional 4-speed transmission through a single dry-disc clutch. A vacuum operated servo disengages and engages the clutch in response to the control valve.

When the driver moves the gearshift lever longitudinally, a contact in the lever operates the cotnrol valve solenoid. The control valve supplies engine vacuum from the intake manifold to the clutch servo, which disengages the clutch. Since power flow is interrupted, the driver can continue to move the gearshift and manually select the desired gear.

The control valve engages the clutch automatically after an interval determined by engine load. A cam on the throttle valve shaft indicates engine load and opens or closes Valve II on the control valve. If engine load is low, the throttle valve is closed or nearly so, and Valve II remains closed. If engine load is high, the throttle valve is fully open and Valve II opens. When the driver releases the gearshift, the solenoid closes Valve I. The vacuum in the servo "bleeds off" to atmospheric pressure quickly through Valve II which is open or slowly opening through Orifice III. The rate at which the servo returns to atmospheric pressure controls the speed of clutch engagement.

Removal/Installation

Remove the engine/transaxle as a unit, then separate them. See Chapter Four or Five for details.

Clutch Removal

Refer to **Figures 16 and 17** for the following procedure.

1. Remove transaxle as described above.

2. Disconnect clutch operating rod from bellcrank. See **Figure 18**.

3. Remove 4 outer nuts (**Figure 19**) and 2 inner nuts (**Figure 20**) holding torque converter housing to transaxle.

4. Pull torque converter housing free of transaxle. See **Figure 21**. Rotate the release bearing to clear the release fork.

5. Remove pressure plate bolts. See **Figure 22**. Loosen diagonally opposite bolts a few turns at a time to prevent warpage due to spring pressure.

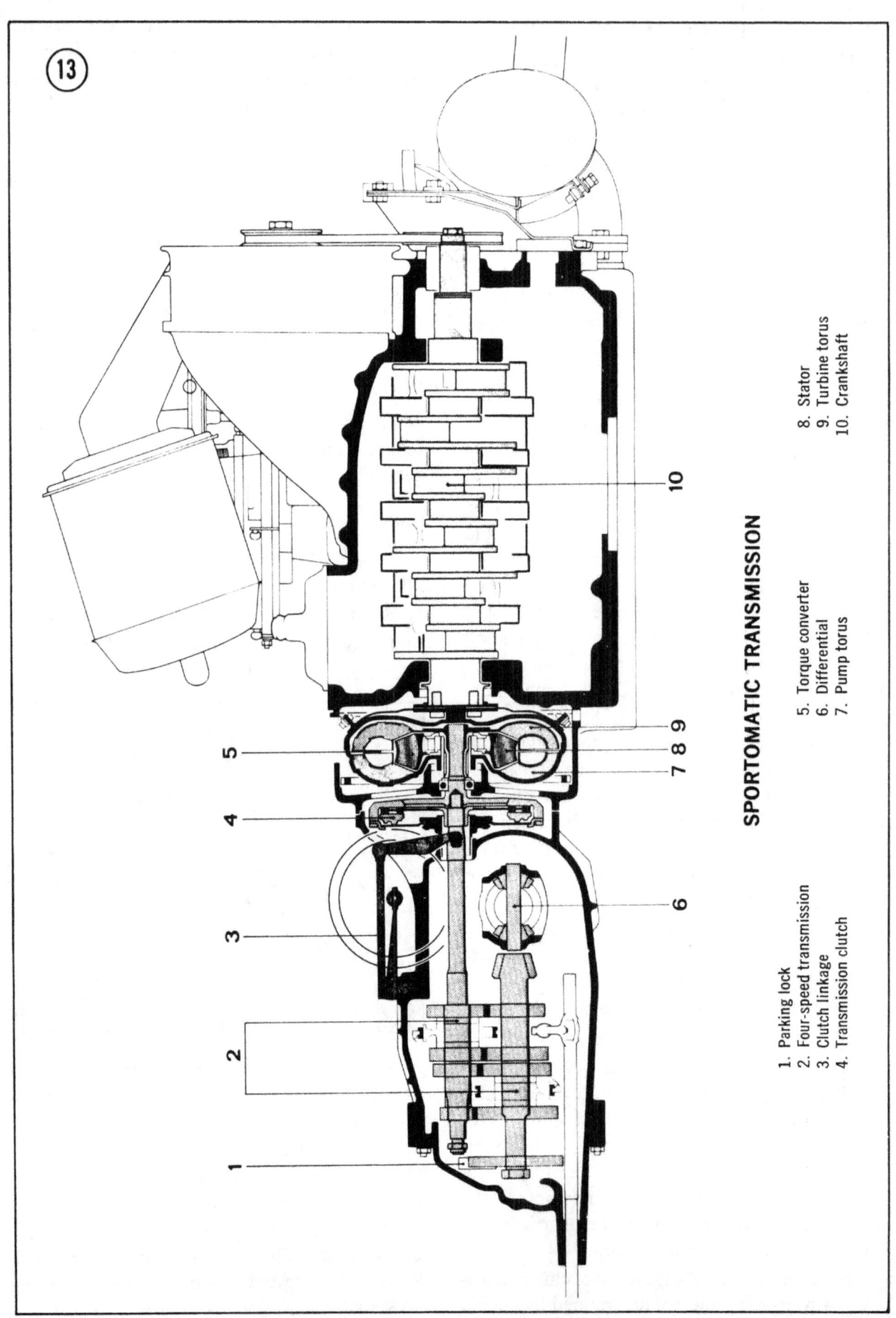

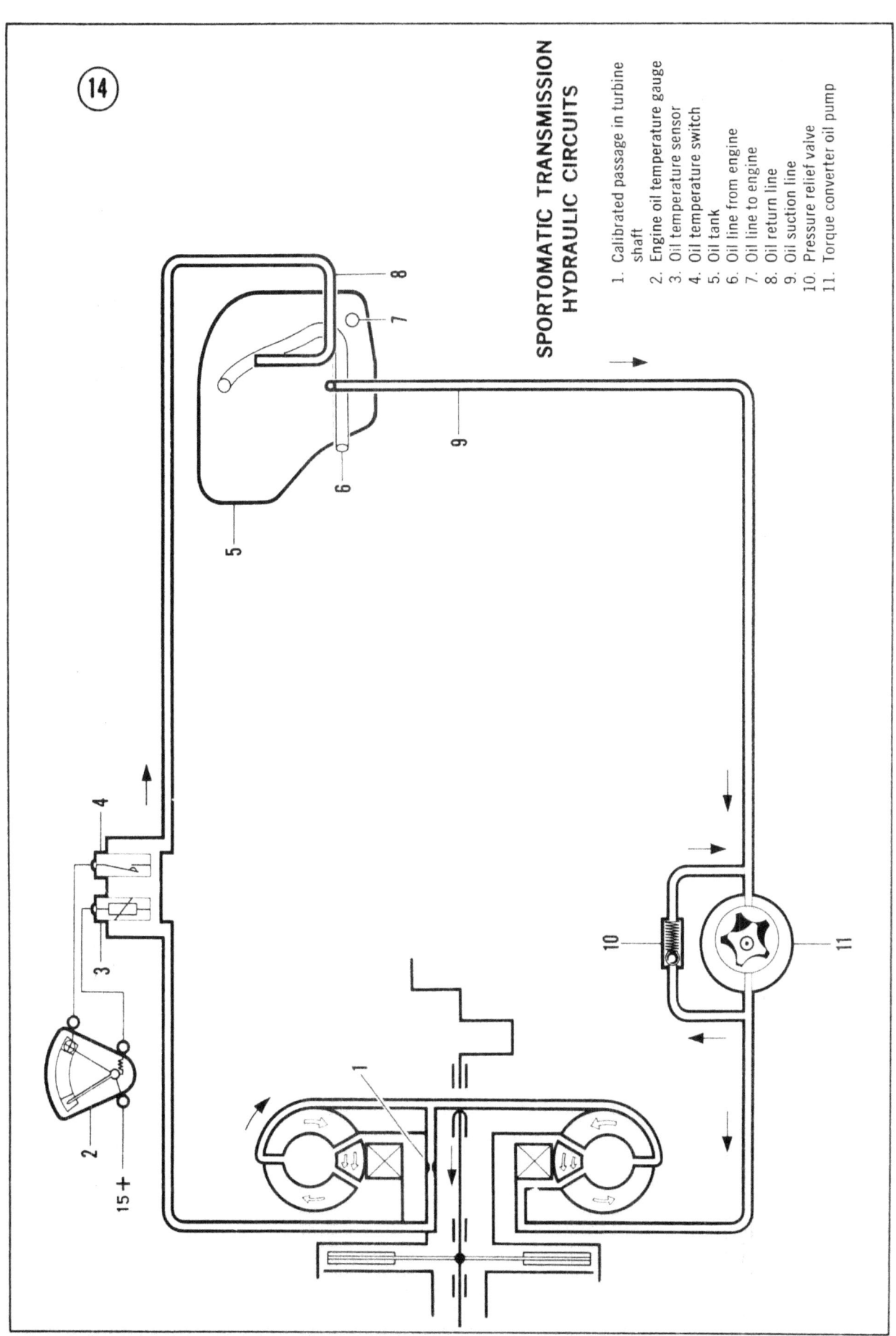

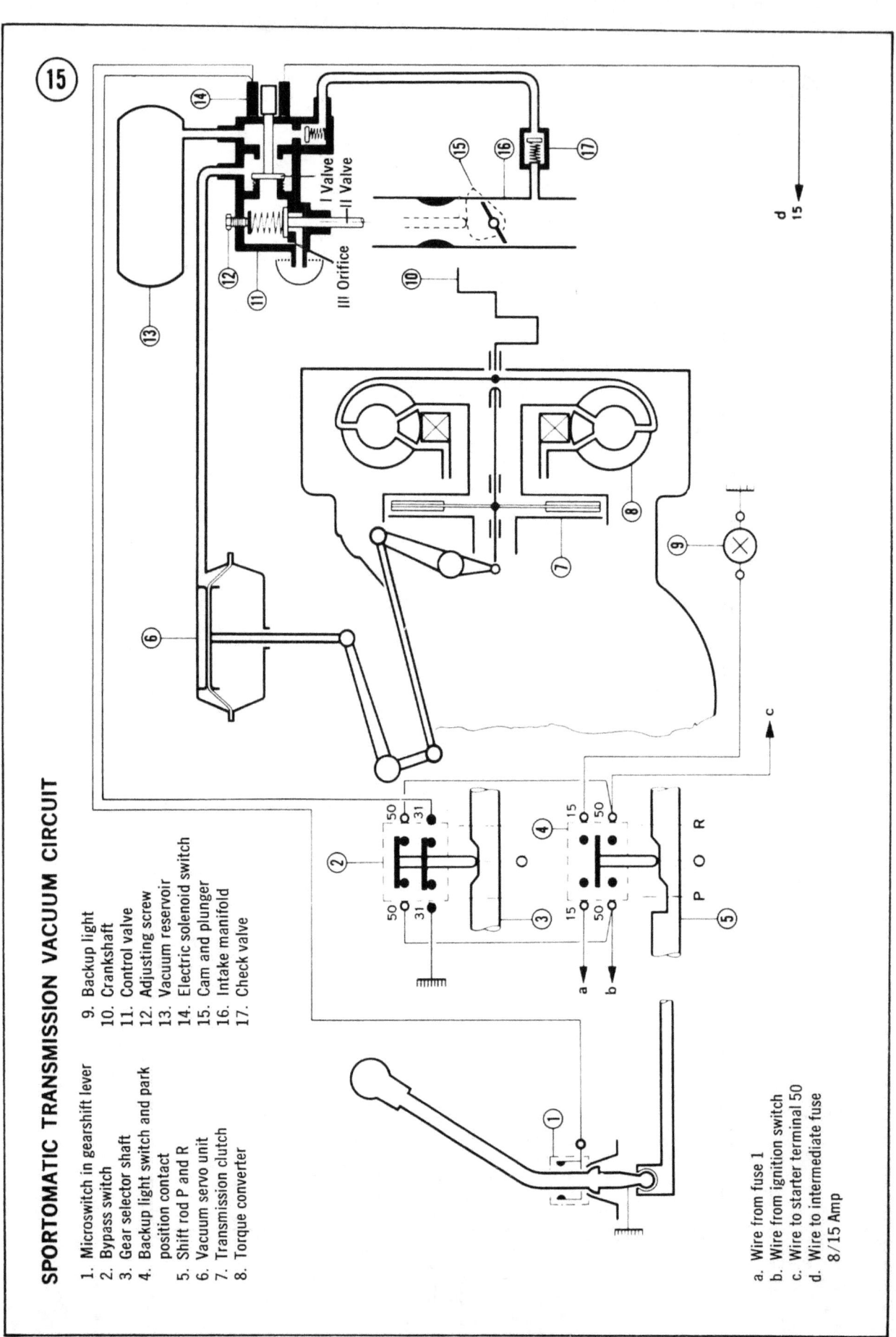

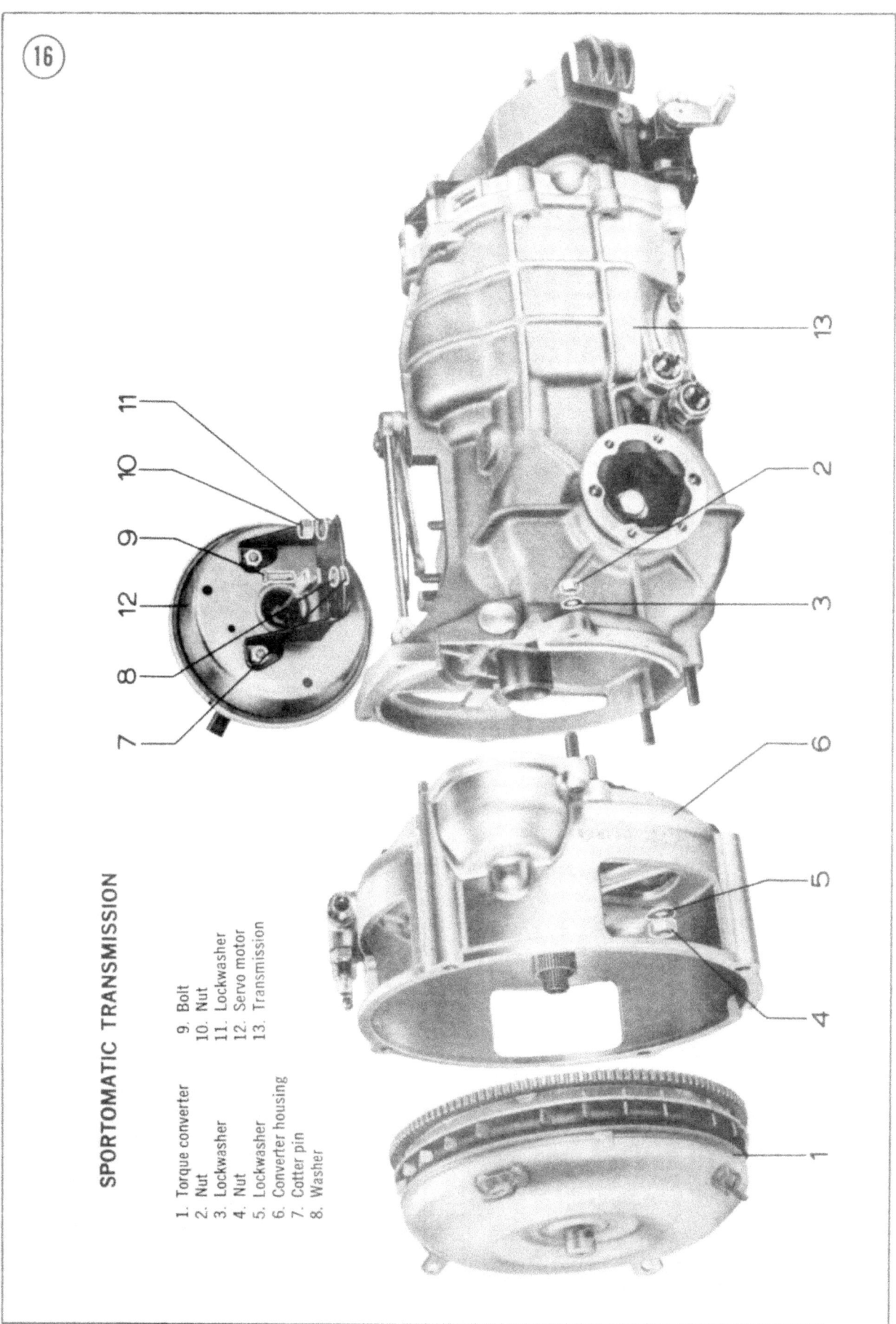

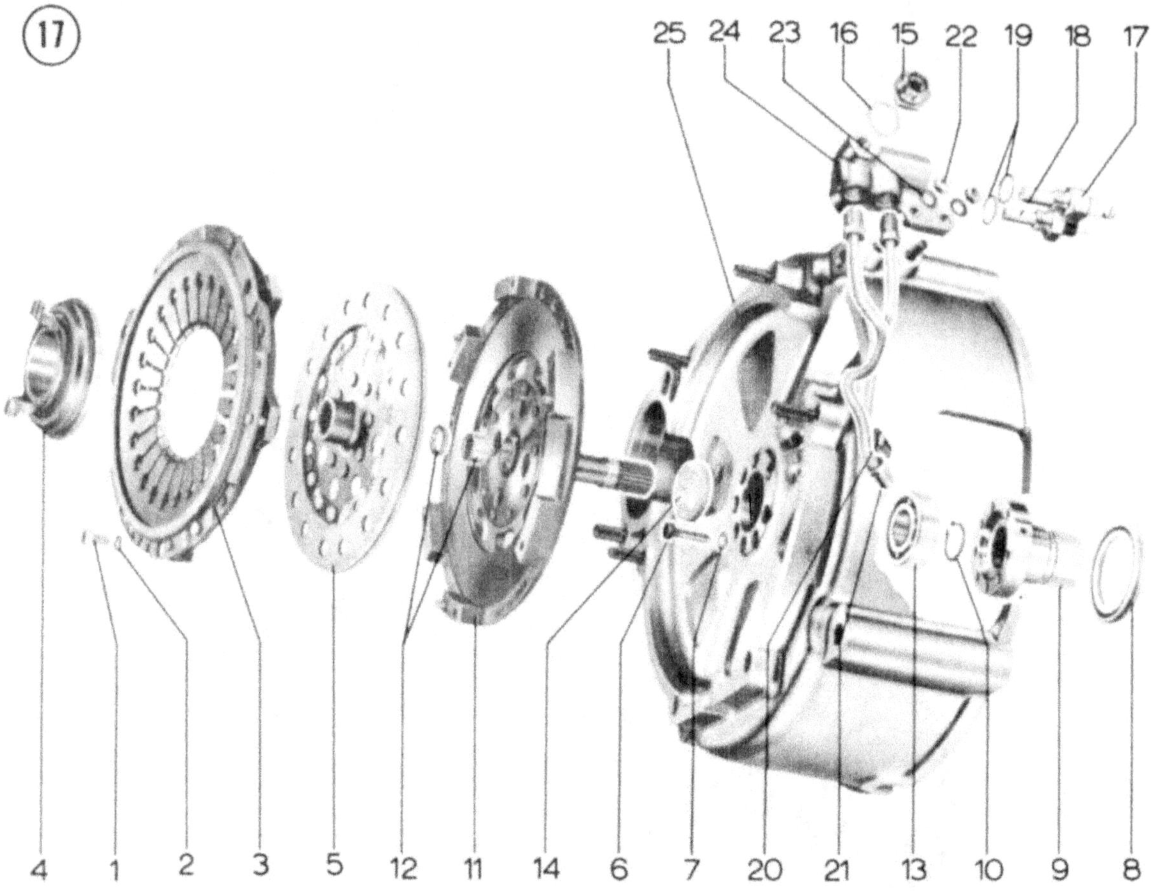

SPORTOMATIC CLUTCH

1. Internal multitooth screw
2. Spring ring
3. Plate spring clutch with pressure plate
4. Throwout bearing
5. Clutch plate
6. Internal multitooth screw
7. Sealing washer
8. Sealing ring
9. Freewheeling unit
10. Locking ring
11. Carrier plate
12. Sealing ring and needle bearing
13. Grooved ball bearing
14. Sealing ring
15. Double connection
16. Sealing ring
17. Tele-thermometer transmitter
18. Temperature switch
19. Sealing ring
20. Hydraulic line
21. Tubing nut
22. Nut
23. Lockwasher
24. Sensor housing
25. Converter housing

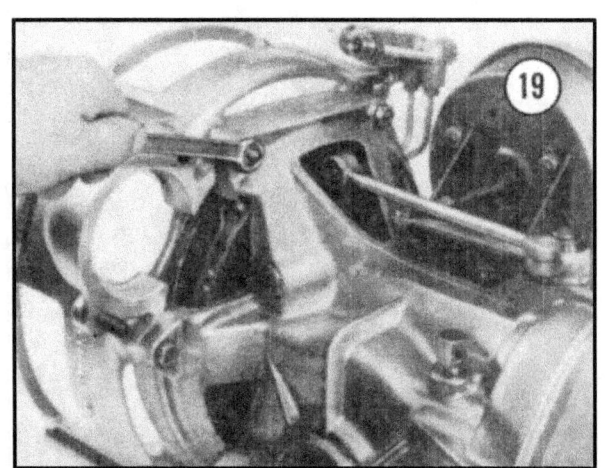

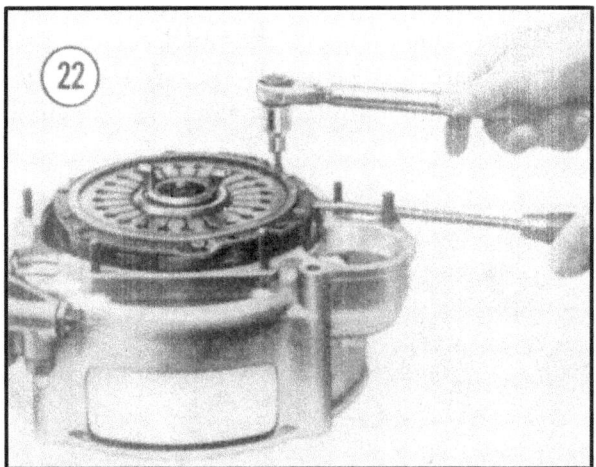

6. Remove release bearing. Do not wash bearing in solvent. Wipe with a clean, dry cloth.
7. Remove clutch disc.

Clutch Inspection

1. Clean the clutch plate carrier and pressure plate in non-petroleum base cleaner such as trichlorethylene.
2. Check the friction surface of the clutch plate carrier for cracks and grooves. If worn, replace as described in a later procedure.
3. Check the pressure plate for cracked or broken spring fingers, cracked or scored friction surface, and evidence of heat (bluish tint). Replace if necessary.

4. Check the clutch disc lining for wear, cracks, oil, and burns. The assembled thickness of the disc must be at least 0.36" (9mm). Check for loose rivets and cracks in the spring leaves or carrier plate. Ensure that the disc slides freely on the transmission main shaft spline without excessive radial play. Replace disc if necessary.
5. Check the release bearing for noise or excessive wear. It's good practice to replace an inexpensive part like this, regardless of condition, to prevent having to tear the transmission down again. If other clutch parts are worn, it's very likely the release bearing is also worn.

Clutch Installation

Refer to Figures 16 and 17 for the following procedure.

1. Lubricate the release bearing guide on the transmission case and both lugs of the release bearing (see **Figure 23**) with lithium grease. Insert the bearing into the clutch pressure plate.

2. Apply lithium grease to the needle bearing in the clutch carrier plate.
3. Install the clutch disc and pressure plate with release bearing into the clutch housing. Center the clutch disc with a pilot cut from a scrap main shaft. See **Figure 24**. Ensure that the release bearing is properly centered in the diaphragm spring. Tighten diagonally opposite pressure plate bolts a few turns at a time until all are tight. Torque to 10 foot-pounds (1.4 mkg).

3. Screw in 2 bolts (6x60mm) diagonally opposite one another. Carefully tap on the bolt heads and drive out freewheeling support with oil seal. See **Figure 26**.

4. Assemble the transmission and clutch housing. Ensure that the release fork engages behind the release bearing lugs. Tighten all nuts evenly, a few turns at a time, then torque to 14 foot-pounds (2 mkg).

5. Reconnect clutch operating rod bellcrank. Adjust the clutch as described later in this chapter.

6. Install the torque converter. Rotate until the converter seats fully into the turbine shaft.

Clutch Carrier Plate Replacement

Refer to Figures 16 and 17 for the following procedure.

1. Remove the clutch as described previously.
2. Remove 8 Allen screws securing the one-way clutch support through any of 4 holes in the carrier plate. See **Figure 25**.

4. Remove the C-ring on the clutch carrier plate turbine shaft. See **Figure 27**. Knock the carrier plate out with a rubber hammer as shown in **Figure 28**.

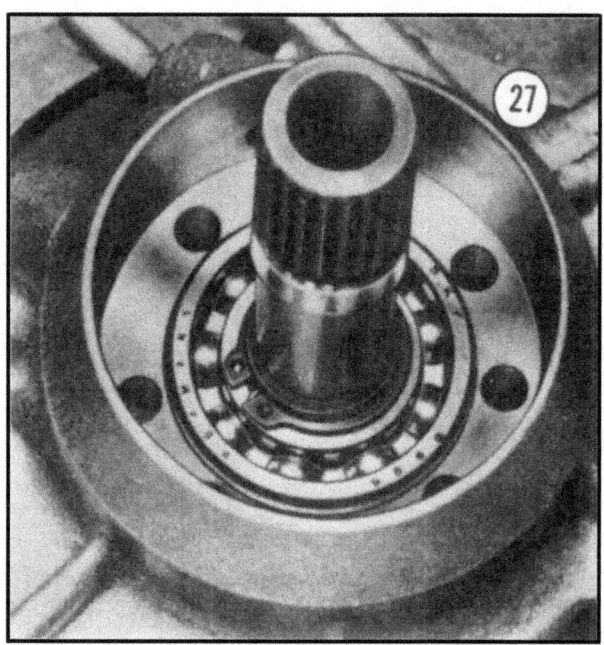

5. Pull the seal and needle bearing out of the carrier plate with a puller. See **Figure 29**. If a puller cannot be substituted, take the carrier plate to the dealer.

6. Knock the ball bearing and seal out of the clutch housing with suitable drifts (**Figure 30**).

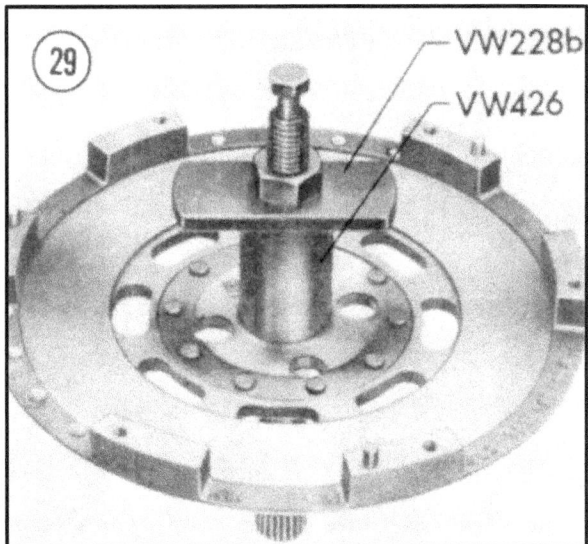

7. Heat the clutch housing to about 250°F (120°C). Insert the new ball bearing in the clutch housing with a drift as far as the stop on the housing. See **Figure 31**. Support the bottom of the housing near the bearing on a small sleeve so the studs and housing are not damaged by the pounding.

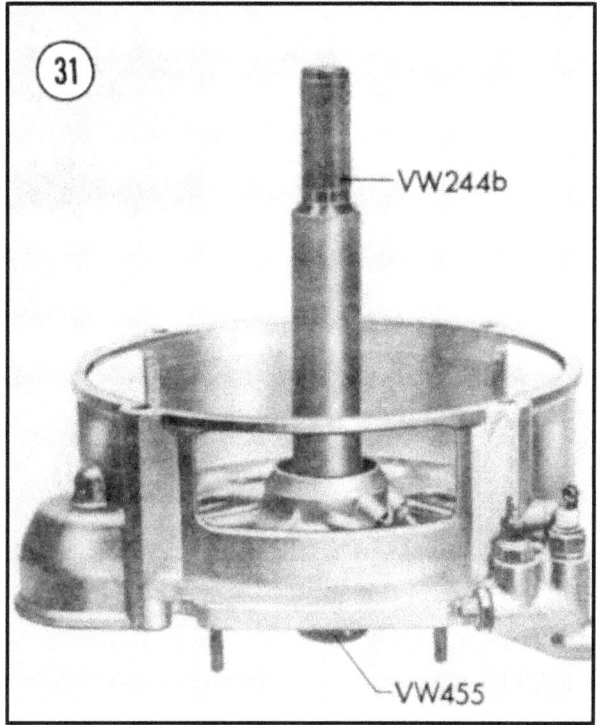

8. Drive the seal in with the sealing lip towards the torque converter. See **Figure 32**.

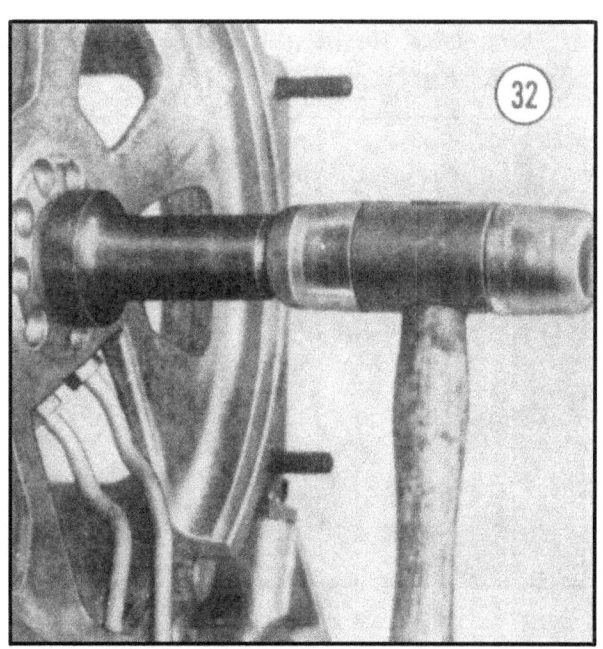

9. Drive the turbine shaft of the carrier plate into the ball bearing and install the C-ring.
10. Install the freewheeling support into the

clutch housing. Install the Allen screws through holes in the carrier plate with new O-rings.

11. Lubricate the needle bearing with lithium grease and install needle bearing and seal in the carrier plate as shown in **Figure 33**.

12. Reinstall clutch as described earlier.

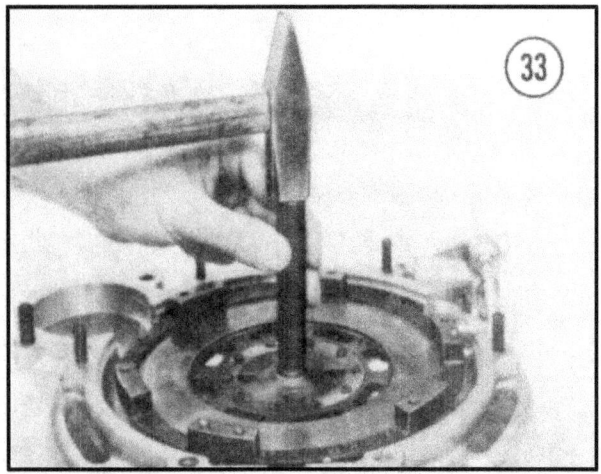

Basic Clutch Adjustment

These adjustments are performed whenever the clutch or servo are disassembled. See the next procedure for clutch free-play adjustment.

1. Install the clutch servo on the mounting bracket.
2. Disconnect servo rod from intermediate lever. See **Figure 34**.

1. Servo rod
2. Lock nut
3. Clevis
4. Intermediate lever

3. Pull servo out as far as possible. Push intermediate lever toward servo as far as possible. The hole in the servo rod must extend 0.5″ (10-12mm) past the hole in the intermediate lever (A, **Figure 35**).

4. If adjustment is incorrect, loosen locknut and turn clevis on servo rod to obtain correct rod length. Tighten locknut.

5. Reconnect servo rod and intermediate lever.

Control Valve Replacement (914/6)

The control valve is located on the right side of the left intake manifold. It cannot be repaired.

1. Disconnect battery ground cable(s).
2. Remove air cleaner assembly. See Chapter Eight.
3. Pull rubber boot off control valve connector. Remove cotter pin and disconnect electrical connector. See **Figure 36**.

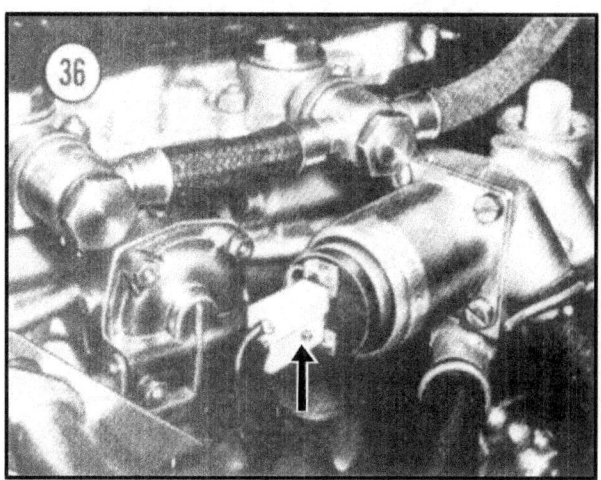

4. Disconnect vacuum lines from control valve.
5. Unbolt control valve bracket from carburetor.
6. Remove control valve from bracket.
7. Installation is the reverse of these steps. Smear multipurpose grease on the throttle cam where it contacts the control valve.
8. Adjust control valve as described below.

Control Valve Adjustment (914/6)

This procedure assumes that throttle linkage and idle speed are correctly adjusted. See Chapter Two.

To adjust for upshifts:

1. With throttle in idle position, insert feeler gauge under control valve cam follower. See

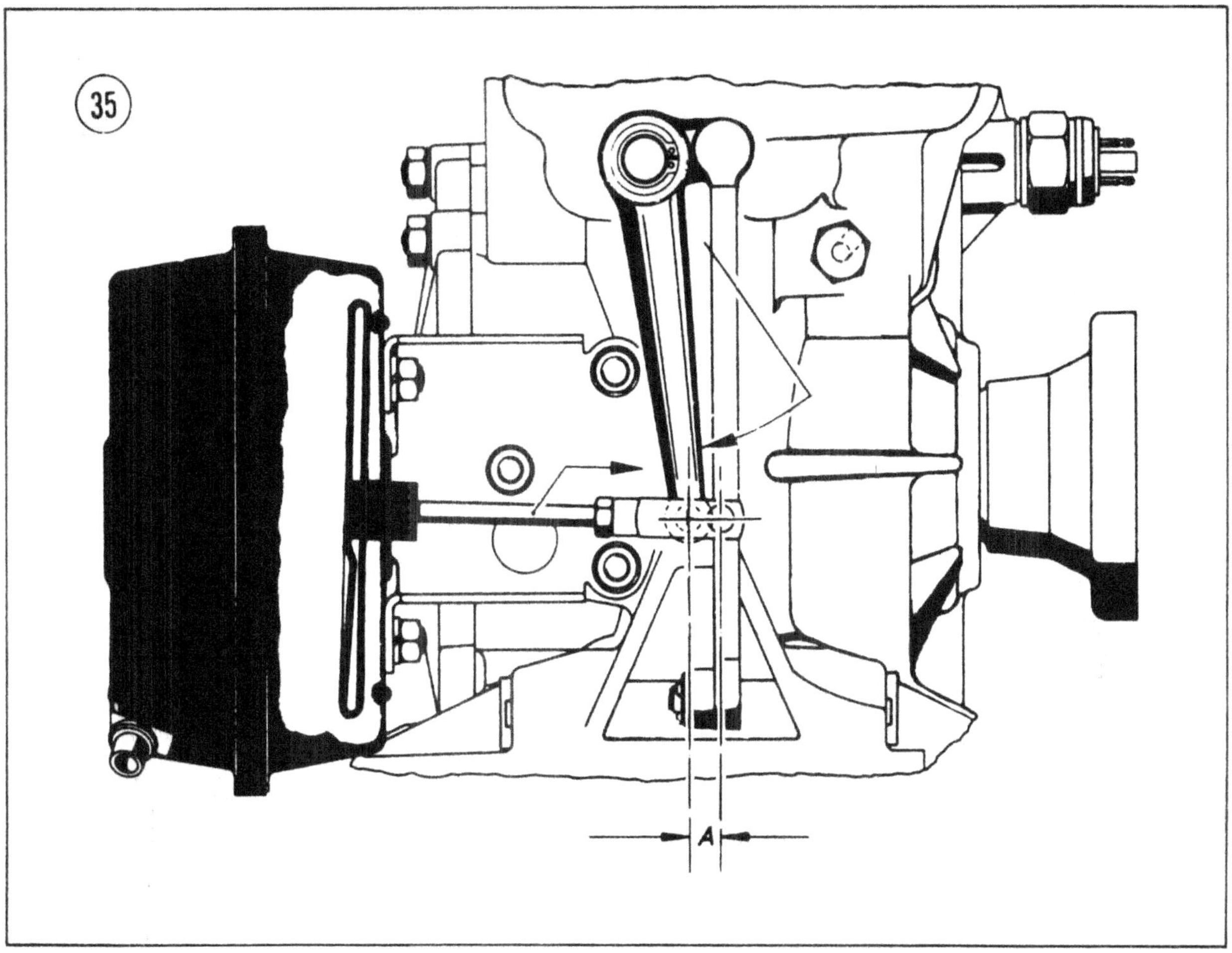

Figure 37. Adjust length of follower so that clearance is 0.04-0.06" (1-1.5mm).

2. Insert shim(s) 0.12" (3mm) thick under left idle speed adjustment (see **Figure 38**). Loosen Allen bolt on cam so that the drag spring (see **Figure 39**) just touches the control valve cam follower.

3. Depress accelerator to full throttle. Ensure

that the cam follower is not fully depressed. It should be possible to depress the follower an additional 0.012" (0.3mm) by inserting a feeler gauge. See **Figure 40**.

To adjust for downshifts:

Adjust the control valve so that the clutch smoothly engages after a downshift without substantial time lag (0.3-0.5 seconds), yet does not cause rear wheels to lock and cause tire chirp.

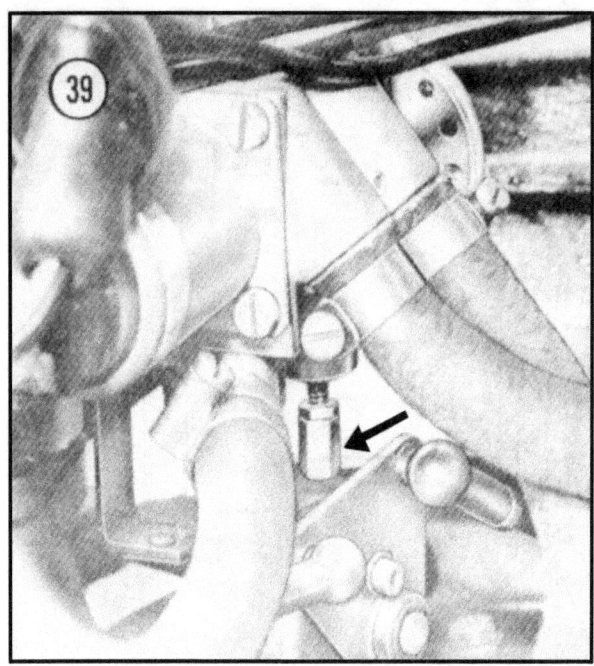

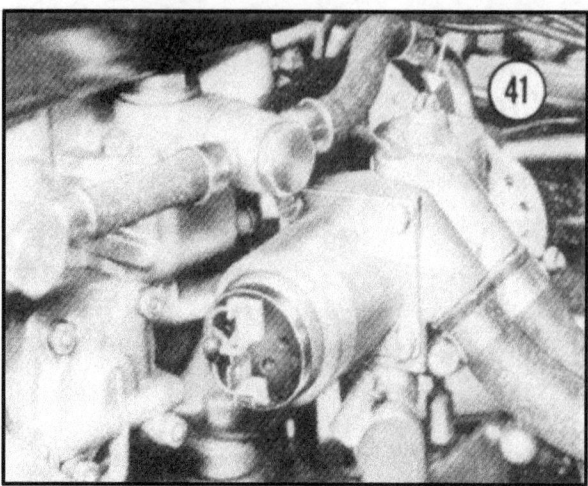

2. Remove center tunnel covering.

3. Remove 5 bolts securing gearshift base and lift base slightly. See **Figure 42**.

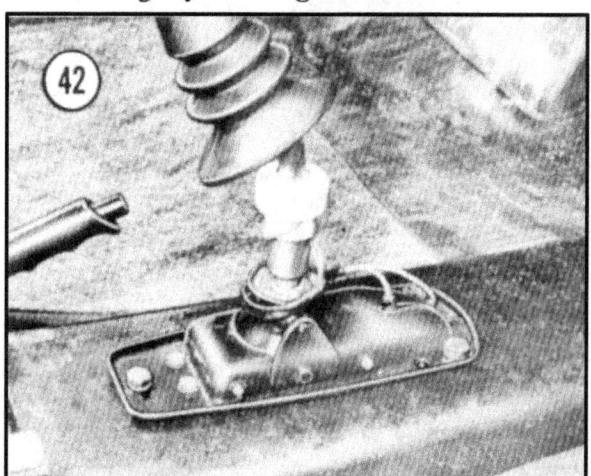

4. Disconnect microswitch wire and lift entire base out.

5. Hold lever in a vise with soft jaws and remove knob with a fork-shaped tool. See **Figures 43 and 44**. Pull locking sleeve out of knob.

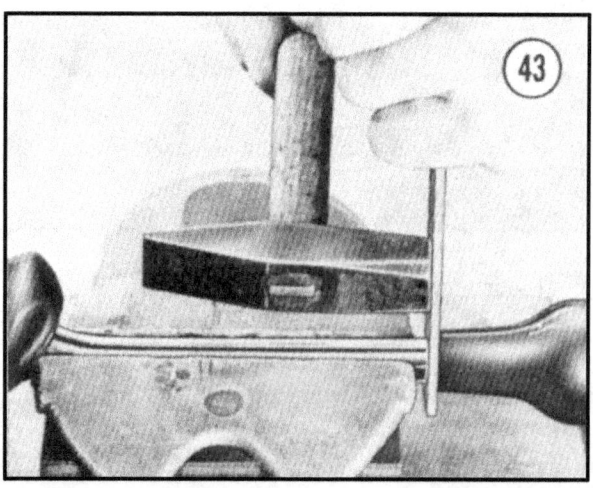

1. Select D and drive at 4,500 rpm.
2. Take foot off throttle and shift to L.
3. If clutch engages too fast or too slow, stop the car and remove the air cleaner. Remove the plastic cover over the control valve adjustment. See **Figure 41**. Turn screw clockwise if clutch engages too fast. Turn screw counterclockwise if clutch engages too slowly.

> NOTE: *Turn screw ¼-½ turn, then repeat procedure.*

4. When adjustment is correct, reinstall plastic cover and air cleaner.

Gearshift Lever Microswitch Replacement

1. Push both front seats back as far as possible.

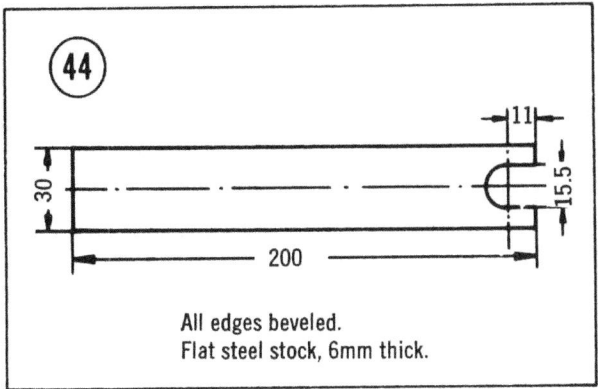

All edges beveled.
Flat steel stock, 6mm thick.

6. Pull dust boot and switch off lever.

7. Slide bottom of new microswitch onto lever with slit facing forward. See **Figure 45**.

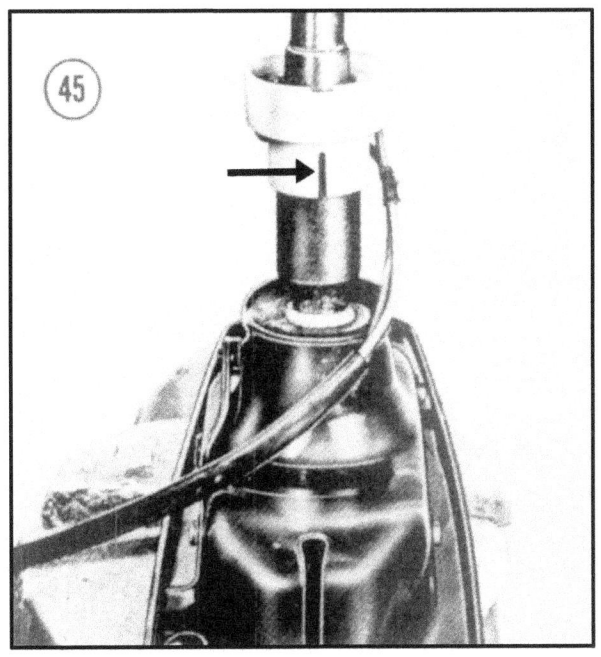

8. Install top of switch and rubber boot.

9. Push new locking sleeve into knob. Hold lever in a vise with soft jaws and drive the knob on with a plastic or hardwood tool (**Figure 46**).

10. Reconnect microswitch wire in center tunnel and install base. The ground wire goes under the left front retaining bolt. Torque large bolts to 18 foot-pounds (2.5 mkg) and small bolts to 7 foot-pounds (1.0 mkg).

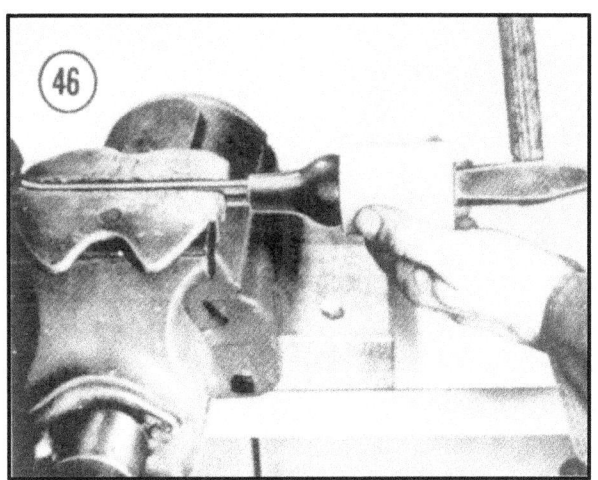

Table 1   SPECIFICATIONS

MANUAL TRANSAXLE	
Gear ratios	*
Oil capacity	
with limited slip	3.17 quarts (3 liters)
without limited slip	2.6 quarts (2.5 liters)
Oil type	
with limited slip	SAE 90 (MIL-L-2105B)
without limited slip	SAE 90 hypoid gear oil
SPORTOMATIC	
Gear ratios	
1st	2.400
2nd	1.550
3rd	1.125
4th	0.858
Reverse	2.533
Final drive ratio	3.857
Oil capacity	2.6 quarts (2.5 liters)
Oil type	SAE 90 hypoid gear oil

*See "Determining Transmission Gear Ratios" in text.

Table 2   TIGHTENING TORQUES

	foot-pounds	mkg
Transmission-to-frame bolts		
Sportomatic pressure plate bolts	10	1.4
Sportomatic transaxle-to-clutch housing bolts	14	2.0
Temperature switch or sender	33-36	4.5-5.0
Engine mounting bolts	69	9.5
Gearshift bolts (large)	18	2.5
Gearshift bolts (small)	7	1.0

CHAPTER TWELVE

REAR AXLE AND SUSPENSION

The 914 and 914/6 have independent rear suspension with trailing arms. See **Figure 1**. The two trailing arms are sprung by separate coil springs. Double-articulated drive shafts with constant velocity joints drive the rear wheels.

Table 1 includes specifications, while **Table 2** provides tightening torque values for mounting hardware. Both are at the end of the chapter.

WHEEL ALIGNMENT

Wheel alignment on an independent rear suspension is as important to handling and tire wear as front wheel alignment. Camber and toe-in on the 914 are adjustable and should be checked every 6,000 miles.

Camber and Toe-in Adjustments

It is not possible to adjust camber and toe-in without an alignment ramp. If you have disassembled the trailing arms, take the car to your dealer or other suspension specialist immediately after reassembly.

WARNING
Drive slowly and carefully, as handling is affected. Don't drive too far as tires can wear extremely quickly when scrubbed sideways by a misaligned suspension.

DRIVE SHAFTS

Refer to **Figure 2** for the following procedures.

Removal

1. Put the transmission in gear and pull up the handbrake.

2. Loosen the wheel lug bolts.

3. Remove the cotter key in the castellated hub nut and loosen the nut with a 36mm socket and a long breaker bar. The nut is torqued to 217 foot-pounds (30 mkg).

CAUTION
Never loosen the nut unless all 4 wheels are firmly on the ground. The force required to loosen the nut is sufficient to knock the car off the jackstand.

4. Raise rear of car on jackstands. Remove rear wheels.

5. Remove heat exchanger(s). See Chapter Six.

6. Remove the castellated hub nut.

7. Remove Allen bolts at inner flange. See **Figure 3**.

8. Carefully knock inner end of shaft loose from its seat with a rubber or plastic mallet and pull the outer end out of the wheel hub.

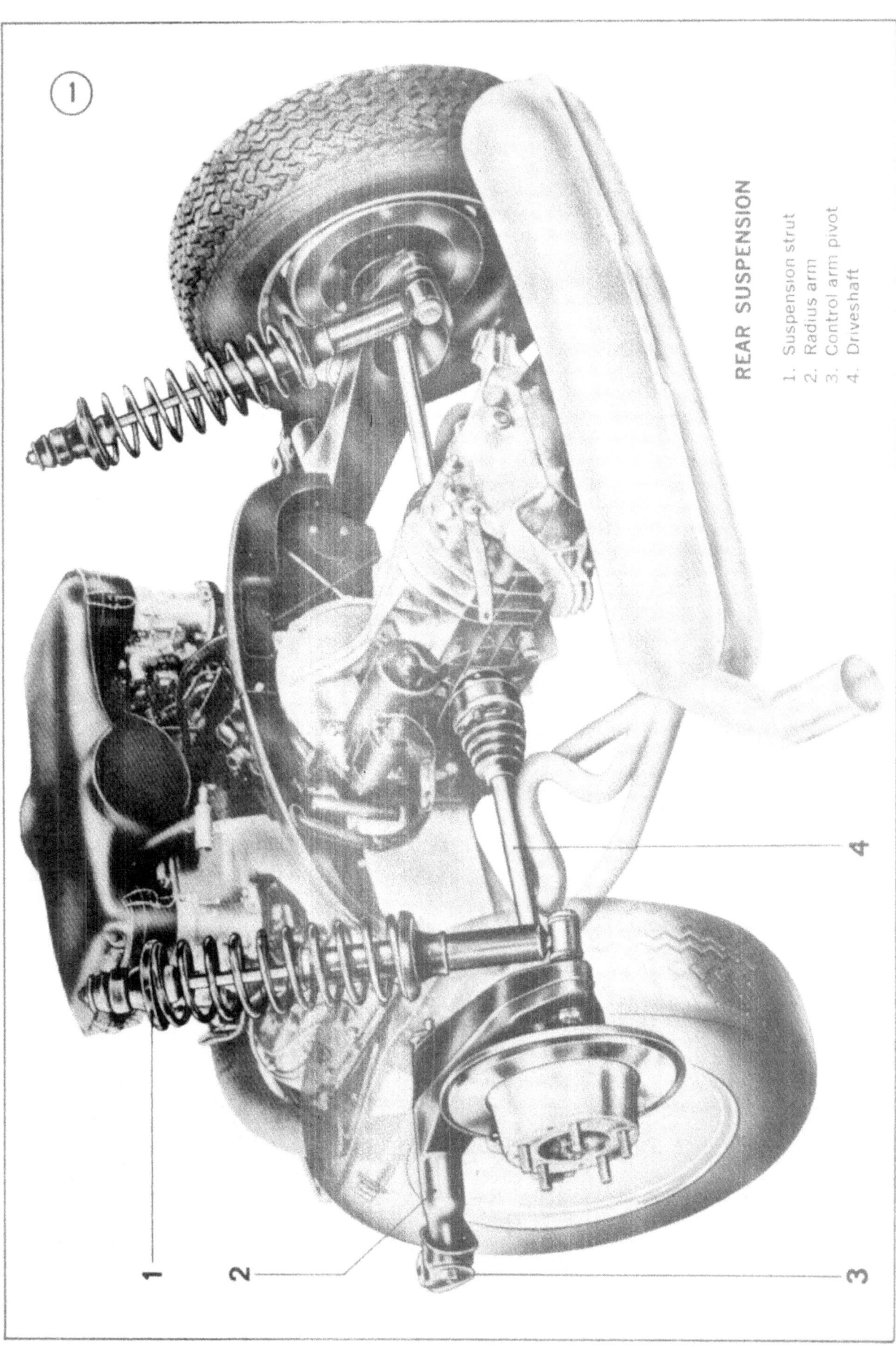

REAR SUSPENSION

1. Suspension strut
2. Radius arm
3. Control arm pivot
4. Driveshaft

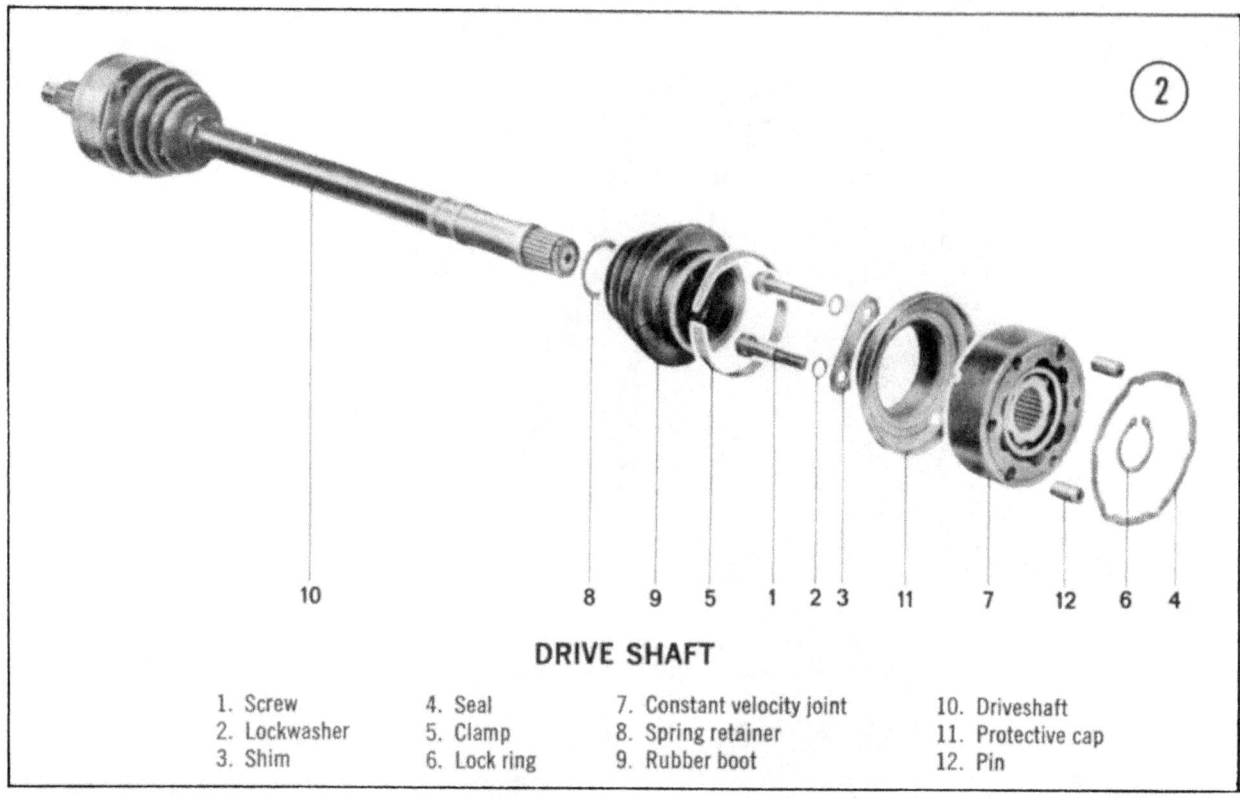

DRIVE SHAFT

1. Screw
2. Lockwasher
3. Shim
4. Seal
5. Clamp
6. Lock ring
7. Constant velocity joint
8. Spring retainer
9. Rubber boot
10. Driveshaft
11. Protective cap
12. Pin

CAUTION
Do not damage flange surfaces.

Inspection

1. Check constant velocity joints for excessive play. If worn, entire shaft must be replaced.
2. Check shaft for nicks and bends. Replace if necessary.
3. Check rubber boots for deterioration. Replace as described below.

Installation

1. Lightly oil the splines and insert the shaft into wheel hub.

2. Connect inner end to transaxle. Make sure mating surfaces are thoroughly clean. Use a new gasket. Tighten Allen bolts to 31 foot-pounds (4.3 mkg).

3. Install washer and castellated nut on outer end of shaft. Tighten to 20-30 foot-pounds (2.8-4.2 mkg).

4. Lower car.

5. Tighten castellated hub nut to 217-253 foot-pounds (30-35 mkg). Secure the nut with a new cotter pin.

REAR AXLE BOOTS

Refer to Figure 2 for the following procedure.

Removal/Installation

1. Remove drive shaft as described previously.
2. Remove hose clamps from boot.
3. Remove lock ring from end of shaft (see **Figure 4**) and press constant velocity joint off. See **Figure 5**.
4. Remove rubber boots.
5. Clean all parts in solvent.
6. Slide new boot onto shaft.
7. Slide constant velocity joint onto shaft and secure with lock ring.

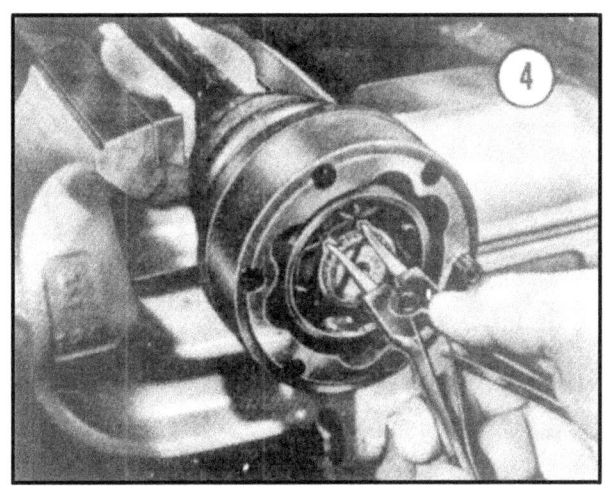

8. Pack multipurpose molybdenum disulphide grease into the inside of the constant velocity joint, boot, and inside flange area. The 914 requires about 3¼ ounces (90 grams); the 914/6, about 2½ ounces (70 grams).

9. Clean area on constant velocity joint on which the rubber boot mounts.

10. Glue boot onto constant velocity joint with gasket compound.

11. Tighten hose clamps with a pliers and bend tap over with small hammer. See **Figure 6**.

> NOTE: *Two small holes must be drilled in clamps as shown in* **Figure 7** *in order to tighten with a pliers.*

12. Install drive shaft.

CONSTANT VELOCITY JOINTS

Removal

1. Remove drive shaft as described previously.

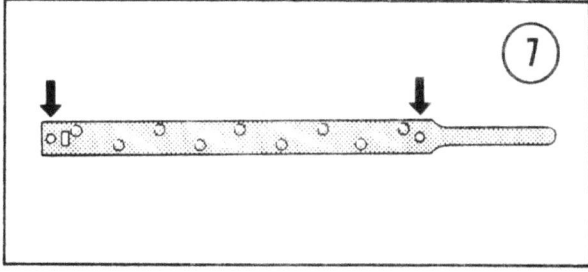

2. Loosen rubber boot clamps and slide the boot back. See **Figure 8**.

3. Drive metal cap off joint with a drift as shown in **Figure 9**.

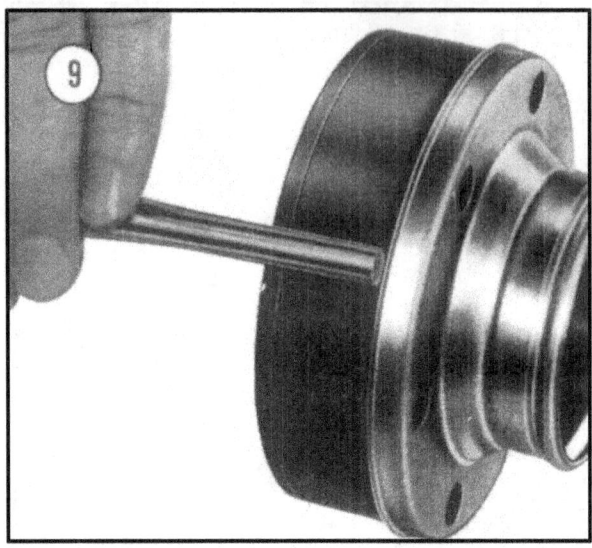

NOTE: *Do not tilt the ball hub more than 20° after removing the cap or the balls will fall out.*

4. Remove circlip from ball hub.
5. Slide outer part with balls onto the ball hub.
6. Press the drive shaft out of the ball hub as shown in **Figure 10**.

7. Support the hub from underneath when doing this.
8. Remove the dished washer from the joint.
9. Slide the rubber boot off drive shaft.

Disassembly/Assembly

1. Remove constant velocity joint as described previously.
2. Press ball hub and cage out of the outer ring as shown in **Figure 11**.

3. Press the balls out of the cage.
4. Tip the ball hub out of the ball cage using the grooves shown in **Figure 12**.

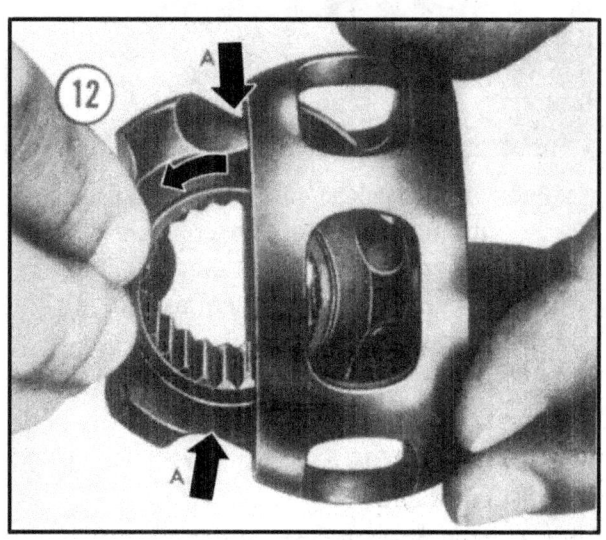

5. Clean all parts in solvent. Check each part for signs of wear or scoring.
6. Install the ball hub in the cage using the grooves in the hub.
7. Press the balls into the cage as shown in **Figure 13**.
8. Hold the outer ring so the large diameter end faces up. Look at the ball groove spacing. Note that the spacing at (a) is wider than at (b), directly opposite. See **Figure 14**.

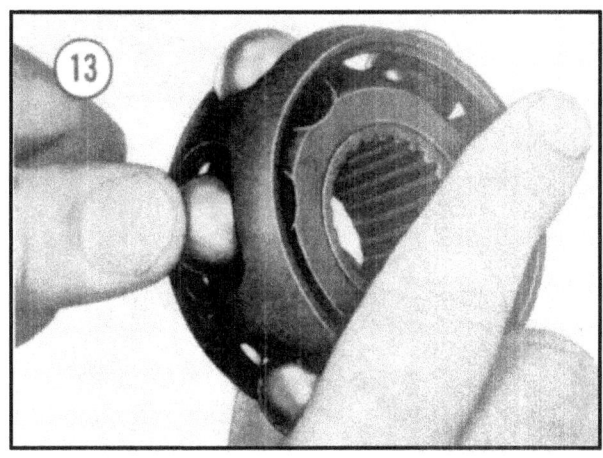

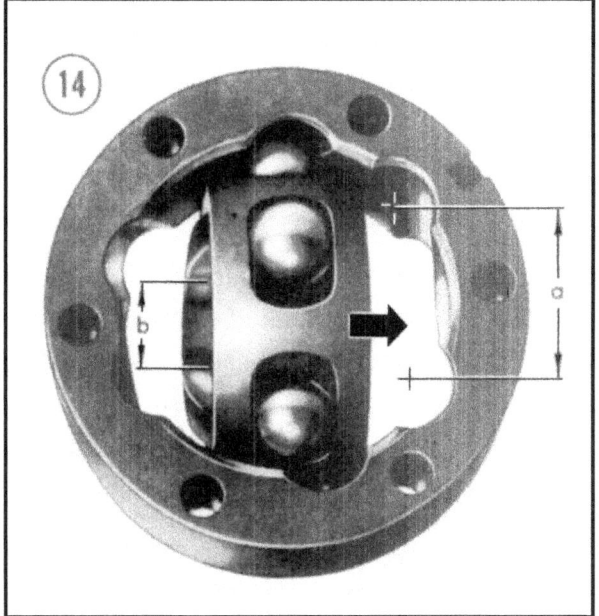

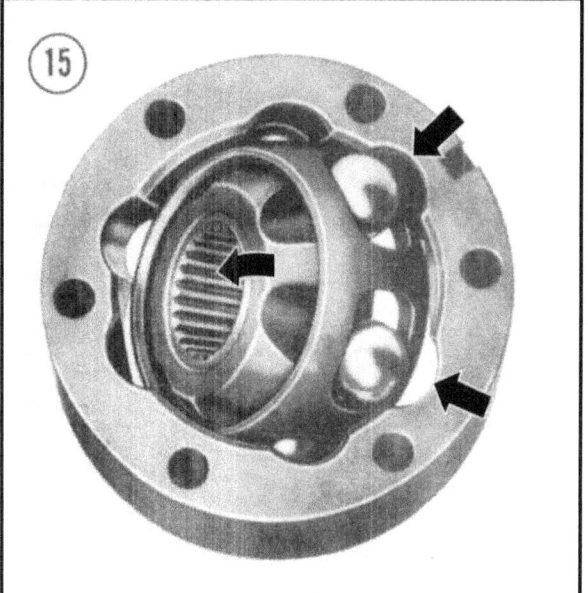

9. Insert the ball hub and cage into the outer ring as shown in **Figure 15**. Ensure that wide spaced balls line up with wide spaced grooves, and that the chamfered end of the hub will face towards the large diameter end of the outer ring when the hub is pivoted.

10. Pivot the ball hub in the hub until the balls fit into their grooves.

11. Press the cage firmly where indicated in **Figure 16** until the hub swings into position.

12. Check the joint before installing. It should be possible to move the hub by hand through its full range.

Installation

1. Inspect all parts for damage and replace if necessary.

2. Install rubber boot over drive shaft. Make sure the boot is not damaged by the splined end.

3. Slide the metal cap, then the dished washer, over the drive shaft.

4. With a hydraulic press, press the joint onto the drive shaft. See **Figure 17**.

NOTE: *The large diameter end (see arrow, **Figure 18**), faces the metal cap.*

5. Install a new circlip on the drive shaft and press it tightly into its groove with water pump pliers. See **Figure 19**.

6. Pack about 2 ounces (60 grams) of lithium grease (with molybdenum disulphide additive) between outer part of joint and metal cap. Do not get any grease on contact surfaces between

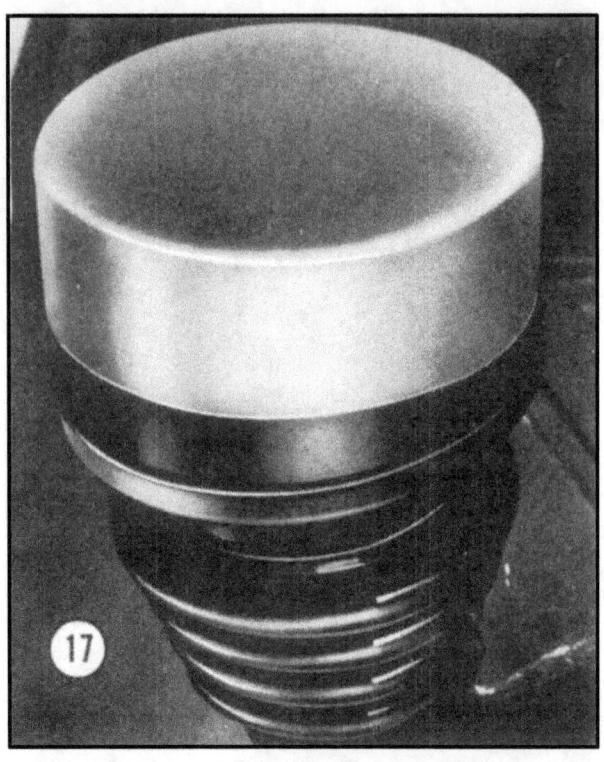

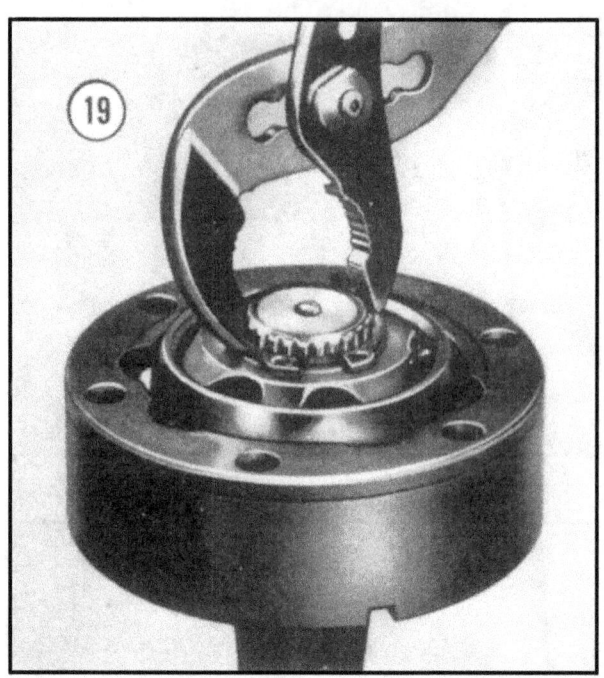

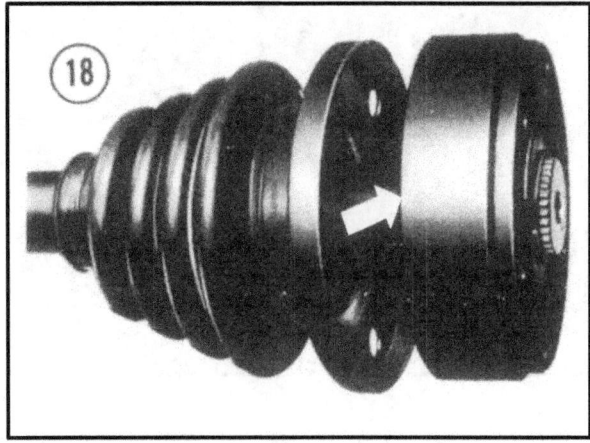

the cap, joint, or rubber boot. Pack another ounce (30 grams) into the end of the joint which faces the wheel.

7. Tap the metal cap into place over the joint.
8. Slide the rubber boot over the metal cap. Tighten both clamps securing the boot.
9. Squeeze the rubber boot by hand to force grease into the rear of the joint.
10. Install drive shaft and tighten Allen bolts to 25 foot-pounds (3.5 mkg).

SHOCK ABSORBERS

The shock absorber and coil spring are removed and installed as a single assembly. See Figure 1 and **Figure 20**.

Removal/Installation

1. Raise rear of car on jackstands.
2. Remove bolt at bottom of shock absorber.
3. Remove nut at top of shock absorber and remove shock absorber downward.
4. Remove coil spring from old shock absorber and install it on new one. See procedure below.
5. Installation is the reverse of these steps. Tighten top nut to 36-43 foot-pounds (5-6 mkg); tighten bottom bolt to 72-87 foot-pounds (10-12 mkg).

COIL SPRINGS

The coil springs are under tension while on the shock absorber. Removal requires a very sturdy tool shown in **Figure 21**. Since this job is potentially very dangerous with makeshift tools, take the shock absorber/coil spring assembly to your dealer and have him transfer the coil for a small bench fee.

If you have the proper tool:

1. Hold tool in a large vise.
2. Clamp coil spring in tool as shown in Figure 21.
3. Alternately tighten bolts on tool to compress coil spring.
4. Remove threaded bushing and top spring retainer.

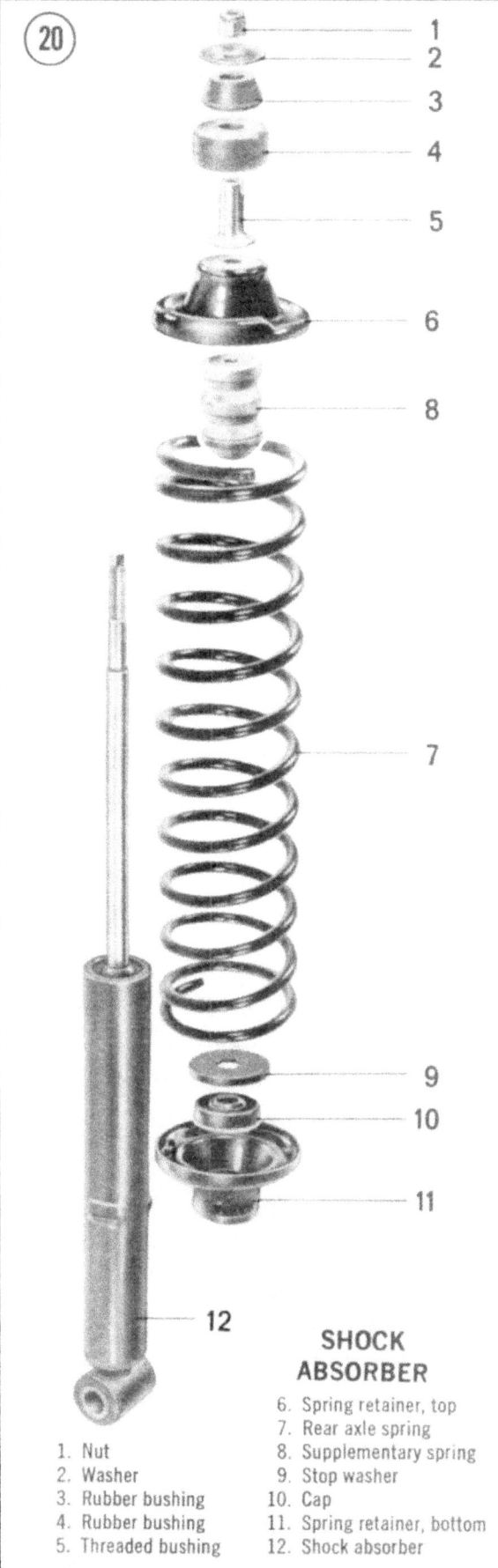

SHOCK ABSORBER

1. Nut
2. Washer
3. Rubber bushing
4. Rubber bushing
5. Threaded bushing
6. Spring retainer, top
7. Rear axle spring
8. Supplementary spring
9. Stop washer
10. Cap
11. Spring retainer, bottom
12. Shock absorber

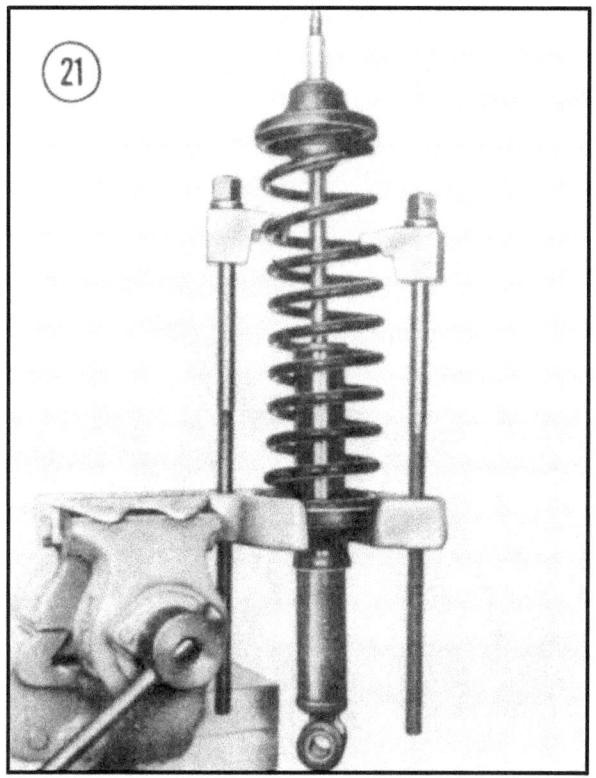

5. Slowly release pressure on spring, then remove the spring.

6. Remove supplementary spring and stop washer, and knock cap off piston shaft.

7. Remove bottom spring retainer.

8. Install bottom spring retainer on new shock absorber so that water drain hole will point towards the center line of the car when installed. See **Figure 22**.

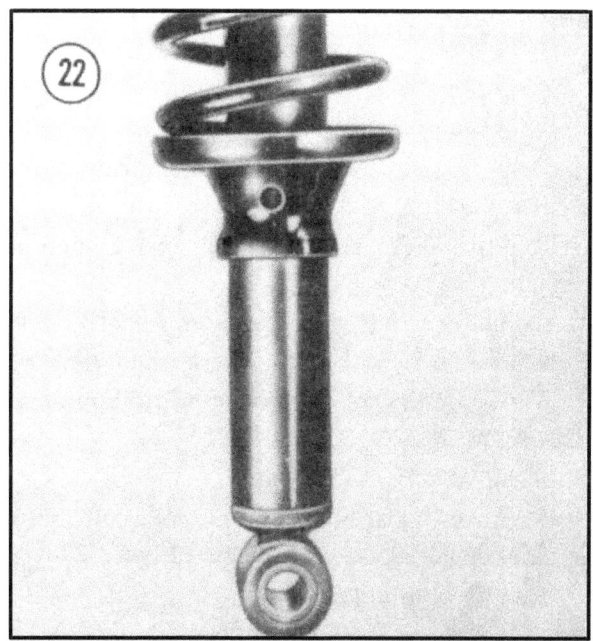

9. Install cap over piston shaft.

10. Install stop washer with grooves down. See **Figure 23**.

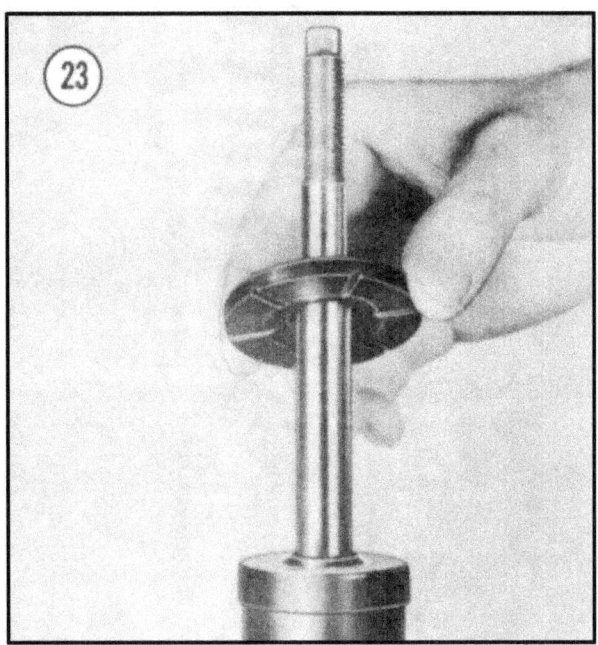

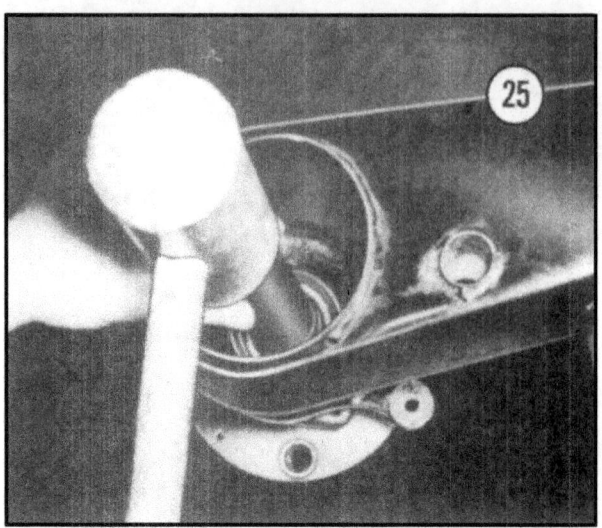

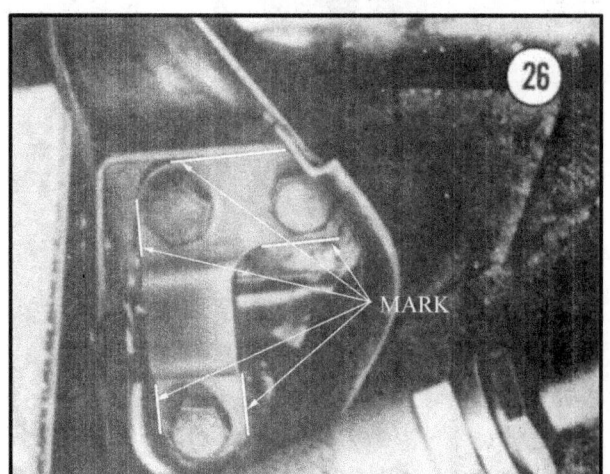

11. Place coil spring over shock absorber. Compress it with special tool.

12. Install supplementary spring, top spring retainer, and threaded bushing. Tighten to 11-14 foot-pounds (1.5-2.0 mkg).

TRAILING ARM

Refer to Figure 1 and **Figure 24** for the following procedures.

Removal

1. Remove rear brake caliper and disc as described in Chapter Fourteen.

2. Remove drive shaft as described earlier in this chapter.

3. Knock out rear wheel hub with a drift. See **Figure 25**.

4. Mark position of shim plate on trailing arm. See **Figure 26**.

5. Remove shock absorber.

6. Remove nut at outer end of pivot and bolts at camber adjusting bracket. See **Figure 27**.

7. Remove trailing arm.

8. Remove camber bracket from trailing arm.

Inspection

1. Remove bearing cover and force tapered roller bearing out of trailing arm. Clean bearing thoroughly in solvent, carefully blow dry with compressed air, and check for wear and pitting.

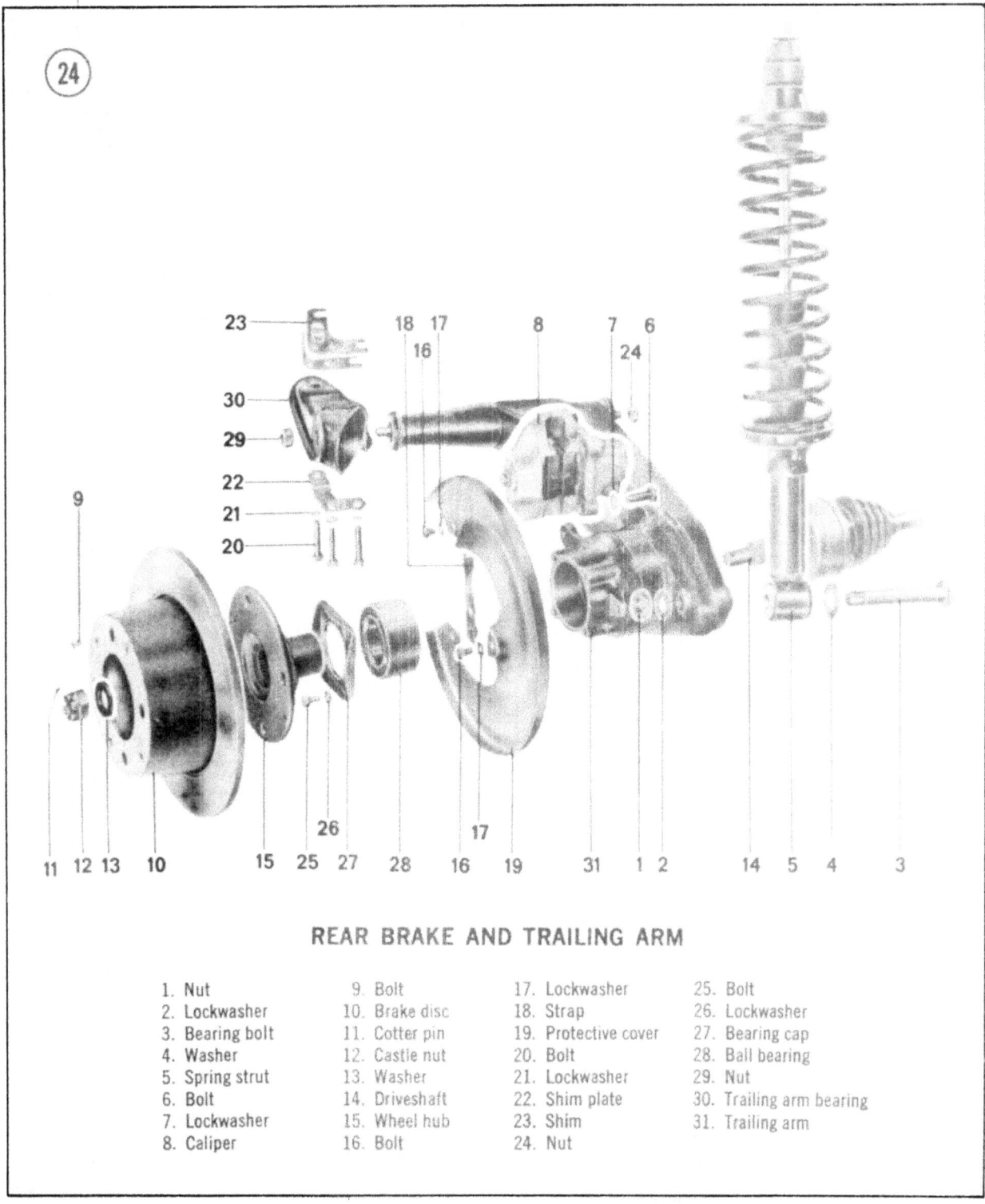

REAR BRAKE AND TRAILING ARM

1. Nut
2. Lockwasher
3. Bearing bolt
4. Washer
5. Spring strut
6. Bolt
7. Lockwasher
8. Caliper
9. Bolt
10. Brake disc
11. Cotter pin
12. Castle nut
13. Washer
14. Driveshaft
15. Wheel hub
16. Bolt
17. Lockwasher
18. Strap
19. Protective cover
20. Bolt
21. Lockwasher
22. Shim plate
23. Shim
24. Nut
25. Bolt
26. Lockwasher
27. Bearing cap
28. Ball bearing
29. Nut
30. Trailing arm bearing
31. Trailing arm

CAUTION

Do not permit bearing to spin while drying. This causes very rapid wear.

2. Check entire trailing arm for bends, cracks, etc. Replace if necessary.

3. Check rubber bushings in trailing arm. If worn or deteriorated, entire trailing arm must be replaced.

4. Install camber bracket on the trailing arm so the 2 are parallel where shown in **Figure 28**. Tighten retaining nut to 108 foot-pounds (15 mkg).

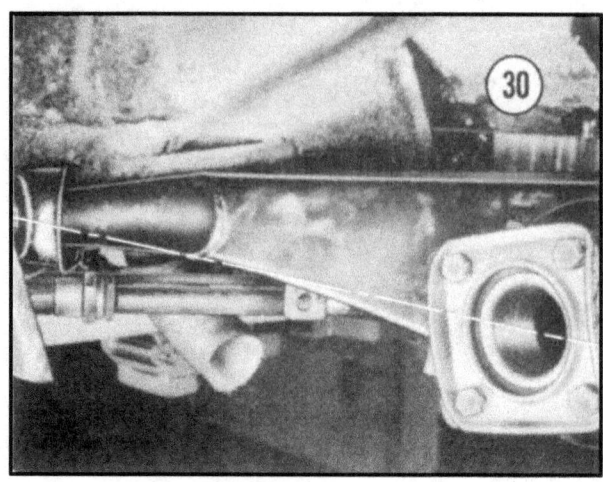

8. Install rear wheel hub.

9. Install shock absorber.

10. Install drive shaft. Tighten castellated nut to 20-30 foot-pounds (2.8-4.2 mkg).

11. Install rear brake calipers and discs as described in Chapter Fourteen.

12. Install rear wheels, lower car, and tighten castellated nut to 217-253 foot-pounds (30-35 mkg).

13. Adjust camber and toe-in on alignment ramp.

5. Press tapered roller bearing into trailing arm. See **Figure 29** for one method.

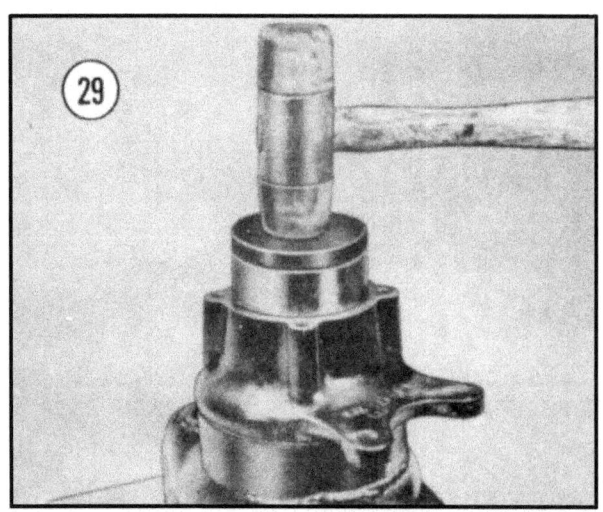

6. Install the bearing cover and tighten bolts to 18 foot-pounds (2.5 mkg).

7. Install trailing arm on body. Keep it horizontal. See **Figure 30**.

Table 1   **REAR SUSPENSION SPECIFICATIONS**

	914	914/6
TYPE	Independent double-jointed half shafts	
SPRINGING	Coil	Coil
REAR TRACK (5½" rims)	54.4" (1383mm)	54.3" (1379mm)
CAMBER (empty)	30'±20'	30'±20'
TOE-IN	0°+15' per wheel	0°+15' per wheel

Table 2   **TIGHTENING TORQUES**

	foot-pounds	mkg
Shock absorber bolt (bottom)	72-87	10-12
Shock absorber nut (top)	36-43	5-6
Shock absorber threaded bushing	11-14	1.5-2.0
Wheel castellated nut	217-253	30-35
Driveshaft bolts(Allen)	31	4.3
Trailing arm-to-body nut	50	6.9
Trailing arm-to-bracket nut	108	15
Bearing cover bolts	18	2.5
Wheel bolts (914)	108	15
Wheel nuts (914/6)	94	13

CHAPTER THIRTEEN

FRONT SUSPENSION AND STEERING

Porsche uses its version of a MacPherson strut suspension on the 914 models. The complete suspension is shown in **Figure 1**.

The front wheels are independently suspended on struts, each consisting of a large shock absorber. The top of each strut is attached to the body through rubber mounts. The bottom of each strut consists of a steering knuckle which connects to a control arm (wishbone) through a ball-joint. The upper mount for the strut is adjustable for camber and caster. Each control arm is sprung by torsion bar running longitudinally through the arm.

Steering is by rack-and-pinion. The rack rides in replaceable bushings in the housing. The floating pinion carrier, located in the housing, supports the pinion which rotates within 2 bearings. Since a pressure block holds the pinion against the rack, there is no free-play in the system.

The steering gear is filled with a permanent lubricant at the factory and requires no periodic maintenance. Drag induced by the steering gear may be adjusted, however.

Front suspension specifications are given in **Table 1**, and tightening torques in **Table 2**, both at the end of the chapter.

FRONT WHEEL ALIGNMENT

Several front suspension dimensions affect running and steering of the front wheels. These dimensions must be properly aligned to maintain directional stability, ease of steering, and proper tire wear.

The dimensions involved define:

  a. caster
  b. camber
  c. toe-in
  d. steering axis inclination
  e. front axle height

All except steering axis inclination are adjustable. Since these adjustments are critical, they must be done by a competent front end alignment shop or your dealer. See **Table 1** at end of chapter for alignment specifications.

Pre-alignment Check

Several factors influence the suspension angles, or steering. Before any adjustments are attempted, perform the following checks:

1. Check tire pressure and wear.
2. Check play in front wheel bearings. Adjust if necessary.
3. Check play in ball-joints or king pins.
4. Check for broken springs or torsion bars.
5. Remove any excessive load.
6. Check shock absorbers.

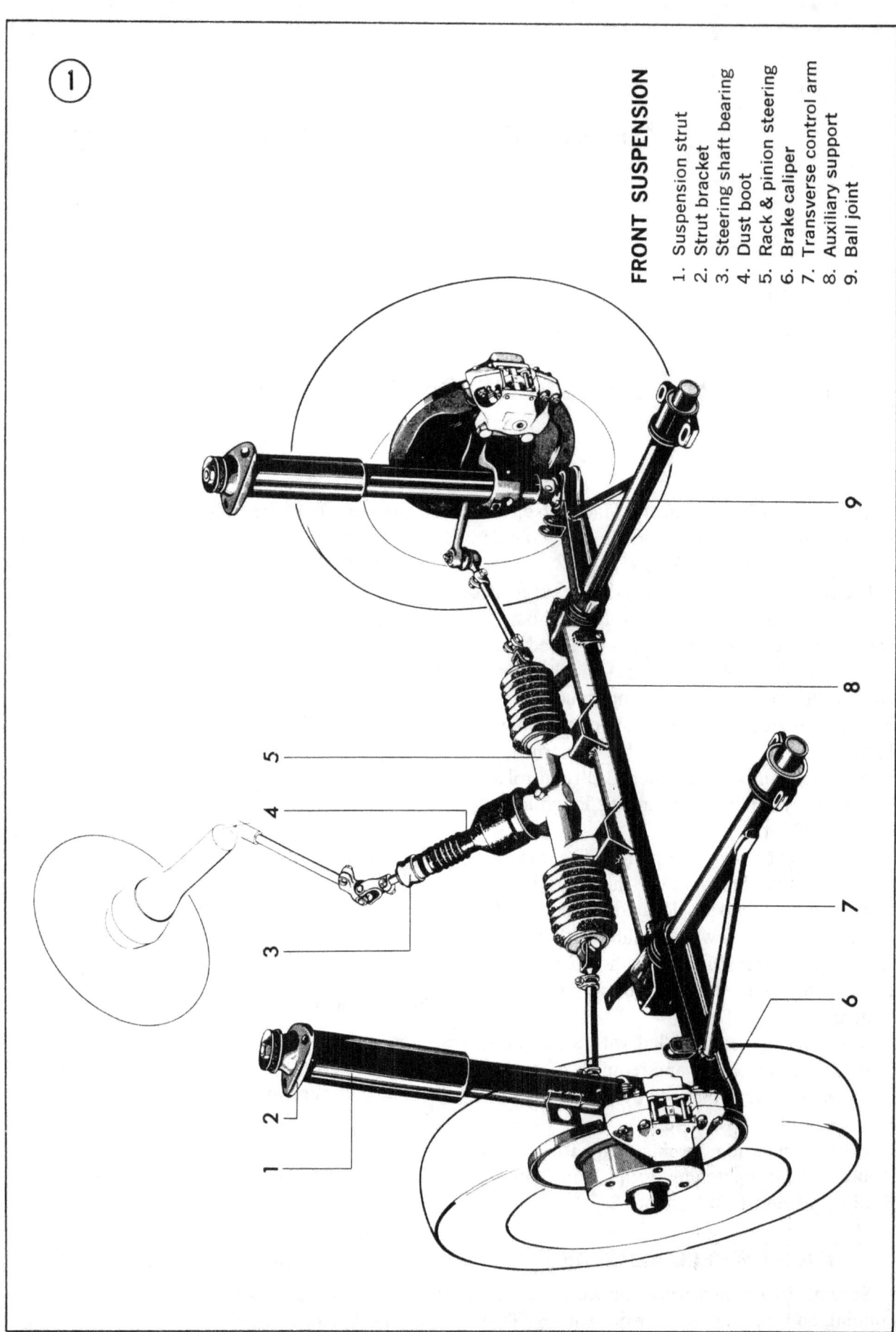

FRONT SUSPENSION

1. Suspension strut
2. Strut bracket
3. Steering shaft bearing
4. Dust boot
5. Rack & pinion steering
6. Brake caliper
7. Transverse control arm
8. Auxiliary support
9. Ball joint

7. Check steering gear adjustments.
8. Check play in pitman arm and tie rod parts.
9. Check wheel balance.
10. Check *rear* suspension for looseness.

A proper inspection of front tire wear can point to several alignment problems. Tires worn primarily on one side show problems with toe-in. If toe-in is incorrect on one wheel, the car probably pulls to one side or the other. If toe-in is incorrect on both wheels, the car probably is hard to steer in either direction. Incorrect camber may also cause tire wear on one side. Tire cupping (scalloped wear pattern) can result from worn shock absorbers, one wheel out of alignment, a bent spindle, or a combination of all. Tires which are worn in the middle, but not the edges, or worn nearly even on both edges, but not in the middle are probably over-inflated or under-inflated, respectively; these conditions are not caused by suspension misalignment.

Camber

Camber is the inclination of the wheel from vertical as shown in **Figure 2**. Note that angle (a) is positive camber, i.e., the top of the tire inclines outward more than the bottom.

Camber is adjusted by loosening Allen bolts and moving the end of the suspension strut inward or outward to decrease or increase positive camber; 1mm movement equals about 6′ change in camber.

Caster

Caster is the inclination of the axis through the strut from vertical. See **Figure 3**. The Porsche has negative caster, i.e., the wheel is shifted rearward. Caster causes the wheels to return to a position straight ahead after a turn. It also prevents the car from wandering due to wind, potholes, or uneven road surfaces.

Caster is adjusted by loosening the same Allen bolts described for camber and moving the strut to the front or rear to decrease or increase caster.

Steering Axis Inclination

Steering axis inclination is shown in Figure 2 and is the inclination of the strut from vertical. This angle is not adjustable, but can be checked

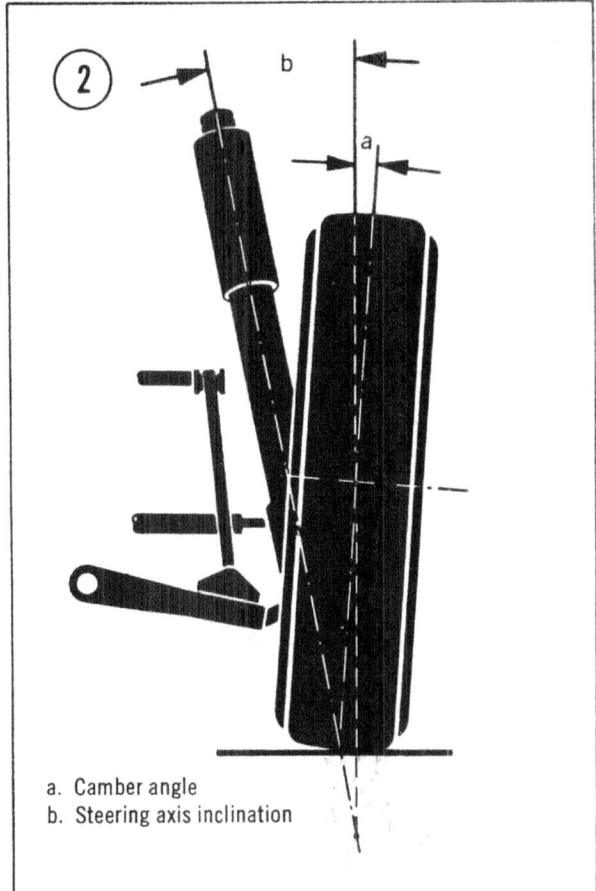

a. Camber angle
b. Steering axis inclination

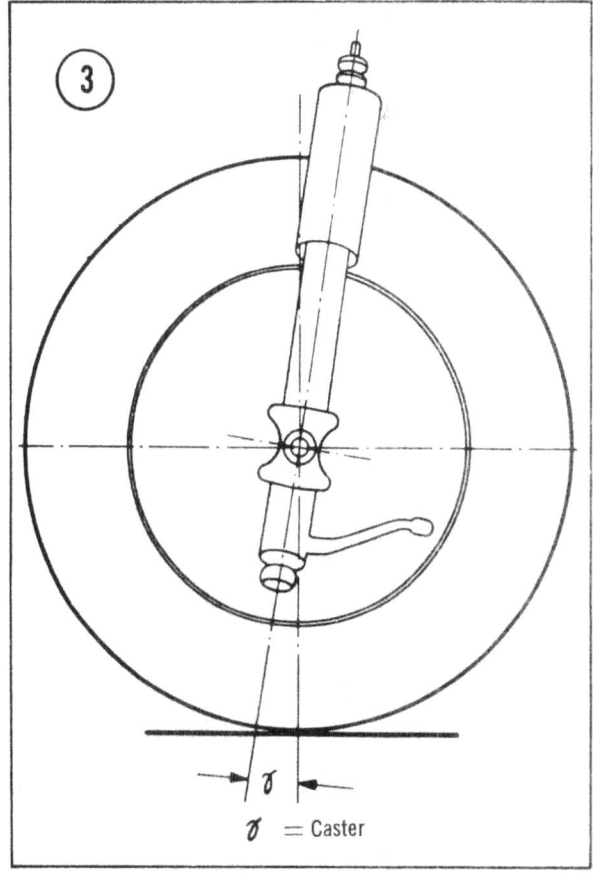

γ = Caster

with proper front-end racks to find bent suspension parts.

Toe-in

Camber and rolling resistance tend to force the front wheels outward at their forward edge. To compensate for this tendency, the front edges are turned slightly inward when the car is at rest. This is toe-in. See **Figure 4**.

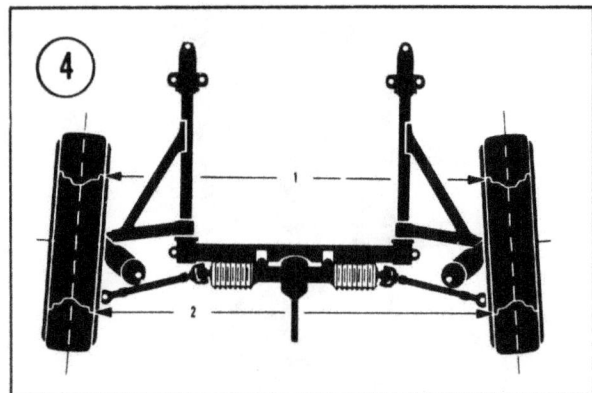

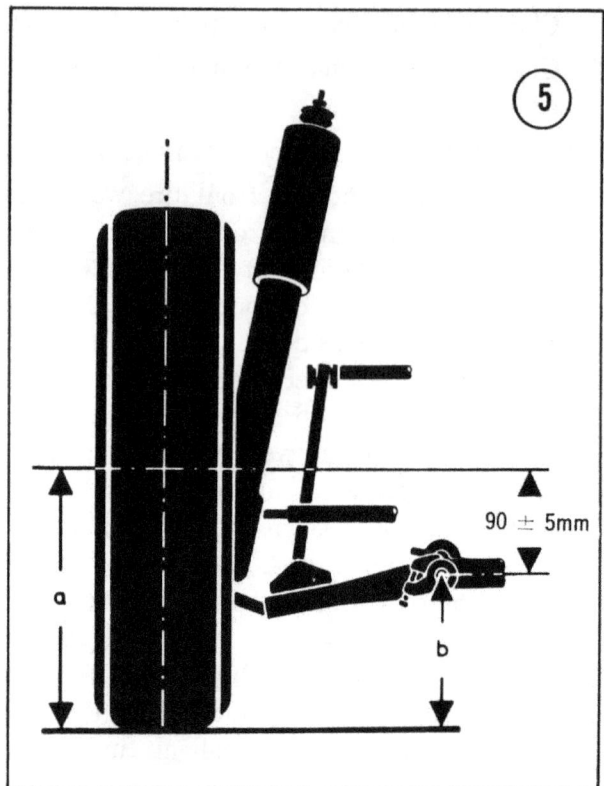

Toe-in is adjusted by lengthening or shortening the tie rods. Each tie rod is threaded so that the center section can be rotated to make the adjustment.

Front Axle Height

Before making any other suspension adjustments, the front axle height must be checked and adjusted if necessary. The measurement requires a full tank of fuel, correct tire pressure (see Chapter Two), spare tire in place, and no other loads. The car must be on an alignment ramp or level floor.

To check front axle height:

1. Mark dead center of dust caps of front wheels.
2. Depress front of car several times by pushing on the bumper guards. Release the guard when the car is down and let it bounce back up by itself.
3. Measure dimension (a), **Figure 5**, from floor to center of dust cover.
4. Subtract 90mm from dimension (a). This new dimension (b) shown in Figure 5 should be 225±5mm. Measure dimension (b) to the center of the torsion bar.

5. If dimension (b) on left side is within tolerance, measure (b) on right side in the same manner. Dimension (b) on right side must be within 5mm of dimension (b) on left side, but in no case can it be less than 220mm or greater than 230mm.

6. If dimension (b) on either side is not 225± 5mm or if dimension (b) on either side is not within 5mm of the other dimension (b), the front axle height must be readjusted.

To adjust front axle height:

1. Remove dust cover over torsion bar adjusting lever. See **Figure 6**.

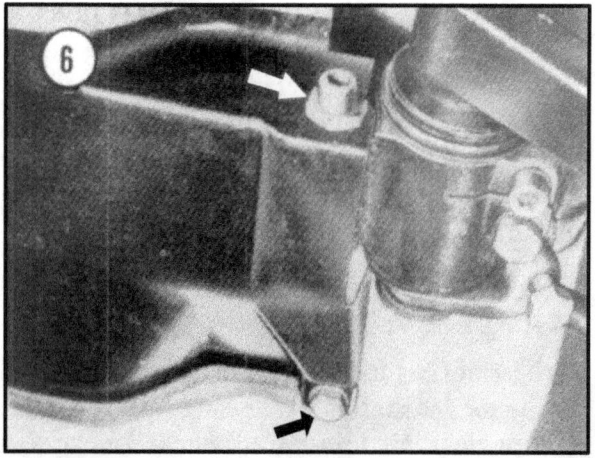

2. Adjust lever adjusting screw until dimension (b) on that side is 225±5mm. See **Figure 7**.

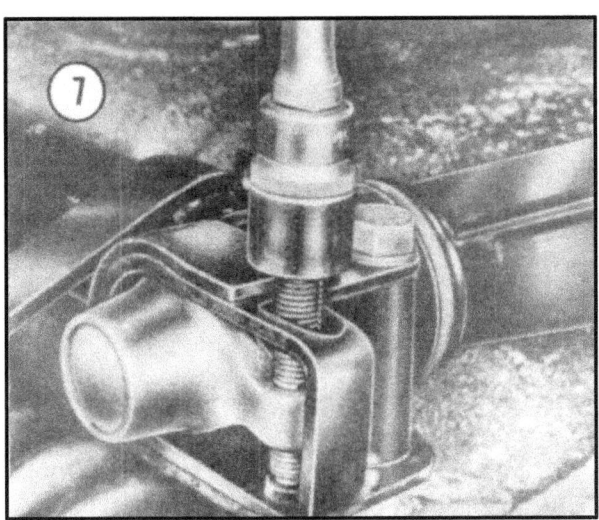

3. Recheck other side to be sure it is within 5mm of the first side. If not, adjust dimension (b) on second side in the same manner as the first side.

4. Install dust cover.

FRONT STABILIZER

The optional front stabilizer bar is 15mm in diameter.

Removal/Installation

1. Raise front of car on jackstands and remove both front wheels.

2. Loosen 2 clamp bolts on each lever arm and pull arms off stabilizer. See **Figure 8**.

3. Remove 3 bolts at the left end of stabilizer securing the rubber bushing and support. See **Figure 9**.

4. Squirt penetrating oil on rubber bushing and support. Pry the 2 parts apart, then remove them.

5. Remove 3 bolts at the right end of stabilizer.

6. Pull stabilizer out from the right side.

7. Remove rubber bushing and support from stabilizer.

8. Remove bolts securing stabilizer shackles to control arms. Remove shackles and lever arms.

9. Check all rubber bushings for deterioration and wear.

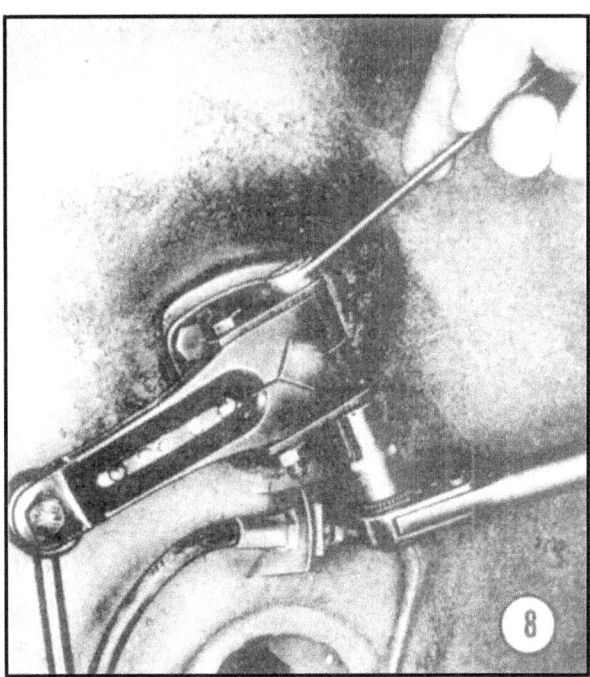

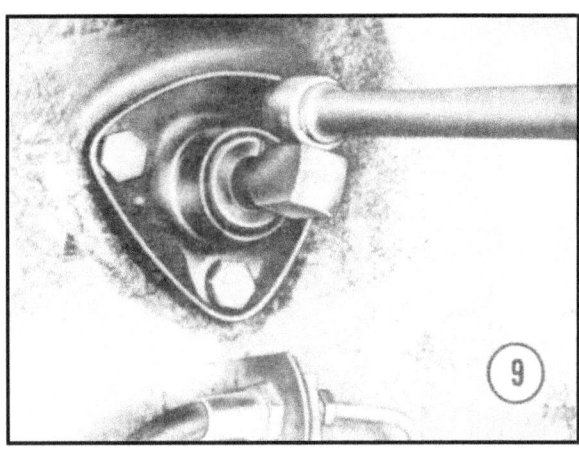

10. Coat rubber bushings with glycerine or similar rubber lubricant.

CAUTION
Do not use petroleum based lubricants. Petroleum based products attack rubber and cause rapid deterioration.

11. Bolt shackles with lever arms attached to the control arms.

12. Install rubber bushing and support on stabilizer.

13. Insert the stabilizer from the right side. Install 3 bolts finger-tight.

14. Install left rubber bushing and support. Install 3 bolts finger-tight.

15. Center stabilizer and tighten all 6 bolts to 18 foot-pounds (2.5 mkg).

16. Attach lever arms to stabilizer ends. About 1mm should protrude past surface of lever arm. Tighten bolts to 18 foot-pounds (2.5 mkg).

FRONT SUSPENSION STRUT

Removal/Installation

1. Raise front of car on jackstands and remove front wheels.

2. Remove brake caliper and disc as described in Chapter Fourteen.

3. Remove backing plate (see **Figure 10**).

4. Disconnect tie rod at strut as described in a later section.

5. On shock absorber struts, loosen torsion bar adjusting screw and pull adjusting arm off. See **Figure 11**.

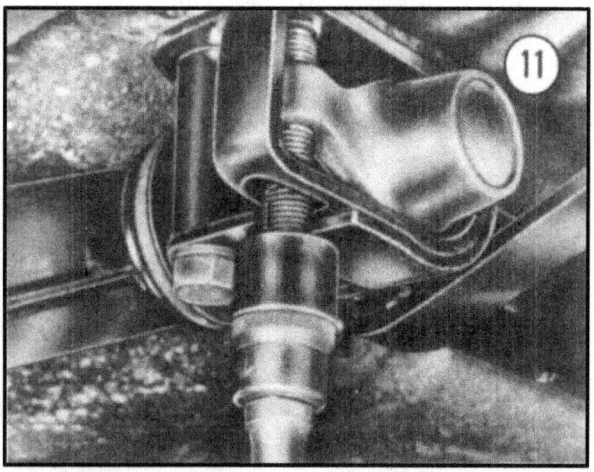

6. Loosen clamp bolt at bottom of strut. See **Figure 12**. Push control arm (wishbone) down until ball-joint is clear of the strut.

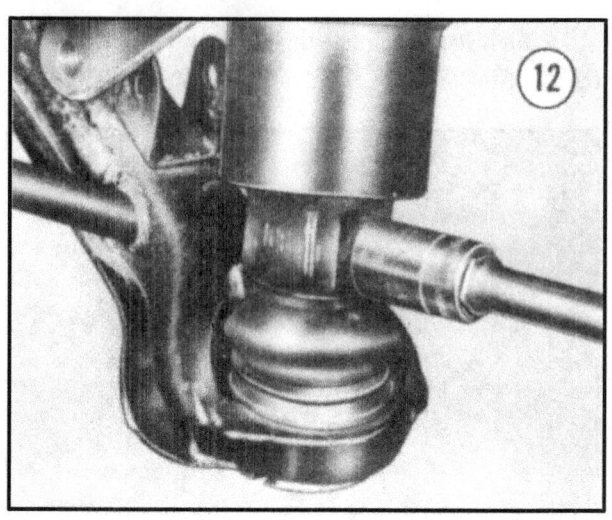

7. Remove nut at top of strut accessible through front luggage compartment. See **Figure 13**.

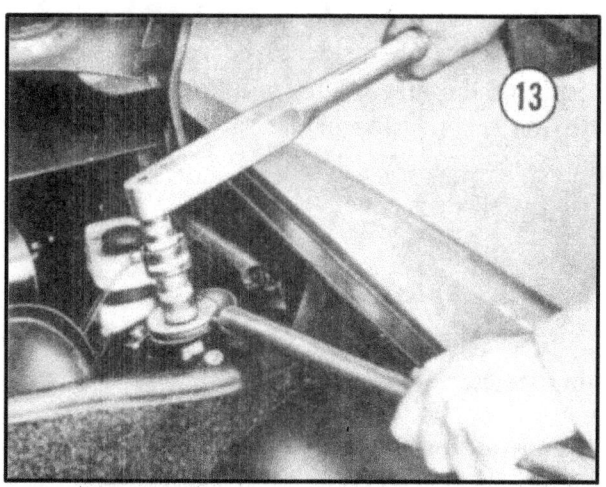

8. Remove strut.

9. Check alignment of strut and steering knuckle. Since this requires special jigs, take the strut to your dealer. Ask him to check alignment and condition of shock absorber (if applicable).

10. Installation is the reverse of these steps. Be sure to reinstall the steel washer on the ball-joint as shown in **Figure 14**. When installing the torsion bar adjusting lever, pry control arm downward with a tire iron or similar tool until it contacts its stop. See **Table 2** at the end of the chapter for proper tightening torques.

TORSION BARS

Removal

1. Raise front of car on jackstands and remove front wheel.

2. Remove nuts and bolts on undershield and remove it. See **Figure 15**.

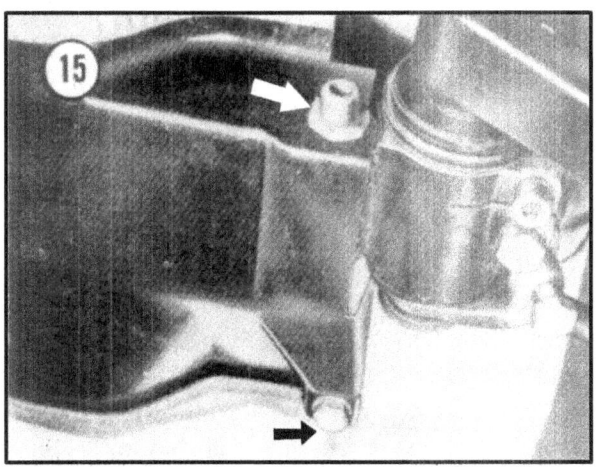

3. Unscrew torsion bar adjustment as shown in Figure 11.

4. Remove torsion bar dust caps. See **Figure 16**.

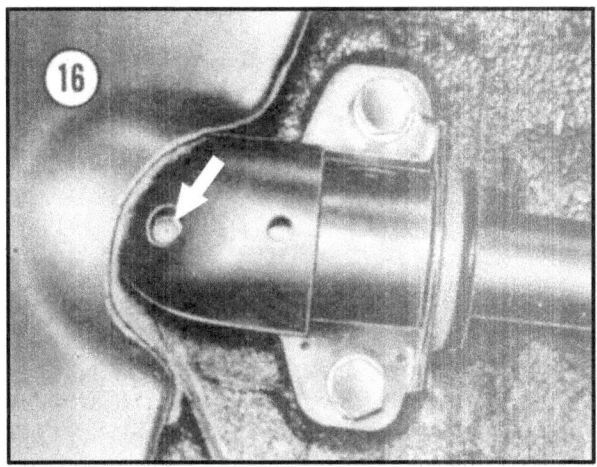

5. Drive torsion bar forward and out using an appropriate punch.

CAUTION
A protective paint covers the torsion bars. Do not nick or scratch this paint. Even slight damage leads to corrosion and eventual fatigue fractures. Touch up with paint if necessary.

Installation

1. Lightly grease torsion bars and particularly the splines with lithium grease.

2. Insert the torsion bar from the rear.

NOTE: *Torsion bars are marked left (L) and right (R) and must not be interchanged. See* **Figure 17**.

3. Install seal on torsion bar. See **Figure 18**.

4. Assuming the shock absorber strut is connected to the control arm, pry the control arm down until strut reaches its stop. See **Figure 19**.

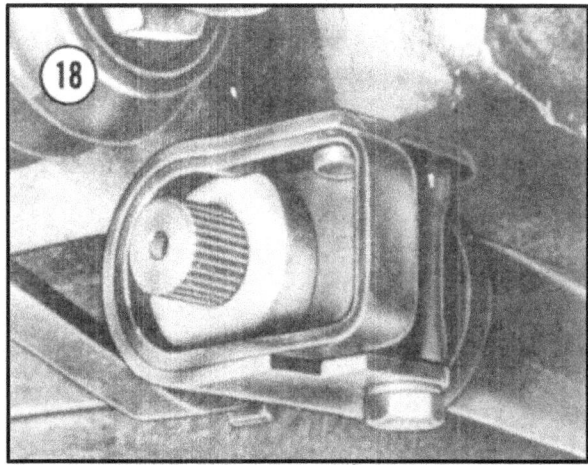

5. Insert torsion bar adjusting lever into cross member and over torsion bar spline with adjusting screw backed off as far as possible. Leave as little clearance as possible between the end of the adjusting screw and the lever.

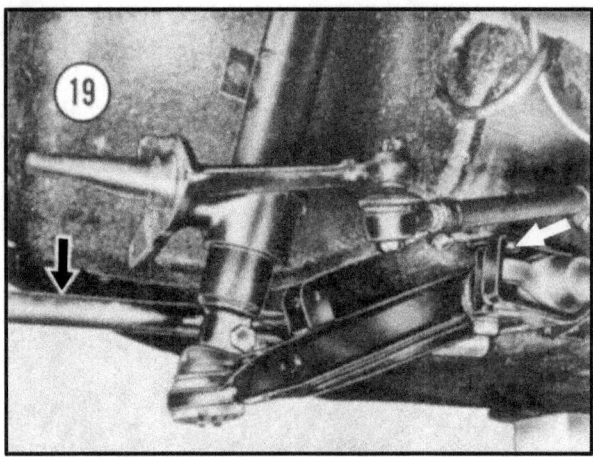

6. Tighten adjusting screw to take up any gap below the screw.

7. Install lock ring and dust cap at front of torsion bar.

8. Adjust front-end height as described in a later section.

9. Have the wheel alignment checked and adjusted by your dealer or other competent wheel alignment expert. Tell him what repairs you have made to help him do a thorough job.

WHEEL BEARINGS

Replacement

1. Raise front of car on jackstands and remove both front wheels.

2. Remove brake calipers as described in Chapter Fourteen.

3. Remove dust cap as shown in **Figure 20**.

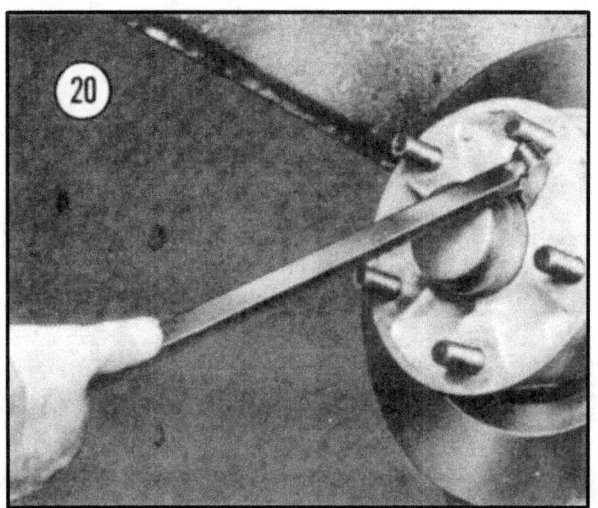

4. Loosen Allen bolt in clamping nut. See **Figure 21**. Remove nut and thrust washer.

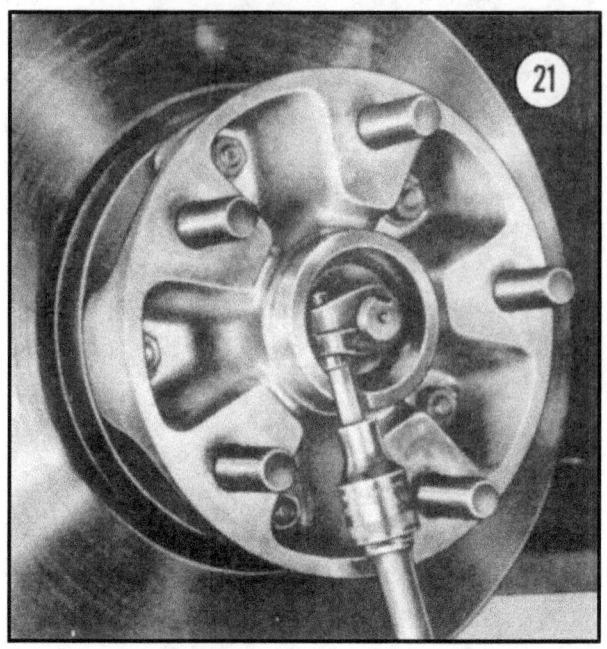

5. Remove wheel hub/brake disc assembly.

6. Remove wheel bearings. To do this, lay the wheel hub assembly over a clean cloth. Tap the lower bearing out from the inside with a hardwood stick and a hammer. Turn the wheel hub over. Tap the other bearing out in the same manner. Do not mix up bearings. Tag them if necessary to mark which wheel they were on.

> NOTE: *In some cases it may be necessary to separate the hub from the disc to remove the bearings. Mark the relationship between the two, then remove bolts joining them.*

7. Clean wheel bearings thoroughly in solvent and blow dry.

CAUTION
Although it is fascinating to watch the bearings rotate rapidly by compressed air, it will ruin a clean, unlubricated bearing in a very short time.

8. Clean bearing races in the wheel hub with solvent.

9. Check rollers for scores, wear, and evidence of overheating (bluish tint). Check bearing races also.

10. If a bearing or bearing race is damaged, the bearing and race must be replaced. Take the

hub to your dealer. For a small bench fee, he will press the old race out and install the new one.

CAUTION
Bearings made by Timken, SKF, and FAG may be used interchangeably on all models and years. Be certain, however, that the bearing and race are of the same manufacture.

11. Insert the inner bearing in the hub.

12. Press the oil seal in carefully and evenly until the seal is flush with the hub housing.

13. Assemble the hub to the disc if they were disassembled in Step 6. Torque bolts to 17 foot-pounds (2.3 mkg).

14. Pack the hub with about 2.1 ounces (65cc) of lithium-based multipurpose grease. Make sure that the bearings are thoroughly coated with grease. Work it in well between rollers. Pack some between the inner seal and bearing.

15. Install brake disc/wheel hub assembly as described in Chapter Fourteen.

16. Adjust wheel bearings as described below.

Adjustment

1. Raise front of car on jackstands.

2. Remove dust covers on hub. See Figure 20.

3. Loosen Allen bolt in clamping nut. See Figure 21.

4. Tighten clamp nut to about 11 foot-pounds (1.5 mkg) while rotating the wheel. This takes all slack out of the bearings.

5. Loosen the clamping nut just to the point when the thrust washer can be moved when pried lightly with a screwdriver. See **Figure 22**.

6. Tighten Allen bolt in clamping nut. Do not move clamping nut while doing this.

7. Recheck adjustment and repeat if necessary.

8. Install dust cap. Do not fill it with grease.

9. Lower car.

STEERING WHEEL

Removal/Installation

1. Disconnect battery ground cable.

2. Twist horn button counterclockwise and remove it. See **Figure 23**.

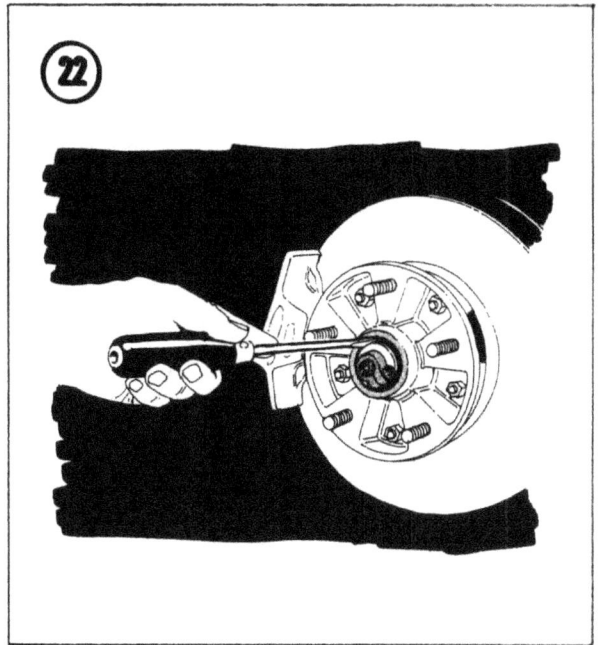

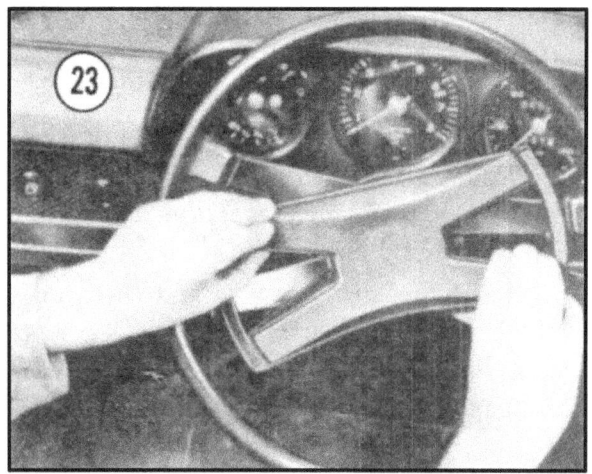

3. Remove horn contact pin.

4. Remove steering wheel retaining nut. See **Figure 24**.

5. Mark relationship between steering wheel and steering shaft.

6. Pull steering wheel off.

7. Remove bearing support ring and spring. See **Figure 25**.

8. Ensure that wheels are straight ahead.

9. Install bearing support ring and spring.

10. Install steering wheel so that spokes are horizontal and align with marks made in Step 5. Tighten nut to 58 foot-pounds (8 mkg).

11. Check that directional lever returns properly when steering wheel is turned.

12. Insert horn contact pin and install horn cap. Turn cap clockwise to lock.

TIE ROD REPLACEMENT

1. Raise car on jackstands and remove front wheels.

2. Remove cotter pins from castellated nuts on tie rod ends.

3. Remove nut on ball-joint at outer end of tie rod.

4. Loosen universal coupling nut and bolt at inner end of tie rod.

5. Press tie rod end out with a special tool as shown in **Figure 26**.

CAUTION
Do not damage rubber seals when removing tie rods.

6. Check tie rods for bends and other damage. Bent tie rods must be replaced, not straightened.

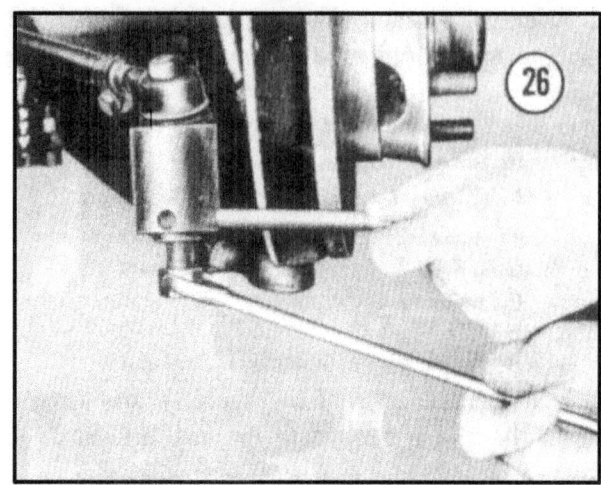

7. Check tie rod pin. If there is any play or the pin is frozen, the tie rod end must be replaced.

8. Check rubber seals. Damaged seals must be replaced.

9. Installation is the reverse of these steps.

10. Adjust toe-in.

STEERING HOUSING

The steering housing contains the rack-and-pinion gears.

Removal/Installation

1. Remove clamp nut and bolt on universal joint at steering housing.

2. Disconnect tie rods at ball-joints. See *Tie Rod Replacement* in the previous section.

3. Remove splash shield over front axle.

4. Loosen steering housing mounting bolts. See **Figure 27**.

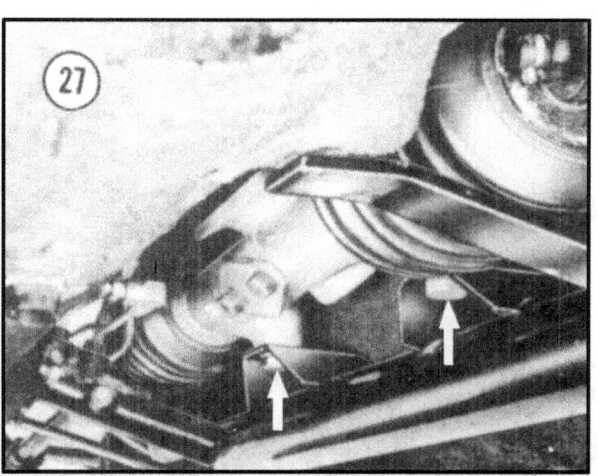

5. Unscrew torsion bar adjusting screws. See **Figure 28**.

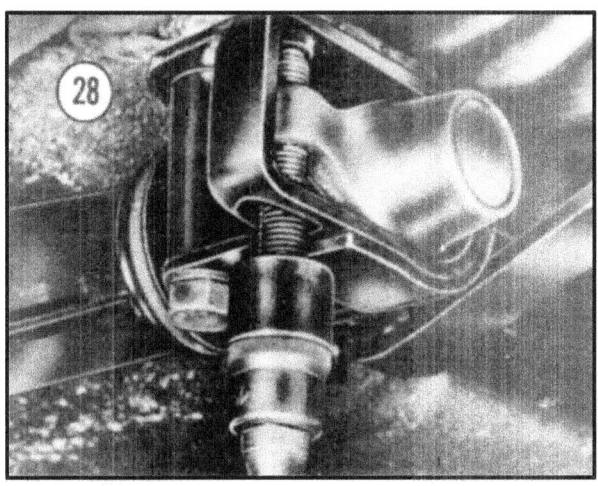

6. Pull adjusting levers off torsion bars and remove seals.

7. Remove bolts securing auxiliary suspension carrier. See **Figure 29**. Remove carrier.

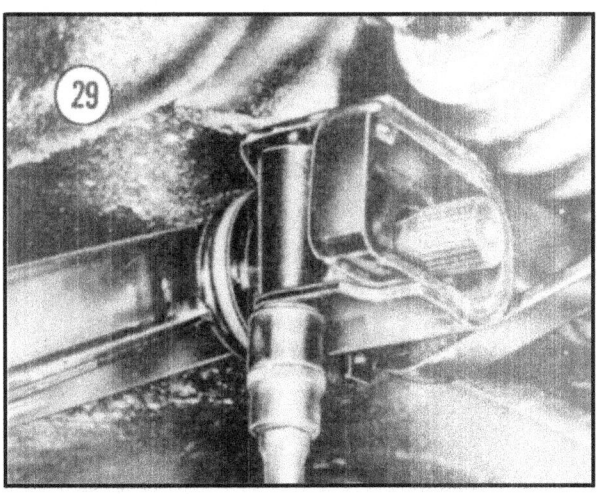

8. Remove steering housing with tie rods.

9. Remove tie rods from steering housing.

10. Installation is the reverse of this procedure. Be sure that universal fits on steering gear splines so that bolt can be inserted before securing the auxiliary carrier.

11. Adjust front axle height and check front end alignment.

Disassembly

Refer to **Figure 30** for the following procedure.

1. Hold steering housing in a vise with soft jaws.

2. Remove base plate, shims, spring, and pressure block. See **Figure 31**.

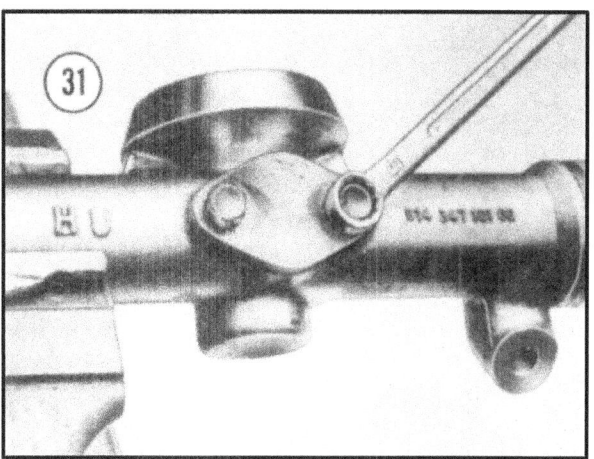

3. Turn housing 90° in the vise.

4. Remove locknut. With a suitable puller (Porsche P293 shown), remove the coupling flange.

5. Carefully pry oil seal out.

6. Remove C-ring and shim(s). See **Figure 32**.

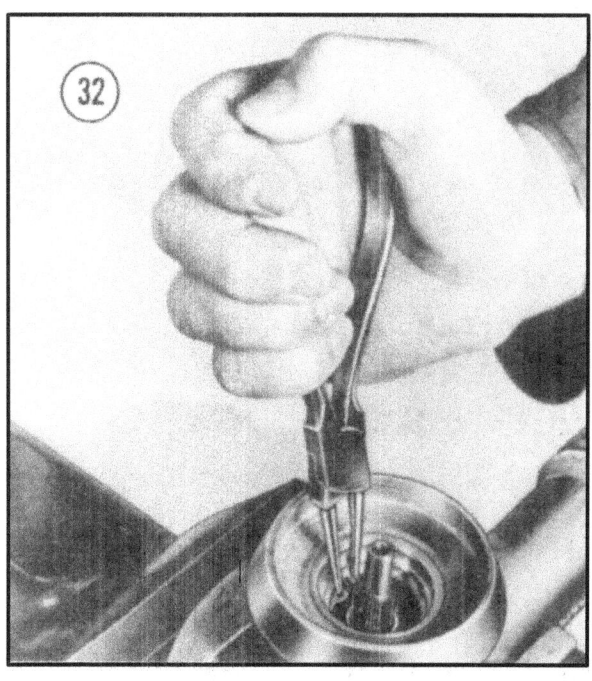

7. Screw locknut on pinion. Pry pinion out with 2 screwdrivers. See **Figure 33**.

CAUTION
Make sure that ball bearing does not bind against housing.

281

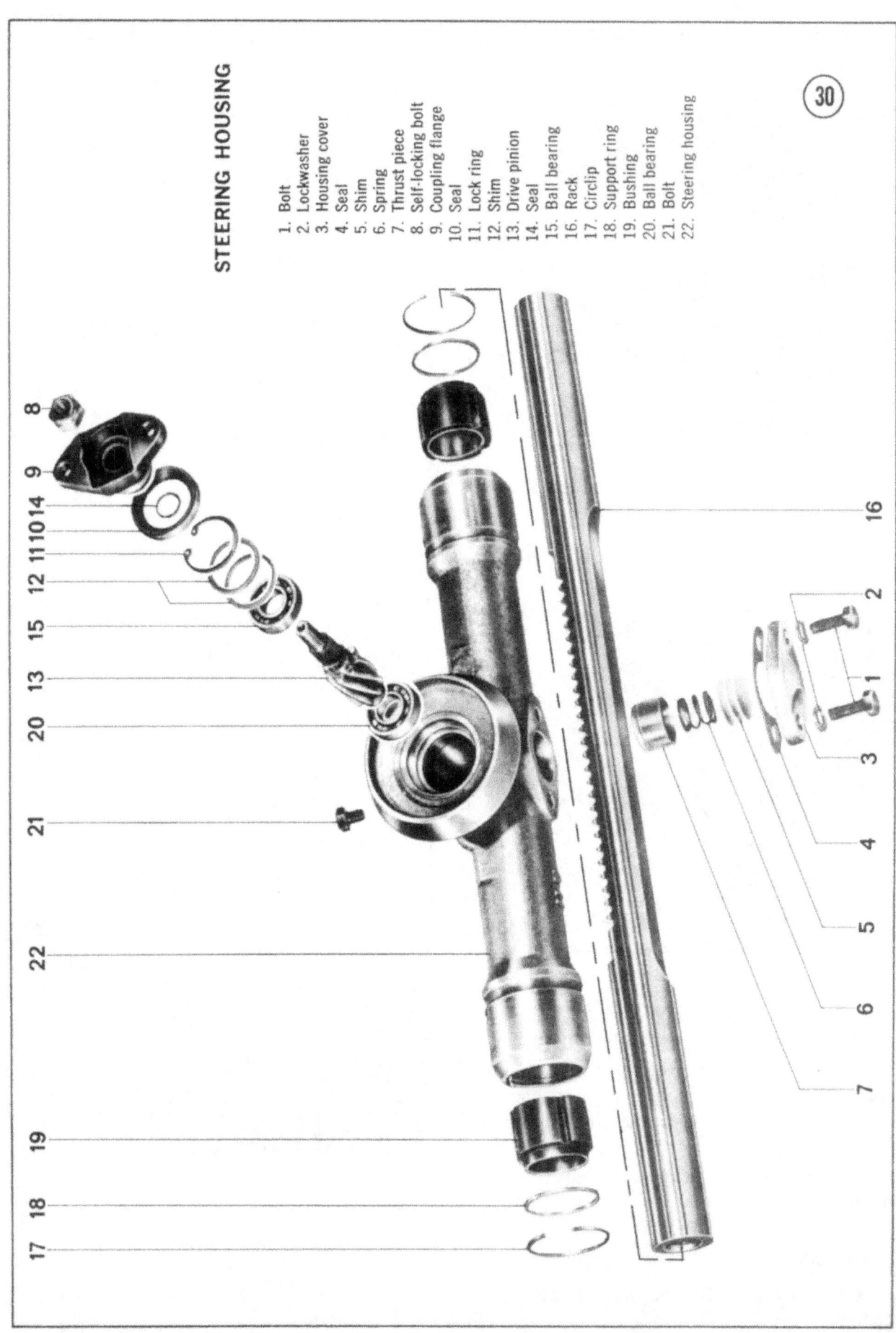

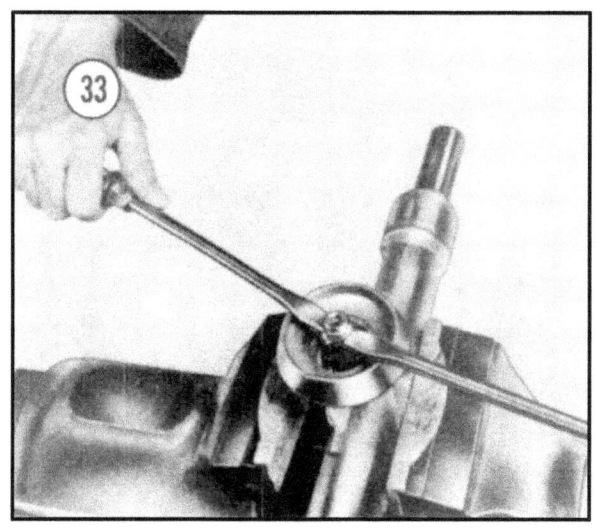

8. Press bearing off pinion.

9. Mark rack so that it can be reinstalled in exactly the same way. Slide it out of the housing. See **Figure 34**.

10. Press ball bearing out of steering housing.

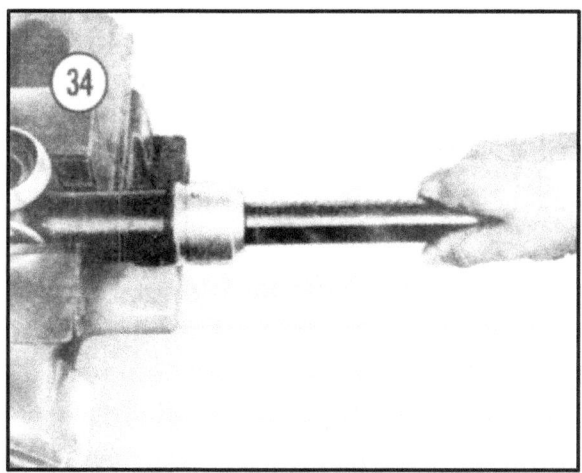

Inspection

1. Clean all parts in solvent.

2. Check rack and pinion for wear or broken teeth.

3. Check bearings for worn or scored balls. Replace if necessary.

4. Check bushings in ends of housing for wear or scoring. If necessary, have your dealer replace the bushings.

Assembly

1. Press bearing into steering housing. Work grease between the balls.

NOTE: *The steering housing is packed with 0.8 oz. (25cc) of multipurpose molybdenum disulphide (MoS_2) grease during the remaining steps. Measure out this quantity beforehand.*

2. Coat the rack thoroughly, using a portion of the total 0.8 oz. of grease mentioned above.

3. Slide the rack into the housing. If reinstalling old rack, install according to marks made during *Disassembly*, Step 9.

4. Press bearing onto pinion. Work some grease between the balls.

5. Pack the remainder of the 0.8 oz. of grease into the steering housing.

6. Insert pinion into housing. Push down until it rests on its seat.

7. Install shim(s) and C-ring. Check end-play of pinion. Change shim(s) if necessary to achieve zero end-play.

NOTE: *Shims are available in the following thicknesses: 0.1, 0.12, 0.15, and 0.30mm.*

8. Install pinion oil seal with sealing lip facing inward.

9. Install the rubber O-ring, then the flange, and secure with self-locking nut. Tighten nut to 34 foot-pounds (4.7 mkg).

10. Install pressure block and spring.

11. Install adjusting nut and adjust as described below.

12. Install cover plate with new paper gasket. Tighten cover bolts to 11 foot-pounds (1.5 mkg).

Adjustment

1. Insert pressure block into housing without spring or shims.

2. Measure distance pressure block protrudes from housing. See **Figure 35**.

3. Measure recess in housing cover plate. See **Figure 36**.

4. Dimension in Step 3 should be 0.008" (0.2mm) larger than dimension in Step 2. If not, add shims as required.

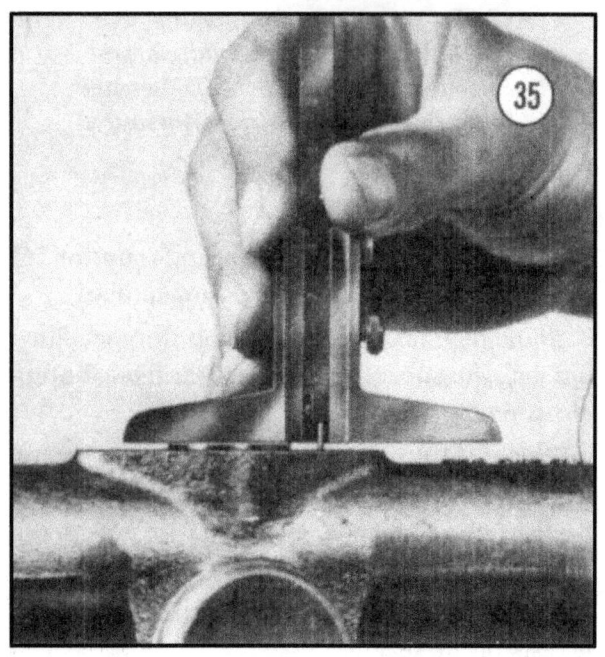

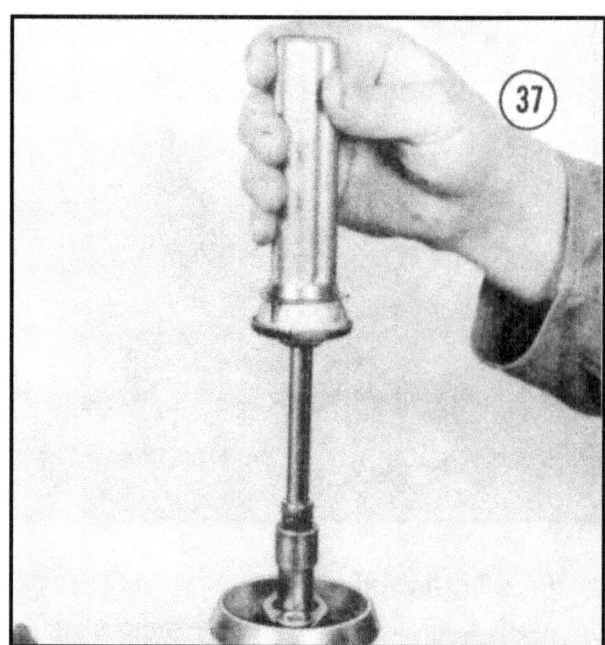

5. Check drag of steering with a torque wrench. See **Figure 37**. Drag should be 5-7 inch-pounds (6-8 cmkg).

Table 1   SPECIFICATIONS (All Models)

Toe-in[1]	20′ ± 10′
Caster	6° ± 30′
Camber	0° ± 20′
Steering gear ratio	17.78
Steering wheel turns lock-to-lock	approx. 3

1. 33 lb. (15 kg) load on front wheels.

Table 2   TIGHTENING TORQUES

	foot-pounds	mkg
Steering coupling bolts	18	2.5
Steering universal clamp nut	34	4.7
Reinforcing brace nut	47	6.5
Reinforcing brace bolt	34	4.7
Steering housing mounting bolts	34	4.7
Steering bushing cap Allen bolts	18	2.5
Tie rod nut	32.5	4.5
Strut clamp bolt	47	6.5
Upper strut nut	58	8.0
Brake backing plate bolts	18	2.5

CHAPTER FOURTEEN

BRAKES

Porsche uses fixed caliper disc brakes on all 4 wheels. All U.S. models have a dual circuit hydraulic system; one circuit operates front brakes, while the other circuit operates rear brakes. See **Figure 1**.

The master cylinder has 2 independent pressure circuits. When the driver depresses the pedal, pressure in the front half of the master cylinder operates both front brakes; pressure from the rear half operates both rear brakes. If one circuit should fail, the other circuit remains intact, permitting a safe stop with 2 wheels. A warning circuit indicates that pressure in one circuit is defective. Increased pedal travel and decreased braking also indicate trouble.

The brake light switch is mechanically coupled to the master cylinder pushrod. It is not operated by hydraulic pressure.

Cable operated mechanical handbrakes act on the rear wheels. When the hand lever is drawn up, a lever on each rear brake caliper forces the inside brake pad against the brake disc.

This chapter describes repair procedures for all parts of the brake system. **Tables 1 and 2** at the end of this chapter list tightening torques and specifications, respectively.

MASTER CYLINDER

Removal

1. Raise front of car on jackstands.

2. Pull accelerator pedal back to disengage it. Remove left front floor mat.

3. Remove retaining bolts and floorboard. See **Figure 2**.

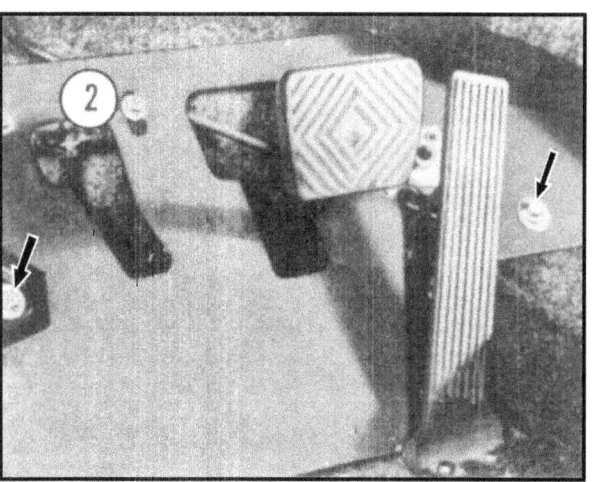

4. Draw brake fluid out of reservoir(s) with a suction pump.

WARNING
Do not siphon by sucking on a length of tubing. Brake fluid is very poisonous.

5. Remove front axle shield over master cylinder. See **Figure 3**.

6. Pull the lines leading from the reservoir out of the master cylinder.

7. Disconnect hydraulic lines. See **Figure 4**.

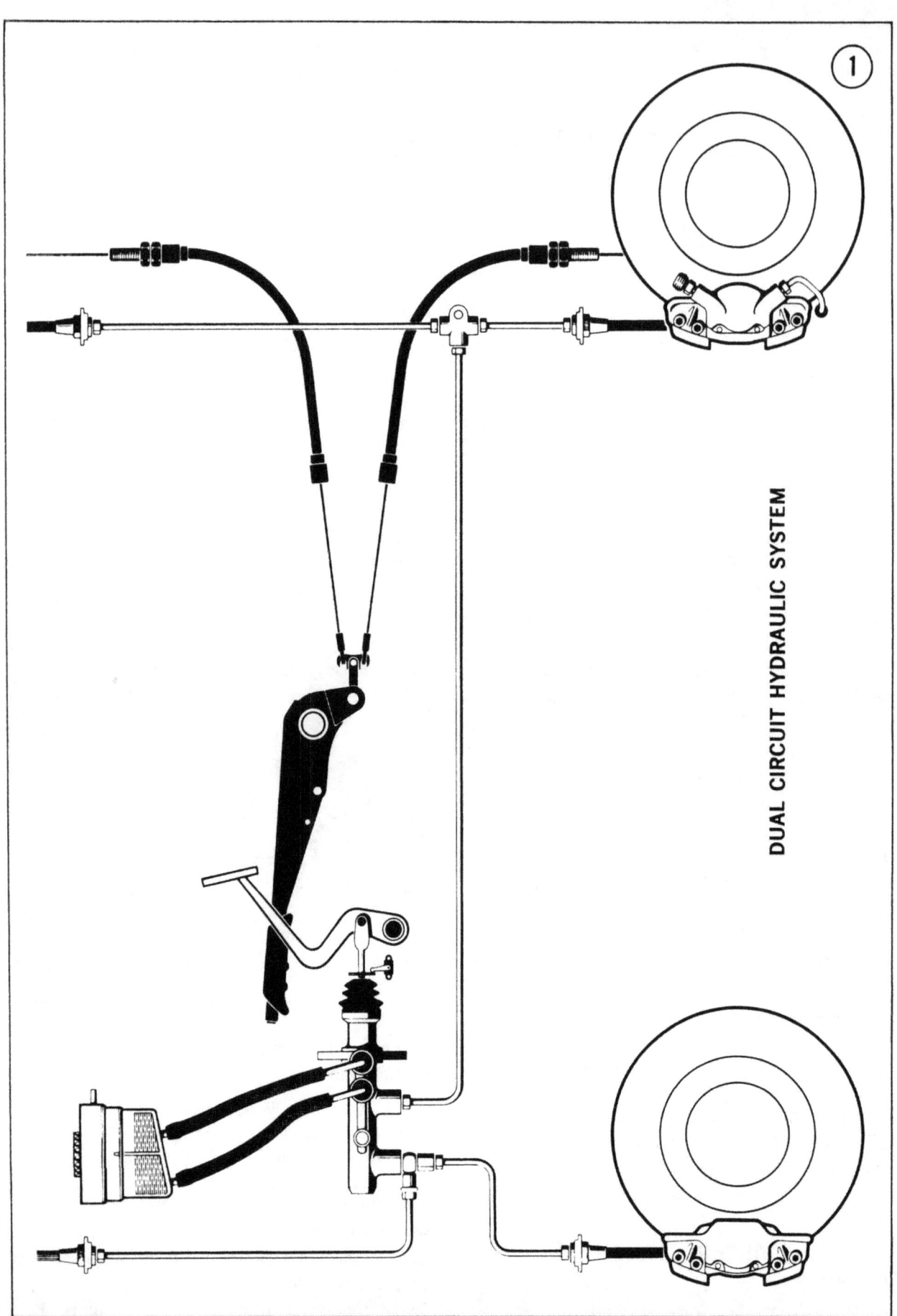

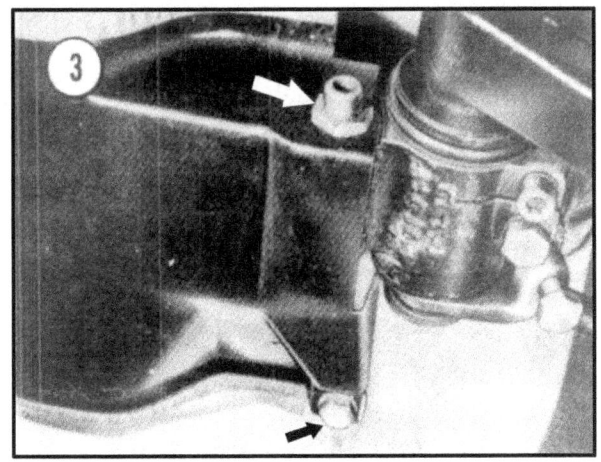

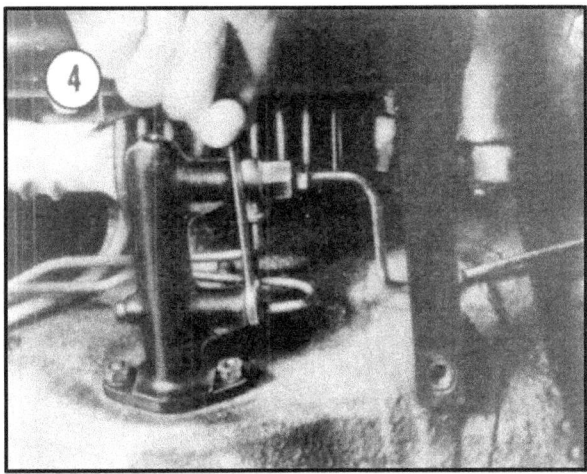

6. Remove stop bolt and gasket.

7. Tap the open end of the master cylinder on a wooden bench or block and the secondary piston will slide out. If it sticks in the bore, plug all holes except the grommeted holes for the secondary circuit (see **Figure 6**). Inject compressed air through the grommet to force the piston out. A bicycle tire pump develops sufficient pressure for this.

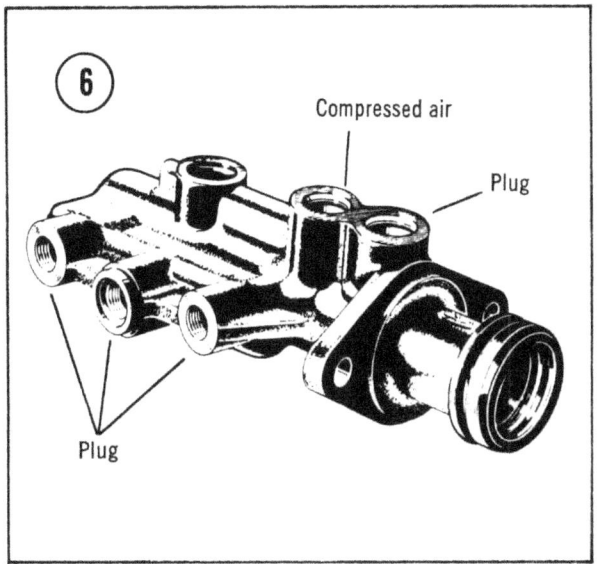

8. Remove spring.

9. Remove circuit failure switch.

10. Unscrew plug and remove 2 springs and pistons for the circuit failure system.

Inspection

1. Clean all parts in denatured alcohol or clean brake fluid.

CAUTION
Never use gasoline, kerosene, or any solvent other than alcohol for rubber brake parts. You may wash metal parts in other solvents if you blow them dry, rinse several times in clean alcohol and blow dry again.

2. Inspect the cylinder bore for scoring, pitting, or heavy corrosion. Very light scratches and corrosion may be removed with *crocus cloth*. Discard the master cylinder if damage is more severe.

3. Run a small, smooth copper wire through the compensating ports and intake ports. See **Figure 7**. Note that dual master cylinders have 4

8. Disconnect electrical wires to circuit failure switch.

9. Pull rubber boot free of master cylinder.

10. Remove retaining nuts and remove master cylinder.

Disassembly

Refer to **Figure 5** for the following procedure. Save *all parts* until master cylinder is reassembled.

1. Scrape off all outside dirt and wash with denatured alcohol.

2. Remove rubber boot.

3. Pry out lock ring with a small screwdriver.

4. Remove stop washer.

5. Remove primary piston and stroke limiter parts (items 3-6 and 8-10). Unscrew stroke limiter screw and remove limiter parts from piston.

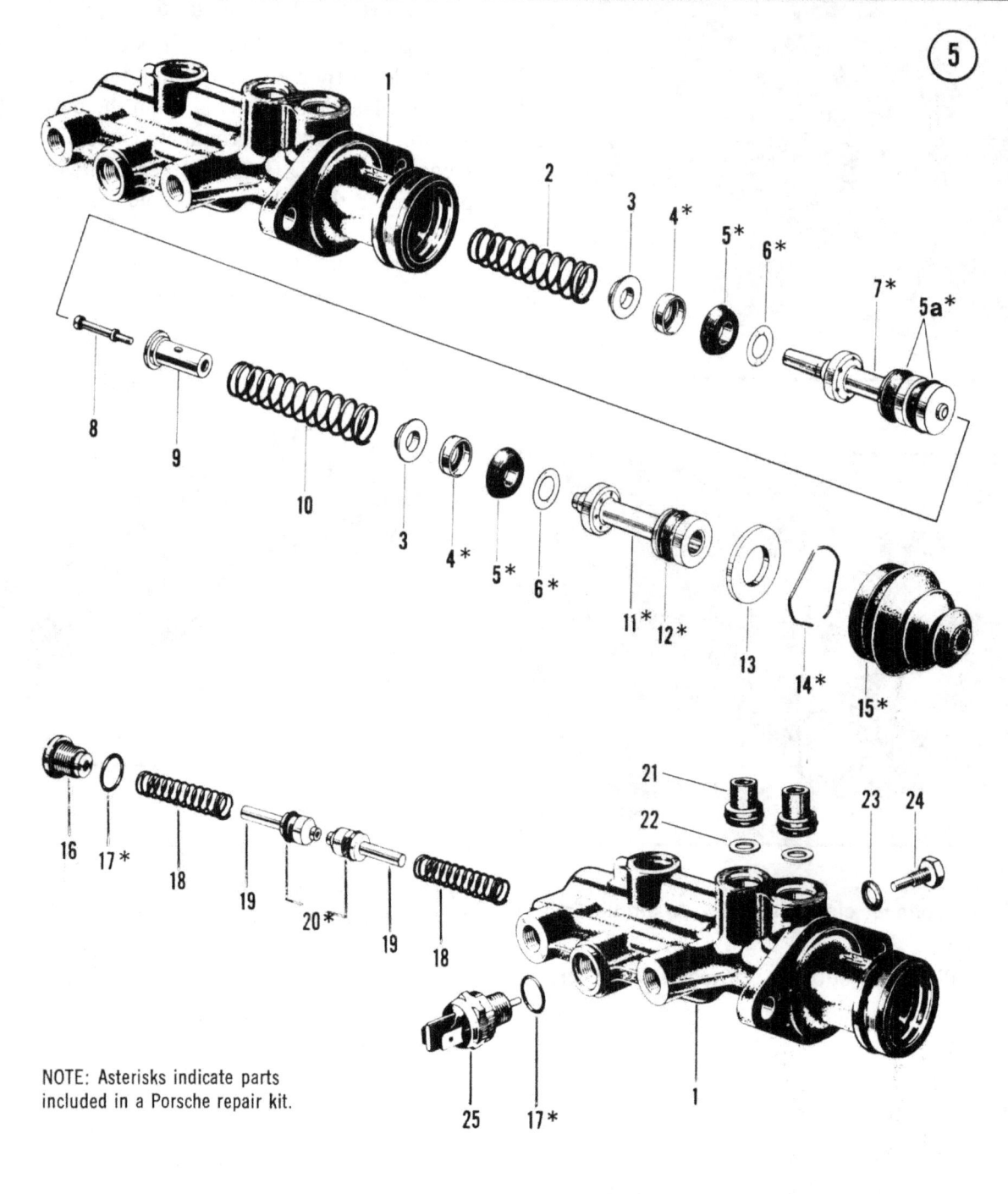

DUAL CIRCUIT MASTER CYLINDER

1. Housing
2. Secondary piston return spring
3. Spring seat
4. Supporting washer
5. Primary cup
5a. Secondary cups
6. Cup washer
7. Secondary piston
8. Stroke limiting screw
9. Stop sleeve
10. Primary piston return spring
11. Primary piston
12. Secondary cup
13. Stop plate
14. Lock ring
15. Dust boot
16. Plug
17. O-ring
18. Spring
19. Piston
20. Piston cup
21. Grommet
22. Washer
23. Gasket
24. Stop bolt
25. Circuit failure switch

NOTE: Asterisks indicate parts included in a Porsche repair kit.

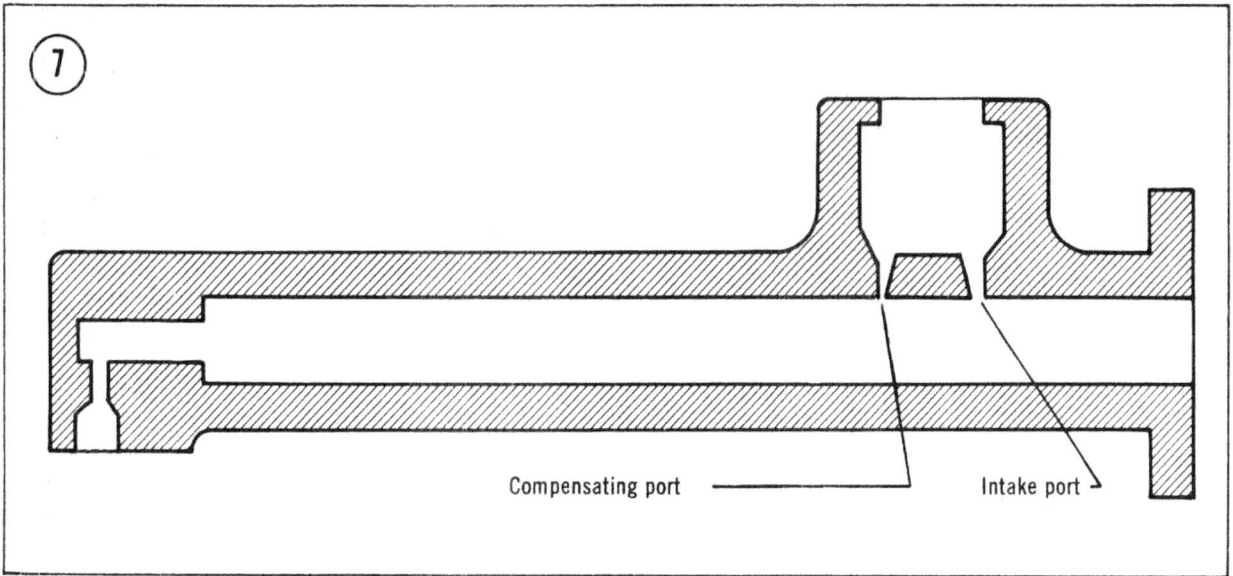

ports in all. Do not use steel or rough wire which may damage the port. Ensure that no burrs exist at the bottom of these ports which may cut the primary cup.

Assembly

When assembling the master cylinder, use parts from a standard Porsche repair kit. Parts included in this kit are indicated in Figure 5 by an asterisk. Never reuse old parts.

1. Clean all parts in alcohol or brake fluid. Blow dry if you use alcohol.
2. Lubricate the cylinder walls and all internal parts with brake fluid.

> NOTE: *VW developed a special brake cylinder paste which may be used to lubricate brake parts. This paste does not attack rubber brake parts; but mineral oil or grease will.*

3. Install new cups on secondary piston. The closed ends should face each other.
4. Assemble the cup washer, primary cup, support washer, spring seat, and spring on secondary piston. Open end of primary cup should face spring.
5. Hold the master cylinder vertically with the open end down. Insert the secondary piston assembly up into the cylinder bore. If you try to install these parts horizontally, they will fall off the piston.
6. Install a new secondary cup on the primary piston. The open end should face the long end of the piston.
7. Install the cup washer, primary cup, support washer, spring seat, spring, stop sleeve, and stroke limiting screw on primary piston. Insert the assembly into the cylinder bore.
8. Install the stop plate and lock ring.
9. Check that the primary piston is not blocking the stop bolt hole and insert the stop bolt and seal. If the hole is blocked, push the primary piston inward until the hole is clear.
10. Install the circuit failure switch with an O-ring.
11. Install top grommets with washers.
12. Install new cups on circuit failure pistons. These are *not* included in a standard repair kit; order them separately.
13. Install springs and pistons in order shown in Figure 5. Install plug with O-ring.

Installation

Master cylinders for disc brake equipped Porsches and VW's are marked by a blue vinyl band around the body of the master cylinder. Master cylinders without this band are for drum brake systems. While outwardly they may look identical, they must not be interchanged.

1. Coat the master cylinder mounting flange with sealing compound to prevent entry of water.

2. Slip a new rubber boot over the pedal-mounted pushrod.

3. Mount the master cylinder from underneath while an assistant guides the pushrod into the master cylinder.

4. Secure the master cylinder with the retaining nuts and new lockwashers. Tighten nuts to 18 foot-pounds (2.5 mkg).

5. Connect hydraulic lines, reservoir line(s), and circuit failure switch wires.

6. Adjust the pushrod length so that there is about 0.040" (1mm) clearance between pushrod and piston. See **Figure 8**. Rock the pedal back and forth by hand; only slight movement should be felt. If movement is excessive, or no movement is detectable, loosen the locknut on the pushrod and turn the rod to lengthen or shorten the rod as required. See **Figure 9**.

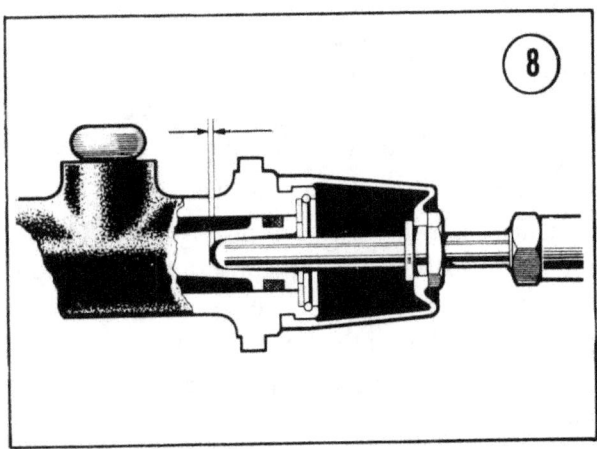

7. Check vent in reservoir cap. Clean it out if clogged.

8. Refill system with brake fluid.

WARNING
Brake fluid must be clearly marked SAE 7OR3, SAE J1703 (which supersedes 7OR3), DOT 3, or DOT 4 only. Do not use SAE 7OR1 or any other brake fluid which can vaporize in disc brake systems.

9. Bleed brakes as described later in this chapter.

10. Check brake light operation.

11. Install front axle shield.

BRAKE PAD REPLACEMENT

Brake pads on all 4 wheels should be inspected every 6,000 miles as described in Chapter Two. Replace brake pads on both front wheels or both rear wheels if pad thickness is 0.08" (2mm) or less. It is rarely necessary to bleed the brake system after a single brake pad replacement.

Porsche offers several replacement brake pad sets for the various years and models. Each consists of 4 brake pads, 4 pin retainers, and 2 expander springs for both front or both rear brakes. When ordering, specify year, model, and presence of solid or ventilated brake discs.

1. Jack up the car on jackstands and remove the wheels.

2. Withdraw pin retainers on 914/6 models. See **Figure 10**.

3. Knock pins out towards the center of the car. See **Figure 11**.

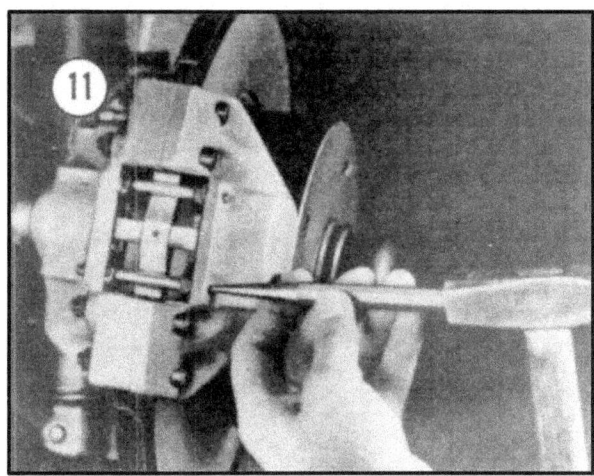

4. Mark original positions of pads which are to be reused.

5. Pull brake pads out as shown in **Figure 12**.

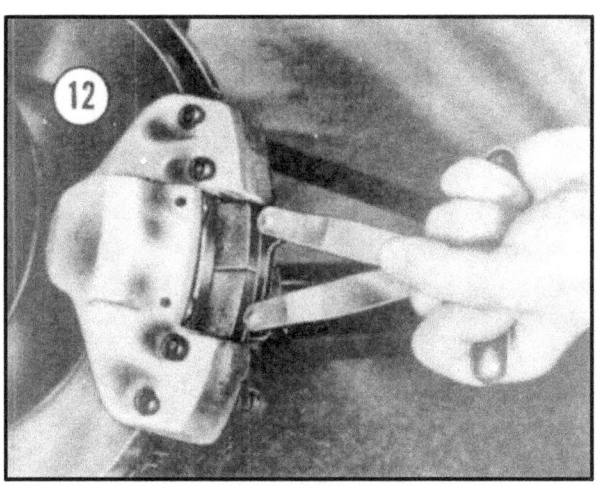

6. Carefully clean out the cavity which holds the brake pads. Do not use solvents other than denatured alcohol and do not use sharp tools.

7. Inspect rubber dust covers; if they are damaged, replace them. If dirt has penetrated cylinders due to a damaged cover, recondition the brake unit as described later.

8. Draw some brake fluid out of the reservoir to prevent overflow while performing the next step. Use a suction pump used exclusively for brake fluid.

9a. Before installing front brake pads, push the pistons in as shown in **Figure 13**. If a special tool is not available, pry the pistons back with

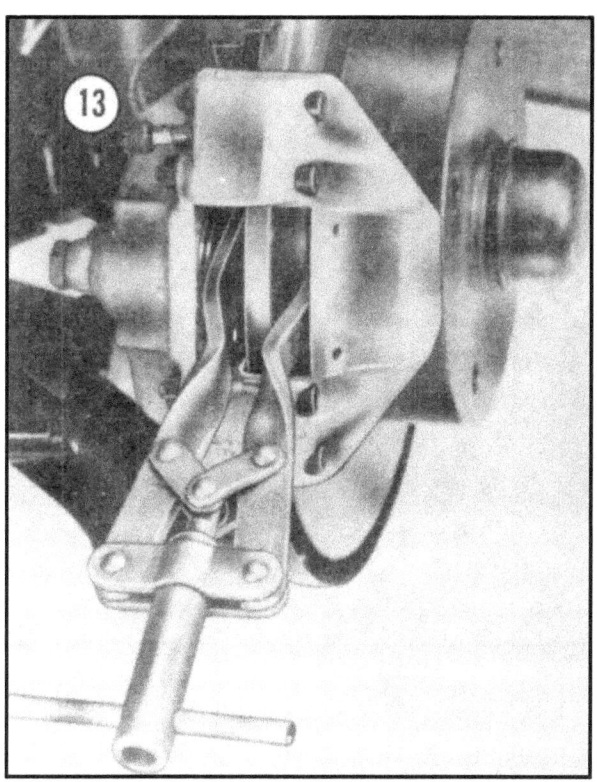

a hardwood block. Do not use metal tools for prying or the piston may be damaged.

9b. Before installing rear brake pads, apply slight tension on pistons with Porsche Tool P83 as shown in **Figure 14**. Remove hex cover to expose Allen bolt shown in Figure 14. Loosen locknut on Allen bolt, then loosen Allen bolt, while maintaining tension on Tool P83. This retracts outer piston. Retract inner piston in the same manner. See **Figure 15**.

10. Clean brake discs with fine emery cloth.

11. Install new brake pads on both front wheels or both rear wheels. Old brake pads which are not excessively worn should be reinstalled only when the other front (or rear) pads are serviceable. Even then, pads should be returned to their original position.

12a. On front brakes, install expander spring, pins, and pin retainers (914/6).

12b. On rear brakes, secure brake pads with pins, but without spreader spring. Insert feeler gauge between outer piston and pad. See **Figure 16**. Adjust clearance with Allen bolt to 0.008" (0.2mm). Adjust clearance between inner piston and pad in a similar manner. Remove pins and reinstall spreader spring and pin retainers. Tighten locknuts on Allen bolts and install hex covers.

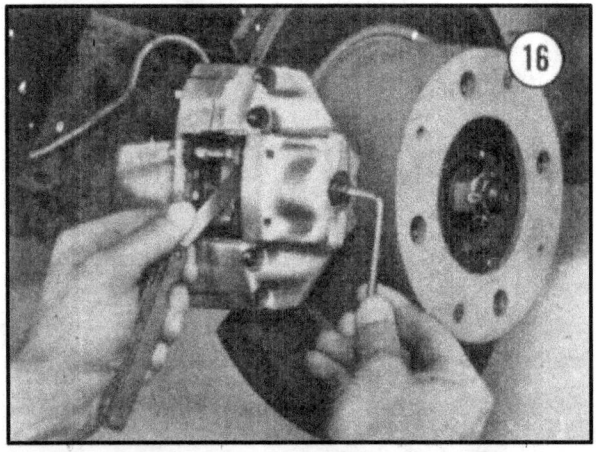

13. Depress the brake pedal several times before driving the car to force the pitsons against the pads and correctly align the pads against the disc.

WARNING
This step is very important. If not done, the brakes could fail on the first few applications.

14. Check level in brake fluid reservoir and top up if necessary.

FRONT BRAKE CALIPERS

Removal/Installation

1. Raise car on jackstands and remove wheels.

2. Remove brake pads as described under *Brake Pad Replacement*.

3. Depress brake pedal about 1" and hold it there to prevent complete loss of brake fluid in next step. Porsche dealers use a special tool shown in **Figure 17**.

4. Disconnect hydraulic line at banjo fitting on brake caliper. Wrap fitting to prevent entry of dirt.

5. Remove caliper retaining bolts and lift caliper off. See **Figure 18**.

6. Installation is the reverse of these steps. Use new lockwashers on caliper retaining bolts; tighten them to 50 foot-pounds (7 mkg).

Reconditioning

Different calipers are used depending on model and options. Gasket kits required for reconditioning are available for front or rear

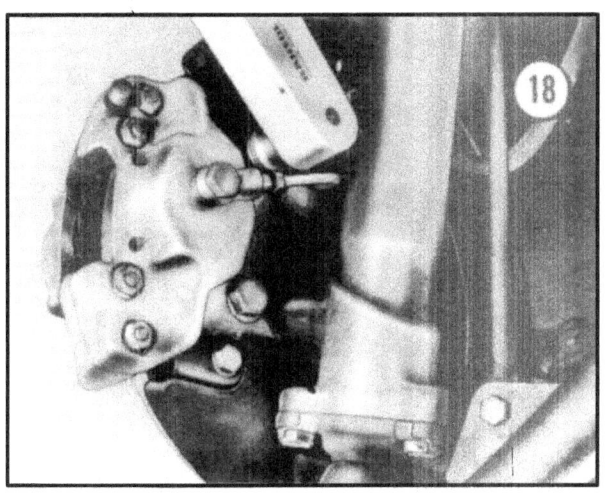

wheels. Each kit does one caliper. Order gasket kits by year and model.

CAUTION
Do not disassemble the caliper any further than described below. If the caliper leaks, take it to your dealer for repair. Alignment of housing parts is very critical.

1. Remove caliper as described earlier.
2. Remove brake pads as described previously.
3. Loosen bleeder valve(s) and blow brake fluid out of caliper.
4. Clamp the caliper in a vise with soft jaws.
5. Remove the piston retaining plate. See **Figure 19**.

6. Pry out retaining ring and rubber boot. See **Figure 20**.

7. Clamp one piston in place as shown in **Figure 21**. Hold a piece of ¼″ thick wood in the housing and force the other piston against it with compressed air.

NOTE: *Once one piston is removed, pressure cannot be built up to force the other out. Therefore, completely rebuild one side before working on the other.*

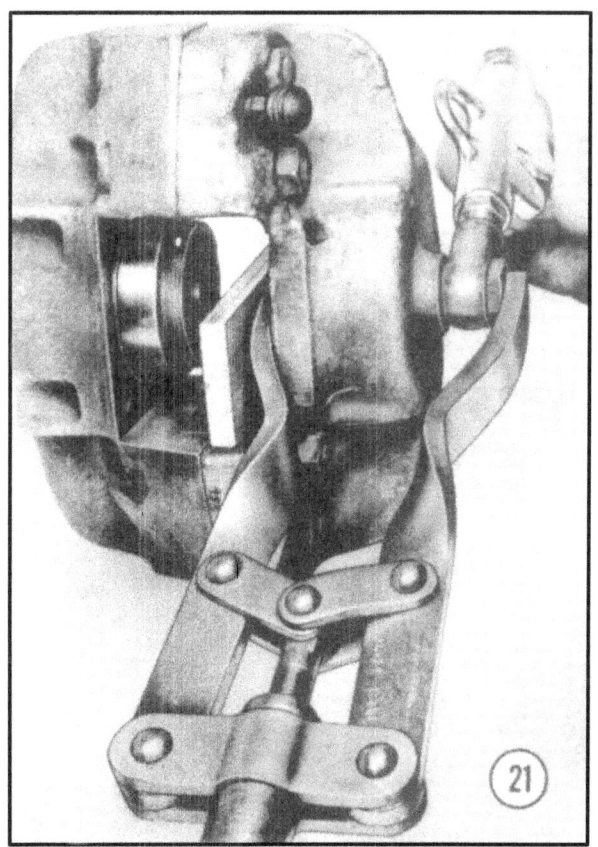

8. Remove rubber seal with a plastic or rubber rod to prevent damage to the housing. See **Figure 22**.

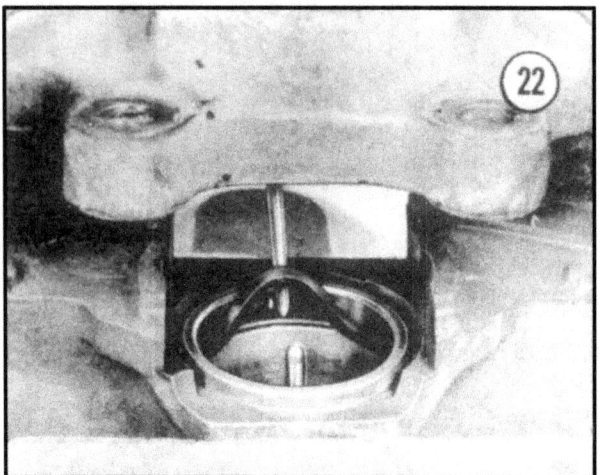

9. Clean all parts in alcohol or clean brake fluid.

10. Check parts for wear. If a cylinder is worn or damaged, the complete caliper must be replaced.

11. Coat the new rubber piston seal with brake cylinder paste. Install the seal and piston. Align the piston in the bore with the tool shown in **Figures 23 and 24** while pressing it in.

CAUTION

The piston must be installed carefully so that it doesn't tilt and jam when pressed in. The piston depressor shown in Figure 21 may be used to press the piston in. If you don't have the proper tools, consider taking the caliper to your dealer.

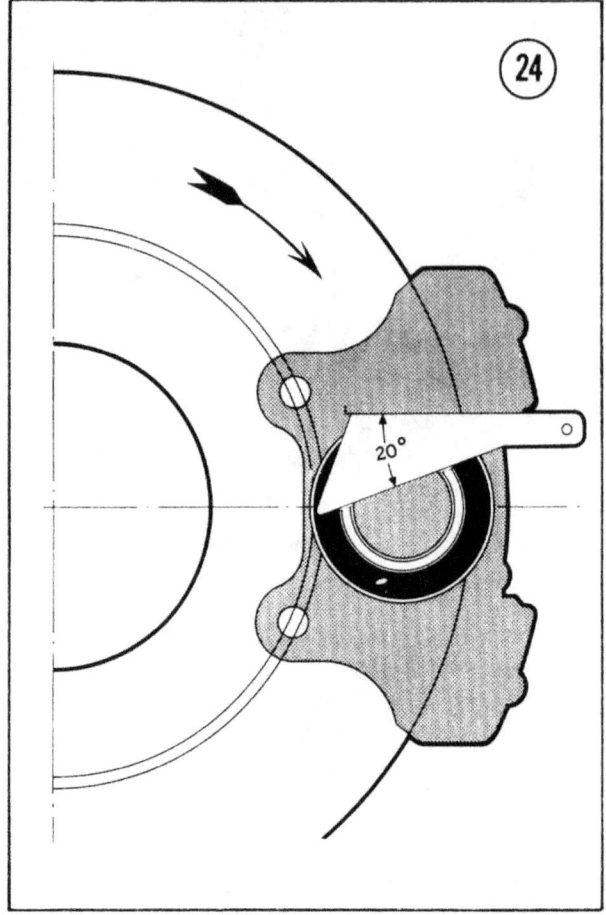

12. Wipe brake cylinder paste (if any) from piston ridge and install new rubber boot without lubricating it in any way. Secure the boot with a new retaining ring.

13. Install piston retaining plate. See Figure 19. Note the circular part of the plate must be firmly pressed into the piston crown. The plate must lie below the recessed part of the piston.

14. Repeat Steps 4-11 for the other piston/cylinder.

REAR BRAKE CALIPERS

Removal/Installation

1. Raise car on jackstands and remove wheels.

2. Remove rubber boot and disconnect handbrake cable from caliper lever.

3. Remove brake pads as described under *Brake Pad Replacement*.

4. Remove bolts securing disc shrouds and remove the shrouds. See **Figure 25**.

5. Depress brake pedal about 1″ and hold it there to prevent complete loss of brake fluid

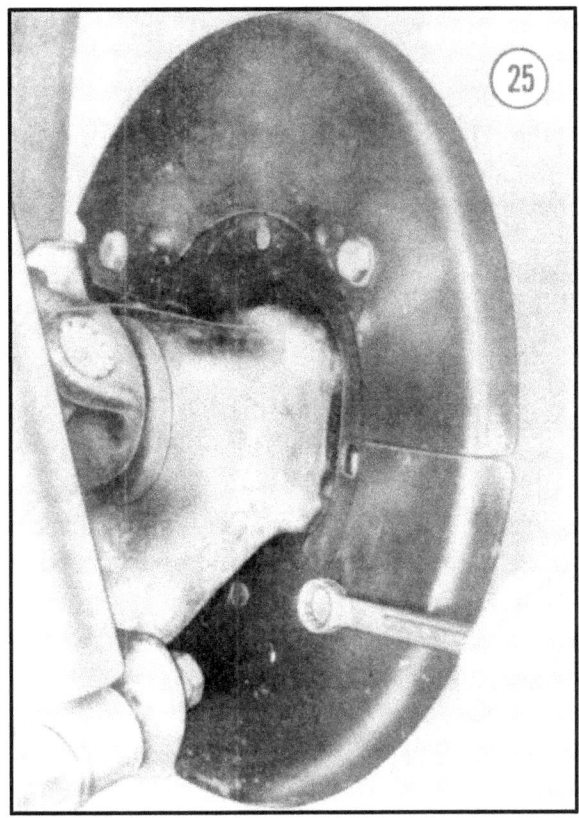

Figure 26; about 0.4-0.6" (10-15mm) from the edge of the disc. Rotate the disc; runout should not exceed 0.008" (0.2mm). In critical applications, such as competition, check runout on both sides of disc.

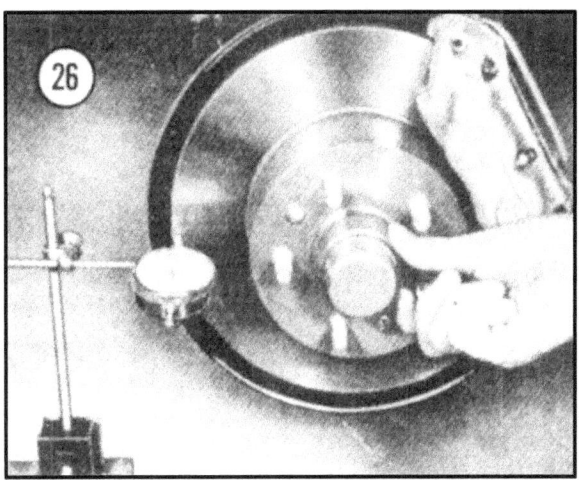

Check disc thickness with a micrometer. Make about 12 measurements around the disc about 1" from the outer edge. Measurements should not vary more than 0.0012" (0.03mm).

If the disc has excessively deep radial scratches, excessive runout, or variation in thickness, renew or replace the disc. See procedure later in this section.

during next step. Porsche dealers use a special tool shown in Figure 17.

6. Disconnect hydraulic line at caliper and plug the line to prevent entry of dirt.

7. Remove caliper retaining bolts and lift caliper off.

8. Installation is the reverse of these steps. Use new lockwashers on caliper retaining bolts; tighten bolts to 43 foot-pounds (6 mkg).

Reconditioning

See *Front Brake Calipers, Reconditioning*.

FRONT BRAKE DISCS

Inspection

The brake discs may be inspected with the caliper mounted, but the front of the car must be raised on jackstands and wheels removed. Small marks on the disc are not important, but radial scratches reduce braking effectiveness and increase pad wear.

Before checking disc runout, check wheel bearing adjustment as described in Chapter Thirteen. Mount a dial gauge as shown in

Removal

1. Remove caliper as described earlier.
2. Remove dust cap as shown in **Figure 27**.

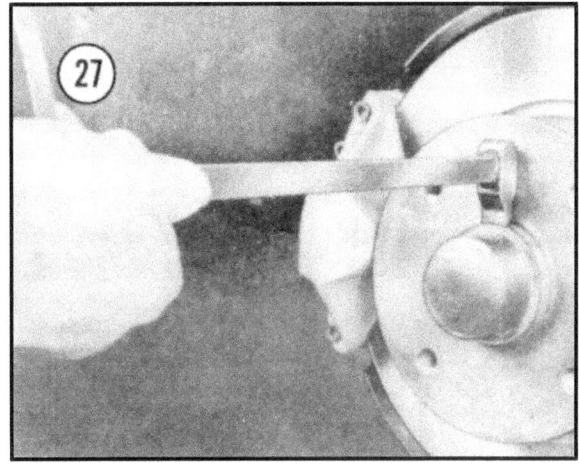

3. Loosen Allen bolt on wheel bearing clamp bolt (see **Figure 28**). Remove clamp nut and thrust washer.

4. Pull brake disc off hub by hand. If necessary, use a standard puller.

CAUTION
Never hit a stubborn disc with any-thing *to remove it.*

Resurfacing

Brake discs should be resurfaced only when absolutely necessary. **Figure 29** shows a disc with rounded ridges on the surface; this disc does *not* require resurfacing. The disc in **Figure 30**, however, has sharp ridges and should be resurfaced or replaced.

If a disc requires resurfacing, take it to your dealer. He will confirm the need for resurfacing and remove the required metal symetrically from both sides of the disc.

Installation

1. Check condition of inner and outer wheel bearings in wheel hub. Replace if necessary as described in Chapter Thirteen.
2. Pack wheel bearings with lithium grease.
3. Install brake disc on hub.
4. Install thrust washer and wheel bearing clamp nut. Adjust wheel bearings as described in Chapter Thirteen.
5. Install dust cap.
6. Install brake caliper as described earlier.

REAR BRAKE DISCS

Inspection

Inspect rear brake discs in exactly the same manner as front disc brakes. See earlier procedure.

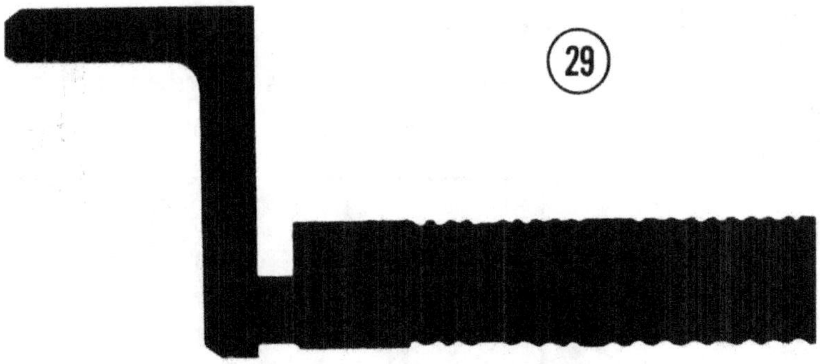

Removal/Installation

1. Remove rear brake caliper as described earlier.
2. Remove 2 screws securing brake disc (see **Figure 31**) and pull disc off.
3. Installation is the reverse of these steps.

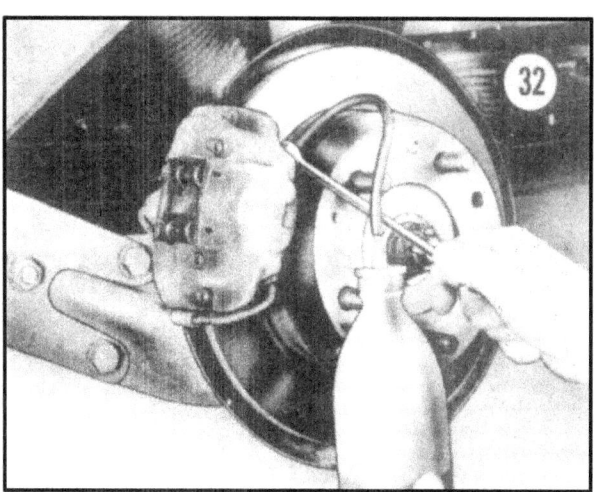

Resurfacing

See *Front Brake Discs, Resurfacing*.

BRAKE BLEEDING

Brakes require bleeding whenever air enters the system, lowering the effective braking pressure. Air can enter when the master cylinder or wheel cylinders are serviced, or if the fluid in the reservoir runs dry. Air can also enter through a leaky brake line or hose. Find the leaky line and replace it before bleeding.

Whenever handling brake fluid, do not get any on the brake pads or body paint. Brake pads will be permanently damaged, requiring replacement. Body paint can be damaged also unless you wipe the area with a clean cloth, then wash it with a soapy solution immediately.

1. Ensure that the brake fluid reservoir is full and that the vent in the cap is open.
2. Connect a plastic or rubber tube to the bleeder valve on the right rear wheel. Suspend the other end of the tube in a jar or bottle filled with a few inches of clean brake fluid. See **Figure 32**. During the remaining steps, keep this end submerged at all times and never let the level in the brake fluid reservoir drop below ½ full.
3. Have an assistant pump the brake pedal quickly several times, then hold the pedal down. Open the outer bleeder valve on the left rear caliper ½ to ¾ turn. Push pedal all the way down quickly. Close the bleeder valve and let the pedal up. Repeat this step as many times as necessary, i.e., until fluid with no air bubbles issues from the tube.
4. Bleed the remaining valves in the same manner described in the preceding steps. Follow the sequence shown in **Figure 33**. Note that the rear calipers have an inner and outer bleeder valve. Keep checking the brake fluid reservoir to be sure it doesn't run out of fluid or you will have to start all over again.

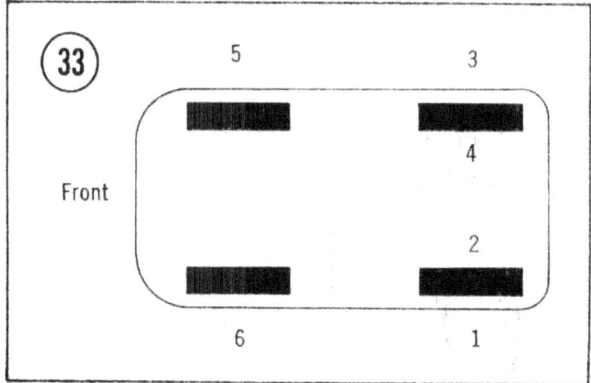

5. When all wheels are bled, discard the brake fluid in the jar or bottle; never reuse such fluid. See Step 8, *Master Cylinder Installation*.

HANDBRAKE

Cable Replacement

1. Remove rubber boot at each rear wheel. Disconnect clevis from lever on each rear brake caliper. See **Figure 34**.

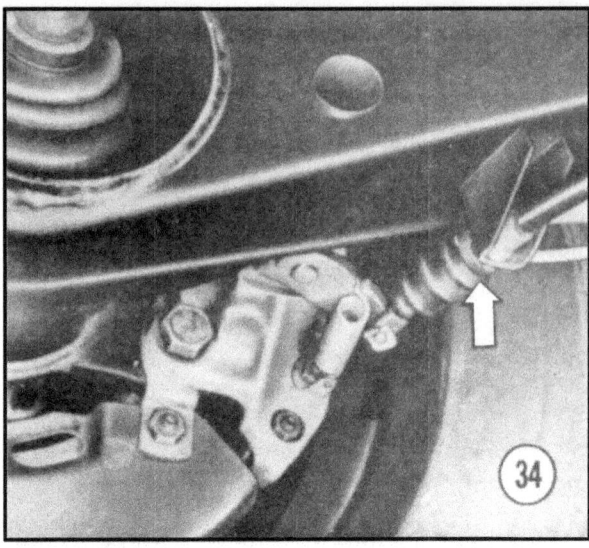

2. Remove driver's seat. See Chapter Fifteen.
3. Remove handbrake lever boot.
4. Unhook cables from cable equalizer.
5. Remove clamps securing cable to body.
6. Remove cable complete with outer sleeve out through the rear.
7. Installation is the reverse of these steps.

Cable Adjustment

This adjustment is required only when the cable or rear caliper has been replaced.

1. Release handbrake lever.
2. Ensure that levers on rear calipers rest against their respective stop pins.
3. Loosen locknuts and tighten adjusting nuts (see **Figure 35**) until the caliper levers just lift from their pins.

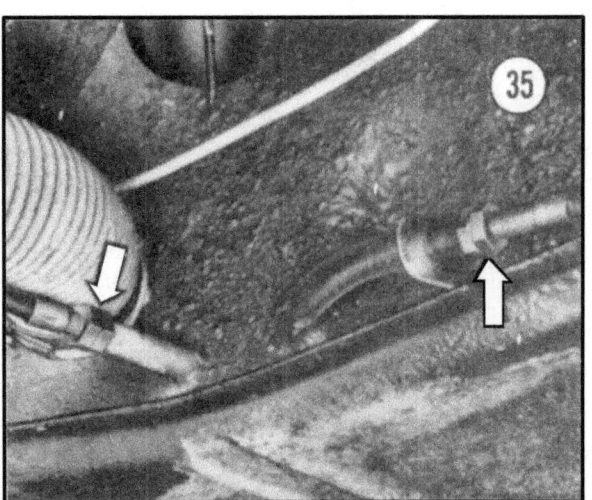

4. Ensure that cable equalizer in passenger compartment is at right angles to the cables.
5. Tighten locknuts.

BRAKE ADJUSTMENT

A self-adjusting device in the brake pistons automatically maintains the proper brake pad-to-brake disc clearance. Therefore, no brake adjustment is necessary.

BRAKE LIGHT ADJUSTMENT

1. Pull accelerator pedal back to disengage it. Remove left front floor mat.
2. Remove floorboard. See **Figure 36**.

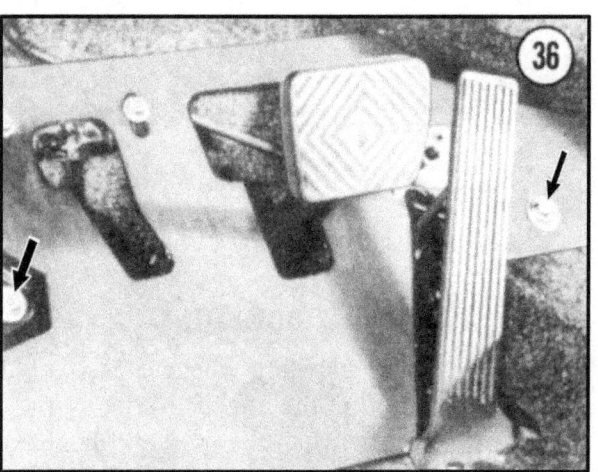

3. Place a 5/32" (4mm) metal gauge between the brake pedal and its stop. See **Figure 37**.

4. Loosen locknut on brake light switch. See **Figure 38**.

5. Move switch until brake lights go out, then back to where they just go on. Tighten locknut.

6. Remove metal gauge and replace floorboard, nut, and accelerator pedal.

Table 1   TIGHTENING TORQUES

	foot-pounds	mkg
Master cylinder mounting bolts	18	2.5
Brake line on master cylinder	11-14.5	1.5-2.0
Caliper bolts	51	7.0
Brake shield mounting bolts	18	2.5
Bleed valve	1.4-2.5	0.2-0.35
Brake disc-to-wheel hub nut	17	2.3
Brake disc-to-wheel hub bolt	3.6	0.5
Castellated hub nut	217-253	30-35

Table 2   BRAKE SPECIFICATIONS

	914	914/6
BRAKE DISC		
Diameter		
Front	11.063" (281mm)	11.122" (282.5mm)
Rear	11.102" (282mm)	11.260" (286mm)
Thickness (new)		
Front	0.433" (11mm)	0.787" (20mm)
Rear	0.374" (9.5mm)	0.414" (10.5mm)
Minimum thickness		
Front	0.374" (9.5mm)	0.732" (18.6mm)
Rear	0.335" (8.5mm)	0.394" (10.0mm)
Thickness variation	0.0008" (0.02mm)	0.0008" (0.02mm)
Lateral run-out (max.)	0.008" (0.2mm)	0.008" (0.2mm)
BRAKE CALIPERS		
Cylinder diameter		
Front	1.7" (42mm)	1.9" (48mm)
Rear	1.3" (33mm)	1.5" (38mm)
BRAKE PADS		
Thickness (new)	0.4" (10.0mm)	0.4" (10.0mm)
Min. thickness	0.08" (2.0mm)	0.08" (2.0mm)
Area (4 pads)		
Front in.^{2} (cm^2)	15.5 (100)	16.4 (106)
Rear in.^{2} (cm^2)	12.4 (80)	16.4 (106)
MASTER CYLINDER		
Bore	0.6874" (17.46mm)	0.7500 (19.05mm)
Stroke	0.7/0.5" (18/13mm)	0.7/0.5" (18/13mm)

CHAPTER FIFTEEN

BODY

This chapter includes replacement or repair procedures for the seats, doors, hoods, fenders, and bumpers. Other body repairs require special knowledge and/or tools and should be done by your dealer or local body repair shop.

SEATS

Driver's Seat Removal/Installation

1. Pull up lever A, **Figure 1** and slide seat all the way forward.

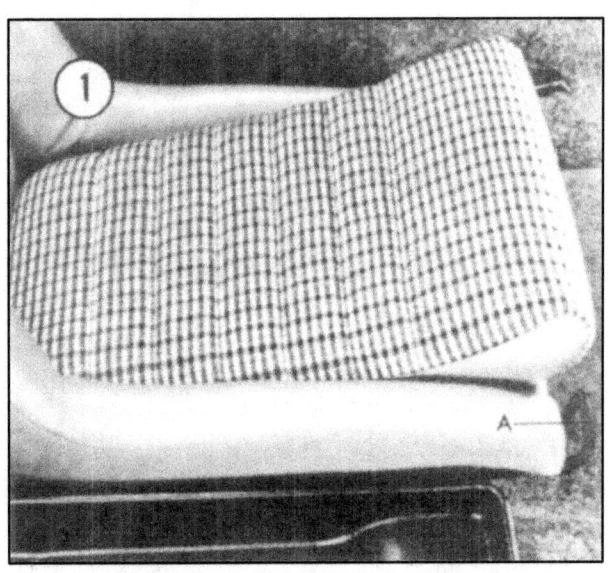

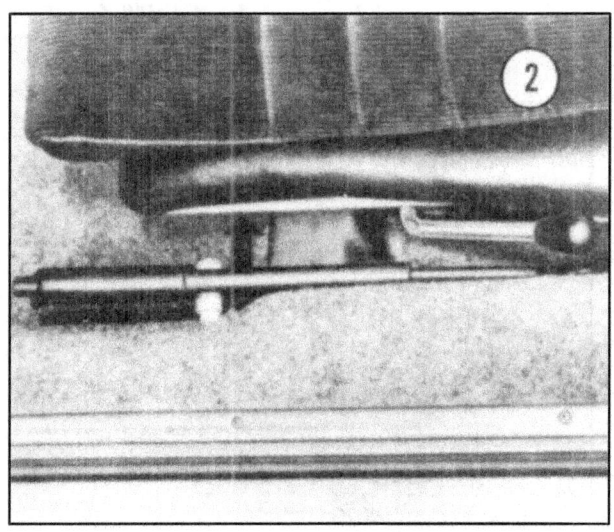

2. Lift leaf spring under left rail and slide seat off rails. See **Figure 2**.

3. Clean rails on seat and body with solvent. Grease lightly with Lubriplate.

4. Slide seat onto runners until leaf spring engages.

Passenger's Seat Removal/Installation

1. Pull seat cushion up at rear. Unhook clip A from seat frame and lift cushion off. See **Figure 3**.

2. Remove 4 nuts and bolts securing seat frame. See **Figure 4**. Lift seat out.

3. Installation is the reverse of these steps.

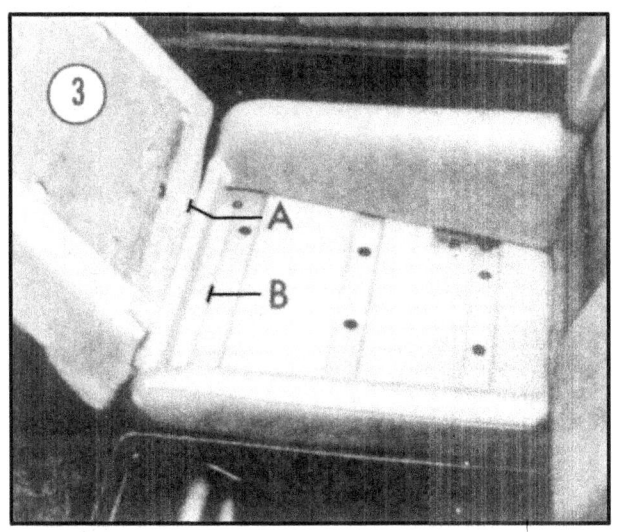

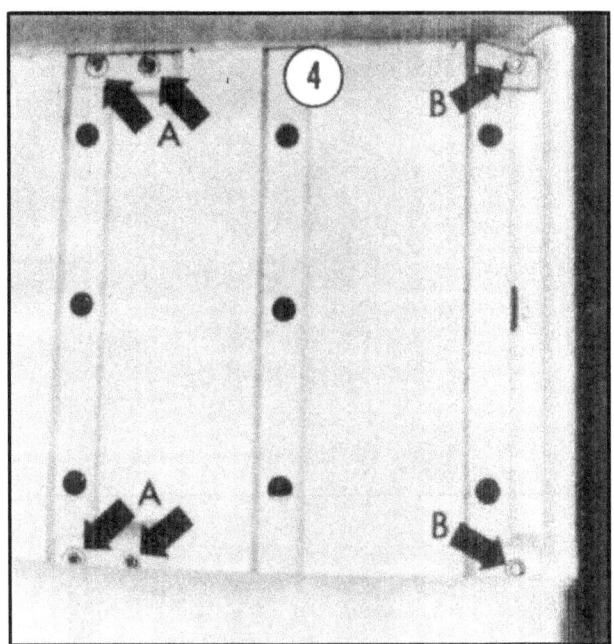

6b. If new door is installed, first remove striker plate. Align door carefully in body opening so that there is a uniform space all around the door. See **Figure 6**. Tighten hinge bolts.

DOORS

Door Removal/Installation

1. Remove cotter pin and disconnect door stop strap. See **Figure 5**.

2. Mark position of hinges on body if same door is to be reinstalled.

3. Unscrew 6 hinge bolts and remove door.

4. Check door seals and replace if necessary.

5. Screw door onto body with hinge bolts. Do not tighten bolts.

6a. If same door is reinstalled, simply align hinges with marks made in Step 2 and tighten bolts.

7. Install striker plate if removed. Adjust striker plate as described in a later procedure.

Striker Plate Adjustment

1. Remove the striker plate. See **Figure 7**.

2. Insert the striker plate pin into the lock latch on the door and press the lock latch down into locking position.

3. Twist the striker plate upwards as shown in **Figure 8**.

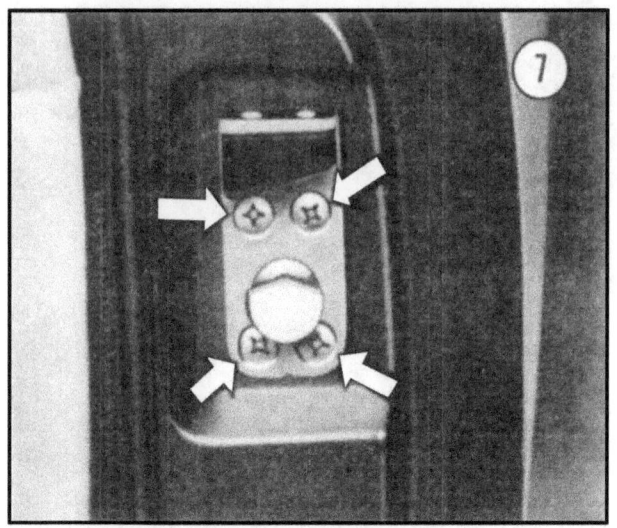

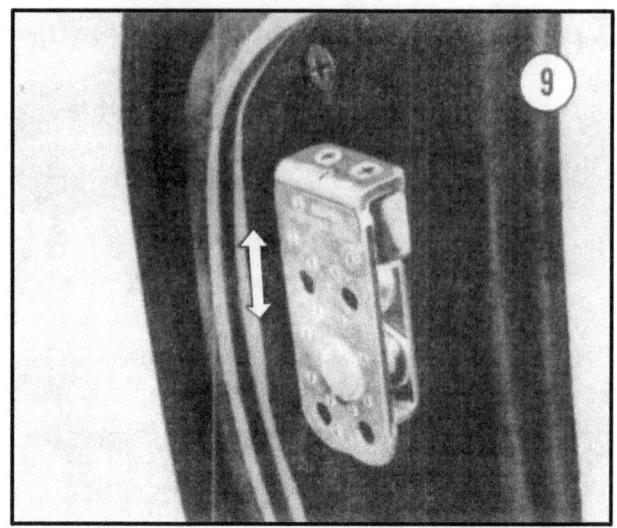

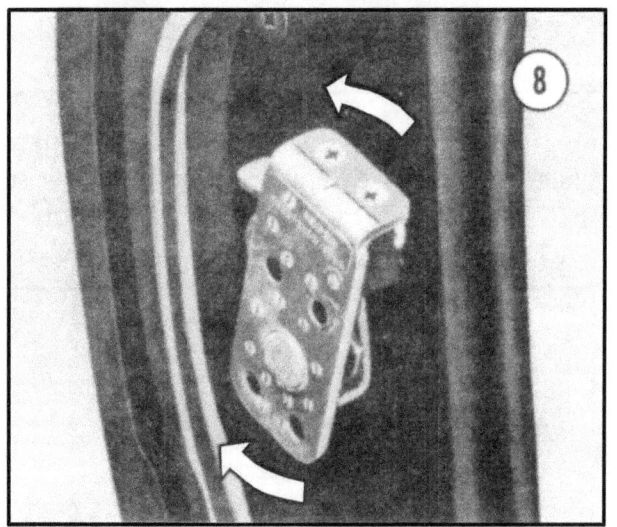

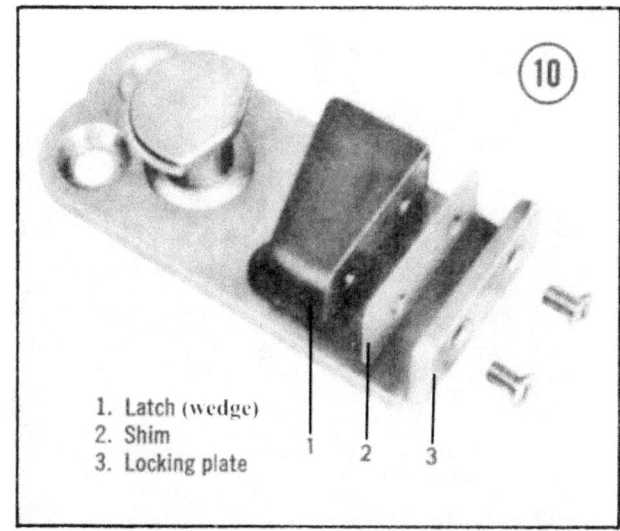

1. Latch (wedge)
2. Shim
3. Locking plate

4. Try to move the striker plate up and down (see **Figure 9**). If there is any play on 1970-1971 models, remove screws securing the wedge (see **Figure 10**), and insert a shim between the wedge and the striker plate. On 1972 and 1973 models, replace the wedge if there is any play. To do this, pull the worn wedge out and press in a new one as shown in **Figure 11**.

5. With the striker plate removed, close the door and check alignment. Adjust door if necessary.

6. Install the striker plate and tighten the screws slightly.

7. Close the door. If the door edge is not flush with the rear quarter panel, move the striker plate in or out.

8. If the door is difficult to close, and the push-button is hard to operate, the top of the striker

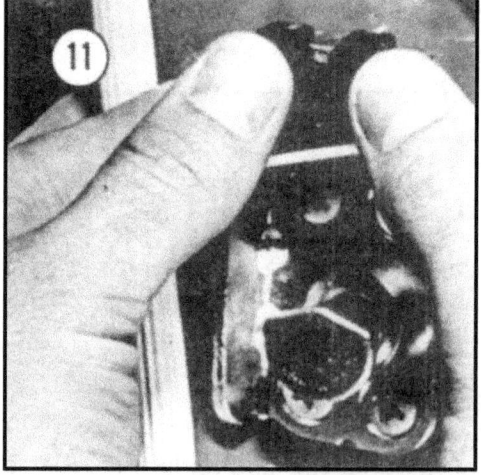

plate may be inclined too far inward. Loosen the screws and properly align the plate.

9. If the door springs back to the safety position when slammed, the top of the striker plate may

be inclined too far outward. It is also possible the striker plate is too low. Realign the striker plate.

10. If the door is difficult to open and drops noticeably when opened, the striker plate is too high. Realign the striker plate.

Door Panel Removal/Installation

1. Pry the plastic trim away from window crank as shown in **Figure 12**. Note the scrap wood used to protect the upholstery. Remove the Phillips screw securing the window crank and remove the crank. See **Figure 13**.

2. Pry the recessed trim plate out as shown in **Figure 14**. Remove the Phillips screw and escutcheon (Figure 13).

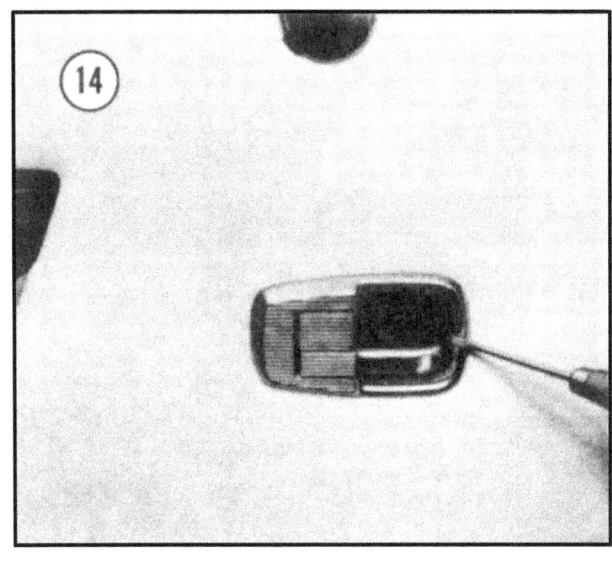

3a. On left door, remove screws marked A and B in **Figure 15**.

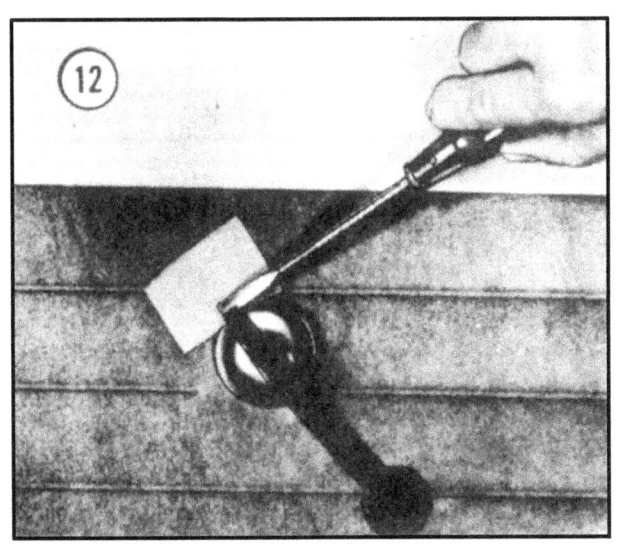

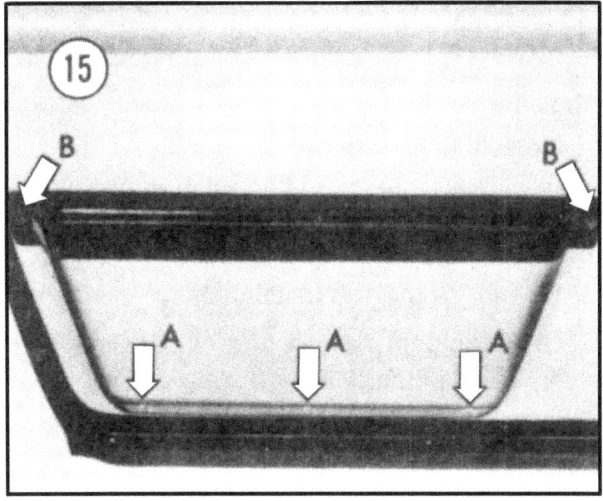

3b. On right door, remove 3 screws from bottom of armrest. See **Figure 16**. Slide bottom portion of armrest forward and remove it. Remove 2 screws shown in **Figure 17**.

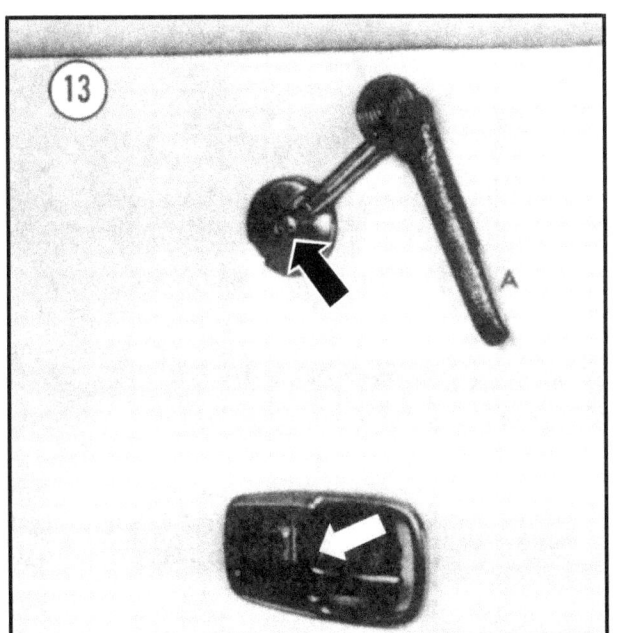

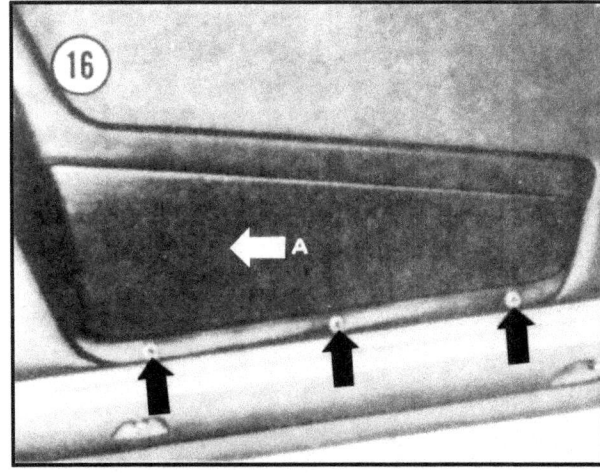

303

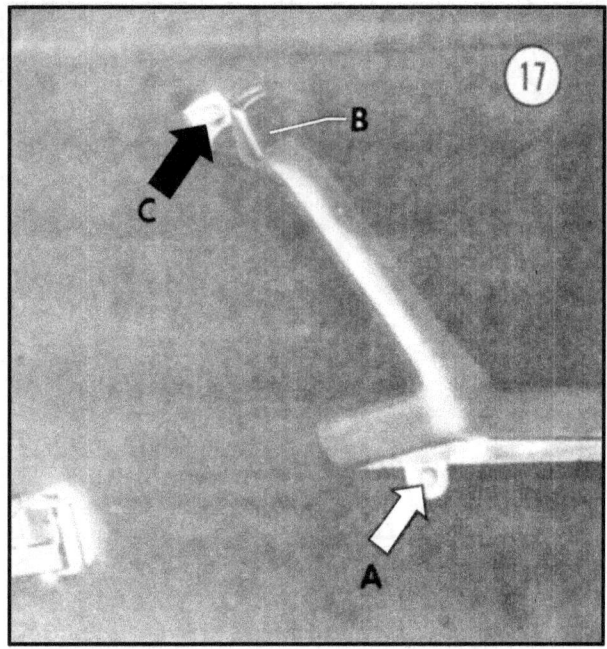

4. Pull bottom edge of door panel outward slightly, then lift up on panel to disengage the top edge clips.

5. Installation is the reverse of these steps. If plastic inner liner is damaged, remove it and glue a new one in.

Door Stop Removal/Installation

1. Remove door panel as described above. Peel away plastic inner liner.

2. Remove cotter pin and disconnect door stop. See **Figure 18**.

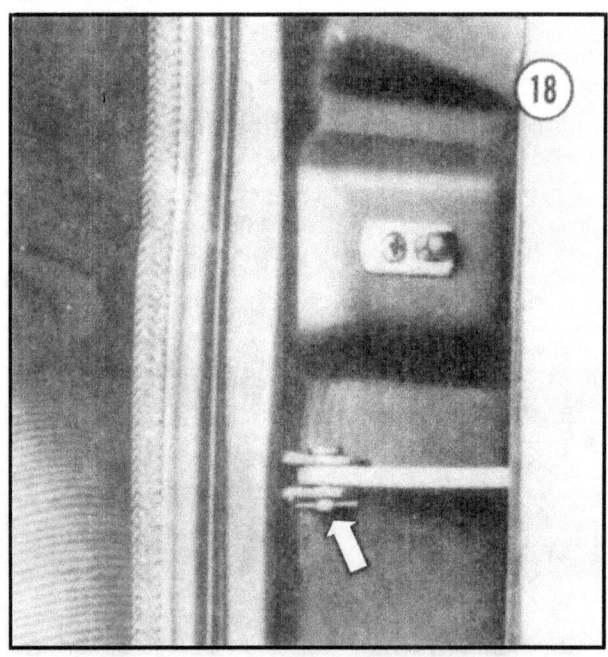

3. Remove 2 bolts securing door stop to door. See **Figure 19**.

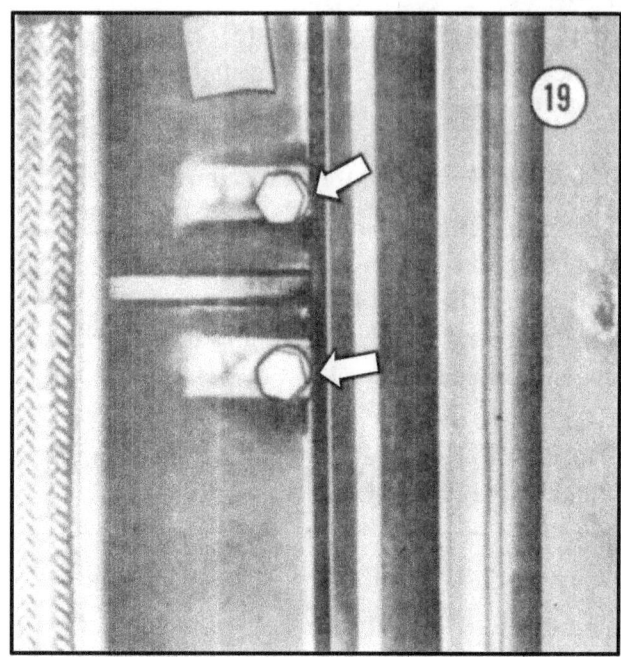

4. Remove door stop from inside door.

5. Clean door stop thoroughly in solvent. Lubricate bearing surfaces with SAE 30 oil.

6. Installation is the reverse of these steps.

Outer Door Handle Removal/Installation

1. Roll door window all the way up.

2. Remove door panel as described earlier.

3. Remove nut and bolt securing door handle. See **Figure 20**.

4. Installation is the reverse of these steps.

WINDOWS

Window replacement requires special skills and equipment. Take these jobs to your dealer or local glass shop.

HOODS AND LOCKS

Front Hood Removal/Installation

1. Open the hood.

2. Scribe marks on the hood around the hinges to aid in reassembly. See **Figure 21**.

3. Remove bolts while a helper supports the hood. See **Figure 22**.

304

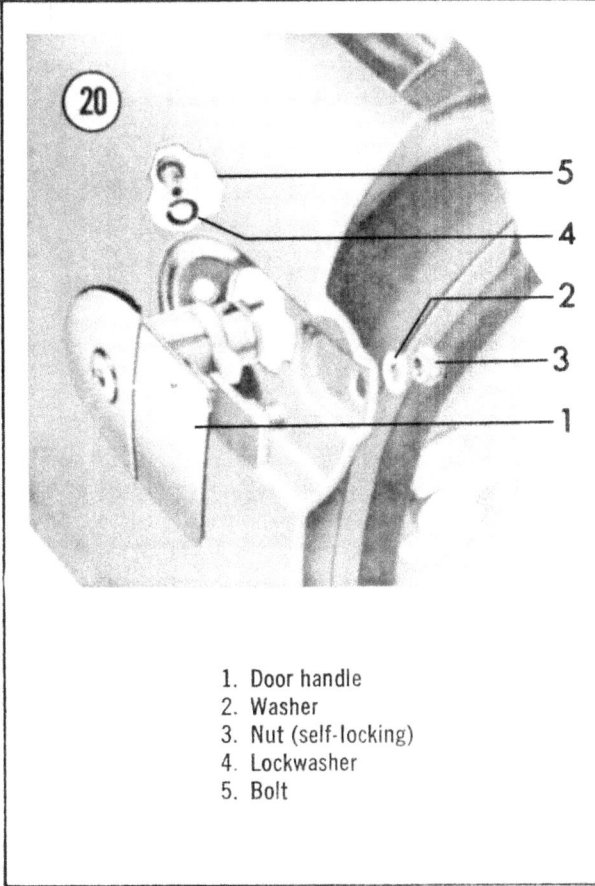

1. Door handle
2. Washer
3. Nut (self-locking)
4. Lockwasher
5. Bolt

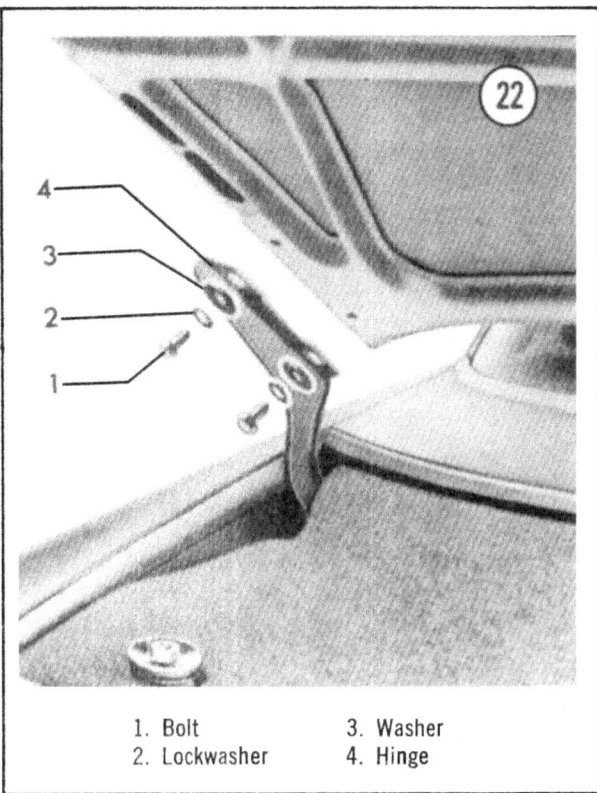

1. Bolt
2. Lockwasher
3. Washer
4. Hinge

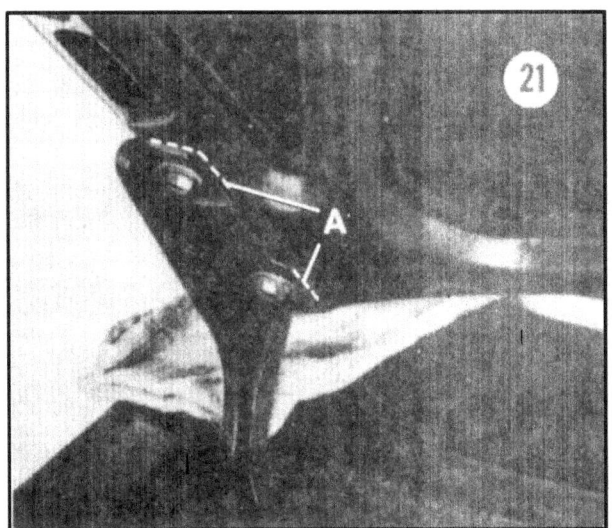

A. Marking point

4. Lift hood off.
5. Installation is the reverse of these steps. Line up scribe marks for proper hood alignment.

Rear Hood Removal/Installation

1. Open the hood.
2. Scribe marks on the hood around the hinges. See **Figure 23**.

A. Marking point

3. Remove bolts while a helper supports the hood. See **Figure 24**.
4. Lift the hood off.
5. Installation is the reverse of these steps. Line up the scribe marks for proper alignment.

Front Hood Lock Replacement

1. Open front hood.

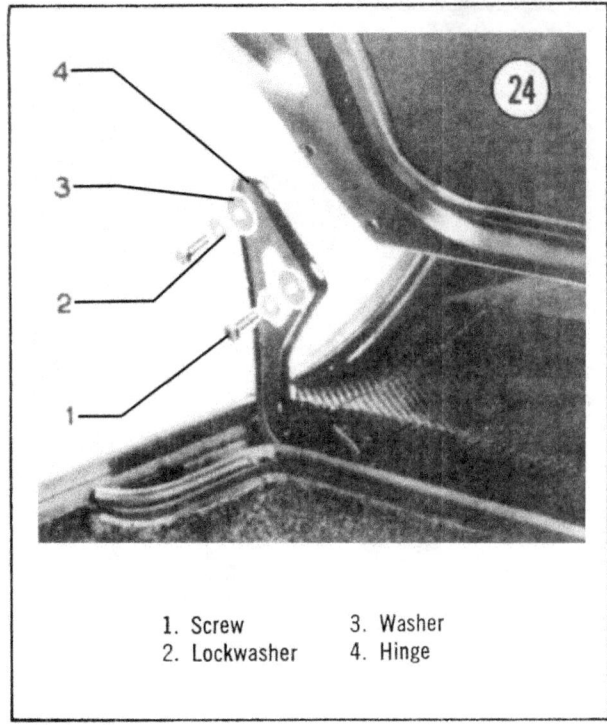

1. Screw
2. Lockwasher
3. Washer
4. Hinge

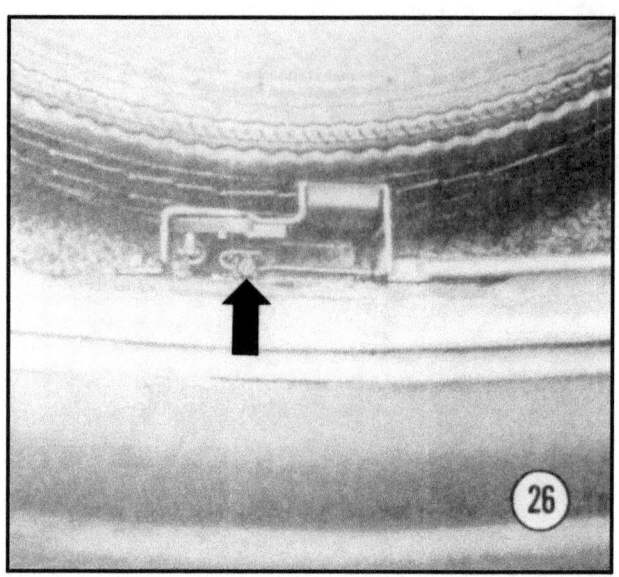

2. Remove bolts securing upper part of lock and remove it. See **Figure 25**.

3. Loosen cable clamp screw on latch plate. See **Figure 26**.

4. Remove bolts holding lower latch in place. See **Figure 27**.

5. Check upper and lower parts for excessive wear. Grease bearing surfaces lightly with Lubriplate.

6. Install lower latch with 2 bolts.

7. Bolt upper part of lock to hood. Adjust its position so that the lock engages smoothly. See **Figure 28**.

Rear Hood Lock Replacement

1. Open hood.

2. Remove bolts holding upper part of lock. See **Figure 29**.

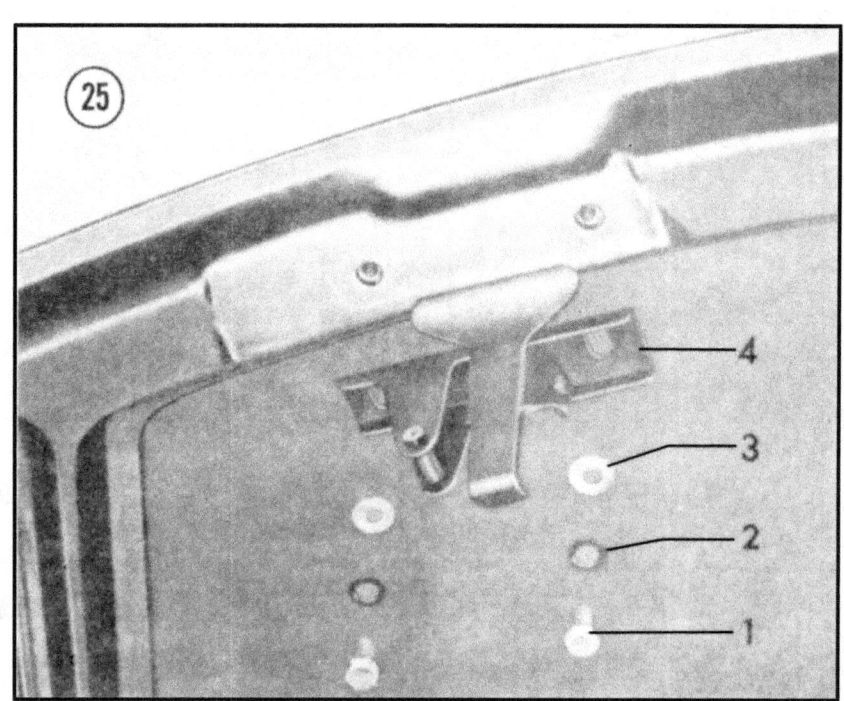

1. Hex screw
2. Lockwasher
3. Washer
4. Lock

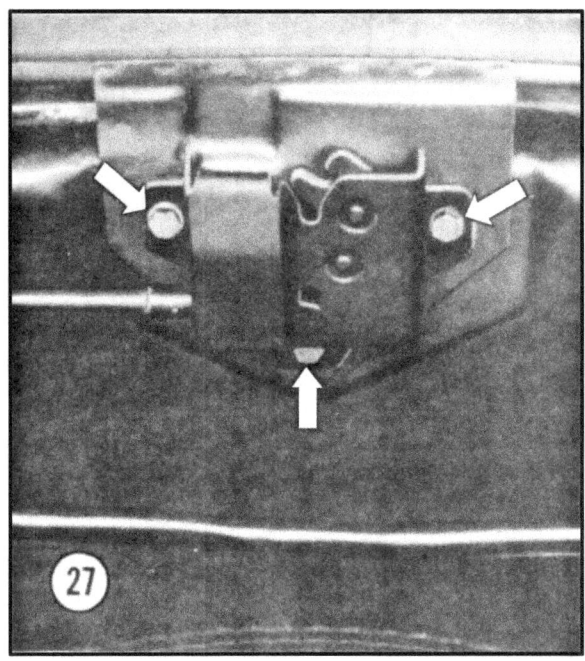

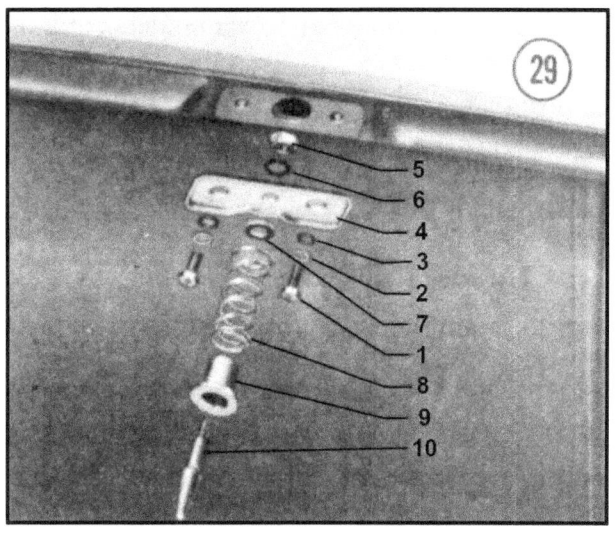

1. Screw
2. Lockwasher
3. Washer
4. Molding
5. Nut
6. Lockwasher
7. Spacer
8. Spring
9. Bushing
10. Lock bolt

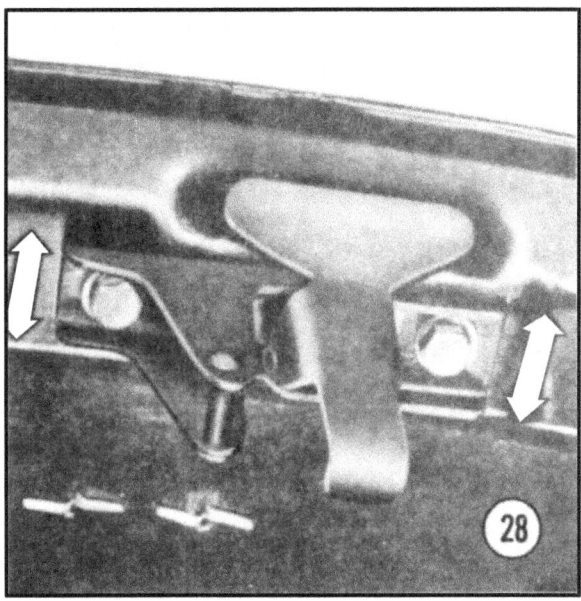

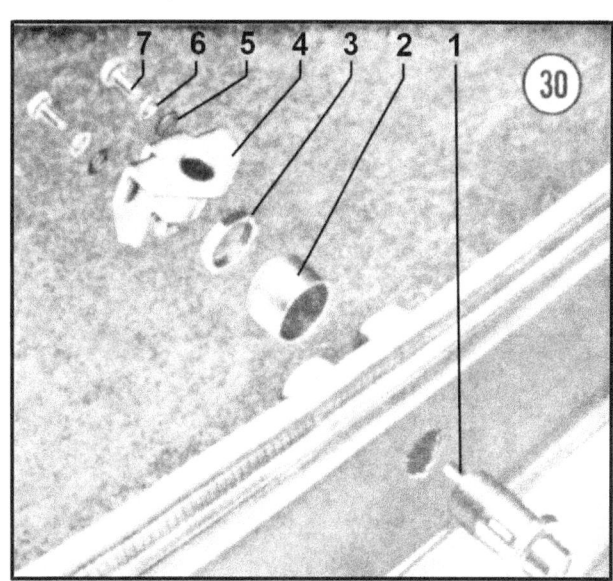

1. Lock tumbler
2. Spacer
3. Nut
4. Lock base
5. Washer
6. Lockwasher
7. Screw

3. Remove 2 bolts securing lower part of lock. See **Figure 30**.

4. Check upper and lower parts for excessive wear. Grease bearing surfaces lightly with Lubriplate.

5. Install lower latch with 2 bolts.

6. Bolt upper part of lock to hood. Adjust its position so that the lock engages smoothly. See **Figure 31**.

Rear Lock Tumbler Replacement

1. Remove 2 screws securing lower latch. See Figure 30.

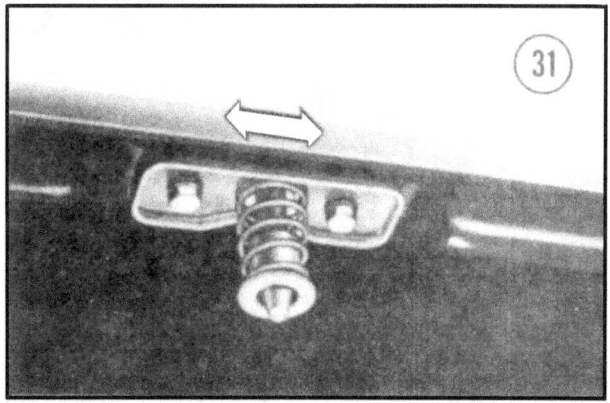

2. Unscrew nut holding lock tumbler in place and remove tumbler.

3. Installation is the reverse of these steps.

BUMPERS

Front Bumper Replacement

Refer to **Figure 32** for the following procedure.

1. Remove bolts accessible from inside wheel wells. See **Figure 33**.
2. Pull bumper out of fenders.
3. Check rubber mounts. If damaged, replace them.
4. Installation is the reverse of these steps.

Rear Bumper Removal/Installation

Refer to **Figure 34** for the following procedure.

33

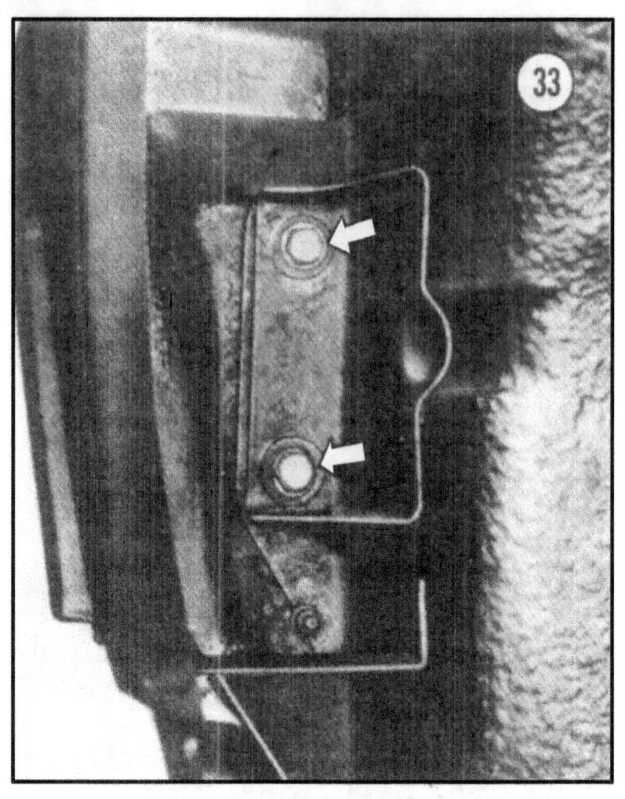

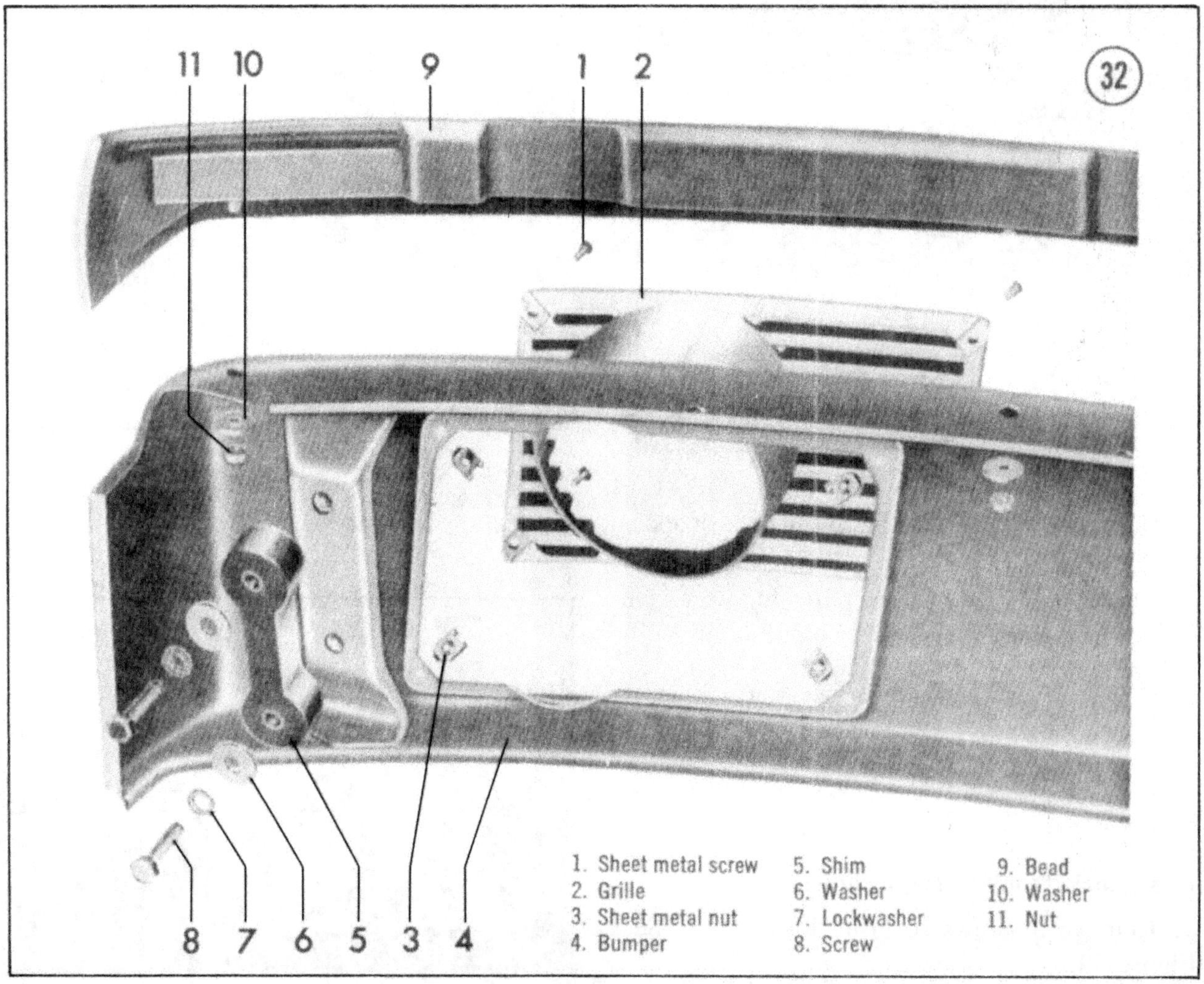
32
11
10
9
1
2
8
7
6
5
3
4
1. Sheet metal screw
2. Grille
3. Sheet metal nut
4. Bumper
5. Shim
6. Washer
7. Lockwasher
8. Screw
9. Bead
10. Washer
11. Nut

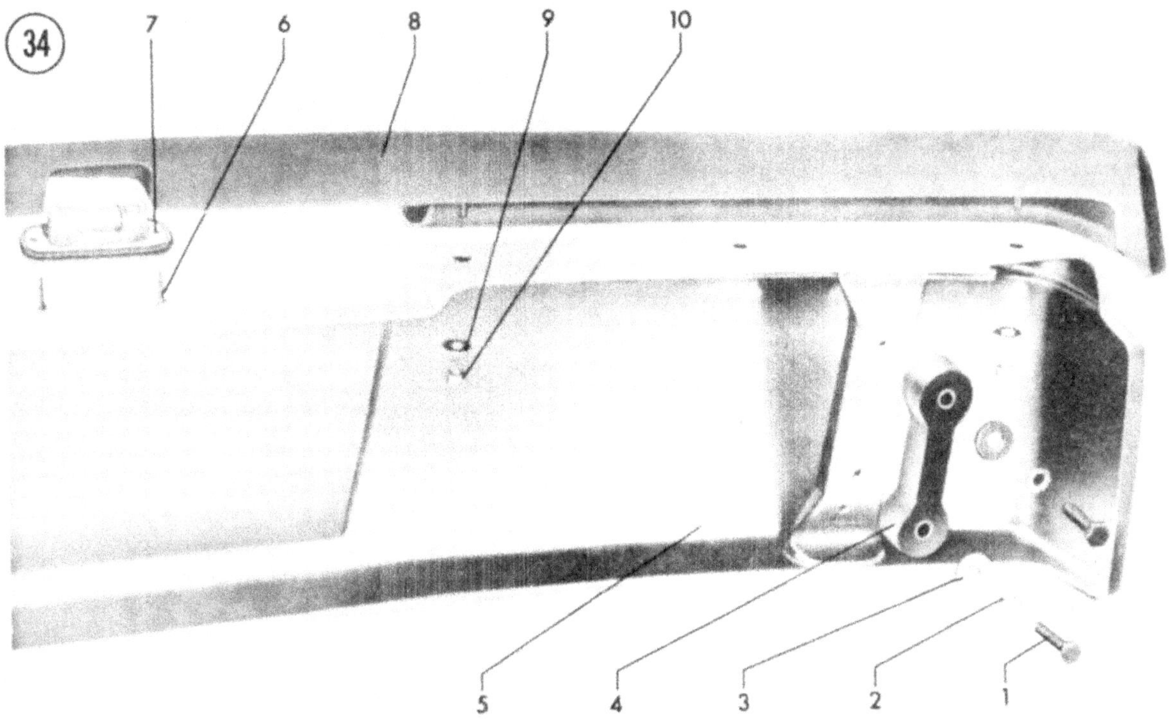

34

1. Screw
2. Lockwasher
3. Washer
4. Shim
5. Bumper
6. Sheet metal screw
7. License plate lights
8. Bead
9. Washer
10. Nut

1. Remove license plate light.
2. Remove bolt in each wheel well. See **Figure 35**.
3. Pull back paneling in rear luggage area (see **Figure 36**) and remove bolt on each side.

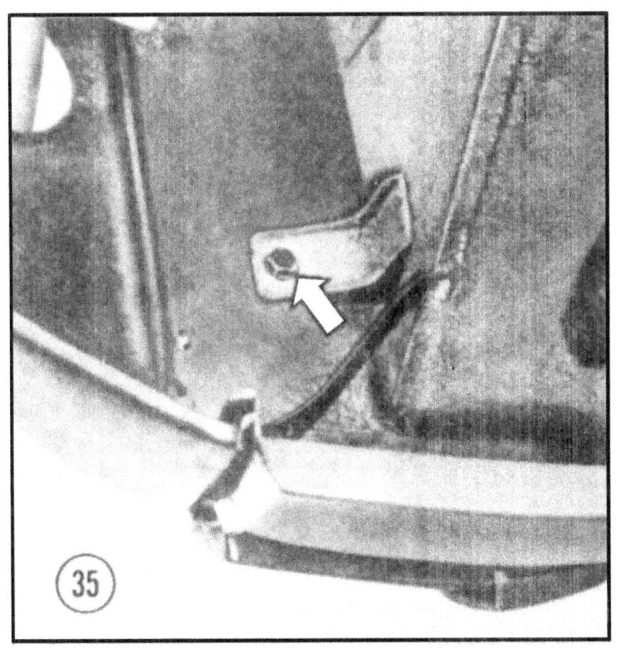

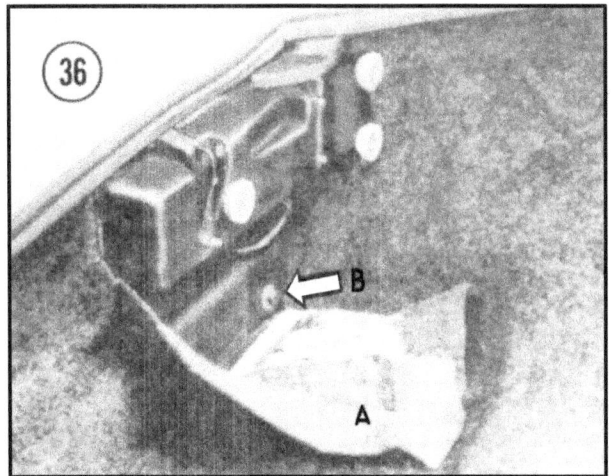

A. Panelling   B. Hex screw

4. Pull bumper out rear.
5. Check rubber mounts. If damaged, replace them.
6. Installation is the reverse of these steps.

309

VELOCEPRESS MANUALS – MOTORCYCLE BY MAKE

AJS 1932-1948 SINGLES & TWINS 250cc THRU 1000cc (BOOK OF)
AJS 1945-1960 SINGLES 350cc & 500cc MODELS 16 & 18 (BOOK OF)
AJS 1955-1965 SINGLES 350cc & 500cc (BOOK OF)
AJS 1957-1966 FACTORY WSM - ALL SINGLES & TWINS
ARIEL UP TO 1932 (BOOK OF)
ARIEL 1932-1939 PREWAR MODELS (BOOK OF)
ARIEL 1933-1951 (WORKSHOP MANUAL)
ARIEL 1939-1960 4 STROKE SINGLES (BOOK OF)
ARIEL 1958-1964 LEADER & ARROW (BOOK OF)
BMW R26 R27 (1956-1967) FACTORY WORKSHOP MANUAL
BMW R50 R50S R60 R69S (1955-1969) FACTORY WORKSHOP MANUAL
BRIDGESTONE 90 SERIES FACTORY WSM & PARTS CATALOGUE
BRIDGESTONE 175 SERIES FACTORY WSM & PARTS CATALOGUE
BRIDGESTONE 350 SERIES FACTORY WSM & PARTS CATALOGUES
BSA SERVICE SHEETS MASTER CATALOGUE ALL MODELS 1945-1967
BSA BANTAM D1 TO D7 1948-1966 FACTORY SERVICE SHEETS MANUAL
BSA BANTAM ALL MODELS FROM 1948 ONWARDS (BOOK OF)
BSA DANDY FACTORY WORKSHOP MANUAL (COMPILATION)
BSA SINGLES & V-TWINS UP TO 1927 (BOOK OF)
BSA SINGLES & V-TWINS UP TO 1930 (BOOK OF)
BSA SINGLES & V-TWINS UP TO 1935 (BOOK OF)
BSA SINGLES & V-TWINS 1936-1939 (BOOK OF)
BSA C10, C11 & C12 1945-1958 FACTORY SERVICE SHEETS MANUAL
BSA OHV & SV SINGLES 250-600cc 1945-1959 (BOOK OF)
BSA C15 & B40 1958-1967 FACTORY SERVICE SHEETS MANUAL
BSA OHV & SV SINGLES 250cc (ONLY) 1954-1970 (BOOK OF)
BSA B31, B32, B33 & B34 1945-60 FACTORY SERVICE SHEETS MANUAL
BSA OHV SINGLES 350 & 500cc 1955-1967 (BOOK OF)
BSA M20, M21 & M33 1945-1963 FACTORY SERVICE SHEETS MANUAL
BSA TWINS A7 & A10 1948-1962 FACTORY SERVICE SHEETS MANUAL
BSA TWINS A7 & A10 1948-1962 (BOOK OF)
BSA TWINS A50 & A65 1962-1965 FACTORY WORKSHOP MANUAL
BSA TWINS A50 & A65 1962-1969 (SECOND BOOK OF)
DOUGLAS 1929-1939 PREWAR ALL MODELS (BOOK OF)
DOUGLAS 1948-1957 POSTWAR ALL MODELS FACTORY SHOP MANUAL
DUCATI 160cc, 250cc & 350cc OHC MODELS FACTORY SHOP MANUAL
HONDA 50cc ALL MODELS UP TO 1970 INC MONKEY & TRAIL (BOOK OF)
HONDA 90cc ALL MODELS UP TO 1966 (BOOK OF)
HONDA 50-65-70-90cc OHC SINGLES 1959-1983 FACTORY WSM
HONDA 100-125cc SINGLES CB/CD/CL/SL/TL 1970-1984 FACTORY WSM
HONDA 125-150cc TWINS C/CS/CB/CA FACTORY WORKSHOP MANUAL
HONDA 125-160-175-200cc TWINS 1965-1978 WORKSHOP MANUAL
HONDA 250-305cc TWINS C/CS/CB 1959-1967 FACTORY WSM
HOHDA 250-350cc TWINS CB/CL/SL 1968-1973 FACTORY WSM
HONDA 450cc CB/CL 1965-1974 K0 TO K7 WORKSHOP MANUAL
HONDA 750cc SHOC 4 CYL 1969-1978 K0~K8 WORKSHOP MANUAL
HONDA C100 SUPER CUB FACTORY WORKSHOP MANUAL
HONDA C110 SPORT CUB 1962-1969 FACTORY WORKSHOP MANUAL
HONDA TWINS & SINGLES 50cc THRU 305cc 1960-1966 (BOOK OF)
HONDA TWINS ALL MODELS 125cc THRU 450cc UP TO 1968 (BOOK OF)
INDIAN PONYBIKE, BOY RACER & PAPOOSE ILL PARTS LIST & SALES LIT
J.A.P. ENGINES 1927-1952 & MOTORCYCLES 1934-1952 (BOOK OF)
MATCHLESS 1931-1939 ALL MODELS 250cc THRU 990cc (BOOK OF)
MATCHLESS 1945-1956 350 & 500cc SINGLES (BOOK OF)
MATCHLESS 1955-1966 350 & 500cc SINGLES (BOOK OF)
MATCHLESS 1957-1966 FACTORY WSM - ALL SINGLES & TWINS
NEW IMPERIAL ALL SV & OHV FROM 1935 ONWARDS (BOOK OF)
NORTON 1932-1939 PREWAR MODELS (BOOK OF)
NORTON 1932-1947 (BOOK OF)
NORTON 1938-1956 (BOOK OF)
NORTON 1955-1963 MODELS 19, 50 & ES2 (BOOK OF)
NORTON 1955-1965 DOMINATOR TWINS (BOOK OF)
NORTON 1960-1970 TWIN CYLINDER FACTORY WORKSHOP MANUAL
NORTON 1970-1975 COMMANDO 850 & 750cc FACTORY WSM
NORTON 1975-1978 MK 3 COMMANDO 850 cc FACTORY WSM
PANTHER 1932-1958 LIGHTWEIGHT MODELS 250 & 350cc (BOOK OF)
PANTHER 1938-1966 HEAVYWEIGHT MODELS 600 & 650cc (BOOK OF)
RALEIGH MOTORCYCLES 1919-1933 (BOOK OF)
ROYAL ENFIELD 1934-1946 SINGLES & V TWINS (BOOK OF)
ROYAL ENFIELD 1937-1953 SINGLES & V TWINS (BOOK OF)
ROYAL ENFIELD 1946-1962 SINGLES (BOOK OF)
ROYAL ENFIELD 1958-1966 250cc & 350cc SINGLES (SECOND BOOK OF)
ROYAL ENFIELD 1962-1970 INTERCEPTOR WSM'S & PARTS (Compilation)
RUDGE 1933-1939 (BOOK OF)
SUNBEAM 1928-1939 (BOOK OF)
SUNBEAM 1946-1957 S7 & S8 (BOOK OF)
SUZUKI 50cc & 80cc UP TO 1966 (BOOK OF)
SUZUKI T10 1963-1967 FACTORY WORKSHOP MANUAL
SUZUKI T20 & T200 1965-1969 FACTORY WORKSHOP MANUAL
SUZUKI TWINS 1962 ONWARDS 125-500cc WORKSHOP MANUAL
TRIUMPH 1935-1949 SINGLES & TWINS (BOOK OF)
TRIUMPH 1937-1951 (WORKSHOP MANUAL)
TRIUMPH 1945-1955 FACTORY WORKSHOP MANUAL
TRIUMPH 1945-1959 TWINS (BOOK OF)
TRIUMPH 1956-1969 TWINS (BOOK OF)
TRIUMPH 1963-1970 UNIT CONSTRUCTION 650cc FACTORY WSM
TRIUMPH 1963-1974 UNIT CONSTRUCTION 350-500cc FACTORY WSM
TRIUMPH 1968-1974 TRIDENT T150 & T150V FACTORY WSM
VELOCETTE 1925-1970 ALL SINGLES & TWINS (BOOK OF)
VELOCETTE 1933-1952 MOV-MAC-MSS RIGID FRAME FACTORY WSM
VELOCETTE 1954-1971 MSS-VENOM-THRUXTON-VIPER FACTORY WSM
VILLIERS ENGINE UP TO 1959 INC. 3 WHEELERS (BOOK OF)
VILLIERS ENGINE UP TO 1969 (BOOK OF)
VINCENT 1935-1955 (WORKSHOP MANUAL)
YAMAHA 1961-1967 YA5 & YA6 (WORKSHOP MANUAL & ILL PARTS LIST)
YAMAHA 1971-1972 JT1& JT2 (WORKSHOP MANUAL & ILL PARTS LIST)

www.VelocePress.com

VELOCEPRESS TECHNICAL BOOKS – MOTORCYCLE

1930'S BRITISH MOTORCYCLE CARBS & ELEC COMPONENTS (BOOK OF)
1930'S BRITISH MOTORCYCLE ENGINES (OVERHAUL & MAINTENANCE)
1930'S BRITISH MOTORCYCLE GEARBOXES & CLUTCHES (BOOK OF)
CATALOG OF BRITISH MOTORCYCLES (1951 MODELS)
LUCAS ELECTRONICS BRITISH M/CYCLES REPAIR & PARTS (1950-1977)
MOTORCYCLE ENGINEERING (P.E. Irving)
MOTORCYCLE ROAD TESTS 1949-1953 (Motor Cycle Magazine UK)
SPEED AND HOW TO OBTAIN IT (Motor Cycle Magazine UK)
TUNING FOR SPEED (P.E. Irving)
WIPAC (COMBO) MANUAL NUMBER 3 + M/CYCLE & SCOOTER MANUAL

VELOCEPRESS MANUALS – SCOOTERS BY MAKE

BSA SUNBEAM SCOOTER WORKSHOP MANUAL 1959-1965
BSA SUNBEAM SCOOTER 1959-1965 (BOOK OF)
LAMBRETTA 1947-1957 ALL 125 & 150cc MODELS (BOOK OF)
LAMBRETTA 1957-1970 LI & TV MODELS (SECOND BOOK OF)
NSU PRIMA 1956-1964 ALL MODELS (BOOK OF)
TRIUMPH TIGRESS SCOOTER WORKSHOP MANUAL 1959-1965
TRIUMPH TIGRESS SCOOTER (BOOK OF)
VESPA 1951-1961 (BOOK OF)
VESPA 1955-1963 125 & 150cc & GS MODELS (SECOND BOOK OF)
VESPA 1955-1968 GS & SS (BOOK OF)
VESPA 1963-1972 90, 125 & 150cc (THIRD BOOK OF)

VELOCEPRESS MANUALS – MOPEDS & MOTORIZED BICYCLES

CYCLEMOTOR (BOOK OF)
NSU QUICKLY 1953-1963 ALL MODELS (BOOK OF)
PUCH MAXI N & S MAINTENANCE & REPAIR (3 MANUAL COMPILATION)
RALEIGH MOPEDS 1960-1969 (BOOK OF)

VELOCEPRESS MANUALS - THREE WHEELER'S

BOND MINICAR THREE WHEELER 1948-1967 (BOOK OF)
BMW ISETTA FACTORY WORKSHOP MANUAL
BSA THREE WHEELER (BOOK OF)
RELIANT REGAL THREE WHEELER 1952-1973 (BOOK OF)
VINTAGE MORGAN THREE WHEELER (BOOK OF)

VELOCEPRESS MANUALS – AUTOMOBILE BY MAKE

ALFA ROMEO GIULIA WORKSHOP MANUAL 1300 TO 2000cc 1962-1975
ALFA ROMEO GIULIA TECH MANUAL CARBURETED CARS FROM 1962
ALFA ROMEO GIULIA TECH MANUAL FUEL INJECTED CARS FROM 1969
ALFA ROMEO GIULIETTA & GIULIA 750 & 101 SERIES 1955-1965 WSM
AUSTIN-HEALEY SPRITE & MG MIDGET WORKSHOP MANUAL 1958-1971
BMW 600 LIMOUSINE FACTORY WORKSHOP MANUAL
BMW 600 LIMOUSINE OWNERS HAND BOOK & SERVICE MANUAL
BMW 2000 & 2002 1966-1976 WORKSHOP MANUAL
CORVAIR 1960-1969 WORKSHOP MANUAL
CORVETTE V8 1955-1962 WORKSHOP MANUAL
FERRARI HANDBOOK ROAD & RACE CARS (SERVICE/SPECS) 1948-1958
FERRARI 250/GT SERVICE & MAINTENANCE MANUAL 1956-1965
FIAT 500 FACTORY WORKSHOP MANUAL 1957-1973
FIAT 600, 600D & MULTIPLA FACTORY WORKSHOP MANUAL 1955-1969
JAGUAR E-TYPE 3.8 & 4.2 SERIES 1 & 2 WORKSHOP MANUAL
JAGUAR MK 7, 8, 9 & XK120, 140, 150 WORKSHOP MANUAL 1948-1961
METROPOLITAN FACTORY WORKSHOP MANUAL
MGA & MGB OWNERS HANDBOOK & WORKSHOP MANUAL
MG MIDGET TC, TD, TF & TF1500 WORKSHOP MANUAL
PORSCHE 356 1948-1965 WORKSHOP MANUAL
PORSCHE 911 2.0, 2.2, 2.4 LITRE 1964-1973 WORKSHOP MANUAL
PORSCHE 911 2.7, 3.0, 3.2 LITRE 1973-1989 WORKSHOP MANUAL
PORSCHE 912 WORKSHOP MANUAL
PORSCHE 914/4 & 914/6 1.7, 1.8, 2.0 LITRE 1970-1976 WSM
TRIUMPH TR2, TR3, TR4 1953-1965 WORKSHOP MANUAL
VOLKSWAGEN TRANSPORTER, TRUCKS & WAGONS 1950-1979 WSM
VOLVO 1944-1968 ALL MODELS WORKSHOP MANUAL

VELOCEPRESS TECHNICAL BOOKS - AUTOMOBILE

HOW TO BUILD A FIBERGLASS CAR
HOW TO BUILD A RACING CAR
HOW TO RESTORE THE MODEL 'A' FORD
MASERATI OWNER'S HANDBOOK
PERFORMANCE TUNING THE SUNBEAM TIGER
SOUPING THE VOLKSWAGEN
SOLEX CARBURETORS (EMPHASIS ON UK & EU AUTOMOBILES)
SU CARBURETORS (EMPHASIS ON UK AUTOMOBILES)
WEBER CARBURETORS (EMPHASIS ON ALFA & FIAT)

VELOCEPRESS BOOKS & GUIDES - AUTOMOBILE

COMPLETE CATALOG OF JAPANESE MOTOR VEHICLES
FERRARI 308 SERIES BUYER'S AND OWNER'S GUIDE
FERRARI BROCHURES AND SALES LITERATURE 1968-1989
FERRARI SERIAL NUMBERS PART I - ODD NUMBERS TO 21399
FERRARI SERIAL NUMBERS PART II - EVEN NUMBERS TO 1050
HENRY'S FABULOUS MODEL "A" FORD
MASERATI BROCHURES AND SALES LITERATURE

VELOCEPRESS BOOKS – RACING

CARRERA PANAMERICANA - MEXICAN ROAD RACE (BOOK OF)
DIALED IN - THE JAN OPPERMAN STORY
VEDA ORR'S NEW REVISED HOT ROD PICTORIAL

Please check our website:

www.VelocePress.com

for a complete
up-to-date list of
available titles

www.ingramcontent.com/pod-product-compliance
Lightning Source LLC
Chambersburg PA
CBHW060245240426
43673CB00047B/1879